# Connecting Children with Classics

# Connecting Children with Classics

## A Reader-Centered Approach to Selecting and Promoting Great Literature

Meagan Lacy and Pauline Dewan

Foreword by Catherine Sheldrick Ross

An Imprint of ABC-CLIO, LLC
Santa Barbara, California • Denver, Colorado

Copyright © 2018 by Meagan Lacy and Pauline Dewan

All rights reserved. No part of this publication may be reproduced, stored in a retrieval system, or transmitted, in any form or by any means, electronic, mechanical, photocopying, recording, or otherwise, except for the inclusion of brief quotations in a review, without prior permission in writing from the publisher.

**Library of Congress Cataloging-in-Publication Data**

Names: Lacy, Meagan, author. | Dewan, Pauline, author.
Title: Connecting children with classics : a reader-centered approach to selecting and promoting great literature / Meagan Lacy and Pauline Dewan ; foreword by Catherine Sheldrick Ross.
Description: Santa Barbara, California : Libraries Unlimited, an imprint of ABC-CLIO, LLC, [2018] | Includes bibliographical references and indexes.
Identifiers: LCCN 2018004745 (print) | LCCN 2017051878 (ebook) | ISBN 9781440844409 (ebook) | ISBN 9781440844393 (paperback : acid-free paper)
Subjects: LCSH: Children—Books and reading. | Children's stories—Bibliography. | Children's stories—Stories, plots, etc. | Children's stories—Themes, motives. | Best books. | Readers' advisory services.
Classification: LCC Z1037.A1 (print) | LCC Z1037.A1 L2195 2018 (ebook) | DDC 028.5/5—dc23
LC record available at https://lccn.loc.gov/2018004745

ISBN: 978–1–4408–4439–3 (paperback)
   978–1–4408–4440–9 (ebook)

22 21 20 19 18   1 2 3 4 5

This book is also available as an eBook.

Libraries Unlimited
An Imprint of ABC-CLIO, LLC

ABC-CLIO, LLC
130 Cremona Drive, P.O. Box 1911
Santa Barbara, California 93116-1911
www.abc-clio.com

This book is printed on acid-free paper ∞

Manufactured in the United States of America

# Contents

*Foreword* vii

*Preface* xi

**Part 1    Foundations**

**Chapter 1**    Matching Each Child with the Perfect Book: Intersections of Interest and Need    3

**Chapter 2**    Why Focus on the Classics?    25

**Chapter 3**    How to Promote the Classics    37

**Part 2    Annotations**

**Chapter 4**    Adventure/Survival    55

**Chapter 5**    Animal    95

**Chapter 6**    Fantasy    131

**Chapter 7**    Fantasy Series    193

**Chapter 8**    Historical Fiction    273

**Chapter 9**    Myth/Legend    335

**Chapter 10**   Realism/Everyday Life    359

**Chapter 11**   Science Fiction    401

**Chapter 12**   Toys/Games    427

Appendix: Key Children's Literature Awards for Fiction in English    453

Themes/Subjects Index    457

Author/Title Index    477

# Foreword

This book is all about how to turn children into enthusiastic readers. Authors Meagan Lacy and Pauline Dewan situate their topic of connecting children to classics within the big picture of how to foster readers. The first three chapters are all about what makes readers and what nourishes them. Chapters 4–12 offer us some three hundred judiciously selected reading gifts, sifted from more than a century's worth of classic children's books and presented with just enough information on both book-centered and reader-centered elements of appeal to help readers make a choice. The organization of the book itself helps readers choose, based as it is on research on how people pick enjoyable books. We know that genre is important but also that readers respond to books based on their own life situations and on their mood at the time of reading. Hence, Lacy and Dewan arrange their selection of titles in chapters according to genres that include survival, animals, fantasy, historical, myth, everyday life, science fiction, and toy/games. And, within each chapter, books are arranged in categories that correspond to readers' needs and motivations for reading. This innovative latter feature gives readers' advisors, teachers, and parents an extra way to narrow down books to those most likely to connect with the individual child.

In the Preface of this book, Meagan Lacy invites us to think about the impact of the first book that we really, really loved. In her case, it was Roald Dahl's *Matilda* that her nine-year-old self heard read aloud by a teacher. This story of inaugural reading highlights some key elements in the making of readers. There is the role of the mentoring adult—whether family member, teacher, or librarian—who reads aloud for no other reason than for the joy of the shared experience itself. Then there is the way in which this particular book about a feisty young girl with a knack for thinking up and executing clever revenge plots keyed into the reader's own life situation, providing her with a helpful model of resilience and agency. This account of reading *Matilda* highlights three aspects of fostering reading that are emphasized within this book itself: access to sure-bet books likely to resonate with many readers; the reader's life situation that makes him or her susceptible to the appeal of particular kinds of stories; and a reading mentor, who introduces the child to the book that produces that eureka moment of discovery of the deep pleasures of reading.

We know that this transformational experience is not unusual. Noted readers' advisor Neal Wyatt once told me in an interview that in her case the magic book was Ellen Raskin's *The Westing Game*, which is included here in Chapter 12 on Toys/ Games as one of the three hundred children's novels selected. Neal Wyatt said: "What turned me into a reader was when I found a book that made me want to read another book just like it—that made me want to continue having those kinds of experiences. It was the process of finding books that made me deeply happy, of exploring the library and finding more books that did the same, and of knowing there were even more to find next time that helped me become a reader." Readers talk about "reading their way into reading." Having read one wonderful book, they want to start on another one right away, so as to repeat the pleasurable experience. *Connecting Children with Classics* provides readers' advisors, teachers, and parents with a multifaceted tool to increase the likelihood of helping a child make a powerful connection with a book that will speak to their interests and needs.

Why classics? Almost any book can perform the magic trick, if the reader connects with it strongly enough and loves it. But, as Lacy and Dewan point out, with classic children's books, there is a higher probability of engagement. That's *why* they are classics—because they address universal themes and make them new for each generation of readers and because they are rich enough to connect with readers in multiple ways using multiple hooks. This richness makes them great candidates for reading aloud with children, who will be able to enjoy stories more complex than they could read on their own. Quite often, books that children have heard read aloud become the first chapter books that they read independently. One reader told me that her earliest reading memory was her mother reading her *The Secret Garden*, night after night, in installments. She said, "It was the first book I read to myself once I learned to read when I was about seven. It was my favourite book . . . The first thing I did when I could read to myself was that I read all the books that had been read to me over the past several years, such as *The Secret Garden* and *Heidi* and *Alice in Wonderland*."

In any guide to reading, the more clues to the nature of the reading experience on offer, the better. Lacy and Dewan provide many pathways for readers' advisors and readers to identify a winning book, starting with the arrangement into chapters by genre and within chapters by reader-based appeals. The generous descriptive entry for each book lists appeals, adaptations, translations, read-alikes, and more. And finally the detailed back-of-book index allows for another way to access books with subjects and themes from "abandoned children" and "abolitionism" to "wrongly accused," "youngest sibling," and "Yukon territory." *Connecting Children with Classics* is like a Swiss Army officer's knife for readers' advisors: compact but equipped with the multiple tools needed for helping children become avid readers.

Catherine Sheldrick Ross, Professor Emerita<br>
The Faculty of Information and Media Studies<br>
The University of Western Ontario

# Preface

Think for a moment about the first book you ever really loved—that book you didn't want to end, that after you finished, you wanted to reread, the book that makes you wonder, had you never discovered it, whether you would be the same reader, or person, you are today.

For me, that book was Roald Dahl's *Matilda*. I was nine years old, and it was the summer before the fourth grade. I was in daycare, and my teacher read it to us during afternoon story time. I was immediately drawn to this gifted girl genius whose parents did not appreciate her, who, rather, only noticed her to criticize her. At the time, I did not understand all of the reasons I identified so much with her, but as an only child growing up in a single-parent household, I certainly understood her loneliness. After my teacher finished reading us the story, I persuaded my dad to buy me my own copy, and I read it again, on my own.

Before I discovered *Matilda*, however, I wasn't much of a reader. Though I always loved stories, I much preferred television, cartoons and sit-coms, to the printed text. During required "Silent Sustained Reading" periods in the classroom, I read the Baby Sitters Club "Little Sister" series. But outside of class, I never read for pleasure.

Growing up with busy, single parents in a relatively rural town, I wasn't exposed to many books, either. I never saw my mom or dad sit down with a novel, and there were few books in either of their homes. Although a public library was within a short, seven-minute drive, we rarely went.

But, after *Matilda*, I sought my own books. I took advantage of my elementary school's library, and I checked out everything available by Roald Dahl. Although I enjoyed *Charlie and the Chocolate Factory*, *James and the Giant Peach*, and *The Witches*, none of these characters touched me quite like Matilda.

Then, in middle school, without a literary-minded parent, teacher, or librarian to guide me, and not knowing whom to ask, I had difficulty finding other novels to read. At my middle school library, I chose titles somewhat randomly, based on subjects I was interested in or titles I recognized. *Little Women* had just been made into a film starring Winona Ryder and so I checked it out. I found it to be an instant snooze. Disappointed with my search, I switched to magazines and didn't discover novels again until I was in high school.

Today, I regret this lost time. I think of all of the books I could have read that might have changed my life the way *Matilda* had but that I did not know existed until now. To put it into Craigslist parlance: so many "missed connections!" While I can rattle off many titles that have affected me and my life as an adult, *Matilda* was all I had as a child, one of the most difficult times in my life, a time when I know I could have greatly benefited from the friends to be found in books.

But what made *Matilda* so special? Certainly, I was drawn to Dahl's writing style, his humor, and his inventiveness. Thanks to him, "scrumdiddlyumptious" is now in the *Oxford English Dictionary*. However, though I enjoyed his other stories, I never identified with them in quite the same way. Clearly, it wasn't just his writing style.

Genre, then. Yes, genre was definitely a part of it. I liked the fantasy elements, how Matilda was able to fool and outsmart her abusers with her extraordinary ability to move objects with her mind. But I wanted to possess her power, not her magic. I knew we lived in the "real world," and I wanted to learn how to live and survive in *it* and not make-believe ones. Because I did not understand all of the elements that characterize this genre, I'm sure if someone had asked me back then if I would be interested in trying another "fantasy" novel, I would have said, "No thanks." This world was challenging enough. I wasn't interested in adding made-up "fantastic" ones into the mix.

So there had to have been something more to this book-reader connection than the author and genre, but what? Luck? Yes, a little bit. Of course, there is no perfect equation, no algorithm, that will fully and consistently match a reader with his or her ideal book. But it takes away power from the reader to reduce such interactions down to luck. Surely, there has to be some way to speed up serendipitous discovery.

Then, at this thought I suddenly recalled Catherine Sheldrick Ross's study on avid readers,[1] which I had come across a few years earlier while writing and researching another book. After 194 interviews with avid book readers, Ross discovered that readers read books not only for their entertainment value but also for the information, or insight, they could offer into their own lives. As readers discussed significant books or books that changed their lives, Ross noticed several themes emerge. She then organized and coded these themes, identifying a total of seven ways readers use narratives for information. They read to: (1) awaken new perspectives, (2) find models for identity, (3) find reassurance, comfort, confirmation of self-worth, or strength, (4) find connection with others, (5) find courage to make a change, (6) find acceptance, and/or (7) obtain a disinterested understanding of the world.[2]

*Aha!* I thought. I was finally able to articulate why *Matilda* had been so significant to my nine-year-old self. In mirroring some of my own feelings and experiences, the story had offered me both "connection with others" and an "awareness of not being alone." Matilda was also a model I could draw upon for "comfort" and "strength" as she manages to prevail in her life despite almost no emotional support or nurturing. Matilda showed me that while I was not omnipotent, I did have some power and some choice. I could decide the kind of life I wanted to live, the kind of person I wanted to be . . . and I could pursue it on my own. Matilda helped me recognize that I had agency, that I was not helpless in the world. No wonder I wanted to keep reading! I was beginning to understand the power of words.

As we already know, reading is an acquired skill that takes *lots* of practice. We also know that the roots of literacy are grounded in childhood. The earlier we can help children make the kind of connection with a book like I made with *Matilda*, the more likely they will develop into readers and enjoy all of the benefits associated with literacy. Some of these benefits—academic and career success, creativity, and empathy—are also crucial to their economic and human flourishing.

Studies on children's reading have shown that negative attitudes toward reading correlated with weaker reading ability, with the least able readers being the least interested in reading.[3] Not surprisingly, as children grew older, these negative attitudes worsened. In other words, the longer a child goes without liking to read, the less likely he or she will ever become a reader, and the less likely he or she will obtain the levels of proficiency needed to handle today's complex literacy demands.

Adding to this challenge is our culture's growing dependency on digital technologies. Computers, tablets, and smartphones, while expanding access to ideas and to what can be thought, have also changed how and what we read. Their anti-linear structure, created by hyperlinks, popups, and other visual and noise distractions, makes online screen-reading difficult. These technologies encourage a kind of reading behavior characterized by skimming and information retrieval and actually *deter* the kind of focused reading novels, or any text that is lengthy and complex, require. Yet, again, this ability to follow a sustained line of thought is needed if one is to handle modern society's complex literacy demands. A lack of literacy skills, including reading literacy, writing literacy, and information literacy, means disenfranchisement. It means being shut out of jobs and opportunities, which in turn further creates and reinforces economic and class divisions. Thus, books remain superior to digital technologies at least in this respect: they help readers develop the skills and habits for focused, sustained reading and thinking.

It is, therefore, all the more important to teach young readers the value of books and the pleasures of reading. Children begin to discover the pleasures of books when they see their librarians, teachers, and parents reading themselves, modeling, and then when they begin to read stories to them. But children don't become readers themselves until they find a book that actually interests them. As one reading researcher points out, "Pleasure is the spur that motivates beginning readers to spend the thousands and thousands of hours reading that it takes to become a proficient reader."[4] But how can librarians, teachers, and parents help children effectively connect with books when their own knowledge of children's literature will necessarily be limited?

The book in your hands now responds to this challenge. While there are plenty of excellent reference works and comprehensive encyclopedias about children's literature (e.g., *Best Books for Children*, *The Cambridge Guide to Children's Books in English*), they are designed primarily for information retrieval, not necessarily to help readers find books they would want to read. This book is different in that it organizes children's classics by how they can appeal to readers. In other words, instead of organizing entries by subject headings (e.g., books about dogs) or by genre, the thematic categories derived from Catherine Sheldrick Ross's research are used to group books according to reading appeal. If these are the reasons booklovers read, then librarians, educators, and parents ought to be tapping into them when suggesting books for children who are developing as readers. In doing so, you might "speed up serendipity," that is, spark a child's interest in a book and a deeper connection with and appreciation for reading that may eventually grow into a lifelong reading habit.

*Meagan Lacy*

## Notes

1. Catherine Sheldrick Ross, "Finding Without Seeking: What Readers Say about the Role of Pleasure Reading," *Aplis* 13, no. 12 (2000): 72–80.
2. Ibid., 77–79.
3. Michael C. McKenna, Dennis J. Kear, and Randolph A. Ellsworth, "Children's Attitudes towards Reading: A National Survey," *Reading Research Quarterly* 30, no. 4 (1995): 934–56.
4. Catherine Ross, "The Company of Readers," in *Reading Matters: What the Research Reveals about Reading, Libraries, and Community*, eds. Catherine Sheldrick Ross, Lynne (E. F.) McKechnie, and Paulette M. Rothbauer (Westport, CT: Libraries Unlimited, 2006), 45.

# PART 1

# Foundations

CHAPTER ONE

# Matching Each Child with the Perfect Book: Intersections of Interest and Need

### A New Approach to Readers' Advisory

For those of you who are not librarians, "readers' advisory" (RA) service simply refers to the "the act of putting people together with the books they love."[1] RA can occur through direct means, that is, through a one-on-one interaction, or indirect means (e.g., book displays, promotional brochures, and online forums). Obviously, parents and teachers do this kind of work, too, not just librarians, but it is important to note that most public and school librarians receive some kind of training in RA, and most of the RA tools available to them are focused on the *book's* appeal elements, not reader-driven (reader-motivated) appeals, which is problematic since book appeals aren't necessarily what motivates a reader to want to read.

Examples of book appeal elements include the type of book (fiction or nonfiction), author, genre (e.g., fantasy or memoir), length, pacing, characterization, story line, setting, writing style, language, subject matter, and the author's treatment of the subject matter. Certainly, these elements are important to consider when readers' advisors are trying to match books with readers, and readers often have preferences regarding them. But book appeal elements do not take into account the reader's mood or the kind of reading experience the reader wants. For example, just because I like realistic and historical fiction (genres), does not mean I am in the *mood* to read, for example, *Little Women*. If I am feeling sad or lonely, I would rather read something that would make me feel connected with others and less alone. Under these circumstances, Peter Dickinson's *Eva*, a science fiction novel about a girl who becomes disfigured after a tragic accident, may better serve this need. Compared to *Little Women*, this novel reflects much more deeply on the situation of the outsider and themes of alienation. Recognizing some of my own experience in Eva's, I can identify with and relate to and, feel less alone.

Unfortunately, though, most RA tools (including indexes in print RA reference books such as Diana Tixier Herald's *Genreflecting* and Joyce Saricks' *The Readers' Advisory Guide to Genre Fiction* and also online databases like Novelist) are organized by book appeal elements and not by reader-driven appeals. Of course, this is partly because it is so much easier to organize literature by book appeal elements. Book appeal elements like genres or subjects can be quickly identified, divided up, and adapted for information retrieval. Organizing books this way does not require one to have read or even have that much familiarity with the stories themselves. But the limitations of these tools become obvious when one tries to search for books that will fulfill a certain curiosity, need, or motivation. As LIS scholar Keren Dali deftly points out, "[T]he process of readers' advisory is not identical to the process of retrieving information about fiction or nonfiction titles . . . while book characteristics are instrumental in facilitating such information retrieval, they are less effective for the process of advisory."[2] In other words, a better RA tool would take into account not only the books but also the *readers* themselves.

What is the reader seeking? What does he or she need, in terms of a reading experience? The aim of these questions is to determine more than just what the reader might like to read. Of course, you want your readers to *like* the books you suggest and hope they will. But readers do not necessarily have to like a book in order for it to be important or influential in their lives. For example, some readers, adults and children alike, read because of social pressure, that is, they choose to read a bestseller because everyone they know is reading it, and they want to read it because they want to feel socially included. But readers always read for some anticipated effect—instrumental (i.e., for the purposes of obtaining information about something or about how to do something), psychological (e.g., for pleasure, for relaxation, or for escape), or both—and matching them with relevant titles will obviously depend on what those expectations are. For this reason, we embrace Dali's more expansive definition of reading appeal "as 'the power to invoke interest in reading and set off an action of reading' (as opposed to an established definition of 'appeal as the elements/characteristics of books')."[3] By taking into account the individual's psychological state, emotional needs, and personal motivations for reading, readers' advisors are much better equipped to make suggestions and much more likely to choose titles that will actually invoke this interest and help our readers connect with books.

We suspect, also like Dali, that the reason RA fails is largely because the reader's mood has either been minimized or ignored completely.[4] When working with adults, the potential consequences of a failed interaction are minor. The reader might be disappointed, but having already established a reading habit, it is unlikely he or she will stop reading or seeking books. With children, though, the stakes are much higher. Research shows that the longer a child goes without having made a connection to a book, the less likely he or she is to develop into a reader and therefore to enjoy the benefits associated with reading proficiency.[5] These benefits are significant. For example, pleasure readers have been shown to perform better academically,[6] think more creatively,[7] and behave more empathetically.[8] Moreover, we live in the Information Age, in a world that is "permanently permeated by texts."[9] From news media, to advertisements, to job applications: the ability to navigate this complex information landscape depends totally on one's reading, writing, and information literacy skills. It is not enough to be able to read. One needs to know how to read *well*, and in order for children to develop this level of proficiency, they must read *a lot*. Hours and hours. But it isn't likely that children will invest this time and effort until they have discovered a book they love, a story they can connect to, and learned the pleasures to be found in thinking about and analyzing literature.

However, the glaring problem with a reader-centered approach to RA is that it requires making judgments about the type of reader to whom a story would most appeal, and such judgments are difficult, if not impossible, to make if one has not read the title himself or herself. And yet, it is virtually impossible for librarians, teachers, and parents to obtain enough knowledge of children's literature to be able to suggest titles in every kind of genre, for every kind of reader. Even the most devoted reader of children's literature would still never possess exhaustive knowledge. Given this challenge, it's no wonder why book appeal has dominated the RA literature. Categorizing titles by genre or subject requires a lot less interpretative effort.

Our guide addresses this problem. We have organized children's literature titles in terms of not only book appeal elements but also reader appeal elements, that is, in terms of Catherine Sheldrick Ross's categories. Again, these categories are derived directly from her research on avid readers.

Throughout nearly 200 interviews, Ross discovered that avid readers read in order to find:

(1) new perspectives;
(2) models for identity;
(3) reassurance, comfort, confirmation of self-worth, or strength;
(4) connection with others or awareness of not being alone;
(5) courage to make a change;
(6) acceptance; and/or
(7) a disinterested understanding of the world.[10]

So, in reading, interpreting, and categorizing novels by reader motivations, we offer librarians, teachers, and parents a means of inspiring children's interest in books even when your own background in children's literature is limited or you have not read the titles yourself. This guide helps you identify titles that you can suggest or read to children that are more likely to satisfy their *needs* and *mood*. For a reader to connect to a book, both of these conditions must be met. As Ross explains, the impact of a book depends on the life experiences that the reader brings to it.[11] This, of course, accounts for how a book can completely captivate one reader and immediately repel another. It also underscores the importance of taking the time to learn about the reader. The more you know about his or her personality, needs, preferences, and mood, the more able you are to translate these details into relevant appeal factors and read or suggest books to children that are more likely to gratify and make a lasting, positive impact on their development as readers.

## Why *Reading* Appeal

It's important to note that this book is not intended to diminish the role of book-related appeals. They are not only important but also necessary factors to consider in reading decision making. Reading appeal is not in competition with book-related appeals. Rather, as Dali puts it, it is a "two-dimensional concept—a function of both book related and reader-driven appeal elements."[12] These factors are intertwined and will simultaneously guide one's decision to read or not to read a book. For example, I might choose to read Karen Cushmen's *The Midwife's Apprentice* because I love historical fiction and character-driven novels (book-related appeal elements) and also because it is the only book that happens to be in my tote bag when I am bored and waiting for the subway to arrive (a reader-driven appeal). Then again, I might choose to read it because I liked the blurb on the back cover (another book-related appeal element), and I thought I would *connect* with the main character because I was also going through a challenging time in my own life and feeling alone (a reader-driven appeal). I may not be consciously aware of all of the factors that are informing my decision, but they are nonetheless there.

Of course, in the process of reading, a book may surprise a reader, for good or for bad, and play a very different role from the one anticipated. It may be that I read *The Midwife's Apprentice* for the former reason (because I was bored and in need of distraction) but discovered (serendipitously!) that it also gave me comfort because I was feeling sad and lonely at that particular moment in my life. In this way, I was matched with just the right book, at just the right time. Making this emotional connection is part of what made reading it such a pleasure. It is our belief that when children also make this kind of connection, they begin to discover the pleasures of literature, and for this reason, it is one of the first and most important steps in their becoming readers.

In her research, Catherine Sheldrick Ross defines a comprehensive model for the process of choosing books for pleasure, which is based on five related elements that take into account both book- and reader-related appeals. The elements are:

(1) the reading experience wanted by the reader (reader-driven appeal),
(2) alerting sources the reader uses (e.g., recommendations from friends, books that have become movies, both of which are also types of reader-driven appeals),
(3) elements in a book (book appeals such as genre, length, writing style, etc.),
(4) clues on the book itself (book appeals such as cover art, prizes, and summary blurbs), and
(5) costs to the reader in getting access to a particular book (i.e., the amount of effort required to obtain a copy, a reader-driven appeal).[13]

Although this model is based upon interviews with adult readers rather than child readers, it remains relevant since her interviewees were all committed readers, many of whom discovered their love for reading and began to develop their leisure reading habit as children. In other words, they offer a lot of insights into the kinds of reading experiences that the average or reluctant reader may lack and need before he or she can find reading pleasurable and an activity worth pursuing. It takes many experiences and many personal connections before readers can cross the threshold from perceiving reading as work, as a means to an end, to reading as pleasure, as an end in itself.

With respect to her model, Ross concluded that the reader's *mood* is the "bedrock for choice."[14] In other words, desired reading experience is the main determining factor for committed readers when they are making decisions about what to read. Based on these observations, it is reasonable to infer that developing readers, which all children are, also need to experience stories that suit *their* mood in order to find reading interesting and worth pursuing. To put it another way, if the primary means children encounter books is in school (as assigned reading) or as prescribed by some other adult in their lives, then it is safe to say they have had few opportunities to encounter stories that speak to them personally, and it is no wonder that so many children think that they do not like reading or do not take to a reading habit.

Besides needing to make personal connections to their reading, this research also suggests that children need autonomy, freedom to make choices about their reading. Reading researcher Stephen Krashen, author of *The Power of Reading*, also explains that "free voluntary reading" (FVR), that is, "reading because you want to," is critical to one's reading development as it lays down the groundwork needed in order for higher levels of proficiency to be achieved.[15] So, one of the best and easiest ways librarians, teachers, and parents can help children's reading development is by allowing them and helping them to make their own choices.

But even after accepting that children are more inclined to read when they are allowed to choose titles for themselves and that this freedom is key to their discovering the inherent pleasure in reading, there still remains the challenge of helping them identify potential matches in the first place. Obviously, it's not helpful to tell children they can choose when they have no idea what they are choosing *from*. Letting them roam freely and browse the library stacks, although a worthy activity, won't offer them much help in the way of sifting through all of the possibilities. It is at this point that your role as a librarian, teacher, or parent can become instrumental. Since librarians and teachers often have intimate knowledge of the lives of the children they serve, and parents definitely do, you can use this information and other details you learn to assess what the child might be in the mood for and then use this guide to help them find potential titles.

## How to Use a Reader-Centered Approach

Of course, assessing a reader's mood, whether the reader is an adult or a child, is easier said than done. As a parent, teacher, or librarian, you might know if your child (or student, or patron) is feeling anxious about his or her first day of school, or struggling with a death in the family, or grieving over his or her parents' divorce. This is helpful information that can certainly give insight into their mood. But these details are not sufficient in themselves. For example, just because a child's parents are getting divorced does not mean he or she wants to read a book about another child encountering or coping with divorced parents. Children's librarian Maeve Knoth observes this problem in her *Hornbook* editorial, "What Ails Bibliotherapy?" She explains how often parents and teachers come to her asking for book recommendations that exactly mirror their children's lives or emotional experience. However well intentioned, the problem with this approach is that it is too literal. It makes the false assumption that in order for a child to connect to a book, the story must closely reflect his or her life. But actually, it is just as possible that such reading may make him or her feel *worse*. As Knoth explains, such reading may be "*too* close" to the situation.[16] Or, as one of Ross's interviewees puts it, "Sometimes you have to be ready for a book. There are some books it's not your time to read, or it's not their time be read by you."[17] Maybe the child whose parents are divorcing is feeling lonely and insecure, and what they really crave, what they are in *the mood* for, is a story that gives them strength and reinforces their own sense of agency. In other words, the book need not have anything to do with divorce. Consider the characters and books to which you yourself have made personal connections. How many of them resemble you or your actual life? If the goal were merely to provide the child with information, then this literal approach would be adequate. But if your goal is to "invoke" children's interest in reading and "set off the action" of reading, then we as librarians, teachers, and parents would all do better to ask children what they might like rather than *presume* we know better than them.

More concretely, a reader-centered approach means that you talk less and listen more. By honoring and taking into consideration the individual child's personality, interests, and life circumstances, you can better feel out his or her book-related preferences as well as better interpret his or her present mood or state of mind. Ask open-ended questions that prompt the reader to talk more. For example, "Tell me about a story (a book, a movie, a TV show) that you enjoyed . . . Tell me what you enjoyed or liked about it . . ." Complete guidance on how to conduct an RA interview is beyond the scope of this book, but Keren Dali's recent article, "Hearing Stories, Not Keywords: Teaching Contextual Readers' Advisory,"[18] provides an excellent framework as well as practical suggestions for this approach. In this article, she stresses that "no single question or limited set of questions should be prescriptive," but she did discover that asking readers how they came across the last book they liked almost always succeeded in initiating a conversation. The vagueness of this question helps prompt respondents to interpret it in their own way and "impose their own system of relevancy on a fuzzy possibility."[19] Since most children are new to reading and therefore may not have "a last book they liked," it may be more fruitful to ask instead about a "story" they liked and broaden the question to include other narrative-based media such as comics, television, and film.

Once you have started the conversation, encourage the reader to do most of the talking by actively listening and resisting the urge to interrupt. If the child is shy or reluctant to speak, encouraging this kind of dialogue can be difficult. In such cases, readers' advisors may want to draw upon Dali's other strategies for supporting the reader. Although she was researching adult readers, these strategies still apply. They include:

> smiling, avoiding an annoyed or hurried facial expression during the pauses, and encouraging nodding; a frank verbal confirmation that the readers' advisor really does not wish to steer the reader in a certain direction; a verbal expression of confidence in the reader's ability to deliver the best description and story; reassurance that the reader cannot give wrong answers or talk beyond the point; a verbal expression of acceptance of everything that the reader says as valid and relevant; and so on.[20]

By letting the reader talk, you can listen for clues that reveal their needs (book-related appeal elements) and mood (reader-driven appeal elements). A few follow-up questions may be necessary, but keep them to a minimum so as not to slide into asking leading questions that divert attention away from the reader. Remember, your goal as a readers' advisor is not to be a mind reader but to help your readers articulate their own thinking about their own needs and preferences. The more you can support and reassure your readers that their interests and needs are valid, the more likely they are to gain the confidence and ability to recognize and express them on their own.

Applying Ross's "What Mood Am I In?" test can help you further reflect on your knowledge about the reader and better gauge the kind of reading experience he or she might be looking for. Consider whether the child would prefer a story that is:

- familiar or novel,
- safe or risky,
- easy or challenging, or
- upbeat and positive or hard-hitting, ironic, or critical.

*Matching Each Child with the Perfect Book*

Also, ask yourself:

- Does the reader want to be reassured/stimulated/frightened/amazed?
- Does the reader want his/her values confirmed, or does he or she want to be challenged by an uncomfortable but stimulating new perspective?[21]

With this information, you can identify reader-driven appeals (defined more fully in the next section) and book-related appeals that are the most relevant and appropriate, and then you can use this guide to find potential matches. For example, a child who craves familiarity will most likely be drawn to stories that provide "reassurance, comfort, confirmation of self-worth, [and/or] strength," while a child who wants something novel would be better matched with stories that provide new "models for identity" or "a disinterested understanding of the world." A child who seems willing to have his or her views challenged will likely match well with stories that provide "awakening," while the child who wants his or her values confirmed would be better paired with stories that provide "reassurance" or "connection with others." Considering both the reading experience wanted and the child's needs and preferences should help you hone in on potential titles. For example, if the child seeking connection with others would also like something "easy" and "upbeat," you might suggest Michael Bond's *Paddington Bear* instead of Jack London's *White Fang*.

Of course, to glean even a basic understanding of the reader, one needs time. Fortunately, parents and teachers have the advantage of spending a lot of time with their children and students and so are probably able to answer a lot of these questions (about the child's interests, life circumstances, etc.) already. Librarians, on the other hand, do not usually have this luxury. In addition, they are more frequently approached by a teacher, parent, or parent and child rather than by the child alone, by himself or herself. Obviously, under these circumstances, the children's actual needs and interests may be easily eclipsed and so limit the librarian's ability to provide a reader-centered approach. But even in the ideal situation when the librarian is speaking to a child one-on-one, the child may still struggle to articulate his or her needs or interests, or the librarian may not have the time to devote to adequately find out.

For librarians facing such limitations, we offer a few suggestions to help you preserve a more reader-centered approach. First, in the instance of a parent-child interaction, try as much as possible to direct your questions to the child. In other words, convey to both the child and the parent that you are primarily interested in the reading experience that *the child* wants. If the child is not available to speak, ask the parent or teacher the questions you would ask if he or she were. In other words, model reader-centered questions to encourage them to think and speak from their child's perspective. Another easy solution, and perhaps the most effective, especially given the importance of FVR, is to place a copy of this guide on a shelf that is easy for both parents *and* children to see and access. Obviously, no one knows better than the readers themselves what titles would interest them. While this guide would not be helpful or appropriate for very young children, older and middle-grade children could easily learn how to use this guide to browse and search for titles on their own. In introducing them to systems of knowledge organization, it would also offer children the added benefit of teaching them information retrieval, helping them practice and develop information literacy skills so that they can gain confidence and ability to continue to choosing books for themselves throughout their lifetime.

## Reader-Driven Appeals

The problem with categorizing books in any way, whether by book appeals or by reader-driven appeals, is that categorization, by definition, is reductive. In fact, most of the titles listed in this book have more than one, and some possess virtually *all* of these reader-driven appeals. In addition, reader appeals are necessarily going to vary reader by reader. While I found in *Matilda* "reassurance, confirmation of self-worth, and strength," another reader may find "connection with others/awareness of not being alone." It is impossible to know *exactly* what in a story will resonate with each and every reader.

However, it is not impossible to make some educated predictions. For every title in this guide, we assessed which reader appeals stood out the most and then tried to imagine the kind of reader who would most benefit from it. This process wasn't always clear and straightforward. Again, most novels have several kinds of readers. For example, *The Secret Garden* could provide one reader with a "connection with others/awareness of not being alone" as Mary, who has become suddenly orphaned, exists as an outsider, completely dependent on her new guardian, a distant relative, but with no clear status within his residence at Misselthwaite Manor. Then again, another reader might find in it "reassurance, confirmation of self-worth, and strength" as Mary demonstrates perseverance despite her grief and neglect. Still other readers might find Mary herself a "model for identity," as she finds agency (by escaping to and cultivating her garden) in the face of these difficult life circumstances.

A great novel has *many* potential readers—that's part of what makes it so great, part of what makes it, as the next chapter explains, a *classic*.

Categorizing these titles often results in oversimplification, or diminished nuance. Therefore, a secondary reader appeal is included in each annotation. This addition will hopefully help expand each novel's audience and also help librarians, teachers, and parents to identify additional titles to read or recommend to children.

Nonetheless, to provide helpful guidance to readers, some judgment calls were needed. You may disagree with some of them. But keep in mind that assigning these categories is not a precise science. Rather, it requires weighing textual evidence with that nebulous, hard-to-define feeling called intuition. Always when making these judgments, we tried to answer the question, *Which reader is this book most suited to? What need does it fill best?*

You, the librarian, teacher, or parent, will obviously know your readers better than we do! You can better anticipate how a book might appeal to them, what they might hook into. But most librarians, teachers, counselors, and parents do not have an endless reserve of knowledge about children's books. They can only know and be familiar with so much, and that is why we created this tool. It's meant to help you connect children with books, even if you have not read the books yourself. Each annotation provides enough summary and analysis that you could quickly gauge how well it might match a particular child's mood.

As you learn more about your readers—what they are curious about, what their motivations are for reading, what their mood is, and what their personal needs and social situation are—you can better determine which reader appeal elements might be relevant. In this section, each of Ross's categories are examined. For further definition, think about books you have read (children or adult) that have affected you in each of these ways. Doing so will provide a frame of reference that will help you better recognize these needs in others so you can determine which reader appeal elements might apply.

### Awakening/New Perspective/Enlargement of Possibilities

Books that "awaken" expand the reader's perception or outlook on life. Perhaps the reader is feeling helpless, scared, stubborn, or resistant to change. These books provide access to alternative viewpoints, prompting them to examine *how* they are seeing and to consider the potential limitations of that point of view. They provoke questions about perspectives they might have ignored or might not have considered at all.

Characters in these stories tend to be nonconformists. Relative to the reader, they deviate in some way from social or cultural norms. For example, Astrid Lindgren's Pippi Longstocking is an ultra-independent, super creative, freethinking nine-year-old girl who lives alone and doesn't go to school. Inventing the term, "Thing-Finder," Pippi goes about life actively imagining new uses for ordinary objects or new purposes for junk. A rusty, old tin becomes a jar without cookies or something to put over her head so she can "pretend its midnight." A "Thing-Finder," in other words, is someone who can think flexibly, shift perspective, and recognize multiple possibilities. A "Thing-Finder" is someone who is able to exercise her autonomy even within limited spaces. For readers who are too dependent on others, or risk adverse, or overly rule regimented, Pippi can challenge their points of view and also offer alternative ways of thinking. As is the case in this book, the possibilities do not have to be real or realistic. They simply have to offer readers another lens. By expanding their frame of reference, and by helping them to think imaginatively, these books also help readers understand and empathize with others, strengthen and nourish their curiosity, and build resiliency.

### Models for Identity

"Models for identity" refer to stories that feature protagonists who model agency and perseverance in the face of difficult situations. The term "model" does not necessarily mean "moral" or "virtuous"; this category is not meant to prescribe a certain kind of child or child behavior. Rather, the characters in these stories may be flawed and complex but nonetheless remain "models for identity" because they possess some trait or excellence that readers may internalize for their own growth or preservation of self. These characters are "models" in that they usually leave readers feeling, as one of Ross's interviewees puts it, that the book is "secretly about [them]."[22]

Finding the right "model," again, depends on the child. If he is feeling powerless, or helpless, he may find a model in James in *James and the Giant Peach* as James's life circumstances force him to draw upon his strengths and become a leader. If the child lacks confidence or seems insecure in her own ideas, then Avi's Poppy may serve as a model of independent thinking and self-assurance as she questions authority figures rather than blindly accepting what she has been told. Though James and Poppy are very different from each other, they both demonstrate individual agency and serve as reminders to readers that they also have the ability to choose and shape their own lives.

### Reassurance, Comfort, Confirmation of Self-Worth, and Strength

Stories that provide "reassurance, comfort, confirmation of self-worth, and/or strength" tend to be stories about bullying, abuse, or neglect.

The protagonists in these stories are unrecognized for their talents and therefore must achieve a sense of self-worth on their own, often with very little external support or influence. Think J. K. Rowling's *Harry Potter and the Sorcerer's Stone* and Roald Dahl's *Matilda*. In both of these stories, the characters manage to maintain a sense of self-worth in the face of constant criticism and degradation from others.

In this way, the protagonists in these stories often provide "Models for Identity" as well, though not always. The main distinction is that these stories primarily offer *hope* that readers can persevere over adversity. They suggest the possibility, but they do not necessarily provide a concrete means of taking action as "Models for Identity" do. For example, the "trouble twins" in Sharon Creech's *Ruby Holler*, Florida and Dallas, having spent most of their lives in and out of foster care, spend most of the novel resisting and trying to run away from their new foster parents, Tiller and Sairy. After years and years of neglect, the twins doubt their foster parents' motives. Tiller and Sairy are the twins' first experience of nurturing love, and only because Tiller and Sairy remain committed, unwavering in their demonstrations, do the twins begin to change, trust, receive their love, and reciprocate it. In this way, the story may reassure readers who feel neglected or unwanted as it might help them recognize that they are worthy and deserving of love and attention, too.

### Connection with Others/Awareness of Not Being Alone

Stories that provide connection with others closely mirror the reader's feelings of rejection, loneliness, or isolation. Feeling like an outsider and struggling to belong are common elements to these stories. Paradoxically, in reflecting the readers' feelings of loneliness or alienation, these stories also serve as reminders that they are not alone. *Everyone* feels like an outsider at some point in his or her life.

For example, Jerusha "Judy" Abbott, in Jean Webster's *Daddy-Long-Legs*, is a teenaged orphan who lucks out when a mysterious benefactor gives her a full scholarship to college. Composed as a collection of letters to her donor, this novel captures Judy's feelings of alienation and inadequacy as she is plunged into the new and unfamiliar world of privilege. Unable to match her classmates' level of education, wealth, or experiences, she works doubly hard to compensate and "catch up" with them. Lacking the support of parents or family, she finds resolve on her own, almost entirely within herself. In this way, she provides both "connection with others" and models strength. After reading her story, one is likely to not only feel less alone but also inspired by her determination and resolve.

## Courage to Make a Change

In these stories, the protagonist faces some kind of personal struggle or moral dilemma that he or she must overcome. Ultimately, these characters "do the right thing" or, in the case of a tragic dilemma, make the best choice they possibly can. But they are heroes not so much because they "do the right thing" as because they do the right thing *despite internal resistance*. It is *difficult* for them to do the right thing. Thus, they model the humility that character building requires and inspire readers to also find the "courage to make a change." Admitting faults or flaws is hard for everyone, not to mention changing them. In reflecting this challenge, these characters help readers recognize that while virtue is difficult, it is not impossible to obtain. They always have a choice. As one of Ross's interviewees explains how she relates to these types of books, "I look to see if there is something about my life or somebody else's that I can pull out of it,"[23] that "something" being courage.

For example, when Charlotte Doyle, the daughter of a noble English family in Avi's *The True Confessions of Charlotte Doyle*, first boards the *Seahawk* to sail to the United States, readers find her blindly following the conventions of her class. Her privilege is betrayed in the entitled way she acts and also in the way she treats the crew, who she perceives as being beneath her. However, when she witnesses the cruelty and violence of Captain Jaggery, a supposed gentleman, she is forced to examine her classist assumptions. She begins to doubt the social hierarchy and, as she colludes with the crew to overthrow the captain, eventually rejects it. As a result, she grows. She discovers her own agency. She learns to think for herself and to choose her own destiny. In this way, readers can see that while choosing virtue is difficult, it is also worthwhile as it is key to one's ability to flourish and fully realize themselves.

## Acceptance

When life is not going according to plan, and one is powerless to change it (as children, by nature of being dependents, often are), then a story that illustrates acceptance may be the best match for this reader. William Steig's *Abel's Island* is a good example. After a violent storm, Abel, a mouse, becomes stranded on an island far away from his beloved wife, Amanda. As he tries to figure out a way to return home, he is forced to become more resourceful and more self-reliant than his previous life of privilege required of him. This long period of loneliness also prompts him to reflect on himself and reassess his priorities. Though this transformation is meaningful and important, in the end, it is not Abel's ingenuity that saves him but luck.

Thus, Abel demonstrates how not all situations can be changed or helped through effort. Being neither all-knowing nor all-powerful, there is only so much human beings can do, and sometimes there is nothing. Sometimes, one must simply accept this reality and endure. Just acknowledging this truth can provide some comfort.

## Disinterested Understanding of the World

When the readers want to be transported, moved into a world that is different or outside of themselves, then they might be looking for books that provide a "disinterested understanding of the world." Readers value these books for the escape they provide, the way they can help them forget themselves and redirect their attention on someone or someplace else.

For example, Anna Sewell's *Black Beauty*, written as an autobiography of a horse, allows readers to perceive the world, its humanity and cruelty, from the perspective of an animal. In enlarging the readers' perspective, these books may offer "awakening" as well. The main distinction is that books in the "awakening" category provide readers with additional lenses with which to perceive their world, while books in this category carry them *out* of their present, away from their culture or current moment in history. As a result, they stretch readers' empathetic imaginations and thus help deepen their understanding of their own world.

Historical novels are good examples, since by definition they depict another time and place. Think Mildred Taylor's *Roar of Thunder Hear My Cry*, which portrays the South's Jim Crow era from the point of view of a young, African American girl, or Lois Lowry's *Number the Stars*, which gives insight into what it would be like to grow up under authoritarian, Nazi rule. Such perspectives add dimension to historical events, make them "come to life" in ways that cannot be captured in textbooks.

## How to Use This Book

As mentioned earlier in this chapter, reader-driven appeal elements should be considered in addition to, and not in lieu of, book appeal elements. Genre, setting, pacing, and other book appeals frequently matter to readers, and taking them into account will strengthen one's ability to match readers with the right book. But the goal of librarians, teachers, and parents is usually to expand children's worlds and their ways of seeing and not to merely indulge their reading preferences and confirm preexisting worldviews. Helping readers discover and love books or genres that they would not have otherwise discovered is part of the pleasure and satisfaction of doing RA, and for this reason it is all the more important that readers' advisors take readers into deeper consideration. Since their personality, private experiences, and social situation all frame their reasons for reading, an awareness of them can help readers' advisors identify other possible entry points in which to introduce new genres, authors, or characters to their readers.

As mentioned previously, "reading appeal" is a two-dimensional concept, a function of both book-related and reader-driven appeal elements. Readers' advisors need to consider both of these factors if they want to invoke the reader's interest in reading and set off the action of reading. This book supports a reading appeal approach to RA by referencing *both* book appeal and reader-driven appeal elements. Since genre is one of the most important book appeal elements, and a helpful means of providing information retrieval, chapters are divided first by genre: Adventure, Animal, Fantasy, Historical, Myths and Legends, Everyday Life, Science Fiction, and Toys. Then, within each genre, titles are categorized by Catherine Sheldrick Ross's reader-driven appeals ("Awakening," "Connection with Others," and so on).

Each annotation is headed with the author's name and necrology, the title of the book, the date of its original publication, and a citation to a recommended edition. In many cases, there is only one edition in print, but for those that have multiple imprints and editions, we recommended editions that we judged offered the best features (e.g., prefaces, helpful appendices, and/or illustrations). In addition, any novels that are out of copyright and therefore freely available in the public domain (e.g., Frances Hodgson Burnett's *The Secret Garden* and Edith Nesbit's *The Railway Children*) will have the abbreviation "PD" listed at the end of the citation. Many classic works of children's literature that are in the public domain can be found online through digital collections such as The Hathi Trust and Project Gutenberg.

The citation is followed by the annotation, which consists of two parts: a summary of the book and a critical evaluation. The summaries are written as "book talks," intended to give enough information to entice a reader's interest without spoiling the story. The analysis, which, it should be noted, often does give away the ending is intended to help you understand how the title fits the reader-driven appeal to which it has been categorized and possibly any other ways it might appeal to readers.

The annotation concludes with a list of reader-driven and book appeal elements. Each field is intended to help the user quickly determine the reading appeal of a particular book for a particular reader. Each of these fields is described in more detail below.

### "For Those Who Also Seek"

This phrase refers to alternative or secondary reader-driven appeals. As mentioned earlier, most titles have more than one reader-driven appeal element, sometimes several. But we only included one since we knew that, in order to provide helpful guidance, we needed to be discerning.

### "For Those Drawn To"

This phrase refers to key book-related appeal elements. More precisely, we borrow from Nancy Pearl's "four experiential elements,"[24] identifying books with strong stories, characters, settings, and/or language. In other words, some readers want page-turners, that is, fast-paced, action-packed plots. These readers are looking for a strong narrative, or *story*. Others may prefer interesting and/or complex *characters* (such as Grandma Dowdel, the iconoclast in A Long Way from Chicago) or unique *settings* that will transport them to other dimensions (such as the imaginary universe in A Wrinkle in Time). Still others may require creative and skillful use of *language*, for instance, the poetry and nonsense in Roald Dahl's *Charlie and the Chocolate Factory*.

While good books, particularly classics, tend to have *all* of these elements, we tried to narrow and select the categories for which they are the most outstanding. To avoid confusion, no more than two book-related appeal elements are given per title.

### Themes/Subjects

While other book appeals were assigned with great selectivity, the subjects and themes listed in this field are an exception. Because headings can help capture elements of the story that cannot be fully detailed in the annotations, we included any and all that might apply. This field may be useful when you are trying to identify books on a particular subject (death) or theme (good and evil). These subjects and themes are fully indexed in the subject index.

Please keep in mind that these subject headings are not applied with the same level of specificity as the Library of Congress subject headings. Rather, they have been assigned more like online tags. These tags help identify the many possible doorways that could lead one into a particular book. For example, *The Witches* by Roald Dahl is not *about* grandmothers, but "grandmothers" is listed as a subject because a grandmother plays a significant role in the story. Other stories that prominently feature a grandmother are also given this heading.

### Reading Interest Level

This category was one of the trickiest, mostly because narrowing a book's audience to a certain age group invites problems. After all, a good book is a good book regardless of who its intended audience is. If an eighth grader wants to read *Charlotte's Web*, why should you discourage them? On the other hand, some content is going to be too mature, or advanced, for younger audiences, and some content is going to be too simple for more mature audiences. As a compromise, instead of age, grade levels K–8 have been assigned. Since this is a book about connecting *children* with the classics, the eighth grade was chosen somewhat arbitrarily as the cut-off, even though childhood doesn't automatically end then and even though many of these books would be of interest to young adult and adult readers as well.

Finally, "reading interest level" is meant to capture audiences who may be interested in the story. Therefore, this term does not necessarily designate books that would be at an appropriate reading level for the reader. Rather, this field was used to identify the range of children who might be drawn into the story whether they read it themselves or had it read to them. For example, a second grader might enjoy reading and discussing *The Yearling* with a parent, although the language would be too archaic and complex for most second graders to read and enjoy on their own.

### Curricular Tie-Ins

Recognizing the growing movement toward interdisciplinarity in K–8 schools, lessons and activities are suggested to provide instructors opportunities to use these titles to complement their curriculum and enhance student learning. For example, reading Roald Dahl's *George's Marvelous Medicine* might be a great way for a fourth-grade teacher to segue into a mathematics unit on fractions and proportions. Assigning Mildred Taylor's *Role of Thunder, Hear My Cry* would enhance studies about African American history and the post–Civil War era in the American South. In this field, you'll find ideas to stimulate thinking and ways of approaching interdisciplinary instruction.

### Adaptations and Alternate Formats

There are many ways to enter a story. Some prefer to listen to a story rather than to read it. Some might like to compare the movie version of a novel to the text version. You'll find important adaptations and alternative formats noted for each title, so you can provide children with as many entry points into a story as possible. Note that this list is not comprehensive.

Rather, the focus is on adaptations that we thought would generate the most interest.

## Translations

In light of growing immigrant populations in the United States and Canada, translated Spanish and French titles are cited whenever applicable. Besides the fact that developing and strengthening reading literacy skills in one's native language places English language learners at an advantage, reading classics in translation can also help immigrant children learn more about Anglo-American culture. Native English speakers who are trying to learn Spanish or French may also find this information helpful. Depending on the populations they serve, public libraries may or may not have these translated titles, but they can easily been found for purchase online.

## Read-Alikes

Read-alikes are books that in some way resemble the title being described in the annotation. If the reader says he or she wants to read another story just like it, then this field is useful for quickly finding suggestions that are based primarily on book appeal elements (genre, author, etc.).

## Conclusion

This guide is intended to further enhance RA service by recognizing and prioritizing the reader's mood. Doing so provides a more holistic approach to RA and is more likely to lead to recommendations that will help children connect to their reading on an emotional level. This emotional connection helps children realize the pleasures of reading, which is essential to their development as lifelong readers.

On a personal note, I can say that while I am grateful to Roald Dahl's *Matilda* for helping shape me into the reader I am today, I also regret that I missed out on L. M. Montgomery's *Emily of New Moon*, Jean Webster's *Daddy-Long-Legs*, and Dodie Smith's *I Capture the Castle* and that I was already an adult when Kate DiCamillo's *Because of Winn-Dixie* and Sherman Alexie's *The Absolutely True Diary of a Part-Time Indian* were published. While I can appreciate and love these novels now, I *needed* them then. We hope this tool will help young readers by giving them more options and speed up serendipitous discovery so that they do not sit wanting for years, like I did, for the next great book.

## Notes

1. Diana Tixier Herald, *Genreflecting* (blog), as quoted by Jessica Moyer, "Readers' Advisory: The Most Important Class for New Librarians," *NMRT Footnotes* 36, no. 2 (2006), accessed July 13, 2017, http://www.ala.org/nmrt/news/footnotes/november2006ab/readersadvisorymostimp06.
2. Keren Dali, "From Book Appeal to Reading Appeal: Redefining the Concept of Appeal in Readers' Advisory," *Library Quarterly* 84, no. 1 (2014): 24.
3. Ibid.
4. Keren Dali, "Hearing Stories, Not Keywords: Teaching Contextual Readers' Advisory," *Reference Services Review* 41, no. 3 (2013): 481.
5. Catherine Sheldrick Ross, Lynn E. F. McKehnie, and Paulette M. Rothbauer, *Reading Matters: What the Research Reveals about Reading, Libraries, and Community* (Westport, CT: Libraries Unlimited, 2006), 45.
6. Jude D. Gallik, "Do They Read for Pleasure? Recreational Reading Habits of College Students," *Journal of Adolescent & Adult Literacy* 42, no. 6 (1999): 484.
7. Kathryn E. Kelly and Lee B. Kneipp, "Reading for Pleasure and Creativity among College Students," *College Student Journal* 43, no. 4 (2009): 1137–1144.
8. David Comer Kidd and Manuele Castano, "Reading Literary Fiction Improves Theory of Mind," *Science* 342 (2013): 377–380.
9. Ross, McKehnie, and Rothbauer, *Reading Matters*, 3.
10. Catherine Sheldrick Ross, "Finding Without Seeking: The Information Encounter in the Context of Reading for Pleasure," *Information Processing & Management* 35, no. 6 (1999): 793–795.
11. Catherine Sheldrick Ross, "Finding Without Seeking: What Readers Say about the Role of Pleasure Reading as a Source of Information," *Australasian Public Libraries and Information Services* 13, no. 2 (2000): 80.
12. Dali, "From Book Appeal to Reading Appeal," 41.
13. Catherine Sheldrick Ross, "Making Choices," *Acquisitions Librarian* 13, no. 25 (February 2001): 16–19.
14. Ibid., 115.
15. Stephen D. Krashen, *The Power of Reading* (Westport, CT: Libraries Unlimited, 2004), x.
16. Maeve Visser Knoth, "What Ails Bibliotherapy," *Horn Book* 82, no. 3 (2006): 275.
17. Ross, "Making Choices," 114.
18. Dali, "Hearing Stories, Not Keywords," 474–502.
19. Tom Wengraf, *Qualitative Research Interviewing*, as quoted by Dali, "Hearing Stories," 496.
20. Ibid., 494.
21. Ross, "Making Choices," 17.
22. Ross, "Finding without Seeking: The Information Encounter in the Context of Reading for Pleasure," 793.

23. Ibid., 794.

24. Nancy Pearl, "Check It Out with Nancy Pearl: Finding That Next Good Book," *Publishers Weekly* (blog), accessed March 16, 2012, http://www.publishersweekly.com/pw/by-topic/columns-and-blogs/nancy-pearl/article/51109-check-it-out-with-nancy-pearl-finding-that-next-good-book.html.

CHAPTER TWO

# Why Focus on the Classics?

This book is not intended as merely a list of classic works of literature for children. Such a list might be useful for reference or for developing library collections, but it wouldn't necessarily explain why anyone would want to read them. Instead, the goal is to excite readers and provide bridges to fulfilling reading experiences. The focus is on classics because they exemplify the pleasures of children's literature, and by helping children discover these pleasures, librarians, teachers, and parents can encourage a love of reading.

But what makes a classic *classic*? What does that word even mean, and why is it applied to works like *Peter Pan* and *Alice in Wonderland*, but not *Captain Underpants*? Are the classics better than other kinds of books? Are they the only books worth reading?

In this chapter, you'll find our definition of "classic" and an explanation of why classic literature is worthy of promotion. However, in emphasizing the classics, we do not intend to discourage readers from reading other kinds of books. Far from it! Based on both what the research says and our own personal experience as readers, it is evident that all reading is good reading. Choice, in fact, is crucial. As Stephen Krashen, author of *The Power of Reading*, explains, free voluntary reading, that is, "reading because you want to,"[1] plays a fundamental role in one's development as a reader. This practice lays down the groundwork "so that higher levels of [reading] proficiency may be reached."[2]

On the other hand, too, often books described as classic are dismissed as being too old or too boring to interest children and thus are not even presented as options. But, these assumptions—both about classics and about children—are not only unfortunate but also wrong. Classics are defined as classic precisely because they stand the test of time, and the reason they stand the test of time is because they continue to connect with readers. In other words, the classics wouldn't *be* classics if they didn't appeal to readers in at least one of the ways that Catherine Sheldrick Ross identifies in her research.[3] Therefore, in the effort to create a tool that matches children to stories based upon their reading motivations, the classics were an obvious starting point. But we hope as you use this guide, you will begin to recognize reader-driven appeal elements in other books and keep them in mind as you suggest titles to children.

## What Is Children's Literature?

The first challenge that arises when defining classic children's literature is first defining children's literature. A convenient definition would be "books written for children." But many books (e.g., *Little Women* and *The Adventures of Huckleberry Finn*) were written before the concept of "children's literature" really existed. And, even today, much of what is considered children's literature is not written exclusively for the child audience. Yet, children still read these books. Or at least children are thought to read them, as they are almost always housed in the juvenile collections at public libraries or in the children's literature sections at bookstores. So perhaps, "books that are read by children" would be a better definition. But then that means *any* book could be a children's book.

For this reason, some have gone so far as to say that there is no "children's literature," that it simply doesn't exist. In his essay collection, *Sticks and Stones*, children's literature scholar Jack Zipes explains that because "children" and "childhood" are social constructs, defined differently across cultures and throughout history, "the concept of a children's literature is also imaginary, referring to what specific groups composed mostly of adults construct as their referential system."[4] Children do not "own" their literature the way adults do. In other words, "there has never been a literature conceived *by* children *for* children, a literature that belongs to children, and there never will be."[5] Rather, it is what adults—editors, agents, publishers, librarians, teachers, and parents—decide it is, or should be. Thus, what really distinguishes a children's book from literature intended primarily for an adult audience "is the fact that the writer must take into account many more audiences and censorship than a writer of a work intended for adults does."[6] The writer must conceptualize what the child as implied reader is. In this way, children's literature *is* imaginary.

An awareness of how children's literature is written and produced is needed in order to understand how it shapes and defines our conception of children and childhood. The genre, as normally thought about, is a relatively new invention of commercial publishing. It began to develop during the eighteenth century, with the publication of serious, religious and morally didactic texts, and it exploded during the twentieth century with the kinds of books that we recognize as "children's books" today. While the creation of this genre has certainly changed and expanded the variety of writing available to children, making a book like this one even possible, it is also limiting. The publishers' need to maximize profits necessarily limits what books are available to children, as publishers will only want to publish what they think will sell. But this need, in turn, also shapes and defines our conception of children. To put it another way, when you visit a children's bookstore, the reason you see the shelves filled with flashy, illustrated covers is because the publisher knows that this packaging will help their books sell. But, at the same time, you become conditioned to believe that this is what a children's book is, that if it does not have a flashy, colorful cover, children would not be interested in reading it. Thus, the children's literature marketplace has determined what you think children need and therefore what you think of children.

This phenomenon brings to the surface and challenges many assumptions made about children. In particular, it challenges the assumption that children can't or won't find the classics interesting or worth reading. It is certainly fair to say that no child will like every classic included in this book. It is also fair to say that the publishers' assumptions are sometimes right—some children *do* like and prefer books with flashy, contemporary visuals. But not *all* children require them. The point is to be aware of the assumptions you are making because, as children's literature scholars Perry Nodelman and Marvis Reimer point out:

> Far too many children learn to be exactly as limited as adults expect them to be—and if they don't, they often learn to respect the tyranny of the norm, and hide their lack of limitations from others, both from adults and other children. They understand that knowing or being more than others expect them to be is likely to cause them serious social problems. They pretend to be "childlike."[7]

In other words, the way adults imagine children and childhood can become self-fulfilling prophecies, manifested in the way in which they are treated and the literature that is created for them. Consider, for example, Heinrich Hoffman's humorous book of nursery rhymes *Struwwelpeter*

(1845), or *Slovenly Peter* in the United States.[8] This picture book portrays children as beastly, feral, and cruel. While the tone may be humorous, these depictions nonetheless betray an attitude that children are inherently wild and lacking in self-control and this, in turn, is what is meant to be "childlike." On the other hand, imagining children as innocent is no better. As Nodelman and Reimer also point out:

> When people speak of the innocence of childhood, they forget about the 40 million children in the world who are living on the streets, without homes or parents or enough food. Most of the generalizations about the kind of literature children can "relate" to imply the degree to which people assume that all children live the comfortable, protected lives of white, middle-class North Americans.[9]

Since it is our intention with this book to help children, *all* children, find stories they can relate to, it is important to be conscious of assumptions when choosing books for them because very often assumptions are *wrong*. Without this awareness, you may choose books that, at best, fail to meet their emotional needs and, at worst, actually deny their experience.

Self-awareness is at the core of a reader-centered approach to readers' advisory. In questioning assumptions, you can shift our thoughts about what children *should* be and what they *should* read to instead focus on the unique individual who stands before you and what *he or she* needs. Shifting your thoughts in this direction, you are much more likely to learn about the reader and his or her emotional state and be able to make better judgments about how to match him or her to the right books.

## Why the Classics?

The hallmark of a classic is that it stands the test of time. It is the kind of story that, though it may have been published over a hundred years ago, in some way continues to resonate with readers today.

Therefore, part of the reason for focusing on the classics was to ensure that this book would have a longer shelf life. After going through the work of reading, annotating, and categorizing more than 300 novels, it is important that our work endure and not just cater to current trends.

Another practical reason for focusing on the classics is to provide *focus*. The children's literature marketplace is massive. It is daunting to try to identify criteria that help prioritize and select novels for inclusion. The emphasis on classics naturally eliminates many books, making the work more manageable.

However, focusing on classics has a downside as well. The first issue is the lack of diversity in the classics, both in terms of authorship and representation within the texts themselves. In other words, because a lot of the books that have stood the test of time were written during a time when white, middle- and upper-class voices dominated, this point of view necessarily becomes overrepresented and consequently privileged.

In addition, publishers know that parents, and not their children, are their real audience, as they are the consumers with the actual purchasing power. They also know that parents tend to buy the books they think will entertain or bring pleasure. So, bookstores and publishers have responded by focusing on books in three categories:

1. reprints and new editions of favorite books (i.e., the classics, *Charlotte's Web* and *Anne of Green Gables*),
2. movie and TV tie-ins, and
3. new series.[10]

Books in all of these categories have brand recognition and therefore wide commercial appeal. While this strategy ensures that books sell, it also means that new, more daring books and books with more diverse perspectives have a harder time making it into the market. Again, as Jack Zipes critiques, it has also led to the cultural homogenization of children's literature and, therefore, children.[11] In other words, publishing practices maintain and reinforce a mostly white, middle-class perspective.

Consequently, focusing on children's classics held the danger of participating in this homogenization process and tacitly consenting to it. Perpetuating old ideologies and failing to recommend titles to which *all* readers could relate would undermine the intent of this book. However, this very tension provides a good rationale for focusing on books considered classic. As a reader, you know that the primary reason you enjoy reading is because of what a story can make you *think* and *feel*. However, the reason readers respond to a story isn't necessarily because they *like* the characters, or the ending, or the genre within which it is written. You also do not have to *agree* with an author's philosophical worldview in order to enjoy reading his or her book. And this is because the principal pleasure of reading is interrogating the text. The thinking *is* the pleasure.

The classics, by virtue of their contentious status as canonical "children's literature," provide so much opportunity to reveal this pleasure to young readers. Consider, for example, the 1936 Newbery Medal winner *Caddie Woodlawn*. Set in the 1860s, Carol Ryrie Brink's historical novel depicts frontier life in Wisconsin from the perspective of a white family. While the novel attempts to position the Woodlawn family equally with their Native American neighbors and promote peaceful attitudes, Brink's language—for example, her frequent and condescending use of the word "savage" in her descriptions of Native Americans—betrays an assumed position of superiority. Although well intentioned (Brink is clearly trying to portray a compassionate view of Native Americans), her descriptions nonetheless reinforce stereotypes of Native Americans (as primitive and uncivilized) and help justify the Woodlawns' presence and minimize their harm as settlers on their land.

Certainly, Brink's point of view is neither admirable nor should it be perpetuated. But the question then becomes, do you expose children *only* to stories that align with present-day attitudes? Should you just ignore history and introduce the world only as you want them to see it? Or, do you do the work of teaching children how to read critically so that they can interrogate the texts for themselves? Obviously, by engaging children in dialogue, that is, a *real* discussion in which adults not only share their interpretations but also listen to their children's questions and responses, you can help young readers discover the pleasures of *thinking* about literature. Furthermore, in teaching children how to identify, question, and evaluate ideological assumptions, you can empower them to subvert these assumptions rather than passively accept them.

While it would be a lot easier to avoid problematic classics, either by willfully ignoring these details or by not reading them altogether, doing so ultimately does children a disservice.[12] It limits their experience and therefore their ability to navigate and understand the world around them. As Nodelman and Reimer also observe:

> Many people emerge from their childhood exposure to literature with simplistic interpretative strategies that prevent them from getting much pleasure from their own reading and that often lock them inside a narrow vision of themselves and the world they live in.[13]

By helping children to recognize their authority as readers, that is, by helping them develop the confidence to make their own meaning of texts, they can begin to experience and appreciate the deeper pleasures of reading and thinking about literature. Although entertainment and escapism are often thought of as the reasons why reading is pleasurable, readers develop into avid readers because they also enjoy how and what their reading makes them think. As children's literature scholar Roderick McGillis puts it, "Reading critically is a liberating activity. It is also fun."[14]

*Why Focus on the Classics?*

So, put simply, the classics are the chosen focus of this guide because they have multiple reader-driven appeal elements and also because they can provide the fodder for lively discussions with children, which could then reveal the pleasures of literature and of reading.

## Defining Classics

In this section, you'll explore what makes a classic different from other kinds of books and the criteria were used for selecting books to include in this guide. We borrowed and adapted many of the categories that Tina Frolund outlines in her book *Genrefied Classics: A Guide to Reading Interests in Classic Literature*.[15]

A couple of caveats: approximately 300 titles are included in this book, but it is still in no way comprehensive. For one, the focus is mainly on American and British writers. Again, the conditions of children's writing differ from country to country, and these cultural differences determine the nature of writing for children. Because it is written in English, American and British children's literature is what is most available and accessible to us. We are also challenged by our own limited knowledge and our personal reading biases. We cannot deny that these challenges have led to some authors (e.g., Roald Dahl and Edith Nesbit) receiving more attention than others. There are a lot of other kinds of children's literature out there, even within the realm of the English language that we have not included here. That does not mean we don't think they are great. It might mean that those other titles just didn't get enough visibility to really be dubbed a classic. It might also mean we just didn't know about them. Some titles were also eliminated simply for lack of time and space, and only novels have been included, which eliminated many classic picture books from consideration. This decision was based not only on time and space limitations but also on the more important issue that for children to obtain advanced reading proficiency, they need *lots* of practice, and novel-length reading represents the point in their development when they begin to read on their own. So, the sooner you can help children discover a love of novel-length reading, the more likely they are to continue reading, and the more likely they will achieve the kind of reading proficiency needed to flourish in our information society.

Finally, while the titles annotated meet the following selection criteria, they do not always meet them in equal measure. For instance, some titles, *The Black Stallion* or *Where the Red Fern Grows*, are not as literary as, say,

*The Animal Family* or *Charlie and the Chocolate Factory*. But they remain so popular and beloved by audiences that we would be remiss to not include them.

So what do the classics selected for this reference book have in common?

## Timelessness

Something about the book—a character, a conflict, or a theme—continues to resonate with readers, whether or not it was published 25 years ago or 125 years ago. Classics are old books that, because of their enduring quality, manage to still stay in print, or at the very least are easy to access. While the lives of Jo March in *Little Women* and Anne Shirley in *Anne of Green Gables* are (thankfully!) very different from the lives of young women today, readers continue to connect to their stories because they can still appreciate these characters' freethinking, rebellious attitudes. In other words, Jo and Anne continue to model resistance to oppressive social norms, even if those norms have changed.

## Age

For a book to endure, it has to have been around for a long time, long enough for it to be told, retold, and possibly adapted in new ways. That Madeleine L'Engle's *A Wrinkle in Time*, published over 50 years ago, has been recently adapted into a graphic novel and a new film or that L. M. Montgomery's *Anne of Green Gables*, published over 100 years ago, continues to be adapted for film and TV (most recently as a Netflix series called *Anne with an E*) is a testament to their lasting appeal. Also for this reason, it is often the mark of a classic when you know the story even before you have read it. In light of the fact that time must pass before a book can be truly regarded as a classic, selections (with a few exceptions) are limited to titles published in 2007 or earlier, assuming that a period of at least 10 years is needed to reasonably judge whether or not a book will endure.

## Universal Themes

Classics are *about* something. They are written with a purpose, to convey meaning about some aspect of the human condition. For this reason alone, readers can find some way, on some level, to relate to them, no matter who they are. For example, on the surface Michael Bond's *Paddington Bear* might seem like it is just a funny story about a clumsy bear adapting to his new family and new way of life in England. But, though Paddington is a bear,

# Why Focus on the Classics?

he is an anthropomorphized bear and an immigrant from "darkest Peru." He appeals to readers because they can easily relate to his fears and anxieties as an outsider. Readers, young and old, can all relate to his small humiliations, his insecurities, and his loneliness.

## Language and Craft

While some classics are classics simply because they are such good stories, most of them are classics because they are also well written, that is, literary. Authors use language imaginatively, intentionally, in order to shape and structure their narratives in a way that enhances and reinforces their stories' meaning. Consider E. B. White's *Charlotte's Web*: the plot, characters, and the setting, which begins and ends in spring, are all used to reinforce themes about death and rebirth. These literary elements all fit together in service to the story and its meaning.

Unlike a lot of formulaic fiction, which is essentially produced like Ford Model T's, that is, by applying the principles of mass production, literary writing is inventive. This does not mean writing does not make use of some formulaic conventions—that would be impossible. But the author respects the principles of originality; he or she tweaks and reinvents the formula to say something new. Generic, mass-produced fiction, on the other hand, by virtue of being mass-produced, necessarily conforms to mechanical, predictable rules and is therefore also predictable to read. Such works do not introduce new ideas or new perspectives so much as maintain and reinforce an established worldview. But for a classic to become a classic, it must possess some degree of artistry and originality of perspective. The titles chosen for this guide were chosen because of their potential to introduce new ideas and excite new thought.

## *Multiple Levels of Meaning*

Related to language and writing craft, classics have depth. They are stories that invite conversation, "excite thought," because they are open to multiple interpretations. For instance, some might say that Sara Crewe in Frances Hodgson Burnett's *A Little Princess* is a model of strength and virtue. On the other hand, some might find her cloying optimism to be delusional and her generosity classist and condescending. But, either way, whether or not the reader likes Sarah Crewe or despises her, *A Little Princess* remains a good book and a classic precisely because it is so provocative.

Books that have multiple levels of meaning also read differently at different stages in one's life. For example, in William Steig's *Abel's Island*, young readers can certainly appreciate the frustration, anxiety, and loneliness that Abel experiences once he becomes stranded and separated from his wife, Amanda. But to older readers, who have had more opportunities to experience loneliness, loss, and grief, his suffering resonates more deeply.

Again, though it would be nice if readers *liked* all of the stories they read or the characters they read about, liking or relating to a book's story or characters isn't the only pleasure to be found in literature. Ultimately, the greater concern is in developing young readers' desire to *talk* and to *think* about the stories they read. As asserted earlier in this chapter, this is what is meant by the pleasures of reading.

### Honors/Awards

Classics are books that have been recognized. The children's division of the American Library Association has awarded the Newbery Medal to authors who have made distinguished contributions to American literature for children since 1922, and it is one of the highest distinctions a children's book can earn. It is, therefore, indicative of its groundbreaking achievement. But obviously many books that have not earned this award are included in this guide, because they were published before the award existed (e.g., *Little Women, The Adventures of Huckleberry Finn*), they earned other awards (see Appendix), and/or they received other important distinctions (e.g., a popular audience reception, scholarly attention). Again, classics are classics because they generate discussion. Honors and awards signify this.

### Conclusion

For the past two years, I have spent every free moment reading children's books. I have read them on the subway going to and from work. I have read them on airplanes visiting friends and family. I have read them while standing in one of New York City's many lines—at Whole Foods, at the post office, or at the pharmacy. And what would continue to amaze me were the people who would notice me reading and react to the titles I held. When I pulled out *A Wrinkle in Time*, a woman standing nearby eyed it, smiled, and nodded approvingly. When I sat with *Watership Down* on an airplane, the passenger next to me, a middle-aged man, told me it was one of his favorite stories. On the subway, a young man, probably in his early 20s, half asleep, cracked open his eyes when I pulled out *Where the Red Fern Grows*, smiled fondly, and said, "I remember reading that book."

I won't pretend that you or your readers will like every book listed in this guide. In fact, I know you won't because *I* didn't like every book I had to read and annotate for it. But this isn't a book about books I like; it's a book about helping other people find books *they* might like. If you doubt whether children will find the classics interesting, then think of these strangers and their reactions. Each of them reminded me, and I hope they will remind you, too, that we should never presume to know what someone else will or will not like. But also consider that most early readers need to be *taught* to appreciate literature. It is part of *your job* as a librarian, teacher, or parent to help them discover the pleasures of reading literature. In the next chapter, you'll explore ways in which librarians, teachers, and parents can promote the classics and thus do this job better.

## Notes

1. Stephen D. Krashen, *The Power of Reading* (Westport, CT: Libraries Unlimited, 2004), x.
2. Ibid.
3. Catherine Sheldrick Ross, "Finding without Seeking: What Readers Say about the Role of Pleasure Reading as a Source of Information," *Australasian Public Libraries and Information Services* 13, no. 2 (2000): 72–80.
4. Jack Zipes, "Why Children's Literature Does Not Exist," in *Sticks and Stones* (New York: Routledge, 2001), 39–60, 40.
5. Ibid.
6. Ibid., 44.
7. Perry Nodelman and Marvis Reimer, "Common Assumptions about Childhood," in *The Pleasures of Children's Literature*, 3rd ed. (Boston, MA: Allyn and Bacon, 2003), 95.
8. For illustrations, see the digitized version available through the Hathi Trust: Heinrich Hoffman, *Struwwelpeter or Merry Rhymes and Funny Pictures* (New York: E.P. Dutton & Co.), https://babel.hathitrust.org/cgi/pt?id=nc01.ark:/13960/t55d9xf27;view=1up;seq=5.
9. Nodelman and Reimer, "Common Assumptions about Childhood," 90.
10. Perry Nodelman and Marvis Reimer, "Children's Literature in the Marketplace," in *The Pleasures of Children's Literature*, 3rd ed. (Boston, MA: Allyn and Bacon, 2003), 116.
11. Jack Zipes. "The Cultural Homogenization of American Children," in *Sticks and Stones* (New York: Routledge, 2001), 1–23.
12. For an extended discussion of this topic, see: Stephen Marche, "How to Read a Racist Book to Your Kids," *New York Times*, June 15, 2012, http://www.nytimes.com/2012/06/17/magazine/how-to-read-a-racist-book-to-your-kids.html.

13. Perry Nodelman and Marvis Reimer, "Teaching Children Literature," in *The Pleasures of Children's Literature*, 3rd ed. (Boston, MA: Allyn and Bacon, 2003), 33.

14. Roderick McGillis, "The Delights of Impossibility: No Children, No Books, Only Theory," *Children's Literature Association Quarterly* 23, no. 4 (Winter 1998): 204, doi: 10.1353/chq.0.1257.

15. Tina Frolund, *Genrefied Classics: A Guide to Reading Interests in Classic Literature* (Westport, CT: Libraries Unlimited, 2007).

CHAPTER THREE

# How to Promote the Classics

You likely know children who consider classic books dull and interesting. You are probably also aware of the large selection of notable books available to children and would like them to consider these books when making reading choices. But if you tell children what to read, it can backfire. Children want to choose their own books. So how can you encourage them to read books written by talented writers? Research on child readers offers a number of clues.

Gay Ivey and Karen Broaddus surveyed 1,700 sixth-grade students about their reading. Comments such as "Nothing usually makes me want to read" and "It stinks and I don't like to read anyway" indicate the strong negative feelings that some children harbor toward books in general and classic books in particular.[1] Attitudes such as these do not develop overnight. By the time children start school, they have already developed deeply ingrained ideas about reading.

Young readers who enjoy classic novels are first and foremost children who enjoy reading. To encourage a love of great books, you need to do so in the context of reading in general. Parents and caregivers need to lay the groundwork and promote books of all kinds—including highbrow and lowbrow material as well as fiction and nonfiction. This chapter explores ways that parents, caregivers, teachers, and librarians can help develop lifelong readers who enjoy a wide range of books, including the classics.

The goal should not be for children to read classic books exclusively, but rather to enjoy the ones that address their interests and needs.

## The Relationship between Skill and Enjoyment in Reading

Positive and negative attitudes toward books are shaped by the skills children develop in reading. Some children become fluent readers who find the activity effortless while others find it a chore. In her study of avid readers, Catherine Ross observes, "Nonbook readers find any kind of reading hard work and view book reading in particular as something to be prepared for psychologically and performed only when long blocks of time are available. Confident readers, in contrast, say that they find book reading easy, something they can do 'just about anytime.' "[2]

Effortless readers are not born with the skill. Becoming a reader involves a long apprenticeship in the activity. Children's author and education professor, Mem Fox, maintains that children need to hear a thousand stories before they enter kindergarten.[3] The more stories they hear, the easier they find reading on their own. As children's writer Aidan Chambers points out, "We cannot easily read for ourselves what we haven't heard said. We learn to read by joining in with those who know how to do it, and gradually taking on all of it for ourselves."[4] When we read, we encounter vocabulary and syntax only found in print. So reading fluency hinges on reading widely. "Every time we read," observes cognitive neuroscientist, Mark Seidenberg, "we update our knowledge of language. At a conscious level we read a text for its content: because it is a story or a textbook or a joke. At a subconscious level our brains automatically register information about the structure of language ... Developing this elaborate linguistic network requires exposure to a large sample of texts."[5]

Unless children are exposed to stories, they will not discover their attraction. Finding pleasure in books is key to developing lifelong readers. Research has shown that children whose early encounters with literacy are pleasurable are more likely to read frequently and broadly as they get older.[6] Unless children enjoy reading, they do not pursue the activity and never read enough books to become effortless at it. If reading is fun, it is done more often, and if it is done more often, it produces fluent readers who love to read. Catherine Ross speaks of reading fluency in terms of Malcolm Gladwell's claim that it takes 10,000 hours of practice to become good at anything.[7]

Adults who work with or care for children can have a profound effect on their development of the skill. Teachers, librarians, parents, and caregivers take on the role of an enabling adult, facilitating the development of skills in reading and attitudes toward it. This role, as Aidan Chambers argues in his book,

*The Reading Environment: How Adults Help Children Enjoy Books*, is so important that "all other obstacles in the way of learner readers can be overcome if they have the help and example of a trusted, experienced adult reader."[8]

Promoting a love of reading takes the combined efforts of all adults who work with and care for children. The goal of the enabling adult is to instill a love of reading in children. Those who love to read expect pleasure from books and maintain an open mind to the experience.

## Promoting Reading and the Classics in the Home

Before children start school, they spend many years listening to stories, an activity that is cumulative in its effect. These years are crucial in forming ideas about books and reading. As Mem Fox observes, "Reading problems are difficult to fix but very easy to prevent. Prevention happens *long before a child starts school*. In fact, the first day of school is almost too late for a child to begin to learn to read."[9] Parents and caregivers lay the foundation that teachers and librarians build upon.

### Creating a Book-Rich Environment

Research shows that avid readers grow up in homes that contain a lot of books. According to a recent study by Scholastic, children who are frequent readers live in places that contain on average 141 children's books, while infrequent readers live in places that contain 65 children's books.[10] Likewise, Catherine Ross's study found that adult book lovers were raised in book-rich environments. One respondent commented, "Our house had lots of books spread around. I know I began indiscriminately reading. It was never guided reading. Mother just left books around." Not all respondents in this study could afford books but this fact did not impede them. One reader reported, "There [were] about 50 books on the hall table every week or every two weeks from the library."[11] If books are not easily available, children are less likely to read. Out of sight is indeed out of mind. A place filled with books can remind children to read and, in fact, motivate them to do so. Also, ensure that books are available in places where children would otherwise be bored, places such as the car.[12]

### Finding the Right Book

You know that there is nothing more tedious than reading something that you have no interest in. Children are no different. All readers have personal preferences in reading. No more do all children like the same books than all of them enjoy the same food. One child in the Scholastic survey observed, "Those who say reading is boring simply haven't found a book they like."[13] Some children like scary stories, others humorous ones; some enjoy novels about wizards, others soccer players; some prefer fast-paced novels, others gradually enfolding stories; some look for reassurance in a story, others role models. Children can also outgrow their reading interests and develop new ones as they grow or the circumstances in their lives change. And like adults, one day they are in the mood for a story about survival and the next day a novel about coping with failure.

A personal connection to a story makes it the perfect choice for one reader and not another. Commenting about a book she enjoyed, one middle-school student said, "it related to me," while another student said about the protagonist, "he reminds me of myself."[14] The closer the connection between a reader's life and a character's life, the greater the impact of that book for that reader. Stories that contain a connection to the reader have a personal significance for him or her.

Research shows that children acquire more books as gifts than by any other method. Parents, grandparents, aunts, uncles, friends, and teachers are the major gift-givers.[15] No one is in a better position than parents or caregivers to choose books that match their child's tastes and current needs. Asking booksellers and librarians for help in finding a book your child will like is an effective strategy; they make it their business to know their collections. Librarians can also show you reference books and online tools to help you make a decision. Using this book will help you find a book that matches your child's favorite genre or topic. It will also hopefully assist you in finding a novel that meets your child's emotional and psychological needs. For example, your daughter might want a book that helps her accept something she cannot alter or give her courage to make a change in her life. Starting your child on a book in a series is another great way to keep him or her reading.

As young children get older, they increasingly like to pick their own books. In a recent study, 89 percent of children aged 6–17 years agreed with the statement "My favorite books are the ones that I have picked out myself."[16] Giving gift certificates for books is a useful way of promoting reading while providing choice.

Many parents underestimate how difficult it is for children to choose books. While 42 percent of children (57 percent infrequent readers and 26 percent frequent readers) agreed with the statement, "I have trouble finding books that I like," only 29 percent of parents thought so.[17] Helping children with their choices by suggesting a few possibilities and relying on the expertise of librarians and booksellers can make the process more manageable for a child.

## Prioritizing Reading

If you want your child to enjoy reading and increase the likelihood that he or she will enjoy great literature, prioritize reading-related activities. Children need to know that their parents and caregivers value reading as an essential activity. In *Raising Kids Who Read*, Daniel T. Willingham reminds parents that family traditions reveal what they value enough to repeat. He advises parents to "communicate in words and actions that reading and learning about the world are family values."[18] For example, display books in prominent places in your home; read the newspaper together on Sunday mornings; buy a bookcase for your children.[19] Reading should be part of the family routine, something engaged in daily such as reading before going to bed. Visiting the library frequently, not just for books but also for children's programs and activities, could become part of the family tradition. Giving books, ebooks, or bookstore gift certificates as presents shows children how much you value reading. Attending book signings, author readings, and plays are also activities that promote reading. These traditions are one of the best ways for creating positive attitudes toward reading.[20] Research has also shown that children of parents who focus on reading as fun score higher on a reading motivation scale than do children whose parents focus on reading as a skill.[21]

Providing a setting that facilitates reading increases the likelihood that your child will engage in it.[22] It is difficult to read in a noisy environment. Children need a place to read that is relatively free of distractions, especially the sound of televisions or other devices. Whether a chair in a room or a nook in a corner, such a place can become part of a child's reading routine. Reading takes time. Busy families who schedule many activities for their children should not let reading fall between the cracks.

Facilitating an informal forum for discussing books is also important. Talking about stories at mealtime is a practice that extends the enjoyment of reading in the same way that book clubs do.

Encourage your child to keep track of his or her reading. Doing so provides a sense of accomplishment that motivates readers. Children can keep reading diaries, either noting the author and title of the book or adding their personal responses to a story. Like adults who use sites such as Goodreads, some children like to keep track by creating their own online bookshelves. Biblionasium, which describes itself as "the alternative, safe Goodreads for Kids," is one such reading tracker for children.

## Modeling Reading

"Readers are made by readers," writes Aidan Chambers. "Without saying anything at all, our behaviour will communicate the place and importance reading holds in our private lives."[23] We cannot expect our children to read if they do not see us doing so. Research confirms this connection. In 2009, the Organisation for Economic Co-operation and Development (OECD) administered a multicountry study about reading to 15-year-olds and their parents. Results showed that children whose parents read and have a positive attitude toward reading score higher on reading comprehension tests and are more likely to say they enjoy reading.[24]

One respondent in Catherine Ross's study of avid readers explained how reading became second nature to her:

> Both of my parents are great readers. I don't remember either of them saying, "You should read" or "Reading is a wonderful thing." I think we all just did it by following their example.... My mother was the sort who went to the library every week and got five books out and read them. And then, as soon as we were old enough, we had library cards and we would go with her. I just took [reading] for granted. I thought everybody did it. It didn't have to be sold to me.[25]

Enthusiasm for books is contagious. Do not worry, though, if you do not enjoy fiction; read what you do like. As the OECD advises, if you "prefer to read newspapers and magazines, that's fine. What is important is showing children—of all ages—that reading is a daily, enjoyable, valuable activity, and that it is made even more pleasurable when people discuss what they have read with others."[26]

### Reading Aloud or Listening to Audiobooks

Long before your child can read, he or she needs to hear stories. The OECD has shown that children who are read to before entering school are more likely to attain higher reading scores and greater reading enjoyment when they are older.[27]

The first of Mem Fox's "Ten Read-Aloud Commandments" is: "Spend at least ten wildly happy minutes every single day reading aloud."[28] Reading aloud exposes your child to stories in a fun and enjoyable environment. Children who have never had stories read to them miss out on such fun, and find it more difficult to acquire a taste for books later on. These children also find it harder to learn how to read on their own, which in turn puts them behind in school and makes them less likely to pursue the activity. "The ultimate goals," according to the OECD, "are that parents begin to regard reading to their young children as essential as feeding and clothing them, and that the children grow up with the deeply ingrained sense that reading is both a valuable pursuit and a pleasure."[29]

Reading is pleasurable when it is not too difficult. Children must have a broad foundation of words and knowledge of the world in order for reading to be enjoyable.[30] Studies have shown that children need to know at least 98 percent of the words in a story or reading will be a chore. One of the best ways to increase your child's vocabulary and knowledge of the world is to read aloud to her.

Just as important as reading aloud to preschoolers is reading aloud to older children. The Scholastic survey found that 59 percent of parents read aloud to children under five, 38 percent to their six- to eight-year-olds, and 17 percent to their nine- to eleven-year-olds.[31] Parents often stop reading aloud because they think that once their children know how to do it themselves, they do not need them. But for many years, children are still fledgling readers. Bernice Cullinan points out that "No matter how much your child reads alone, it's still important for you to read aloud to him. . . . He needs to hear what reading sounds like when it is done by a competent reader." Children can also understand more sophisticated books when they are read to them.[32] An eight-year-old in the Scholastic study said, "I like it when my mom reads to me. I enjoy the time together and we get to read harder chapter books. I can't wait to see how the story ends."[33] Reading aloud to older children is a perfect opportunity to introduce them to classic books that are suited to their tastes and needs.

Listening to audiobooks is another way of experiencing stories. Professional readers bring books to life and can engage the most reluctant reader. "Some people say they don't like reading stories," says Aidan Chambers, "but I've never come across anyone who doesn't like hearing one."[34] Books that contain dialect or long descriptive passages are often easier to comprehend and more engaging when listened to. Most public libraries contain robust audiobook collections—CDs as well as downloadable books.

## Promoting Reading and the Classics in School

The OECD found that in all 65 countries it surveyed "students who enjoy reading the most perform significantly better than students who enjoy reading the least."[35] Indeed, if there is one skill that can make a significant difference in a child's academic life, it is reading. While parents and caregivers lay the foundation for reading, teachers extend and reinforce children's reading capabilities.

## Reading Aloud by the Teacher

The reading activity that students report enjoying the most is listening to their teacher read aloud.[36] One student commented, "When the teacher reads to our class, he does all of the voices in the story," while another observed, "She makes it sound so interesting. If there's complicated words instead of us trying to figure it out she'll be reading it and she'll understand what the works mean."[37] Hearing a story told by a competent reader not only brings it to life but also takes the hard work out of deciphering language, which in turn allows students to be more easily drawn into the story. There is no age when students outgrow their need to hear stories in school. Mem Fox writes that when she taught teacher candidates in college, she often read them a novel. All her students loved this read-aloud time: "Even the football players in my class loved being read aloud to. They'd sit like silent mice, rapt in spite of themselves, drawn in by the pull of the story."[38]

### Independent Reading Time

The reading activity that students report enjoying almost as much as being read to by their teacher is independent reading time. Programs such as D.E.A.R. (Drop Everything and Read) set aside class time for independent reading on a regular basis. Children choose their own book and are given quiet time each day to read them. For children who do not read at home, such school programs give them reading opportunities they would otherwise not have. If home is typically a noisy place, independent reading time provides students with a time and place conducive to the activity. As one student said, "I get to read without being disturbed."[39] Independent reading also allows for variation in reading pace and comprehension. Students who need more time than their classmates to read a story or those who want to reread sections can set their own pace.

### Teacher as a Reading Model and Source of Encouragement

Never underestimate a teacher's power and influence on their students' attitude toward reading. Children benefit by seeing examples of readers who love the activity. It helps them to know that their teachers read in their personal lives and that reading is an activity that they enjoy. Teachers who are enthusiastic about books motivate students to follow their example. And teachers who are passionate about classic books will inspire followers. Students need to know that notable books can be enjoyable before they hear otherwise.

The more teachers are familiar with children's literature, the more they can offer book suggestions. Teachers can hook readers by tempting them with an excerpt from a story or a comment about a book that they think will interest them. Discussing books with students, not just in class time, but informally on a one-to-one basis, can be highly motivational.

Rewarding students by praising their reading accomplishments can encourage even the most reluctant readers. As one teacher says, "I celebrate any reading my students do. When students see that I value their reading choices, they begin to trust themselves to select their own reading material and trust me to suggest more books. I tap into this reading relationship to move students toward more challenging, meatier books over time."[40] Offering upbeat support and setting a positive emotional tone go a long way to creating positive reading experiences.[41]

"If 'reader' is part of your self-concept," observes Willingham, "it will occur to you as a viable activity more often."[42] Research has shown that helping students create a positive reader identity improves their motivation. Asking them what kind of reader they would like to become gives them a sense of agency and ownership over their own learning.[43]

### Choice of Materials and Access to Them

Like home, school should be a book-rich environment. When choosing books for the school library or classroom, nothing is more important than including a wide variety of genres and formats. Whether large or small, the collection should reflect a broad spectrum of readers' interests in order to attract their attention. Some schools create surveys that ask students what they like to read. Doing so helps meet local needs.[44] Classics can be introduced by purchasing media adaptations as well as the books. Children who might not read *The Hobbit* may watch the three movies.

No matter how robust the collection, the books will sit on the shelf if they are not easy and convenient to access. School libraries with limited hours frustrate readers who may turn to another activity instead. Finding the right book in a large collection can be a daunting task that discourages potential readers. As one 14-year-old girl said, "I don't like reading because I cannot find the right book for me to read."[45] The Scholastic survey found that 51 percent of children get ideas about books to read from teachers and school librarians.[46]

### Classics in the Curriculum

One of the best opportunities to promote classics is through novel study in Language Arts class. But teaching whole-class novel units has the built-in challenge of lack of choice. When Ivey and Broaddus, for example, asked respondents about their reaction to *Slake's Limbo*, a book they read in class, one student said, "I got hooked on *Slake's Limbo*. It was just so interesting," while another said, "It was boring, No action whatsoever. It was just dull."[47] Although not always possible, it is preferable to give students choice of texts, even if it is between two options. Dividing students into groups and providing a few choices from which to pick is ideal. One teacher, who gave up whole-class novel units, redesigned her instruction around the skills and competencies that students need to learn but let each group of students choose their own book.[48]

Novels used as accompanying texts to social studies units can be a powerful strategy. Since fiction appeals to emotions as well as intellect, novels can draw students into issues and inspire them in a way that nonfiction does not usually do. Linda Sue Park's *A Long Walk to Water*, for example, creates a more powerful impact on students than a lesson on Sudan by itself. As students read about the harsh lives of Salva and Nya, they experience the same emotions as the characters and learn what it is like to "walk in their shoes." Classic books are particularly skilled at bringing social studies topics to life. Classic books, in fact, address a wide variety of topics and can be used in a number of subject areas. Consult the subject/theme index of this book to find a novel on a particular topic.

In *Ban the Book Report: Promoting Frequent and Enthusiastic Reading*, Foster and Mototsune argue that, to inspire lifelong reading, teachers should go beyond assigning book reports and encourage students to make personal connections with novels in the same way that avid adult readers do.[49] Unless students see the relevance of a story to their own lives, they will not enjoy it. Asking students to record their impressions, emotional connections, and ideas in a reader response journal can help them become thoughtful and reflective readers. Teachers could design prompts and questions for these journals to help readers make connections between texts and their own lives. Reader response journals can also give students insight into their identity as readers. Foster and Mototsune describe additional activities that deepen students' engagement with texts and help them see the relevance of books to their lives. Asking students to prepare book talks that focus on what they like about a novel gives them insight into their reading selves as well as tempt other students to read the stories. Consult the following chapters in this book for additional curricular tie-in activities for each novel.

## A Culture of Reading

Developing a culture of reading in a school creates an enthusiastic atmosphere that inspires readers. Consider facilitating an after-school book club or inviting parents to an author's tea in which students read excerpts from their creative writing. Class trips to a book-related event or a publisher's office can also inspire students to read. Teachers could also follow the example of one school that creates a calendar of yearly reading events such as Family Literacy Day and Science Fiction Day, events that they enthusiastically celebrate.[50]

## Promoting Reading and the Classics in the Library

A low-risk way of finding a classic book to read is to borrow a selection of choices from a library. But for some parents and children, libraries are unfamiliar, even intimidating places. In Pew's 2016 survey of Americans, 17 percent of 16- to 29-year-olds said they have never been inside a public library.[51] These adults made it all the way through childhood without visiting their local library.

### Creating an Inviting Library Environment

If librarians want to facilitate reading, they should take whatever steps they can to create an inviting and welcoming environment, one that will attract nonreaders as well as readers. Granted, many libraries must make do with aging infrastructures and tight budgets, but anything that can be done to improve the atmosphere of a building can attract people to reading. No one will be tempted to borrow books if the library is drab and forbidding, and the books worn and shabby. Good lighting, attractively displayed books, and comfortable places to read in areas that are conducive to the activity are essential.

Library consultant, Rachel Van Riel, argues that libraries should follow the example of retail to attract more readers. Library books, like merchandise in a store, should be displayed to tempt customers to select them. Yet the layout of most libraries discourages all but the most committed customers from finding what they want. Surveys from Van Riel's company show that three out of every four people who visit a library are "impulse" customers; the rest are "destination" customers who know what book or item they want. Impulse customers are unsure what they are looking for, hoping that they will spot a book that helps them make a decision.[52] Traditional library layouts that feature long rows of bookshelves discourage impulse customers. The newer "discovery" layout, in which curved bookshelves staggered throughout a space, makes books more visible and the space more inviting to explore.[53]

### Tempting Readers with an Attractive Collection

If a library's editions of the classics are worn and the covers outdated, children will be discouraged from choosing them. As publishers and bookstore owners know, appearance matters with books. Publishers invest considerable money in cover designs because they know that attractive book covers sell books. Book jackets are created by professional designers who are skilled at tempting readers to buy them. Replacing older editions of classics with newer versions, and deselecting tattered books in the surrounding area will create a more attractive, eye-catching display.

Also consider buying copies of a text when a movie is released. Heavily advertised films can reinterest children in the original story.

### Finding the Right Book

A child looking for a classic book will find it harder to find in a public library than in a bookstore. Children who are used to bookstores are sometimes daunted by the larger collections in public libraries. Readers' advisors are trained to match readers with the books they want. By questioning the child, parent, or teacher asking for a book, they learn what is wanted and make suggestions. Skilled readers' advisors know that to suggest an assortment of titles rather than recommend avoids putting pressure on readers. They also know that providing a manageable number of choices for readers is an effective way of helping them. Knowledge of the classics and an enthusiasm for them is an obvious asset in making suggestions that include them. But readers' advisors do not have to be limited to their own reading. Fortunately readers' advisory reference books such as those published by Libraries Unlimited or the American Library Association and by online databases such as NoveList can help identify choices.

Libraries can and should make it easy and convenient for readers to find what they want. Librarians can follow the example of bookstores and create displays that attract children by their visibility in high traffic areas. Displaying a book in a select group calls attention to it, preventing it from going unnoticed in the book stacks. Although choice in reading material is important, too much choice can be overwhelming. Impulse customers in particular rely on book displays to make decisions. Turning a book face out in the book stacks also makes the invisible, visible and offers a focal point for users. Doing so with classic books is an effective way of highlighting them.

### Promoting the Books

Annotated book lists, read-alike lists (if you like this book, try these . . .), bookmarks with title suggestions, blogs, tweets, and book covers displayed on scrolling shelves on the library website give children ideas about reading choices and a manageable number of books from which to select. All of these promotional tools can be used to focus attention on classic books, either entirely or partially.

Creating posters that promote readers and the reading experience rather than books and authors can be an effective strategy. "Clever advertisers promote their products and services" observe Van Riel, Fowler, and Downes "by helping consumers imagine themselves using them."[54] Moving from a book-centric to a reader-centric perspective will entice young readers by focusing on their needs. Displaying posters of children lost in reading a timeless book, for example, can be a powerful incentive.

Creating library programming that involves one or more classic books is a fun way of introducing them to children. Facilitating in-person or online book clubs, or hosting local author events, can change reading from an invisible activity to a visible and social one. One library system makes it an annual practice to visit grade four classes to give them a package called "Operation Super Sleuth." The purpose of this package is to reinterest children in the library at a time when reading interest typically wanes. Children then visit their local branch and solve missions such as finding a book by its call number. Children who "pass" are given an invisible ink pen.[55] Such an activity could involve searching for a classic book.

Avid book lovers, according to Ross, weave reading into the texture of their lives and the fabric of their identities. They cannot imagine life without books.[56] Helping a child to do the same increases the likelihood that he or she will read widely and expect pleasure from great literature. Parents, caregivers, teachers, and librarians have the opportunity to inspire, facilitate, and support reading in children's lives.

## Notes

1. Gay Ivey and Karen Broaddus, "'Just Plain Reading': A Survey of What Makes Students Want to Read in Middle School Classrooms," *Reading Research Quarterly* 36, no. 4 (2001): 362, doi:10.1002/pits.21593.

2. Catherine Ross, "Finding Without Seeking: What Readers Say about the Role of Pleasure Reading as a Source of Information," *Australasian Public Libraries and Information Services* 13, no. 2 (2000): 73.

3. Mem Fox, *Reading Magic: Why Reading Aloud to Our Children Will Change Their Lives Forever* (San Diego: Harvest, 2001), 17.

4. Aidan Chambers, *The Reading Environment: How Adults Help Children Enjoy Books* (York, ME: Stenhouse, 1996), 48.

5. Mark S. Seidenberg, *Language at the Speed of Sight: How We Read, Why So Many Can't, and What Can Be Done about It* (New York: Basic Books, 2017), 82–83.

6. Linda Baker, Deborah Scher, and Kirsten Mackler, "Home and Family Influences on Motivations for Reading," *Educational Psychologist* 32, no. 2 (1997): 69–82, doi:10.1207/s15326985ep3202_2.

7. Malcolm Gladwell, *Outliers: The Story of Success* (London: Allan Lane, 2008), quoted in Catherine Sheldrick Ross, "Reader on Top: Public Libraries, Pleasure Reading, and Models of Reading," *Library Trends* 57, no. 4 (2009): 651, doi:10.1353/lib.0.0059.

8. Chambers, *The Reading Environment*, 11.

9. Fox, *Reading Magic*, 13.

10. Scholastic, "Kids and Family Reading Report." 6th ed. Accessed January 13, 2017, http://www.scholastic.com/readingreport/downloads.htm.

11. Lynne (E. F.) McKechnie, "Becoming a Reader: Childhood Years," in *Reading Matters: What the Research Reveals about Reading, Libraries, and Community*, eds. Catherine Sheldrick Ross, Lynne (E. F.) McKechnie, and Paulette M. Rothbauer (Westport, CT: Libraries Unlimited, 2006), 72.

12. Daniel T. Willingham, *Raising Kids Who Read: What Parents and Teachers Can Do* (San Francisco: Jossey-Bass, 2015), 66.

13. Scholastic, "Kids and Family Reading Report," 36.

14. Ivey and Broaddus, "Just Plain Reading," 363.

15. Lynne E. F. McKechnie, " 'I'll Keep Them for My Children' (Kevin, 9 Years): Children's Personal Collections of Books and Media," *The Canadian Journal of Information and Library Science* 28, no. 4 (2004): 82.

16. Scholastic, "Kids and Family Reading Report," 10.

17. Ibid. 5.

18. Willingham, *Raising Kids Who Read*, 59.

19. Ibid., 60.

20. Ibid., 59.

21. Baker, Scher, and Mackler, "Home and Family Influences," 77.

22. Chambers, *The Reading Environment*, chap. 6.

23. Ibid., 78.

24. OECD, "Let's Read Them a Story! The Parent Factor in Education, PISA," 2012, 53, http://www.oecd-ilibrary.org/education/let-s-read-them-a-story-the-parent-factor-in-education_9789264176232-en;jsessionid=2hmcxud54fm8.x-oecd-live-02.

25. McKechnie, "Becoming a Reader," 72.

26. OECD, "Let's Read them a Story!" 55.

27. Ibid., 18.

28. Mem Fox, "Ten Read-Aloud Commandments," accessed September 26, 2013, http://memfox.com/for-parents/for-parents-ten-read-aloud-commandments/.

29. OECD, "Let's Read them a Story!" 27.

30. Willingham, *Raising Kids Who Read*, 20.

31. Scholastic, "Kids and Family Reading Report," 55.

32. Bernice E. Cullinan, *Read to Me: Raising Kids Who Love to Read* (New York: Scholastic, 2000), 27–28.

33. Scholastic, "Kids and Family Reading Report," 48, 55.

34. Chambers, *The Reading Environment*, 41.

35. OECD, "Pisa 2009 Results: Executive Summary," 2010, 12, http://www.oecd.org/pisa/pisaproducts/46619703.pdf.

36. Ivey and Broaddus, "Just Plain Reading," 350–77; Jessie de Naeghel and Hilde Van Keer, "The Relation of Student and Class-Level Characteristics to Primary School Students' Autonomous Reading Motivation: A Multi-Level Approach," *Journal of Research in Reading* 36, no. 4 (2013): 351–70, doi:10.1111/jrir.12000; Linda B. Gambrell, "Creating Classroom Cultures That Foster Motivation," *The Reading Teacher* 50, no. 1 (1996): 14–25.

37. Ivey and Broaddus, "Just Plain Reading," 361.

38. Fox, *Reading Magic*, 27.

39. Ivey and Broaddus, "Just Plain Reading," 361.

40. Donalyn Miller, "Creating a Classroom Where Readers Flourish," *The Reading Teacher* 66, no. 2 (2012): 92, doi:10.1002/TRTR.01109.

41. Willingham, *Raising Kids Who Read*, 118–27.

42. Ibid., 24.

43. Ibid., 25; Leigh A. Hall, "Rewriting Identities: Creating Spaces for Students and Teachers to Challenge the Norms of What It Means to Be a Reader in School," *Journal of Adolescent & Adult Literacy* 55, no. 5 (2012): 368–73, doi:10.1002/JAAL00045.

44. Kevin Thomas and April Burke, "Building a World of Frequent Readers: How Can Teachers Encourage All Students to Read?" *The Looking Glass: New Perspectives on Children's Literature* 19, no. 1 (2016), https://www.lib.latrobe.edu.au/ojs/index.php/tlg/article/view/763/708.

45. Scholastic, "Kids and Family Reading Report," 38.

46. Ibid., 40.

47. Ivey and Broaddus, "Just Plain Reading," 364.

48. Miller, "Creating a Classroom Where Readers Flourish," 90–91.

49. Graham Foster and Kat Mototsune, *Ban the Book Report: Promoting Frequent and Enthusiastic Reading* (Markham, ON: Pembroke, 2012).

50. Nicole N. (Simon) Guldager, Karla Steele Krueger, and Joan Bessman Taylor, "Reading Promotion Events Recommended for Elementary Students," *Teacher Librarian* 43, no. 5 (2016): 13–19.

51. John B. Horrigan, "Libraries 2016: Trends in Visiting Public Libraries Have Steadied, and Many Americans Have High Expectations For What Their Local Libraries Should Offer," Pew Research Report, 15, http://pewinternet.org/2016/09/09/libraries-2016/.

52. Rachel Van Riel, "All Set to Change: Challenging Traditional Practice in Library Design" (conference presentation, Ontario Library Association's Super Conference, Toronto, ON, February 1, 2017), http://www.olasuperconference.ca/event/all-set-to-change-challenging-traditional-practice-in-library-design/.

53. See, for example, the discovery layout designed by Opening the Book: http://www.openingthebook.com/ca/library-design.

54. Rachel Van Riel, Olive Fowler, and Anne Downes, *The Reader-Friendly Library Service* (Newcastle upon Tyne, UK: The Society of Chief Librarians, 2008), 10.

55. Toronto Public Libraries, "Mission Possible: Get Kids Running to the Library," 2017, http://tplfoundation.ca/stories/grade-4/.

56. Ross, "Finding without Seeking."

# PART 2

# Annotations

CHAPTER FOUR

# Adventure/Survival

In his introduction to *The Swiss Family Robinson*, Jon Scieszka writes, "Living in a giant tree house in a tropical jungle. Catching monkeys. Shooting sharks. Lassoing sea turtles. Exploring. Hunting. Fishing, Surviving. If you are not interested yet, you don't need to read any further." In identifying the multiple attractions of Wyss's novel, Scieszka also highlights the attractions of adventure/survival fiction. Stories in this genre appeal to children because they are fast-paced, plot-driven, action-filled, and suspenseful. These novels can be plotted on a continuum of danger from low risk (adventure stories) to high risk (survival stories)—ranging from playful to dangerous to life-threatening.

Although adventure/survival stories are distinguished by their fast-paced, action-dominated plots, they are also remarkable for their exotic, remote, or extreme landscapes—places such as desert islands (*The Coral Island, The Swiss Family Robinson, Island of the Blue Dolphins*), stormy seas (*The Wanderer, We Didn't Mean to Go to Sea*), the wild West (*Bandit's Moon*), wilderness landscapes (*Hatchet, Julie of the Wolves, My Side of the Mountain*), and remote, inaccessible environments (*King Solomon's Mines, The Twenty-One Balloons*). In *Swallows and Amazons,* John observes that "all the most exciting charts and maps have places on them that are marked 'Unexplored.'" Many adventure/survival novels were written during or set at a time when unmapped places still existed.

Children in these novels have minimal if any adult supervision. Most of the protagonists must cope on their own in highly dangerous situations.

In reading these novels, children can try out adult roles and experience vicariously what it would be like to be completely independent, in charge of their own decisions. The protagonists leave home, temporarily or permanently, for the wider world and develop a hardier, more independent self as a result of their experiences. As Claudia insists in *From the Mixed-Up Files of Mrs. Basil E. Frankweiler*, "I didn't run away to come back home the same."

Although adventure stories were initially written for boys and began as stories of empire, they have become more inclusive, many of them exploring issues of race, culture, and gender.

Wilderness survival stories often question the value of money and possessions, reconsidering the assumptions of modern civilization. The appeal of simplifying life, stripping down to essentials, getting rid of extraneous baggage, and starting over in harmony with the natural world is a strong attraction in such novels.

### Awakening/New Perspectives/Enlargement of Possibilities

**Falkner, J. Meade** (1858–1932)
**Moonfleet** (1898). London: Vintage Books, 2011. 256pp. 978-0099541127. PD.

When John Trenchard discovers a tunnel underneath the village church that leads to the Mohune family burial chamber, he also learns that the vault serves as a hiding spot for smugglers. Exploring the vault one day, he suddenly hears voices. John hides behind a rotting casket, upsetting it by mistake when the people leave. Finding a locket on the corpse of Colonel John Mohune, he is deeply disappointed that it does not contain the legendary diamond that the Colonel is believed to have stolen. But it does contain a message, one that John tries to decipher.

John's obsession with the fabled diamond becomes an all-consuming passion. Even when he is warned that the diamond is "evilly come by, and will bring evil with it," he cannot forget about it. An orphan who becomes a smuggler and an exile, John chooses a life of great danger. Turned out of the house by his guardian aunt, convicted of murder, swindled by a diamond-buyer, and sent to prison, John's life is filled with high drama and adventure.

After discovering that the smugglers are not evil and the magistrate is not ethical, readers may reframe their ideas about moral behavior, realizing that

Adventure/Survival

it is more complex than they previously assumed. The novel will especially resonate with those who are obsessed with a strong desire. Set in an eighteenth-century English village, the novel also introduces readers to the fascinating details of daily life in this period.

**For those also seeking**: disinterested understanding of the world
**For those drawn to**: story
**Themes/subjects**: buried/hidden treasure, outlaws, adventure, father-son relationships, outcasts/misfits, obsessions, orphans, cemeteries/tombs, village/small-town life, British history, nurturers, inns/taverns, clues/riddles, romance, smugglers
**Reading interest level**: grade 6 and up
**Curricular tie-ins**: Ask students to research the everyday lives of people in mid-eighteenth-century England or smuggling in eighteenth-century England. They could present their findings in written, pictorial, or audio form.
**Adaptations & alternative formats**: television mini-series directed by Andy De Emmony (2013); movie directed by Fritz Lang (1955); audiobook read by Peter Joyce (2010)
**Translations**: Spanish: *Moonfleet*
**Read-alikes**: Readers who enjoy adventure novels about buried treasure will also like Robert Louis Stevenson's *Treasure Island* and H. Rider Haggard's *King Solomon's Mines*. Murder and swindling also dominate Avi's *Murder at Midnight*.

**Fleischman, Sid** (1920–2010)
**Bandit's Moon** (1998). New York: Greenwillow Books, 2008. 184pp. 978-0061450969.

When 11-year-old Annyrose moves from Louisiana to California with her family, her mother dies of jungle fever, bandits steal their money, and Annyrose breaks her ankle. Her brother Lank decides to travel to the gold-rush area of Mariposa to become rich but is unable take Annyrose with him because of her injury. He leaves his sister at the nearest farmhouse with O. O. Mary, a woman who steals her clothes and treats Annyrose like a slave. Hearing that an infamous outlaw named Joaquin Murieta is in the area, O. O. Mary steals away, leaving Annyrose alone to face him. When Joaquin and his men break into the farmhouse, Annyrose asks if they will take her with them so she can escape from the cruel woman. Joaquin agrees because he wants Annyrose to teach him how to read.

Little is she prepared for the dangers she must endure and the moral dilemmas she must face in traveling with a band of notorious outlaws. An exuberant, plot-driven novel, *Bandit's Moon* will appeal to readers who enjoy lively, fast-paced stories. The twists and turns of the plot are clever and filled with high drama.

Joaquin Murieta was an actual outlaw who lived during the time of the California Gold Rush. But, as Fleischman writes in an afterward to the novel, Joaquin's life was transformed into "flamboyant legend" in the newspapers of his day. Called "the Robin Hood of the Mountains," he sought revenge for racially motivated wrongs committed against him. Like Annyrose, readers will reconsider their assumptions about outlaws once they hear his story. As Annyrose observes, "I wondered what sort of man he would have been now if he hadn't been so cruelly wronged." The moral complexities and ironies of the novel turn an exciting story of a bandit into a thought-provoking critique of a historical era. Readers will gain a deep understanding of a fascinating time in American history by reading *Bandit's Moon*.

**For those also seeking**: disinterested understanding of the world
**For those drawn to**: story, setting
**Themes/subjects**: California, Gold Rush, frontier and pioneer life, outlaws, criminals/thieves, racism, stealing, greed, siblings and sibling issues, orphans, moral dilemmas, revenge, literacy/illiteracy, justice and injustice, wrongfully accused, disguises, missing persons
**Reading interest level**: grades 3–6
**Curricular tie-ins**: Ask students to create a wanted poster for Joaquin Murieta. This book would also be an excellent resource for a lesson on the California Gold Rush.
**Adaptations & alternative formats**: audiobook read by Julia Gibson (2002)
**Translations**: Spanish: *La Luna del Bandido*
**Read-alikes**: Karen Cushman's *The Ballad of Lucy Whipple* and Sid Fleischman's *By the Great Horn Spoon!* also depict the California Gold Rush. Leon Garfield's *Black Jack* features a child who travels with a larger-than-life villain similar to Joaquin Murieta. Like Fleischman, Garfield uses gusto and exaggeration in his depiction of the past. Literacy and alleged crimes feature prominently in Avi's *Murder at Midnight*.

**Horvath, Polly** (1957–)
***My One Hundred Adventures*** (2008). New York: Yearling Books, 2010. 260pp. 978-0375855269.

*Adventure/Survival*

Jane Fielding and her three siblings live with their poet mother in a run-down house near the sea. The summer after she turns 12, Jane longs for something different in her life, and even prays that she will experience a hundred adventures. After Jane finishes her prayer, Preacher Nellie asks her to help give out bibles. The preacher hijacks a hot-air balloon and persuades Jane to get in and then drop bibles from above. When Jane accidentally hits a youngster on the head with one of the bibles, his mother accuses her of causing permanent brain damage. Horrified, Jane offers to babysit her five unruly children, an offer that Mrs. Gourd exploits. Although Jane participates in many additional adventures, few of them are what she expects and all of them help her mature.

Winner of the National Book Award, and a runner up for the Newbery Award, *My One Hundred Adventures* is a heart-warming, character-driven story. Encountering a number of eccentric characters who take advantage of her lack of sophistication, Jane must deal with what she calls "the mysterious workings of adults," and learn how to cope with all types of characters. Like her mother, who has been let down and used by a number of people, Jane develops compassion and understanding for them. Readers who have been disappointed by or mistreated by others will reframe their ideas and find a new way of responding to them after reading the story. A novel filled with irony, insight, and wry observations, it will appeal to anyone looking for a witty, thought-provoking story.

**For those also seeking**: reassurance/comfort/confirmation of self-worth/strength
**For those drawn to**: character
**Themes/subjects**: single-parent families, poverty, summer vacations, aiding/helping, adventure, secrets, sea and seashore, village/small-town life, imposters, New England
**Reading interest level**: grades 4–7
**Curricular tie-ins**: Ask students to pick a secondary character from the novel and write a diary entry about his or her life, focusing on one of the days depicted in the novel.
**Adaptations & alternative formats**: audiobook read by Alexandra Ricci (2008)
**Read-alikes**: Readers who would like to follow Jane's life will enjoy the sequel to the novel: *Northward to the Moon*. Jeanne Birdsall's *The Penderwicks* is also about the adventures of a single-parent family during a summer vacation.

**Key, Watt** (1970–)
**Alabama Moon** (2006). New York: Square Fish, 2010. 294pp. 978-0312644802.

From the very first sentence—"Just before Pap died, he told me that I'd be fine as long as I never depended on anybody but myself"—the novel captures our attention. Moon is only 10 years old and living in a dugout in an Alabama forest. After describing how he manages to bury his only living parent, Moon describes the events that led to his father's death. Pap breaks his leg but refuses to get medical attention. Squatting on land and living like a hermit, Pap does not want anyone's help. Eventually he realizes that he is dying and advises Moon to travel to Alaska and find like-minded people. He especially warns his son to stay clear of the government. The story of how this 10-year-old boy tries to survive on his own is deeply moving.

Because readers sees everything through Moon's eyes, they soon realize that they cannot trust his naive perception of events. Moon's unquestioning acceptance of his father's advice is called into doubt once he leaves home. Added to his grief and fear are creeping reservations about his father's ideas.

After reading the novel, children will realize that some adults may have misguided, even dangerous ideas, and that society's rules do not always benefit everyone. The novel gives readers insight into the effects of war on members of the armed forces. It also helps them understand what it would like to be raised in an institution.

**For those also seeking**: disinterested understanding of the world
**For those drawn to**: story
**Themes/subjects**: orphans, survival, wilderness survival, bullying, self-reliance, friendship, resourcefulness, loneliness, dead or absent father, father-son relationships, war (psychological effects), forests, southern United States
**Reading interest level**: grades 6–8
**Curricular tie-ins**: Moon's father returns from the Vietnam War a changed man. Ask students to research the Vietnam War, focusing on how it was perceived by the American public and how this perception affected those who fought in it. Students could present their findings as a script for a podcast.
**Adaptations & alternative formats**: movie directed by Tim McCanlies (2009); audiobook read by Nick Landrum (2007)
**Translations**: French: *Alabama Moon*

Adventure/Survival

**Read-alikes**: Felice Holman's *Slake's Limbo*, Gary Paulsen's *Hatchet*, and Jean Craighead George's *My Side of the Mountain* are also about boys who learn to survive on their own. Marjorie Kinnan Rawlings's *The Yearling* is about a boy who grows up in a similarly remote environment. Like Moon's father, Peter's guardian in Kate DiCamillo's *The Magician's Elephant* and the recluse in Lauren Wolk's *Wolf Hollow* are also negatively affected by war.

**Thurber, James** (1894–1961)
**The Wonderful O** (1957). Illustrated by Marc Simont. New York: New York Review Books, 2009. 72pp. 978-1590173091.

When Littlejack enters a tavern, a stranger called Black suspects that the pirate has a map of an island containing hidden treasure. When Littlejack discovers that Black has a ship and a crew, they form a partnership. The men set sail for the island of Ooroo and once there, scour the island for treasure. Finding nothing, Black turns his attention to a preoccupation of his and issues an edict banning the letter "O." "I've had a hatred of that letter," he tells Littlejack, "ever since the night my mother became wedged in a porthole. We couldn't pull her in and so we had to push her out." The pirates and their crew start by banning words that contain the letter O. Then they banish musical instruments, statues, animals, flowers, food, games, and just about anything on the island that contains the letter "O" in its name.

A very funny book, *The Wonderful O* takes the idea of banishing a letter and carries it to absurd extremes ("O-lessness is now a kind of cult in certain quarters" says Hyde, the pirate lawyer). Filled with wordplay, alliteration, and rhyme, the book is an excellent choice for reading aloud. Readers will view language with fresh appreciation after reading this novel.

The book will also appeal to readers who love exciting stories about pirates and buried treasure. A language- and plot-driven novel, *The Wonderful O* contains high drama, thrilling scenes, and an imaginative portrayal of an unusual subject. Marc Simont's original, offbeat illustrations are an added appeal.

**For those drawn to**: language, story
**Themes/subjects**: pirates, wordplay, language/communication, buried/hidden treasure, islands, humor
**Reading interest level**: grades 3–6

**Curricular tie-ins**: Ask students to create a billboard advertisement for the novel. They should only use words that do not contain the letter "o" (with the exception of the title of the book).
**Adaptations & alternative formats**: audiobook read by Melissa Manchester (2011)
**Translations**: Spanish: *La Maravillosa O*
**Read-alikes**: Jon Scieszka's *The Not-So-Jolly Roger* is a humorous book about pirates while Norton Juster's *The Phantom Tollbooth* is a funny story about a boy who visits places such as the language-dominated Dictionopolis.

## Models for Identity

**Fleischman, Sid** (1920–2010)
**The 13th Floor: A Ghost Story** (1995). Illustrated by Peter Sis. New York: Greenwillow Books, 2007. 228pp. 978-0061345036.

When Buddy Stebbins's parents die in a plane crash, Buddy and his sister are left in deep debt. Faced with the prospect of selling the family home, and left with no one but his older sister, 12-year-old Buddy is deeply worried about the future. After receiving a mysterious call from a stranger telling him to go to the 13th floor of an old law building, Buddy is not able to ask his sister what to do. He is unable to locate her. Suspecting that she has gone to the law building, he does too. When he gets off the elevator on the thirteenth floor, he is amazed to find that he is on a pirate ship run by an ancestor from the seventeenth century. Buddy must deal with dangerous pirates, possible starvation and dehydration, and a witch trial.

In an afterward to the novel, Fleischman points out that because the age of piracy coincided with the age of witchcraft, he created a novel about both. An exciting swashbuckling tale, *The 13th Floor* combines an action-filled plot with historical events. Fleischman's trademark humor and exuberance make this fast-paced story lively and entertaining. After reading this novel, children will understand how ordinary people could have been accused of being witches.

Buddy copes successfully with the loss of his parents, the threat of losing his home, and highly dangerous adventures at sea. His resourcefulness, courage, and calm acceptance of all challenges make him a truly inspirational character. Readers who have faced the death of family members or those who have lost their homes will find Buddy's story a source of strength.

Adventure/Survival

Illustrations by award-winning artist, Peter Sis, evoke an old-world charm that will attract readers to the past.

**For those also seeking**: disinterested understanding of the world
**For those drawn to**: story, setting
**Themes/subjects**: pirates, witch hunting, orphans, time travel, adventure, mystery/suspense, superstitions, colonial New England, Puritans, buried/hidden treasure, boats and ships, sea voyage, ghosts, justice and injustice, missing persons, money/debt, wrongfully accused
**Reading interest level**: grades 3–6
**Curricular tie-ins**: Divide students into three groups for a jigsaw activity. Groups are responsible for finding out information about one of the following topics: Puritanism in New England, seventeenth-century witch hunting, or everyday life in colonial New England.
**Translations**: French: *Le Treizième Étage: Une Histoire de Fantôme*
**Read-alikes**: Those who love stories about pirates will enjoy Robert Louis Stevenson's *Treasure Island*, Kenneth Oppel's *Airborn*, and Leon Garfield's *Jack Holborn*, while those who like stories about witch hunting should read Diana Wynne Jones's *Witch Week* or Elizabeth George Speare's *The Witch of Blackbird Pond*. Avi also depicts mysteries, ghosts, superstitions, and historical matters in *Midnight Magic* and *Murder at Midnight*.


**Ibbotson, Eva** (1925–)
**Journey to the River Sea** (2001). New York: Puffin Books, 2003. 298pp. 978-0142501849.

After her parents die in a train crash, Maia's guardian looks for relatives to look after her. In the meantime, Maia attends the Mayfair Academy for Young Ladies in London. When the Carters are located in Brazil, these distant relatives agree to give Maia a home. Scared about living in the dangerous Amazon region but excited at the prospect of a home and family, Maia travels across the ocean by boat with Miss Minton, her newly hired governess. Maia instantly falls in love with the landscape but is surprised at the cool reception she receives from Mr. and Mrs. Carter and their twin daughters. The English Carters barely tolerate the Brazilian people and the South American environment. Mr. Carter had hoped to make his fortune in Brazil by harvesting rubber. Maia discovers that he only agreed to take her in because his business has been failing and he needs extra income. Maia must learn to cope with her cruel relatives and their prison-like home.

Runner up for three awards (the Carnegie Medal, the Whitbread Children's Book of the Year, and The Guardian Fiction Award), *Journey to the River Sea* is an exciting story set in an exotic locale. It is also a though-provoking exploration of the exploitation of indigenous peoples during the age of empire-building.

Maia's journey is one of discovery as she learns about new places, new ways of life, and her own goals. An inspirational character who must cope with the unexpected death of her parents, the dangers of the jungle, and the cruelty of her relatives, Maia serves as a role model for readers who must face adversity. Those who have suffered the loss of a parent or experienced the cruelty of people close to them will find encouragement and comfort in Maia's story.

**For those also seeking**: reassurance/comfort/confirmation of self-worth/strength
**For those drawn to**: story, character
**Themes/subjects**: adventure, Amazon region, orphans, colonialism, ethnocentrism, governesses, indigenous peoples (Brazil), cultural differences, class differences, cruelty, education, courage, twins
**Reading interest level**: grades 5–8
**Curricular tie-ins**: The Amazon region is a place that fulfills Maia's and Finn's dreams while England is Clovis's ideal place to live. Ask students to write a reflection in their reader response journals about where they would like to live and why. The novel would also be an ideal resource for a lesson on rain forests or the Amazon jungle.
**Adaptations & alternative formats**: audiobook read by Penelope Rawlins (2014)
**Translations**: Spanish: *Maia se Va al Amazonas*; French: *Reine du Fleuve*
**Read-alikes**: Readers who enjoy adventure stories with female protagonists will like Sharon Creech's *The Wanderer*, Jean Craighead George's *Julie of the Wolves*, and Scott O'Dell's *Sarah Bishop*.

## Reassurance/Comfort/Confirmation of Self-Worth/Strength

**Ballantyne, R. M. (1825–1894)**
**The Coral Island** (1858). Doylestown, PA: Wildside Press, 2002. 291pp. 9781592245062. PD.

Attracted to the sea, Ralph has always possessed a roving disposition. When the 15-year-old hears stories about the idyllic islands in the South

*Adventure/Survival* 65

Pacific, he joins a crew bound for the area. But once the ship approaches the south-sea islands, a violent storm hits and the vessel sinks. When Ralph awakens after falling unconscious, he discovers that he has landed on an island with two of his shipmates: 18-year-old Jack and 14-year-old Peterkin. The sole survivors of the shipwreck, they are afraid of starving to death if the island is uninhabited and being eaten by cannibals if it is occupied.

Ralph faces disaster on a colossal scale including the loss of virtually everyone he knows and everything he owns. Once on the island, he confronts threats from natural disasters, wild animals, pirates, and cannibals. Ralph's story is still popular a century and a half after publication because it arouses primal fears in readers, as they imagine what it would be like to lose everything and live on a remote desert island. Although a tale of daring exploits and grave dangers, *The Coral Island* reassures readers that no disaster is insurmountable. The novel will resonate with readers whose families have experienced economic challenges or those who have experienced homelessness.

**For those also seeking**: acceptance
**For those drawn to**: story
**Themes/subjects**: castaways, shipwrecks, wilderness survival, survival, islands, indigenous peoples (South Pacific), nature, tornados, caves, colonialism, cultural differences, Christianity, civilization, sailing
**Reading interest level**: grades 5–8
**Curricular tie-ins**: In small groups, students could discuss Ballantyne's depiction of indigenous peoples. Ask them to consider whether or not the novel is the product of a colonial mentality. Volunteers could then share their responses with the entire class.
**Adaptations & alternative formats**: audiobook read by Peter Joyce, 2010
**Translations**: Spanish: *La Isla de Coral*; French: *L'Île de Corail*
**Read-alikes**: Readers who enjoy island adventure stories will also like Dan Gemeinhart's *Scar Island*, Johann David Wyss's *The Swiss Family Robinson*, Robert Louis Stevenson's *Treasure Island*, Scott O'Dell's *Island of the Blue Dolphins*, Kenneth Oppel's *Airship*, and J. M. Barrie's *Peter Pan*.

**Haggard, H. Rider** (1856–1925)
**King Solomon's Mines** (1885). London: Penguin, 2007. 260pp. 978-0141439525. PD.

When Sir Henry Curtis learns that the elephant hunter, Allan Quatermain, had once met his missing brother, he is deeply interested in pairing up with him to find the lost man. Quatermain tells Sir Henry that his brother was rumored to have gone in search of King Solomon's Mines. Sir Henry asks Quatermain to accompany him and Captain John Good on a journey to the African interior in search of his brother. The three men also plan to look for the legendary diamond mines, a place of immense treasure from which no one has ever returned alive. If they manage to bring back diamonds from these mines, they will be the richest men in the world. With an ancient treasure map to guide them, the trio must cross 130 miles of grueling desert, a feat few have ever accomplished.

Inspired by Robert Louis Stevenson's *Treasure Island*, *King Solomon's Mines* is an exciting plot-driven novel. From the beginning of their journey, the men feel doomed to disaster and believe that they have little chance of success or even survival. Readers who feel pessimistic about the future will find hope and encouragement in this story. Even when the men are doomed, they act nobly and courageously, providing models of identity for readers.

**For those also seeking**: models for identity
**For those drawn to**: story
**Themes/subjects**: wilderness survival, buried/hidden treasure, missing persons, mines/mining, indigenous peoples (Africa), cultural differences, colonialism, friendship, deserts, battles/wars, courage, journeys, wealth, hunger
**Reading interest level**: grade 6 and up
**Curricular tie-ins**: Ask students to create an extra scene for the novel. Imagine Sir Henry and Quatermain leaving the mine with sacks of diamonds. They meet a group of indigenous men who accuse them of stealing.
**Adaptations & alternative formats**: television mini-series directed by Steve Boyum (2004); movie directed by J. Lee Thompson (1985); audio-book read by Simon Prebble (2011); graphic novel by C. E. L. Welsh and illustrated by Bhupendra Ahluwalia (2011)
**Translations**: Spanish: *Las Minas del Rey Salomon*; French: *Les Mines du Roi Salomon*
**Read-alikes**: Readers who enjoy novels about treasure hunting will like William Pène Du Bois's *The Twenty-One Balloons*, J. Meade Falkner's *Moonfleet*, and Robert Louis Stevenson's *Treasure Island*.

Adventure/Survival

**Otis, James** (1848–1912)
**Toby Tyler; or, Ten Weeks with a Circus** (1881). Victorville, CA: Pulpville Press, 2013. 171pp. 978-0983185789. PD.

When the circus comes to town, the candy vendor, Mr. Lord, offers young Toby a permanent job. Unhappy with his foster father and fascinated with circuses, Toby agrees to run away from home to join the traveling show. But once he does so, the candy vendor reveals his true nature, beating the boy and treating him cruelly. Toby soon realizes how much he misses home and what a big mistake he made in running away from it. Unable to leave the circus, Toby creates a new life for himself, making friends with unusual characters as well as with a monkey named Mr. Stubbs.

Seeing the world through Toby's eyes, the reader realizes before the boy does that his naiveté will lead him into trouble. Toby is tricked by cunning adults and is too trusting of the monkey, Mr. Stubbs. Attributing human emotions and altruistic ideas to the monkey, Toby does not anticipate the trouble that the animal will cause him. Readers who are harshly or unfairly treated will find strength in Toby's story.

Ironically, when Toby lives in foster care, he dreams of an exciting life in the circus, and when in the circus, he yearns to return home. Readers who think "the grass is greener on the other side" may see their lives differently and recognize the value of their present circumstances after reading the novel.

**For those also seeking**: awakening/new perspectives/enlargement of possibilities
**For those drawn to**: story
**Themes/subjects**: circuses (animal), runaway children, monkeys/apes, abused children, abuse (physical), adventure, foster care, orphans, corporeal punishment, cruelty, friendship, homesickness, mistakes
**Reading interest level**: grades 3–5
**Curricular tie-ins**: Ask students to create a collage about circuses. Alternatively, ask them to pair with another student and discuss the benefits and drawbacks of circuses.
**Adaptations & alternative formats**: Disney movie directed by Charles Barton (1960); audiobook read by Amon Purinton (1999)
**Read-alikes**: Readers who enjoy stories about circuses should also read Kenneth Oppel's *The Boundless*, Hugh Lofting's *Doctor Dolittle's Circus*, and Astrid Lindgren's *Pippi Goes to the Circus*. Gilly in Katherine Paterson's *The*

*Great Gilly Hopkins* is another character who is initially unhappy with her foster care situation.

**Ransome, Arthur** (1884–1967)
**Swallows and Amazons** (1930). Illustrated by the author. Boston, MA: David R. Godine, 1985. 351pp. 978-1567924206.

While on summer holidays at a farm in the English Lake District, the four Walker children find a small island that they know is not "just an island. It was *the* island, waiting for them." Highly imaginative children, they decide to sail there, pretending to be explorers on their way to a desert island. Mother facilitates their journey—sewing tents, supplying provisions, and visiting them periodically. As the children sail to their island, they pass a man they call Captain Flint and suspect him of being a retired pirate. Once on the island, they are surprised to find evidence of previous inhabitants. A few days later a boat with a skull-and-crossbones flag draws near. When two "Amazons" shoot arrows at them, they meet the fearless Blackett sisters.

This first of 12 novels in the *Swallows and Amazons* series is about the children's adventures on a desert island. It will appeal to readers who enjoy humorous stories about outdoor adventures. Nancy Blackett, who introduces herself as "master and part owner of the Amazon, the terror of the seas," is a particularly feisty and engaging character. Ordering her sister about ("Avast there, Peggy, you goat") and taking to heart her role as pirate, she is lively and entertaining.

Although the children play at occupations such as explorer and pirate, they also acquire practical skills, becoming more independent in the process. Readers who are interested in managing on their own in a remote location will learn a host of survival skills. The novel will appeal to children who would like to be more self-sufficient, and will reassure them that they too can be resourceful and self-reliant. The winsome illustrations by the author evoke a world of guileless, childlike innocence.

**For those also seeking**: disinterested understanding of the world
**For those drawn to**: story
**Themes/subjects**: adventure, islands, sailing, boats and ships, camping, friendship, self-reliance, utopian places, summer vacations
**Reading interest level**: grades 4–7

*Adventure/Survival*

**Curricular tie-ins**: Create either a comic strip of the Walkers and the Blacketts or a map of the island and surrounding area.
**Adaptations & alternative formats**: movie directed by Philippa Lowthorpe (2016); audiobook read by Alison Larkin (2008)
**Translations**: French: *Hirondelles et Amazones*
**Read-alikes**: Readers who enjoy sea adventures will also like Avi's *The True Confessions of Charlotte Doyle*, Sharon Creech's *The Wanderer*, Jules Verne's *Twenty Thousand Leagues under the Sea*, and Arthur Ransome's 11 sequels to *Swallows and Amazons* (*Swallowdale, Peter Duck, Winter Holiday, Coot Club, Pigeon Post, We Didn't Mean to Go to Sea, Secret Water, The Big Six, Missee Lee, The Picts and the Martyrs, Great Northern?*).

**Ransome, Arthur** (1884–1967)
**We Didn't Mean to Go to Sea** (1937). Illustrated by the author. Jaffrey, NH: David R. Godine, 2014. 333pp. 978-1567924879.

When Jim Brading invites the four Walker children to join him onboard the Goblin for a few days, their mother insists they confine their sailing to the harbor and not to go near the sea. After the first night, Jim leaves the boat anchored at port so that he can buy fuel. Once he leaves, everything goes wrong. Jim fails to return, dense fog suddenly emerges, and the anchor does not hold when the tide rises. Before they know it, the Walker children are out to sea in the midst of an impenetrable fog. They are forced to steer blindly because of the fog; they have no idea where they are going, and the weather deteriorates quickly. When night arrives, their lights fail to work, making the vessel invisible to other boats.

The most exciting story in the *Swallows and Amazons* series, *We Didn't Mean to Go to Sea* is a heart-pumping tale of survival at sea. The Walker children must cope with a series of disastrous scenarios, ones over which they have no control. Although there is little that the Walker children can do to change the circumstances they are in, they learn to be resilient and resourceful during the crisis. Readers who must face frightening or intimidating situations will find inspiration in this story.

**For those drawn to**: story
**Themes/subjects**: sea voyage, boats and ships, sailing, adventure, survival, self-reliance
**Reading interest level**: grades 4–8

**Curricular tie-ins**: Ask students to pretend they are journalists and must write a front-page news story about the crossing of the North Sea by the Walker children.
**Adaptations & alternative formats**: audiobook read by Alison Larkin (2009)
**Translations**: French: *Nous ne Voulions pas Aller en Mer*
**Read-alikes**: Avi's *The True Confessions of Charlotte Doyle*, Sharon Creech's *The Wanderer*, Sid Fleischman's *The 13th Floor* are also survival stories that take place at sea. Ransome wrote 11 additional adventure stories in the *Swallows and Amazons* series (*Swallows and Amazons, Swallowdale, Peter Duck, Winter Holiday, Coot Club, Pigeon Post, Secret Water, The Big Six, Missee Lee, The Picts and the Martyrs, Great Northern?*).

**Stevenson, Robert Louis** (1850–1894)
**Treasure Island** (1883). New York: Knopf, 1992. 319pp. 978-0679418009. PD.

When Billy Bones arrives at the Admiral Benbow Inn, the old pirate is worried that a seafaring man with a wooden leg may appear. He even pays young Jim Hawkins, the innkeeper's son, to look out for the man. When a blind beggar named Pew arrives and gives Billy Bones the dreaded "black spot" summons, Bones dies of a stroke. Upon searching Billy Bones's sea chest, Jim finds a treasure map. When he shows it to Doctor Livesey and Squire Trewlaney, the men decide to hire a ship and search for the treasure. Hiring a sea cook named Long John Silver who suggests the names of many of the crew members, Squire Trewlaney outfits the ship to sail to Treasure Island. While they are at sea, Jim overhears a conversation that reveals the real identity and motivation of the crew members.

Jim's perception of Treasure Island changes dramatically from initial dreams of joyful anticipation to final nightmares of mutiny, deceit, double-crossing, and murder. As he admits at the end of the story, "Oxen and wain-ropers would not bring me back again to that accursed island." A swashbuckling sea adventure, *Treasure Island* with its pirates, treasure maps, and threats of mutiny will appeal to fans of derring-do novels. Long John Silver, the self-serving pragmatist who survives by his wits, resiliency, and ingenuity, is charming, irresistible, and unforgettable. The book will reassure readers who are fearful of the unknown that they, like Jim Hawkins, can survive. And those who wish for great wealth may think twice about the value of riches after reading the novel.

**For those also seeking**: awakening/new perspectives/enlargement of possibilities
**For those drawn to**: story, setting
**Themes/subjects**: sea voyage, pirates, buried/hidden treasure, boats and ships, greed, islands, inns/taverns
**Reading interest level**: grades 6–8
**Curricular tie-ins**: Ask students to create a slideshow presentation about piracy in the nineteenth century.
**Adaptations & alternative formats**: television movie directed by Steve Barron (2012); Disney movie directed by Byrin Haskin (1950); audiobook read by Neil Hunt (2009); graphic novel by Andrew Harrar (2010); graphic novel by Tim Hamilton (2005)
**Translations**: Spanish: *La Isla del Tesoro*; French: *Île au Trésor*
**Read-alikes**: Those who enjoy books about pirates will like Sid Fleischman's *The 13th Floor: A Ghost Story* and Kenneth Oppel's *Airship*, while those who love novels about treasure hunting should read J. Meade Falkner's *Moonfleet* and Scott O'Dell's *The King's Fifth*. Dan Gemeinhart's *Scar Island* is an island adventure story about a boy who must survive in the midst of dangerous, criminal characters.

## Connection with Others/Awareness of Not Being Alone

**Konigsburg, E. L.** (1930–2013)
**From the Mixed-Up Files of Mrs. Basil E. Frankweiler** (1967).
Illustrations by the author. New York: Aladdin, 2007. 162pp. 978-1416949756.

The eldest of four children, 12-year-old Claudia feels underappreciated and unjustly treated by her parents. She is also "bored with simply being straight-A's Claudia Kincaid." Deciding to run away from her suburban Greenwich home, she plans to go to "a comfortable place, an indoor place, and preferably a beautiful place." Claudia persuades her 9-year-old brother, Jamie, to run away with her to the Metropolitan Museum of Art in neighboring New York City. However, hiding out in a museum for a week is much more difficult than either of them suspect.

Adamant that she must not return home until she can come back changed somehow, Claudia undertakes a journey that is as much a psychological exploration as a geographical and educational one. When she first arrives at the museum, Claudia is determined to learn "everything about everything." Her intellectual curiosity is infectious and readers too will learn fascinating facts about the museum, the Italian renaissance, and Michelangelo. But her attention then focuses on an alleged secret about a sculpture recently acquired by the museum.

Those who feel taken for granted at home, or tired of the responsibilities of being the eldest will not feel so alone after reading the novel. Claudia's story will also resonate with readers who are tired of the monotony of their lives. A witty, light-hearted novel, this Newbery Award Winner depicts humorous scenes such as Claudia and Jamie bathing in the museum fountain, sleeping in a sixteenth-century bed in a furniture exhibit, and worrying if they forget to brush their teeth before going to bed in the museum.

**For those also seeking**: disinterested understanding of the world
**For those drawn to**: character, setting
**Themes/subjects**: museums, secrets, runaway children, siblings and sibling issues, New York City, education, identity, anger/hostility, eldest siblings, Italian Renaissance, Michelangelo, city life, journeys, perseverance/determination, boredom, humor
**Reading interest level**: grades 4–7
**Curricular tie-ins**: The novel could be used as a motivational resource for classes visiting New York City, The Metropolitan Museum of Art, or indeed any museum. The book would also work well as a resource for a lesson on the Italian Renaissance or Michelangelo.
**Adaptations & alternative formats**: movie by Fielder Cook (1973); audiobook read by Jill Clayburgh (2009)
**Translations**: French: *Fugue au Metropolitan*
**Read-alikes**: Readers who identify with Claudia will like Hermione Granger in the Harry Potter books. Another novel set in New York City, Louise Fitzhugh's *Harriet the Spy*, features a strong female character who is eager to learn all about the world.


**Paulsen, Gary** (1939–)
*Hatchet* (1987). New York: Simon and Schuster Books for Young Readers, 1999. 186pp. 978-1416936473.

After the divorce of Brian's parents, a pilot flies the 13-year-old to the Canadian bush so that he can spend the summer with his father. During the flight, the pilot has a heart attack and dies, leaving Brian alone to manage the plane. With no knowledge of flying, Brian must keep the plane in the air until he finds a place to land it. He crashes in a lake but manages to escape and survive. Landing in the middle of a dense forest in northern Canada with no way of being tracked and nothing to eat, Brian must figure out how to stay alive.

True to his name, Brian Robson is a literary descendant of *Robinson Crusoe* and *The Swiss Family Robinson*. Stripped of everything but his hatchet and the clothes on his back, and forced to manage without food, shelter, people, or civilization, Brian experiences repeated failures and serious setbacks. Unlike his Robinsonnade predecessors, Brian is a city boy who possesses no skills or talents that would help him survive in a remote wilderness landscape. What makes the story so compelling is that he does manage, providing an example that ordinary readers today could follow. By refusing to give in to the depression, loneliness, fear, and self-pity that overwhelm him at times, and by learning from his mistakes, he slowly and steadily makes progress. In doing so, he develops mentally, emotionally, and psychologically.

The theme of separation and division is highlighted in the title of this Newbery Honor book. Calling his parent's divorce, "the big split," and feeling cut off from humanity, Brian starts making connections in the natural world, ones that help him heal. Readers who have experienced emotional pain because of parental dissension or divorce will realize that others have experienced the same emotions. Children who live in poverty will also find strength in this coming-of-age story.

**For those also seeking**: models for identity
**For those drawn to**: story, character
**Themes/subjects**: wilderness survival, survival, plane crashes, coming of age, divorce, forests, adaptation/adjusting to change, accidents (major), natural disasters, tornados, urban versus rural living, loneliness, secrets, self-reliance, resilience, independence, civilization, hunger, anxiety/fears, Northern Canada, northern settings
**Reading interest level**: grade 6 and up
**Curricular tie-ins**: At the end of the novel, Brian is interviewed by the media. Ask students to write a script of an interview with Brian in the style of published interviews—asking and answering the questions that readers would want to know.
**Adaptations & alternative formats**: movie called *A Cry in the Wild* directed by Mark Griffiths (1990); audiobook read by Peter Coyote (2002)
**Translations**: Spanish: *El Hacha*; French: *Crash en Forêt*

**Read-alikes**: Readers who enjoyed Brian's story will want to read the sequels to it: *The River, Brian's Winter, Brian's Return, Brian's Hunt*. Older readers may enjoy William Golding's *Lord of the Flies*, a story of children who survive in a remote environment after their plane crashes.

**Twain, Mark** (1935–1910)
**The Adventures of Tom Sawyer** (1876). New York: Dover Publications, 1994. 220pp. 9780486280615.

When mischief-maker, Tom Sawyer, plays hooky from school, his aunt makes him whitewash the fence as punishment. But Tom gets out of it by outwitting his friends, conning them into doing the work for him. Life in the sleepy village of St Petersburg is too dull and too strict for Tom so he and his friends run away and set up camp on a nearby island. Although they lead a carefree life filled with pranks and adventures, they also witness something traumatic: the murder of a local doctor. When an innocent man is framed for the murder, Tom is tormented with the knowledge that he knows the real murderer.

Although action and adventure dominate the novel, Tom Sawyer's character is its chief attraction. An anti-hero, Tom shirks his responsibilities, plays pranks on others, disobeys authority, and delights in outwitting the adults in his life. Avoiding work and doing as he pleases, Tom Sawyer leads a fun-filled, carefree life that readers can experience vicariously.

Tom is particularly envious of his friend Huckleberry Finn, the outsider in the novel. As the son of a drunkard, Huck "never had to wash, nor put on clean clothes; he could swear wonderfully. In a word, everything that goes to make life precious, that boy had. So thought every harassed, hampered, respectable boy in St Petersburg." Although Tom rebels against society and its restrictions, he, unlike Huck, is very much a part of it and dearly wants its approbation. Imagining himself in outcast roles such as pirate, savage, and outlaw, Tom is knowledgeable about the conventions of each character type, information that he has ironically gained from books. The humorous depiction of the young rogue will especially appeal to readers who feel like misfits. Those who do not fit society's standards of conventional behavior will not feel as solitary or unusual after reading the novel, and will regard their differences and shortcomings with more compassion and understanding.

Adventure/Survival

**For those drawn to**: character
**Themes/subjects**: adventure, prank tricks and mischief, rebelliousness, idleness, challenging authority figures, insiders/outsiders, conformity and nonconformity, moral dilemmas, village/small-town life, runaway children, siblings and sibling issues, half siblings, buried/hidden treasure, camping, murder, humor
**Reading interest level**: grade 5 and up
**Curricular tie-ins**: Ask students to choose five books or movies that Tom Sawyer would like, and provide reasons for these choices.
**Adaptations & alternative formats**: audiobook read by Nick Offerman (2016); graphic novel by Matt Josdal (2010)
**Translations**: Spanish: *Las Aventuras de Tom Sawyer*; French: *Les Aventures de Tom Sawyer*
**Read-alikes**: Those who want to read more about Tom Sawyer will enjoy the sequels to the novel: *The Adventures of Huckleberry Finn*, *Tom Sawyer Abroad*, and *Tom Sawyer, Detective*. The children in Arthur Ransome's *Swallows and Amazons* series (*Swallowdale*, *Peter Duck*, *Winter Holiday*, *Coot Club*, *Pigeon Post*, *We Didn't Mean to Go to Sea*, *Secret Water*, *The Big Six*, *Missee Lee*, *The Picts and the Martyrs*, *Great Northern?*) also lead adventurous lives and pretend to be characters from books.

## Courage to Make a Change

**Du Bois, William Pène** (1916–1993)
**The Twenty-One Balloons** (1947). Illustrations by the author. New York: Puffin Books, 2005. 179pp. 978-0142403303.

Retired Professor Sherman is found stranded and half-dead in the Atlantic Ocean after traveling around the world in a hot air balloon. Rescued by a captain and asked to tell his story, the professor says that he will not divulge any details until he first tells them to the Western American Explorer's Club in San Francisco. The press, then the mayor of New York, and finally the President of the United States ask him to tell his story but the professor refuses to do so until he first tells his fellow explorers. Anticipation mounts as he is given a hero's welcome in San Francisco. The tale that he tells is a strange mixture of fact and fantasy, involving volcanic blasts, diamond mines, peculiar inventions, and a utopian landscape. The professor's bizarre adventures both in the balloon and on the strange island of Krakatoa keep readers in a state of high suspense.

Newspaper headlines such as "PROFESSOR SHERMAN IN WRONG OCEAN WITH TOO MANY BALLOONS," and activities such as washing dishes by hanging them outside the balloon from a fishing rod are some of the delightful touches in the novel. In his introduction to the story, Du Bois writes, "half of this story is true and the other half might very well have happened." A humorous and highly original tall tale, *The Twenty-One Balloons* won the Newbery Medal for the best American children's novel in 1884.

Children who are tired of the routine and monotony of their lives will be inspired to try something adventurous after reading the novel. The fact that Professor Sherman survives his amazing feats and is ready to tackle additional ones is reassuring for those who are anxious about trying new things in their lives.

**For those also seeking**: awakening/new perspectives/enlargement of possibilities
**For those drawn to**: story, setting
**Themes/subjects**: balloons (hot-air), earthquakes/volcanoes, adventure, accidents (major), journeys, islands, inventing/creating, utopian places, greed, secrets, explorers, survival, teachers, wealth, humor
**Reading interest level**: grades 4–6
**Curricular tie-ins**: Ask students to pretend they are journalists for the *New York Times* during the famous volcanic eruption at Krakatoa in 1883. Their assignment is to research the volcano and write a news story about it.
**Adaptations & alternative formats**: audiobook read by Hal Hollings (2008)
**Translations**: Spanish: *Los 21 Globos*; French: *Les 21 Ballons*
**Read-alikes**: Matt in Kenneth Oppel's *Airship* also travels across oceans in a flying machine. Readers who enjoy adventure stories set in unusual places will also like Jules Verne's *Journey to the Center of the Earth* and his *Twenty-Thousand Leagues under the Sea*.


**Fleischman, Sid** (1920–2010)
**The Whipping Boy** (1986). Illustrated by Peter Sis. New York: Greenwillow Books, 2003. 90pp. 978-0060521226.

Prince Horace is called Prince Brat by everyone because he continually misbehaves. Since in his kingdom it is forbidden to spank or hit a prince,

Adventure/Survival 77

Jeremy, the whipping boy, bravely accepts the punishment every time Prince Brat does something wrong. One night the prince awakens Jeremy to tell him that he is running away and needs a servant to accompany him. The boys are captured by outlaws, who discover the prince's identity and plan to hold him for ransom.

A humorously told story with whimsical illustrations by Peter Sis, *The Whipping Boy* will appeal to readers who enjoy fast-paced, plot-driven narratives. This Newbery Award–winning book cleverly introduces parallel episodes and ironic reversals as the haughty prince and likable rat-catcher's son bridge the gap between their very different lives. Readers who would like to make changes in their lives but do not have the confidence to do so will find inspiration in the prince's story. They may also be surprised that, by the end of the novel, they quite like Prince Brat, a character who initially appears detestable. This discovery will help them see that it is possible to like unlikable people if they learn to understand them.

**For those also seeking**: awakening/new perspectives/enlargement of possibilities
**For those drawn to**: story
**Themes/subjects**: princes, royalty, runaway children, adventure, corporeal punishment, spoiled children, class differences, outlaws, stealing, justice and injustice, friendship, humor
**Reading interest level**: grades 3–5
**Curricular tie-ins**: Sid Fleischman uses humor throughout this story. Ask students to create a humorous cartoon related to the book.
**Adaptations & alternative formats**: movie directed by Sydney Macartney (1994); audiobook read by Spike McClure (1993)
**Translations**: Spanish: *El Niño que Pagaba el Pato*; French: *Le Souffre-Douleur*
**Read-alikes**: Sharon Creech's *Castle Corona* is another story about peasant children who move into a castle. Mark Twain's *The Prince and the Pauper* is also a story about a prince and a peasant, one that will appeal to older middle schoolers. Like Jeremy, Fabrizio in Avi's *Midnight Magic* and *Murder at Midnight* is a poor boy trying to survive harsh circumstances in a past era.

**Holman, Felice** (1919–)
**Slake's Limbo** (1974). New York: Aladdin Paperbacks, 1986. 117pp. 978-0689710667.

Considered a "worthless lump," neglected by his guardian, bullied by his classmates, and chased by authorities, 13-year-old Aremis Slake descends into the tunnels of the New York subway. When he finds a hole in a tunnel that leads to an abandoned storage area, he makes this four- by eight-foot cavern his new home. A boy who has never known kindness or care, and who owns nothing in the world but the clothes on his back, Slake learns to manage for himself in a hostile world.

A moving story of urban survival, the novel also depicts Slake's life before he moves into the subway. Sleeping in a cot in his aunt's kitchen, never having enough to eat, slapped into wakefulness in the morning, growing up in a neighborhood of boarded-up buildings and junk-filled vacant lots, Slake has no friends, parents, siblings, role models, or support from anyone. Although he has little insight into his own psyche, readers realize that going underground is his way of burying his fears and hiding from his plight.

Like protagonists in desert-island stories, Slake learns how to find food, create a home for himself, take stock of his environment, find and use tools, discover a way to light his dwelling, make friends with an animal, and prepare ahead for times of need. Readers who have suffered neglect, bullying, abuse, or abandonment will find inspiration and courage to change in Slake's example.

**For those also seeking**: reassurance/comfort/confirmation of self-worth/strength
**For those drawn to**: story, setting
**Themes/subjects**: abused children, abuse (physical), abuse (emotional), trains/subways, homelessness, runaway children, bullying, survival, orphans, underground, city life, child neglect, loneliness, New York City, inventing/creating
**Reading interest level**: grades 6–8
**Curricular tie-ins**: As a class, decide on something students could do to help homeless and disadvantaged children.
**Adaptations & alternative formats**: audiobook read by Neil Patrick Harris (2009)
**Translations**: Spanish: *El Robinson del Metro*; French: *Le Robinson du Métro*
**Read-alikes**: Living alone in a train station, Hugo Cabret learns to survive on his own in Brian Selznick's *The Invention of Hugo Cabret*. Children manage to survive without parents or guardians in Cynthia Voigt's *Homecoming* and Paula Fox's *Monkey Island*.

Adventure/Survival

**Twain, Mark** (1835–1910)
**The Adventures of Huckleberry Finn** (1885). New York: Aladdin Paperbacks, 1999. 978-0689831393. PD.

Seeking escape from his greedy and abusive alcoholic father, Huck Finn fakes his own death and retreats quietly to the Mississippi River in his canoe. He passes the days in hiding, alone and lonely, until he chances upon Jim, an escaped slave he recognizes from his home in St. Petersburg, Missouri. Joined in their pursuit for freedom, they drift peacefully toward Cairo, where the Mississippi meets the Ohio, so that they can paddle their way to a free state. But, just when they are on the cusp of freedom, a thick fog, followed by a series of catastrophes, sets them off course.

Although the contemporary reader may find it difficult to stomach the racial epithets of African Americans and the mawkish depictions of women, this novel is a satire, intended to reflect and critique the social and political evils present in the Heartland during the mid-nineteenth century. As a historical document, it is as important to cultural history of the United States as to its literary history. (Hemingway famously wrote that all modern literature is derived from *The Adventures of Huckleberry Finn*.) It is also still a powerful, character-driven novel about a young boy (Huck is around the age of 12 or 13 when he runs away) faced with a difficult moral dilemma—to help or betray an escaped slave. His conscience, schooled by his society, urges him to turn in Jim, but his reason, and heart, refuses. Like many abused children, Huck struggles with self-doubt. Ultimately, though, he overcomes his uncertainty and chooses to follow his own ethical conclusions.
In this way, Huck Finn remains a national model of courage and civil disobedience.

**For readers also looking for**: disinterested understanding of the world
**Book appeal elements**: setting, language
**Themes/subjects**: abused children, abuse (physical), abuse (emotional), adventure, African American history, alcohol/alcoholism, anxiety/fears, boats and ships, camping, child neglect, coming of age, criminals/thieves, dead or absent mother, depression, disguises, etiquette and customs, escape, father-son relationships, feuds, freedom, friendship, gender roles, greed, guns, humor, hypocrisy, journeys, literacy/illiteracy, low self-esteem, Midwestern United States, mob mentality, money/debt, moral dilemmas, narcissistic parents, only children, orphans, outcasts/misfits, poverty, prank tricks and mischief, resourcefulness, runaway children, satire, slavery, superstitions, survival, wrongfully accused

**Reading interest level**: grades 4–8
**Curricular tie-ins**: Use this book to explain the concept of public domain. Ask students to adapt a part of the story (into a graphic novel, found poem, song, etc.) and share it with the class. Discuss potential ways copyright law can both enable and hinder creativity.
**Adaptations & alternative formats**: audiobook read by Tom Parker (1997)
**Translations**: Spanish: *Las Aventuras de Huckleberry Finn*; French: *Les Aventures de Huckleberry Finn*
**Read-alikes**: Readers who enjoy Twain's sense of humor should also check out *The Prince and the Pauper*. A good companion read is also *Little Women* as Alcott and Twain were contemporaries.

### Acceptance

**Creech, Sharon** (1945–)
**The Wanderer** (2000). New York: HarperTrophy, 2002. 305pp. 978-0064410328.

Thirteen-year-old Sophie decides to join her cousins and uncles in a sailing voyage across the Atlantic. Although everyone but Uncle Dock in this all-male group would rather sail without her, they grudgingly accept her. The story is told from two alternating points of view: Sophie's and her cousin Cody's. Suspense increases as Cody reveals facts about Sophie that she does not disclose or seem to be aware of. And all are puzzled when Sophie tells stories about Bompie's past, stories that the others know cannot be true since she has never met Bompie.

Although the sea voyage is filled with pulse-pounding adventures and very real dangers, what sets the novel apart is the fascinating portrayal of Sophie, a character who experienced trauma in her past. Sophie is both attracted to and fearful of the sea. Like the giant wave that recurs in her nightmares, she feels "torn, as if something is pushing and pulling." A psychologically complex character, Sophie tries to hide painful facts from herself. But once at sea, she is unable to maintain her defense mechanisms. "The sea, the sea, the sea. It thunders and rolls and unsettles me; it unsettles all of us," writes Sophie in her journal. The lyrical language of this Newbery Honor book evokes the rhythmic action of the waves, inspiring readers to view the maritime world with fresh eyes.

Adventure/Survival

Those who have endured trauma may be able to understand and accept it better after reading Sophie's story. The novel will also resonate with those who have experienced the death of a loved one. Readers will gain valuable insight into the psychology of others who have suffered traumatic experiences.

**For those also seeking**: disinterested understanding of the world
**For those drawn to**: character, language
**Themes/subjects**: sea voyage, sailing, boats and ships, adoption, orphans, repression (psychology), projection (psychology), trauma, death, stories and storytelling, grandparents, feminism, dreams, adventure, anxiety/fears, phobias
**Reading interest level**: grade 5 and up
**Curricular tie-ins**: Sophie keeps a journal and Cody, a ship's log. Ask students to create a journal for Brian, recording his thoughts and reflections about one day onboard *The Wanderer*.
**Adaptations & alternative formats**: audiobook read by Dana Lubotsky and John Beach (2009)
**Translations**: Spanish: *A Bordo de el Vagabundo*; French: *Les Voix de l'Océan*
**Read-alikes**: Avi's *The True Confessions of Charlotte Doyle*, Sid Fleischman's *The 13th Floor: A Ghost Story*, and Richard Peck's *Secrets at Sea* are also about characters who make sea voyages across the Atlantic.


**O'Dell, Scott** (1898–1989)
**Island of the Blue Dolphins** (1960). New York: Houghton Mifflin Harcourt, 2010. 177pp. 978-0547328614.

When the Russian Aleuts arrive on the Island of the Blue Dolphins and demand to fish otter, Karana's father—the chief of the tribe—allows them to do so if they pay for the otter in goods. The Aleuts agree to these terms, set up camp, fish for the season, then try to leave the island without paying. Fighting ensues and many islanders, including Karan's father, are killed. Because there are few remaining islanders, the new chief leaves to look for a more hospitable site for the remaining islanders to live. When he finds a place, he sends a ship for his people. Twelve-year-old Karana boards the vessel but realizes that her young brother has been left behind. Jumping off the ship, she finds Ramo but the pair are left stranded on the island. Wild dogs kill Ramo the next day and Karana is left by herself to wait year after year for the ship to return.

Based on the true account of a young nineteenth-century woman who was stranded on a Pacific island for 18 years, this intensely moving story will not easily be forgotten. The twists and turns of the narrative are poignant and compelling, stirring something deep within readers. The events are related in spare, unsentimental, even matter-of-fact prose that reflects the lifestyle and thinking of a stoic people who value simplicity and integrity. The rhythmic language is calm and reassuring—instilling in readers a sense of peace and serenity in the face of calamity. Navigating by the stars, and measuring time by suns, moons, and seasons, Karana lives in harmony with the natural world. A character who makes us question the dominant values of modern society, Karana does so with simple yet profound insights.

At the end of the novel, Karana looks back on her life, realizing how different it has been from the one she had wished for and expected to have. Her story will resonate with readers struggling to accept things that cannot be changed. Published more than half a century ago, this Newbery Award–winning story of courage, determination, and hope still remains an Amazon bestseller today.

**For those also seeking**: models for identity
**For those drawn to**: story, language
**Themes/subjects**: castaways, wilderness survival, survival, adaptation/adjusting to change, loneliness, indigenous peoples (South Pacific), cultural differences, environmentalism, nature, death, accidents (major), revenge, courage, self-reliance, islands, natural disasters, civilization, caves, fish and sea animals, dolphins
**Reading interest level**: grades 4–8
**Curricular tie-ins**: The novel could be used as a resource for a unit on environmentalism. In small groups, students could discuss Karana's attitude toward the environment. The novel would also work well as a springboard to a lesson on nineteenth-century indigenous peoples.
**Adaptations & alternative formats**: movie directed by James B. Clark (1964); audiobook read by Tantoo Cardinal (2000)
**Translations**: Spanish: *La Isla de los Delfines Azules*; French: *L'île des Dauphins Bleus*
**Read-alikes**: Karana's niece travels in search of her aunt in *Zia*, the sequel to *Islands of the Blue Dolphins*. Scott O'Dell's *Sing Down the Moon* is another story about the adventures of an indigenous girl. Readers who enjoy books about survival in remote places will also enjoy Terry Pratchett's *Nation*, R. M. Ballantyne's *The Coral Island*, Gary Paulsen's *Hatchet*, and Scott O'Dell's *Sarah Bishop* and *Streams to the River, River to the Sea*.

**Voigt, Cynthia** (1942)
**Homecoming** (1981). New York: Atheneum Books for Young Readers, 2012. 388pp. 978-1442428782.

When Mrs. Tillerman leaves her four children in a car at a mall, she does not return. Her parting words are, "You little ones, mind what Dicey tells you." Thirteen-year-old Dicey, who is left in charge of ten-year-old James, nine-year-old Maybeth, and six-year-old Sammy, is not sure how long to wait for their mother or what she should do if she does not return. Abandoned years ago by their father, and with no one to turn to except a great-aunt whom they have never met, Dicey is afraid the siblings will be split up if they ask the authorities for help. The siblings decide to travel from Provincetown, Massachusetts, to Bridgeport, Connecticut, in search of Great Aunt Cilla but, with less than twelve dollars to spend, must do so on foot. When they set out, the children have no idea of the length of time it will take to walk across the state or of the difficulties they will encounter along the way.

A National Book Award finalist, this riveting story of survival will appeal to both eager and reluctant readers. Viewing the adults in the novel through the eyes of the children, readers experience the same confusion and lack of comprehension that they do. Maybeth explains their mother as "not lost from anyone. Just lost." Although numerous adults let the children down, they persevere against all odds. Their resourcefulness transforms what could have been a bleak, pessimistic novel into one of hope.

Readers will not forget the psychologically penetrating portraits of the siblings, their cousin, or their grandmother. Although Dicey is afraid, unsure, and confused, she is also tenacious and determined. She is an inspirational role model for readers who have been neglected, wronged, or deserted by parents or guardians. The novel will also resonate with readers whose parents have experienced mental illness.

**For those also seeking**: reassurance/comfort/confirmation of self-worth/strength
**For those drawn to**: story, character
**Themes/subjects**: abandoned children, survival, homelessness, poverty, independence, resilience, resourcefulness, perseverance/determination, grandmothers, family, mental illness, non-traditional families, eldest siblings
**Reading interest level**: grade 6 and up

**Curricular tie-ins**: Ask students to form small groups, find information about homelessness (causes, prevention, and remedies), and create a poster about it.

**Adaptations & alternative formats**: movie directed by Mark Jean (1996); audiobook read by Barbara Caruso (2008)

**Translations**: Spanish: *La Familia Tillerman Busca Hogar*; French: *Les Enfants Tillerman*

**Read-alikes**: Readers interested in the Tillerman children will enjoy the six sequels: *Dicey's Song, A Solitary Blue, The Runner, Come a Stranger, Sons from Afar,* and *Seventeen Against the Dealer*. Katherine Paterson's *The Same Stuff as Stars* and Paula Fox's *Monkey Island* also depict children who have been abandoned by parents.

### Disinterested Understanding of the World

**George, Jean Craighead** (1919–2012)
**My Side of the Mountain** (1959). Illustrated by the author. New York: Puffin Books, 2004. 177pp. 978-0142401118.

When 15-year-old Sam Gribley decides to leave his family and their overcrowded New York apartment, he travels to the Catskill Mountains to live in the wilderness. With only a penknife, a ball of cord, an axe, forty dollars, and some flint and steel, Sam finds his way to land owned by his ancestors. A city boy, he knows very little about surviving in the wilderness. After he manages to catch fish and start a fire, he finds an ancient tree that is hollow at the base. Figuring out how to expand the hole, Sam creates a home for himself inside the base of the tree. With fall and winter approaching, Sam must learn how to stock provisions, survive the cold, make himself winter clothes, evade hunters and tourists, and become totally self-reliant.

A book that appeals to readers of all ages, this survival story is also a fascinating guide to living in the wilderness without money, a home, or other people. Readers who love the outdoors and yearn for adventures will enjoy this story written by an acclaimed naturalist.

In her introduction to the novel, Jean Craighead George writes that "it is very pleasant to run away in a book" and live vicariously through a character like Sam. Even though he has many failures, and despite the fact that he does not possess extensive knowledge of the wilderness, his yearning to succeed outweigh these limitations. Sam's courage, ingenuity, and desire to

Adventure/Survival

live in harmony with the natural world can serve as a role model for readers with similar interests.

**For those also seeking**: models for identity
**For those drawn to**: story, setting
**Themes/subjects**: wilderness survival, runaway children, civilization, urban versus rural living, self-reliance, falcons, mountains, conformity and nonconformity, inventing/creating
**Reading interest level**: grade 3 and up
**Curricular tie-ins**: Ask students to create a travel brochure advertising the Catskill Mountains.
**Adaptations & alternative formats**: movie directed by James B. Clark (1969); audiobook read by Christian Rummel (2007)
**Translations**: Spanish: *Mi Rincon en la Montana*; French: *Ma Montagne*
**Read-alikes**: Readers interested in Sam's story will want to read the four sequels to the novel: *On the Far Side of the Mountain*, *Frightful's Mountain*, *Frightful's Daughter*, and *Frightful's Daughter Meets the Baron Weasel*. Readers will also enjoy the wilderness survival novels: *The Sign of the Beaver* by Elizabeth George Beaver, *Julie of the Wolves* by Jean Craighead George, and *Hatchet* by Gary Paulsen. Brian, in *Hatchet*, is a city boy like Sam.


**George, Jean Craighead** (1919–2012)
**Julie of the Wolves** (1972). New York: Harper & Row, 1972. 170pp. 978-0064400589.

Lost in the Arctic, 13-year-old Julie tries to attract the attention of nearby wolves. She knows that she will starve to death unless the wolves befriend and help her. Having run away from her 13-year-old husband, Julie had planned on journeying to Port Hope. From there she thought she could work aboard a ship and travel to San Francisco, the home of her pen pal. But when she becomes hopelessly lost in the Arctic Tundra, she must figure out how to survive in this inhospitable environment.

*Julie of the Wolves* is a story of a girl as well as people who are caught between worlds: traditional and modern, as well as Inuit and non-native. Known as Julie in English and Miyaz in Inuit, the protagonist is a child on the brink of adulthood, trying to reconcile her past and present. Through Julie's relationships with others, readers learn about the Inuit people and the issues they face—knowledge that will impact readers emotionally as well as intellectually. An exciting tale of survival, this Newbery Award–winning novel also teaches readers about the Arctic environment, the ecosystem, and wild animal's methods of communication. The book will especially appeal to readers whose family members are from two different cultures or races.

Julie patiently watches how the wolves communicate with one another and imitates them to make her needs known. Her desire is to live "in rhythm with the animals and the climate."

Julie's courage, ingenuity, and integrity will provide models of meaning for readers caught between competing forces in their lives.

**For those also seeking**: models for identity
**For those drawn to**: character, setting
**Themes/subjects**: Inuit, Arctic, Alaska, cultural differences, wilderness survival, survival, wolves, father-daughter relationships, indigenous peoples (United States), adaptation/adjusting to change, runaway children, non-traditional families, hunting, hunger, northern settings, winter, environmentalism, ecosystems
**Reading interest level**: grades 5–8
**Curricular tie-ins**: Ask students to form small groups and create poster presentations on one of the following topics: wolves, animals and birds that live in the Arctic, or the adaptation of Inuit people to modernization.
**Adaptations & alternative formats**: audiobook read by Christina Moore (2014)
**Translations**: Spanish: *Julie y los Lobos*; French: *Julie des Loups*
**Read-alikes**: George wrote two sequels to the novel: *Julie* and *Julie's Wolf Pack*. Readers who enjoy books about survival in remote environments will also want to read Jean Craighead George's *My Side of the Mountain*, Gary Paulsen's *Hatchet*, and Scott O'Dell's *Island of the Blue Dolphins* and *Streams to the River, Rivers to the Sea*. The latter two also depict the survival of an indigenous girl in a remote environment. Jack London's *The Call of the Wild* features wolves living in the Yukon.

**Morpurgo, Michael** (1943–).
**Kensuke's Kingdom** (1999). New York: Scholastic Press, 2003. 164pp. 978-0439591812.

When Michael's parents lose their jobs, his father sells the family car and buys a yacht, convincing his wife that their misfortune is an opportunity to see the world. Michael and his parents take sailing lessons and then embark on their

Adventure/Survival 87

world tour. All goes well until Michael and his dog get swept overboard during a violent storm. Hanging on to his football, Michael tries to stay afloat. But as time passes, he is unable to keep fighting and drifts off to sleep.

Awakening on a strange beach, Michael realizes that he and his dog have somehow managed to survive. But unable to find anything to eat or drink on this desert island, he worries that he will die. Awakening the following morning, Michael finds food and bowls of water waiting for him. When he tries to make a fire, a strange old man appears and angrily puts it out. The man draws a picture of the island in the sand and makes it clear that Michael is to stay on one side, and he on the other. In order to survive, Michael knows that he will have to cope with this seeming mad man.

This exciting story of adventure at sea and survival on a desert island will appeal to readers who enjoy action-filled stories. *Kensuke's Kingdom* is also a thought-provoking exploration of the effects of the atomic bombing at Nagasaki. After reading Kensuke's story, readers will understand the events at Nagasaki in a way that touches them deeply. Michael's growing friendship with Kensuke, and his discovery of a way of life that is very different from his own challenges his assumptions and helps him mature. The novel will resonate with readers who have experienced a life-altering event and those whose parents are unemployed.

**For those also seeking**: acceptance
**For those drawn to**: story
**Themes/subjects**: castaways, islands, survival, adventure, atomic bombing (Japan), friendship, cultural differences, Japanese social life and customs, accidents (major), monkeys/apes, anger/hostility
**Reading interest level**: grades 4–8
**Curricular tie-ins**: This novel could accompany a unit on World War II. Students could have a debate about the bombing at Nagasaki. Do they think it was justified or not?
**Adaptations & alternative formats**: audiobook read by Derek Jacobi (2011)
**Translations**: Spanish: *El Reino de Kensuke*; French: *Le Royaume de Kensuké*
**Read-alikes**: Laurence Yep's *Hiroshima* also explores the consequences of the atomic bombing of Japan. Scott O'Dell's *Island of the Blue Dolphins* is about a girl who is stranded on an island in the south Pacific, while Sharon Creech's *The Wanderer* is about a girl who sails across the Atlantic with relatives. Terry Pratchett's *Nation* is another story about castaways on a remote island.

**Mowat, Farley** (1921–2014)
**Lost in the Barrens** (1956). New York: Bantam, 1984. 192pp. 978-0553275254.

When Uncle Angus invites his 16-year-old orphan nephew to live with him in a cabin in northern Manitoba, Jamie happily leaves his Toronto boarding school. Uncle Angus, an Arctic trader and trapper, lives four hundred miles from civilization. After he introduces Jamie to his Cree friend Meewasin and his son, Awasin, the two adolescents become friends. When representatives from a northern Chipewyan tribe visit and ask for help, the boys are keen to assist and prepare for the hundred-mile journey to their camp. Once they arrive at the Chipewyans' home, they are asked to go on a second journey to an area in the Arctic called the Barrens. Eager to comply, the boys accompany the Chipewyans on their journey. But they become separated from their guides and wreck their canoe in a cataract. Realizing that they are in dangerous Inuit territory in one of the world's most inhospitable environments, the boys must figure out how to survive.

Winner of the Governor General's Award for the best Canadian children's novel, this fast-paced book is filled with high adventure and death-defying heroics. The daring feats of the boys land them in serious trouble, but in coping with disaster, they come of age. This compelling novel is also about making connections—with the land as well as with different ethnic groups.

Readers who are interested in how native peoples have managed to survive for centuries in inhospitable environments will find this narrative gripping. The boys' story will also reassure those who are fearful of taking risks that they too can manage in dangerous situations.

**For those also seeking**: reassurance/comfort/confirmation of self-worth/strength
**For those drawn to**: story, setting
**Themes/subjects**: survival, wilderness survival, adventure, Northern Canada, Arctic, indigenous peoples (Canada), coming of age, Inuit, cultural differences, courage, accidents (major), hunting, orphans, winter, inventing/creating, hunger, non-traditional families, northern settings
**Reading interest level**: grade 5 and up
**Curricular tie-ins**: Ask students to form groups for a jigsaw activity. The groups could research subjects depicted in the book such as Crees, Chipewyans, Inuit people, Vikings, and the Arctic Barrenlands.

Adventure/Survival

**Adaptations & alternative formats**: movie directed by Michael Scott (1990)
**Translations**: French: *Perdus dans le Grand Nord: Roman*
**Read-alikes**: Gary Paulsen's *Dogsong* and Jean Craighead George's *My Side of the Mountain* are also about boys who survive in the wilderness.

**Park, Linda Sue** (1960–)
**A Long Walk to Water** (2009). Boston: Clarion Books, 2010. 121pp. 978-0547577319.

Told in alternating chapters, *A Long Walk to Water* is a story about the lives of two 11-year-old Sudanese children. Salva's story begins in 1985 and Nya's, years later in 2008. Salva's class is suddenly interrupted one day by the sound of gunfire. His teacher instructs the students to hide in the bush rather than return home. The Sudanese people are in the midst of civil war, and the violence of the fighting forces villagers to leave their homes and flee their country. Salva does not know where his family is, but must flee south with strangers. Lonely and afraid, he eventually runs into his uncle, a man who helps him escape to Ethiopia. The story of Salva's dangerous journey alternates with the story of Nya's long arduous trips to get drinking water for her family. Walking back and forth to a pond twice daily takes her all day, every day.

A compelling and incredibly moving tale, *A Long Walk to Water* is based on the true story of Salva Dut, a person who endured separation from his family, homelessness, and life in refugee camps. As the narrative progresses, readers wonder if Salva's family survives the violent civil war, and if so, whether Salva ever finds them. They also wonder how Nya and her family can survive in unhealthy, primitive conditions. The two separate plots increase the suspense in the novel as each plot breaks off at key points and turns to the other story. The final chapters of the novel in which the two narratives converge are poignant and powerful, ones that remain with readers long after they finish the novel.

The simplicity of the language helps convey the outlook of a people who endure unbearable trials "bit by bit, one step at a time." Following his uncle's example, Salva tells himself, "*I need only to get through the rest of this day.*" The perseverance of Salva and Nya in the face of incredible adversity will motivate readers who are facing their own problems. By deciding to work on a project that will benefit Sudanese people, Salva transforms his suffering into something truly inspirational.

Readers who want to know what it is like to be a Sudanese child today and what it was like to be a child during the Sudanese Civil War will experience the hopes and suffering of such children by reading the stories of Salva and Nya.

**For those also seeking**: models for identity
**For those drawn to**: story, character
**Themes/subjects**: survival, battles/wars, refugees, Sudan, water shortages (drinking), perseverance/determination, cultural differences, family
**Reading interest level**: grades 5–8
**Curricular tie-ins**: Students can research one of the following topics: the history, customs, politics, refugees, social conditions, and geography of Sudan and present their findings as pages on a class Web site about Sudan. They could also decide as a class on an action that would help victims such as Salva and Nya.
**Adaptations & alternative formats**: audiobook read by David Baker and Cynthia Bishop (2013)
**Read-alikes**: Andrea Davis Pinkney's *The Red Pencil* is about another Sudanese refugee, while Beverley Naidoo's *The Other Side of Truth* is about a girl who must flee her worn-torn country. Gill Lewis's *Gorilla Dawn* is a story set in African country disrupted by war. Like Salva, Serafina in Ann E. Burg's *Serafina's Promise* is uprooted from her home, and like Nya, she must make daily trips for water.


**Paulsen, Gary** (1939–)
**Dogsong** (1985). New York: Simon Pulse, 2007. 162pp. 978-1416939191.

Russel, a 14-year-old Inuit boy, tells his father that he is dissatisfied with life but does not know what to do about it. His father directs him to Oogruk, the elderly village shaman. When Oogruk tells Russel about traditional Inuit ways, the boy realizes that he wants to practice them. Russel learns to hunt using Oogruk's dogsledding team, an activity that prepares him for the epic journey he makes across the inhospitable lands of the Arctic. In traveling to the far north, he must learn how to survive a severe winter with no one to help him but the dogs. Russel is unprepared for what he finds on his journey.

Adventure/Survival

Written in spare language well suited to a people who value simplicity, this Newbery Honor book is a moving account of a boy caught between modern and traditional ways of life. Readers who wonder what it would be like to be Inuit will gain a deep understanding of these people and their lifestyle.

Not finding meaning in modern practices, Russell turns to the past for a more holistic lifestyle. His dogsledding journey to the far north is a rite of passage that tests his survival skills and teaches him how to live off the land. Readers who are dissatisfied with life and are looking for something meaningful will find in Russel's story the courage to make a change.

**For those also seeking**: courage to make a change
**For those drawn to**: character, setting
**Themes/subjects**: survival, wilderness survival, Inuit; indigenous peoples (United States), dogsledding, coming of age, identity, purpose in life, Arctic, winter, hunting, colonialism, conformity and nonconformity, journeys, dreams, northern settings, dogs
**Reading interest level**: grades 6–8
**Curricular tie-ins**: Ask students in small groups to create a book trailer for the novel, one that will interest potential readers to choose the book.
**Adaptations & alternative formats**: audiobook read by Robert Ramirez (2009)
**Read-alikes**: Scott O'Dell's *Black Star, Bright Dawn* is also about indigenous peoples and dogsledding. The Inuit protagonist of Jean Craighead George's *Julie of the Wolves* is another character who is caught between modern and traditional ways of life. Readers who enjoy wilderness survival stories will like Farley Mowat's *Lost in the Barrens*, Gary Paulsen's *Hatchet*, Scott O'Dell's *Island of the Blue Dolphins*, and Jean Craighead George's *My Side of the Mountain*.

**Sachar, Louis** (1954)
**Holes** (1998). New York: Yearling, 2000. 233pp. 978-0440414803.

Finding a pair of running shoes, Stanley races home to give them to his father, a man who is working on an invention for recycling them. But Stanley is stopped by the police and charged with stealing. He is sent to a juvenile detention center called Camp Green Lake. Situated in the middle of a Texas desert and run by an abusive warden, this detention center is a child's worst nightmare. Every day the boys must dig a grave-size hole in the midst of suffocating heat. Befriending a boy named Zero who is insulted and abused by Camp Green Lake workers, Stanley worries when the boy runs away. Stanley goes in search of his friend, but no one expects either boy to survive the desert heat or return alive.

Winner of both the Newbery Medal and the National Book Award for Young People's Literature, *Holes* is a compelling story about boys who have fallen through the cracks of society. Although Sachar explores issues such as poverty, abuse, injustice, juvenile delinquency, racism, illiteracy, homelessness, and abandonment, the novel is witty and hopeful in tone, not gloomy and oppressive as one might expect.

Believing that he is ill-fated, Stanley comes to realize that he is actually a fortunate boy—blessed rather than cursed by the circumstances in his life. A bullied boy who was not happy with himself before going to Camp Green Lake, Stanley grows into the person he wants to be. The ending of the novel in which interconnections between the past and the present and between supposed strangers is cleverly conceived and immensely satisfying.

*Holes* will provide readers with a personal understanding of children who suffer injustice, homelessness, and illiteracy as well as those who end up in juvenile correction facilities. Readers will gain a new perspective on those charged with crime and those who are raised in poverty. The book will resonate with children who have lived in foster homes, have been in trouble with the law, or have experienced any form of injustice.

**For those also seeking**: awakening/new perspectives/enlargement of possibilities
**For those drawn to**: story, character
**Themes/subjects**: prison/incarceration, imprisonment/entrapment, justice and injustice, poverty, stealing, luck/chance, fate/destiny, homelessness, racism, cruelty, abused children, deserts, survival, bullying, agency and powerlessness, reptiles, buried/hidden treasure, literacy/illiteracy
**Reading interest level**: grades 4–7
**Curricular tie-ins**: Sachar explores poverty, homelessness, racism, child abandonment, juvenile delinquency, and illiteracy in the novel. Ask students to divide into groups, pick one of these issues, and create the script for a radio commercial to raise public awareness about it.
**Adaptations & alternative formats**: Disney movie directed by Andrew Davis (2003); audiobook read by Kerry Beyer (2003)
**Translations**: Spanish: *Hoyos*; French: *Le Passage*

*Adventure/Survival*

**Read-alikes**: Dan Gemeinhart's *Scar Island* is about a boy who is sent to a detention center while Katherine Applegate's *Crenshaw* is about a family coping with poverty. In Watt Key's *Alabama Moon*, the boys that Moon meets experience many of the same problems as the boys do in the detention center in *Holes*.

**Wyss, Johann David** (1743–1818)
**The Swiss Family Robinson** (1812). Translated from the German by William H. G. Kingston. Introduction by Jon Scieszka. London: Puffin, 2009. 471pp. 978-0141325309. PD.

When a storm hits the ship that the Robinson family is traveling on and the ship begins to sink, the Crusoes and their four sons are stranded without lifeboats. Managing to float in tubs, they wash up on a remote island. Father, mother, and sons must manage to survive and make a life for themselves in this uninhabited corner of the world. Their major threats are from the wildlife on the island: bears, buffalo, lions, sharks, and even boa constrictors. The family members must use all their ingenuity and courage to survive on their own on this primitive tropical island.

Never safe from threats, the family continually faces the possibility of extinction. Like other desert-island stories, *The Swiss Family Robinson* is filled with daring adventures and high drama. And no one who reads the novel will forget the family's magnificent tree house—the dream habitation of many children.

But what particularly captures the reader's imagination in this Noah's ark story is the loss and rebuilding of a civilization. Stripped of everything, the family has to start life over in this "New Switzerland." The novel will particularly appeal to readers who wonder how they would survive in a remote environment. Depicting how the family members are able to find and grow food, protect themselves from wild animals, create one house and then a second winter dwelling, make clothing, tame animals, and gradually turn a primitive landscape into a civilized environment, the novel is a primer for wilderness survival. The Robinsons even build a library and a budding museum of natural history within their winter home. Characters invent, adapt, reuse, and make do, inspiring readers to do the same.

**For those also seeking**: reassurance/comfort/confirmation of self-worth/strength

**For those drawn to**: story
**Themes/subjects**: castaways, shipwrecks, wilderness survival, survival, islands, adaptation/adjusting to change, boats and ships, inventing/creating, brothers, colonialism, Christianity, wilderness, civilization, caves, fish and sea animals, reptiles
**Reading interest level**: grades 3–6
**Curricular tie-ins**: Ask students to identify 10 things they would take with them to a desert island, and give reasons for their choices.
**Adaptations & alternative formats**: movie directed by Ken Annakin (1960); audiobook read by Jack Sondericker (2012); graphic novel by Richard Blandford (2011)
**Translations**: Spanish: *El Robinson Suizo*; French: *Le Robinson Suisse*
**Read-alikes**: Readers who enjoy island adventure stories will also like R. M. Ballantyne's *The Coral Island*, Robert Louis Stevenson's *Treasure Island*, Scott O'Dell's *Island of the Blue Dolphins*, Terry Pratchett's *Nation*, Kenneth Oppel's *Airship*, and J. M. Barrie's *Peter Pan*. Family members survive by creating a temporary shelter in an abandoned railway car in Gertrude Chandler Warner's *The Boxcar Children*.

CHAPTER FIVE

# Animal

Put simply, an animal story is a story about animals. It doesn't necessarily feature an all-animal cast of characters, but at least one animal features prominently as a main character who is integral to the overall narrative.

Though this definition seems straightforward enough, it doesn't fully capture the diversity to be found within this genre. On one end of the spectrum, we have such writers as Felix Salten whose animal characters in *Bambi* are described realistically, from a third-person, observational perspective. Then, on the other end, we have writers like Michael Bond and characters like Paddington Bear who are so completely anthropomorphized that their animal bodies seem only incidental to the plot. Most fall somewhere in between: E. B. White's farm animals in *Charlotte's Web* still behave like farm animals, and the rabbits in Richard Adam's *Watership Down* still act like rabbits, even though in both stories they seem to possess human consciousness.

Some of the stories are written from the animal's point of view, as in Anna Sewell's *Black Beauty*, Jack London's *Call of the Wild* and *White Fang*, and Sheila Burnford's *The Incredible Journey*. In others, the animals have no voice at all, rather function as foils to the central child character as in *Shiloh*, *The Yearling*, and *Because of Winn Dixie*. Still other writers combine and blend genres: science fiction in Terry Pratchett's *The Amazing Maurice and His Educated Rodents*, fairytale in Kate DiCamillo's *The Tale of Despereaux*, and fantasy in Kenneth Oppel's *Silverwing* trilogy.

Despite this variety, the vulnerability of the animal is always a key element of the animal story. This vulnerability can manifest itself in different ways. In some stories, the animals are hunted or abused; in others, abandoned, lost, or neglected. While some children can unfortunately relate to these experiences, all children, being dependent on adults for their welfare and safety, can relate to these animal characters' subordinate status. It is no wonder that so many children's stories fall into this genre.

A note on series: only one series is included in this section, Kenneth Oppel's *Silverwing* trilogy. This series includes *Silverwing* (1997), *Sunwing* (2000), and *Firewing* (2002). It should be noted that while these novels can be read as their own stand-alone stories, reading them out of order will spoil some plot points, so reading them chronologically is recommended.

## Awakening/New Perspectives/Enlargement of Possibilities

**Dahl, Roald** (1916–1990)
**Fantastic Mr. Fox** (1970). Illustrated by Quentin Blake. New York: Puffin Books, 2007. 81pp. 978-0142410349.

Boggis, Bunce, and Bean, three greedy, rotten lowdown farmers are outraged when they discover that their chickens and ducks are disappearing from their estates. They suspect, correctly, that the culprit is a clever fox. In fact, Mr. Fox, who is indeed very clever, regularly pilfers their houses in order to feed his wife and their four pups.

The farmers, though, are indifferent to the dietary needs of Mr. Fox and his family, and so they hatch a plot to destroy him. But things don't quite go according to plan, and the feud escalates into an all-out war: Mr. Fox loses his tail in a shooting, the woods are destroyed, and all of the animals begin to starve. Desperate, Mr. Fox devises a plan that he hopes will outsmart the farmers and save everyone.

Although Mr. Fox's actions are questionable—he does, after all, steal—they are also what give this fun adventure story its complexity. Is Mr. Fox's stealing for the sake of his family as bad as the farmers' vengeance and greed-motivated violence? In the end, Mr. Fox is rewarded for his tenacity and ingenuity and in this way inspires readers to use their creativity to think of alternative possibilities and persevere.

**For those drawn to**: story, character
**Themes/subjects**: badgers, battles/wars, food, forests, foxes, greed, humor, moral dilemmas, prank tricks and mischief, predators, stealing, underground
**Reading interest level**: grades K–3
**Curricular tie-ins**: This story would complement basic science studies on predator-prey relationships and could be expanded for more advanced studies by asking how agribusiness (as represented by Boggis, Bunce, and Bean) complicates these relationships.
**Adaptations & alternative formats**: first edition published by Alfred Knopf features adorable illustrations by Donald Chaffin; audiobook, *Fantastic Mr. Fox and Other Animal Stories*, read by Chris O'Dowd, Geoffrey Palmer, Stephen Fry, and Hugh Laurie (2013); movie directed by Wes Anderson (2009)
**Translations**: Spanish: *El Superzorro*; French: *Fantastique Maître Renard*
**Read-alikes**: Roald Dahl's *The Twits* also features animals who outwit cruel humans and *Danny, the Champion of the World*, follows a similar plot, but no animal characters, and would appeal to slightly older readers.

**Jarrell, Randall** (1914–1965)
**The Animal Family** (1965). Illustrated by Maurice Sendak. New York: HarperCollins, 1996. 179pp. 978-0062059048.

A hunter lives alone in a log cabin, hidden in the forest, on the edge of the sea. He leads a peaceful, but lonesome existence until he discovers, one day, a beautiful mermaid singing on the shore. The hunter goes to her, and they fall in love. They tell each other stories; they give each other gifts; and they make each other laugh. Their family begins and grows as they adopt new members—first a cub, then a lynx, and then a baby boy who has tragically become orphaned. Although the family is an unusual one, it is loving, supportive, and happy. The animal family is an ideal family.

Randall's spare, lyrical language is both haunting and beautiful and lends to this story a dreamy, fairytale-like quality. While recalling and confirming our basic human need for love and companionship, Randall's odd family also suggests that relations are not always inherited, but forged and built. It awakens readers to the idea that they can seek their own relationships, *choose* both whom they love and support and who loves and supports them.

**For those also seeking**: connection with others/awareness of not being alone
**For those drawn to**: language, setting
**Themes/subjects**: babies, bears, death, fish and sea animals, language/communication, loneliness, love, mermaids, nontraditional family, sea and seashore, translation/translators, wild cats
**Reading interest level**: grades 5–8
**Curricular tie-ins**: As a language activity, use the chapter, "The Mermaid," to segue into a discussion about the limits of language and translation as well as the relationship between language and culture.
**Translations**: Spanish: *La Familia Animal*; French: *Des Animaux Pour Toute Famille*
**Read-alikes**: In Rudyard Kipling's *The Jungle Book*, Mowgli makes his home with animals of different types. Patricia MacLachlan's *Sarah, Plain and Tall* is another book about building a family and the challenges of uniting family members who are different from one another. Also *The Witch Family* by Eleanor Estes features another non-traditional family.


**Lofting, Hugh** (1886–1947)
**The Voyages of Doctor Dolittle** (1922). Illustrated by the author. New York: Dell Publishing, 1988. 316pp. 978-0440400028.

Tommy Stubbins is not quite 10 years old when he begins to apprentice under the famous Doctor Dolittle. It is the early nineteenth century in some place in England called Puddleby-on-the-Marsh. Stubbins's family can't afford to give him a formal education, so instead he assists the naturalist and famous animal doctor so that he can learn, like him, to speak the language of animals and cure them of their ailments.

Apprenticing under Doctor Dolittle is a tall order as he can speak virtually every animal language: parrot, dog, duck, everything except shellfish. Determined to learn this language, too (as shellfish are some of the oldest living creatures on earth and therefore probably very knowledgeable about the Earth's natural history), Doolittle takes Tommy and also his friends Bumpo, Polynesia the parrot, and Jip the dog on a discovery voyage to Spidermonkey Island. The journey, however, is not easy. They encounter bad weather, shipwrecks, and wars—not to mention the fact that the doctor has never been very good with money.

*Voyages* is actually the second book in the series of Doctor Doolittle stories, but it is superior to the others in terms of its narrative shape and its depth of social critique. Awarded the Newbery Medal in 1923 in part, no doubt, to Loftings's satirizing and challenging of Western-centric views on culture and civilization, education, and ways of knowing. He achieves this effect primarily by depicting the world from outsiders' perspectives, animals as well as indigenous peoples living on the fictional Spidermonkey Island. While still a product of his time (Lofting attempts to celebrate the knowledge and culture of indigenous peoples that in some ways perpetuates stereotypes), he nonetheless succeeds at expanding readers' awareness of other points of view.

**For those drawn to**: story
**Themes/subjects**: adventure, battles/wars, birds, boats and ships, class differences, dogs, colonialism, cooperation and teamwork, critical thinking/strategy, cultural differences, fish and sea animals, humor, indigenous peoples, language/communication, malapropisms, money/debt, nature, poverty, sea voyage, shipwrecks, survival
**Reading interest level**: grades K–6
**Curricular tie-ins**: To introduce/encourage critical reading, draw students' attention to Loftings's depiction of indigenous peoples in parts four and five of the novel and ask them what cultural and ideological assumptions are underlying the text (e.g., the notion that they are "primitive").
**Adaptations & alternative formats**: audiobook read by William Sutherland (2004)
**Translations**: Spanish: *Los Viajes Del Doctor Dolittle*; French: *Les Voyages Du Docteur Dolittle*
**Read-alikes**: In addition to the other books in the series, readers who enjoy both the humor of the story and young and independent protagonist may also like Astrid Lindgren's *Pippi Longstocking*.


**Smith, Dodie** (1896–1990)
**The One Hundred and One Dalmatians** (1956). New York: Puffin Books, 2002. 184pp. 978-0140340341.

Pongo and Missus Pongo are a newly wedded Dalmatian dog couple, basking in matrimonial bliss in their new London home, outside Regent's Park. They like to take their "pets," a human couple named Mr. and Mrs. Dearly, there for afternoon strolls. Pongo and Missus think it's impossible to be any happier, but then they discover they are soon-to-be parents, and Missus gives birth to a litter of fifteen puppies!

But their happiness is quickly shadowed by Cruella De Vil, the Dearlies' fiendish, furs-obsessed neighbor. Cruella is a strange vision, who stands out not only because of her hair, which is all white on the one side and all black on the other, but also because of her costume. She never leaves the house without her white mink shawl or one of her other furs. When she sees the newborn puppies, she is suddenly struck by an idea—a Dalmatian coat for her collection—and so she steals them away from the Dearlies. Pongo and Missus must find them—but how?

While a suspenseful, adventuresome story, the best part of this novel is its humor. Smith's language reveals her originality of perception and keen wit. By examining man from the point of view of man's best friend, she exposes human weakness and suggests to readers that these four-legged creatures may have something to teach them about love, loyalty, and friendship; about hospitality and cooperation; and about sacrifice.

**For those drawn to**: language, story
**Themes/subjects**: animal abuse, birth, cooperation and teamwork, criminals/thieves, cruelty, dogs, family, gender roles, greed, hospitality, journeys, London, love, stealing
**Reading interest level**: grades 3–6
**Curricular tie-ins**: Use this novel to segue into a unit on animal rights and introduce the concept speciesism. Challenge students to compare and contrast real dogs to the anthropomorphized Dalmatians and to consider whether or not these differences entitle humans to greater moral rights than nonhuman animals.
**Adaptations & alternative formats**: audiobook read by Martin Jarvis (2003); animated film *101 Dalmatians* directed by Clyde Geronimi (1961)
**Translations**: French: *Les Cent Un Dalmatiens*
**Read-alikes**: Humor and journeys also combine in E. B. White's *The Trumpet of the Swan*. Felix Salten's *Bambi* is also about humans who are enemies to animals.

## Models for Identity

**Avi** (1937– )
***Poppy*** (1995). Illustrated by Brian Floca. New York: HarperCollins, 2006. 176pp. 978-0380727698.

Poppy, a deer mouse and spirited teenager, sneaks out one night with her rebellious boyfriend, Ragweed, to Bannock Hill. The problem is that Bannock Hill is in Dimwood Forest, an area ruled by a ruthless, horned owl named Mr. Ocax. Mr. Ocax has promised to protect the mice so long as no one enters his forest without first obtaining his permission. Those who violate this agreement, however, are subject to death.

Tempting fate, Poppy and Ragweed go anyway and, upon discovering them, Mr. Ocax attacks. Poppy manages a narrow escape, but Ragweed is not so lucky. When Poppy returns home though, her family blames her for angering Mr. Ocax, who has, out of retaliation, denied them their request to move to New House, an area of the forest that promises a new and much needed food supply. Poppy, distrustful of Mr. Ocax, and determined to prove she is not at fault, sets off for New House to discover what Mr. Ocax is hiding.

In this suspenseful story, Poppy stands out not only for her courage in the face of adversity but also for her resistance to and willingness to challenge authority. Rather than blindly accept what she is told (by her father, by Mr. Ocax), Poppy makes up her own mind and discovers the truth out for herself. In this way, she is a model of independent thinking and self-empowerment.

**For those also seeking**: awakening/new perspectives/enlargement of possibilities
**For those drawn to**: story, character
**Themes/subjects**: challenging authority figures, courage, death, deception, forests, mice, owls, porcupines, perseverance/determination, predators, rebelliousness, self-confidence, self-reliance, survival, underground
**Reading interest level**: grades 3-6
**Curricular tie-ins**: Bring examples of children around the world who, like Poppy, challenge the status quo. Ask students to reflect on ways they can empower themselves to be leaders.
**Adaptations & alternative formats**: audiobook read by John McDonough (2013)
**Read-alikes**: In addition to the other five books in the series, Richard Peck's *Secrets at Sea* is similar in that Helena, like Poppy, worries about her mouse family and undertakes dangerous adventures on behalf of them.

**Gipson, Fred** (1908–1973)
**Old Yeller** (1956). New York: Perennial, 2001. 132pp. 978-0060935474.

Thankfully, the Civil War has ended, but Travis and his family still struggle to make ends meet on their farm near Birdsong Creek in central Texas. When Travis's dad sets off to Kansas on a cattle drive, he leaves 14-year-old Travis to manage the farm and look after his mother and younger brother, Arliss. Travis does not mind the responsibility. He wants to prove his strength, especially since his father has promised to bring him his own horse when he returns. But sometimes he can't help getting irritated with little Arliss, who dirties up their drinking water by swimming in it or chases off good game by making a loud fuss.

When Arliss convinces their mother to let him keep a stray dog that has stolen some of their meat, Travis rolls his eyes. It's just one more thing he has to worry about. But when the dog proves himself to be fiercely loyal and a brave protector, Travis warms to him. They call him "Old Yeller," not only because of his scrappy, yellow-colored coat but also because of the yowling bark he makes whenever he is defending them from danger. Old Yeller can stand up to bears, wild pigs, and mad cows, but when hydrophobia, or rabies, begins to plague the area, it becomes a constant, looming threat. If he were to become infected with this virus, it would be dangerous, and therefore, Travis shudders to think, fatal.

Travis stands out as a model of maturity, demonstrated not only by his willingness to shoulder familial responsibilities but also in his tenderness and compassion. When he is forced to put Old Yeller down, Travis does not put up a pretense of stoicism, but performs his duty with committed, painful awareness. Through this experience he discovers that pain and heartache are part of the beauty of life and the happiness of living, and he responds to this paradox by acting with more love and tolerance (especially for Arliss). In changing his attitude, he also models the courage of making a change.

**For those also seeking**: courage to make a change
**For those drawn to**: story, character
**Themes/subjects**: accidents (major), aiding/helping, American Civil War, animal instinct, brothers, community, courage, coming of age, death, diseases/viruses, dogs, duty, eldest siblings, farm life, food, gender roles, grief, guns, horses, hunting, moral dilemmas, poverty, responsibility, siblings and sibling issues, southern United States, survival
**Reading interest level**: grades 3–7

**Curricular tie-ins**: Connect with a unit on infectious disease and/or disaster response.
**Adaptations & alternative formats**: audiobook read by Peter Francis James (2010); film directed by Robert Stevenson (1957)
**Read-alikes**: Marjorie Kinnan Rawlings's *The Yearling* is an ideal companion read as it follows a similar plot. William H. Armstrong's *Sounder* also takes place in the South during the reconstruction and features a dog character.

**Naylor, Phyllis Reynolds** (1933–)
**Shiloh** (1991). New York: Aladdin Paperbacks, 2000. 137pp. 978-0689835827.

Eleven-year-old Marty Preston is out wandering the hills near his home in a small town Friendly, West Virginia, when he realizes he is being followed—not by a person, but by a dog. Slightly skittish, the beagle keeps his distance, and yet he dutifully trails Marty all of the way home. Marty soon finds out that the dog belongs to their neighbor Judd, who is known to starve and beat his dogs, which he believes is how obedience is taught.

It breaks Marty's heart to have to return the dog, but he yields, knowing that Shiloh is not lawfully his. But, when the dog escapes a second time, and again returns to Marty, Marty vows this time to protect him and not hand him back to his vicious owner. He names the dog Shiloh, and figures out a way to take care of him by himself. But doing so requires keeping Shiloh a secret, and therefore lying to his parents. In this way, Marty must decide what is the greater wrong: deception or not helping a helpless creature?

As Marty demonstrates, sometimes there is no right choice, only good judgment. While his deception cannot be condoned, Marty remains a model of courage and wisdom as he thinks through the dilemma and ultimately does what *he* thinks is best. Readers who becoming aware of such moral ambiguity may take comfort in his example.

**For those also seeking**: connection with others/awareness of not being alone
**For those drawn to**: story, character
**Themes/subjects**: animal abuse, challenging authority figures, country life, courage, deception, dogs, empathy, gender roles, moral dilemmas, poverty, perseverance/determination, responsibility, rural life, secrets

**Reading interest level**: grades 3–7
**Curricular tie-ins**: Connect with a service-learning activity in which students volunteer at an animal shelter (visit humanesociety.org for a list of possible projects).
**Adaptations & alternative formats**: audiobook read by Peter MacNicol (2002); film directed by Dale Rosenbloom (1997)
**Read-alikes**: In addition to the novel's sequels (*Shiloh Season*, *Saving Shiloh*, and *Shiloh Christmas*), Sharon Creech's *Love That Dog* is about a boy's love for a dog. Readers drawn to animal welfare issues should also check out Anna Sewell's *Black Beauty*.


**Oppel, Kenneth** (1967–)
**Sunwing** (2000). New York: Aladdin Paperbacks, 2008. 311pp. 978-1416949978.

Because of Goth and Throbb, two vicious, murderous, jungle bats, birds and bats are warring with each other over the sky. Believing that humans are their only hope for survival, the bats speed to a "Human building," a laboratory, seeking refuge. Shade also hopes to find his father, Cassiel, who had gone missing since before he was born.

At first, the laboratory seems like a paradise; it is warm, lush, and bountiful with insects to eat. But soon, the ever-suspicious and shrewd Shade discovers the humans' sinister motivations in providing them with such comfortable accommodations. Once he makes this discovery, it is up to him to save his colony. Although he is small and scrappy, the runt of the bunch, he possess a keen intellect as well as a special gift—the ability to move objects with sounds he creates.

Lacking in both physical strength and beauty, Shade appears to be an unlikely hero. But, in recognizing and using the virtues he does possess—intelligence, courage, and a strong sense of justice—he leads like a true diplomat. By forming alliances with rats and owls, former enemies of the bats, he leads the war against the cannibals and saves his colony. In this way, Shade models strength and perseverance in the face of adversity.

**For those also seeking**: reassurance/comfort/confirmation of self-worth/strength
**For those drawn to**: setting, language

Animal

**Themes/subjects**: animal abuse, bats, battles/wars, body image, cemeteries/tombs, cooperation and teamwork, courage, critical thinking/strategy, crushes, diplomacy, friendship, good and evil, heroism, jealousy, leadership, low self-esteem, loyalty, moral dilemmas, mythology, omens/prophecies, owls, quests, rats, super powers (magical)
**Reading interest level**: grades 3–8
**Curricular tie-ins**: Have students do some basic Internet research about Project X-Ray (the secret weapons program on which the novel is based). Ask them to explain how it illuminates the text and/or offers insight into current political events.
**Adaptations & alternative formats**: audiobook read by John McDonough (2010)
**Translations**: Spanish: *Sunwing* (translated by Alejandro Palomas); French: *Sunwing* (translated by Luc Rigoureau)
**Read-alikes**: The sequel, *Firewing*, continues the saga. Another unexpected hero who would appeal to younger audiences is the mouse Despereaux in Kate DiCamillo's *The Tale of Despereaux*.

**Rawls, Wilson** (1913–1984)
**Where the Red Fern Grows** (1961). New York: Laurel Leaf Books, 2001. 249pp. 978-0553274295.

Ten-year-old Billy lives with his parents and three sisters on a remote farm in the Oklahoma Ozarks. Although few people inhabit the land, it nonetheless brims with life: deer, mountain lions, raccoons. Billy loves his life in the outdoors, but it would be better if he had a couple of hunting dogs of his own. But not just any dogs—Billy is desperate for a pair of long-faced hound puppies that he can raise and train to hunt raccoons.

Hound dogs, however, are expensive to come by, and Billy's family is poor and already struggling to make ends meet. Although his parents want to give him his dogs, they can't afford them. Discouraged, but still determined, Billy decides he will find a way to earn the dogs himself. For two years, he works and saves. Finally, he is rewarded with two pups who turn out to be two of the best hunting hounds the country has seen.

As Billy comes of age, he models agency and reveals the deep satisfaction that can be found in exercising one's initiative and achieving a goal on one's own. For readers who may often feel like they do not have a lot of freedom, they may take comfort in the knowledge that they, like Billy, can take actions to shape their own fate. Of course, Billy also demonstrates the realities that such self-determination requires patience, hard work, and sacrifice. Although the dialogue is at times cloying, the story nonetheless pulls on readers' heartstrings. It is easy to connect to Billy's deep ache—first for not having his dogs and then for his losing them.

**For those also seeking**: connection with others/awareness of not being alone
**For those drawn to**: story, setting
**Themes/subjects**: bullying, class differences, coming of age, competition, country life, death, dogs, education, hunting, pain/suffering, poverty, perseverance/determination, raccoons, responsibility, school, self-reliance, southern United States, sportsmanship
**Reading interest level**: grades 3–8
**Curricular tie-ins**: Since this story centers so much on hunting, it provides a great springboard into a student debate in which students research and debate the ethics of hunting and killings animals.
**Adaptations & alternative formats**: audiobook read by Anthony Heald (2003); film directed by Norman Tokar (1974)
**Read-alikes**: William H. Armstrong's historical novel *Sounder* features another outstanding coon dog while also depicting the horrific treatment of African Americans in the South after the Civil War. Marjorie Kinnan Rawlings's *The Yearling* is also about a boy growing up in rural landscape and his love for his pet.

### Reassurance/Comfort/Confirmation of Self-Worth/Strength

**DiCamillo, Kate** (1964–)
**The Tale of Despereaux** (2003). Illustrated by Timothy B. Ering. Cambridge, MA: Candlewick Press, 2015. 267pp. 978-0763680893.

When Despereaux is born, he is tiny, even for a mouse. His parents and siblings, with whom he lives in a giant, medieval castle, as well as the entire mouse community constantly criticize his strange appearance, especially his "obscenely large ears." But Despereaux doesn't just look different, he acts different, too. Unlike his brothers and sisters, he doesn't like to scurry, or compete for leftover crumbs. He would rather read a story or listen to the music, activities that are not, according to his family, very mouse-like. Despereaux is punished for his behavior, sent to the castle dungeon to die because of his unwillingness to conform.

*Animal*

However, driven by his chivalrous love for the castle's princess, Princess Pea, Despereaux manages a clever escape—only to find that the princess's safety is also in peril. As Despereaux attempts to save her, his story intersects with that of Chiaroscuro, an embittered and vengeful rat, and a slow, plodding, servant girl, Miggery Sow, who hopes to escape her abusive childhood by one day becoming a princess like Princess Pea.

More than a touching story about an unlikely hero, this story takes up difficult themes about neglect and abuse, death and grief, and good and evil, without resorting to cloying sentimentalism or cliché happy endings. Although one may not be able to control the darkness in the world, as Despereaux demonstrates, one always has within his or her power some ability to shape his or her own story, to drive his or her own narrative, and that is some comfort.

**For those also seeking**: acceptance
**For those drawn to**: story, language
**Themes/subjects**: abused children, being different, betrayal, child neglect, conformity and nonconformity, dreams, empathy, good and evil, heroism, hope, love, low self-esteem, Middle Ages, mice, music, pain/suffering, princesses, rats, stories and storytelling
**Reading interest level**: grades K–6
**Curricular tie-ins**: This story would complement a unit on the Middle Ages. Ask students to research topics related to the story (treatment of children, castles, clothing, music, etc.) and to compare them to the text.
**Adaptations & alternative formats**: hardcover, special edition contains colored illustrations (978-0763629281), audiobook read by Graeme Malcolm (2003); film directed by Rob Stevenhagen and Sam Fell (2008)
**Translations**: Spanish: *Despereaux: Es La Historia De Un Rátón, Una Princesa, Un Cucharada De Sopa Y Un Carrete De Hilo*; French: *La Quête De Despereaux, Ou, L'histoire D'un Souriceau, D'une Princesse, D'un Bol De Soupe Et D'une Bobine De Fil*
**Read-alikes**: Richard Peck's *Secrets at Sea* is also a tale about resourceful mice and is written in a humorous tone.

**Oppel, Kenneth** (1967–)
**Silverwing** (1997). New York: Aladdin Paperbacks, 2007. 216pp. 978-1416949985.

When Shade, a newly born Silverwing bat, learns the reason that he and the others in his colony are confined to the nocturnal darkness, his curiosity possesses him, and he is determined to see the sun. But, this action is a direct violation of the treaty between the Silverwings and the owls and constitutes an act of war. The Silverwings flee to Hibernaculum, where they can escape the owls at Tree Haven and hibernate for the winter.

But on the way, Shade is separated from the others and must find his way to Hibernaculum on his own. Luckily, he meets Marina, a Brightwing bat who is just a little older than him and just as shrewd. Marina has been banished from her colony because of her being tagged with a silver ring by humans, which the other Brightwings believed was a sign of bad luck. Marina joins Shade on his journey, and on their way they discover the evil cannibal jungle bats, Goth and Throbb, who are wreaking havoc and spreading a bad name for bats everywhere. When Shade and Marina learn that Goth and Throbb are following them to Hibernaculum in order to enslave the colony and kill and harvest them as food, it is up to them to find a way to stop them.

Although Shade is the runt in his colony, what he lacks in might he makes up for in intelligence. Because of his keen observational skills and good judgment, he is able to lead his colony to safety. In this way, he provides comfort and reassurance to readers who are experiencing a similar feeling of weakness or powerlessness. As Shade demonstrates, there is more than one way to measure strength.

**For those also seeking**: connection with others/awareness of not being alone
**For those drawn to**: story, character
**Themes/subjects**: adventure, bats, being different, cooperation and teamwork, courage, critical thinking/strategy, dead or absent fathers, forests, gods, good and evil, low self-esteem, mythology, omens/prophecies, owls, religion, winter
**Reading interest level**: grades 3–7
**Curricular tie-ins**: Religion is a major theme in this series. Ask students to compare and contrast religious customs and conflicts in the text with real life current and/or historical examples.
**Adaptations & alternative formats**: audiobook read by John McDonough (2009); animated TV series directed by Keith Ingham (2003)
**Translations**: Spanish: *Silverwing* (translated by Alejandro Palomas) French: *Silverwing* (translated by Luc Rigoureau)

**Read-alikes**: In addition to the sequel, *Sunwing*, another story with a cunning hero is *The Amazing Maurice and His Educated Rodents* and Randall Jarrell's *The Bat-Poet* is another story about a bat.

**White, E. B.** (1899–1995)
**The Trumpet of the Swan** (1970). Illustrated by Fred Marcellino. New York: HarperCollins, 2000. 978-0064410946.

When Louis, a trumpeter swan, is born mute, his father assures him that he will overcome it and that, by compelling him to become a good listener, this flaw may even prove to be to his advantage. Buoyed by this advice, Louis travels to Montana in search of his only human friend, 11-year-old Sam Beaver, in hopes that he will help him learn how to read and write. He does, but when Louis discovers this mode of expression fails to help him communicate with other swans—a particular problem during mating season—he learns to play the trumpet as well. Using this skill, he bugles at a boy's camp in Montana, serenades on a swan boat in Boston, and solos at a nightclub in Philadelphia. He also woos his beloved, a beautiful swan named Serena. Thus, in choosing to overcome the adversity in his life, Louis is led on a unique journey that expands and enriches his world.

This humorously told, character-driven novel was White's third and last children's book, and it is perhaps his most political. While Louis primarily serves as a model for children who are also overcoming adversity in their lives, there is also a clear subtext referencing American racial injustice at the time. For instance, when Louis tries to reserve a room at the Ritz, a desk clerk shakes his head and says, "No birds"—an especially poignant scene when one considers that Louis's name is an allusion to famous African American jazz trumpeter, Louis Armstrong.

**For those also seeking**: connection with others/awareness of not being alone
**For those drawn to**: story, language
**Themes/subjects**: being different, disability, humor, love, music, otherness, father-son relationships, prejudice, romance, swans
**Reading interest level**: grades 3–5
**Curricular tie-ins**: Use this book to segue into a short introduction to American jazz by showcasing selections by major trumpeters (e.g., "Struttin' with Some Barbecue" by Louis Armstrong, "So What" by Miles Davis, and "Salt Peanuts" by Dizzy Gillespie).

**Adaptations & alternative formats**: audiobook read by E.B. White (2000); first edition illustrated by Edward Frascino (1970).
**Translations**: Spanish: *La Trompeta Del Cisne*; French: *La Trompette Du Cygne*
**Read-alikes**: *The Cricket in Time Square* also features another musically gifted creature.

## Connection with Others/Awareness of Not Being Alone

**Bond, Michael** (1926–2017)
**A Bear Called Paddington** (1958). Illustrated by Peggy Fortnum. New York: HarperCollins, 2006. 198pp. 978-0062312181.

While waiting for their daughter's train to arrive at London's Paddington Station, Mr. and Mrs. Brown are stunned by a curious sight. A small, furry, brown bear, in "a funny kind of hat," sits on his suitcase, looking lost and forlorn on the train's platform. Introducing themselves, the Browns quickly learn that this tiny bear has traveled to London all the way from "Deepest Peru," in search of a new home. Charmed by his sweet appearance and polite demeanor, the Browns invite him to become a part of their family, renaming him Paddington in honor of the place they first met.

Paddington is lucky to have joined the Browns' household. The whole family, including the Browns' two children, love and pamper him. They fix him marmalade sandwiches, Paddington's favorite, and buy him a handsome suit of clothes. They take him on trips to the theater and to the seaside. Although Paddington's adventures never quite go as planned (he is a bit clumsy and tends to court disaster), somehow he "always seems to land on his feet."

Character-driven and episodic in style, these stories are laugh-out-loud funny. Bond draws on Paddington's outsider status for much of this humor, using his unique perspective to reveal the peculiarity of many of England's manners and customs. As an immigrant, Paddington also arouses sympathy from anyone who has ever experienced the loneliness of being a stranger or remembers the loneliness of being a child.

**For those also seeking**: reassurance/comfort/confirmation of self-worth/strength
**For those drawn to**: character, language

Animal                                                                                     111

**Themes/subjects**: adaptation/adjusting to change, adoption, anxiety/fears, bears, being different, city life, family, food, humor, (the) immigrant experience, London, mistakes, otherness
**Reading interest level**: grades 2–5
**Curricular tie-ins**: Use this book to complement studies about immigration and other cultures. As an activity, ask students to write a story in which they imagine one of the Brown children trying to adapt to life in Peru.
**Adaptations & alternative formats**: movie *Paddington* directed by Paul King (2014); audiobook read by Stephen Fry (2005)
**Translations**: Spanish: *Un Oso Llamado Paddington*; French: *Paddington*
**Read-alikes**: Besides Bond's many sequels, similar titles include A. A. Milne's *Winnie-the-Pooh* and *The House at Pooh Corner*, which also describe animal mishaps, and E. B. White's story about a boy mouse, *Stuart Little*, which features many of Paddington's absurdist elements.

**London, Jack** (1876–1916)
**White Fang** (1906). London: Puffin Books, 2008. 307pp. 978-0141321110.

White Fang, the only wolf cub to survive his litter, loses both of his parents before a family of American Indians takes him in. Although he is only a pup, White Fang is still wild, and he must adapt to the humans' way of living or face the brutal Yukon wilderness alone. Too young to survive on his own, White Fang learns their rules and submits to their demands.

Protection, though, is *all* they offer him. His human family never shows signs of tenderness or affection, and so he does not understand what love is or what it feels like to be loved. Rather, after he is sold to a cruel new owner, all he comes to know is hate. White Fang's new owner exploits, beats, and torments him to the point of despair. He is nearly dead when a kind man named Weedon Scott rescues him and shows him the possibility of human goodness.

This is a heartbreaking story that is not only about survival but also about the transformative power of love. White Fang is the definition of "lone wolf." He is domesticated, and therefore unfit to run in the wild with a pack. But he is still different from domestic breeds and so he cannot connect with them either. Readers who have experienced or are experiencing such feelings of isolation will immediately connect to White Fang and find strength in his ability to endure and survive life's tragedies.

**For those also seeking**: reassurance/comfort/confirmation of self-worth/strength
**For those drawn to**: story, language
**Themes/subjects**: adaptation/adjusting to change, animal abuse, animal instinct, death, dogs, anxiety/fears, food, indigenous peoples (Canada), laws, justice and injustice, loneliness, love, nature versus nurture, northern settings, otherness, pain/suffering, predators, rebirth, survival, wilderness survival, Yukon Territory, wolves, dogsledding, evolution
**Reading interest level**: grades 4–8
**Curricular tie-ins**: Use this text to enhance science-based discussions about evolution and the debate of nature versus nurture.
**Adaptations & alternative formats**: audiobook read by John Lee (2001)
**Translations**: Spanish: *Colmillo Blanco*; French: *Croc-Blanc*
**Read-alikes**: Jack London's *The Call of the Wild* is a companion to White Fang. Jean Craighead George's *Julie of the Wolves* is another story of wolves in the far north.


**Oppel, Kenneth** (1967–)
**Firewing** (2007). New York: Harper Collins, 2010. 374pp. 978-1554686131.

Griffin doesn't quite fit in with the other bats in his colony. Unlike his friends, who are so eager for excitement that they invent risky games just for the thrill of it, Griffin is paralyzed by anxiety. All he can do is to think of the potential consequences and worst-case scenarios. Adding to his shame, Griffin's dad, Shade, is a war hero, revered throughout Tree Haven for his bravery, and Griffin feels like he can never live up to his father's name.

So, to try to prove himself and also to impress his friends, he tries to steal fire. But in the attempt, he accidentally burns his best friend, Luna, and the damage is so severe, she may not live. Wracked with guilt—how could he ever forgive himself?—he hides himself away, deep in the forest, to mourn. Then, suddenly, the earth shakes and opens. Griffin falls through the fissure and is sucked into another dimension, the Underworld. Though his heart is still beating—he is alive—he finds no obvious way to escape and return to the world of the living. With no water to drink or life to feed on, Griffin fears he will be trapped there forever.

This action-packed, odyssey-like adventure confronts difficult topics about guilt, death, and faith and contemplates them with exceptional clarity.

Readers who are grieving a loss or who are distressed by a mistake they've made themselves may find comfort in Griffin, to whom they can easily relate. As Griffin begins to realize that no one, including himself, is beyond love and redemption, he also offers comfort and strength.

**For those also seeking**: reassurance/comfort/confirmation of self-worth/strength
**For those drawn to**: story, character
**Themes/subjects**: accidents (major), adventures, anxiety/fears, bats, caves, courage, critical thinking/strategy, death, earthquakes/volcanoes, escape, faith, father-son relationships, friendship, guilt, gods, good and evil, grief, heroism, immortality, journeys, love, pain/suffering, magical transformations, mythology, omens/prophecies, revenge, sacrifice, self-blame (psychology), survival, underworld
**Reading interest level**: grades 3–7
**Curricular tie-ins**: To complement units on Greek mythology and emphasize its relevance to contemporary Western culture, ask students to compare and contrast Oppel's underworld with the afterlife described in Homer's *Odyssey*.
**Adaptations & alternative formats**: audiobook read by John McDonough (2009)
**Translations**: Spanish *Firewing: La Saga De Los Murciélagos*; French: *Firewing*
**Read-alikes**: The prequel, *Darkwing* (2007), expands the saga. Those who enjoy the Odyssey-like structure may also enjoy Richard Adams's *Watership Down*.

## Courage to Make a Change

**Adams, Richard** (1920–2016)
**Watership Down** (1972). New York: Scribner, 2005. 476pp. 978-0743277709.

When Fiver, an unusual rabbit with psychic abilities, tries to warn the other rabbits in his warren that their home is in danger, few believe him. Those that do, however, decide to flee, narrowly escaping death. Even so, they must still wander the English countryside in search of a new home, and obstacles and dangers are at every turn. Fortunately, Fiver's brother, the quick-thinking and competent Hazel, is their leader, and with his direction they manage to survive a river crossing and a host of predators (cats, humans, other rabbits even) before they discover Watership Down, the perfect place to settle.

But only then do they realize that in order for their warren to grow and flourish, they need more rabbits and, therefore, does. Without them, the bucks are forced to dig and burrow homes for themselves, a job they have never been tasked with before. While they learn to adapt, they still must find does to ensure that the warren will thrive. So, the search is on, and the danger and adventure continue.

Although the rabbits resemble humans in this *Odyssey*-like tale, it is important to remember that Adams is still writing about animal nature, both its beauty and its brutality. He develops and uses a lexicon of "Lapine terms" to emphasize this difference between animal nature and human free will. In this way, Adams reveals how our ability to overcome fear is uniquely human and also how, without it, there would be no such thing as courage. In helping readers recognize this truth, Adams inspires them to take heart and to live their lives not fearlessly, but courageously.

**For those also seeking**: disinterested understanding of the world
**For those drawn to**: story, language
**Themes/subjects**: adaptation/adjusting to change, battles/wars, co-operation and teamwork, critical thinking/strategy, cultural differences, dreams, environmentalism, extrasensory perception, faith, good and evil, gods, language/communication, leadership, predators, mythology, quests, rabbits, stories and storytelling, survival, underground
**Reading interest level**: grades 3–8
**Curricular tie-ins**: In this story, Adams explores big ideas about cultural traditions, both how they can empower and how they can divide. To explore these ideas, ask students to retell a part of the story from the point of view of one of the lesser characters—for example, one of the does or an enemy rabbit from Efrafa.
**Adaptations & alternative formats**: film directed by Martin Rosen (1978) is part of the Criterion Collection; audiobook read by Ralph Cosham (2010).
**Translations**: Spanish: *La colina de Watership*
**Read-alikes**: Animals must leave their homes and search for a new place to live in Kenneth Oppel's *Silverwing* and Cornelia Funke's *Dragon Rider*.

**Byars, Betsy** (1928–)
**The Midnight Fox** (1968). New York: Puffin Books, 1996. 135pp. 978-0140314502.

Animal    115

Ten-year-old Tom is not an outdoors kind of guy. He'd rather build models, or watch TV, or invent pranks to pull on his best friend Petie. So when his parents decide to take a two-month bicycle tour of Europe and leave him with his Aunt Millie and Uncle Fred at their farm for the summer he is less than thrilled.

While he is relieved to find out that Aunt Millie and Uncle Fred are good and generous and do not expect him to spend his days baling hay and milking cows, he is, at first, bored by the quiet and the slow pace of life. Quickly, though, he discovers how it can stimulate creativity and strengthen one's powers of observation. He starts to write long letters to Petie filled with all of the things he has never noticed before—the way butterflies move in flight, the shape of a hornet's nest.

The sight that most captivates him, however, is a mother fox with a striking black coat. He is so enchanted by this rare and beautiful sight that he spends the rest of the summer trying to spot her and her babies. But when she is discovered to have stolen one of Aunt Millie's chickens, Uncle Fred resolves that he will have to hunt her down and kill her. Tom is horrified by the thought and wants to save her but feels powerless.

While some readers will certainly connect to Tom's feeling like a black sheep (or a black fox!) among his athletic family, almost all readers can connect to Tom's fear of the unknown. As he learns to adapt to his rural surroundings, and then to love them, he is a reminder to us all that trying new things, while sometimes uncomfortable, is almost always worthwhile.
Furthermore, his decision to obey his conscience and save the fox, rather than passively submit to his aunt and uncle's wishes, demonstrates moral courage.

**For those also seeking**: connection with others
**For those drawn to**: story, character
**Themes/subjects**: adaptation/adjusting to change, anxiety/fears, being different, body image, country life, courage, empathy, extended families, forests, foxes, friendship, games, humor, hunting, idleness and creativity, imagination, letters, moral dilemmas, nature, only children, summer vacations, homesickness
**Reading interest level**: grades 1-5
**Curricular tie-ins**: Because this contrasts modern life and nature, it is especially relevant in today's Age of Distraction. Use this story as a springboard into an observational activity. Ask students to observe something in

nature (as in the story) or a work of art for a set length of time. As they are observing, ask them to record what they see and at what point in time, *how long it took*, before they noticed it.

**Adaptations & alternative formats**: audiobook read by Joshua Swanson (2008)

**Translations**: Spanish: *La Zorra Negra*

**Read-alikes**: Laura Ingalls Wilder's *Farmer Boy* is about another boy on a farm, and Marjorie Kinnan Rawlings's *The Yearling* is also about a boy who copes with loneliness by befriending an animal.


**Pratchett, Terry** (1948–2015)
**The Amazing Maurice and His Educated Rodents** (2001). New York: HarperCollins, 2008. 340pp. 978-0060012359.

An ordinary day of scavenging in the trash leads a stray cat and a pack of rats into the oozing remains of a science experiment, and suddenly they find themselves "changed." The stray cat is no longer just a stray cat but Maurice, a thinking, *talking* cat. The rats, too, are transformed. They are intelligent, thoughtful.

Sly and street-smart, a con artist, Maurice finds a musical orphan boy and persuades him and the rats to join him in a brilliant, moneymaking scheme. Moving from town to town, Maurice sends the rats out in swarms to create a "pest problem." Then, by posing the boy as a "Pied Piper," he uses him to sell his pest control services. The plan works perfectly, over and over again—until they come to the impoverished town of Bad Blintz. There they stumble upon something much more sinister, which only Maurice and his team can expose and put a stop to.

Part animal story and part fantasy and science fiction, this novel centers primarily on Maurice, who transforms from a self-interested egoist into a loyal friend, capable of self-sacrifice. As Maurice learns to suppress his selfish, animal instincts, he reveals the moral responsibility that comes with being human, with having, in other words, intelligence and free will. Readers can relate to Maurice's struggle and find comfort in it as he demonstrates that one can always make the choice to change and be better.

**For those also seeking**: disinterested understanding of the world
**For those drawn to**: story, character

**Themes/subjects**: animal abuse, battles/wars, cats, civilization, courage, diplomacy, faith, free will, greed, good and evil, humor, moral dilemmas, prejudice, rats, responsibility, sacrifice, stories and storytelling, self-interest
**Reading interest level**: grades 5–7
**Curricular tie-ins**: Ask students to do some basic Internet research about the legend of the Pied Piper and then, as a class, discuss how this knowledge illuminates or changes their reading of the text, especially with regard to the morality of major characters.
**Adaptations & alternative formats**: audiobook read by Stephen Briggs (2013)
**Translations**: Spanish: *El Asombroso Mauricio Y Sus Roedores Sabios*; French: *Le Fabuleux Maurice Et Ses Rongeurs Savants*
**Read-alikes**: Robert C. O'Brien's *Mrs. Frisby and the Rats of NIMH* is another story of clever rats. Madeleine L'Engle's *A Wrinkle in Time* also takes up similar questions about free will and responsibility.


**Selden, George** (1929–1989)
**The Cricket in Times Square** (1960). Illustrated by Garth Williams. New York: Square Fish, 2008. 132pp. 978-0312380038.

A Connecticut cricket named Chester takes an accidental ride in a New Yorker's picnic basket and finds himself suddenly lost in the Times Square subway station. Chester's cricket chirp is a peculiar sound in the city, where there is more mortar and concrete than wildlife, and so he quickly attracts the attention of Mario, a young boy who is working at his family's nearly bankrupt newsstand. Led by Chester's song, Mario discovers him hidden under piles of paper litter.

Mario begs his parents to allow him to keep Chester as a pet, and they agree on the condition that he remains at the newsstand in the subway station. But Chester does not spend his nights alone, as he soon befriends Tucker, a street-smart mouse, and Harry, a stray yet refined and gentlemanly tabby cat. Together, they figure out a way to use Chester's musical gifts to help save Mario's family's newsstand business.

But, despite his new friends and despite Mario's careful supervision, Chester finds himself longing for the country, for natural landscapes, for home, and he must make the difficult decision of whether to stay or to go. Readers may find a model of strength in Chester who finds the courage to listen to and follow his own heart.

**For those also seeking**: connection with others/awareness of not being alone
**For those drawn to**: setting, story
**Themes/subjects**: cats, Chinese Americans, city life, courage, friendship, insects, Italian Americans, mice, music, New York City, responsibility, (the) immigrant experience, urban versus rural living, trains/subways, underground, homesickness
**Reading interest level**: grades 3–4
**Curricular tie-ins**: This book would be an excellent complement to or means of introducing classical music. Play the "Blue Danube," a South American rumba, Mozart's "A Little Night Music," etc. as they appear in the story. Discuss the power of music, especially in the context of New York City and the story's immigration themes.
**Adaptations & alternative formats**: audiobook read by Tony Shalhoub (2008)
**Translations**: Spanish: *Un Grillo en Times Square*; French: *Un Grillon Dans Le Métro*
**Read-alikes**: Readers drawn to Chester and Tucker's miniature world may also enjoy Mary Norton's *The Borrowers*.

## Acceptance

**DiCamillo, Kate** (1964–)
**Because of Winn-Dixie** (2004). Cambridge, MA: Candlewick Press, 2015. 182pp. 978-0763680862.

When Opal Buloni goes to Winn-Dixie to pick up a couple of groceries, she doesn't expect to come home with a dog. But when she gets there, she can't help but notice the mangy animal running amok in the produce section, knocking down vegetable displays and sending the store's manager into a tizzy. Skinny and dirty, the dog is clearly a stray. The manager threatens to call animal control, but Opal, thinking quickly, stops him by claiming that the dog is hers. She names him Winn-Dixie, saying the first thing that pops into her head, calls him over, and saves him from the pound.

She leads Winn-Dixie back home to Friendly Corners Trailer Park, where she just moved with her Baptist minister father, who she calls "the preacher." Because Opal is new to town, and because the preacher is always preoccupied, acting "like a turtle hiding inside its shell," she often finds herself feeling lonely and alone. She longs for friends and also for her mother who had left her years ago, who she never really knew.

But, because of Winn-Dixie, Opal's world begins to expand. The dog leads her to new places and new people in town, helping her to find and build community. He also becomes the reason that Opal and her father are finally able to discuss, and accept, her mother's absence. In gorgeous language, DiCamillo captures both the beauty and peril of rural life in the American South.

**For those also seeking**: connection with others/awareness of not being alone
**For those drawn to**: story, language
**Themes/subjects**: abandoned children, alcohol/alcoholism, child neglect, community, country life, dead or absent mothers, disability, divorce, dogs, father-daughter relationships, friendship, humor libraries/librarians, loneliness, love, missing persons, only children, poverty, preoccupied parents, resilience, southern United States, single-parent families
**Reading interest level**: grades 4–7
**Curricular tie-ins**: Read this story while comparing and contrasting urban and rural life (especially in the United States).
**Adaptations & alternative formats**: audiobook read by Cherry Jones (2001), film directed by Wayne Wang (2005)
**Translations**: Spanish: *Gracias a Winn-Dixie*; French: *Le Chien Qui Souriait*
**Read-alikes**: Susan Patron's *The Higher Power of Lucky* is about another motherless girl living in a trailer park and also features eccentric characters. Gary Paulsen's *Harris and Me* is about a boy who learns to cope with his parents' alcoholism while visiting relatives in the rural, American Midwest.

**Grahame, Kenneth** (1859–1932)
**The Wind in the Willows** (1908). New York: Penguin Books, 2012. 157pp. 978-0143106647.

Set in the wilderness, along the River Bank, this story follows a mole, a river rat, a badger, and a toad, who are all overcome with a vague dissatisfaction. They sense an incompleteness in their lives that they yearn to fill. In the opening chapter, Mole realizes that he can no longer tolerate the dark confines of his underground home, so he crawls out into the world, where he meets the friendly River Rat. The two become fast companions and embark on several adventures together—some fun, some dangerous—along with Mr. Badger and Toad.

Although *The Wind and the Willows* takes place in post-Victorian England, it is a surprisingly contemporary story about friendship and acceptance. Profound questions about human existence and relationships are explored as each character responds to his wanderlust. Toad particularly suffers as he wrestles with an addictive personality and an insatiable lust for driving automobiles—a combination that eventually parks him in the clinker. But Toad, though irresponsible, conceited, and spoiled-rich, is not without his redeeming qualities; he is charming and generous. The other characters, too, are good but flawed: Mole is loyal and trustworthy, but naïve and easily manipulated. Rat is a dreamer and a poet but, like many artists, sometimes falls into self-absorption. While their imperfections do not go unscrutinized, they nonetheless tolerate, accept, and help each other—demonstrating the work of true love and friendship.

**For those also seeking**: courage to make a change
**For those drawn to**: character, language
**Themes/subjects**: badgers, friendship, addiction, civilization, class differences, existentialism, forests, humor, industrialization, modernization, moles, narcissism, prison/incarceration, river rats, toads, underground
**Reading interest level**: grades K–8
**Curricular tie-ins**: For an interdisciplinary study, have students compare the characters in the novel to the real-life animals and habitats that inspired them. As a challenge, ask students to reflect on how these attributes are reflected in the personalities of Grahame's characters.
**Adaptations & alternative formats**: audiobook read by Michael Hordern (2007)
**Translations**: Spanish: *El Viento en los Sauces*; French: *Le Vent Dans Les Saules*
**Read-alikes**: E. B. White's *Charlotte's Web* contains characters with similar depth and consciousness. A. A. Milne's *Winnie-the-Pooh* and *The House at Pooh Corner* are also light-hearted novels about friendship among animals.

**London, Jack** (1876–1916)
**Call of the Wild** (1903). London: Puffin Books, 2008. 133pp. 978-0141321059.

Buck, a Saint Bernard-Scotch Sheepdog mix, was born into a comfortable life, spending his days sunning himself in the warm California sun outside his master's estate. But, it is the time of the Yukon Gold Rush, and, with everyone rushing to Yukon Territory, sled dogs are in high demand. Buck is stolen from his home and sold from one sled driver to another. Some of these drivers are stern, but fair, while others lead with force, literally beating Buck and the other sled dogs into submission.

Unlike some of the other sled dogs, who know nothing but harsh winters and hard work, Buck must adapt to his new, primitive surroundings. While difficult at first, he discovers after a time that he actually loves the work, takes pride in it, and does not miss the idleness or comforts of civilized life—that is until a particularly foolish and brutal driver threatens to crush his spirit.

In this novella, London vividly depicts the bleak, violent realities of the cold, isolation, and lawlessness that is pioneer life in the Yukon. Removed from civilized society, and forced to adapt to the wild, Buck realizes that his identity and morals are shaped not only by internal forces but also by his external environment. In this way, he calls readers to question their own sense of self, of right and wrong, and their limits, helping to broaden self-awareness and capacity for empathy.

**For those also seeking**: connection with others/awareness of not being alone
**For those drawn to**: story, language
**Themes/subjects**: adventure, animal abuse, dogs, food, good and evil, Gold Rush, greed, imagination, journeys, love, northern settings, wilderness survival, Yukon Territory, wolves, dogsledding
**Reading interest level**: grades 4–7
**Curricular tie-ins**: Use this text to enhance studies about the Klondike Gold Rush. Ask students to research the event and plot Buck's route on a map, using archival photographs from the University of Washington's digital collections (http://content.lib.washington.edu/extras/goldrush.html) to create a visual presentation.
**Adaptations & alternative formats**: audiobook read by John Lee (2001)
**Translations**: Spanish: *La Llamada De Lo Salvaje*; French: *L'appel De La Forêt*
**Read-alikes**: London's next novel, *White Fang*, tells the story of wolf born into the wild and becomes domesticated and, in providing a mirror to Buck,

is a great companion read. Gary Paulsen's *Dogsong* is also about dogsledding in the far north.

**Rawlings, Marjorie Kinnan** (1896–1953)
**The Yearling** (1938). New York: Aladdin, 2001. 513pp. 978-0689846236.

Jody Baxter is a young boy living in the southern backwoods of Florida in the 1870s, shortly after the American Civil War. Although he is Ora and Erza "Penny" Baxter's only surviving son, he hardly fits the spoiled, only-child stereotype. He spends his days working hard, not at school, but on his family's farm since the Baxters' very survival depends on its prospering. The crops they produce are not only their only source of income but also their main source of sustenance. Thus, they live in constant fear of environmental threats: hurricanes that can destroy their crops and hungry wolves and bears. They particularly fear a giant bear called "Old Slewfoot," who is missing a toe on one foot and notorious for killing farmers' livestock.

But Jody's life is not all fear and toil. When he finishes his chores, the surrounding creeks and forests, teeming with natural life and beauty, become his playground. There he likes to go "rambling." He weaves aimlessly through trees and bramble on his bare, calloused feet.

But, most of all, he likes to go hunting alongside Penny. Jody adores Penny and cherishes their time together in the woods. On one such trip, Penny is struck and bitten by a rattlesnake. Seeing his father's life in peril, Jody runs for help and discovers in the commotion an orphaned fawn. Jody saves the fawn and brings him back to the Baxter farm where he loves and tends to him like a pet. Jody soon learns, though, the problems of keeping an animal not meant to be tamed. As the fawn grows bigger, he becomes more destructive, and Jody must make a difficult decision about what to do with him.

This is a haunting story that captures the painful paradox of living, how its beauty is rooted in and shaped by suffering. Rawlings's language is stunning; the dialogue, written in Southern dialect, sparkles. Although some readers may find that the language and its nineteenth-century setting challenging, it is still worth attempting (especially if you are an adult reading aloud) as it can stimulate rich discussions about grief, loss, and acceptance.

This novel is also remarkable in that it is one of the very few that portrays a strong father figure. Penny fulfills the typical gendered roles as Jody's father and as the family's primary provider. But, surprisingly, he is also the primary nurturer. Although Jody's mother is not unkind, she is rather grave and distant so that Penny's loving patience and gentleness toward Jody really stands apart.

**For those also seeking**: connection with others/awareness of not being alone
**For those drawn to**: setting, language
**Themes/subjects**: alcohol/alcoholism, bears, camping, coming of age, community, death, deer, disability, empathy, farm life, forests, gender roles, hurricanes/cyclones, moral dilemmas, feuds, father-son relationships, food, grief, hunting, literacy/illiteracy, loneliness, natural disasters, neighbors, only children, pain/suffering, poverty, wolves, southern United States, nurturers
**Reading interest level**: grades K-8
**Curricular tie-ins**: Education is a central theme in this novel. Ask students to research the history of public education and compare and contrast rural and urban education, historically, as in the story, and today.
**Adaptations & alternative formats**: audiobook read by Tom Stechschulte (2012); film directed by Clarence Brown (1946)
**Translations**: French: *Jody et le Faon*
**Read-alikes**: Sara Pennypacker's *Pax* is also about a boy who tames a wild animal (a fox), and William H. Armstrong's *Sounder*, which is about a dog, is set in a similar time and place but depicts the African American perspective, providing a good point of comparison.

**Steig, William** (1907–2003)
*Abel's Island* (1976). Illustrated by the author. New York: Square Fish, 2007. 117pp. 978-0312371432.

Abel and his elegant wife Amanda, both mice from the upper crusts of Victorian society, are enjoying an afternoon of leisure, picnicking in the park, when a rainstorm descends unexpectedly upon them. As the storm becomes more violent, they race for cover, and on the way Amanda's scarf is taken by a sudden gust of wind. Abel, in a gallant effort, tries to reach for it, but he loses his footing and because swept away by the hurricane. He loses consciousness as a result of his fall, and when he finally comes to he discovers himself alone and "marooned" on an island, unable to cross the rushing river that surrounds him so that he can reunite with his beloved Amanda.

Born and accustomed to an aristocratic way of life, Abel doesn't know the first thing about how to rescue himself or survive on the island.

But, trapped, he must learn. He invents and attempts several escapes, but fails to get off the island. When the winter weather comes, making travel impossible, Abel is forced to accept and adapt to his new surroundings. Though he isn't sure he will ever see her again, he still dreams of and aches for his lovely Amanda.

As time passes, Abel becomes more thoughtful and introspective. He learns who he is and what he can do, and he also learns self-reliance. However, in the end it is not his ingenuity that saves him, but, rather, a simple change in the weather and a little bit of luck. In this way, Abel demonstrates the importance of independence and self-sufficiency, but he also shows that such strengths are not always enough. While one may be able to survive alone no one can expect to truly flourish alone. And yet, such circumstances are not always within one's individual control.

**For those also seeking**: reassurance/comfort/confirmation of self-worth/strength
**For those drawn to**: character, language
**Themes/subjects**: adaptation/adjusting to change, art (as coping mechanism), castaways, class differences, courage, existentialism, humor, identity formation, loneliness, love, luck/chance, mice, natural disasters, pain/suffering, rain/storms, resilience, stories and storytelling, survival, homesickness
**Reading interest level**: grades 3–7
**Curricular tie-ins**: On the island, Abel passes the time by reading literature and making sculptures of his loved ones and, through these activities, learns to embrace his solitude. To encourage students to develop their own independent thinking skills, invite them to reflect on and write about the activities they can do, or like to do, on their own and discuss as a class, drawing out patterns in their responses.
**Adaptations & alternative formats**: audiobook read by George Guidall (2013); short film directed by Michael Sporn (1988)
**Translations**: Spanish: *La Isla de Abel*; French: *L'ile D' Abel*
**Read-alikes**: Roald Dahl's *The Witches* is also about adaptation but with a much more unexpected ending. E. B. White's *Stuart Little* and Richard Peck's *Secrets at Sea* are other adventures of mice.

**White, E. B.** (1899–1985)
**Stuart Little** (1945). Illustrated by Garth Williams. New York: HarperCollins, 2005. 131pp. 978-0064400565.

When Stuart Little is born, his parents are surprised to find him looking more like a mouse than a baby boy. He is two inches high with a mouse's tail and a mouse's whiskers as well as "the pleasant, shy manner of a mouse." Nonetheless, the Littles love and adore Stuart. They carefully tend to him and make special accommodations—a bed from a cigarette box, a pair of ice skates from two paperclips—so that he can live happily and comfortably in their home. The family, which also includes Stuart's older brother George and a villainous housecat named Snowball, live in a spacious apartment in New York City.

White invented the character Stuart Little to entertain visiting nieces and nephews who would beg for him to tell them a story. Unable to deliver a tale impromptu, he wrote a series of episodes over a long period of time so that he would always be prepared. Not surprisingly, the novel reflects this episodic approach. Each chapter is its own stand-alone adventure, full of wonderful, absurd humor. While there is a narrative (Stuart leaves New York to search for his missing friend, a beautiful bird named Margalo), it is a bit unformed and does little to move the action forward. The real pleasure is derived from the nonsense elements (when Stuart chases after an invisible car, for instance, or tries a stint as a substitute school teacher) as well as the piquant personality of Stuart himself. Throughout the novel, Stuart is unfazed by his apparent differences and models self-acceptance, self-confidence, and a fearless capacity to follow his own heart.

**For those also seeking**: reassurance/comfort/confirmation of self-worth/strength
**For those drawn to**: character, language
**Themes/subjects**: being different, courage, family, friendship, loyalty, mice, New York City, otherness
**Reading interest level**: grades 3–5
**Curricular tie-ins**: As a literary activity, ask students to write an original *Stuart Little* episode of their own.
**Adaptations & alternative formats**: audiobook read by Julie Harris (2000); film directed by Rob Minkoff (1999)
**Translations**: Spanish: *Stuart Little*; French: *Petit Stuart*
**Read-alikes**: Michael Bond's *Paddington Bear* also captures the feelings of being an outsider, and William Steig's *Abel's Island* and Richard Peck's *Secrets at Sea* are also adventures of mice.

**White, E. B.** (1899–1985)
**Charlotte's Web** (1952). Illustrated by Garth Williams. New York: HarperCollins, 2012. 184pp. 978-0064400558.

After an impassioned plea to her father, eight-year-old Fern Arable saves the life of a sickly runt in a litter of piglets. Naming him Wilbur, "the most beautiful name she can think of," Fern tends to him and nurses him to good health. But once Wilbur is five-weeks-old—no longer a baby—and his appetite begins to cost the Arables, Fern is forced to sell him to her uncle, whose farm is just down the street from hers. While this arrangement allows Fern to continue to visit and tend to Wilbur, his fate remains uncertain. The other animals on the farm, which include horses, cows, geese, sheep, and a rat named Templeton, warn him that he is to be fattened up, slaughtered, and served for Christmas dinner. But hope is preserved when Wilbur meets Charlotte, a shrewd and sophisticated spider, who intervenes and devises a clever plan to save his life.

*Charlotte's Web* is probably most remembered for its careful character studies: the anxious but loyal and tenderhearted Wilbur, the friendless and egocentric Templeton, and Charlotte—beautiful, cunning, heroic. But the language, too, is just stunning and exceptionally crafted. Beginning and ending in the springtime, the novel structures itself along the seasons and mirrors the birth, death, and rebirth inherent in living. Coupled with White's originality of perception, it's hard to finish this book and not see the natural world differently—and to not feel an especial gratitude for the friendships and relationships that make this unpredictable world worth living.

**For those also seeking**: disinterested understanding of the world
**For those drawn to**: character, language
**Themes/subjects**: aiding/helping, animal ethics, anxiety/fears, competition, empathy, food, friendship, love, loyalty, nature, farm life, environmentalism, death, interconnectedness, nurturers, rats, rebirth, self-centeredness, pigs, spiders
**Reading interest level**: grades K–6
**Curricular tie-ins**: Read in conjunction with a unit on biological life cycles. As a challenge, ask students to reflect on how the biological life cycle is reflected in the structure of this book.
**Adaptations & alternative formats**: audiobook read by E. B. White (2006); movie directed by Gary Winick (2006)
**Translations**: Spanish: *La Telarana De Carlota*; French: *La Toile De Charlotte* and also *Le Petit Monde de Charlotte*

**Read-alikes**: Roald Dahl's *James and the Giant Peach* features a cast of colossal insects whose unique personalities are reminiscent of White's farm animals. Arnold Lobel's *Frog and Toad Are Friends* is about friendship between animals. In Natalie Babbitt's *Tuck Everlasting*, interconnectedness of the natural world is also a key theme.

## Disinterested Understanding of the World

**Burnford, Sheila** (1918–1984)
**The Incredible Journey** (1961). Illustrated by Carl Burger. New York: Yearling Books, 1997. 145pp. 978-0440413240.

A homely old bull terrier named Bodger, a young lab called Luath, and a sweet but slightly supercilious Siamese known as Tao set off across the Canadian wilderness in search of their owners in Western Ontario. Because the animals' family needed to leave the country for a year, for the father's work, and could not bring the animals along, the trio was left with a friend of the family who lives 150 miles away. For eight months, the animals live peacefully with their new friend, Mr. Londridge. Although time passes easily with the kind man, they do not forget their family and remain homesick for them throughout their stay. So when Mr. Londridge takes off for a hunting trip, they take advantage of his absence and escape. The wilderness, though, is full of danger. Bad weather, natural disasters, animal predators, and unfriendly humans constantly threaten their survival.

While the animals are to some extent anthropomorphized, Burnford nonetheless succeeds in providing a realistic account of the wilderness from their perspective. As speechless, domesticated pets, the dangers of the wild, are thrown into sharper relief. At the same time, their reliance on human beings also reveals the potential of human goodness and the kindness strangers. Anyone who has ever longed for home will appreciate Bodger's, Luath's, and Tao's loyalty and perseverance.

**For those drawn to**: story
**Themes/subjects**: adventure, aiding/helping, cats, dogs, friendship, homesickness, hospitality, hunger, hunting, indigenous peoples (Canada), journeys, loyalty, northern settings, predators, wilderness survival
**Reading interest level**: grades K–6
**Curricular tie-ins**: The animals' survival largely depends on the kindness of strangers. Extend this conversation by asking students to reflect and write

about the role of hospitality in their own lives (on either a personal or political level) to draw out conclusions about its fundamental importance to society.
**Adaptations & alternative formats**: audiobook read by Megan Fellows (2003); film directed by Fletcher Markle (1963) and adaptation, *Homeward Bound: The Incredible Journey*, directed by Duwayne Dunham (1993)
**Read-alikes**: For another odyssey-like animal adventure story, check out Richard Adams's *Watership Down* or, for a shorter journey, Kenneth Oppel's *Silverwing*.

**Farley, Walter** (1915–1989)
**The Black Stallion** (1941). New York: Random House, 2016. 224pp. 978-0679813439.

After spending his summer vacation with his missionary uncle in India, 14-year-old Alec Ramsay sails back to his home in New York City aboard the *Drake*. But halfway through his journey, a storm capsizes and sinks his ship. Alec would have perished had he it not been for the stallion who, freed from his stable in the cargo cabin, swims for shore. By holding onto his mane, the stallion carries him to a nearby island. The only ones to survive the wreck, Alec and the horse wait several months on the deserted island before they are rescued.

During this time, the two develop a special bond. Although the stallion is wild and skittish around most people, he trusts and listens to Alec, and he is also the only person the stallion will permit to ride him. When Alec returns to New York, he brings the stallion with him and discovers the horse's potential to race. The two of them then begin an ambitious journey to compete and break the world's record.

Written in simple, plain language, this novel is as accessible today as it was when it was published, and it continues to appeal to equine enthusiasts as it captures the unique relationship that sometimes exists between humans and their animals.

**For those drawn to**: story
**Themes/subjects**: adventure, castaways, competition, friendship, horses, islands, perseverance/determination, responsibility, sea voyage, shipwrecks, survival, self-reliance
**Reading interest level**: grades 3–5

**Curricular tie-ins**: As Alec travels halfway across the world, ask students to research and create a map of the locales that make up his and the stallion's journey.
**Adaptations & alternative formats**: audiobook read by Frank Muller (2010); film directed by Carroll Ballard (1979)
**Read-alikes**: Farley wrote 20 novels about Black, the first sequels *The Black Stallion Returns* and *Son of the Black Stallion* are probably the most popular. Mary O'Hara's *My Friend Flicka* and Laura Ingalls Wilder's *Farmer Boy* also both feature boys who are passionate about horses.

**Salten, Felix** (1869–1945)
**Bambi: A Life in the Woods** (1923; trans. 1928). Illustrated by Richard Cowdrey. New York: Aladdin Paperbacks, 2013. 262pp. 978-1442467453.

When the story opens, Bambi is just a newborn fawn, discovering the forest for the first time. He explores the woods with his mother, who teaches him about butterflies, and squirrels, and rabbits, and all of the other creatures they meet along the way. Through the warm spring and summer, life is happy in the woods. Bambi visits with the other animals and plays with his twin cousins and best friends, Gobo and Faline. But when winter comes, Bambi learns painful truth of man and the depth of his violence: His mother is hunted, and killed, and Bambi must now take care of himself.

An Austrian novelist and exceptional observer of the natural world, Salten gives a faithful, unsentimental glimpse into life in the wilderness but in gorgeous, lyrical language. It will be hard for readers to look at the physical world the same way after reading this story. Salten's critiques of man and his brutal dominance over nature are sadly as relevant today as they were almost a century ago.

**For those also seeking**: acceptance
**For those drawn to**: setting, language
**Themes/subjects**: birds, death, deer, forests, foxes, guns, environmentalism, grief, hunting, nature, owls, pain/suffering, predators, rabbits, rebirth, squirrels, self-reliance, wilderness survival
**Reading interest level**: grades 3–7
**Curricular tie-ins**: Because this book is written from the perspective of the forest animals, it would complement and enhance understanding of virtually any unit focused on environmental issues.

**Adaptations & alternative formats**: audiobook read by Frank Dolan (2002); animated film produced by Disney (1942)
**Read-alikes**: Readers who enjoy vivid descriptions of nature should also check out Sheila Burnford's *The Incredible Journey*.

**Sewell, Anna** (1820–1878)
**Black Beauty** (1877). New York: Penguin Books, 2011. 203pp. 978-0143106470.

Cast as an autobiography, *Black Beauty* recounts the experiences of a horse living in the late nineteenth-Century England. As Black Beauty is sold from one owner to another, again and again throughout his life, he experiences a series of different landscapes and living conditions, from quiet countryside pastures to bustling London. Originally intended to educate adult readers of animal abuses and to inspire sympathy for animals' suffering, this novel quickly gained popularity with children who were drawn to its subject matter.

Written in a plain, episodic style, which some scholars attribute to Sewell's Quaker background, this story is not only an autobiography of a horse, but also a meditation on human behavior. Through Black Beauty, the reader is able to see human kindness, and human cruelty, from the perspective of a vulnerable outsider. Thus it teaches much about empathy for animals and for others. Although at times excessively pedantic and moralistic, it is also a vivid and haunting novel, and it is no wonder why it has stood the test of time.

**For those drawn to**: story
**Themes/subjects**: alcohol/alcoholism, animal abuse, country life, city life, death, empathy, England, horses, industrialization, London, modernization, pain/suffering
**Reading interest level**: grades 3–7
**Curricular tie-ins**: Assign students to research contemporary examples of animal abuse and compare and contrast them with the novel.
**Adaptations & alternative formats**: audiobook read by Ralph Cosham (2011); movie directed by Caroline Thompson (1994)
**Translations**: Spanish: *Belleza Negra*
**Read-alikes**: Walter Farley's *The Black Stallion* and Margaret Marshall Saunders's *Beautiful Joe* are also books about horses.

CHAPTER SIX

# Fantasy

The major distinguishing feature of fantasy is magic—that extraordinary power, influence, or skill that defies the laws of reality. Some fantasy novels introduce elements of magic into the real world (*The Little Prince*); others open in the real world, move to a magical world, and then return to the real world (*Peter Pan*); while still others are set entirely in a magical realm (*The Light Princess*). Fantasy novels can provide a rational explanation for the magic (*Alice's Adventures in Wonderland*) or expect readers to believe the magic (*The Ropemaker*); they can be comic in tone (*The 13 Clocks*) or serious (*The Blue Sword*); and they can contain magic that is strange and arresting (*The Wonderful Wizard of Oz*) or closer to a heightened ordinariness (*The Princess Academy*).

When fantasy worlds are separated from real ones, they are cordoned off in a variety of ways: by geography (*Sabriel*), by consciousness (*Jacob Two-Two and the Hooded Fang*), by time (*The Phoenix and the Carpet*), and even by books (*Inkheart*). Fantasy realms in children's literature are located in a variety of unusual places: underground (*Dorothy and the Wizard in Oz*), inside a mirror (*Through the Looking-Glass*), in a graveyard (*The Graveyard Book*), over the edge of the wild (*The Hobbit*), in a garden after midnight (*Tom's Midnight Garden*), on a remote island (*The Thief Lord*), even underwater (*Wet Magic*). Many fantasy realms are named and these places remain some of the memorable places in children's literature (Wonderland, Narnia, the Hundred Acre Wood, Oz, Inkworld, Neverland, Earthsea, Fantastica, Looking-Glass World). Characters get to these realms through unusual portals such as magical wardrobes (*The Lion, the Witch, and the Wardrobe*), mysterious doors (*Coraline*), caves (*The Enchanted Castle*), paintings (*The Voyage of the Dawn Treader*), and enchanted tollbooths (*The Phantom Tollbooth*).

Entering one of these portals is crossing a physical and psychological threshold. In Michael Ende's *The Neverending Story*, the Childlike Empress says of Fantastica, "Every human who has been here has learned something that could be learned only here, and returned to his own world a changed person." When Bastian returns from Fantastica, he sees his world "with new eyes. Where he had seen only dull, everyday reality, he now discovered wonders and mysteries." Readers too, as Tolkien observes, are freed "from the drab blur of triteness or familiarity" when they read such works, and are able to regain a clearer view of their own world.[1]

Fantasy novels, points out Ursula Le Guin, are journeys "into the subconscious mind."[2] Indeed, Mrs. Darling finds Neverland inside the minds of her children. Although setting is important in these books, landscapes are typically mindscapes. In fantasy realms, characters face dangers and undergo trials that help them mature. Fantasy kingdoms are coming-of-age places in which children gain insight into self, discover talents, cope with problems, rehearse adult roles, and accept limitations.

Since many of the novels in the toys/games and myth/legend chapters contain magic, fantasy enthusiasts will also enjoy them. Readers who like fantasies typically love books that are driven by character and dominated by setting. Because fantasy novels create new and unfamiliar worlds, they place high initial demands on readers and are best appreciated by those willing to invest the effort. Not typically fast-paced, fantasy novels appeal to readers who love the exoticism of magical realms and the strangeness or complexity of characters. Those who enjoy fantasy books find them transformative. As Ursula Le Guin contends, they *"will change you."*[3]

## Awakening/New Perspectives/Enlargement of Possibilities

**Babbitt, Natalie** (1932–2016)
**Tuck Everlasting** (1975). New York: Square Fish, 2007. 148pp. 978-0312369811.

Frustrated by her overprotective parents, 10-year-old Winnie Foster contemplates running away from home. When she enters the woods by her house, she sees a teenage boy drinking from a spring of water. After they introduce themselves, 17-year-old Jessie Tuck tries to dissuade Winnie

Fantasy                                                                                       133

from drinking from this spring. When his mother and older brother appear, they kidnap Winnie and take her to their house. Explaining to her that the spring confers immortality on anyone who drinks from it, they tell Winnie their story. Eighty-seven years ago, they drank from this magical spring and have not aged a day since then. The Tucks want to keep the spring a secret but a strange man in a yellow suit follows them, trying to find information about it.

This action-filled story about secrets, kidnapping, betrayal, and killing is also a thought-provoking exploration of death and immortality—one that is surprisingly accessible to middle-school-aged children. The lyrically described, forest and pond settings are a perfect backdrop for ideas about life and death, and will make readers look at the natural world with new appreciation.

Although Winnie feels smothered by her protective parents, she does not realize how insulated her life has been until she lives with the Tucks. Once she leaves home, she is exposed to new ideas and confronted with difficult moral decisions. Readers who are afraid of death will look at it differently after reading the novel. The story will also resonate with children who wish they had more freedom.

**For those also seeking**: connection with others/awareness of not being alone
**For those drawn to**: character, setting
**Themes/subjects**: immortality, death, overprotective parents, secrets, kidnapping, forests, nature, imprisonment/entrapment, moral dilemmas, ecosystems, interconnectedness
**Reading interest level**: grades 4–7
**Curricular tie-ins**: The novel explores death as part of the natural cycle of life. As such, it could accompany a science lesson on the ecosystem.
**Adaptations & alternative formats**: movie directed by Jay Russell (2002); audiobook read by Peter Thomas (2007)
**Translations**: Spanish: *Tuck Para Siempre*; French: *La Source Enchantée*
**Read-alikes**: E. B. White's *Charlotte's Web* is another book about the cyclicality of life and the interconnectedness of the natural world. Gail Carson Levine's *Ever* also explores the topic of immortality.

**Dahl, Roald** (1916–1990)
**The BFG** (1982). Illustrated by Quentin Blake. New York: Puffin Books, 2007. 207pp. 978-0142410387.

It's the "witching hour," and young Sophie, unable to sleep at the orphanage where she lives, wanders to her window to take a peek outside. To her horror, she discovers an enormous man, a real-life giant, staring back at her through the glass. The giant plucks her from her bedroom and takes her back to his home, where other, bigger, bloodthirsty giants also live.

Lucky for Sophie, the giant who snatches her is kind (even if he does talk a little funny). His name is the BFG, which stands for the Big Friendly Giant. He spends his time collecting beautiful dreams, and then blows them into the ears of children as they sleep at night. But, even though the BFG is good and Sophie doesn't have to worry about him eating her, the BFG refuses to return her to London for fear that the humans, which he mistakenly calls "human beans" (the BFG regrets that he does not have a formal education), will capture and imprison him in a zoo. Sophie, however, being extremely clever, comes up with the perfect plan that will allow her to return home *and* put a stop to the other giants' murderous rampage.

In experiencing the new world of the giants, Sophie begins to see her own world differently and examine it more critically. The BFG admits that although his fellow giants are savage toward human beings, they never hurt each other. Humans, he says, are "the only animals that is killing their own kind." Thus, the novel invites readers to consider their own culture and habits from an outsider's perspective and at the same time reveals the importance of tolerance and empathy—how, without them, conflicts, big and small, can develop.

**For those also seeking**: models for identity
**For those drawn to**: story, language
**Themes/subjects**: adventure, critical thinking/strategy, cultural differences, dreams, education, giants, good and evil, heroines, humor, kings/queens, London, malapropisms, misanthropes, missing persons, nonsense, orphans, palaces, royalty, tolerance
**Reading interest level**: grades K–5
**Curricular tie-ins**: To stretch students' empathetic imaginations, ask them to retell a scene, or write an additional chapter, from one of the giants' perspectives.
**Adaptations & alternative formats**: audiobook read by David Walliams (2013); film directed by Steven Spielberg (2016)
**Translations**: Spanish: *El Gran Gigante Bonachón*; French: *Le Bon Gros Géant: Le BGG*
**Read-alikes**: Another story about a giant is Holly Black's *A Giant Problem*.

*Fantasy*

**Dahl, Roald** (1916–1990)
**Charlie and the Great Glass Elevator** (1972). Illustrated by Quentin Blake. New York: Puffin Books, 2013. 159pp. 978-0142410325.

When we last left Charlie Bucket and his family, they were blasting off to Willy Wonka's factory in his magic glass elevator. But, like many of Wonka's inventions, his elevator has a few mechanical flaws. Aboard the elevator, they wind up off course, so that what should have been a simple hop across town becomes a circuitous outer space adventure, in which they have to negotiate with the President in a made-up alien language, escape shapeshifting, "vermicious knids," and rescue a group of American astronauts.

Similarly, the narrative structure of Charlie's new adventures follows a very different course than those in *Charlie and the Chocolate Factory*. Whereas the first book sticks to a tight plot, this story is much more episodic and meandering. Except for the characters, little connects the two novels. Rather, Dahl uses variety of settings, outer space as well as the extraordinary chocolate factory, with its surreal laboratories and ever-expanding chambers. All of these episodes, however, contribute to a repeated theme about challenging assumptions: about authority (the President and Secretary of War are heavily satirized), about knowledge and self-knowledge, about how we choose to live, and about what we perceive as limitations to living well. This novel stands out for its ability to pose complex, philosophical questions, and prompt reflection in a way that is fun and engaging.

**For those drawn to**: setting, language
**Themes/subjects**: adventure, challenging authority figures, critical thinking/strategy, cultural differences, good and evil, humor, madmen, math/numbers, magic potions, magical transformations, nonsense, politics, satire, space and time, wordplay
**Reading interest level**: grades K–5
**Curricular tie-ins**: As a language activity, show students how a word's meaning is conveyed not only by letters but also by sound. Ask them to make up their own language, like Willy Wonka does in chapters 5 and 6, or make up their own nonsense poems.
**Adaptations & alternative formats**: first edition illustrated by Joseph Schindelman; audiobook read by Douglas Hodge (2013)
**Translations**: Spanish: *Charlie Y El Gran Ascensor De Cristal*; French: *Charlie Et Le Grand Ascenseur De Verre*

**Read-alikes**: Readers who enjoy Dahl's nonsense writing should check out how all the nonsense really got started and read Lewis Carrol's *Alice in Wonderland*.

**DiCamillo, Kate** (1964–)
**The Magician's Elephant** (2009). Somerville, MA: Candlewick Press, 2015. 201pp. 978-0763680886.

When 10-year-old Peter is sent to the market to buy bread and fish for dinner, he spends the money on a fortuneteller. Although he knows that his guardian will be angry, his desire to find information about his missing sister is too strong to ignore. The fortuneteller tells him that his sister is alive and that he must follow an elephant to find her. Peter does not know now who to believe since his guardian has always said that his sister died when she was born. But that very night, an elephant falls through the roof of the local opera house during a magician's show.

Peter wishes to do what is "honorable and true," but has been influenced, even brainwashed, by his guardian, an old soldier who today would be diagnosed with post-traumatic stress syndrome. Raised as a soldier-in-training, Peter now questions his way of life. Left on his own to figure out the world, he trusts his intuitions, dreams, and deepest feelings. Although DiCamillo portrays various forms of physical and psychological captivity in the novel, she also depicts characters who free themselves from their bonds.

The magical elements in the novel highlight the wondrous nature of life. What particularly distinguishes *The Magician's Elephant* is the presence of the miraculous in mundane and unexpected places. Those who believe that magic and miracles are just wishful thinking may reframe their ideas after reading this story of hope. The novel will resonate with readers whose parents have fought in war or those who have been affected in some way by war.

**For those also seeking**: reassurance/comfort/confirmation of self-worth/strength
**For those drawn to**: character, language
**Themes/subjects**: orphans, missing persons, elephants, hope, magicians, quests, war (psychological effects), dreams, non-traditional families, animals in captivity
**Reading interest level**: grades 4–6

**Curricular tie-ins**: When Peter introduces himself to the fortuneteller, he says that he is "a soldier, brave and true." Facilitate a class discussion about the role of war in the novel and the effects it has on individuals. Alternatively, ask students to research elephants and their habitats.
**Adaptations & alternative formats**: audiobook read by Juliet Stevenson (2010)
**Translations**: Spanish: *La Elefanta del Mago*; French: *L'Éléphant du Magicien*
**Read-alikes**: Brothers are also deeply concerned about their baby sisters in David Almond's *Skellig* and Kenneth Oppel's *The Nest*. Katherine Applegate also writes about an animal in captivity in *The One and Only Ivan*.


**Ende, Michael** (1929–1995)
**The Neverending Story** (1979). Translated from the German by Ralph Manheim. New York: Puffin Books, 1997. 444pp. 978-0140386332.

Bastian enters an old bookstore to escape classmates who are trying to bully him. Once inside, he becomes fascinated with the books. Irresistibly drawn to a fantasy novel called *The Neverending Story* and not having the money to pay for it, Bastian steals it. He returns to his school, sneaks into the attic, and starts reading it. The novel is about a dying realm called Fantastica and the ailing Childlike Empress who rules it. Both are fading away because humans have forgotten how to get to Fantastica. The Childlike Empress appoints a boy named Atreyu to find a cure for herself and her waning kingdom. Bastian becomes so absorbed in Atreyu's quest that he enters the story himself. And once inside Fantastica, Bastian decides he will never return home.

This story, the narrator tells us, is for readers like Bastian who forget cold and hunger, and in fact, the entire world when immersed in a book. Those who enjoy vividly imagined supernatural worlds will lose themselves in breathtaking places such as Perilyn, the Night Forest; Goab, the Desert of Colors; and the Silver City of Amarganth. Fantastica is as much an exploration of an inner landscape as an outer one. In fact, its very geography is determined by Bastian's wishes. When he wants to be tough and persevering, for example, a desert appears for him to cross.

Bastian learns to cope in the real world by doing so first in a land of fantasy. Discovering his special talents and learning how to cope with adversity prepare him for the harsh realities that he must face when he returns home. A though-provoking story that can be appreciated on a variety of levels by readers of different ages, *The Neverending Story* will especially resonate with children who have been bullied, those who have lost a loved one, and readers with a poor self-image. The novel will open children's eyes to both the power of fantasy and the importance of failure in life. When Bastian admits he has done everything wrong thus far, Dame Eyola tells him that all paths in life are the right ones: "You went the long way around, but that was *your* way."

**For those also seeking**: reassurance/comfort/confirmation of self-worth/strength
**For those drawn to**: setting
**Themes/subjects**: quests, adventure, bullying, dead or absent mother, father-son relationships, stories and storytelling, stealing, identity formation, dragons, overweight children, body image
**Reading interest level**: grade 5 and up
**Curricular tie-ins**: Ask students to create a travel brochure of Fantastica, highlighting some of its most interesting places.
**Adaptations & alternative formats**: movie directed by Wolfgang Petersen (1984); audiobook read by Gerard Doyle (2006)
**Translations**: Spanish: *La Historia Interminable*; French: *L'Histoire sans Fin*
**Read-alikes**: Meggie also enters a fantasy novel in Cornelia Funke's *Inkheart* books (*Inkheart*, *Inkspell*, and *Inkdeath*). Like Bastian, Rendi in Grace Lin's *Starry River of the Sky* must come to terms with a father who does not seem to care for him.

**Gaiman, Neil** (1960–)
**Coraline** (2002). Illustrated by Dave McKeon. New York: HarperTrophy, 2002. 162pp. 978-0380807345.

When Coraline moves to a new flat, she is intrigued with a locked drawing-room door that opens onto a brick wall. An only child of preoccupied parents, Coraline tries the door again while her mother and father are out. Amazingly, it opens this time to a flat that seems to replicate her own. She meets a couple inside the flat who introduce themselves as her "other mother" and "other father." Although they look like her parents, their eyes are large black buttons. They devote all their attention to Coraline, fill her room with enchanting toys, and cook delicious meals for her. However, as Coraline starts to notice eerie details about this world, she becomes increasingly uneasy and suspicious.

Fantasy 139

Winner of the Bram Stoker Award for Best Work for Young Readers and the Hugo Award for Best Novella, this book will appeal to readers who enjoy strange and scary stories. The "other world" is a chilling Gothic mirror of Coraline's everyday existence—a dream world turned nightmare.

*Coraline* is a novel well suited to readers who are apprehensive about significant changes in their lives or feel lonely, neglected, or unsupported during stressful periods. Opening the door to the other world, Coraline unlocks a psychological portal to a place where her dreams and fears are fully realized. Entering the other world becomes a turning point in Coraline's life, an event that changes her ideas about her parents and awakens new insight into her own desires. Readers who think that life would be perfect if their wishes were granted will think differently after reading this psychologically penetrating novel. They will also feel less unusual when they read about Coraline's hidden anxieties. Dave McKean's spidery, elongated illustrations perfectly capture the eerie atmosphere of the book.

**For those also seeking**: connection with others/awareness of not being alone
**For those drawn to**: story, setting
**Themes/subjects**: preoccupied parents, moving houses (relocating), loneliness, courage, games, anxiety/fears, only children, portals/thresholds
**Reading interest level**: grades 4–7
**Curricular tie-ins**: Ask students to create a scrapbook of the novel, cutting out or drawing objects that Coraline notices or would be interested in.
**Adaptations & alternative formats**: movie directed by Henry Selick (2009); audiobook read by the author (2002); graphic novel by P. Craig Russell (2008)
**Translations**: Spanish: *Coraline*; French: *Coraline*
**Read-alikes**: Odd, unexplained events also encroach on the everyday world in Philippa Pearce's *Tom's Midnight Garden* and Jonathan Auxier's *The Night Gardener*. N. D. Wilson's *100 Cupboards* contains a house with magical cupboards that lead to fantasy places. The children in *The Field Guide* by Holly Black and Tony DiTerlizzi move to an eerie home that contains a secret room.

**Juster, Norton** (1929–)
**The Phantom Tollbooth** (1961). Illustrated by Jules Feiffer. New York: Yearling, 1961. 255pp. 978-0394820378.

Bored and dissatisfied with everything, Milo longs to be outside when he is inside, and inside when he is outside. "It seems to me," he admits, "that everything is a waste of time." In addition, he does not see the point of anything he learns at school. When he arrives home one day, he finds a large, mysterious package in the corner of his room. The envelope indicates that it is a tollbooth that is "EASILY ASSEMBLED AT HOME, AND FOR USE BY THOSE WHO HAVE NEVER TRAVELLED IN LANDS BEYOND." Intrigued, Milo assembles the tollbooth and drives through it in his toy electric car. Arriving in the magic land of Expectations, Milo asks the Whether—not Weather—Man how to get to Dictionopolis. Taking the wrong turn, Milo ends up in Doldrums, a pointless, colorless place where nothing happens or changes. Once he manages to escape, he undertakes a quest to rescue the princesses, Rhyme and Reason, who are imprisoned in the Castle in the Air.

An excellent choice for a read-aloud book, *The Phantom Tollbooth* is a witty, whimsical story that uses wordplay and nonsense in a highly original and engaging way. Combining humor and allegory, Juster makes abstract ideas concrete as he plays upon the metaphorical basis of numerous words and phrases. Conveying the humor, strangeness, and marvels of language and mathematics, Juster gives readers a fresh appreciation of both.

Accompanied on his quest by Tock, the Watchdog, and the irascible Humbug, Milo meets a host of eccentric characters on his way to the Castle in the Air. The strange fantasy world defamiliarizes the ordinary and inspires Milo, upon his return home, to view everything in a new light. Readers who are bored in school or dissatisfied with life in general will be reenergized after reading this story. Illustrations by Jules Feiffer, the Pulitzer Prize–winning cartoonist, highlight the humorous absurdity of the fantasy world.

**For those also seeking**: connection with others/awareness of not being alone
**For those drawn to**: language, setting
**Themes/subjects**: boredom, language/communication, math/numbers, journeys, nonsense, wordplay, adventure, education, struggling or disinterested students
**Reading interest level**: grades 3–7
**Curricular tie-ins**: *The Phantom Tollbooth* would work well in conjunction with a Math or Language Arts lesson. For a think-pair-share activity, ask

Fantasy

students to discuss the following question: if they could live in Dictionopolis or Digitopolis, which one would they choose and why?
**Adaptations & alternative formats**: audiobook read by David Hyde Pierce (2008)
**Translations**: Spanish: *La Cabina Mágica*; French: *Le Royaume Fantôme*
**Read-alikes**: Lewis Carroll's *Alice's Adventures in Wonderland* and *Through the Looking-Glass* also take place in a strange world filled with nonsense. James Thurber's *The Wonderful O* is a witty exploration of our use of language.

**Lin, Grace** (1974–)
**Where the Mountain Meets the Moon** (2009). Illustrated by the author. New York: Little, Brown and Co. Books for Young Readers, 2009. 278pp. 978-0316038638.

Living in the shadow of Fruitless Mountain, in a village where everything is the color of dried mud, Minli works in the rice fields with her parents. Desperately poor, the Chinese family has barely enough to eat. Wishing that she could change their fate, Minli uses one of the family's two coins to buy a goldfish from a man who says it will bring good luck. When her mother discovers Minli's purchase, she is very upset. Although Minli regrets her decision, she wishes that she could find the Old Man of the Moon to ask him to change their fate. The goldfish surprises her by giving directions to the old man's home on Never-Ending Mountain. After Minli leaves her home in search of the Old Man of the Moon, she meets a dragon who cannot fly. Together they begin a dangerous quest.

A Newbery Honor book and Mythopoeic Award winner, *Where the Mountain Meets the Moon* is interspersed with stories from Chinese folktales. These enchanting tales echo the themes of the central narrative and provide an enriching cultural context for them.

By the time Minli makes her wish, she realizes that her desires have changed. Ironically, the treasure she seeks has been with her all along. Readers who wish for great riches and those living in poverty will think differently about the value of money after reading the novel. Lin's poetic use of language and rich, full-color illustrations evoke a mesmerizing world of wonder and magic.

**For those also seeking**: reassurance/comfort/confirmation of self-worth/strength

**For those drawn to**: setting, story
**Themes/subjects**: quests, adventure, dragons, stories and storytelling, gratitude, poverty, greed, Chinese social life and customs, family, fate/destiny, mountains, selflessness, parental disapproval
**Reading interest level**: grades 3–6
**Curricular tie-ins**: This novel will stimulate interest in Chinese customs and ways of life. Divide students into groups for a jigsaw activity and ask each group to research an aspect of China such as its culture, traditions, social customs, folklore, and economy.
**Adaptations & alternative formats**: audiobook read by Janet Song (2010)
**Translations**: French: *Là où la Montagne Rejoint la Lune*
**Read-alikes**: Readers who enjoyed this story will love the two companion novels: *Starry River of the Sky* and *When the Sea Turned to Silver*. Lloyd Alexander's *Dream-of-Jade: The Emperor's Cat*, although about a cat, depicts the cultural richness of China in a fairy-tale-style story. Like Minli, Sunflower in Cao Wenxuan's *Bronze and Sunflower* grows up in a poverty-stricken Chinese village. Elodie in Gail Carson Levine's *A Tale of Two Castles* also befriends a dragon.

**Lindgren, Astrid** (1907–2002)
**Pippi Longstocking**, translation of *Pippi Langstrump* (1945). New York: Puffin Books, 2013. 160pp. 978-0142427521.

Nine-year-old Pippi Longstocking stands out in a crowd. Her bright red hair is braided into two braids that stick straight out from her head, and she wears mismatched stockings and shoes way too big for her feet. She also possesses exceptional physical strength. But, even more unusual, she lives alone, without a mother and father, in her own house in Villa Villekulla—unless you count her pet monkey, Mr. Nilsson and her horse, which lives on her porch. While Pippi doesn't go to school like other children, she does befriend two of the children in her new neighborhood, Tommy and Annika, whom she impresses with her home cooking, games and, most of all, her unexpected, unpredictable point of view.

Pippi is striking in both her confidence and strength of mind. Although an orphan, she never pities herself but instead finds ways to make her own fun. As a devoted "Thing-Finder," that is, a person who studies the world around her and "hunts for things," Pippi is ever creative and on the look for new possibilities. While to most of us an empty can is *just* an empty can, thoughtful Pippi wears one over her head so that she can "pretend that it is midnight." Written in playful, often subversive language, one hilarious episode follows another.

**For those also seeking**: models for identity
**For those drawn to**: character, language
**Themes/subjects**: dead or absent father, dead or absent mother, friendship, humor, imagination, independence, inventing/creating, money/debt, only children, pets, redheads, self-confidence, Sweden
**Reading interest level**: grades 3–6
**Curricular tie-ins**: Tie to a theme about sustainability for younger students by asking them to be "Thing Finders" and find creative, new uses for discarded objects. For older students, reread chapter four, in which Pippi attends school for a day before deciding she does not want to be a student, as a class and use it to segue into a lecture about the history of public schools/public education. Challenge students to identify the advantages and disadvantages of formal education (as in a classroom debate).
**Adaptations & alternative formats**: new translation by Oxford University Press edition published in the United Kingdom (published by Viking in the United States) includes whimsical illustrations by Lauren Child; movie directed by Olle Hellbom (1969)
**Translations**: Spanish: *Pippi Calzaslargas*; French: *Fifi Brindacier*
**Read-alikes**: Roald Dahl's *Matilda* also features a strong, independent female protagonist.


**MacDonald, George** (1828–1905)
**The Light Princess** (1864). Illustrated by Maurice Sendak. New York: Farrar, Straus and Giroux, 1977. 110pp. 978-0374444587. PD.

When the king and queen christen their baby, they forget to invite the king's sister, a witch called Princess Makemnoit. In revenge, the witch deprives the baby of gravity, a curse that causes her to float in the air and fly off with the breeze. As well as no bodily gravity, the light princess possesses no mental gravity, and can never take anything seriously. A light-hearted character, she spends all her time laughing. Although the king and queen foresee the problems that her lack of gravity will cause throughout life, they do not know how to remedy the situation.

When the princess turns 17, she meets a prince who falls in love with her. He discovers that when she swims—an activity that she adores—she is more like other people. But after a witch casts a spell on the lake that causes it to die, the princess starts to pine away.

Filled with puns and wordplay, this whimsical story is amusing for children of all ages. "Sliding and flitting and gliding from one piece of furniture to another," this weightless princess appears to lead a joyous, carefree life. But as the story shows, being merry and happy-go-lucky does not always result in happiness. Readers who think that their lives would be perfect if they had no cares or concerns will reconsider this idea after reading *The Light Princess*. Maurice Sendak's enchanting, amusing illustrations are outstanding additions to the text.

**For those drawn to**: character, language
**Themes/subjects**: princesses, spells/curses, wordplay, love, romance, sacrifice, royalty, humor
**Reading interest level**: grades K–6
**Curricular tie-ins**: This novel could accompany a science lesson on forces and motion. Ask students to create poster presentations about the subject of gravity.
**Adaptations & alternative formats**: audiobook read by Nicki White (2014)
**Translations**: Spanish: *La Princesa Ligera*
**Read-alikes**: Characters who enjoy fairy-tale fantasies with a light, humorous tone will also like Gail Carson Levine's *Ella Enchanted* as well as her six princess tales (*The Fairy's Mistake, The Princess Test, Princess Sonora and the Long Sleep, Cinderellis and the Glass Hill, For Biddle's Sake, The Fairy's Return*).


**MacDonald, George** (1828–1905)
**The Princess and the Goblin** (1872). Illustrated by Arthur Hughes. London: Puffin, 2010. 234pp. 978-0141332482. PD.

When Princess Irene explores the upper stories of her castle/farmhouse, the eight-year-old discovers a beautiful elderly woman working at a spinning wheel. The woman introduces herself as her great-great-grandmother, and tells Irene that, although no one in the castle knows she is there, she has come to take care of her. However, the next time that Irene searches for her, she cannot find her and begins to doubt her existence.

Leading a sheltered life in the mountains, Princess Irene is never allowed outside after the sun goes down. Because the grotesque goblins who live inside the mountains spend their time creating trouble for the people who live aboveground, Irene's King Papa warns his servants to keep Irene out of their way. Curdie, a 12-year-old miner who works inside the mountain, overhears goblins speak about a plot that will cause mass destruction. He suspects that the goblins also want to kidnap Princess Irene.

"Ludicrously grotesque" in appearance, the goblins are dwarfed and debased versions of their former selves. While everything on the surface of the world seems secure, goblins undermine the foundations of the castle, invading it by digging a tunnel beneath the building. Their hidden presence and secret activities create a menacing atmosphere in the novel.

Counterbalancing these hideous, subterranean creatures is Irene's great-great-grandmother, a healing and guiding figure who can only be seen by people who believe in her. Associated with light, the moon, and her spinning wheel, great-great-grandmother represents the transformative power of both faith and the imagination. Irene's advice to Curdie—"you must believe without seeing"—may open reader's eyes to a new way of looking at life. The novel will reassure readers who have many fears in life that they will be able to cope. The original illustrations by the pre-Raphaelite artist, Arthur Hughes, highlight the haunting atmosphere of the novel.

**For those also seeking**: reassurance/comfort/confirmation of self-worth/strength
**For those drawn to**: setting
**Themes/subjects**: princesses, goblins, mines/mining, mountains, grandmothers, faith and skepticism, imagination, good and evil, caves, underground, castles, overprotective parents
**Reading interest level**: grades 3–7
**Curricular tie-ins**: Curdie is a 12-year-old miner. Ask students to create a poster about some aspect of mines and mining (e.g., the products of mines, changes in mining over the last century, the different types of mining, the work of a miner).
**Adaptations & alternative formats**: movie directed by József Gémes (1991); audiobook read by Brooke Heldman (2014)
**Translations**: Spanish: *La Princesa y los Trasgos*; French: *La Princesse et le Goblin*
**Read-alikes**: Wicked characters try to kidnap a princess in Lloyd Alexander's *The Castle of Llyr*, while evil creatures build a secret tunnel to the Emerald City in L. Frank Baum's *The Emerald City of Oz*. Readers who are interested in stories about faith in the unseen will enjoy C. S. Lewis's

*Chronicles of Narnia* (*The Lion, the Witch and the Wardrobe*; *Prince Caspian*; *The Voyage of the Dawn Treader*; *The Silver Chair*; *The Horse and His Boy*; *The Magician's Nephew*; *The Last Battle*).

**Nesbit, Edith** (1858–1924)
**The Enchanted Castle** (1907). London: Puffin, 1994. 291pp. 978-0140367430. PD.

When siblings Gerald, Jimmy, and Kathleen are forced to remain at school during the holidays because of a measles threat at home, they explore a nearby cave in search of adventure. The cave leads to a beautiful castle and gardens. Finding a young princess asleep in a maze of yews, the children believe that they have stumbled upon a fairy-tale realm. When they awaken the princess, she says, "Then the hundred years are over?" The princess, who acts just like a fairy-tale princess, invites them into the enchanted castle and shows them a treasure chamber. After she tries on a magic ring, she turns invisible. Astounded by her own invisibility, the princess confesses that she is an ordinary girl named Mabel and is the housekeeper's niece. She admits that she was just pretending to be magical. However, once the children realize that the ring is actually enchanted, they encounter endless complications as they try to understand and control the magic.

The real and the magical, although juxtaposed throughout the novel, are not mutually exclusive. Nesbit depicts the extraordinariness of the ordinary as a type of magic. Characters experience the wonder and magic of music, fairy tales, stories, art, and dreams. The music that the goddess Phoebe plays, for example, stirs visionary thoughts of the world's goodness and beauty. The narrator observes that when people are exposed to magic of any kind, they "are never quite the same again."

Readers who love stories of fantasy and make-believe and those who enjoy daydreaming about far-off realms or far-fetched scenarios will not think such pursuits are merely escapist after reading *The Enchanted Castle*. They will find comfort in the fact that stories of magic and enchantment serve an essential function by inspiring readers to dream about ideals.

**For those also seeking**: reassurance/comfort/confirmation of self-worth/strength
**For those drawn to**: story, setting

**Themes/subjects**: castles, adventure, invisibility cloaks and rings, wishes and wishing, magical transformations, mythology, summer vacations
**Reading interest level**: grades 3–6
**Curricular tie-ins**: The statues that come to life are replicas of Greek gods and goddesses. Ask students to find information about one of them and write an epilogue to the novel that includes the god or goddess.
**Adaptations & alternative formats**: audiobook read by Virginia Leishman (2013)
**Translations**: Spanish: *El Castillo Encantado*
**Read-alikes**: Edith Nesbit's *Five Children and It* (another book about wishes) and Lynne Reid Bank's *The Indian in the Cupboard* also explore the comic complications of magic in the real world.

**Nesbit, Edith** (1858–1924)
**The House of Arden** (1908). New York: New York Review Children's Collection, 2006. 242pp. 978-1590172025. PD.

Bandits capture and kill the father of Edred and Elfrida as he prepares to return home from South America. Now Edred will be the new Lord Arden. The siblings and their guardian, Aunt Edith, move into the Arden family castle, but do not have the money to restore the dilapidated structure. Old Beale, the caretaker of the property, tells the children that their ancestors hid the family treasure somewhere in the castle during a war. A book in the castle library contains the spell that will lead to the treasure. The children discover the spell, and Edred reads it aloud. The spell calls forth the Mouldiwarp, an eccentric magical being who says that the children will discover a magical door, but only after they learn to be kind and wise. Edred and Elfrida eventually find this door, and time travel to different eras to look for clues to the treasure.

Meeting historical personages such as Sir Walter Raleigh and Anne Boleyn, the children experience what it would have been like to live during earlier eras. Readers who enjoy learning about the past will find the historical narratives that are interwoven into the children's story interesting and informative.

The emphasis on magic and enchantment in the novel highlights the wonder of life itself. The narrator observes, "if you sit perfectly silent for a long time and look at the sea, or the sky, or the running water of a river, something happens to you—a sort of magic." This inside magic "makes things clear and shows you what things are important, and what are not." Like the natural world, imaginative literature unlocks the door to life's marvels. Edred and Elfrida, for example, must say lines of poetry in order to summon the magical Mouldiwarp.

As Edred and Elfrida search for treasure, they change their ideas about its value. After reading the novel, readers who wish they were wealthy will realize that they already possess a myriad of treasures.

**For those also seeking**: disinterested understanding of the world
**For those drawn to**: setting
**Themes/subjects**: castles, time travel, buried/hidden treasure, adventure, dead or absent father, siblings and sibling issues, kindness
**Reading interest level**: grades 4–7
**Curricular tie-ins**: Ask students to choose one of the historical persons in the book (King James III, Napoleon Bonaparte, Guy Fawkes, Sir Walter Raleigh, Anne Boleyn) and find information about him or her. They can pretend to be that person and write either a speech or a diary entry by him or her.
**Adaptations & alternative formats**: audiobook read by Cathy Dobson (2012)
**Read-alikes**: Readers who enjoy time-travel stories will also like Edith Nesbit's *Harding's Luck* (the sequel to the novel) and *The Story of the Amulet*. In Lloyd Alexander's *Time Cat*, Jason and Gareth also visit a variety of historical periods.


**Pearce, Philippa** (1920–2006)
**Tom's Midnight Garden** (1958). New York: HarperTrophy, 1992. 229pp. 978-0064404457.

When Peter contracts measles, his brother Tom is sent to stay with his aunt and uncle, a childless couple who live in a small flat with no garden. Upset that his plans to build a tree house with his brother are ruined, and confined indoors with adults who know nothing about children, Peter is bored and frustrated. Unable to sleep one night, he hears the grandfather clock unexpectedly strike 13. Wandering downstairs, he opens the door to the backyard. Shocked to find a beautiful garden when he was told that there was nothing in the yard, Tom investigates. Night after night, he waits for the clock to strike 13 and then visits the garden, a place that lures him inside.

Although he initially thinks the garden is a real place, he starts to wonder why time moves backward and forward in a strange and unpredictable way. Meeting a girl named Hatty in the garden, he befriends her but later wonders if she is a ghost.

Winner of the Carnegie Medal for the best British novel, *Tom's Midnight Garden* is a compelling story about a boy's obsession with an imaginary world. Tom's life in the garden becomes so all-consuming that he asks to extend his stay with his uncle and aunt. Home starts to seem "like a long, long misty way, away." Tom lives "his real and interesting life" at nighttime when he goes into the garden, while during the day, he thinks backward and forward to his time in the garden. Hatty, an orphan girl who is cruelly treated by her guardian aunt, also lives so much in her imagination that she almost believes she is a real princess. Readers who prefer fantasy to reality—whether in games, media, or books—may think about the amount of time they spend in imaginary pursuits after reading Peter's story.

**For those also seeking**: connection with others/awareness of not being alone
**For those drawn to**: setting
**Themes/subjects**: obsessions, imagination, time travel, gardens/gardening, ghosts, secrets, elderly, brothers, boredom
**Reading interest level**: grades 4–7
**Curricular tie-ins**: Tom visits the Victorian era via time travel. Ask students to write a reflection in their reader response journals, answering the question, "If you could magically travel to another time or place, when or where would it be and why?"
**Adaptations & alternative formats**: movie directed by Willard Carroll (1999); audiobook full-cast dramatization by the BBC (2006); graphic novel by Edith (2016)
**Translations**: Spanish: *El Jardin de Medianoche*; French: *Tom et le Jardin de Minuit*
**Read-alikes**: J. M. Barrie's *Peter Pan* also travels to an imaginary place that he does not want to leave, while Mary Lennox in Frances Hodgson Burnett's *The Secret Garden* becomes entranced with a garden that she discovers. A mysterious tree and a ghostly gardener exert a powerful influence over the inhabitants of a house in Jonathan Auxier's *The Night Gardener*. A boy is unhappy about the prospect of living with relatives for the summer in Betsy Byars's *The Midnight Fox*.

**Pratchett, Terry** (1948–2015)
**The Wee Free Men** (2003). New York: HarperCollins, 2015. 342pp. 978-0062435262.

At age nine, dairymaid Tiffany Aching begins seeing supernatural beings. Tiffany tells Miss Tick, a witch who has taken notice of the girl, about these strange sightings. Miss Tick is immediately worried, believing that monsters and nightmarish beings may be planning to invade the area. After the witch leaves to get help, the Wee Free Men—"the most feared of all the fairy races"—appear in increasingly numbers. Then Tiffany's baby brother goes missing. Armed with a frying pan to use as a weapon, Tiffany joins forces with the Wee Free Men to search for her brother.

The Fairyland that Tiffany enters is filled with nightmares that entrap and ensnare characters. However, the horrors of the fairy world are mitigated by Pratchett's offbeat humor and his eccentric characters. Pipe-smoking Granny Aching, the witty talking toad, and the rebellious Wee Free Men keep the story lively and light-hearted.

Gifted with "first sight and second thoughts," Tiffany Aching is spunky, fearless, and precocious. Looking forward to attending a school for witches, she must abandon her plans in order to search for her brother. Later she discovers that witchcraft is like life: "First you get the test and then afterwards, you spend years findin' out how you passed it." Tiffany learns to become a witch by simply acting as one in the midst of a crisis. Readers will realize that, like people in life, Tiffany develops her talents through life's experiences. Her story will resonate with children who must come to terms with the death of a loved one and readers who do not recognize their strengths and talents.

**For those also seeking**: reassurance/comfort/confirmation of self-worth/strength
**For those drawn to**: character
**Themes/subjects**: witches, fairies, dreams, kidnapping, missing persons, grandmothers, grief, quests, humor
**Reading interest level**: grades 5–7
**Curricular tie-ins**: Ask students to write a letter from Tiffany to Miss Tick describing how she feels about being a witch.
**Adaptations & alternative formats**: audiobook read by Stephen Briggs (2004)

Fantasy

**Translations**: Spanish: *Los Pequeños Hombres Libres*; French: *Les Ch'tits Hommes Libres*
**Read-alikes**: The sequels to the Tiffany Aching novels are *A Hat Full of Sky*, *Wintersmith*, *I Shall Wear Midnight*, and *The Shepherd's Crown*. Laura Amy Schlitz's *The Night Fairy* is another novel about fairies, while Diana Wynne Jones's *Witch Week* and Eleanor Estes's *The Witch Family* are about young witches discovering their power.


**Schlitz, Laura Amy** (1956– )
**The Night Fairy** (2010). Illustrated by Angela Barrett. Somerville, MA: Candlewick Press, 2010. 117pp. 978-0763636746.

When a bat crushes the wings of a three-month-old fairy named Flory, she is no longer able to fly. Fearful of bats and stranded in a cherry tree far from her fellow fairies, Flory decides to become a day fairy. However, changing from a night fairy is not at all easy: "She had to make a whole new life for herself, with no one to show her how." Attacked by predators, Flory must survive in a world that is both unfamiliar and hostile.

Winner of a number of prestigious awards for children's literature, Laura Amy Schlitz is particularly skilled at creating psychologically convincing characters. Alone and unsupported, the injured Flory does not give in to self-pity and fear, but remains spunky, resilient, and headstrong. She figures out how to survive in an alien world and learns how to adapt, socially and psychologically. Those who live in a dysfunctional family, endure a disability, believe that they are misfits, or feel lonely or unsupported by those who care for them will discover a new way of viewing the world and coping with challenges. This story will also resonate with readers who try to be like others, even though they would rather remain unique.

The dreamlike quality of Angela Barrett's beautiful watercolor illustrations highlights the strangeness of this world to Flory. An excellent read-aloud book, *The Night Fairy* is a lyrically written story about an unforgettable character and the interconnected natural world she inhabits.

**For those also seeking**: disinterested understanding of the world
**For those drawn to**: character
**Themes/subjects**: fairies, birds, bats, spiders, disability, adaptation/adjusting to change, empathy, courage, identity formation, accidents (major),

friendship, conformity and nonconformity, being different, homelessness, self-reliance, resilience, flying magically, outcasts/misfits

**Reading interest level**: grades 1–4

**Curricular tie-ins**: This novel could be used as a resource for a lesson on hummingbirds or bats, and in particular, how these creatures depend upon their environment. Students could create a bird house for the lesson.

**Adaptations & alternative formats**: audiobook read by Michael Friedman (2010)

**Read-alikes**: The protagonist in Carolyn Sherwin Bailey's *Miss Hickory* also creates a home for herself in the natural world and learns to cope on her own. Terry Pratchett's *The Wee Free Men* depicts a fairy protagonist who is spunky and unconventional. And like Flory, Luna, in Kelly Barnhill's *The Girl Who Drank the Moon*, is a plucky magical being who is separated from her family and relocated to an unfamiliar setting.


**Travers, P. L.** (1899–1996)
**Mary Poppins** (1934). Illustrated by Mary Shepard. Boston: Houghton Mifflin Harcourt, 2015. 191pp. 978-0544439566.

When Mr. Banks tells his wife that she should advertise for a new nanny, a blustery east wind blows in a most unusual woman named Mary Poppins. Immediately taking charge of both the children and their mother, this new nanny inverts the customary norms of the household. Sliding up bannisters, pulling a folding armchair out of an apparently empty carpetbag, entering a picture, pasting gingerbread stars in the sky, and conversing with animals in their own language, Mary Poppins introduces unconventionality, eccentricity, and mystery to a bourgeois, middle-class household. Although she is gruff and cantankerous, the children immediately love her. When John asks, "Mary Poppins, you'll never leave us will you?" she will only reply, "I'll stay till the wind changes."

A curious combination of haughty superiority, stern curmudgeon, and plucky adventurer, Mary Poppins is a character with wide reader appeal. Although she appears to be prim and proper, her conventional appearance belies her strange magical talents. Adding to the mystery surrounding her is her curious reticence about her feelings, her past, and her acquaintances.

*Mary Poppins* does not begin in a magical world or leave a realistic one for a fantasy realm but rather introduces elements of magic into the everyday world—a somewhat unsettling experience for Jane and Michael as well as readers. Blowing in with the wind, Mary Poppins shakes up life as the children know it. And after magical events occur, Mary Poppins vehemently denies their taking place, leaving the children unsure what to believe. Mary Poppins's cosmic connections and mysterious relationships with a variety of creatures hint at a much larger reality than the prosaic one inhabited by the Banks. Readers, like the children in the novel, sense the presence of a mysterious otherworld that lies just beyond their consciousness. The novel will resonate with children who feel constrained by their circumstances and believe that there is more to life than the everyday.

Editions today still contain the iconic line drawings by Mary Shephard, daughter of the renowned illustrator of *Winnie-the-Pooh* and *The Wind in the Willows*.

**For those also seeking**: reassurance/comfort/confirmation of self-worth/strength
**For those drawn to**: character
**Themes/subjects**: nannies and caregivers, adventure, otherness, London, city life, conformity and nonconformity, language/communication
**Reading interest level**: grades 3–6
**Curricular tie-ins**: Ask students to choose five picture books that Mary Poppins might pick to read to the Banks' children. They should provide reasons for their choices. Alternatively show the Disney movie in class and initiate a class discussion about the differences between the movie and the book.
**Adaptations & alternative formats**: Disney movie starring Julie Andrews directed by Robert Stevenson (50th anniversary edition, 2013); audiobook read by Sophie Thompson (2009)
**Translations**: Spanish: *Mary Poppins*; French: *Mary Poppins*
**Read-alikes**: Louise Fitzhugh's *Harriet the Spy* and Lois Lowry's *The Willoughbys* also feature a beloved nanny. Readers will enjoy the sequels to *Mary Poppins*: *Mary Poppins Comes Back*, *Mary Poppins Opens the Door*, *Mary Poppins in the Park*, *Mary Poppins in Cherry Tree Lane*, and *Mary Poppins and the House Next Door*.

## Models for Identity

**Dahl, Roald** (1916–1990)
**James and the Giant Peach** (1961). Illustrated by Quentin Blake. New York: Puffin Books, 2007. 146pp. 978-0142410363.

When Henry James Trotter is just four years old, his parents are tragically eaten by an enormous rhinoceros escaped from the London zoo. Orphaned, he is sent to live with his wicked aunts, Aunt Sponge and Aunt Spiker. They mistreat him, call him names, and employ him like their personal servant. For three years, James endures this abuse until a chance encounter with a magical stranger sends him on a journey inside a giant peach, along with seven, giant insect companions. On their way, they confront several obstacles—shark infested waters, a gauntlet of creepy cloud creatures—and narrowly escape death. However, thanks to James's excellent leadership, they make safe passage to New York City, where they all settle into happy, successful lives.

In this fast-paced, narrative-driven story, James stands out as an example of a child overcoming both grief and adversity. Plunged into difficult, frightening situations, James responds with courage and creativity and develops into a fearless and dependable leader. By the end of the story, he is his own agent, living happily, by himself, in a home of his own carved out of the stony remains of his giant peach.

**For those also seeking**: connection with others/awareness of not being alone
**For those drawn to**: character, language
**Themes/subjects**: abused children, abuse (emotional), cooperation and teamwork, courage, food, friendship, leadership, magical transformations, misopedists, resilience, insects, orphans, only children, pain/suffering
**Reading interest level**: grades K–5
**Curricular tie-ins**: Read this novel in conjunction with a science unit on insects. Assign students an insect to research and ask them to compare how the biological features of the insects are manifested in their fictionalized personalities.
**Adaptations & alternative formats**: Penguin Classics Deluxe Edition (2011; ISBN: 978-0143106340) contains cover art by Jordan Crane and the original interior art from the 1961 edition; audiobook read by Julian Rhind-Tutt (2004); play adapted by Richard George (1982); film directed by Henry Selick (1996)
**Translations**: Spanish: *James Y El Melocotón Gigante*; French: *James Et La Grosse Pêche*
**Read-alikes**: Christopher is another innocent boy taken advantage of by a wicked relative in Diana Wynne Jones's fantasy novel, *The Lives of Christopher Chant*.

**Hale, Shannon** (1974– )
**The Goose Girl** (2003). New York: Bloomsbury, 2005. 383pp. 978-1582349909.

As the Crown Princess of Kildenree, Ani spends her life preparing to be queen of the kingdom one day. After her father dies, her mother announces that Ani's brother is next in succession for the throne. Ani is confused and upset at this unexpected turn of events. When she asks for an explanation, the queen says that she has secretly betrothed her daughter to a prince in the neighboring kingdom of Bayern. Ani must leave home to become queen in an unfamiliar land. Ani is then betrayed for a second time by someone close to her, this time when she travels to Bayern. Selia, her lady-in-waiting, convinces a group of guards to kill Ani so that Selia can pretend to be the princess and betroth the Bayern prince. Although Ani escapes and hides, she must disguise herself as a goose girl and elude Selia's guards. While she works as a goose girl, she meets and falls in love with the crown prince who has also disguised his identity.

This first book in the Bayern series is filled with intrigue, suspense, and secrets. Continually hunted by Selia's guards and always in danger of being recognized, Ani is never sure who she can trust.

Expanding upon the fairy tale *The Goose Girl*, Shannon Hall creates a large cast of fully realized, psychologically complex characters. In this coming-of-age novel, the goose girl grows into her role as future queen. Ani, who always felt she lacked the social graces of her mother, must recognize the gifts she possesses and accept herself as she is.

Her loss of social status opens her eyes to the suffering of working-class people and makes her aware of the social injustices in her kingdom. As her empathy grows, so too does her magical ability to communicate with nature. Readers who feel awkward in social situations or those who do not recognize their own strengths will find in Ani, a role model to follow.

**For those also seeking**: reassurance/comfort/confirmation of self-worth/strength
**For those drawn to**: character, story
**Themes/subjects**: princesses, betrayal, outcasts/misfits, coming of age, royalty, inheritance and succession, romance, poverty, class differences, courage, empathy, battles/wars, geese, justice and injustice
**Reading interest level**: grade 6 and up

**Curricular tie-ins**: Ask students to create a banner or a coat of arms for the royal kingdom.
**Adaptations & alternative formats**: audiobook read by Cynthia Bishop (2012)
**Translations**: Spanish: *La Princesa que Hablaba con el Viento*
**Read-alikes**: The sequels to this novel are *Enna Burning*, *River Secrets*, and *Forest Born*. Robin McKinley's *Spindle's End* and Gail Carson Levine's *Ella Enchanted* are also fairy-tale-inspired fantasies about princesses. A budding romance is also hindered by characters who disguise themselves as other people in Garth Nix's historical fantasy, *Newt's Emerald*.

**Levine, Gail Carson** (1947–)
**Ella Enchanted** (1997). New York: HarperCollins, 1997. 232pp. 978-0064407052.

During Ella's christening, a fairy foolishly bestows on her the gift of obedience. Since anyone is able to control Ella with a direct order, the gift becomes a curse. When Ella is 15 years old, her mother dies. Since she was always close with her mother and distant with her self-centered father, the event is especially tragic for her. Her father sends her off to finishing school and then tries to trick her into marrying a repellent older man for his money. Ella's father then marries an odious woman who is cruel and abusive to Ella. Although her two stepsisters are mean and controlling, Ella's fairy godmother and Prince Char are friends that she can rely on.

Not until well into the story do readers suspect that Ella is a Cinderella character. Levine does not retell the fairy tale but rather reinterprets and elaborates on it. In the original tale, Cinderella is a subservient character who is preyed upon by bullies. In Levine's novel, Ella's obedient nature becomes her curse. Although the characters share the same psychological profile, Ella is a more richly imagined character than her fairy-tale predecessor. Her feisty resistance to orders, her optimism in the face of adversity, and her creative resilience make her an inspiring role model for readers. Those who believe that obedience is always a virtue may realize that it can border on submissive docility. The novel will resonate with readers who feel constrained by misfortune as well as those who have experienced the death of a parent.

**For those also seeking**: awakening/new perspectives/enlargement of possibilities

Fantasy                                                                                              157

**For those drawn to**: character
**Themes/subjects**: fairies, dead or absent mother, stepparents, stepsisters, spells/curses, obedience, challenging authority figures, agency and powerlessness, romance, love, princes, father-daughter relationships, resourcefulness, school, fairy godmothers, etiquette and customs
**Reading interest level**: grades 5–8
**Curricular tie-ins**: Ask students to compare Perrault's "Cinderella" with the novel.
**Adaptations & alternative formats**: movie directed by Tommy O'Haver (2004); audiobook read by Eden Riegel (2004)
**Translations**: Spanish: *El Mundo Encantado de Ela*; French: *Ella, l'Ensorcelée*
**Read-alikes**: Readers who enjoy fairy-tale-inspired stories will also like Gail Carson Levine's *Fairest* and Robin McKinley's *Beauty* and *Spindle's End*.


**McKinley, Robin** (1952–)
**The Blue Sword** (1982). New York: Puffin Books, 2000. 272pp. 978-0141309750.

After her father dies, Harry goes to live with Sir Charles and Lady Amelia in Istan, the British Homelanders' outpost in the kingdom of Damar. Although she is grateful to both her military brother for arranging a home for her and the kind couple for taking her in, she suffers from a "vague restlessness" and longing for adventure. When King Corlath of the native Hillfolks visits the Homelanders' military leaders, he asks for their help in closing mountain passes against the barbaric Northerners. Sir Charles is suspicious of the Hillfolks and refuses to help.

As Corlath leaves, he sees Harry for the first time. Her presence stirs something deep within him, and he returns to the outpost to kidnap her. Although she is treated with great respect, Harry is devastated at being taken away against her will. After she sees strange visions of the past and the future, she is baffled, not sure where she belongs or even if she wants to return home. This gradually unfolding story gains great force as characters converge later in the novel.

Harry's story is one of displacement and estrangement. Not conforming to the standards expected of her gender and class, Harry has never quite fit in with family and friends. If she feels like a stranger in Sir Charles's home, she considers herself a complete outsider in the tightly knit Hillfolk community.

*The Blue Sword* will resonate with anyone who feels different, unusual, or unconventional.

Losing her parents, moving in with strangers at the outpost, and forcibly taken away from her people, Harry must cope with severe loss and adversity. Thoughtful, reflective, independent, and courageous, she grows into her role as an epic heroine. Female readers with high ambitions will find her story particularly inspirational.

**For those also seeking**: connection with others/awareness of not being alone
**For those drawn to**: character
**Themes/subjects**: adventure, kidnapping, courage, coming of age, identity formation, identity, outcasts/misfits, insiders/outsiders, independence, conformity and nonconformity, battles/wars, romance, love, orphans, gender roles, knives/daggers/swords
**Reading interest level**: grades 6–8
**Curricular tie-ins**: In their reader response journals, students could answer the question: Would they like to live in Damar? Why or why not?
**Adaptations & alternative formats**: audiobook read by Diane Warren (2013)
**Read-alikes**: Readers who enjoyed this novel will like its prequel, *The Hero and the Crown*. Heroines also battle against forces of evil in Garth Nix's The Old Kingdom Series (*Sabriel, Lirael, The Abhorsen, Clariel, Goldenhand*). Like Harry, Serafina in Robert Beatty's *Serafina and the Twisted Staff* is torn between two worlds.

**McKinley, Robin** (1952–)
**The Hero and the Crown** (1984). New York: Puffin Books, 2000. 246pp. 978-0141309811.

Aerin's mother was a witchwoman who allegedly enspelled her king father into marrying her. When her mother gave birth to her, she was so upset at having a girl that she turned her head to the wall and died. Her daughter, who is never really accepted by the people in her kingdom, takes little part in the life of the castle. Her only friend is Tor, the cousin who will succeed her father as king. Wanting to prove herself useful, Aerin learns how to ride her father's lame war horse, and experiments with an ointment that insulates against dragon fire. Once she perfects the ointment, she teaches herself how to kill dragons. But when she tries to save a village from the deadly dragon,

Maur, she almost dies. Never fully recovering, she leaves to find the man who has appeared in her dreams, one that she believes might be able to save her.

Winner of the Newbery Medal, *The Hero and the Crown* is a compelling, character-centered story about a girl treated as an outsider by her own people. A strong female protagonist who is not accepted because of her parentage, her gender, and her failure to develop the royal Gift, Aerin works hard to make a name for herself. Her story will resonate with those who have felt left out or not respected by others. It will also strike a chord with readers who view gender as a barrier to their ambitions.

When Aerin kills her first dragon, she expects it to be easy. Those who are impatient for results will see that in Aerin's case, change is very slow, almost imperceptible. Persistent, courageous, and independent, Aerin is an inspirational role model for readers.

**For those also seeking**: reassurance/comfort/confirmation of self-worth/strength
**For those drawn to**: character
**Themes/subjects**: princesses, inheritance and succession, dragons, witches, quests, adventure, gender roles, romance, love, coming of age, father-daughter relationships, castles, immortality, perseverance/determination
**Reading interest level**: grades 6–8
**Curricular tie-ins**: The mortal Tor marries the immortal Aerin. Ask students to write an epilogue to the novel explaining what happens to the pair over time.
**Adaptations & alternative formats**: audiobook read by Roslyn Alexander (2013)
**Read-alikes**: *The Hero and the Crown* is the prequel to *The Blue Sword*. Shannon Hale's *The Goose Girl* is also about a crown princess who loses her queenship to someone else, while Garth Nix's *Lirael* is about a girl who feels like an outsider among her own people.

### Reassurance/Comfort/Confirmation of Self-Worth/Strength

**Dahl, Roald** (1916–1990)
**Matilda** (1988). Illustrated by Quentin Blake. New York: Puffin Books, 2007. 240pp. 978-0142410370.

Matilda is only three years old when she teaches herself how to read. By five, she has already completed classics written by famous authors like Charles Dickens and Jane Austen. See, Matilda is not just exceptionally bright. She is a genius. Unfortunately, her crooked car salesman father and her bingo-obsessed mother could care less. They often leave her home alone. In fact, the only time they pay attention to her is to criticize her. They do not understand Matilda's intelligence or curiosity, and they actively *discourage* her from reading.

At least when she starts school, she finds some relief. She makes friends easily and has an excellent teacher, Miss Honey. Still, the headmistress, Miss Trunchbull, is a terrifying woman who casts a perpetual shadow on the school. She actually takes pleasure in threatening and tormenting children, in wielding her adult power. She is a bully who cannot be stopped—that is, until she crosses paths with the super crafty and brilliant Matilda.

Readers who have ever felt neglected or underappreciated will find a kindred spirit in Matilda. In standing up to Trunchball, she models strength and conviction in her own ideas and also provides confirmation that authorities can be wrong. As children are vulnerable to their judgments and opinions, this discovery can offer some comfort and encourage them to find self-worth within themselves.

**For those also seeking**: connection with others/awareness of not being alone
**For those drawn to**: story, character
**Themes/subjects**: abused children, abuse (emotional), abuse (physical), authoritarian figures, being different, books, bullying, challenging authority figures, child neglect, gifted children, greed, heroines, humor, libraries/librarians, misopedists, moving houses (relocating), narcissistic parents, super powers (magical), nurturers, resilience, stories and storytelling, teachers
**Reading interest level**: grades K–5
**Curricular tie-ins**: Matilda cultivates her own curiosity by going to the public library to find books. As an information literacy exercise, ask students to identify something they would like to personally know about and show them how to look it up the subject in a library catalog and find it in the library.
**Adaptations & alternative formats**: audiobook read by David Ian Davies; film directed by Danny DeVito (1996)
**Translations**: Spanish: *Matilda*; French: *Matilda*

**Read-alikes**: Jonathan Stroud's *The Amulet of Samarkand* is about another brilliant child, a boy, whose intelligence is not recognized by adults. Lemony Snicket's *The Bad Beginning* also features clever children who triumph over wicked adults. Kate DiCamillo's *Flora and Ulysses* features another character with super powers (in this case, a squirrel).

**Funke, Cornelia** (1958–)
**Dragon Rider** (1997). Illustrated by the author. Translated from the German by Anthea Bell. 523pp. New York: Chicken House, 2011. 978-0545316484.

Dragons discover that humans plan to invade their territory and destroy their valley. Firedrake decides to search for a place for the dragons to relocate. He then remembers the story about a legendary valley called the Rim of Heaven, a place that may not even exist. Little is known about the place except that it lies in the highest mountain range in the world and was home to dragons when the wise old dragon, Slatebeard, was born. Sorrel, a bad-tempered brownie, insists on accompanying the dragon Firedrake on the journey. Along the way, they meet Ben, an orphan boy who joins the pair. When an evil dragon named Nettlebrand discovers that Firedrake is searching for the Rim of Heaven, he sends a creature known as a homunculus to spy on him. During their search, Firedrake, Ben, and their allies must outwit such creatures as mountain dwarfs, a blue djinn, a basilisk, and a sea serpent.

Humorous dialogue and a richly described fantasy world distinguish this novel. The unusual traveling group of dragon, boy, brownie, and homunculus set this fantasy apart from traditional quest stories. Engaging, one-of-a-kind creatures such as Sorrel, Twigleg, and Nettlebrand will appeal to readers who enjoy unique characters and witty dialogue. Ben, as an orphan child who makes new friends and a better life for himself, provides a reassuring role model for readers who feel lonely or unsupported by others.

**For those also seeking**: models for identity
**For those drawn to**: setting, characters
**Themes/subjects**: dragons, valleys, orphans, quests, friendship, co-operation and teamwork, omens/prophecies, mythological creatures, spies and spying, dwarfs, genies
**Reading interest level**: grades 4–6

**Curricular tie-ins**: Ask students to find information about one of the following topics: alchemy in the middle ages, mythological animals, or belief in magic in the middle ages. They could compose an encyclopedia entry for Wikipedia.
**Adaptations & alternative formats**: audiobook read by Brendan Fraser (2004)
**Translations**: Spanish: *El Jinete del Dragón*; French: *Le Cavalier du Dragon*
**Read-alikes**: Readers who enjoy stories about dragons would like Edith Nesbit's *The Book of Dragons* and Gail Carson Levine's *A Tale of Two Castles*. In Kenneth Oppel's *Silverwing* and Richard Adams's *Watership Down*, animals are forced to search for a new place to live because their homes are destroyed.

**Funke, Cornelia** (1958–)
**The Thief Lord** (2000). Translated from the German by Oliver Latsch. New York: Scholastic, 2010. 349pp. 978-0545227704.

After the mother of 12-year-old Prospero and 5-year-old Bo dies, Aunt Esther decides to adopt Bo, but not his older brother. Distraught at the idea of being separated from his brother, Prospero runs away with Bo to Venice, a place their mother loved. Once the boys arrive in the city, they meet a girl named Hornet. She and three homeless boys live in an abandoned movie theatre. A mysterious boy who calls himself the thief lord steals goods for them so that the children can survive. Meanwhile, when Aunt Esther discovers that the brothers have fled Hamburg, she hires a detective to find them. The boys' dangerous life on the streets, including a job that changes all their lives, involves secrets, magic, and betrayal. A story with many unexpected twists and turns, *The Thief Lord* will appeal to readers who enjoy exciting, action-filled stories.

Exploring the lives of characters who have no one to look after them, the novel is a poignant depiction of homeless, orphaned, wronged, and forsaken children. Readers who have been neglected by parents or caregivers will find reassurance and hope in the novel.

The haunted Isola Segreta—a place from which no one has ever returned to tell the tale, the enchanted merry-go-round that transforms children into adults and vice versa, and the magic and the mystery of Venice are all strong appeals in the novel.

**For those also seeking**: connection with others/awareness of not being alone
**For those drawn to**: story, setting
**Themes/subjects**: runaway children, criminals/thieves, brothers, adventure, Venice, homelessness, stealing, orphans, non-traditional families, poverty, detectives
**Reading interest level**: grades 5–8
**Curricular tie-ins**: Ask students to research Venice and create a travel poster about the city.
**Adaptations & alternative formats**: movie by Richard Claus (2006); audiobook read by Oliver Latsch (2005)
**Translations**: Spanish: *El Señor de los Ladrones*; French: *Le Prince des Voleurs*
**Read-alikes**: Brian Selznick's *The Invention of Hugo Cabret*, Felice Holman's *Slake's Limbo*, and Paula Fox's *Monkey's Island* are also stories about homeless boys who must cope on their own. Rendi in Grace Lin's *Starry River of the Sky* is also a runaway boy.


**Goudge, Elizabeth** (1900–1984)
**The Little White Horse** (1946). New York: Puffin Books, 2001. 238pp. 978-0142300275.

Maria Merryweather, a recently orphaned 13-year-old, must leave her London home and move in with her second cousin, Sir Benjamin. Because her mother died when she was a baby and her soldier father was rarely home, Maria is only close to one person: her beloved governess, Miss Heliotrope. Although Maria finds it difficult to leave behind everything she has ever known and move to the countryside after living in London, she is supported by her governess, befriended by Sir Benjamin, and protected by a trio of strange, magical animals. Expecting to find her new home rough and unsophisticated, she is unexpectedly charmed by it. However, as she learns about the Moonacre estate and her Merryweather ancestors, she discovers many secrets, mysteries, and troubling circumstances.

Maria discovers that once in every generation, the Moon Princess returns to Moonacre Manor. According to local legend, one day the Moon Princess will deliver the valley from the wickedness of a band of locals known as the Men from the Dark Woods. The weight of ancestral history hangs heavily on Maria's shoulders. Her job is to discover the secrets of the family, mend divisions within it, and right social injustices that have been committed.

This 1947 Carnegie Medal winner was made popular again after J. K. Rowling said that it was her favorite childhood book. The world of the novel is suffused with an atmosphere of wonder and enchantment—a skillful intermingling of the ordinary and the extraordinary, the everyday and the magical. The quaint nineteenth-century village of Silverydew that lies in a sheltered valley, the 600-year-old manor that was "almost more of a castle than a house," the enchanted silvery landscape, and Maria's child-sized bedroom at the top of a turret all provide strong appeals for readers who enjoy richly detailed settings.

This novel of mystery and magic will appeal to readers whose lives have been uprooted, whether due to a death, parental divorce, or changed family circumstances. A deeply reassuring novel in which divisions are mended and misfortunes conquered, *The Little White Horse* will comfort children experiencing hardship.

**For those also seeking**: models for identity
**For those drawn to**: setting
**Themes/subjects**: orphans, secrets, moving houses (relocating), governesses, country life, quarrels/fights, village/small-town life, valleys, forests, romance
**Reading interest level**: grades 5–8
**Curricular tie-ins**: Ask students to choose a symbol in the book that could be used for the cover. They should provide reasons for their choice.
**Adaptations & alternative formats**: *The Secret of Moonacre*, a movie directed by Gábor Csupó (2008); audiobook read by Juliet Stevenson (2008)
**Translations**: Spanish: *El Pequeño Caballo Blanco*; French: *Le Secret de Moonacre*
**Read-alikes**: Irene Hunt's *Up a Road Slowly*, Eva Ibbotson's *Journey to the River Sea*, and Frances Hodgson Burnett's *The Secret Garden* are also stories about girls who must move in with relatives after the death of a parent. Maryrose Wood's *The Mysterious Howling* also contains an uprooted heroine, a mysterious mansion, a local mystery, and a governess.

**MacDonald, George** (1828–1905)
**The Princess and Curdie** (1883). London: Puffin, 1994. 256pp. 978-0140367621. PD.

Fantasy

A year after the events in *The Princess and the Goblin*, the young miner Curdie believes that Irene's great-great-grandmother must have been a dream. As his faith in the unseen dwindles, so too does his idealism: "On his way to and from the mine he took less and less notice of bees and butterflies, moths and dragonflies, the flowers and the brooks and the clouds. He was gradually changing into a commonplace man." After killing a pigeon, something stirs within Curdie and he searches for and finds great-great-grandmother. She tests Curdie before giving him a strange magical gift: the ability to detect the hidden nature of a person through touch. She sends him on a quest to the court of the kingdom, assuring him that he will discover what he needs to do as he goes. When he arrives at the court, he finds the king is gravely ill and suspects that someone is poisoning him.

Few characters are what they seem in the novel. Great-great-grandmother appears in many guises; many seemingly noble people are beastly; and grotesque-looking creatures prove to be noble. Curdie's task is to distinguish between good and evil in order to uncover the duplicity and political corruption in the kingdom. Readers who worry about appearances will be reminded that the true value of a person lies within. The novel will appeal to readers who enjoy richly detailed descriptions and a slowly enfolding story.

**For those also seeking**: connection with others/awareness of not being alone
**For those drawn to**: characters
**Themes/subjects**: princesses, faith and skepticism, appearance versus reality, poisoning, royalty, leadership, political corruption, good and evil
**Reading interest level**: grades 4–7
**Curricular tie-ins**: Some readers feel the ending of the novel is too bleak. Ask students to rewrite it.
**Adaptations & alternative formats**: audiobook read by Ian Whitcomb (2004)
**Translations**: Spanish: *La Princesa y Curdie*
**Read-alikes**: Ojo the Unlucky in L. Frank Baum's *The Patchwork Girl of Oz* and Inga in L. Frank Baum's *Rinkitink in Oz* must also save adults who have been tricked or captured by evildoers.

**Nesbit, Edith** (1858–1924)
**Wet Magic** (1913). Hollywood, CA: Aegypan Press. 185pp. 978-1598181746. PD.

When siblings Mavis, Francis, Bernard, and Mavis go on vacation to the sea, they are excited at the prospect of seeing a mermaid. Once they arrive in Beachfield, they attend a local fair and view a mermaid on display. She asks them to return in the dead of night to rescue her. The children do so with a wheelbarrow and take the mermaid to her home in the sea. The next day, the children jump in the sea and go down with the mermaid to her underwater realm. They discover that the mermaid is a princess and that the underground kingdom is filled with marine splendors. But Kathleen violates an interdiction and the children become embroiled in a war between the Mer-people and the Under Folk.

When the children enter the underwater world, they visit enchanting places such as the pearl and turquoise Museum of Foreign Curiosities, the submerged palace of pearl and gold, the Cave of Learning in which the darkest part is the beginning, and a mother-of-pearl terrace that leads to "the most beautiful garden ever imagined or invented." Populated by such creatures as the friendly Mer-people, the Book People who walk out of their texts, the Lobster Battalion, the Crustacean Brigade, and the frivolous Thin-Skins who live near the surface of the water, the mermaid kingdom is a richly imagined submarine world.

Readers who would like to step outside their comfort zone but are fearful of doing so will find inspiration and reassurance in the siblings' story.

**For those also seeking**: models for identity
**For those drawn to**: setting
**Themes/subjects**: sea and seashore, underwater exploration, mermaids, adventure, princesses, circuses (animal), imprisonment/entrapment, battles/wars, missing persons, courage, magic potions
**Reading interest level**: grades 3–6
**Curricular tie-ins**: For a unit on aquatic life, students could visit an aquarium. Ask them to identify fish that are mentioned in the novel.
**Read-alikes**: L. Frank Baum's *The Sea Fairies* and Jules Verne's *Twenty Thousand Leagues under the Sea* also explore the wonders of aquatic life. Readers who enjoy stories about mermaids will also like Randall Jarrell's *The Animal Family* and Hans Christian Andersen's *The Little Mermaid*.

**Pullman, Philip** (1946–)
**Count Karlstein** (1982). New York: Knopf, 2000. 243pp. 978-0375803482.

Count Karlstein, who made a pact with Zamiel the Demon Huntsman in order to get riches, must pay for them by offering up his two orphan nieces as prey on All Souls' Eve. When a Castle Kalstein servant named Hildi overhears this nefarious plan, she tries to save the girls by hiding them in a hut on the mountains. At the same time, a mysterious Doctor Cadaverezzi appears with his strange Cabinet of Wonders. Then the girls' feisty teacher turns up, and concocts a counterplot to defeat the wicked Count Karlstein. The three-part story is told first by the servant Hildi; then, by a variety of narrators; and lastly, by Hildi again.

A humorous thriller that will remind readers of Lemony Snicket's *A Series of Unfortunate Events*, it contains brooding Gothic elements such as an isolated castle on a high precipice, a supernatural legend, a long-lost heir, hunted females, and an evil villain. The gloomy, haunting atmosphere evokes as well as parodies Gothic conventions. The novel will appeal to those who enjoy thrillers and horror stories.

The legend of the Daemon Huntsman blurs the boundary between supernatural events and the superstitious nature of the villagers, causing readers to wonder what really happened on All Soul's Eve. The novel's intricate plotting and clever interconnections between various strands of the story are other strong appeals. The theme of hunting, for example, ties together the characters, events, and themes in the novel.

Most of the narrators give away more about themselves than they are aware of, and all of them have distinct and engaging voices. Charlotte, for example, presents herself in terms of the Gothic heroines she reads about; the language she uses is filled with the artifice of the novels she loves. The comic expose of many of the so-called horrors in the novel will reassure readers who are fearful and anxious by nature.

**For those drawn to**: setting, story
**Themes/subjects**: adventure, mystery/suspense, superstitions, ghosts, orphans, servants, hunting, castles, inns/taverns, village/small-town life, humor
**Reading interest level**: grades 5–8
**Curricular tie-ins**: For a write-pair-share activity, ask students to identify Gothic elements in the novel and consider why readers would like them.
**Adaptations & alternative formats**: audiobook read by Jo Thurley (2006); graphic novel by Patrice Aggs (1992)

**Translations**: Spanish: *El Conde Karlstein*; French: *La Comte Karlstein*
**Read-alikes**: Readers who enjoy humorous Gothic novels will also enjoy the six novels in Maryrose Wood's *The Incorrigible Children of Ashton Place* series (*The Mysterious Howling, The Hidden Gallery, The Unseen Guest, The Interrupted Tale, The Unmapped Sea, The Long-Lost Home*) and the 13 novels in Lemony Snicket's *A Series of Unfortunate Events* (*The Bad Beginning, The Reptile Room, The Wide Window, The Miserable Mill, The Austere Academy, The Ersatz Elevator, The Vile Village, The Hostile Hospital, The Carnivorous Carnival, The Slippery Slope, The Grim Grotto, The Penultimate Peril, The End*). Sid Fleischman's *The Midnight Horse* and Avi's *Midnight Magic* contains superstition, magic, and Gothic villains. Like Hildi, Conrad in Diana Wynne Jones's *Conrad's Fate* is a servant in an eerie, Gothic dwelling. Serafina also works in a mysterious mansion in Robert Beatty's *Serafina and the Black Cloak*.


**Pullman, Philip** (1946–)
**Clockwork, or, All Wound Up** (1998). London: Corgi Yearling, 2004. 99pp. 978-0440866381.

On the eve of the unveiling of a new clockwork figure for a community clock, the apprentice who made it sits glumly by himself in the White Horse Tavern, a place in a little German village. Instead of looking forward to the unveiling, an event that traditionally marks the end of a clockmaker's apprenticeship, Karl dreads it, since in his idleness, he never actually made the figure. While he sits despondently, the other customers listen to a story that Fritz the writer has just composed.

The strange story that he tells concerns a prince, his young son, and Dr. Kalmenius—a man skilled at creating clockwork figures. When Fritz gets to the point in his story where Dr. Kalmenius enters, the door to the White House Inn creaks open, and the doctor himself materializes, astonishing the tavern customers.

Every element in the novel and each component of the narrative is interconnected like clockwork and tied to the theme of clockwork, either literally or figuratively. Older readers will appreciate the philosophical ideas in the novel, ideas presented in concrete and accessible ways. Pullman explores the nature of humanity, reality, time, stories, and human agency ("Our lives are clockwork," observes Dr. Kalmenius). Younger readers will delight in the strange and scary story about a prince, a knight, and a spine-chilling doctor who comes to life. Readers who feel powerless will find hope and optimism in the example of Gretl, the servant girl.

**For those drawn to**: story, setting
**Themes/subjects**: clockwork and mechanical figures, love, stories and storytelling, mystery/suspense, knights, princes, apprentices, agency and powerlessness, inns/taverns, idleness
**Reading interest level**: grades 4–8
**Curricular tie-ins**: This novel could be used in conjunction with a science lesson on levers, pulleys, and gears. Ask students to work in groups and create a collage of clockwork items.
**Adaptations & alternative formats**: audiobook read by Anton Lesser (2013)
**Translations**: Spanish: *El Reloj Mecánico*; French: *La Mécanique du Diable*
**Read-alikes**: Pullman's *Count Karlstein* is a scary story about a character who makes a deal with a devil-like figure, while John Bellairs's *The House with a Clock in Its Walls* is a Gothic horror story about a mysterious clock. In Cornelia Funke's *Inkheart*, characters from a book also appear in the real world. The same mysterious, brooding atmosphere dominates Laura Amy Schlitz's *Splendors and Glooms*.

### Richler, Mordecai (1931–2001)
**Jacob Two-Two Meets the Hooded Fang** (1975). Toronto: Tundra Books, 2009. 85pp. 978-0887769252.

The youngest of five children, six-year-old Jacob Two-Two repeats everything he says. "I am the littlest," he explains. "Nobody hears me the first time." Whenever he tries to play with his siblings or help around the house, he is turned down because of his age and size. Sympathizing with his son, Jacob's father allows him to run his first errand. When Jacob goes to the store to buy two tomatoes for his father, the grocer teases him for repeating everything, and he does so in front of the local policeman. Thinking he is trouble, Jacob runs outside into the fog and finds himself in a dark cell beneath the courthouse. Jacob's worst fears materialize when characters and creatures that he encountered earlier reappear in nightmare form. The judge, Mr. Justice Rough, charges Jacob with insulting behavior "to a big person" and sends him to a children's prison on Slimer's Isle.

A very humorous story with a fast-paced plot, *Jacob Two-Two and the Hooded Fang* depicts life as it appears to a six-year-old who feels unfairly treated by older siblings and adults. The judge warns Jacob that "in this court, as in life, little people are considered guilty, unless they can prove themselves innocent, which is just short of impossible." He also insists that children must be taught that "BIG PEOPLE ARE NEVER, NEVER WRONG." Once Jacob arrives in the children's prison, he relies on the assistance of "Child Power" advocates, two rescuers in capes who turn out to be his brother and sister. This empowering story will appeal to young children who feel small and helpless in a world of older people.

**For those also seeking**: connection with others/awareness of not being alone
**For those drawn to**: character, story
**Themes/subjects**: youngest sibling, imprisonment/entrapment, agency and powerlessness, dreams, families, anxiety/fears, humor
**Reading interest level**: grades JK–3
**Curricular tie-ins**: Ask students to draw a picture of their favorite character or setting in the book.
**Adaptations & alternative formats**: movie directed by George Bloomfield (1999); audiobook read by Rick Miller (2015)
**Translations**: French: *Jacob Deux-Deux et le Vampire Masqué: Roman*
**Read-alikes**: Readers who enjoyed the novel will like its sequels: *Jacob Two-Two and the Dinosaur* and *Jacob Two-Two's First Spy Case*. Like Jacob Two-Two, James in Roald Dahl's *James and the Giant Peach* initially feels small and powerless.

**Thurber, James** (1894–1961)
**The 13 Clocks** (1950). Illustrated by Marc Simont. Introduction by Neil Gaiman. New York: New York Review Books, 2008. 124pp. 978-1590179376.

Once upon a time, a Princess called Saralinda lived in a gloomy castle with her cold-hearted uncle, the Duke. To win her hand, suitors of the princess must perform impossible tasks. No one has yet succeeded. When the Duke's spies discover that a ragged minstrel named Xingu is in fact Prince Zorn of Zorna, the Duke captures him and throws him in the castle dungeon. The Duke tells Prince Zorn that, in order to win the hand of Princess Saralinda, he must go on a quest in search of a thousand gems and then restart the 13 castle clocks. The Duke warns the prince that, if he fails, he will slit him from his "guggle" to his "zatch."

Readers who enjoy stories that are humorous and ridiculous will love this original fairy tale. Funny villains ("We all have flaws," says the Duke, "and mine is being wicked"), absurd situations (Hagga laughs so hard that she produces a thousand gems), light-hearted dialogue ("The fat is in the fire," says the Golux, "the die is cast, the jig is up, the goose is cooked, and the cat is out of the bag"), and humorous use of language ("taverners, travelers, tale-tellers, tosspots, troublemakers, and other townspeople" gather at an inn) make this fairy tale fun to read. In Neil Gaiman's introduction to the novel, he observes that Thurber uses words which "glitter and gleam, tossing them out like a happy madman."

Combining the comic with the philosophical, the story contains thought-provoking metaphorical details such as the stopped clocks in the castle. ("Time lies frozen there. It's always Then. It's never Now.") Readers who have ambitious goals will be reassured that, no matter how daunting, they can be achieved. Marc Simont's whimsical, original illustrations convey both the charm and absurdity of this eccentric world.

**For those drawn to**: language
**Themes/subjects**: quests, princesses, princes, castles, love, wordplay, humor
**Reading interest level**: grades 3–7
**Curricular tie-ins**: Ask students to create a wanted poster for the Duke.
**Adaptations & alternative formats**: audiobook read by Edward Woodard (2009)
**Translations**: Spanish: *Los 13 Relojes*
**Read-alikes**: James Thurber's *The White Deer* and Jon Scieszka's *The Stinky Cheese Man and Other Fairly Stupid Tales* are also humorous fairy tales. A cruel duke tries to steal the throne from a princess in Garth Nix's *Frogkisser!* Clocks and time dominate in Garth Nix's *Mister Monday*.

## Connection with Others/Awareness of Not Being Alone

**Dahl, Roald** (1916–1990)
**Danny the Champion of the World** (1975). Illustrated by Quentin Blake. New York: Puffin Books, 2007. 205pp. 978-0142410332.

Danny is an only child who lives in a tiny, old gypsy caravan with his father, who owns the filling station next door. Although Danny doesn't have a mother (she died when he was only four months old) and Danny and his father live alone out in the country and don't have much money, their life together is actually quite happy and rich. They are always making and inventing things to do, and Danny's father, who is an excellent storyteller, amuses him with fantastic stories.

Despite their close bond, Danny is nine years old before he learns his father's secret. Sometimes, at night, he sneaks onto the greedy Mr. Hazell's estate (which includes almost all of the land in the country where Danny and his dad live), and poaches (steals!) the pheasants that he keeps in his woods. Although Danny worries about his father's thievery, he is not convinced that the mean Mr. Hazell doesn't deserve it. So, in order to spoil Mr. Hazell's annual pheasant shooting party, Danny conceives of a brilliant plan that will embarrass Mr. Hazell in front of all of England's rich and famous.

Full of humor and mischief, this story challenges universal standards about right and wrong. While it is, of course, always wrong to steal, who is more blameworthy: Poor Danny's father or the greedy Mr. Hazell? While, in the end, the moral stands that "It never pays to eat more than your fair share," readers can relate to these dilemmas and empathize with Danny and the power imbalance inherent in his situation.

**For those also seeking**: awakening/new perspectives/enlargement of possibilities
**For those drawn to**: story, language
**Themes/subjects**: adventure, anxiety/fears, class differences, corporeal punishment, critical thinking/strategy, dead or absent mother, father-son relationships, food, greed, hunting, inventing/creating, justice and injustice, moral dilemmas, nurturers, only children, poverty, secrets, stealing, stories and storytelling, wealth
**Reading interest level**: grades K–5
**Curricular tie-ins**: Offer a basic overview of consequentialism and rule-based ethics and ask students to try to apply them to the story. Discuss how the rightness of Danny and his father's actions shifts depending on the theory being applied.
**Adaptations & alternative formats**: audiobook read by Peter Serafinowicz (2013)
**Translations**: Spanish: *Danny El Campeón Del Mundo*; French: *Danny, Le Champion Du Monde*

**Dahl, Roald** (1916–1990)
**Charlie and the Chocolate Factory** (1964). Illustrated by Quentin Blake. New York: Puffin Books, 2007. 155pp. 978-0142410318.

Charlie Bucket lives in a shabby, one-room house in the outskirts of a big city along with his mom, dad, and grandparents. While his family is kind and loving to each other, they are very poor, and life is hard. Charlie and his parents sleep on mats on the floor, and his grandparents share their only bed. There is also never enough food to eat, and to add insult to injury Charlie lives next door to Willy Wonka's famous chocolate factory. Every time he steps outside, he can't help but breathe in the sweet chocolate fragrance.

But then, Willy Wonka, who no one has seen or heard for years, announces he has hidden golden tickets inside five of his candy bars, and the five children who find them will be invited to tour his factory. Charlie finds one of them, but his tour turns into a mixed experience. While the things he sees, tastes, and experiences far exceed anything Charlie could have imagined, Wonka himself is a dubious, somewhat sinister character. The other four children, who, unlike Charlie, are all terribly spoiled and headstrong, and do not heed Mr. Wonka's warnings for their safety, start to go missing, one-by-one.

While fun and imaginative, this story is also a dark morality tale about the consequences of intemperance. While Charlie Bucket doesn't have enough of anything (food, wealth, and entertainment), the other children have too much and are spoiled and dulled as a result. While these children represent extremes, their faults are very human. Readers can recognize their own weaknesses in them, see that they are not alone, and also, hopefully, learn from them.

**For those also seeking**: models for identity
**For those drawn to**: story, character
**Themes/subjects**: candy/chocolate, class differences, family, food, grandparents, greed, hope, hunger, humor, imagination, intellectual property, justice and injustice, love, luck/chance, madmen, magic potions, magical transformations, only children, poverty, spoiled children, stories and storytelling, wealth, wordplay, indentured servitude
**Reading interest level**: grades K–5

**Curricular tie-ins**: In the first edition of this novel, Willy Wonka's workers, the Oompa Loompas, are essentially indentured servants from Africa. Ask students why they think Dahl revised this detail in subsequent editions. To broaden their understanding, ask students to research the production of chocolate, from cacao bean to processed chocolate bar, to uncover the traces of fact in Willy Wonka's fantasy factory.
**Adaptations & alternative formats**: first edition illustrated by Joseph Schindelman; audiobook read by Douglas Hodge (2013) and Eric Idle (2004); films directed by Mel Stuart (1971) and Tim Burton (2005)
**Translations**: Spanish: *Charlie Y La Fábrica De Chocolate*; French: *Charlie Et La Chocolaterie*
**Read-alikes**: Chris Grabenstein's *Escape from Mr. Lemoncello's Library* is about another boy who wins a contest to view a new high-tech library designed by the Willy-Wonky-like billionaire game-maker Luigi Lemoncello.

**Hale, Shannon** (1974-)
**Princess Academy** (2005). New York: Bloomsbury, 2015. 314pp. 978-1619636132.

When the chief delegate of the King of Danland visits the outlying village of Mount Eskel, he announces that the prince's future bride, according to divine prediction, will come from this village. Tradition dictates that all females between the ages of 12 and 17 will be princess candidates and must attend the Academy for a year. Although 14-year-old Miri feels like an outsider in this closely knit mountain village, she does not want to leave her father and sister to attend the Academy. Forced to go, she is even more upset when cruel Tutor Olana treats all the girls as if they were stupid and uncivilized. And when Miri's classmates shun her and leave her out of activities, she is devastated. Lonely and homesick, Miri throws herself into her studies.

The mountain landscape is inextricably linked with Miri's identity and choices. The stunningly beautiful scenery, the isolating power of the mountains, and their potential for lethal accidents make them a memorable backdrop to the action. Torn between two ways of life represented by two romantic choices, Miri does not know what she wants. An outsider and misfit in both her village and her class, she wishes with all her heart to fit into a community.

Before Miri attends the Princess Academy, she dreamt "of nothing grander than working in the quarry. But now she was aware of the kingdom beyond her mountain, hundreds of years of history, and a thousand things she could be." Although Miri is unjustly treated by Tutor Olana and deeply unhappy at school, she learns about the wider world, an experience that provides her with opportunities she never considered before, choices that both enrich and complicate her life. Readers who feel pulled in two directions, are unsure about their future, or see themselves as outsiders will not feel so alone or so different after reading Miri's story.

**For those also seeking**: reassurance/comfort/confirmation of self-worth/strength
**For those drawn to**: character, setting
**Themes/subjects**: princesses, schools, quarries, mountains, royalty, kings/queens, identity formation, dead or absent mother, father-daughter relationships, romance, homesickness, cliques (in school), friendship, prejudice, village/small-town life, tutors, telepathy, etiquette and customs
**Reading interest level**: grade 5 and up
**Curricular tie-ins**: This novel could be used as a resource for a geology lesson. Ask students to create a project about quarries and how they tie in with the lithosphere. Alternatively, students could research trade in their country—specifically, the products that their country produces, the partners they trade with, and changes in trading patterns over the years. Students could present their findings as slide presentations.
**Adaptations & alternative formats**: audiobook read by Laura Credidio (2012)
**Translations**: Spanish: *Academia de Princesas*; French: *Le Collège des Princesses*
**Read-alikes**: Readers who enjoy Miri's story will also like the two sequels to the novel—*Princess Academy: Palace of Stone* and *Princess Academy: The Forgotten Sisters*. Like Miri, Ella in Gail Carson Levine's *Ella Enchanted* goes unwillingly to a finishing school for girls, while Heidi, in Johanna Spyri's novel by the same name, is another mountain girl who leaves her beloved home for school. Like Miri, Po communicates telepathically in Kristin Cashore's *The Graceling*, while both the heroines of these novels must find their place in their kingdoms.

**Stroud, Jonathan** (1970)
**The Amulet of Samarkand** (2003). New York: Hyperion Books for Children, 2003. 462pp. 978-0786852550.

In a modern-day London ruled by magicians, the government advertises for a young child to become an apprentice magician. Nathaniel's parents give up their son in exchange for money. Nathaniel is trained by Arthur Underwood, a middle-ranking magician in the Ministry of Internal Affairs. "Your true life begins now," Underwood tells the five-year-old boy. A mediocre government official, Underwood is an indifferent guardian and harsh disciplinarian. Tutors provide Nathaniel with a demanding and rigorous education, something he excels at.

When Simon Lovelace, the Junior Minister for Trade, meets Nathaniel, he belittles his intelligence and humiliates the boy in front of a group of magicians. From that point on, Nathaniel's mind is "fired by hate," and he becomes obsessed with revenge. Little does the 12-year-old boy know what kind of political intrigue he gets himself involved in when he summons a 5000-year-old djinni to steal an amulet from Lovelace.

Readers who love exciting thrillers and those who enjoy magical fantasies will both like this fast-paced, action-dominated novel. Although magicians appear in many novels, magicians as politicians are unique to the Bartimaeus series. Underwood tells Nathaniel that a magician is "a wielder of power," and as such, magicians are "the most influential people in London." Believing themselves to be "the greatest magical elite on earth," the politicians discriminate against the non-magical "commoners." The corrupting influence of power is a key theme in the novel.

By alternating between Bartimaeus's point of view and Nathaniel's, and by breaking off the story at crucial points in each narrative, Stroud intensifies the suspense. Bartimaeus as a haughty genie is a particularly strong voice—droll, witty, and engaging. Nathaniel's character is another strong appeal in the novel. Rejected by his parents, dismissed by his guardian, and not recognized for his intellectual talents, he has many strikes against him. Turning to revenge, Nathaniel becomes obsessed with it. Readers who are gifted, those whose abilities have not been recognized by adults, and anyone who has felt hatred for another will not feel so alone after reading Nathaniel's story.

**For those also seeking**: reassurance/comfort/confirmation of self-worth/strength
**For those drawn to**: story, character
**Themes/subjects**: genies, wishes and wishing, apprentices, magicians, mystery/suspense, revenge, hatred, stealing, gifted children, amulets,

*Fantasy*

obsessions, political corruption, politics, prejudice, disguises, education, tutors, England, London, city life, mysteries
**Reading interest level**: grades 5–8
**Curricular tie-ins**: Bartimaeus often refers to his time with Ptolemy; Nathaniel, on the other hand, is interested in Benjamin Disraeli. Ask students to find information about one of these historical figures and write a short biographical sketch about him.
**Adaptations & alternative formats**: audiobook read by Simon Jones (2004); graphic novel by Jonathan Stroud and Andrew Donkin (2010)
**Translations**: Spanish: *El Amuleto de Samarkanda*; French: *L'Amulette de Samarcande*
**Read-alikes**: *The Golem's Eye* and *Ptolemy's Gate* are sequels to the story while *The Ring of Solomon* is a prequel. Ged in Ursula K. Le Guin's *A Wizard of Earthsea* is another precocious magician who causes great turmoil by summoning a figure of immense power. Adults also underestimate Matilda's intellectual brilliance in Roald Dahl's novel by the same name. In Kelly Barnhill's *The Girl Who Drank the Moon*, a child is separated from her parents by a corrupt regime that promotes such practices. Like Nathaniel, Annabelle in Karen Foxlee's *A Most Magical Girl* must save London from an evil magician.


**Thurber, James** (1894–1961)
**The White Deer** (1945). Illustrated by the author. San Diego: Harcourt Brace, 1973. 115pp. 978-0156962643.

King Clode has three sons: Thag and Gallow are hunters like their father, while Jorn is a poet and musician. The King tells his sons the story of how he and his two brothers entered an enchanted forest and were about to kill a deer. But the deer transformed into a princess and gave each of the three brothers a perilous task to perform to win her hand. King Clode won the competition and the princess became the mother of Thag, Gallow, and Jorn. Amazingly, the three sons also find a white deer in an enchanted forest, and this deer similarly transforms into a lovely princess. She, in turn, gives the three brothers perilous tasks to perform to win her hand. This princess does not know her name or who she is.

Wit and wordplay transform the fairy-tale plot into a humorous, whimsical story filled with quirky characters, nonsensical dialogue, and ridiculous incidents. Alliterative descriptions such as the white deer "climbed a ruby ridge, flung across a valley of violets, and sped along the pearly path leading to the myriad mazes of the Moonstone Mines" change a conventional incident to a highly engaging one.

Reason and factual knowledge are satirized throughout the tale. When the castle's Royal Recorder discovers that the white deer is Princess Rosanore, he complains, "The case lacks precedent . . . and lacking precedent, is difficult, if not, indeed, impossible, to classify, co-ordinate, and catalogue. We have here terms of two distinct and unrelated sets of spells which overlap. Overlapping, in the legal sense, I heartily deplore."

Entering the enchanted forest changes characters' perspectives: "nearby things sound far away and far things near." The forest is associated with magic, imagination, and love—all of which, according to the story, are more important than facts and logic. Readers who feel different from others because they do not conform to the status quo may feel less strange and unusual after reading Jorn's story.

**For those drawn to**: language
**Themes/subjects**: magical transformations, wordplay, quests, princesses, princes, forests, romance, love, wizards, deer
**Reading interest level**: grade 6 and up
**Curricular tie-ins**: *The White Deer* is a tongue-in-cheek fairy tale. Ask students to identify the characteristics of a traditional fairy tale and explain how they are used in the story. This book would also make an excellent resource for a language lesson on sound devices such as alliteration and assonance.
**Translations**: French: *Le Conte de la Biche Blanche*
**Read-alikes**: Norton Juster's *The Phantom Tollbooth* and James Thurber's *The Wonderful O* are also witty, whimsical stories featuring wordplay and nonsense.

## Courage to Make a Change

**Dahl, Roald** (1916–1990)
**George's Marvelous Medicine** (1981). Illustrated by Quentin Blake. New York: Puffin Books, 2015. 88pp. 978-0142410356.

Eight-year-old George is stuck at home with his nasty, old grandmother. Although she acts civil in the presence of his parents, George's grandmother becomes simply beastly when they are gone. She calls George mean names, belittles him, and bosses him around. When she demands that he bring her medicine, George decides he will serve her one of his own concoctions, instead. He mixes a variety of household products—from shaving cream to flea powder—that produce fantastic results. Indeed, an actual doctor may not have done any better.

While pure fantasy, this short novel ultimately offers a liberating tale of a child finding the courage to challenge authority. Although George's grandmother is grown and supposedly a "grown-up," she is actually quite vicious—moody, unpredictable, impossible to be around. Children who are confronting similar kinds of authority figures may connect with George's plight, and recognize, like him, that they have agency and possess the power to stand up for themselves.

**For those also seeking**: Connection with others/awareness of not being alone
**For those drawn to**: story
**Themes/subjects**: abuse (emotional), challenging authority figures, food, grandmothers, humor, magic potions, magical transformations, math/numbers, misopedists, narcissism
**Reading interest level**: grades K–5
**Curricular tie-ins**: George's medicine is "marvelous" because he keeps mixing up the proportions of ingredients with different results. Thus, this story would provide great examples with which to introduce a basic mathematics lesson on proportions and ratios.
**Adaptations & alternative formats**: audiobook read by Derek Jacobi (2013)
**Translations**: Spanish: *La Maravillosa Medicina De Jorge*; French: *La Potion Magique De Georges Bouillon*


**Gaiman, Neil** (1960–)
**The Graveyard Book** (2008). Illustrated by Dave McKean. New York: HarperCollins, 2010. 313pp. 978-0060530945.

After the man Jack murders a mother, father, and their daughter, he plans to kill the toddler son. Not finding him, the murderer walks to the nearby graveyard where he thinks the toddler might be. In the meantime, the spirit of the murdered mother asks two inhabitants of the grave—the ghostly Mr. and Mrs. Owen—to raise and protect her son. Naming the baby "Nobody" ("Bod" for short), the Owens keep him safe within the gates of the graveyard.

Silas, a wise character who straddles the border between life and death, becomes Bod's guardian. Although Bod grows up in a protected and nurturing environment, he is, unbeknownst to him, relentlessly pursued by the killer Jack.

Like Gaiman's earlier novel *Coraline*, *The Graveyard Book* is a Gothic fantasy—a genre which Gaiman excels at. Winner of three prestigious awards—the Newbery Medal, the Carnegie Award, and the Hugo Award—*The Graveyard Book* is by turns eerie, humorous, terrifying, moving, and quirky. Lyrical language, endearing characters, a suspenseful plot, and a witty tone ("It will take a graveyard" to raise the child), unite to produce this richly imagined best-seller.

The story will resonate with readers who feel stifled in an over-protective environment. Even though Bod knows that the safest place for him is the cemetery, he constantly defies his parent's rules and travels beyond the protective gates. An outsider to both the world of the dead and the world of the living, he comes of age when he decides where he will live. Readers looking for courage to make a significant change in their lives will find it in Bod's example. Illustrations by Gaiman's long-time collaborator, Dave McKean, evoke the eerie, other worldly atmosphere of the novel.

**For those also seeking**: reassurance/comfort/confirmation of self-worth/strength
**For those drawn to**: story, setting
**Themes/subjects**: cemeteries/tombs, ghosts, murder, death, coming of age, identity formation, orphans, witches, education, revenge, independence, non-traditional families, overprotective parents
**Reading interest level**: grades 5–8
**Curricular tie-ins**: Ask students to pretend they are social workers and write a report on Bod's adaptation to his new foster family.
**Adaptations & alternative formats**: audiobook read by the author (2008); graphic novel by P. Craig Russell (2 vols; 2014)
**Translations**: Spanish: *El Libro del Cementerio*; French: *L'Étrange Vie de Nobody Owens*
**Read-alikes**: Gaiman has said that the novel was inspired by Rudyard Kipling's *The Jungle book* but with a graveyard setting. J. K. Rowling's *Harry Potter and the Sorcerer's Stone* is about a boy whose family is murdered, while Garth Nix's *Sabriel* is about the borders between life and death.

**Levine, Gail Carson** (1947–)
**The Two Princesses of Bamarre** (2001). New York: HarperCollins, 2001. 241pp. 978-0064409667.

Princess Meryl, who revels in swordplay, adventure, and danger, is the diametrical opposite of her sister, Princess Addie, who is afraid of "almost everything—from monsters to strangers to spiders." Meryl is Addie's protector and promises her that she will stay home and keep her safe until Addie decides to marry. Although their kingdom is plagued with monsters and specters, its real danger lies in a fatal sickness called the Gray Death. When Meryl contracts the disease, Addie is devastated. Their mother had died of it when the girls were young, and there is no known cure. After the girl's father makes a half-hearted attempt to save his daughter by looking for a cure for it, Addie realizes that it is up to her to save Meryl. To do so, she must brave the dangerous world beyond the castle walls. Ironically, the sister who has prepared her entire life for dangerous quests is not the one who must go on one.

Not knowing where to search for a cure and feeling deeply afraid, Addie nevertheless begins her quest. Readers who are fearful of many things, those who have phobias, and anyone who has experienced anxiety will find strength and encouragement in Addie's tale. Readers wishing to make a difficult change in life and lacking the courage to do so will also find inspiration in the novel.

Levine began the book with the idea of adapting the fairy tale, *The Twelve Dancing Princesses*. Although she eventually abandoned this idea, the fairy-tale elements within the novel will appeal to those who love the genre. From the burnished gold of the dragon's lair to the coral-colored marble of the fairy castle, the settings are highly distinctive and mesmerizing. And although the story is gripping and suspenseful, it is the psychologically convincing characterization that distinguishes the novel. The surprise ending is an added appeal, one that is both fitting and original.

**For those also seeking**: reassurance/comfort/confirmation of self-worth/strength
**For those drawn to**: character, setting
**Themes/subjects**: princesses, sisters, illness, dragons, courage, self-confidence, anxiety/fears, phobias, omens/prophecies, romance, fairies, castles, courage, adventure, quests

**Reading interest level**: grades 4–8
**Curricular tie-ins**: The Gray Death in the novel has overtones of the actual Black Death of the fourteenth century. Ask students to research and create the script for a commercial warning people about the Black Death.
**Translations**: Spanish: *Dos Princesa Sin Miedo*; French: *Les Deux Princesses de Bamarre*
**Read-alikes**: The prequel to the novel is *The Lost Kingdom of Bamarre*. Readers who enjoy fairy-tale-inspired fantasies will also like Gail Carson Levine's *Ella Enchanted* and *Fairest*, Shannon Hale's *The Goose Girl*, and Robin McKinley's *Beauty*.


**Tolkien, J. R. R.** (1892–1973)
**The Hobbit, or, There and Back Again** (1937). Illustrations by the author. Boston: Houghton Mifflin Harcourt, 2012. 300pp. 978-0547928227.

When the wizard Gandalf visits Bilbo Baggins, he asks the hobbit if he would like to go on an adventure. Bilbo tells him that he has no use for adventures: "Nasty disturbing uncomfortable things! Make you late for dinner! I can't think what anybody sees in them." The next day, 13 dwarfs appear on his doorstep and expect to be entertained. When the dwarf Thorin sings about adventures, Bilbo forgets everything else and is "swept away into dark lands under strange moons." Something awakens deep within him, and he agrees to search for a dragon and steal his treasure horde. Leaving home with Gandalf and the dwarfs, Bilbo begins a long and dangerous quest. Once they leave the safety of the Hobbit lands, Gandalf warns the group, "There are no safe paths in this part of the world. Remember you are over the Edge of the Wild now."

A novel that provides enjoyment on many levels, *The Hobbit* can be read by young readers as an exciting story of survival and magical adventures. Bilbo's journey takes him farther and farther away from the security of civilization. Places such as the nightmarish Misty Mountains, the menacing Mirkwood Forest, the Last Homely House, Beorn's Wide Wooden Halls, and the dragon's Lonely Mountain are among the most memorable settings in literature and will appeal to fans of imaginative fantasy realms.

Older readers will also recognize Bilbo's journey as a symbol of his psychological development. Facing such creatures as trolls, goblins, wolves, giant

Fantasy

183

spiders, and a dragon, the hobbit grows into his role as hero. Bilbo's earlier encounters with evil prepare him for later more difficult ones. The mind games he plays with Gollum, for example, are a prelude and rehearsal for his psychological warfare with the dragon Smaug.

What appeals to readers of all ages is the fact that Bilbo is an unlikely and unpromising hero. His fellow dwarves do not think he is capable of the quest and Bilbo does not believe in himself. Gandalf, the only character who sees potential in the hobbit, tells the skeptical dwarfs, "There is a lot more in him than you guess, and a deal more than he has any idea of himself." The story will appeal to readers who possess untapped potential, those who are afraid of leaving their comfort zone, and anyone who would like to change but is afraid of the difficulties of doing so.

**For those also seeking**: connection with others/awareness of not being alone
**For those drawn to**: setting, story
**Themes/subjects**: quests, adventure, self-confidence, dwarfs, buried/hidden treasure, greed, stealing, wizards, goblins, wilderness survival, clues/riddles, forests, mountains, invisibility cloaks and rings
**Reading interest level**: grade 3 and up
**Curricular tie-ins**: Many characters in the novel long for the dragon's treasure. In a write-pair-share activity, students could consider how the treasure should be divided, who should receive it, and why.
**Adaptations & alternative formats**: three-part movie directed by Peter Jackson (2012, 2013, 2014); audiobook read by Rob Inglis (2012); graphic novel by Chuck Dixon (1989)
**Translations**: Spanish: *El Hobbit*; French: *Bilbo le Hobbit*
**Read-alikes**: Lloyd Alexander's *The Chronicles of Prydain* (*The Book of Three*, *The Black Cauldron*, *The Castle of Llyr*, *Taran Wanderer*, and *The High King*) feature another unlikely hero who accomplishes great things, while Robert Louis Stevenson's *Treasure Island* is a story about a quest for treasure. Older readers will enjoy *The Lord of the Rings* books (*The Fellowship of the Ring*, *The Two Towers*, and *The Return of the Ring*). These sequels to *The Hobbit* follow the life of Frodo Baggins, Bilbo's younger cousin.

## Acceptance

**Barrie, J. M.** (1860–1937)
**Peter Pan** (1911). In Peter Pan: Peter and Wendy and Peter Pan in Kensington Gardens. New York: Penguin Books, 2004. 234pp. 978-0142437933. PD.

When Peter Pan and the fairy, Tinkerbell, fly into the Darling nursery, Peter leaves without his shadow. Returning to get it, he shows Wendy, John, and Michael how to fly and then takes them to Neverland. Once the Darling children arrive, they meet the lost boys who create a house for Wendy and invite them into their own underground home. The children participate in a series of adventures with mermaids, fairies, Captain Hook and his pirates, and Tiger Lily and her tribe.

Few fantasy places are as memorable as Neverland, the island located "second to the right and straight on till morning." Mrs. Darling first finds a map of Neverland in her children's minds, and the island is as much a psychological state as an imaginary realm. Unlike the drab world of adults, in which grown-ups work in offices and Mr. Darling calculates expenses, Neverland is filled with adventure, play, and endless fun. A place where children rehearse roles that prepare them for adulthood, Neverland is an interim landscape rather than a permanent dwelling. But Peter Pan, who refuses to leave Neverland, tries to prevent the children from returning home and becoming adults. Readers who are anxious about growing up or feel reluctant about taking on adult responsibilities will find both easier to accept after reading about a boy who has remained forever childish and immature.

The edition of the novel currently in print contains two versions of the Peter Pan's story: *Peter and Wendy* and *Peter Pan in Kensington Gardens*. The story that readers are familiar with today is *Peter and Wendy* (often re-titled *Peter Pan*). This story was performed as a play in 1904 and then published as a novel in 1911. An earlier version of the tale, *Peter Pan in Kensington Gardens*, is chiefly remembered for its illustrations by Arthur Rackham.

**For those also seeking**: reassurance/comfort/confirmation of self-worth/strength
**For those drawn to**: story, setting
**Themes/subjects**: adventure, growing up (apprehension), fairies, islands, pirates, mermaids, imagination, stories and storytelling
**Reading interest level**: grades 3–6
**Curricular tie-ins**: *Peter Pan* was performed as a play before it was published as a novel. Ask students to build a replica of the island stage setting. Alternatively, the novel could be used as a springboard to an art lesson. The narrator observes that the Neverlands vary a great deal. John's Neverland, for example, is quite different from Peter's. Ask students to draw their version of the island.

Fantasy

**Adaptations & alternative formats**: movie directed by P. J. Hogan (2003); movie called *Hook* directed by Steven Spielberg (1991); Disney movie directed by Clyde Geronimi and Wilfred Jackson (1953); audiobook read by Jim Dale (2006)
**Translations**: Spanish: *Peter Pan*; French: *Peter Pan*
**Read-alikes**: Although R. L. Stevenson's *Treasure Island* and R. M. Ballantyne's *Coral Island* are realistic novels, they also feature island adventures. Sid Fleischman's *The 13th Floor: A Ghost Story* is a story about pirates and magical adventures. Geraldine McCaughrean's *Peter Pan in Scarlet* is the official sequel to *Peter Pan*.


**Craik, Dinah Maria Mulock** (1826–1887)
**The Little Lame Prince** (1875). Amsterdam: Fredonia Books, 2001. 216pp. 978-1589632905. PD.

During Prince Dolor's christening, the lady carrying the baby stumbles and drops him. Although not known at the time, the accident causes long-term damage and prevents the prince from walking. On the same day, the baby's mother unexpectedly dies, and a few years later, his father passes away. Prince Dolor's then uncle usurps the throne and hides his nephew—the rightful crown prince—in a tower with a nurse. As a toddler and then a young child, he does not realize his plight, but once he learns about the world, he understands what he is missing by not being able to walk. Later, when the nurse tells him about his uncle's usurpation of the throne, Prince Dolor is angry and upset.

However, the prince has a fairy godmother who gives him a magic traveling cloak so that he can fly and see the world. Although the fairy godmother is able to help him with some things, she cannot bring back his parents or cure his disability. He must learn to accept these misfortunes. Prince Dolor experiences sadness, anger, and hopelessness, but his sorrows open his eyes to the sufferings of others, which in turn increases his wisdom and compassion. The story, although sentimental at times, will resonate with readers who struggle to accept hardships. Readers who have been wronged or have experienced trauma will be reassured by Prince Dolor's story.

**For those also seeking**: acceptance
**For those drawn to**: story
**Themes/subjects**: princes, disability, flying magically, fairy godmothers, inheritance and succession, entrapment/imprisonment, royalty, kings/

queens, wishes and wishing, orphans, justice and injustice, accidents (major), deception
**Reading interest level**: grades 1–5
**Translations**: French: *Le Petit Prince Paralysé*
**Curricular tie-ins**: In their reader response journals, students could consider the question: If they could ask for one wish from a fairy godmother, what would it be and why would they wish for it?
**Read-alikes**: Like the fairy godmother in *The Little Lame Prince*, the Psammead grants wishes in Edith Nesbit's *Five Children and It*. Shannon Hale's *The Goose Girl* is about a crown princess who has her queenship stolen away from her. Kip must also come to terms with his lameness in Jonathan Auxier's *The Night Gardener*.

**Dahl, Roald** (1916–1990)
**The Witches** (1983). Illustrated by Quentin Blake. New York: Puffin Books, 2015. 206pp. 978-1101996997.

A seven-year-old English boy moves in with his Norwegian grandmother after his parents are tragically killed in a car accident. Although stricken by grief, he finds comfort in his warm and affectionate "Grandmamma," who tells him stories to try to take his mind of his sadness. Although an excellent storyteller, it isn't until she reaches the subject of witches, which she insists are *real*, that he becomes really enthralled. Drawing on firsthand encounters, Grandmamma explains how real witches don't look like witches, but rather like nice women, and how this makes them especially dangerous as they despise children and live their lives to harm them.

Although it is impossible to spot a witch just by looking at her, Grandmama explains that there are signs to look out for and beware of; for instance, witches must wear gloves at all times, even in the summer, to hide the fact that they don't have fingernails. The good news is that there are not that many witches in the world, and so no reason to be really afraid. But, unfortunately for Grandmama and her grandson, they decide to vacation at the hotel where, coincidentally, the witches of England are holding their annual conference. Because Grandmamma has told him all about how to identify a witch he is able to detect the Grand High Witch herself—but not, unfortunately, before he can escape her spell. Now he must stop her evil plot before she hurts any more children.

While the story of the parents' death is not explored, this remains a story largely about acceptance and adaptation. Once the boy, who is unnamed throughout the story, becomes transformed, he does not return to his human body. But he does not dwell on his misfortune, but instead learns to appreciate the opportunities his new body affords him. In this way, he models resilience in the face of seemingly hopeless situations.

**For those also seeking**: awakening/new perspectives/enlargement of possibilities
**For those drawn to**: story, language
**Themes/subjects**: adaptation/adjusting to change, challenging authority figures, death, good and evil, grandmothers, grief, heroism, magical transformations, mice, misopedists, moving houses (relocating), nurturers, orphans, resilience, spells/curses, spoiled children, stories and storytelling, witches
**Reading interest level**: grades K–6
**Curricular tie-ins**: Even though this is a work of fiction, the narrator insists that witches are "real." As an information literacy exercise, teach students ways of evaluating information, focusing on information genre (fiction versus nonfiction), type (books, news, social media), and authority (level of expertise). Ask students to develop their own criteria for determining whether information is "true" or not.
**Adaptations & alternative formats**: audiobook read by Miranda Richardson (2013); film directed by Nicolas Roeg (1990)
**Translations**: Spanish: *Las Brujas*; French: *Sacrées Sorcières*
**Read-alikes**: John Masefield's *The Midnight Folk* features another coven of witches.


**Dickinson, Peter** (1927–2015)
**The Ropemaker** (2001). New York: Delacorte Press. 375pp. 978-0385730631.

When Tilja awakens one morning, she senses that something is wrong in the Valley. Already uneasy about suspicious signs in nature, she is upset when the family horse returns home without her mother. Tilja's father is unable to enter the forest to look for his wife because a strange sickness overcomes any male who ventures into it. Instead, Tilja and her grandmother search for her. Finding Ma half dead, they bring her back to the farm. Grandmother Meena suspects that the magic that has protected the Valley from the evil

Empire for 18 generations is now running out. When she uses her enchanted wooden spoons to look into the future, she discovers that she and Tilja must go on a journey. Once Ma regains her strength, Meena and Tilja join forces with a boy named Tahl and his grandfather to travel in search of Faheel, an old magician who may be able to renew the magic in the Valley. Tilja's journey introduces her to the treachery, corruption, and evil of the Empire.

Tilja is also deeply concerned about her lack of magical ability. Her female ancestors, including her grandmother, mother, and sister, are magically connected to the landscape, a talent that Tilja would dearly love to possess. An essential step in accepting herself is to recognize and nurture her own special gifts, something she learns on her journey. She is helped by her grandmother, a stoic but crotchety character. Tilja's story will resonate with readers who have a poor self-image and those who covet talents that they do not possess.

**For those also seeking**: reassurance/comfort/confirmation of self-worth/strength
**For those drawn to**: character, setting
**Themes/subjects**: spells/curses, magicians, identity formation, identity, good and evil, grandmothers, grandfathers, political corruption, journeys, stories and storytelling, omens/prophecies, blindness, disability, valleys, elderly, spies and spying
**Reading interest level**: grade 7 and up
**Curricular tie-ins**: Political corruption is a key theme in the novel. Ask students to form small groups to research a corrupt regime, comparing it to the Empire in the novel. Each group could present their work in a blog format.
**Translations**: Spanish: *La Cuerda del Tiempo*
**Read-alikes**: Garth Nix's *Lirael* is another novel about a character who must come to terms with talents she will never possess, while Susan Collins's *The Hunger Games* and Jonathan Stroud's *The Amulet of Samarkand* are books about powerful empires that control their citizens.

**Levine, Gail Carson** (1947–)
**Fairest** (2006). New York: HarperTrophy, 2008. 326pp. 978-0060734107.

Although Aza is gifted with a beautiful voice and lives in a realm that cherishes song, she is deeply unhappy about her appearance. Describing herself

Fantasy

as "an unsightly child" who longs to be pretty, Aza tries to hide from guests who stay at the family inn. When a visiting duchess asks her to accompany her to Ontonio Castle, Aza is thrilled at the opportunity but also afraid of encountering others. Meeting Ivi, the betrothed queen to the king of the realm, Azi is impressed with her beauty and delighted when asked to become her lady-in-waiting. Ivi discovers that Aza can sing as a ventriloquist and asks her to make it look as if Ivi has Aza's amazing voice. When Aza refuses, Ivi threatens to put her in jail and jeopardize her family's livelihood. As Ivi's attendant, Aza also becomes embroiled in the affairs of the royal family and their leadership of the kingdom.

Not until well into the story will readers suspect that the plot is based upon the fairy tale, "Snow White." As the parallels between the two stories become evident, the novel resonates with the insights of a familiar and enduring tale.

An engaging story about a girl who "aches" to be pretty, *Fairest* will appeal to readers who struggle with self-acceptance and body image. Aza must come to terms with not just her appearance but also her self-confidence. Her story is a reassuring one for readers who desire gifts and talents that they do not possess.

**For those also seeking**: reassurance/comfort/confirmation of self-worth/strength
**For those drawn to**: character, story
**Themes/subjects**: beauty/ugliness, body image, appearance (physical), jealousy, music, deception, royalty, kings/queens, omens/prophecies, gnomes, self-acceptance, self-confidence, princes, romance, inns/taverns, moral dilemmas
**Reading interest level**: grade 6 and up
**Curricular tie-ins**: Ask students to compare the fairy tale *Snow White* with the novel.
**Adaptations & alternative formats**: audiobook read by Soneela Nankani (2015)
**Translations**: French: *Belle Comme le Jour*
**Read-alikes**: Readers who enjoy fantasies based upon fairy tales will also like Robin McKinley's *Beauty* and *Spindle's End*, Shannon Hale's *Goose Girl*, and Gail Carson Levine's *Ella Enchanted*. R. J. Palacio's *Wonder* is a story about a boy who must come to terms with his appearance. Joan also worries about body image in Laura Amy Schlitz's *The Hired Girl*.

## Disinterested Understanding of the World

**Dahl, Roald** (1916–1990)
**The Twits** (1980). Illustrated by Quentin Blake. New York: Puffin Books, 2007. 76pp. 978-0142410394.

Mr. and Mrs. Twit are ugliest couple in the world. Mr. Twit's beard is always tangled with crumbs, and Mrs. Twit looks as though all of her meanness has been etched into her haggish face. See, they are not only ugly on the outside, but on the inside, too. The Twits live inside a dark, windowless house, and all they do is bicker and play tricks on each other. When they're not tormenting one another, they are trapping birds (in a very unsportsmanlike way) for bird pie or mistreating their pet monkeys, the Muggle-Wumps, that is, until the Muggle-Wumps have their fill of abuse and decide to take their revenge on the Twits.

For being a short story with such a loose narrative structure, *The Twits* is a surprisingly philosophical work. In the first few pages, Dahl exposes the fallacy of adulthood: that just because someone is grown-up and old that he or she is automatically good, smart, or wise. By calling into question the authority of the Twits, Dahl encourages readers to question and analyze the authorities in their own lives: parents and family members, teachers, and politicians. Developing such habits has lifelong applications as they are essential to individual and social survival.

**For those also seeking**: courage to make a change
**For those drawn to**: character
**Themes/subjects**: anger/hostility, beauty/ugliness, birds, challenging authority figures, cruelty, guns, humor, hunting, misanthropes, misopedists, monkeys/apes, prank tricks and mischief, revenge
**Reading interest level**: grades K–4
**Curricular tie-ins**: To further develop children's ability to question authority, ask them to identify a figure (someone they know, or a notorious celebrity/public figure) and ask them to compare them to the Twits. Give particular focus to the figure's age, and ask students to reflect on how aging may or may not coincide with maturation or wisdom.
**Adaptations & alternative formats**: audiobook read by Simon Callow (2006)
**Translations**: Spanish: *Los Cretinos*; French: *Les Deux Gredins*
**Read-alikes**: Animals outwit wicked adults in Roald Dahl's *Fantastic Mr. Fox*.

**Norton, Mary** (1903–1992)
**Bed-Knob and Broomstick** (1957). San Diego: Harcourt, 2000. 227pp. 978-0152024567.

Siblings Carey, Charles, and Paul are sent to stay with an elderly aunt for the summer. While playing outside, they discover a neighbor, Miss Price, sitting on the ground complaining of pain in her ankle. Six-year-old Paul tells Miss Price that he knows she has fallen off her broomstick. When she tries to deny it, he insists that he has seen her practicing on it many times. Not happy about being discovered as a witch, Miss Price tells the children that she will give them something magical if they keep quiet about her identity. After showing them her magical workroom, Miss Price gives them a bed-knob that, once they screw it into Paul's bed, will take them wherever they wish. If they want to visit a place in the present, they turn the bed-knob one way; a place in the past, the opposite way. Carey and her brothers engage in a number of magical adventures and bring back a necromancer from the seventeenth century.

The humorous complications that arise from these travels will appeal to readers who love comic adventures. When, for example, a policeman finds the children in the magical bed in the midst of a London street, the children have great difficulty explaining the situation and extracting themselves from it.

Traveling to the seventeenth century, the children discover what life was like for people believed to be witches. Readers who are curious about life in this century and those who are interested in witch hunting will be fascinated by the second half of the novel. Children who are hesitant to take chances will be motivated to do so after reading the children's story.

**For those also seeking**: reassurance/comfort/confirmation of self-worth/strength
**For those drawn to**: setting
**Themes/subjects**: witches, time travel, adventure, flying magically, witch hunting, British history, summer vacations
**Reading interest level**: grades 5–7
**Curricular tie-ins:** This novel will stimulate interest in life in seventh-century England. Ask students to research English social life in this era and create a display of texts and images related to aspects of this century.
**Adaptations & alternative formats**: Disney movie directed by Robert Stevenson (1971); audiobook read by Anna Massey (2008)

**Translations**: French: *L'Étrange Histoire de L'Apprentie Sorcière*
**Read-alikes**: The characters in Edith Nesbit's *The Phoenix and the Carpet* and *The Story of the Amulet* also fly magically to other times and places.

## Notes

1. J. R. R. Tolkien, "On Fairy-Stories," in *The Monsters and the Critics and Other Essays*, ed. Christopher Tolkien (London: George Allen and Unwin, 1983), 146.

2. Ursula K. Le Guin, "From Elfland to Poughkeepsie," in *The Language of the Night: Essays on Fantasy and Science Fiction* (New York: Putnam, 1979), 93.

3. Le Guin, "From Elfland to Poughkeepsie," 93.

# CHAPTER SEVEN

# Fantasy Series

Series novels have always appealed to children and adults—and for good reason. Once readers make that special connection with the perfect book, they want to repeat the experience. Series books are especially popular with fantasy readers. These readers invest considerable time and effort in acquainting themselves with a world that is very different than their own. To be able to return to that fantasy world and the characters that they have come to know is an experience that they eagerly anticipate.

Before looking into individual novels, you'll find brief overviews of the twelve series in this chapter.

**Baum, L. Frank**
**The Oz Series** (1900–1920)

*The Wizard of Oz* and its thirteen sequels are set in and around the fairy lands of Oz. Baum also wrote a book of short stories called *Little Wizard Stories of Oz*. Each book in the series is self-contained and can be read in isolation. Editions by the original illustrators are still in print and popular today. W. W. Denslow's illustrations for *The Wizard of Oz* were inspired by Japanese woodcuts, while John R. Neill's illustrations for all subsequent Oz books remind readers of Arthur Rackham's more detailed style. After Baum's death, other writers continued the series, most notably Ruth Plumly Thompson (21 books) and John R. Neill (3 books).

Baum said that his aim in the series was to create "a modernized fairy tale in which the wonderment and joy are retained." The books are indeed fairy-tale-like but very different from the traditional tales. The biggest appeal of these books is the Land of Oz itself—a happy, child-centered world unlike any other fictional realm. Populated with a menagerie of one-of-a-kind, eccentrics, Oz and its neighboring realms are a testament to Baum's fertile imagination. Children who feel different than others will feel at home in a world where everyone is accepted, no matter how unusual or unique. In "A Modern Fairy Tale," Baum observed that children like plenty of action: " 'something doing every minute'—exciting adventures, unexpected difficulties to be overcome, and marvelous escapes." Each Oz book is based on a magical-quest narrative structure and is filled with thrilling adventures.

**Funke, Cornelia**
**Inkheart Trilogy** (2003–2007)

The three books in this fantasy series present characters who cross the boundary line between fiction and reality by entering and exiting a novel called *Inkheart*. Each chapter in the three novels begins with a quotation from literature, often one about the wonder of stories and the imagination. Readers are, in fact, surrounded by stories, mesmerized by their seductive charm, and inspired to read them.

Called "the German J. K. Rowling," Cornelia Funke has also been identified as one of *Time*'s 100 most influential people. Achieving both popular and critical success, the Inkheart books remained on the *New York Times* bestseller lists for months when they were first published and received starred reviews from *Kirkus Reviews*, *Booklist*, and *Publisher's Weekly*. *Inkheart* is the only one of the three books that can be read as a stand-alone novel.

**Jansson, Tove**
**The Moomin Series** (1945–1971)

Tove Jansson's Moomins are small roundish creatures who resemble two-legged hippopotami. These part human/part animal/part fantasy characters are lovable, funny, and unique. Jansson's insight into human nature and her recognition of the absurdities of the human condition are particularly evident in her depiction of these childlike characters. Her whimsical illustrations for each of the novels are humorous and lighthearted.

A dazzling Finnish world of lofty mountains, stormy seas, and hidden caves is the lyrically described backdrop to the stories. Tucked within this landscape is Moominvalley, a snug retreat and idyllic home base. A sunny realm where all are welcomed, no matter how strange or idiosyncratic, the Moomin world is friendly, hospitable, and carefree. When life becomes difficult, the characters turn to Moominmamma, the voice of wisdom and comfort in the novel. As Moomintroll says, "Mother's sure to know."

The nine books in the Moomin series include the now out-of-print introductory volume, *Moomin and the Great Flood*, and the last three books that are of greater interest to adults than children. Although the other five novels can be read as stand-alone books, they are even more engaging when read as a series in chronological order. In 1966, Jansson won the Hans Christian Andersen Award, the highest international honor given to an author whose complete works have made a lasting contribution to children's literature.

**Jones, Diana Wynne**
**Chrestomanci Series** (1977–2006)

Set in a one-of-a-kind multiverse, the six novels and book of short stories in the Chrestomanci series are highly original works of fantasy. Each book functions as a stand-alone story and is populated with its own set of characters. What unites the texts is the multiverse framework and the character of Chrestomanci—a powerful enchanter whose job is to control witchcraft in the parallel worlds.

Characters in the novels often find themselves in comic situations as magic gets out of hand and troubles multiply. Set in places such as mysterious castles with gateways to elsewhere, boarding schools for witch-orphans, Italian mesas with golden pear trees appearing inside the home, mansions situated on fault lines between worlds, and strange regions called The Anywheres, these quirky, offbeat worlds run side by side with other universes. Characters have doubles in other worlds and even switch places in one of the novels.

What distinguishes the series is the psychologically astute way Jones depicts neglected, bullied, and troubled children who, in the process of self-discovery, learn to deal effectively with their situations. Protagonists are often unaware of their talents and must learn to accept not only abilities they never anticipated but also intensely desired skills they will never possess and ambitions they will never realize.

## Jones, Diana Wynne
## The Land of Ingary Trilogy (1986–2008)

These vividly imagined novels are set in and around Ingary—an enchanted, fairy-tale realm. What readers remember long after finishing the series are the mysterious and magical buildings of the titles. Defying the laws of gravity and physics, these curious structures are situated in a protean, unstable world in which nothing is what it appears. Because disguises and deceptions abound, characters do not know whom to trust.

As in Jones's Chrestomanci series, the protagonists are gifted, young witches and enchanters who are unaware of their talents. They cannot rely on wise, parental figures to help them cope; parents are either dead or an impediment to their child's well-being. Magic often spirals out of control, resulting in wild adventures. Each novel is self-contained and can be read on its own.

## Le Guin, Ursula K.
## The Earthsea Series (1968–2001)

Set in an archipelago, *A Wizard of Earthsea, The Tombs of Atuan*, and *The Farthest Shore* are epic fantasy novels similar in scope and tone to Tolkien's *The Lord of the Rings*. Decades after the initial trilogy was published, Le Guin wrote two more novels (*Tehanu* and *The Other Wind*) and a book of short stories (*Tales from Earthsea*). These latter books are of greater interest to young adults than children. Like the Oz series, the Earthsea books are united through their geography. Although the Archmage, Ged, appears throughout, he is the central protagonist in only the first novel. Each of the books can be read without knowing the others. The novels are incredibly moving and deeply memorable coming-of-age stories about characters who make a serious mistake, one that causes the death or near-death of others.

Language also plays a crucial role in Le Guin's novels; to name something is to gain mastery over it. The nameless shadow in the first novel and gods called the Nameless Ones in the second novel are much more frightening and powerful because they remain nameless. Highly quotable books filled with words of wisdom and insight, the Earthsea novels are notable for spare, poetic prose that resonates with readers of all ages.

## Lewis, C. S.
## The Chronicles of Narnia (1950–1956)

Although published in the 1950s, the imaginative fantasy world of Narnia continues to attract readers to the series. Narnia's uniqueness lies in its curious assortment of anthropomorphised animals, trees, rivers, magical beings, and mythological creatures. Although some of the characters reappear in various novels, the series introduces new characters in each book. The enchanted kingdom of Narnia is the common feature of the novels. The many portals to the kingdom suggest that the otherworld lies just beyond our own and is accessible to those who believe in it. The books are biblical allegories, and although children do not have to read them as such, those who do will find an added layer of meaning in the Christian symbolism.

Although each book in the series can be read as a stand-alone novel, both *Prince Caspian* and *The Magician's Nephew* have added impact if read as sequels to *The Lion, the Witch and The Wardrobe*. Likewise, *The Last Battle* is more engaging if read after all the novels.

## Nesbit, Edith
## The Psammead Trilogy (1902–1906)

Siblings Anthea, Cyril, Jane, and Robert participate in exciting adventures and amusing mishaps when their wishes are magically granted in the Psammead trilogy. Readers who enjoy comic fantasies will love the witty narrator and humorous incidents in the three books. The curmudgeon-like Psammead and the egotistical phoenix are eccentric wish-granting beings. Although the texts follow a loose chronological order, they can easily be read in isolation from one another.

Readers will readily identify with the high-spirited, well-meaning siblings who, despite their best efforts, continually find themselves in serious trouble. Nesbit draws upon some of the deepest longings of children—to have their wishes granted, to fly on magic carpets, to satisfy their heart's desire—but then enhances and enlarges their ideas about such wishes. Her depiction of the thoughts, feelings, and anxieties of children is one of her greatest strengths as an author. She seems to have remembered just how it felt to be a child and is especially perceptive about children who view life through the lens of their imagination.

**Nix, Garth**
**The Old Kingdom Series** (1994–2016)

These deeply engaging, character-driven books are set in a mysterious, foreboding world reminiscent of Le Guin's Earthsea and Tolkien's Middle Earth. Dividing the world into a magical, primitive realm in the north and an ordinary, civilized country in the south, the medieval stone Wall introduces themes of thresholds, boundaries, and barriers. In a world where the living dead roam the landscape and haunt its peoples, the Abhorsen maintains the borders of life and death.

The first three novels appeal to both children and young adults; the audience for the next two novels (*Clariel* and *Goldenhand*) is young adults. Although the first book in the series can be read as a stand-alone novel, *Lirael: Daughter of the Clayr* is continued in *The Abhorsen* and needs to be read with it. The series has won three prestigious Australian book awards: the Aurealis Award for Excellence in Australian Speculative Fiction (for *Sabriel*), the Ditmar Award for Achievement in Australian Science Fiction (for *Lirael*), and the Aurealis Award for Best Fantasy Novel (for *Lirael*).

**Norton, Mary**
**The Borrowers Series** (1952–1982)

The five books in the Borrowers series form one long story about a miniature family's search for a home and a daughter's quest for independence. The Clock family lives under the floorboards of an English country house and hides from its human occupants. Their story is set within a frame narrative that extends the meaning and significance of the inset story. Taken together, the five novels form a pattern that balances themes of security and freedom and indoors and outdoors. In each of the novels, a male is introduced who upsets the balance and challenges borrower assumptions.

Ingenious details of miniaturization create a strong appeal in each of the novels. Survival takes on a new meaning when characters are only six inches tall but live in a world designed for regular human beings. Impressive too is Norton's use of the environment as a determinant of character. Because the books form a single narrative, they should be read in chronological order.

## Pullman, Philip
## His Dark Materials (1995–2000)

According to an ancient prophecy, the fate of the world rests on the actions of a 12-year-old girl named Lyra. The three books take place in a number of parallel worlds, populated by a variety of different creatures such as armoured bears, witches, specters, angels, scientists, theologians, and wheeled beings called mulefa. In Lyra's world, each person is accompanied throughout life by a daemon that represents his or her soul. This daemon takes the form of an animal or bird and does not stabilize as a specific creature until after the child reaches puberty.

These novels are distinguished for their sweeping, larger-than-life stories; evocative use of language; and controversial ideas about God, organized religion, and the afterlife. These *New York Times*'s bestsellers won both the Carnegie Medal for best British children's book and the Whitbread Book of the Year Award. The three novels form a continuous story and should be read in chronological order.

## Rowling, J. K.
## The Harry Potter Series (1997–2007)

The highest-grossing and most popular series of all time, the seven Harry Potter books continue to perform unprecedented magic on their followers, appealing to both readers and nonreaders, males and females, young and old. Although the books can be described as fantasy novels, they are also a unique combination of mystery, coming of age, thriller, school story, and adventure—resulting in a one-of-a-kind magical brew. Rowling spent five years carefully planning the series and considers it a single interconnected narrative rather than seven separate novels. The books span seven years of Harry Potter's life (from 10 to 17) and should be read in chronological order.

One of those rare series of books that appeals to readers in a variety of ways, the Harry Potter books contain psychologically convincing characters, pulse-pounding plots, spell-binding settings, a sinister atmosphere, and unforgettable humor. Winner of numerous literary honors, including four Whitaker Platinum Awards and the Mythopoeic Fantasy Award, the Harry Potter books were also shortlisted for two Carnegie Medals for best British children's book. In 2016, *Harry Potter and the Cursed Child*—the eighth story in the series—was presented on stage in London's West End and published as a play.

## Awakening/New Perspectives/Enlargement of Possibilities

**Funke, Cornelia** (1968–)
**Inkheart** (2003). Translated from the German by Anthea Bell. New York: Scholastic, 2003. 534pp. 978-043953164.

When Meggie was three years old, her mother inexplicably disappeared. Then nine years later, a mysterious stranger named Dustfinger appears and talks to Meggie's father in private. The next morning Mo tells his daughter that they must pack their bags and leave at once for Great-Aunt Elinor's house. Dustfinger accompanies them, bringing with him a strange bird with horns.

While Dustfinger performs fire-eating stunts for Meggie, a band of outlaws breaks into Elinor's house and kidnaps Mo. When Meggie, Elinor, and Dustfinger travel in search of him, Meggie discovers that nine years earlier her father had read Dustfinger and the band of outlaws out of a book called *Inkheart*. Meggie suspects that her mother magically entered the story when the others came out of it.

Funke's novel is an exciting tale of adventure and survival. Those who feel trapped in hopeless situations will identify with Meggie and her feisty great-aunt, Elinor. A strong role model for girls, Meggie is determined and courageous in the face of adversity. The novel is also a thought-provoking exploration of the role of stories in life. Richly detailed and poetically written, this book will enlarge readers' worlds by rekindling their appreciation of the wonders of the imagination.

**For those also seeking**: models for identity
**For those drawn to**: story, language
**Themes/subjects**: stories and storytelling, imagination, courage, survival, father-daughter relationships, kidnapping, missing persons, jealousy, libraries/librarians, books, only children, outlaws, criminals/thieves, mysteries
**Reading interest level**: grades 4–7
**Curricular tie-ins**: *Inkheart* celebrates the magic of books. Ask students to give a book talk about novel they would like to enter.

*Fantasy Series*

**Adaptations & alternative formats**: movie directed by Iain Softley (2008); audiobook read by Lynn Redgrave (2003)
**Translations**: Spanish: *Corazón de Tinta*; French: *Coeur d'Encre*
**Read-alikes**: Michael Ende's *The Neverending Story* is about another character who enters the story he is reading. Garth Nix's *Sabriel* and Michael Chabon's *Summerland* are also about children who search fantasy lands for their missing fathers. Grace Lin's *When the Sea Turned to Silver* is also about the kidnapping of a family member. The theme of stories is integral to both these novels.

**Funke, Cornelia** (1968–)
*Inkspell* (2005). Translated from the German by Anthea Bell. New York: Scholastic, 2005. 635pp. 978-0439554008.

A year after the events in *Inkheart*, Meggie and her parents are back in the real world living with Great-Aunt Elinor. But Meggie longs for the excitement of Inkworld and cannot stop thinking about it. When Farid appears and asks her to read him back into this enchanted realm, Meggie decides to go with him. Devastated by her disappearance, Mo follows his daughter into Inkworld and is shot by the evil old woman, Mortola. Back at home, Great-Aunt Elinor and her librarian Darius are captured by men from *Inkheart* and imprisoned in Elinor's cellar.

The Inkworld with its Wayless Wood, glass men, Laughing Prince, silvery Castle of Night, blue fairies, and trees growing up to the sky casts a powerful spell on readers. The novel is also a survival story in which the danger of stories poses a major threat to characters lured into their snares. Even though the plot is action-filled, it is not fast-paced. *Inkspell* is suited to readers who enjoy gradually enfolding stories filled with strikingly descriptive details.

Ignoring the council of adults, Meggie relies on an inner voice to guide her courageous actions. The novel will appeal to readers who are strong-willed, driven more by personal vision than by others' advice. Those who feel pressured to conform to conventional standards will identify with Meggie and may see her story as a turning point in their lives.

**For those also seeking**: connection with others/awareness of not being alone
**For those drawn to**: setting, language

**Themes/subjects**: stories and storytelling, imagination, courage, survival, father-daughter relationships, castles, libraries/librarians, books, death, immortality, only children, romance, fate/destiny, self-reliance, outlaws, criminals/thieves, mysteries
**Reading interest level**: grades 6–8
**Curricular tie-ins**: Ask students to choose a paragraph from the novel that is descriptively written. In small groups, each person can read his or her choice out loud and comment on the reasons that they chose it.
**Adaptations & alternative formats**: audiobook read by Brendan Fraser (2005)
**Translations**: Spanish: *Sangre de Tinta*
**Read-alikes**: Like Meggie, Sabriel and Lirael in Garth Nix's The Old Kingdom series and Lyra Belacqua in Philip Pullman's His Dark Materials series enter a dangerous otherworld and fight forces of evil.


**Funke, Cornelia** (1968–)
**Inkdeath** (2007). Translated from the German by Anthea Bell. New York: Scholastic, 2008. 683pp. 978-0439866293.

Three months after the events of *Inkspell*, Meggie faces even greater dangers in this third novel in the Inkheart trilogy. Although Meggie's father, Mo, has bound a white book that made the evil Adderhead immortal, he secretly wove a spell into it that will cause the despot to suffer and decay. The Adderhead's daughter, Violante, asks Mo to help her kill her father, but he is not sure if he can trust her. Mo allows himself to be captured once the Piper threatens to kidnap the children of Ombra. When Meggie and her mother decide to rescue him, they must travel to Violante's enchanted Castle in the Lake.

As the series progresses, Funke increasingly depicts the dangers of stories. The pictures of painted worlds that replace windows in the Castle in the Lake open readers' eyes to the addicting, inward-focused, and escapist nature of fantasy worlds. The wonderfully ironic ending of the novel reinforces this warning. This novel will resonate with readers who are attracted to fantasy worlds and will prompt them to explore their relationship with the imaginary. Dramatic scenes, poetic language, and a thought-provoking exploration of the role of books in life are strong appeals in *Inkdeath*.

**For those also seeking**: connection with others/awareness of not being alone

**For those drawn to**: language, setting
**Themes/subjects**: stories and storytelling, imagination, courage, survival, death, immortality, kidnapping, only children, romance, jealousy, castles, fate/chance, political corruption, outlaws, criminals/thieves, mysteries
**Reading interest level**: grade 7 and up
**Curricular tie-ins**: Ask students to choose an epigraph to one of the chapters and explain why it is suited to the chapter.
**Adaptations & alternative formats**: audiobook read by Allan Corduner (2008)
**Translations**: Spanish: *Muerte de Tinta*
**Read-alikes**: In Garth Nix's *Sabriel*, a daughter also tries to rescue her father from death and destruction. The dangers of stories are also a key concern in Michael Ende's *The Neverending Story*. Like Meggie, Sophie in Diana Wynne Jones's *Howl's Moving Castle* must survive in a strange fantasy realm.

**Jones, Diana Wynne** (1934–2011)
**Charmed Life** (1977). In The Chronicles of Chrestomanci, Volume 1: *Charmed Life/The Lives of Christopher Chant*. New York: HarperTrophy, 2001. 608pp. 978-0064472685.

The first book in the Chrestomanci series, *Charmed Life*, begins with a tragic accident. The paddleboat that Cat, his sister Gwendolen, and their parents board, sinks. Everyone dies except Cat and Gwendolen, a feat that Cat attributes to his sister's superior powers as a witch. Although the brother and sister are initially cared for by a neighborhood witch, they subsequently move into Chrestomanci castle and are raised by the enchanter, Chrestomanci. Readers who enjoy books set in out-of-the-ordinary fantasy realms will find the world of Chrestomanci castle mesmerizing.

Since no one at the castle seems to appreciate Gwendolen's magical talents, she becomes increasingly angry and casts revengeful spells. When Chrestomanci takes away her magical powers, Gwendolyn leaves for another world. Janet Chant, her double from another universe, takes her place. The switched identities and Cat's growing skill with magic lead to increasing complications in the story.

Winner of the Guardian Children's Fiction Prize for best English children's novel, *Charmed Life* is a riveting, character-driven novel. Growing up as an orphan, Cat reveres his sister and depends upon her for guidance and protection. But readers gradually begin to realize that their perception of

Gwendolen differs from Cat's, a discovery that increases their level of engagement in the novel. Readers who are willing to follow the crowd or may be too acquiescent may change their ideas about the value of doing so after reading the novel. And those who lack confidence in their abilities will be reassured by Cat's story.

**For those also seeking**: reassurance/comfort/confirmation of self-worth/strength
**For those drawn to**: character, setting
**Themes/subjects**: siblings and siblings issues, agency and powerlessness, denial (psychology), child neglect, multiple worlds/universes, adaptation/adjusting to change, orphans, oppressive environments, accidents (major), castles, witches, school, narcissism, anger/hostility, revenge, spells/curses, magical transformations, tutors, deception
**Reading interest level**: grades 5–8
**Curricular tie-ins**: Gwendolen and Janet are doubles in the novel. Ask students to compare and contrast their characters.
**Adaptations & alternative formats**: abridged audiobook read by Tom Baker (2012)
**Translations**: Spanish: *Una Vida Mágica: Los Mundos de Chrestomanci*; French: *Ma Soeur est une Sorcière*
**Read-alikes**: Readers who enjoy novels set in parallel worlds will enjoy Neil Gaiman's *Coraline*. Like Christopher Chant, James Henry Trotter in Roald Dahl's *James and the Giant Peach* and Matilda Wormwood in Roald Dahl's *Matilda* must cope with neglectful guardians.

**Jones, Diana Wynne** (1934–2011)
**Conrad's Fate** (2005). In The Chronicles of Chrestomanci, Volume 3: Conrad's Fate/The Pinhoe Egg. New York: HarperCollins, 2006. 675pp. 978-0061148323.

Whenever 12-year-old Conrad gazes out of his bedroom window, he notices Stallery Mansion. He thinks of it as a fairy-tale castle, one that makes him ponder all the strange and exciting things missing from his life. When his magician uncle tells Conrad that he will die within a year unless he moves to the mansion to put right something that he did in a past life, Conrad is devastated at the thought of leaving school. But obeying his uncle and securing a job as a Stallery servant, he meets the nine-lived enchanter, Christopher Chant.

As Conrad helps Christopher look for his missing friend Millie, he notices a number of strange and unexplained situations. Conrad learns that the mansion is built on a probability fault, "a place where a lot of possible universes are close together and the walls between them are fairly weak." The strange, Gothic-like mansion that interferes with television and computer signals also jerks sideways periodically, shifting events in the world at large.

Presenting the story through the eyes of an innocent narrator, Diana Wynne Jones skillfully draws readers into the narrative by making them question Conrad's observations and judgment. Like Roald Dahl, Jones is skilled and perceptive in her depiction of neglectful and abusive adults. Children who have been wronged or mistreated will find comfort and relief in Conrad's story. They will also realize that not all adults are trustworthy and that children can both question authority and assert their rights.

**For those also seeking**: reassurance/comfort/confirmation of self-worth/strength
**For those drawn to**: character, setting
**Themes/subjects**: appearance versus reality, child neglect, preoccupied parents, betrayal, secrets, class differences, fate/destiny, multiple worlds/universes, disguise, oppressive environments, missing persons, magicians, haunted houses, mansions, servants, mysteries
**Reading interest level**: grades 5–8
**Curricular tie-ins**: There are many secrets in the novel. In a write-pair-share activity, students could discuss the secret that surprised them the most.
**Adaptations & alternative formats**: audiobook read by Gerard Doyle (2005)
**Translations**: French: *Le Destin de Conrad*
**Read-alikes**: A haunted house also dominates *The House of Dies Drear* by Virginia Hamilton. James Henry Trotter in Roald Dahl's *James and the Giant Peach* and Matilda Wormwood in Diana Wynne Jones's *Matilda* must also cope with neglectful and abusive adults. Like Conrad, Hildi in Phillip Pullman's *Count Karlstein* is a servant in an eerie, Gothic dwelling. Serafina also works in a mysterious mansion in Robert Beatty's *Serafina and the Black Cloak* and its sequels: *Serafina and the Twisted Staff* and *Serafina and the Splintered Heart*.

**Jones, Diana Wynne** (1934–2011)
**Castle in the Air** (1977). New York: Eos, 2008. 383pp. 978-0061478772.

This sequel to *Howl's Moving Castle* takes place in Zanzib, an oriental city far south of the magical land of Ingary. Abdullah's father leaves most of his inheritance to relatives but almost nothing to his son. Described by his father as "a great disappointment," Abdullah leads a dull, monotonous life as a carpet merchant. He compensates by creating elaborate "castles in the air," dreams of a better life. After Abdullah buys a magic carpet from a trader, he falls asleep on it and is transported to an exotic land, similar to that of his daydreams. In an enchanted garden he meets a beautiful girl named Flower-in-the-Night, who is later kidnapped by a djinn. When his "castles in the air" continue to materialize, Abdullah must cope with the dangerous complications that arise.

Readers who are drawn to *Arabian Nights* tales will enjoy this story of magic carpets and wish-granting djinns. An imaginative twist on a familiar motif, the "castle in the air" literally appears in the story. The novel highlights the importance of dreams and also underlines the challenges involved in making these dreams come true. Readers who love to daydream will reframe their ideas about its alleged futility. The novel will appeal to those who have not had much encouragement from the adults in their lives.

Jones plays with the conventions of language throughout the story. Characters address each other in humorous, *Arabian Nights*–style phrases such as "oh sheik of shrewdness" and "oh dragon of dubiety."

**For those also seeking**: reassurance/comfort/confirmation of self-worth/strength
**For those drawn to**: setting, language
**Themes/subjects**: castles, spells/curses, romance, omens/prophecies, disguises, parental disapproval, magical transformations, flying magically, wishes and wishing, genies, kidnapping
**Reading interest level**: grades 6–8
**Curricular tie-ins**: Ask students to design a cover for the novel and provide an explanation of their choices on a separate page.
**Adaptations & alternative formats**: audiobook read by Jenny Sterlin (2009)
**Translations**: Spanish: *El Castillo en el Aire*

**Read-alikes**: Readers who enjoy exotic Oriental settings will also like C. S. Lewis's *The Horse and His Boy*. E. Nesbit's Psammead novels and Jonathan Stroud's *The Amulet of Samarkand* are also about the complications that arise from granted wishes.

**Le Guin, Ursula K.** (1929–)
**A Wizard of Earthsea** (1968). New York: Puffin, 2010. 184pp. 978-80140304770.

The man believed by many to be the greatest wizard in all Earthsea grows up as a wild, uncared-for boy, taught rudimentary magic by his aunt, the village witch. When the great mage, Ogion, adopts Ged as an apprentice, the boy thinks he has "a broad bright road" ahead of him. But instead, he finds life with Ogion "a long road towards mastery, a slow bypath to follow." The impatient Ged decides to journey to the renowned school at Roke to continue his education as a wizard. A boy of great talent, Ged flaunts his powers at a school festival by summoning a person from the dead—a foolish, dangerous action that also unleashes a shadow figure from beyond life. The old Archmage of the School, in using all his power to defeat the shadow and save Ged, dies. Although Ged manages to survive, he is hunted from that point on by the shadow—a thing described as a "formless, hopeless horror."

Believing that the purpose of his life is to destroy the shadow, Ged experiences an overwhelming sense of doom once he begins his quest. A book of hard-won wisdom, this Boston Globe-Horn Book Award winner will appeal to readers who have failed, made serious mistakes in life, or been treated as failures. One of the most powerful endings in children's literature, the conclusion will resonate with readers and give them a new way of thinking about themselves.

An integral part of the novel, the setting both shapes and reflects the characters who live in Earthsea. An archipelago, this bracing, nautical world is home to boats such as *Shadow* and *Lookfar* and strange seawinds that prevent ships from docking in certain lands. The remarkable school of wizardry on the Isle of the Wise, the bewitching northerly Court of the Terrenon in which Ged's mind is never clear, Lastland at the world's edge and gateway to the sea from which no one returns, and the path that never reaches the dazzling Immanent Grove for those not ready to enter it are all strange, haunting, and unforgettable places.

**For those also seeking**: connection with others/awareness of not being alone
**For those drawn to**: character, setting
**Themes/subjects**: coming of age, identity formation, wizards, failure, mistakes, self-blame (psychology), ambition, islands, sea voyage, school, pride, agency and powerlessness, resilience, guilt, boats and ships, friendship, apprentices, education, names and naming
**Reading interest level**: grade 6 and up
**Curricular tie-ins**: Taoist philosophy is a strong influence on the novel. Ask students to research it and, in their reader response journals, summarize its main ideas and consider whether it is useful philosophy for their own life.
**Adaptations & alternative formats**: Japanese animated movie called *Tales from Earthsea*, directed by Gorō Miyazaki and based on the first four books in the series (2006, United States 2010); audiobook read by Rob Inglis (2009)
**Translations**: Spanish: *Un Mago de Terramar*; French: *Le Sorcier de Terremer*
**Read-alikes**: Readers who enjoy coming-of-age fantasy novels will like Lloyd Alexander's The Chronicles of Prydain (*The Book of Three, The Black Cauldron, The Castle of Llyr, Taran Wanderer*, and *The High King*). J. R. R. Tolkien's The Lord of the Rings series (*The Fellowship of the Ring, The Two Towers,* and *The Return of the Ring*) will appeal to older readers who enjoy profound, thought-provoking fantasy novels. Like Ged, Matt in Ann E. Burg's *All the Broken Pieces* feels profoundly guilty about an incident that has long-term consequences.


**Le Guin, Ursula K.** (1929–)
**The Tombs of Atuan** (1971). New York: Aladdin, 2001. 180pp. 978-0689845369.

When Tenar is five years old, priestesses from the Place of the Tombs take her away from her family and raise her to be the One Priestess of the Tombs of Atuan. Renamed Arha, "the Eaten One," Tenar loses all remembrance of her family as she grows older. Schooled in the ways of this all-female religious cult, Arha is taught to revere dark gods called the Nameless Ones. Raised in a cruel and repressive environment, the innocent girl eventually becomes as tyrannical as the cold and cruel priestesses who teach her.

*Fantasy Series*

When she turns 14, Arha becomes mistress of the Undertomb and a giant underground labyrinth, both housed below the sacred Place of the Tombs. Light is forbidden in this "home of darkness, the inmost center of the night." Arha spends months exploring her new domain by endlessly feeling her way along the pitch-black corridors of a place described as "always and only night." One day as she crosses the Undertomb, she is shocked to see a man standing in front of her with a lighted staff.

A Newbery Honor book, *The Tombs of Atuan* makes a powerful appeal through choice of setting. The underground that Arha commands is the nightmarish projection of her dark, entangled mind. A deeply affecting, character-driven novel, *The Tombs of Atuan* is the story of an innocent girl trained in the ways of intolerance and hatred. The carefree young girl becomes the harsh priestess who tells a stranger, "All I know is the dark, the night underground. And that's all there really is. That's all there is to know in the end."

Readers who believe they have made poor choices, have gone down the wrong path, or are filled with guilt will find hope and inspiration in Arha's story. The novel will introduce a new way of thinking for readers who believe that they are past hope. It will also show them that their personalities are shaped by a myriad of forces, some of which are beyond their control and might not be fully comprehended by them.

**For those also seeking**: connection with others/awareness of not being alone
**For those drawn to**: character, setting
**Themes/subjects**: coming of age, identity formation, cults/sects, cemeteries/tombs, guilt, self-blame (psychology), cruelty, imprisonment/entrapment, authoritarian figures, oppressive environments, mistakes, resilience, agency and powerlessness, buried/hidden treasure, mazes/labyrinths, names and naming, underground
**Reading interest level**: grade 6 and up
**Curricular tie-ins**: In small groups, students could, first, find information about Stockholm syndrome and, second, discuss whether or not this syndrome applies to the novel.
**Adaptations & alternative formats**: Japanese animated movie called *Tales from Earthsea*, directed by Gorô Miyazaki and based on the first four books in the series (2006, United States 2010); audiobook read by Rob Inglis (2010)

**Translations**: Spanish: *Las Tumbas de Atuan*; French: *Les Tombeaux d'Atuan*

**Read-alikes**: Like Tenar, Louise in Katherine Paterson's *Jacob Have I Loved* also must free herself from the grip of destructive emotions. An adult in Watt Key's *Alabama Moon* and the mothers in Meg McKinlay's *A Single Stone* also try to indoctrinate a child into their way of thinking.


**Le Guin, Ursula K.** (1929–)
**The Farthest Shore** (1972). New York: Aladdin, 2001. 180pp. 978-0689845369.

The King of Enlad sends his son to the Great House at Roke to tell Ged the Archmage that magic is failing in their kingdom. Earthsea itself has not been governed by a king for over 800 years, and many fear that a weakening of power and general want of resolution are starting to destroy the kingdom. After the Archmage holds a council with his nine Masters, he decides that he and Arren—the Prince of Enlad— should set sail to investigate. But as events unfold and the voyage progresses, Arren loses faith in both the mission and the Archmage.

Winner of the National Book Award, this third novel in the Earthsea series is a poignant, coming-of-age story about a prince. Although Arren begins the sea voyage with high hopes and idealistic dreams, hope turns to doubt and then despair as disaster strikes. Readers who have felt creeping doubts destroy their peace of mind, those who have let their friends down, or those who have experienced depression will feel less alone after reading Arren's story. Realizing that a great hero can make serious mistakes and fall prey to despair can be a moment of insight and awakening for readers.

Through her use of poetic language, Le Guin makes readers see familiar things in a new way. In the first novel in the series, she describes Ged's friend Vetch as "keen, shrewd, direct to the center of a thing." Le Guin is skilled at describing the center of things, highlighting their essence and significance.

**For those also seeking**: connection with others/awareness of not being alone
**For those drawn to**: character, language

**Themes/subjects**: coming of age, identity formation, sea voyage, quests, death, immortality, agency and powerlessness, depression, despair, mistakes, resilience, omens/prophecies, dragons, wizards, princes
**Reading interest level**: grade 6 and up
**Curricular tie-ins**: Arren has a number of dreams. Students could create a blog to discuss why they think the author tells us about them.
**Adaptations & alternative formats**: Japanese animated movie called *Tales from Earthsea*, directed by Gorô Miyazaki and based on the first four books in the series (2006, United States 2010); audiobook read by Rob Inglis (2010)
**Translations**: Spanish: *La Costa Más Lejana*; French: *L'Ultime Rivage*
**Read-alikes**: Protagonists in Phillip Pullman's His Dark Materials books and Garth Nix's The Old Kingdom series also undertake dangerous quests to save the world.

**Lewis, C. S.** (1898–1963)
**The Lion, the Witch and the Wardrobe** (1950). New York: HarperTrophy, 1984. 208pp. 978-0064404990.

When siblings Susan, Peter, Edmund, and Lucy evacuate London to escape the bombing of the city that took place during World War II, they move into a large country house owned by an elderly professor. Playing hide-and-seek, Lucy steps into a large wardrobe and finds herself in the fantasy world of Narnia. A fawn named Tumnus invites her into his cozy cave for tea. Discovering that he works for a witch who has been instructed to kidnap any child she meets, Lucy convinces Tumnus to let her go. Despite the fact that her siblings do not believe her story, Edmund follows Lucy into Narnia on her next visit. The White Witch gives Peter enchanted candy that is instantly addictive. She promises him more candy and the kingship of Narnia if he will bring his siblings to her.

Filled with otherworldly castles, curious animal homes, and menacing forests, Narnia is a strangely enchanting realm. Populated with a peculiar assortment of witches, dwarfs, talking animals, and mythological creatures, Narnia continues to lure readers to its kingdom. A story of betrayal and its consequences, this first book in The Chronicles of Narnia is an allegory of the passion of Jesus Christ. Although readers do not need to know the original biblical narrative, a familiarity with it enriches their reading. Readers who feel guilty or sad about something they have done will find hope and a new way of viewing their actions after reading Edmund's story.

**For those also seeking**: reassurance/comfort/confirmation of self-worth/strength
**For those drawn to**: setting
**Themes/subjects**: betrayal, portals/thresholds, faith and skepticism, Bible stories, mistakes, guilt, Christianity, witches, royalty, kings/queens, castles, battles/war, mythology, winter, lions and tigers, addiction, mythological creatures, temptation, sacrifice
**Reading interest level**: grades 3–6
**Curricular tie-ins**: At the beginning of World War II, thousands of British children were evacuated from the cities to the countryside, a move that necessitated leaving their parents and living with strangers. After discussing the historical facts, ask students to write a reflection in their reader response journals about how they would feel if this happened to them.
**Adaptations & alternative formats**: movie directed by Andrew Adamson (2005); audiobook read by Michael York (2005); graphic novel by Robin Lawrie (1995)
**Translations**: Spanish: *El León, la Bruja y el Ropero*; French: *Le lion, la Sorcière Blanche et L'Armoire Magique*
**Read-alikes**: Ged also succumbs to temptation and commits a grievous error in Ursula K. Le Guin's fantasy novel, *A Wizard of Earthsea*. Although a historical novel rather than a fantasy, Kimberly Brubaker Bradley's *The War That Saved My Life* is also the story of children who are evacuated from London during World War II.

**Lewis, C. S.** (1898–1963)
**Prince Caspian** (1951). New York: HarperTrophy, 1994. 238pp. 978-0064471053.

While at a railway station on the way to school, siblings Susan, Peter, Edmund, and Lucy experience a strange pulling sensation before being whisked away to a strange island with a ruined castle. Initially concerned about their survival, the children realize that they are alive and well. They subsequently discover that the castle on the island is Cair Paravel, the one they inhabited as kings and queens in their previous visit to Narnia.

A dwarf lands on the island and tells the story of Prince Caspian, the nephew of the cruel king of Narnia, Miraz. Caspian, who is captivated by the old stories of Narnia in which the four children were kings and queens, is ridiculed by his uncle for his belief in such tales. Caspian is forced to flee his home when the queen gives birth to her first child, an event that changes royal succession plans and endangers his life. Now Caspian and the children must find each other, escape from their mutual enemies, and fight the forces of evil.

A novel about believing in the unseen—magic, fantasy stories, providence, a higher power—*Prince Caspian* is also a story about the power of faith. Prince Caspian insists on believing in stories about Narnia's Golden Age, the children learn to believe in Aslan's guiding power, and Caspian's followers must trust in the power of the magic horn to summon help. As Caspian and the children face challenges and survive life-threatening dangers, they grow into their roles as kings and queens.

Central to the novel is the theme of the power of stories—fantasy stories, stories of survival, biblical narratives, mythological tales—and especially their power to convey profound truths. After reading the novel, children will view fiction in a different light, seeing it as meaningful rather than escapist. Those who are skeptical or pessimistic about the future will be reassured by this compelling story.

**For those also seeking**: reassurance/comfort/confirmation of self-worth/strength
**For those drawn to**: setting, story
**Themes/subjects**: stories and storytelling, faith and skepticism, Christianity, Bible stories, portals/thresholds, princes, kings/queens, royalty, battles/wars, castles, mythology, mythological creatures, dwarfs, tutors, inheritance and succession
**Reading interest level**: grades 4–8
**Curricular tie-ins**: Narnia is populated with mythological characters such as fauns, dwarfs, centaurs, Dryads, and Naiads. Divide students into five groups for a jigsaw activity. Each group is responsible for finding information about one of these types of characters, finding a myth or tale about them, and creating an illustration. The groups could then compile their work into a mythological booklet that could serve as a companion to the novel (in the style of such a text as J. K. Rowling's *Fantastic Beasts and Where to Find Them*).
**Adaptations & alternative formats**: movie directed by Andrew Adamson (2008); audiobook read by Lynn Redgrave (2005)
**Translations**: Spanish: *El Príncipe Caspian*; French: *Le Prince Caspian*
**Read-alikes**: Like Prince Caspian, Septimus Heap and Princess Jenna in Angie Sage's *Magyk* grow up ignorant of both their true role and the identity of their parents. Children are also called upon to help overthrow the forces

of evil in in Susan Cooper's The Dark Is Rising series (*Over Sea, Under Stone, The Dark Is Rising, Greenwitch, The Grey King, Silver on the Tree*).

**Lewis, C. S.** (1898–1963)
**The Voyage of the Dawn Treader** (1952). New York: HarperTrophy, 1984. 256pp. 978-0064405027.

When Lucy and Edmund visit their cousin, Eustace, the three children visit the fantasy kingdom of Narnia by magically entering a painting of a ship. They meet King Caspian who is about to set sail for a year and a day on the *Dawn Treader*, the ship in the painting. His quest is to find seven friends of his father, lords who were sent away to the unknown lands of the east by the cruel king, Miraz. On his coronation, King Caspian promised to find the missing lords or avenge their deaths if they are no longer alive. The children accompany King Caspian on his voyage, encountering enchanting marvels and enduring death-threatening experiences.

Magical and mysterious settings are a strong appeal in this vividly imagined novel. The eastern voyage is an unusual account of a journey toward death, one depicted as a movement toward almost unbearable light. Readers faced with the loss of a loved one will view death in a new light and gain consolation from this story.

Traveling from one curious island to another, the children undergo a series of testing situations, experiences that foster character development. The harsh difficulties that they all face affect Eustace in particular. A pampered and protected child, he becomes more resilient and less egotistical as a result of the adventures. The courageous actions and heroic decisions of the little mouse, Reepicheep, will inspire any child who feels small and powerless.

**For those also seeking**: reassurance/comfort/confirmation of self-worth/strength
**For those drawn to**: setting, story
**Themes/subjects**: boats and ships, sea voyage, quests, death, islands, faith and skepticism, Christianity, Bible stories, portals/thresholds, mice, sea and seashore, narcissism, spoiled children
**Reading interest level**: grades 4–8
**Curricular tie-ins**: Ask students to create a magazine advertisement for a cruise on board the *Dawn Treader*. This cruise will visit the islands described in the novel.

**Adaptations & alternative formats**: movie directed by Michael Apted (2010); audiobook read by Michael Apted (2005)
**Translations**: Spanish: *La Travesia del Viajero del Alb*; French: *L'Odyssée du Passeur d'Aurore*
**Read-alikes**: Ged in Ursula K. Le Guin's *A Wizard of Earthsea* also undertakes an eastward journey to the end of the world. Sophie also makes a voyage of discovery in Sharon Creech's *The Wanderer*.

**Lewis, C. S.** (1898–1963)
**The Silver Chair** (1953). New York: HarperCollins, 1994. 272pp. 978-0064471091.

After Eustace discovers that his classmate, Jill, is crying behind the school gym, the pair runs away from the bullies who are harassing her, escaping through a door that opens to Narnia. After arriving in this enchanted realm, they meet Aslan, the magical lion. He tells Jill that she and Eustace must find the lost prince, Rilian, by following four signs. He asks Jill to repeat the signs daily to herself so that she will not forget them. Jill and Eustace travel to the land of the giants and then to the mysterious world of the Underland, meeting people who keep repeating the ominous phrase, "few return to the sunlit lands." Jill forgets to repeat the signs to herself and does not recognize them when they appear.

One of the most exciting and imaginative books in the Narnia series, *The Silver Chair* is memorable for its strange story and eerie settings. Some of the events in the novel initially deceive the reader as well as the characters. And many characters are not who they seem to be. Readers will find themselves continually reassessing their earlier impressions in this captivating and thought-provoking story. Those who have made a number of mistakes in life will discover that doing so does not make them failures. The story will also resonate with children who have been bullied by others.

**For those also seeking**: reassurance/comfort/confirmation of self-worth/strength
**For those drawn to**: setting, story
**Themes/subjects**: quests, bullying, clues/riddles, underground, giants, faith and skepticism, Christianity, Bible stories, mistakes, disguises, appearance versus reality, witches, portals/thresholds, castles, knights, northern settings
**Reading interest level**: grades 4–8

**Curricular tie-ins**: Jill must look for four signs on her quest. She misses three of them. In a think-pair-share activity, students could brainstorm positive and negative ways of dealing with mistakes.
**Adaptations & alternative formats**: a BBC television production directed by Alex Kirby (2002); audiobook read by Jeremy Northam (2005)
**Translations**: Spanish: *La Silla de Plata*; French: *Fauteuil d'Argent*
**Read-alikes**: Readers who enjoy underground journeys should also read Jules Verne's *Journey to the Centre of the Earth*, L. Frank Baum's *Dorothy and the Wizard in Oz*, and Suzanne Collins's Underland Chronicles (*Gregor the Overlander*, *Gregor and the Prophecy of Bane*, *Gregor and the Curse of the Warmbloods*, *Gregor and the Marks of Secret*, and *Gregor and the Code of Claw*). Like Lewis's Underlanders, the store people in Terry Pratchett's *Truckers* are skeptical about the world outside their familiar environment.

**Lewis, C. S.** (1898–1963)
**The Last Battle** (1956). New York: HarperTrophy, 2002. 240pp. 978-0064471084.

When an ape persuades a donkey to wear a lion skin and impersonate the wise lion, Aslan, the ape is able to take advantage of the gullible Narnians. King Rilian of Narnia is not so easily deceived though. He suspects foul play when he learns that the wood nymphs are dying and the Narnian forests are being destroyed. But King Rilian is captured and imprisoned by the Calormen. After he recalls stories of previous Narnian kings rescued by children from beyond the world, King Rilian calls out for help from these children. Eustace and Jill hear his call, come to his aid, free him from his imprisonment, and fight with him against the false Aslan.

All characters from the previous six books meet and all events culminate in this gripping final volume in the Narnia series. And when the unicorn reaches the final setting in the book, he says, "I have come at last. . . . This is the land I have been looking for all my life, though I never knew it till now." This utopian setting is a captivating and richly imagined fantasy place. What is particularly unique in this novel is the way Lewis presents death and the afterlife. Readers who have faced the death of a loved one can find consolation in Lewis's vision. And those who enjoy stories of epic battles will love the rousing combat scenes in this Carnegie Award–winning novel.

**For those also seeking**: reassurance/comfort/confirmation of self-worth/strength

**For those drawn to**: setting
**Themes/subjects**: battles/wars, utopian places, death, immortality, rebirth, faith and skepticism, Christianity, Bible stories, disguises, portals/thresholds, royalty, kings/queens, castles, lions and tigers, unicorns, donkeys, appearance versus reality, monkeys/apes, political corruption, dwarfs
**Reading interest level**: grades 4–8
**Curricular tie-ins**: Ask students to create a book trailer for the novel, promoting its best features.
**Adaptations & alternative formats**: audiobook read by Patrick Stewart (2005)
**Translations**: Spanish: *La Ultima Batalla*; French: *La Dernière Bataille*
**Read-alikes**: Epic battles also dominate Garth Nix's *Abhorsen*, Lloyd Alexander's *The High King*, and Kevin Crossley-Holland's *Arthur: King of the Middle March*.


**Nesbit, Edith** (1858–1924)
**Five Children and It** (1902). Oxford: Oxford University Press, 2013. 189pp. 978-0192733436. PD.

When five siblings leave London for a holiday in the country, little do they expect to find a sand-fairy in a gravel pit near their vacation house. This ancient Psammead is no ordinary fairy; it is eccentric, cranky, and bad tempered. But the Psammead will grant the children a wish a day, one that lasts until the sun sets. Although the children are incredibly happy at first, they find it much more difficult than they expect to wish for something that they truly want. Their wishes produce a myriad of unanticipated consequences and complications.

Throughout *Five Children and It*, Nesbit juxtaposes the perceptions of children and adults, at the expense of the latter. As the narrator observes, "Grown-up people find it very difficult to believe really wonderful things, unless they have what they call proof." Children, on the other hand, experience a greatly enlarged world because of their belief in magic.

Nesbit skillfully conveys the inner turmoil and anxieties of the five children, doing so with great humor and insight. The conspiratorial narrative tone and lively, engaging characters are strong appeals in the novel. By addressing readers directly, the narrator draws them into the story, reminding them that they know from their own experience what the characters are feeling and thinking. Readers who believe that they would be happy if they were wealthy or beautiful may reconsider their ideas after reading the novel. The book will convince them that the power of happiness lies within them.

**For those also seeking**: reassurance/comfort/confirmation of self-worth/strength
**For those drawn to**: story
**Themes/subjects**: fairies, stories and storytelling, wealth, appearance (physical), siblings and siblings issues, wishes and wishing, flying magically, urban versus rural living, humor
**Reading interest level**: grades 3–5
**Curricular tie-ins**: Read the fairy tale "The Three Wishes" to the class. Ask students to compare and contrast the two stories.
**Adaptations & alternative formats**: movie directed by John Stephenson (2004); audiobook read by Johanna Ward (2012)
**Read-alikes**: In Edith Nesbit's Bastable novels (*The Treasure Seekers*, *The New Treasure Seekers*, and *The Woodbegoods*), the well-intentioned children also find themselves in unanticipated predicaments. Like the Psammead, the ancient djinni in Jonathan Stroud's *The Amulet of Samarkand* grants magical wishes.

**Nesbit, Edith** (1858–1924)
**The Phoenix and the Carpet** (1904). London: Puffin Books, 2012. 282pp. 978-0141340869. PD.

A sequel to *Five Children and It*, *The Phoenix and the Carpet* is another novel about wishes and wishing. As in the earlier book, siblings Anthea, Cyril, Jane, and Robert find a magical object, this time a flying carpet with an egg wrapped inside it. After the egg accidentally roles into the fireplace, it catches fire and hatches a phoenix. The bird tells the children that the carpet is enchanted and will take them anywhere they wish. As in *Five Children and It*, the granting of wishes leads to unforeseen consequences and unexpected disasters. The magical adventures that the children experience are exciting, unpredictable, and funny.

Like the Psammead, the phoenix is a wish-granting creature with a decidedly eccentric personality. Despite the fact that it can help the children escape from predicaments, it does so only after they are truly desperate and have tried to manage the situation themselves. Although the children have great fun flying all over the world, they begin to realize that life in a magical world is not what they expected. Children who spend time imagining themselves in different circumstances will look at their desires differently after reading about the adventures of the four children. As the novel makes clear, having one's wishes granted may not be as desirable as expected.

A strong appeal of the book is the voice of the narrator—witty, confiding, playful, and comforting. As in all her children's books, Nesbit depicts the thoughts and emotions of children with great perceptiveness.

**For those also seeking**: reassurance/comfort/confirmation of self-worth/strength
**For those drawn to**: story
**Themes/subjects**: fairies, stories and storytelling, siblings and sibling issues, wishes and wishing, flying magically, time travel, humor, adventure
**Reading interest level**: grades 4–7
**Curricular tie-ins**: Ask students to videotape people's response to the question, "Where they would like to go on a magic carpet and why?"
**Adaptations & alternative formats**: movie directed by Zoran Perisic (1995); audiobook read by Johanna Ward (2014)
**Read-alikes**: A bed in Mary Norton's *Bed-Knob and Broomstick* takes the children to different places; a clock in Mrs. Molesworth's *The Cuckoo Clock* magically transports Griselda to a variety of places; and a traveling cloak in Dinah Maria Mulock Craik's *The Little Lame Prince* takes the boy on a variety of adventures.

**Norton, Mary** (1903–1992)
**The Borrowers Afield** (1955). Orlando, FL: Harcourt, 1998. 215pp. 978-0152047320.

After Arrietty and her parents—the miniature people introduced in *The Borrowers*—are forced to move out of Firbank Hall, they begin the hazardous journey in search of their relatives. Robinson Crusoe–like, they take stock of their hastily packed provisions and realize that they possess almost nothing. Life, they realize, will be very different from now on. Moreover, finding their relatives will be a nearly impossible task. When rain forces them to take refuge in an old boot, they decide to make it their temporary home. But once they settle in, the boot is invaded by other creatures. Items are stolen, food starts running out, and winter approaches.

Sequel to *The Borrowers*, this novel is another thrilling survival story. But despite the hardships that Arrietty faces, she thrives in this outdoor world. "This is what I have longed for," she thinks when she first emerges from the boot. Arrietty felt stifled and entrapped in their home below the floorboards of Firbank Hall. In opposition to the wishes of her protective parents, she continues to take risks. When she tells her father she sees no threats in their new environment, he insists that danger is everywhere: "Before and Behind, Above and Below." Readers who fear difficulties and those who are afraid of change will look at both differently after reading the novel. Arrietty's story will resonate with children who feel stifled by overprotective parents.

The humorous tone of the novel is another strong appeal. The discrepancy between the miniature size of the borrowers and the life-sized world they inhabit is often amusing. When, for example, Pod finds the boot that they use as shelter, Homily says, "Oh, my goodness me . . . I wonder who ever wore it . . . I'm not going in no further: there might be something in the toe."

**For those also seeking**: courage to make a change
**For those drawn to**: character, setting
**Themes/subjects**: miniature beings, moving houses (relocating), independence, imprisonment/entrapment, overprotective parents, only children, parental disapproval, survival, poverty, adaptation/adjusting to change, greed, nature, country life, humor
**Reading interest level**: grades 4–8
**Curricular tie-ins**: Arrietty keeps a diary and proverb book. Ask students to create diary entries for either Homily or Pod, noting things that are important to them.
**Adaptations & alternative formats**: audiobook read by Rowena Cooper (2009)
**Read-alikes**: Adventurous heroines who thrive in dangerous environments are also the subject of Scott O'Dell's *Island of the Blue Dolphins* and Eva Ibbotson's *Journey to the River Sea*.


**Norton, Mary** (1903–1992)
**The Borrowers Aloft** (1961). Orlando, FL: Harcourt, 1998. 224pp. 978-0152047344.

This fourth novel in the Borrowers series begins with a description of two model villages: Little Fordham, a work of love created by a retired railway employee, and Ballyhoggin, an imitation of Little Fordham created by

Mr. and Mrs. Platter to make money. When the miniature Clock family arrives in Little Fordham, they move into Vine Cottage and work hard at making it a suitable home. As profits shrink at Ballyhoggin, the Platters decide to kidnap the Clock family and put them on display in a glass cage.

Readers who enjoy model trains, miniature villages, and dollhouses will love *The Borrowers Aloft*. The sheer joy of invention is a dominant theme and attraction in the novel. But surprisingly, when the kindly creators of Fordham Village finish renovating the house for the Clocks, Pod announces, "It won't do." Readers who believe they would be happy if their dreams were realized and their problems solved may think differently after reading the novel. They will also find comfort in a story in which the miniature underdogs outwit their human opponents.

As in the earlier novels in the series, Arrietty continues to struggle with her parents as she tries to gain independence from them. Children who have strained relationships with their parents or feel overprotected by them will identify with Arrietty's struggles.

**For those also seeking**: reassurance/comfort/confirmation of self-worth/strength
**For those drawn to**: setting, character
**Themes/subjects**: miniature beings, moving houses (relocating), utopian places, independence, imprisonment/entrapment, agency and powerlessness, adaptation/adjusting to change, balloons (hot air), kidnapping, only children, overprotective parents, parental disapproval, inventing/creating, adventure, humor
**Reading interest level**: grades 4–8
**Curricular tie-ins**: In small groups, students could find information about hot-air balloons: who invented them, when they were invented, and how successful they have been as a means of travel. They could then create a commercial about hot-air balloons.
**Adaptations & alternative formats**: audiobook read by Rowena Cooper (2009)
**Translations**: Spanish: *Los Incursores en el Aire*; French: *Les Chapardeurs en Ballon*
**Read-alikes**: Readers who enjoy stories about hot-air-balloon adventures will also like William Pène du Bois's *The Twenty-One Balloons*, while those who love stories about miniature villages will also enjoy Edith Nesbit's *The Magic City*.

**Norton, Mary** (1903–1992)
**The Borrowers Avenged** (1982). Orlando, FL: Harcourt, 1998. 289pp. 978-0152047313.

Like the previous four books in the series, *The Borrowers Avenged* opens with the Clock family searching for a new home. On the run from the Platters—a couple who earlier kidnapped them in order to put them on public display—Arrietty and her parents are continually hunted by them. When the Clocks find a suitable place to live, they meet a new borrower and discover relatives inside the nearby church. But can they remain safe with the Platters threatening to recapture them?

The ingenious contrivances that the borrowers create and the miniature houses that they furnish are a source of great interest in the novel. The close ties between a borrower's environment and his or her character are both telling and humorous. The Overmantels, for example, are haughty and class conscious.

Although the Clocks hope that they have finally found a permanent home, their constant moving suggests that they there is no such thing as permanence in life. Readers who believe that they will be happy once they reach their goal may reconsider this idea after reading the novel. Arrietty's focus on the journey rather the goal will reduce tension for readers who are driven by end points and finales. Children who are afraid of change will also find Arrietty's story as a source of comfort and support.

**For those also seeking**: reassurance/comfort/confirmation of self-worth/strength
**For those drawn to**: setting, character
**Themes/subjects**: miniature beings, moving houses (relocating), independence, adaptation/adjusting to change, only children, parental disapproval, inventing/creating, disability, humor
**Reading interest level**: grades 4–8
**Curricular tie-ins**: Norton frequently depicts close connections between characters and their environments. Ask students to describe how the place that Lupy, Peagreen, or Spiller inhabits affects or reflects their character.
**Adaptations & alternative formats**: audiobook read by Rowena Cooper (2009)
**Translations**: Spanish: *Los Incursores Vengados*; French: *Les Chapardeurs Sauvés*

*Fantasy Series* 223

**Read-alikes**: Like the Clock family, the Ingalls in Laura Ingalls Wilder's Little House books (*Little House in the Big Woods, Farmer Boy, Little House on the Prairie, On the Banks of Plum Creek, By the Shores of Silver Lake, The Long Winter, Little Town on the Prairie, These Happy Golden Years, The First Four Years*) continually search for a suitable house. The nature-loving heroines in both books struggle with the domestic role that their mothers espouse for females.

**Pullman, Philip** (1946–)
**The Amber Spyglass** (2000). New York: Dell Yearling, 2000. 518pp. 978-0440418566.

Drugged by her mother and held captive in a remote cave near a Himalayan valley, 12-year-old Lyra only wakes long enough to be drugged again. While she sleeps, she is hunted by three groups of people, each of whom plans to capture or kill her. When Lyra finally awakens, she does not know whom to trust; the forces of evil disguise themselves as the forces of good. Her dreams guide her to the land of the dead, a place that is highly dangerous to the living. Together with her friend Will, Lyra must save the world from complete annihilation.

A larger-than-life epic in which the fate of the universe rests on the actions of Lyra and Will, this third book in Pullman's His Dark Materials trilogy is an emotionally intense, pulse-pounding story conveyed in lyrical, evocative language. Facing impossible choices, Lyra and Will are forced to leave their childhoods behind in this coming-of-age story. Readers who must confront situations in which change is not possible will gain inspiration from the ending of the novel.

From the highest ramparts of Lord Asriel's adamant tower in the saw-toothed mountains to the terrifying abyss that Lyra and Will climb out of, the settings in *The Amber Spyglass* are vividly imagined and highly memorable. The book is also renowned for its controversial ideas, ideas that will make readers examine their assumptions about spiritual matters and organized religion. The novel will resonate with those who are grappling with their identity and their beliefs.

**For those also seeking**: acceptance
**For those drawn to**: setting, language
**Themes/subjects**: death, immortality, Christianity, multiple worlds/universes, romance, sacrifice, omens/prophecies, authoritarian figures,

challenging authority figures, angels/cherubs, witches, mother-daughter relationships, underground, coming of age, faith and skepticism, political corruption, spies and spying
**Reading interest level**: grade 7 and up
**Curricular tie-ins**: In their reader response journals, students could discuss whether or not they agree with Pullman's ideas about spirituality, organized religion, and the afterlife.
**Adaptations & alternative formats**: audiobook read by the author and a full cast (2003)
**Translations**: Spanish: *El Catalejo Lacado*; French: *Le Miroir d'Ambre*
**Read-alikes**: In C. S. Lewis's *The Magician's Nephew*, Digory also experiences temptation during a quest in an alternate world. Like Lyra and Will, Ged and Arren in Ursula K. Le Guin's *The Farthest Shore* must try to fix a world that is slowly dying.

## Models for Identity

**Baum, L. Frank** (1856–1919)
**Rinkitink in Oz** (1916). Illustrated by John R. Neill. New York: Dover, 1993. 336pp. 978-0486277561. PD.

Young Prince Inga lives on the island of Pingaree, a land of costly pearls and widespread contentment. But one day, invaders storm the island, demolish the buildings, and capture everyone except Prince Inga, the visiting king Rinkitink, and his talking goat, Bilbil. The prince watches from a tree-top perch as his father, mother, and fellow islanders are forced onto enemy ships and taken away. Initially devastated, Prince Inga takes stock of his situation and remembers that his father has hidden three magical pearls in the royal palace. The pink pearl provides safety from danger; the blue pearl, superhuman strength; and the white pearl, words of wisdom. Once Prince Inga finds these pearls in the demolished palace, he convinces King Rinkitink and Bilbil to accompany him on a dangerous sea voyage to rescue his parents and the inhabitants of Pingaree. *Rinkitink in Oz* is a story of intense suspense and excitement.

Stranded on a ruined island without family and friends, Prince Inga reacts with resourcefulness, courage, and wisdom. The ship that he summons is black on the outside and silver on the inside, suggestive of the silver lining that can accompany difficulties. This story will motivate readers who are facing painful losses or insurmountable difficulties to accept their challenges with confidence and courage.

*Fantasy Series*

Despite the fact that King Rinkitink and Bilbil are odd, unusual characters, they each have their part to play in rescuing the island people. Readers who feel isolated because of their uniqueness will gain comfort from their example.

**For those also seeking**: connection with others/awareness of not being alone
**For those drawn to**: character, story
**Themes/subjects**: being different, inclusiveness, battles/wars, friendship, resilience, optimism, courage, only children, islands, sea voyage, princes, royalty
**Reading interest level**: grades 3–8
**Curricular tie-ins**: Ask students to engage in a debate about whether an invasion into another country's territory is ever justified or not.
**Adaptations & alternative formats**: audiobook read by Ron Knowles (2011)
**Read-alikes**: Invaders also attack island people in Scott O'Dell's *Island of the Blue Dolphins*. Amira's village is attacked by militants in Andrea Davis Pinkney's *The Red Pencil*.

**Baum, L. Frank** (1856–1919)
**Glinda of Oz** (1920). Illustrated by John R. Neill. New York: Books of Wonder, 2000. 283pp. 978-0688149789. PD.

When Ozma discovers that two groups of Oz inhabitants—the Flatheads and the Skeezers—are using magic illegally and are about to fight each other, she and Dorothy travel to a remote corner of Gillikin Country to educate them. The Flatheads, who carry their brains in a can, will not listen to reason and try to entrap Ozma and Dorothy on top of a secluded mountain. The Skeezers, who live in a glass-domed city on a magic island, submerge the city below water, imprisoning the girls indefinitely.
The submerged, domed city and the saucer-like area atop an isolated mountain are singular and memorable fantasy settings, ones that are characteristic of Baum's best work.

Ozma's magic is powerless to free the girls from their glass prison. Because the dangers that Ozma and Dorothy face seem insurmountable, the suspense is intense and the story compelling. This last book in the Oz series is one of Baum's most exciting stories and imaginative fantasies.

*Glinda of Oz* is also an inspirational exploration of the theme of effective governance. As a wise and benevolent ruler, Ozma cares for her people and works tirelessly to establish peace throughout her kingdom. The novel will particularly appeal to readers who aspire to leadership positions and those who are attracted to stories about compelling leaders.

**For those also seeking**: courage to make a change
**For those drawn to**: setting, story
**Themes/subjects**: being different, leadership, inclusiveness, spells/curses, underwater exploration, battle/wars, imprisonment/entrapment, islands, princesses, royalty
**Reading interest level**: grades 3–8
**Curricular tie-ins**: As a worksheet activity, ask students to compare and contrast two different rulers in the novel. They could also compare one of these rulers to a current head of state.
**Adaptations & alternative formats**: audiobook read by Karen White (2012)
**Read-alikes**: Characters in E. Nesbit's *Wet Magic* and L. Frank Baum's *The Sea Fairies* also live in underwater environments. Readers who enjoy such settings will also like Jules Verne's *Twenty Thousand Leagues under the Sea*.

## Reassurance/Comfort/Confirmation of Self-Worth/Strength

**Baum, L. Frank** (1856–1919)
**The Wonderful Wizard of Oz** (1900). Illustrated by W. W. Denslow. New York: Dover, 1996. 140pp. 978-0486291161. PD.

When a cyclone hits Kansas, Dorothy's house is swept away, landing in the magical world of Oz. Although Oz is a wondrous world unlike the colorless, arid prairies, Dorothy wants nothing more than to return home. The good witch, Glinda, instructs her to follow the yellow brick road to the City of Emeralds where the powerful Wizard of Oz may be able to grant her wish. While on her journey to the city, she befriends a talking scarecrow who wants brains, a tin woodman who wants a heart, and a cowardly lion who wants courage. When these four characters arrive in Oz, the Wizard tells them that he will grant their wishes on one condition: they must first kill the Wicked Witch of the West.

The vibrant world of Oz, with its jewel-laden city center and color-coded countries, is strange, enchanting, mesmerizing. A vividly imagined fantasy

*Fantasy Series*

land, it is filled with such singular places as sleep-inducing fields of poppies, enchanted trees whose branches capture people, and a land of miniature china figures.

The dangerous journey in search of the Wizard of Oz prepares Dorothy and her friends for the much more difficult quest of conquering the evil witch. Children who lack faith in their own abilities will find comfort in the story of the four friends, all of whom discover talents they already possess. Readers who love richly imaginative fairy-tale worlds, unconventional characters, and exciting quest adventures will enjoy this first book in the Oz series. W. W. Denslow's original illustrations are an added appeal in the novel.

**For those also seeking**: connection with others/awareness of not being alone
**For those drawn to**: setting, character
**Themes/subjects**: self-confidence, spells/curses, castles, courage, empathy, intelligence, quests, witches, friendship, lions and tigers, natural disasters, hurricanes/cyclones, balloons (hot-air), cowardice
**Reading interest level**: grades 3–8
**Curricular tie-ins**: Students could compare the book with the Disney movie. Ask them which one they like best and why.
**Adaptations & alternative formats**: movie directed by Victor Fleming and others (75th anniversary edition of the 1939 MGM movie starring Dorothy Garland, 2013); audiobook read by Robin Field and Kathy Aughenbaugh (2010); graphic novel by Eric Shanower (2010)
**Translations**: Spanish: *El Maravilloso Mago de Oz*; French: *Le Magicien d'Oz*
**Read-alikes**: Readers who love stories that feature magical castles will also enjoy E. Nesbit's *The Enchanted Castle*, E. Nesbit's *The House of Arden*, Diana Wynne Jones's *Howl's Moving Castle*, and J. K. Rowling's Harry Potter books. Like Dorothy, Elodie in Gail Carson Levine's *A Tale of Two Castles* also befriends unusual creatures.

**Baum, L. Frank** (1856–1919)
**The Road to Oz** (1909). Illustrated by John R. Neill. New York: Dover, 1986. 261pp. 978-0486252087. PD.

When a stranger called the Shaggy Man asks Dorothy for directions to Butterfield, she takes him to a crossroad near her home. Strangely enough, the roads seem to multiply and she becomes lost and disoriented. Unable to find her way back home, Dorothy decides to accompany Shaggy Man on his journey. They visit fairy lands such as the enchanting Foxville with its marble houses and civilized foxes, the frightening land of the head-throwing Scoodlers, and the magical Truth Pond. During their travels, Dorothy and the Shaggy Man meet Polychrome—the daughter of the rainbow—in addition to all their old friends. Road adventures are juxtaposed with Oz adventures, while the folly of the foxes, donkeys, and Scoodlers is counterbalanced by the wisdom of Ozma.

*The Road to Oz* is a story about the true nature of intelligence, a theme that is highlighted by the many unusual heads in the novel. Dorothy meets characters who remove their heads, transform their heads from human to animal, throw their heads, and even grow new heads. Readers who may feel inferior to intelligent classmates will find that this novel not only resonates with them but also reassures them. Intelligence manifests itself in a myriad of ways in the story. No two characters possess the same type of mind, a fact that is celebrated throughout.

Children who have read the four previous Oz books will recognize many of the beloved Oz inhabitants. The novel is also memorable for its plethora of unique characters who reunite at Ozma's festive birthday celebrations. However, readers looking for a suspenseful story will find the meandering plot weak in comparison with the other Oz books.

**For those also seeking**: acceptance
**For those drawn to**: setting, character
**Themes/subjects**: intelligence, being different, inclusiveness, journeys, foxes, donkeys, road trips, adventure
**Reading interest level**: grades 3–8
**Curricular tie-ins**: On chart paper, ask students to draw a large map of the places visited in the novel. Each place could include a suitable image.
**Adaptations & alternative formats**: audiobook read by Ron Knowles (2010); graphic novel by Eric Shanower (2013)
**Translations**: Spanish: *El Camino de Oz*
**Read-alikes**: William Steig's *Dominic* is another lighthearted fantasy novel that features road adventures. Milo also travels around a strange and unusual fantasy world in Norton Juster's *The Phantom Tollbooth*.

**Jansson, Tove** (1914–2001)
**Comet in Moominland** (1946). Illustrated by the author. Translated from the Swedish by Elizabeth Portch. New York: Square Fish, 2010. 175pp. 978-0312608880.

When a young creature called Moomintroll notices comet-like patterns in nature, he and his friend, Sniff, travel to the Observatory on the Lonely Mountains to ask professors about the possibility of a comet attack. During this peril-filled journey, Moomintroll and Sniff encounter a series of life-threatening situations that prepare them for an impending catastrophic event—a comet heading for their valley. They also meet a number of odd, one-of-a-kind creatures who become fellow travelers and best friends.

*Comet in Moominland*, as Jansson's playful illustrations suggest, is funny, endearing, and reassuring. Although Moomintroll and Sniff undergo one calamitous event after another, their lighthearted dispositions and adventurous spirits keep the tone of the novel cheerful and optimistic. Jansson depicts the follies and foibles of Moomintroll, Sniff, and their friends in such a way that readers smile at their shortcomings and recognize them in themselves. Children who feel anxious about the future will identify with Moomintroll. And those who like to acquire and collect things will relate to Sniff.

The idyllic Moominvalley, a strong attraction in the novel, is taken for granted by Moomintroll until he leaves it. As he discovers, "You must go on a long journey before you can really find out how wonderful home is."

**For those also seeking**: connection with others/awareness of not being alone
**For those drawn to**: character, story
**Themes/subjects**: journeys, anxiety/fears, courage, survival, natural disasters, comets, being different, inclusiveness, tolerance, humor
**Reading interest level**: grades 1–6
**Curricular tie-ins**: The novel works well as an accompanying resource for a lesson on comets. Ask students to create either an infographic or poster on comets.
**Adaptations & alternative formats**: audiobook read by Hugh Dennis (2012)

**Translations**: French: *La Comète Arrive!*
**Read-alikes**: Anne Fine's *The Jamie and Angus Stories* and A. A. Milne's *Winnie-the-Pooh* and *The House at Pooh Corner* are also lighthearted books about the anxieties and concerns of young children.

**Jansson, Tove** (1914–2001)
**Finn Family Moomintroll** (1948). Illustrated by the author. Translated from the Swedish by Elizabeth Portch. New York: Square Fish, 2010. 160pp. 978-0312608897.

When Moomintroll and his friends awaken from hibernation, they are surprised to find a top hat sitting on a mountain. The hat belongs to the feared Hobgoblin, and it magically transforms whatever is placed inside it. The hat provides endless fun and adventures for Moomintroll and his friends. But it also causes so many problems that Moominmamma and Moominpappa get rid of it by throwing it in the river. Snufkin and Moomintroll secretly rescue the hat, an action that precipitates a series of dangerous and exciting adventures.

When Moomintroll and Snufkin retrieve the Hobgoblin's hat, Moomintroll says, "You know . . . it's the first time we have done anything that we couldn't tell mother and father about." *Finn Family Moomintroll* is a psychologically penetrating story about a character growing up and becoming less reliant on his parents. The magical transformations in the novel highlight the theme of personal change and development. The book will appeal to readers who would like to be more independent but are cautious about change. The story is, by turns, exciting, scary, and funny, one that appeals to wide array of young readers.

**For those also seeking**: models for identity
**For those drawn to**: character, setting
**Themes/subjects**: journeys, being different, inclusiveness, self-reliance, independence, nature, identity formation, magical transformations, tolerance, humor, goblins
**Reading interest level**: grades 1–6
**Curricular tie-ins**: Ask students to draw a picture of the magic hat. On the one side, draw an object they would like to change, and on the other side, draw it transformed.
**Adaptations & alternative formats**: audiobook read by Hugh Dennis (2012)

*Fantasy Series*

**Translations**: Spanish: *La Familia Mumin*
**Read-alikes**: William Steig's Dominic is another carefree character who travels in search of adventures. Sara Pennypacker's *Clementine* is also about an endearing character who continually finds herself in trouble.

**Jansson, Tove** (1914–2001)
**Moominpappa's Memoirs** (1966). Illustrated by the author. Translated from the Swedish by Thomas Warburton. Revised edition of *The Exploits of Moominpappa* (1950). New York: Square Fish, 2010. 167pp. 978-0312625436.

Moominpappa, a character who views himself as a hardworking, respectable father, writes his memoirs about his "stormy youth." Dropped off on the doorstep of an orphanage, he starts life as a misfit among 12 obedient foundlings. Not understood or appreciated by the others, he decides to leave. "I shall return one day," he writes in his farewell note, "crowned with laurel leaves." Moominpappa's adventures take him to sea where he meets the fathers of Moomintroll's friends.

One of the funniest books in the series, *Moominpappa's Memoirs* is narrated by someone who is oblivious of his true character. Moominpappa believes he is descended from royalty, "born under special stars," and destined to be heroic. But his romantic vision of himself stands in stark contrast to reality. Another amusing character in the novel is the domineering, rule-bound Aunt Hemulin. A caricatured villain who is driven by a sense of oppressive duty, she is humorously juxtaposed to the fun-loving creatures in the novel. Readers who are overly critical of their own faults or lack self-esteem will view their shortcomings in a kindlier way after reading the novel.

The Moomin landscape, with its enchanted islands and stormy seas, is another strong attraction. Jansson's poetic descriptions of the landscape make readers look anew at the familiar world.

**For those also seeking**: connection with others/awareness of not being alone
**For those drawn to**: character, setting
**Themes/subjects**: sea voyage, being different, inclusiveness, tolerance, nature, sea and seashore, islands, orphans, authoritarian figures, outcasts/misfits, memoirs/diaries, humor
**Reading interest level**: grades 1–6

**Curricular tie-ins**: Moominpappa looks back on his life and writes his memoirs. Ask students to write in memoir format about something that happened to them when they were younger.
**Adaptations & alternative formats**: audiobook read by Hugh Dennis (2012)
**Translations**: Spanish: *Papa Mumin y el Mar*
**Read-alikes**: The protagonist in William Steig's *Abel's Island* is another high-spirited character who participates in sea adventures. Kenneth Grahame's *The Wind in the Willows* is also a lighthearted novel about the adventures and mishaps of creatures.


**Jansson, Tove** (1914–2001)
**Moominsummer Madness** (1954). Illustrated by the author. Translated from the Swedish by Thomas Warburton. New York: Square Fish, 2010. 155pp. 978-0312608910.

Forced to move to the second story of their home when floodwaters overtake the main floor, the Moomins eventually evacuate after these waters rise even higher. The troll-like creatures survive by moving into a floating theater, but Moomintroll and the Snork Maiden get left behind by accident. Little My—the miniature Mymble daughter—also encounters a problem when she falls through a trap door in the floating theater and must brave the sea in a tiny sewing basket. The various strands of the suspenseful plot intertwine in a clever and satisfying way.

New creatures such as Little My, Emma the rat, and the 24 Woodies are as humorous, unique, and engaging as the familiar Moomin characters. Little My, in fact, stands out as the most memorable creature in the novel. Only a couple of inches high, she is a miniature tour de force. Plucky, funny, and undaunted by disaster, she is reckless, headstrong, and exuberant. Readers who are anxious about challenges that they must face will find inspiration in this character-driven novel.

**For those also seeking**: connection with others/awareness of not being alone
**For those drawn to**: character, story
**Themes/subjects**: sea voyage, nature, natural disasters, sea and seashore, boats and ships, resilience, being different, inclusiveness, tolerance, humor
**Reading interest level**: grades 1–6

**Curricular tie-ins**: The novel can serve as a springboard to a lesson on safety awareness. Ask students what they should do if their house is threatened by flooding or fire. They could create an advertisement for a children's magazine about fire-safety awareness.
**Adaptations & alternative formats**: audiobook read by Hugh Dennis (2012)
**Translations**: Spanish: *Una Loca Noche de San Juan*
**Read-alikes**: *Secrets at Sea* by Richard Peck and *The Doll People Set Sail* by Ann M. Martin and Laura Godwin are also stories of humorous sea adventures.

**Jansson, Tove** (1914–2001)
**Moominland Midwinter** (1957). Illustrated by the author. Translated from the Swedish by Thomas Warburton. New York: Square Fish, 2010. 141pp. 978-0312625412.

Although the Moomin family hibernates every year, Moomintroll wakes up unexpectedly one winter night and goes outside to explore.

Finding winter strange and unfamiliar, he misses summertime and his hibernating friends. Little My also wakes up, but she is exhilarated by winter, teaching herself to toboggan on Moominmamma's silver tray and to skate with pot lids attached to her feet. The polar opposite of timid Moomintroll, she fashions a pair of improvised skis out of an old barrel and hurtles at "breakneck speed" down a hill. Although Moomintroll yearns for summer and cocoons himself with his ancestor troll in a "thicket of broken chairs, empty boxes, fishing nets, cardboard tubes, old baskets, and gardening tools," he grudgingly participates in a series of winter adventures and learns to face challenges on his own.

*Moominland in Midwinter* is the perfect book for readers who do not like change, reassuring them that they can effectively cope with it. Moomintroll will win children's hearts, and the other lovable, eccentric characters will make them laugh. The novel depicts a magical winter wonderland in simple but poetic language that will renew readers' appreciation of the season.

**For those also seeking**: connection with others/awareness of not being alone
**For those drawn to**: character, setting

**Themes/subjects**: winter, loneliness, nature, resilience, courage, independence, being different, inclusiveness, adaptation/adjusting to change, humor
**Reading interest level**: grades 1–6
**Curricular tie-ins**: This novel could be used in conjunction with a winter field trip to an ice-skating rink.
**Adaptations & alternative formats**: audiobook read by Hugh Dennis (2012)
**Translations**: Spanish: *La Familia Mumin en Invierno*
**Read-alikes**: Readers who love winter stories will also like Carolyn Sherwin Bailey's *Miss Hickory* and Arthur Ransom's *Winter Holiday*.


**Jones, Diana Wynne** (1934–2011)
**The Magicians of Caprona** (1980). In The Chronicles of Chrestomanci, Volume 2: The Magicians of Caprona/Witch Week. New York: HarperTrophy, 2001. 548pp. 978-0064472692.

Like the Capulets and the Montagues in Shakespeare's *Romeo and Juliet*, the great houses of Montana and Petrocchi have been bitter rivals for centuries. The feud between the two families of famous spell-makers involves everyone from the head of the house to the smallest child within them. When the renowned Chrestomanci visits the Montanas, he tells them that he believes a secret enchanter is sapping the strength of their city. Tonino Montana and Angelica Petrocchi are kidnapped from their families and forced to work together to help save the city of Caprona from destruction.

Life in the hectic but loving extended family of the Montanas is portrayed with great humor and warmth. The young Tonino worries about letting his family down because he is a slow learner. His anxiety will resonate with readers who feel unsure of their capabilities or overshadowed by talented family members. Although Tonino remains slow at learning spells, he surprises everyone by developing other talents. The magical Italian setting with its grand scriptorium, luxurious ducal palaces, magnificent cathedrals, and golden streets is richly detailed and imagined.

**For those also seeking**: disinterested understanding of the world
**For those drawn to**: character, setting
**Themes/subjects**: Italian social life and customs, extended families, feuds, quarrels/fights, struggling or disinterested students, spells/curses, anxiety/fears, cooperation and teamwork, tolerance, magicians, magical

transformations, palaces, cats, puppets, oppressive environments, kidnapping
**Reading interest level**: grades 5–8
**Curricular tie-ins**: This novel would be a good choice for broadening children's awareness of other cultures. Ask students how family traditions in this novel differ from those in their family.
**Adaptations & alternative formats**: audiobook read by Gerard Doyle (2006)
**Translations**: French: *Les Magiciens de Caprona*
**Read-alikes**: Ged must also discover why magic is draining out of Earthsea in Ursula K. Le Guin's *The Farthest Shore*, while Will and Lyra must learn why the world is dying in Philip Pullman's *The Amber Spyglass*. The rivalry between two families is the subject of Phyllis Reynolds Naylor's *Boys against Girls*.


**Jones, Diana Wynne** (1934–2011)
**The Pinhoe Egg** (2005). In The Chronicles of Chrestomanci, Volume 3: Conrad's Fate/The Pinhoe Egg. New York: HarperCollins, 2006. 675pp. 978-0061148323.

When Marianne and her brother, Joe, visit their grandmother, they suspect that she has been hexed by visiting neighbors. Gammar starts speaking gibberish that no one can understand. Marianne, who visits her daily, believes that Gammar is also casting evil spells on neighboring clans. Meanwhile, her brother, Joe, is sent to Chrestomanci Castle for the summer, ostensibly as a boot boy, but in reality as a spy for the Pinhoe witches. The Pinhoes and their neighbors do not want the renowned enchanter, Chrestomanci, to know that they possess magical powers that they fear he will control. While these events are taking place, young Cat Chance faces his own troubles at the Chrestomanci Castle. Misdirection spells, a griffin that hatches from a hidden egg, and secret transformations cause complications for Cat, Marianne, and Joe.

Like the five previous novels in the Chrestomanci series, *The Pinhoe Egg* is noteworthy for its quirky humor and exuberant use of magic. Jones is skilled at depicting talented children who are undervalued by adults and unaware of their true talents. The stories of Marianne, Joe, and Cat will comfort readers who do not believe in themselves or are not valued by those close to them. As in many of Jones's works, malicious adults are responsible for many of the problems in the novel.

Although the narrative brings together the castle characters and the Pinhoe witches in a satisfying conclusion, its focus on feuding families may not be as interesting to children as the events in the previous novels. Readers do not need to have read other books in the Chrestomanci series before reading this one.

**For those also seeking**: connection with others/awareness of not being alone
**For those drawn to**: character
**Themes/subjects**: witches, extended families, feuds, quarrels/fights, magical transformations, castles, unicorns, horses, secrets, magicians, deception, spies and spying
**Reading interest level**: grades 4–8
**Curricular tie-ins**: Ask students to create an "elevator speech" for the novel, identifying its best features in 30 seconds or less (the time it would take to ride an elevator).
**Adaptations & alternative formats**: audiobook read by Gerard Doyle (2007)
**Read-alikes**: Most of the adults in the book do not recognize Marianne's talents or have faith in her opinions. Harry in *Harry Potter and the Order of the Phoenix* is not believed by others or respected by them. Similarly, Nathaniel in Jonathan Stroud's *The Amulet of Samarkand* is not recognized for his abilities.


**Jones, Diana Wynne** (1934–2011)
**Howl's Moving Castle** (1986). New York: Eos, 2008. 429pp. 978-0061478789.

Sophie Hatter, the eldest of three sisters, lives in the land of Ingary—a realm where "such things as seven-league boots and cloaks of invisibility really exist." Believing that she will be the first in her family to fail since all firstborn heroines do in fairy tales, Sophie is not surprised when the dreaded Witch of the Waste enters her stepmother's hat shop and transforms her into an old hag. Deciding to leave the shop, Sophie travels toward the surrounding hills and sees a strange castle that continually moves. She recognizes it as Howl's moving castle, the home of a wizard who sucks the souls out of young girls. Less fearful in the disguise of an old hag than she would be otherwise, Sophie enters this mysterious castle and confronts Howl and his fire demon.

Howl's moving castle contains a door that opens on four different worlds, depending which of doorknob's four colors faces downward. Like the setting, the people in this world are strange, protean, and deceptive. Sophie, as well as the reader, is not sure whom to trust.

She is unaware of her true talents and lacks self-confidence. Before she is transformed into an old crone, she is afraid of attracting attention by dressing attractively. Readers who are shy, fearful of others, or suffer from a negative body image will find hope in Sophie's story. Winner of the Phoenix Award, *Howl's Moving Castle* will appeal to readers who enjoy richly imagined, character-driven fantasies.

**For those also seeking**: connection with others/ awareness of not being alone
**For those drawn to**: setting, character
**Themes/subjects**: fate/destiny, castles, stepparents, magical transformations, eldest siblings, witches, romance, body image, disguises, shyness, self-confidence, stores
**Reading interest level**: grades 6–8
**Curricular tie-ins**: There are many references to fairy tales in the novel. As a worksheet activity, ask students to read the fairy tale "Bluebeard," and then compare Howl with Bluebeard.
**Adaptations & alternative formats**: Japanese animated movie dubbed in English, directed by Hayao Miyazaki (2004); audiobook read by Jenny Sterlin (2008)
**Translations**: French: *Le Château Ambulant*; Spanish: *El Castillo Ambulante*
**Read-alikes**: The protagonists in Garth Nix's *Lirael* and L. Frank Baum's *The Patchwork Girl of Oz* also lack confidence in their abilities.


**Lewis, C. S.** (1898–1963)
**The Horse and His Boy** (1954). New York: HarperTrophy, 1994. 241pp. 978-0064471060.

Son of an abusive fisherman, Shasta is chastised for dreaming about the life he imagines beyond the hill. When his father is about to sell him into slavery, Shasta meets a talking horse named Bree who suggests they escape to the north toward a land called Narnia. Shasta agrees to go, admitting, "I've been longing to go north all my life." On his journey, he meets a girl named

Aravis who is fleeing from an impending forced marriage. When Shasta is captured by authorities and mistaken for a prince, he overhears a plot to kidnap Queen Susan of Narnia. His plan of personal escape enlarges to become a quest to save the queen and the northern peoples.

Readers who enjoy *Arabian Nights* tales will love the exotic eastern setting of this fairy-tale-based story. Shasta and Aravis visit extravagant oriental cities, luxurious palaces, haunting ancient tombs, and perilous deserts. The movement in the novel from poverty to prosperity, from tyranny to freedom, and from ignominy to honor is deeply satisfying. Shasta's story as well Aravis's will resonate with children from dysfunctional families or those who suffer from oppression or abuse. Aslan's presence as a providential figure guiding Shasta and Aravis to safety is reassuring for young readers.

**For those also seeking**: connection with others/awareness of not being alone
**For those drawn to**: setting, story
**Themes/subjects**: quests, identity formation, faith and skepticism, Christianity, Bible stories, horses, battles/wars, royalty, deserts, omens/prophecies, northern settings
**Reading interest level**: grades 4–8
**Curricular tie-ins**: Ask students to create a collage of the settings in the novel.
**Adaptations & alternative formats**: audiobook read by Alex Jennings (2005).
**Translations**: Spanish: *El Caballo y el Muchacho*; French: *Le Cheval et Son Écuyer*
**Read-alikes**: Readers who enjoy books about the hidden identity of a protagonist will also like T. H. White's *The Sword and the Stone*, Angie Sage's *Magyk*, and Leon Garfield's *Devil in the Fog*.


**Lewis, C. S.** (1898–1963)
**The Magician's Nephew** (1955). New York: HarperCollins, 2007. 202pp. 978-0060234973.

When Polly meets Digory, a row-house neighbor staying with his aunt and uncle because his mother is dying, the pair decides to explore a passageway that connects their attics. The passage leads them to the secret study of Digory's magician uncle, a room that Digory is forbidden to enter. When his uncle unexpectedly appears at the study door, he sends the children off to another world, a place where Digory breaks an ancient spell, awaking the evil witch, Jadis. Together with Jadis, the children travel across worlds and witness the creation of Narnia. Narnia's creator sends the characters on a quest to Archenland in search of a magical fruit that will heal Digory's mother.

A prequel to *The Lion, the Witch and the Wardrobe*, *The Magician's Nephew* is a richly detailed novel that depicts strange and wondrous magical worlds. Although the book can be read on its own, it has greater impact if read after *The Lion, the Witch and the Wardrobe*. The reader discovers, for example, that the boy, Digory, becomes the beloved Professor Kirke in *The Lion, the Witch and the Wardrobe*. Readers who feel alone or confused about life will find reassurance and comfort in the guiding figure Aslan. Those who have experienced the grave illness of a parent will relate to Digory's story.

**For those also seeking**: connection with others/awareness of not being alone
**For those drawn to**: setting
**Themes/subjects**: quests, multiple worlds/universes, magicians, faith and skepticism, Christianity, Bible stories, witches, death, immortality, forests, portals/thresholds, moral dilemmas, spells/curses
**Reading interest level**: grades 4–8
**Curricular tie-ins**: Read the biblical story of the creation of the world to the class. Ask students in a large group how this narrative is similar with the account in *The Magician's Nephew*.
**Adaptations & alternative formats**: audiobook read by Kenneth Branagh (2005)
**Translations**: Spanish: *El Sobrino del Mago*; French: *Le Neveu du Magicien*
**Read-alikes**: Children in Edith Nesbit's *The Story of the Amulet* travel between two worlds and experience the complications that arise when magical beings cross into the real world. Like Digory, Conor in Patrick Ness's *A Monster Calls* must endure the grave illness of his mother.


**Norton, Mary** (1903–1992)
**The Borrowers Afloat** (1959). Orlando, FL: Harcourt, 1998. 191pp. 978-0152047337.

Although the miniature Clock family arrives safely at their relatives' home after being forced to leave their own place, relations between the two families are tense. Since resources are scarce and must now be shared, the relationship between the two is further strained. Lupy and Hendreary provide the Clocks with the necessities to set up house but do so from leftovers they do not want. When Arrietty discovers that the human inhabitants of their house plan to leave, the borrower families realize that their food supply will be soon cut off. Once again, the Clocks must leave their home to fend for themselves in the large world outdoors. Although their goal is to live in a model village called Little Fordham, it is far away. They find and move into a kettle, one that becomes dislodged from its mooring on the bank of a stream and sends them on a precarious voyage.

The pivotal third novel of the series, *The Borrowers Afloat* presents a goal for the Clocks: to live in the utopian world of Little Fordham. The move to this legendary place, the Clocks believe, should end their troubles.

The conflict between mother and daughter, the former who loves the indoors and the latter, the outdoors, continues as a source of tension in the novel. Readers who do not meet their parent's expectations or are anxious about difficult problems will find this book a source of comfort.

Part of the charm of the novel is the creative use that borrowers find for such odds and ends as a wooden cutlery drawer that is used as a boat and a butter knife that is used as a paddle. Children should read *The Borrowers* and *The Borrowers Afield* before turning to this novel.

**For those also seeking**: courage to make a change
**For those drawn to**: character, setting
**Themes/subjects**: miniature beings, moving houses (relocating), independence, imprisonment/entrapment, overprotective parents, only children, parental disapproval, adaptation/adjusting to change, utopian places, poverty, nature, humor
**Reading interest level**: grades 4–8
**Curricular tie-ins**: Arrietty thrives outside; Homily inside. Ask students to write a reflection in their reader response journals about where they feel most suited and why.
**Adaptations & alternative formats**: audiobook read by Rowena Cooper (2009)
**Translations**: Spanish: *Los Incursores Navegan*
**Read-alikes**: Sharon Creech's *The Wanderer* and Avi's *The True Confessions of Charlotte Doyle* also depict the sea adventures of female protagonists.

*Fantasy Series* 241

**Rowling, J. K.** (1965–)
**Harry Potter and the Sorcerer's Stone** (1997). New York: Arthur A. Levine Books, 1998. 309pp. 978-0590353403.

Uncle Vernon—a man who leads a very predictable, conventional life—starts to notice odd, unexplained things one day. The next morning his wife, Petunia, opens the door and finds a basket with a baby boy inside. The baby turns out to be their orphaned nephew, a dependent they raise grudgingly. Ten years later, when a letter arrives for the boy, Uncle Vernon refuses to give it to him. More and more letters arrive in a variety of unexpected ways, including pouring down the chimney. Although Uncle Vernon takes the family to a deserted hut on a remote island to escape the letters, the strategy fails. A giant appears at the hut door and tells 11-year-old Harry that he is a famous wizard. Harry's life radically changes after he moves to a magnificent castle-school called Hogwarts School of Witchcraft and Wizardry. But this mesmerizing world of enchanted sorting hats, invisibility cloaks, moving staircases, and magic mirrors hides secrets and lurking horrors.

The enigmatic opening chapter establishes the magical and mysterious atmosphere that dominates the novel. A blockbuster of a book, *Harry Potter and the Sorcerer's Stone* (U.K. title: *Harry Potter and the Philosopher's Stone*) continues to enchant, scare, enthrall, and amuse readers.

Harry Potter, the likable underdog who is bullied and abused by relatives and enemies, appeals to a wide variety of readers, both young and old. Harry's experiences with the Dursleys prepare him for his encounters with his enemies at school, which in turn equip him for his meeting with the villainous Lord Voldemort. Children who have experienced injustice, intimidation, or lack of recognition for their talents will especially enjoy the novel. Identifying with Harry's difficulties, they too will learn how to cope with evil and injustice. Shortlisted for the Carnegie Medal, this richly imagined novel introduces a memorable cast of characters, a highly suspenseful plot, and a dazzling magical world.

**For those also seeking**: connection with others/awareness of not being alone
**For those drawn to**: character, setting
**Themes/subjects**: wizards, school, mystery/suspense, abused children, self-knowledge, self-confidence, justice and injustice, friendship, bullying,

rejection, orphans, immortality, wordplay, disguises, invisibility cloaks and rings, sports, mysteries

**Reading interest level**: grade 4 and up

**Curricular tie-ins**: Ask students to form three groups. The first group should decide upon three characters they like best; the second group, three events; the third group, three settings. Then each group could create a YouTube video to publicize their choices and promote the strengths of the book.

**Adaptations & alternative formats**: Warner Bros. movie directed by Chris Columbus (2001); audiobook read by Jim Dale (1999); fully illustrated print edition by Jim Kay (2015); enhanced animation e-book edition through iBooks (2015)

**Translations**: Spanish: *Harry Potter y la Piedra Filosofal*; French: *Harry Potter a L'Ecole des Sorciers*

**Read-alikes**: Ursula K. Le Guin's *A Wizard of Earthsea*, Angie Sage's *Magyk*, and Diana Wynne Jones's *The Lives of Christopher Chant* are also books about the education of a wizard or enchanter.

**Rowling, J. K.** (1965–)
**Harry Potter and the Chamber of Secrets** (1998). New York: Arthur A. Levine Books, 1999. 341pp. 978-0439064866.

At great risk to himself, a house-elf named Dobby not only warns Harry Potter of impending disaster but also tries to prevent him from returning to Hogwarts School of Witchcraft and Wizardry. Harry ignores the warning, returns to school, and, once there, hears an icy voice deliver a bone-chilling message: "Come . . . come to me . . . let me rip you . . . let me tear you . . . let me kill you . . ." In the following months, this voice keeps interrupting Harry's thoughts. Meanwhile threatening messages appear on the walls of the school, and one student after another is turned into stone. Many Hogwarts pupils believe that the legendary Chamber of Secrets has been reopened after 50 years, an event that has unleashed a dangerous monster. To make matters worse, classmates witness Harry communicating with a snake and suspect him of being involved.

This suspense-filled plot will appeal to readers who love mysteries and scary stories. The narrative is filled with magical features such as flying cars, violent trees that attack humans, hidden castle chambers, diaries that magically reveal their secrets, and deadly reptile monsters.

*Fantasy Series* 243

This second novel in the series introduces themes of prejudice, slavery, and racism. *Harry Potter and the Chamber of Secrets* will resonate with readers who have suffered discrimination or been unfairly judged, reassuring them that eventually justice will prevail.

**For those also seeking**: connection with others/awareness of not being alone
**For those drawn to**: setting, story
**Themes/subjects**: wizards, school, clues/riddles, vanity and pompousness, justice and injustice, secrets, prejudice, racism, slavery, reptiles, memoirs/diaries, castles, sports, mysteries
**Reading interest level**: grade 4 and up
**Curricular tie-ins**: The novel can be used as a springboard to a social studies lesson on slavery. In a literature circle, students can compare the plight of the house elves with that of historical slaves.
**Adaptations & alternative formats**: Warner Bros. movie directed by Chris Columbus (2002); audiobook read by Jim Dale (2012); fully illustrated print edition by Jim Kay (2016); enhanced animation e-book edition through iBooks (2016)
**Translations**: Spanish: *Harry Potter y la Cámara Secreta*; French: *Harry Potter et la Chambre des Secrets*

Read-alikes: Neil Gaiman's spooky novel, *The Graveyard Book*, is also about a murderer who kills a boy's family when he is a baby and pursues the boy when he grows up. Jonathan Auxier's *Night Gardener* is a scary story about a house's secret curse.

**Rowling, J. K.** (1965–)
**Harry Potter and the Prisoner of Azkaban** (1999). New York: Arthur A. Levine Books, 1999. 435pp. 978-0439136358.

When Aunt Marge says something insulting about Harry's parents, Harry becomes so angry that he casts an inflating spell on her, packs his bags, and leaves the Dursleys. After the Knight Bus appears out of nowhere and drives Harry to Diagon Alley, the Minister of Magic arranges for him to stay in the magical district until school begins. Harry cannot understand why people are so protective of him until he discovers that a dangerous serial killer has escaped Azkaban prison and is stalking him. Azkaban guards called Dementors are subsequently stationed around the school to protect the students. Harry is violently affected by their presence; they seem to suck the life out of him, causing him to pass out. And on top of all this, he repeatedly sees a death omen called the Grim.

In this third novel in the Harry Potter series, Harry must come to terms with the longing and depression he feels whenever he thinks of his dead parents. After discovering that his father's best friend betrayed his dad to Lord Voldemort, he is obsessed with thoughts of revenge. In coming to terms with his father's murder, Harry is supported by a number of reassuring paternal figures in the novel: Professor Lupine, Professor Dumbledore, and the mysterious Sirius Black. Winner of the Bram Stoker Award for Best Work for Young Readers and the Whitbread Book of the Year, *Harry Potter and the Prisoner of Azkaban* will appeal to children who are suffering from depression, anger, or the loss of a loved one. This character-driven novel will also appeal to readers who like fast-paced, suspenseful plots.

**For those also seeking**: connection with others/awareness of not being alone
**For those drawn to**: character, story
**Themes/subjects**: wizards, school, friendship, magical transformations, omens/prophecies, revenge, betrayal, depression, grief, death, imprisonment/entrapment, prison/incarceration, orphans, obsessions, sports, mysteries
**Reading interest level**: grade 4 and up
**Curricular tie-ins**: Ask students to research prison conditions in their country and create a podcast from the point of view of the inmates.
**Adaptations & alternative formats**: Warner Bros. movie directed by Alfonso Cuarón (2004); audiobook read by Jim Dale (2000); enhanced animation e-book edition through iBooks (2015)
**Translations**: Spanish: *Harry Potter y el Prisionero de Azkaban*; French: *Harry Potter et le Prisonnier D'Azkaban*
**Read-alikes**: In Ursula K. Le Guin's *A Wizard of Earthsea*, the wizard, Ged, is also stalked throughout the novel by an evil force. The main characters in Garth Nix's *Sabriel* and Marjorie Kinnan Rawlings's *The Yearling* must come to terms with the death of a parent.

**Rowling, J. K.** (1965–)
**Harry Potter and the Goblet of Fire** (2000). New York: Arthur A. Levine Books, 2000. 734pp. 978-0439139595.

At the end of the Quidditch World Cup, the Dark Mark (the symbol of Lord Voldemort) terrifies everyone by appearing in the sky. Ministry of Magic

*Fantasy Series* 245

officials suspect Harry Potter of creating the spell since his wand produced it. Back at Hogwarts, Harry is also suspected of illegally applying to the Triwizard Tournament, a dangerous competition only open to older students. When he is chosen to compete, Professor Dumbledore believes that someone is trying to harm, even kill him. Thirteen-year-old Harry must compete with two 17-year-olds in a series of three tasks, each of which is more hazardous than the previous one. Harry discovers that he cannot trust those whom he thought were trustworthy and that there is a deadly plot lurking in wait for him.

Midbook and narrative turning point of the series, *Harry Potter and the Goblet of Fire* depicts the rebirth of Lord Voldemort, a pivotal event foreshadowed by phoenix imagery throughout the earlier books. The intricately designed, pulse-pounding plot and continued strong characterization combine to produce a compelling novel. Harry's story will particularly resonate with readers who have been falsely judged or unfairly treated. *Harry Potter and the Goblet of Fire* was shortlisted for the prestigious Hugo Award for best fantasy novel of the year.

**For those also seeking**: connection with others/awareness of not being alone
**For those drawn to**: character, story
**Themes/subjects**: wizards, school, friendship, magical transformations, spells/curses, rebirth, justice and injustice, wrongfully accused, competition, clues/riddles, mazes/labyrinths, sportsmanship, sports, mysteries
**Reading interest level**: grade 4 and up
**Curricular tie-ins**: Ask students to create a commercial advertising either the Quidditch World Cup or the Triwizard Tournament.
**Adaptations & alternative formats**: Warner Bros. movie directed by Mike Newell (2005); audiobook read by Jim Dale (2000); enhanced animation e-book edition through iBooks (2015)
**Translations**: Spanish: *Harry Potter y el Cáliz de Fuego*; French: *Harry Potter et la Coupe de feu*
**Read-alikes**: Lyra Belacqua and Will Parry also face life-threatening dangers in Philip Pullman's *His Subtle Knife* and *The Amber Spyglass*. The fate of the world rests on the actions of these characters.

**Rowling, J. K.** (1965–)
**Harry Potter and the Order of the Phoenix** (2003). New York: Arthur A. Levine Books, 2004. 870pp. 978-0439358071.

During the summer holidays, Harry and his cousin, Dudley, are attacked by a pair of terrifying creatures called Dementors. Harry saves Dudley's life as well as his own by using the Patronus charm, an action that is declared illegal by the Ministry of Magic. Back at school, Harry is mocked by his classmates, maligned by the media, vilified by the Ministry of Magic, and abused by the new Defense against the Dark Arts teacher, Dolores Umbridge. Almost no one believes that Harry saw Lord Voldemort, or that the Dark Lord is back in power. Moreover, Harry's terrifying nightmares about long corridors, locked doors, and a secret weapon hint at a mysterious connection with the Dark Lord.

The injustice that Harry has faced throughout the series reaches new heights in this novel, and the villains that he has encountered have become more heinous, cunning, and guileful. Dolores Umbridge, a tour de force of characterization, shares the spotlight with Lord Voldemort as a vile, malicious villain. Evil to the core but appearing docile and mild-mannered, Umbridge is cruel and sadistic to Harry. Cut off from almost all support and increasingly isolated, he faces his greatest challenges yet, experiences that prepare him for an almost unbearable loss at the end of the novel.

At the mercy of a myriad of forces beyond his control, Harry refuses to be victimized, taking back agency by creating a secret society. The novel will strike a chord with readers who are bitter or angry or those who face injustice or the loss of a loved one. Unrelenting suspense, complex psychological portraits, and mesmerizing magical settings are strong appeals in the novel. *Harry Potter and the Order of the Phoenix* won the Bram Stoker Award for superior achievement in dark fantasy and horror writing.

**For those also seeking**: connection with others/awareness of not being alone
**For those drawn to**: character, setting
**Themes/subjects**: wizards, school, friendship, spells/curses, death, bullying, justice and injustice, wrongfully accused, survival, gossip, omens/prophecies, dreams, sports, mysteries
**Reading interest level**: grade 4 and up
**Curricular tie-ins**: Ask students to research a secret society and compare it to one of the secret societies in the novel. They could also create a pamphlet on one of these fictional societies in the novel or on an actual society.
**Adaptations & alternative formats**: Warner Bros. movie directed by David Yates (2007); audiobook read by Jim Dale (2012); enhanced animation e-book edition through iBooks (2015)

**Translations**: Spanish: *Harry Potter y la Orden del Fénix*; French: *Harry Potter et l'Ordre du Phénix*

**Read-alikes**: Readers who enjoy novels about secret societies will also like Trenton Lee Stewart's *The Mysterious Benedict Society*, *The Mysterious Benedict Society and the Perilous Journey*, and *The Mysterious Benedict Society and the Prisoner's Dilemma*. The notorious secret society, the Ku Klux Klan, dominates the action in Sharon M. Draper's *Stella by Starlight*.

**Rowling, J. K.** (1965–)
**Harry Potter and the Half-Blood Prince** (2005). New York: Arthur A. Levine Books, 2005. 652pp. 978-0439785969.

A darker book than its five predecessors, *Harry Potter and the Half-Blood Prince* begins with the prime minister of England trying to make sense of a series of unexplained disasters. Although stringent safety precautions are adopted at Hogwarts School of Witchcraft and Wizardry as a result of Lord Voldemort's rise to power, one student is poisoned and another almost dies after receiving a package that is cursed. Meanwhile, discovering an old textbook signed by someone called the Half-Blood Prince, Harry starts using the handwritten spells—an activity that his friend Hermione considers dangerous and dishonest. Increasingly Harry becomes obsessed with the behavior of his classmate, Draco Malfoy, warning everyone that he is planning something treacherous. No one believes Harry. This suspense-filled story is fast-paced and expertly plotted.

Harry's hatred for both Draco Malfoy and Professor Snape becomes so intense that it threatens to overtake his better impulses. Harry admits to "a most agreeable feeling of power" over Malfoy when he catches him doing something wrong. Harry is so preoccupied with Draco's activity that he virtually ignores an essential task that Professor Dumbledore assigns him. Harry even uses a dangerous spell from the Half-Blood Prince's book to try and kill Draco. Projecting his darker impulses on to Draco and Professor Snape, Harry fights temptations from both within and without.

Harry's story will resonate with readers who feel intense hatred for another person or are obsessed with any powerful emotion. The novel will also appeal to anyone suffering the loss of a loved one. In this penultimate novel in the series, Rowling also plumbs the dark recesses of the depraved psyche through her astute portrayals of Lord Voldemort and Draco Malfoy.

**For those also seeking**: connection with others/awareness of not being alone

**For those drawn to**: character, story

**Themes/subjects**: wizards, hatred, obsessions, school, spells/curses, death, immortality, clues/riddles, survival, omens/prophecies, projection (psychology), romance, friendship, sports, mysteries

**Reading interest level**: grade 4 and up

**Curricular tie-ins**: Both Harry and Voldemort grow up as orphans, raised by people who do not love or trust them. In a think-pair-square activity, students can discuss why they think one character becomes a hero and the other a villain.

**Adaptations & alternative formats**: Warner Bros. movie directed by David Yates (2009); audiobook read by Jim Dale (2012); enhanced animation e-book edition through iBooks (2015)

**Translations**: Spanish: *Harry Potter y el Misterio del Príncipe*; French: *Harry Potter et le Prince de Sang-Mêlé*

**Read-alikes**: Characters in Ursula K. Le Guin's *The Farthest Shore* and Garth Nix's *Abhorsen* must also prevent a villain from destroying the world.

**Rowling, J. K.** (1965–)
**Harry Potter and the Deathly Hallows** (2007). New York: Arthur A. Levine Books, 2009. 659pp. 978-0545139700.

As one parental figure after another has now died and left Harry alone to face the evil wizard Voldemort, the boy is overwhelmed, pushed beyond the limits of endurance: "There was no map, no plan. Dumbledore had left [him] . . . to grope in the darkness, to wrestle with unknown and undreamed of terrors alone and unaided: nothing was explained, nothing was freely given." Harry must confront not only the terrifying Death Eaters but also the loss of friendship with Ron, the false suspicions of his supporters, and his own doubts about Dumbledore's integrity. Harry's task is to find and destroy the Horcruxes that contain Voldemort's soul—a task that is a prelude to his final charge: to kill Voldemort himself. As the prophecy states: "Neither can live while the other survives."

In no other novel has Harry felt so lost, so deceived by others, and so alone as he does in this seventh and final book in the series. He questions Professor Dumbledore's affection for him and feels betrayed by the man whom he viewed as a wise father figure. Readers who feel isolated, unsupported, or angry about life's unfairness will see themselves in

Harry's predicament. The mysterious connection between Harry and Voldemort strengthens in this final novel, a connection that adds an intriguing psychological dimension to both the novel and the series.

All strands of the plot are tied together, all mysteries solved, and all secrets revealed in this grand culmination.

**For those also seeking**: connection with others/awareness of not being alone
**For those drawn to**: character
**Themes/subjects**: wizards, death, immortality, quests, wizards, good and evil, friendship, sacrifice, secrets, clues/riddles, spells/curses, survival, omens/prophecies, courage, ambition, quarrels/fights, heroism, invisibility cloaks and rings, knives/daggers/swords, sports, mysteries
**Reading interest level**: grade 4 and up
**Curricular tie-ins**: The three deathly hallows (the Elder Wand, the Resurrection Stone, and the Invisibility Cloak) play an important part in the book. In their reader response journals, students could discuss the object they would choose and the reasons they would choose it if they could only acquire one hallow.
**Adaptations & alternative formats**: Warner Bros. movie directed by David Yates (part 1, 2010; part 2, 2011); audiobook read by Jim Dale (2012); enhanced animation e-book edition through iBooks (2015)
**Translations**: Spanish: *Harry Potter y las Reliquias de la Muerte*; French: *Harry Potter et les Reliques de la Mort*
**Read-alikes**: In Lloyd Alexander's *The High King* and J. R. R. Tolkien's *The Lord of the Rings*, the protagonist must also save the world from an evil dictator who plans to take over the realm.

## Connection with Others/Awareness of Not Being Alone

**Baum, L. Frank** (1856–1919)
**The Marvelous Land of Oz** (1904). Illustrated by John R. Neill. New York: Books of Wonder, 1985. 291pp. 978-0688054397. PD.

After a boy named Tip creates a wooden creature with a pumpkin head and brings it to life, the pair runs away from Tip's guardian, the evil sorceress Mombi. When they arrive at the Emerald City, they learn that an all-female army has invaded the area. The army's goal is to overthrow the ruler, the well-loved Scarecrow. Tip, Jack Pumpkinhead, the Scarecrow, the Tin Woodman, a live Saw-Horse, and a human-sized Woggle-Bug participate in a series of dangerous adventures as they attempt to restore the Scarecrow to the throne. *The Marvelous Land of Oz* is a book of magical transformations, perilous journeys, and secrets that emerge from the past.

The most popular sequel in the Oz series, *The Marvelous Land of Oz* is the story about the education of a ruler, a story that will inspire children who want to be leaders. It is also a novel about friendship, the value of riches, and the importance of all people, no matter how different or unique. As the Scarecrow observes, "I am convinced that the only people worthy of consideration in this world are the unusual ones. For the common folks are like the leaves of a tree, and live and die unnoticed." Readers who lack confidence because they are different than others will not feel so isolated after reading the novel. The book will also appeal to those who love dazzling fantasy settings and surprise endings.

**For those also seeking**: models for identity
**For those drawn to**: setting, character
**Themes/subjects**: being different, inclusiveness, tolerance, leadership, spells/curses, secrets, princesses, wealth, feminism, friendship, empathy, intelligence, journeys, battle/wars, magical transformations
**Reading interest level**: grades 3–8
**Curricular tie-ins**: To celebrate Halloween, ask students to create and decorate their own Jack Pumpkinhead figure by joining two miniature pumpkins together to form a body and head.
**Adaptations & alternative formats**: audiobook read by Tara Sands (2013); graphic novel by Eric Shanower (2010)
**Translations**: Spanish: *La Maravillosa Tierra de Oz*; French: *Le Merveilleux Pays d'Oz*
**Read-alikes**: The five books in Lloyd Alexander's The Chronicles of Prydain (*The Book of Three, The Black Cauldron, The Castle of Llyr, Taran Wanderer*, and *The High King*) are also about the growth and education of a leader.

**Baum, L. Frank** (1856–1919)
**Ozma of Oz** (1907). Illustrated by John R. Neill. New York: Books of Wonder, 1989. 272pp. 978-0688066321. PD.

Thrown overboard in a storm while on her way to Australia, Dorothy lands in the magical world of Ev, a neighboring realm to Oz. Captured first by creatures with wheels for hands and feet and then by a princess who wears a different head each day, Dorothy is subsequently rescued by her Oz friends. Dorothy, Ozma, The Tin Woodman, the Scarecrow, and a host of Oz inhabitants then travel to the Nome's underground realm to free the trapped Queen of Ev and her children. The rescuers are forced to play a deadly game of survival in order to save the prisoners. A sense of unease permeates the story since characters and situations are not what they seem.

The enchanting fairyland of Ev and the mysterious Nome underworld are remarkable landscapes that capture the reader's imagination. Like Oz, Ev is filled with odd, unique creatures that remain memorable long after readers finish the novel. Ozma, the child ruler of Oz; Tik-Tok, the copper wind-up creature; and Billina, the talking hen make their entrance in this third book in the series. After reading the novel, children who feel unusual or atypical will realize that the world is made up of many different individuals.

Inanimate objects that exhibit human qualities and characters who are transformed into objects populate this singular world, prompting readers to question what it is that distinguishes human beings from the rest of creation. Readers who delight in imaginative lands and people will love this fantasy novel. The brave actions of the main characters will inspire young readers to be courageous.

**For those also seeking**: models for identity
**For those drawn to**: setting, character
**Themes/subjects**: appearance versus reality, spells/curses, survival, imprisonment/entrapment, underground, castles, royalty, kings/queens, courage, self-centeredness, clockwork and mechanical figures, magical transformations, deserts, mines/mining, gnomes, games
**Reading interest level**: grades 3–8
**Curricular tie-ins**: This novel would work well as an accompanying text to a social studies lesson about an oppressive ruler. Ask students to find information about a former head of state who persecuted his or her people. They could create an encyclopedic article about this person.
**Adaptations & alternative formats**: audiobook read by Erin Yuen (2014); graphic novel by Eric Shanower (2012)
**Translations**: Spanish: *Ozma de Oz* French: *Ozma, la Princesse d'Oz*
**Read-alikes**: The underground is also a major setting in L. Frank Baum's *Dorothy and the Wizard of Oz*, Jules Verne's *Journey to the Center of the Earth*, and Jeanne DuPrau's *The City of Ember*. Peter Brown's *The Wild Robot* also explores the differences between humans and nonhumans.

**Baum, L. Frank** (1856–1919)
**Dorothy and the Wizard in Oz** (1908). Illustrated by John R. Neill. New York: Books of Wonder, 1990. 262pp. 978-0688098261. PD.

A San Francisco earthquake creates a large fissure in the earth, one into which a horse-drawn buggy carrying Dorothy, her cat, Eureka, and the farm boy, Zeb, plunge. After a long nightmarish fall, they land in a glass city inhabited by people who grow on plants and are picked off when ripe. Lit by six globes in the sky, this Land of the Mangaboos is brilliantly illuminated with continuously changing colors. After the Wizard of Oz arrives, he, Dorothy, Zeb, and their talking animals encounter a series of dangers as they try to return home. They meet invisible people in the Valley of Voe, a man who manufactures holes on the Pyramid Mountain, wooden Gargoyle people in a landscape made entirely of wood, and dragonettes in a hidden cave.

As the nightmarish underside of Oz's fairy-tale countries, the underground places that Dorothy visits are a counterpoint to the utopian world of Oz. The people in each of the subterranean places lack something: the Glass City, empathy; the Valley of Voe, visibility; the home of the Braided Man, substance; the Land of Naught, sound; the Wooden City, love. By juxtaposing underground and above-ground worlds, Baum highlights Oz's distinguishing features.

One of the darker novels in the series, *Dorothy and the Wizard in Oz* will appeal to those interested in strange worlds, one-of-a-kind characters, and peril-filled adventures. The large variety of one-of-a-kind characters in the novel will reassure readers who feel different than others that they are not alone and that there is a place for them in the world.

**For those also seeking**: acceptance
**For those drawn to**: setting, character
**Themes/subjects**: courage, survival, underground, appearance versus reality, journeys, natural disasters, earthquakes/volcanoes, wizards
**Reading interest level**: grades 3–8
**Curricular tie-ins**: During an earthquake, Dorothy falls into a fissure in the earth. Ask students to create a poster about earthquakes.
**Adaptations & alternative formats**: audiobook read by John McDonough (2013); graphic novel by Eric Shanower (2012)
**Translations**: Spanish: *Dorothy y el Mago en Oz*

**Read-alikes**: The underground in Lewis Carroll's *Alice's Adventures in Wonderland* is also depicted as the nightmarish underside of the world above. Readers who like underground settings will also enjoy Jeanne DuPrau's *The City of Ember* and Jules Verne's *Journey to the Centre of the Earth*.

**Baum, L. Frank** (1856–1919)
**The Emerald City of Oz** (1910). Illustrated by John R. Neill. New York: Books of Wonder, 1993. 300pp. 978-0688115586. PD.

Initially intended to be the finale of the series, *The Emerald City of Oz* is one of Baum's most exciting stories. The evil Nome King builds a secret underground tunnel to the Emerald City so that his armies can invade Oz in a surprise attack. Back in Kansas, Dorothy learns that Uncle Henry must give up the farm since he cannot meet the mortgage payments. She asks Princess Ozma if she can bring her uncle and aunt to Oz so that the three of them can live there permanently. Ozma grants Dorothy's wish and finds rooms in the palace for all of them. Baum alternates the Nome King's underground exploits with Dorothy's above-ground adventures. Dorothy, her parents, the Wizard of Oz, and some friends travel around the kingdom and visit a number of unusual, one-of-a-kind communities.

Juxtaposed chapters highlight polar opposites such as utopian/tyrannical kingdoms, caring/cruel rulers, and ferocious/fragile communities. Fantasy readers will be spellbound by the magnificence, variety, and uniqueness of the Land of Oz in this novel. A host of child-centered creatures such as the paper-cut Cuttenclip dolls, the puzzle-pieced Fuddles people, and the high-society Bunnybury animals offset the brutal Whimsies with paste-board heads, the giant-sized, elongated Growleywogs, and the all-powerful, bear-like Phanfasms. Although it is clear who the good characters are, there is great variety within this group. This novel will appeal to readers who wish they were more conventional and conformist, making them feel less isolated in their uniqueness.

**For those also seeking**: acceptance
**For those drawn to**: setting, story
**Themes/subjects**: being different, inclusiveness, tolerance, battles/wars, journeys, leadership, underground, mines/mining, gnomes, good and evil, utopian places

**Reading interest level**: grades 3–8
**Curricular tie-ins**: Ask students to create a travel brochure of the Emerald City.
**Adaptations & alternative formats**: movie directed by Tim Reid (1987); audiobook read by Ron Knowles (2010); graphic novel by Eric Shanower (2014).
**Read-alikes**: Nefarious creatures also dig a tunnel to a castle in order to overtake it in George MacDonald's *The Princess and the Goblin*. Readers who enjoy utopian settings such as the Emerald City will like the island of Krakatoa in William Pène du Bois's *The Twenty-One Balloons*.

**Baum, L. Frank** (1856–1919)
**Tik-Tok of Oz** (1914). Illustrated by John R. Neill. New York: Dover, 1994. 271pp. 978-0486280028. PD.

When Queen Ann Soforth leaves her small kingdom of Oogaboo to conquer the world, she recruits 17 citizens—16 of them as generals. After finding the clockwork man named Tik-Tok at the bottom of a dry well, Queen Ann rescues him and asks the humble creature to join them as the army's only soldier. The army then runs into Shaggy Man, a shipwrecked girl named Betsy Bobbin, and her talking mule, Hank. The two groups join forces in order to find Shaggy Man's missing brother, a man believed to be imprisoned in the fearsome underground caverns of the Metal Monarch. Along the way, the adventurers discover an enchanting fairyland of kings and queens, fall into a hollow tube that takes then to the center of the earth, and wander through a Metal Forest of gold trees, silver bushes, and diamond-strewn paths.

*Tik-Tok of Oz* will especially appeal to readers who feel inferior to others because they do not win awards or stand out as exceptional. After reading the novel, they may identify with Tik-Tok's character and not feel so solitary. The dependable but unpretentious Tik-Tok and Jinjin will help them view unassuming people as extraordinary and self-important people as arrogant.

**For those also seeking**: acceptance
**For those drawn to**: setting, character
**Themes/subjects**: being different, inclusiveness, clockwork and mechanical figures, journeys, vanity and pompousness, feminism, battle/wars,

underground, wealth, appearance versus reality, natural disasters, missing persons

**Reading interest level**: grades 3–8
**Curricular tie-ins**: Ask students to create a diorama of the Metal Forest.
**Adaptations & alternative formats**: audiobook read by Ron Knowles (2010)
**Read-alikes**: Russell Hoban's *The Mouse and his Child* is another fantasy novel about a clockwork figure who goes on a journey. Clockwork figures are also a key feature of Philip Pullman's *Clockwork*. Peter Brown's *The Wild Robot* is about the adventures of a mechanical figure.


**Baum, L. Frank** (1856–1919)
**The Scarecrow of Oz** (1915). Illustrated by John R. Neill. New York: Books of Wonder, 1997. 304pp. 978-0688147198. PD.

*The Scarecrow of Oz* begins as a story about survival in the worst circumstances. Swept into a whirlpool, Trot and the kindly old sailor, Cap'n Bill, find themselves in a frightening underground cavern. Faced with the choice of certain death or descent into a mysterious black hole, the pair chooses the terrifying unknown. As Trot and Cap'n Bill journey toward safety, they encounter a king who wants to destroy them, a lonely desert island with a single inhabitant, a witch who casts magical spells upon them, and a land that rains lemonade and snows popcorn.

One of the most engaging books in the Oz series, *The Scarecrow of Oz* contains spunky, likable characters such as the Bumpy Man and the Ork. The Bumpy Man's continual food-related exclamations ("fruit-cake and applesauce!") endear him to readers. His way of viewing the many bumps on his body as a gift from the fairies—a gift that makes him look rugged like the mountains—is an inspiring example for readers who are unhappy about their appearance.

Children facing challenges in their lives will be encouraged by the resilience and positive attitude of the main characters. Trot, Cap'n Bill, the Bumpy Man, and the Ork all look on the bright side of bleak situations. Polar opposites of the old man on the desert island—a character who is negative and pessimistic about everything—Trot and her friends are stirring role models. Children who feel daunted by problems will feel a sense of kinship with protagonists who face challenges that seem overwhelming.

**For those also seeking**: models for identity
**For those drawn to**: setting, story
**Themes/subjects**: being different, inclusiveness, sea voyage, journeys, friendship, resilience, optimism, courage, natural disasters
**Reading interest level**: grades 3–8
**Curricular tie-ins**: Ask students to create a dust jacket for the book with a summary of the story on the inside flap.
**Adaptations & alternative formats**: audiobook read by Ron Knowles (2011)
**Read-alikes**: Rousing sea adventures also dominate Avi's *The True Confessions of Charlotte Doyle* and Arthur Ransome's *We Didn't Mean to Go to Sea*.

**Baum, L. Frank** (1856–1919)
**The Lost Princess of Oz** (1917). Illustrated by John R. Neill. New York: Dover, 2015. 144pp. 978-1511774383. PD.

The grand ruler of Oz—Princess Ozma—suddenly disappears from her castle in the Emerald City. Ozma's Magic Picture, Glinda's Book of Records, and the Wizard's magical instruments also go missing. Glinda organizes four search parties, each one responsible for investigating a quadrant of Oz. Dorothy and her friends travel through the dangerous Winkie lands, overcoming barriers such as whirling Merry-Go-Round Mountains, a mysterious city on shifting lands, and a room that turns upside down in a wicker castle. Familiar characters meet new ones: the life-size Frogman; the magical, wind-up Pink Bear; and Cakye, the Cookie Cook. The fast-paced, suspenseful plot and enchanting fantasy lands are strong appeals in this novel.

Frogman swims in the Truth Pond and is forever changed by the experience. Before characters can succeed in their quests, they must first distinguish between truth and deception, reality and illusion. The dangers they face on their journey teach them how to recognize truth and not be deceived by appearances. Readers who find it difficult to look beyond surfaces will identify with the characters in this book. Those who feel as if they are the only ones deceived by people who appear admirable but are not may take comfort in the fact that they are not alone.

**For those also seeking**: acceptance
**For those drawn to**: setting, story

**Themes/subjects**: appearance versus reality, journeys, kidnapping, missing persons, truth, being different, inclusiveness, courage, vanity and pompousness, cooperation and teamwork, princesses
**Reading interest level**: grades 3–8
**Curricular tie-ins**: Ask students to paint a picture or create a diorama of the Merry-Go-Round Mountains.
**Adaptations & alternative formats**: audiobook read by Caitlin Davies (2010)
**Read-alikes**: The protagonist in H. Rider Haggard's *King Solomon's Mines* also searches strange lands for a missing brother. The setting in Diana Wynne Jones's *Howl's Moving Castle* is similarly shifting and unstable.

**Baum, L. Frank** (1856–1919)
**The Tin Woodman of Oz** (1918). Illustrated by John R. Neill. New York: Books of Wonder, 1999. 294pp. 978-0688149765. PD.

When Woot the Wanderer visits the Tin Woodman, he asks why he never sought his former sweetheart after he was restored to life. Taken aback, the Tin Woodman realizes that he should have looked for Nimmie and asked her to marry him. He invites Woot the Wanderer and the Scarecrow to travel with him to the Munchkin Country to look for Nimmie. On this dangerous journey across Oz, they meet puffed-up, balloon-like creatures called Loons, visit a giantess who transforms them into different creatures, and travel across an invisible country. Upon arriving at Nimmie's house, the Tin Woodman is surprised at what he finds.

When the Tin Woodman finds his former head in a cupboard, he says to it, "If you are Nick Chopper's Head, then you are Me—or I'm You—or—or—" And when he meets other mirror images of himself such as the Tin Soldier and Chopfyt, the Tin Woodman explores his identity and gains self-knowledge. *The Tin Woodman of Oz* is a character-driven novel that will appeal to readers who feel unsure about their identity. Readers will not feel as isolated in their self-doubts after reading about and identifying with the Tin Woodman. They may experience a sense of relief in realizing that others feel as they do.

Readers who also worry that they are different from their peers will realize that being unique is a strength, not a weakness. As the Scarecrow maintains, "To be like other persons is small credit to one, while to be unlike others is a mark of distinction."

**For those also seeking**: acceptance
**For those drawn to**: character, setting
**Themes/subjects**: journeys, being different, inclusiveness, self-knowledge, identity, giants, magical transformations
**Reading interest level**: grades 3–8
**Curricular tie-ins**: The Tin Woodman goes on a long journey in search of something and does not succeed. Ask students to create the script for a TED talk on how to handle situations in which one does not succeed.
**Adaptations & alternative formats**: audiobook read by Karen White (2013)
**Read-alikes**: Magical transformations and deceptive enchantresses or witches also play an important role in C. S. Lewis's *The Silver Chair* and Diana Wynne Jones's *Charmed Life*.


**Baum, L. Frank** (1856–1919)
**The Magic of Oz** (1919). Illustrated by John R. Neill. New York: Dover, 1998. 288pp. 978-0486400198. PD.

A reckless magician's son named Kiki Aru joins forces with Ruggedo, the former king of the underground Nomes. Their plan is to attack the Emerald City and take over Oz by enlisting an army of wild beasts from the Forest of Gugu. At the same time, Princess Ozma's friends are planning a celebration in honor of their ruler's birthday. Dorothy and the Wizard travel to the Forest of Gugu to borrow a dozen monkeys whom the Wizard will enchant as a surprise gift for Ozma. But when they stumble upon Kiki and Ruggedo, they risk losing their lives.

While these events occur, a third set of characters undertake their own perilous quest. Trot, Cap'n Bill, and the Glass Cat travel to the Isle of the Magic Flower—a secluded island in a northern forest—in search of a magical plant that continuously changes flowers. They believe that it will be a perfect birthday gift for Princess Ozma. But Trot and Cap'n Bill become trapped on the island when their feet grow roots that fasten them to the ground. As the separate plots converge, dangers multiply and suspense increases.

Magical transformations dominate this penultimate novel in the series. Readers who enjoy fairy tales will find this wonder-filled novel simply enchanting. The novel will appeal to children who think they do not conform to conventional standards. They will discover that no character is usual in this novel; each one is unique and therefore special in some way.

**For those also seeking**: acceptance
**For those drawn to**: setting, story
**Themes/subjects**: journeys, being different, inclusiveness, tolerance, spells/curses, magical transformations, imprisonment/entrapment, islands
**Reading interest level**: grades 3–8
**Curricular tie-ins**: Ask students to list five gifts that Ozma would like for her birthday. They should include reasons for their decisions.
**Adaptations & alternative formats**: audiobook read by Johnny Heller (2013)
**Translations**: Spanish: *El Mago de Oz*
**Read-alikes**: Gail Carson Levine's six Princess Tales (*The Fairy's Mistake, The Princess Test, Princess Sonora and the Long Sleep, Cinderellis and the Glass Hill, For Biddle's Sake, The Fairy's Return*) also depict enchanting fairy-tale worlds.


**Jones, Diana Wynne** (1934–2011)
**House of Many Ways** (2008). New York: HarperCollins, 2008. 404pp. 978-0061477973.

Charmain, whose single passion is to read, is told she must look after an old wizard's house while he undergoes treatment for an illness. Although she grumbles about it, Charmain is secretly delighted for the opportunity to get away from her parents. Spoiled and overprotected by them, Charmain is, however, unprepared to perform even the simplest household tasks in the wizard's house. She is also unable to use magic to accomplish anything since she has never studied her. Consequently, when Charmain arrives at the wizard's magical house, she is forced to learn a host of new skills.

The house of many ways that she visits is one of the most peculiar buildings in children's literature. This curious building is far larger in the inside than it is on the outside. It also contains rooms that can only be visited by knowing about the magical entrances to them.

Charmain's character is a strong appeal in the novel. Sheltered by her parents, she has had little experience in dealing with challenges. Doing as she pleases, Charmain has spent all her time reading books rather than engaging with life. In addition, she has a poor opinion of herself and wonders why her parents like her. Readers who feel overprotected by adults or suffer from lack of confidence will realize that others have faced the same challenges. Once Charmain is freed from her overprotective environment, she learns to survive and even thrive.

**For those also seeking**: reassurance/comfort/confirmation of self-worth/strength
**For those drawn to**: setting, character
**Themes/subjects**: self-confidence, overprotective parents, spoiled children, castles, wizards, witches, only children, libraries/librarians, stories and storytelling, flying magically, magical transformations
**Reading interest level**: grade 6 and up
**Curricular tie-ins**: Charmain loves books. Ask students to choose three books she might be interested in and give reasons for these choices. In their reader response journals, students could also identify their own favorite books and the reasons they like them.
**Adaptations & alternative formats**: audiobook read by Jenny Sterlin (2009)
**Translations**: Spanish: *La Casa de los Mil Pasillos*
**Read-alikes**: The protagonist in Garth Nix's *Lirael* also loves books and works in a library. Both characters have little self-confidence in the beginning of the novels. Stallery Mansion in Diana Wynne Jones's *Conrad's Fate*, like the mysterious house of many ways, is strange, unusual, and unstable.

**Norton, Mary** (1903–1992)
**The Borrowers** (1952). Orlando, FL: Harcourt, 1998. 180pp. 978-0152047375.

Thirteen-year-old Arrietty Clock and her parents are "borrowers," miniature characters who borrow food and objects from nearby human beings. Living below the floorboards of an English country house, the Clock family's primary concern is to remain hidden from the people who live upstairs. Despite her parents' efforts to keep her protected in their own space, Arrietty longs for freedom and the outdoors. Because Homily worries excessively about her daughter's safety, she and Arrietty are in constant conflict. When Homily finally relents and lets her daughter go outside with her father, Arrietty is spied by the 10-year-old boy who lives in the house, an event that puts the entire family in danger.

Winner of the Carnegie Medal, *The Borrowers* is an ingenious and engaging story of a girl who longs for freedom. Readers who wish for independence from controlling or overprotective parents will see themselves in Arrietty's plight and feel reassured that they are not alone in their struggles. Norton's depiction of Arietty's parents, especially her mother and her pretensions to gentility, is both humorous and psychologically astute.

The portrayal of the miniature world is richly detailed and highly original. The Clock house includes furnishings such as stamps used as portraits of royalty, blotting paper used as carpets, and a chess piece used as a statue of a knight. Even though the Clocks have perfectly adapted to the world of humans, readers wonder how the Clocks will continue to survive, especially as their race dwindles.

**For those also seeking**: reassurance/comfort/confirmation of self-worth/strength
**For those drawn to**: character, setting
**Themes/subjects**: miniature beings, imprisonment/entrapment, oppressive environments, overprotective parents, family conflict, only children, parental disapproval, independence, freedom, class differences, greed, stories and storytelling, humor
**Reading interest level**: grades 4–8
**Curricular tie-ins**: As a worksheet activity, students can choose three borrower characters or borrower families and discuss why their names are fitting.
**Adaptations & alternative formats**: movie directed by Tom Harper (2011); audiobook read by Rowena Cooper (2001)
**Translations**: Spanish: *Los Incursores*; French: *Les Chapardeurs*
**Read-alikes**: Readers who enjoy stories about miniature characters will also like E. B. White's *Stuart Little*, Terry Pratchett's *The Carpet People*, and his Nome trilogy (*Truckers*, *Diggers*, and *Wings*). Like the Clock family, the dolls in Sylvia Waugh's *The Mennymns* try to hide from human beings and exist in their world.

## Courage to Make a Change

**Baum, L. Frank** (1856–1919)
**The Patchwork Girl of Oz** (1913). Illustrated by John R. Neill. New York: Dover, 1990. 336pp. 978-0486265148. PD.

Ojo the Unlucky undertakes a quest in search of five ingredients that will restore his uncle from marble to human form. Just as importantly, he seeks self-knowledge and self-confidence. A magician's wife tells Ojo, "If, during your travels, you can manage to lose that 'Un' at the beginning of your name 'Unlucky,' you will then become Ojo the Lucky." Traveling with a life-size patchwork doll, a glass cat with a ruby heart and emerald eyes, and a creature with a perfectly square head, Ojo faces a series of dangers as he tries to find the lifesaving ingredients for his uncle. Familiar characters such as Dorothy and Shaggy Man from the previous books join Ojo along the way.

Young readers who face roadblocks in life or lack confidence in their abilities will find inspiration in Ojo's journey. He is prevented from moving ahead by trick roads, magical rivers, and optical illusions. When his path is blocked by a high wall with a padlocked gate, the Shaggy Man tells Ojo to shut his eyes and keep walking. The obstacle, he observes, "is quite real while you have your eyes open, but if you are not looking at it the barrier doesn't exist at all. It's the same way with many other evils in life." Ojo does not find it easy to change from "Ojo the Unlucky" to "Ojo the Lucky," but his story will encourage readers who have self-defeating tendencies that they can follow his example.

The many magical and mysterious lands in *The Patchwork Girl of Oz* will captivate Oz fans. Even though financial pressures and public demand forced Baum to continue writing the Oz series, this seventh novel is one of Baum's most imaginative and engaging books.

**For those also seeking**: reassurance/comfort/confirmation of self-worth/strength
**For those drawn to**: setting, character
**Themes/subjects**: being different, inclusiveness, tolerance, quests, self-confidence, self-knowledge, dolls, magical transformations, luck/chance, magic potions, magicians
**Reading interest level**: grades 3–8
**Curricular tie-ins**: Ask students to write a review of the novel in the style of a movie or book reviews. They should provide a star rating of the novel.
**Adaptations & alternative formats**: audiobook read by Ron Knowles (2010)
**Read-alikes**: Sid Fleischman's *The Midnight Horse* and Susan Patron's *The Higher Power of Lucky* are also stories about luck and chance.

## Acceptance

**Jones, Diana Wynne** (1934–2011)
*Witch Week* (1982). In The Chronicles of Chrestomanci, Volume 2: The Magicians of Caprona/Witch Week. New York: HarperTrophy, 2001. 548pp. 978-0064472692.

The teacher of class 2Y finds between two books a note with the message: "Someone in this class is a witch." Mr. Crossley knows that if he tells the headmistress about the note, inquisitors will be called to Larwood House to investigate. Although the government-run boarding school accepts witch-orphans, there are laws forbidding the use of witchcraft in this alternative world. Anyone identified as a practicing witch must be killed. As fear spreads and more notes appear, students become increasingly cruel and vindictive. What happens in Larwood House is rooted in historical precedent.

As readers identify with the students in Larwood House, they experience the prejudice, oppression, and injustice that historical personages identified as witches must have suffered. Jones is particularly skilled at depicting the destructive cliques and cruel bullying that develop in this threatening environment. She balances these harsh realities with light-hearted humor.

In this character-driven novel, Nan, Charles, and Brian discover and eventually accept their unique talents and powers. *Witch Week* will appeal to readers who feel different from their friends or family and will help them come to terms with their uniqueness. It will also resonate with those who feel left out of groups or bullied by schoolmates.

**For those also seeking**: disinterested understanding of the world
**For those drawn to**: character
**Themes/subjects**: witches, witch hunting, school, cliques (in school), bullying, oppressive environments, being different, identity formation, identity, anxiety/fears, orphans, justice and injustice, flying magically, multiple worlds/universes, teachers
**Reading interest level**: grades 5–8
**Curricular tie-ins**: *Witch Week* is an excellent novel to use in conjunction with a lesson on historical witch-hunts. Ask students to write an editorial about witch hunting for a seventeenth-century newspaper.

**Adaptations & alternative formats**: audiobook read by Gerard Doyle (2005)
**Translations**: Spanish: *Semana Bruja*; French: *La Chasse aux Sorciers*
**Read-alikes**: Hannah and Kit are accused of being witches in Elizabeth George Speare's historical novel, *The Witch of Blackbird Pond*. Phyllis Reynolds Naylor's The Witch Saga contains six entertaining books about witches: *Witch's Sister*, *Witch Water*, *The Witch Herself*, *The Witch's Eye*, *Witch Weed*, and *The Witch Returns*.

**Jones, Diana Wynne** (1934–2011)
**The Lives of Christopher Chant** (1988). In The Chronicles of Chrestomanci, Volume 1: Charmed Life/The Lives of Christopher Chant. New York: HarperTrophy, 2001. 608pp. 978-0064472685.

The son of wealthy parents who are too busy to spend time with him, Christopher Chant routinely dreams about The Place Between, a region that leads to a curious place called the Anywheres. Awakening from these strange dreams, Christopher finds objects that he somehow brought back with him from these dream worlds. When his uncle learns about Christopher's visits, he asks him to conduct experiments for him in the Anywheres. Christopher and a man named Tacroy meet in this dream world and transport parcels for his uncle every week. Christopher is eventually sent to Chrestomanci Castle to apprentice as the future Chrestomanci (a nine-lived enchanter). He continues his experiments for his uncle, despite the fact that he must hide them from everyone in the castle.

A prequel to *Charmed Life*, *The Lives of Christopher Chant* is the story of a boy who struggles with a role that he has no choice but to accept. Told that he will be the next Chrestomanci, Christopher is forced to give up his ambition to be a cricket player. He must also cope with parents who neglect him and other characters who exploit him. With little adult guidance, Christopher finds it difficult to distinguish evil characters from good ones. Seeing the adults in the novel through Christopher's eyes, the reader begins to realize that the boy's impressions are naïve and erroneous. Readers whose parents have little time for them or who feel used by the adults in their lives will be drawn to this novel. Those who struggle to accept situations over which they have little control will also find Christopher's story a source of guidance.

**For those also seeking**: connection with others/awareness of not being alone

**For those drawn to**: character, setting
**Themes/subjects**: betrayal, narcissistic parents, preoccupied parents, child neglect, multiple worlds/universes, portals/thresholds, castles, school, cats, appearance versus reality, agency and powerlessness, stealing, oppressive environments, gods, apprentices, tutors, wizards, deception
**Reading interest level**: grades 5–8
**Curricular tie-ins**: Christopher unwittingly aids a group of smugglers. Ask students to form small groups to find information about a historical smuggler or pirate. Each group can create a slide presentation of their findings.
**Adaptations & alternative formats**: audiobook read by Gerard Doyle (2006)
**Translations**: Spanish: *Las Vidas de Christopher Chant: La Infancia de Chrestomanci*; French: *Les Neuf Vies du Magicien*
**Read-alikes**: Adults do not recognize Nathaniel's magical abilities in Jonathan Stroud's *The Amulet of Samarkand*. Like Stroud's book and *The Lives of Christopher Chant*, J. K. Rowling's Harry Potter books are also about the education of a magical child. Characters in Philip Pullman's His Dark Materials also travel to parallel universes.


**Nix, Garth** (1963–)
**Sabriel** (1995). New York: HarperTrophy, 1996. 491pp. 978-0064471831.

In her last term at Wyverly College, a boarding school that is south of the Wall, 18-year-old Sabriel is visited by a spirit who hands over her father's sword and necromancer tools. Sabriel knows that the only reason these tools would be brought to her is that her father—the famous Abhorsen—is either dead or in grave danger. She leaves Ancelstierre at once, crossing over the Wall that divides the enchanted world from the ordinary one. Once she enters the primitive but magical Old Kingdom, she is attacked by creatures raised from the dead. Her father's job as the Abhorsen is to destroy such half-dead creatures by entering the realm of the dead and using his enchanted bells. Sabriel, who must now take over her father's role, feels unprepared for the dangers and responsibilities she will face.

Readers who cannot change the harsh circumstances of their lives will identify with Sabriel's tale. Confused and anxious about her future, she recalls the Old Kingdom saying, "Does the walker choose the path, or the path the walker?" This coming-of-age story is about crossing thresholds as well as accepting destiny. Daring adventures and a wondrous fantasy world are also strong appeal elements in the novel.

**For those also seeking**: models for identity
**For those drawn to**: character, setting
**Themes/subjects**: death, courage, coming of age, identity formation, portals/thresholds, destiny/fate, father-daughter relationships, self-reliance, romance, missing persons
**Reading interest level**: grade 6 and up
**Curricular tie-ins**: Ask students to create a coat of arms for the royal family or a royal banner for the Old Kingdom. They should explain their choice of image and motto on a separate page.
**Adaptations & alternative formats**: audiobook read by Tim Curry (2003)
**Translations**: Spanish: *Sabriel*; French: *Sabriël*
**Read-alikes**: Meggie in Cornelia Funke's *Inkheart* must also rescue her father. Coraline in Neil Gaiman's novel by the same name must find and rescue both her parents. In Karen Foxlee's *A Most Magical Girl*, Annabelle's life at an ordinary school does not prepare her for the dark forces she must battle in the magical world. In Philip Pullman's *The Ruby in the Smoke*, a daughter must undertake a dangerous mission in order to solve the mystery of her father's past.

**Nix, Garth** (1963–)
**Lirael: Daughter of the Clayr** (2001). New York: HarperTrophy, 2002. 705pp. 978-0060005429.

One of the oldest Clayr to have not yet developed "the Sight," 14-year-old Lirael longs with all her heart to receive this magical foretelling ability. Embarrassed to be a Clayr without the Sight, she asks to become a librarian so that she can hide from others in the Clayr's colossal underground library. Lirael manages to distract herself from her unhappiness by exploring its mysterious depths.

On her 19th birthday, Lirael travels miles below the Clayr's glacier into the library's deepest and most dangerous tunnels. She finds gifts that were prepared for her thousands of years earlier, a discovery that changes the course of her life. At the same time, Prince Sameth of the Old Kingdom almost dies at the hands of the necromancer Hedge, an event that leaves him fearful and traumatized. When Lirael meets Sameth in the boat "the Finder," they discover the interconnections between their lives.

This character-driven book will appeal to a wide variety of readers. Those who are shy around others, feel as if they do not belong, or are unsure about their abilities will relate to Lirael's tale. Sameth's story will appeal to readers who have experienced guilt, trauma, or intense fear. A richly inventive fantasy world of dazzling glaciers, perilous underground tunnels, and horror-filled death realms, *Lirael* is also an epic story with a compelling plot.

**For those also seeking**: connection with others/awareness of not being alone
**For those drawn to**: character, setting
**Themes/subjects**: death, shyness, courage, coming of age, identity formation, identity, trauma, anxiety/fears, phobias, guilt, self-blame (psychology), portals/thresholds, destiny/fate, glaciers, libraries/librarians, omens/prophecies, underground, princes, royalty, outcasts/misfits, conformity and nonconformity
**Reading interest level**: grade 6 and up
**Curricular tie-ins**: Ask students to research glaciers and write an article about them in the style of articles for *National Geographic*.
**Adaptations & alternative formats**: audiobook read by Tim Curry (2008)
**Translations**: Spanish: *Lirael La Guardiana De La Memoria*; French: *Liraël*
**Read-alikes**: Miri in Shannon Hale's *Princess Academy* also feels like an outcast in her community. Like Lirael, Aerin in Robin McKinley's *The Hero and the Crown* and Tilja in Peter Dickinson's *The Ropemaker* feel great anxiety about failing to develop a special gift that is expected of them.

**Nix, Garth** (1963–)
**Abhorsen** (2003). New York: HarperTrophy, 2003. 385pp. 978-0060278250.

South of the Wall in the nonmagical land of Ancelstierre, Sabriel and King Touchstone face a life-threatening situation when they are ambushed by an enemy. North of the Wall in magical territory, Lirael and Prince Sameth learn that someone is unearthing two ancient hemispheres that are buried deep underground. If the hemispheres unite, the consequences will be catastrophic—the end of all life in the kingdom. The only people who can save the world from impending annihilation are Lirael and Sameth.

This plot-driven novel is dominated by harrowing adventures that threaten the existence of the entire kingdom. In this epic struggle against the forces of destruction, Lirael and Sameth grow into roles that neither of them chose. Although Sameth is deeply afraid of the creatures he must face, and Lirael wishes she was back in the Clayr library, they accept their new responsibilities. This novel will appeal to readers who are fearful of the future or find it difficult to accept parts of their life that they cannot change. Since *Abhorsen* continues the narrative begun in *Lirael*, the two novels need to be read together.

**For those also seeking**: connection with others/awareness of not being alone
**For those drawn to**: story, character
**Themes/subjects**: death, courage, coming of age, portals/thresholds, shyness, destiny/fate, anxiety/fears
**Reading interest level**: grade 6 and up
**Curricular tie-ins**: This novel would work well as a springboard to a lesson on the atomic bomb that ended World War II. Students can debate whether the use of a bomb is ever justified.
**Adaptations & alternative formats**: audiobook read by Tim Curry (2008)
**Translations**: Spanish: *Abhorsen: La Novena Puerta*; French: *Abhorsen*
**Read-alikes**: Evil and destructive characters also threaten to overtake the world in Susan Cooper's The Dark Is Rising series (*Over Sea, Under Stone, The Dark Is Rising, Greenwitch, The Grey King, Silver on the Tree*).

**Pullman, Philip** (1946–)
**The Golden Compass** (1995). New York: Alfred A Knopf, 2015. 399pp. 978-1101934661.

Eavesdropping on a meeting of Oxford scholars, 12-year-old Lyra watches the Master of Jordan College attempt to poison her uncle. Although Lord Asriel is her guardian and uncle, he spends little time with her. Most of his life is devoted to secret explorations and affairs of political intrigue. After outwitting his poisoner, Lord Asriel returns to the far north and is captured by armored bears. Lyra worries not only about the safety of her uncle but also about her friend Tony who goes missing. Tony is one of a number of children who have mysteriously disappeared from Oxford and London. In the midst of these events, a beautiful woman named Mrs. Coulter dines with Lyra and the Oxford scholars. The Master of Jordan College tells Lyra that she must move in with Mrs. Coulter to finish her education. Initially mesmerized by this new guardian, Lyra overhears comments about her that cause her to panic.

Winner of the Carnegie Medal, the Guardian Award, and the Carnegie of Carnegies 70th Anniversary Award, *The Golden Compass* (U.K. title: *Northern Lights*) is a novel of high drama and exhilarating adventure. Lyra's journey to a mysterious experimental station in the wild lands of the north is one of survival in an inhospitable landscape. She learns to maneuver in a world of duplicity and deceit where many people are not what they seem. Forced to deal with the neglect and treachery of her parents, Lyra must accept circumstances that she cannot change. Her story will appeal to readers who have suffered neglect or have experienced betrayal by people they trust.

Although she grows up with little adult guidance, Lyra, like everyone else in this world, is paired with a daemon—an animal that represents her soul and accompanies her throughout life. This daemon is her lifelong guide and friend, a creature from which she can never be separated.

**For those also seeking**: awakening/new perspectives/enlargement of possibilities
**For those drawn to**: setting, story
**Themes/subjects**: omens/prophecies, betrayal, child neglect, authoritarian figures, ambition, multiple worlds/universes, father-daughter relationships, kidnapping, missing persons, deception, witches, winter, free will, imprisonment/entrapment, bears, class differences, political corruption, northern settings, poisoning
**Reading interest level**: grade 7 and up
**Curricular tie-ins**: Ask students to write a reflection in their reader response journals about the type of daemon that they would like to have and/or believe would suit them. Alternatively students could choose three adults in the novel and write about the appropriateness of their daemons to their characters.
**Adaptations & alternative formats**: movie directed by Chris Weitz (2007); audiobook read by the author and a full cast (2003); two-volume graphic novel by Stéphane Melchior-Durand (2015–2016)
**Translations**: Spanish: *La Brujula Dorada*; French: *Les Royaumes du Nord*
**Read-alikes**: Like Lyra, Nathaniel in Jonathan Stroud's Bartimaeus series (*The Amulet of Samarkand, The Golem's Eye, Ptolemy's Gate, The Ring of Solomon*) must learn to survive in a world of political intrigue. Serafina notices that children are disappearing and works to find them in Robert Beatty's *Serafina and the Black Cloak*.

**Pullman, Philip** (1946–)
**The Subtle Knife** (1997). New York: A. A. Knopf, 1997. 326pp. 978-0440418337.

Will's mother, a woman who suffers from mental illness, is repeatedly harassed by men who demand information about her missing husband. To keep her safe, her 12-year-old Will asks his piano teacher to look after her while he travels in search of his father. But while he is preparing to leave, the men break into his house. In his desperation to escape, Will crashes into one of them, causing the man to fall down the stairs and die. Will escapes into another world and meets Lyra, a girl who accompanies him on his search. Each of them is pursued by enemies; nowhere are they safe. The action of the novel is intensely dramatic, ending in a heart-wrenching scene reminiscent of Greek tragedy.

Without parents to raise him, Will has had to adopt adult responsibilities early in life. Readers who have had little parental guidance or who are coping with the mental illness of a family member will find strength and encouragement in Will's story. Will must also come to terms with his role as knife bearer, a role he does not want or feel suited to. But as he discovers, the knife chooses the knife bearer, not the reverse.

This epic story is told in lush, poetic language that will remain with readers long after they have finished the novel. The second novel in a trilogy, *The Subtle Knife* is best read after *The Golden Compass*.

**For those also seeking**: reassurance/comfort/confirmation of self-worth/strength
**For those drawn to**: story, language
**Themes/subjects**: multiple worlds/universes, omens/prophecies, knives/daggers/swords, mental illness, authoritarian figures, angels/cherubs, witches, mother-son relationships, self-knowledge, Christianity, faith and skepticism, political corruption
**Reading interest level**: grade 7 and up
**Curricular tie-ins**: Tell students to pretend they have been asked to create a new edition of the novel, one with illustrations and maps of the worlds. In small groups, they could create illustrations and maps for the book.
**Adaptations & alternative formats**: audiobook read by the author and a full cast (2003)
**Translations**: Spanish: *La Daga/The Subtle Knife*; French: *La Tour des Anges*
**Read-alikes**: Like Will, Sameth in Garth Nix's *Abhorsen* must undertake a task he does not want or feel qualified to perform. Christopher Chant in Diana Wynne Jones's *The Lives of Christopher Chant* also travels through different worlds.

## Disinterested Understanding of the World

**Nesbit, Edith** (1858–1924)
**The Story of the Amulet** (1906). London: Puffin Books, 1959. 292pp. 978-0140367522. PD.

While siblings Anthea, Cyril, Jane, and Robert are able to magically visit any place in the world in *The Phoenix and the Carpet*, they are able to visit any time period in *The Story of the Amulet*. Discovering their beloved sand-fairy in a shop, the children learn from the Psammead that the amulet they have found can take them back in time in order to find its missing half. Once the amulet is made whole, it can grant the desire of one's heart. Since the children's father has gone to Manchuria as a war correspondent and their mother has traveled to Madeira to recuperate from an illness, the sibling's greatest wish is to see them again. The amulet takes the children and the Psammead to a variety of places in the past and the future.

After traveling to other times, the children gain a new perspective on their own world, realizing "how very few of the things they had always thought they could not do without were really not at all necessary to life." Readers too will experience what it is like to live in different times and places, encounters that will open their eyes to social inequities. By identifying with historical characters, readers understand their plight in a more deeply felt way than if they had read about the same issues in a nonfiction text.

As unforeseen consequences arise from the magic, the children's lives become increasingly complicated. They find themselves in calamitous situations that are more and more difficult to escape from. The witty narrator, likeable siblings, and wry humor of the novel are additional appeals.

**For those also seeking**: awakening/new perspectives/enlargement of possibilities
**For those drawn to**: story
**Themes/subjects**: fairies, stories and storytelling, wishes and wishing, amulets, portals/thresholds, siblings and siblings issues, time travel, ancient civilizations, British history
**Reading interest level**: grades 4–7
**Curricular tie-ins**: This novel would make an excellent companion for a lesson on ancient Egyptian, Babylonian, or Roman civilizations. Students could consider the following question: If they could visit ancient Egypt,

Babylon, or Roman Britain, which one would they choose and why? They could write a blog discussing their choice.
**Adaptations & alternative formats**: audiobook read by Cathy Dobson (2011)
**Translations**: Spanish: *Historia de un Amuleto*; French: *Le Secret de l'Amulette*
**Read-alikes**: Children also magically visit earlier periods of history in Edith Nesbit's *The House of Arden* and *Harding's Luck* and Mary Norton's *Bedknob and Broomstick*.

CHAPTER EIGHT

# Historical Fiction

At first, the phrase "historical fiction" sounds like an oxymoron. How can something that is supposed to be historical, a factual event of the past, be fiction? But it is indeed its own genre and very distinct from nonfiction. Historical fiction includes stories that take place in a real past—for example, during the Reconstruction era after the U.S. Civil War, during the Great Depression, or during World War II. But the stories themselves are invented, made-up. And, while they allude to actual events, historical fiction does not always report the factual truth because the factual truth may be impossible to discover—as is the case, for example, of Rosemary Sutcliff's novels about Roman Britain.

However, it would be inaccurate to categorize these types of novels as realistic fiction, as writers of realistic fiction write about their present, that is, the time in which they are actually living, while writers of historical fiction write about a past that they could not have actually experienced themselves. This is why Louisa May Alcott's *Little Women*, while offering historical insight, is considered realistic fiction; it takes place during the U.S. Civil War, and it was published around the same time. Christopher Paul Curtis's *Bud, Not Buddy*, on the other hand, is considered historical fiction because the story takes place during the Great Depression, but it was published in the late twentieth century, in 1999, over 50 years after these events took place. Curtis may have been alive during the Great Depression, but he wasn't writing *during* it.

In some historical fiction, like Lois Lowry's *Number the Stars*, major events are woven directly into the narrative. But, in most historical novels, writers merely allude to these events while meticulously attending to the historical accuracy of their fictional details. But, again, historical fiction is not history. Writers use language only to approximate how people really thought and spoke during a particular point in time. Still, as a result, they bring the past to life; they help the reader to imagine what people and living were like at a particular point in time. So while not factual accounts, historical fiction conveys the emotional truth of the past, that aspect of history that sometimes gets lost in the facts.

Because, by definition, historical fiction takes readers to another time and place, all of these novels, to some extent, provide a "disinterested understanding of the world." Any one of these books can take readers outside of their present and give them insight into the past. But historical fiction's focus on the individual's experience means that these novels also tend to be character driven and therefore have just as much potential to possess the other reader-driven appeal factors Ross defines. Consider, for example, Lois Lowry's *Number the Stars* and Jane Yolen's *The Devil's Arithmetic*. Both offer authentic accounts of a girl's experience of authoritarian rule during World War II. But, to use the language of film, where Lowry takes a long shot, Yolen zooms in, diminishing the psychic distance between the character and the reader. Consequently, Lowry gives us an authentic picture of the past and resurrects it, providing more of a "disinterested understanding of the world." Yolen, on the other hand, gets into the mind of the past, and so her novel does more to "awaken" and provide "new perspectives."

Being mostly character-driven novels, historical fiction also tends to explore themes of struggle and survival, though the author's tone and treatment of these themes vary widely. For example, while Richard Peck, in both *A Long Way from Chicago* and *A Year Down Yonder*, and Christopher Paul Curtis, in *Bud, Not Buddy*, use humor while describing the difficulties and hardships brought by the Great Depression, Pam Muñoz Ryan, in *Esperanza Rising*, and Karen Hesse, in *Out of the Dust*, take a much more serious attitude. But in either case, readers are aware that the struggles these characters are facing are real and in relationship to exceptionally difficult circumstances.

Though historical fiction will obviously appeal to readers who are interested in history or the past, it should not be overlooked for readers who are also drawn to character or who are struggling in their own lives and therefore likely to find "connection with others." While these novels, by nature of their focus, can easily integrate and complement classroom studies, one should also not overlook that they are also just good stories, worthy of reading for their own sake, as ends in themselves.

## Awakening/New Perspectives/Enlargement of Possibilities

**Hamilton, Virginia** (1936–2002)
**The House of Dies Drear** (1968). New York: Aladdin Paperbacks, 2006. 244pp. 978-1416914051.

Thomas Small is 13 when he moves from his home in the South to the strange house of Dies Drear, an abolitionist who was murdered long ago for his involvement in the Underground Railroad. Located in a small midwestern town in Ohio, Dies Drear's stately home was once a "station" on the Underground Railroad, the network of secret routes and safe houses that were developed in the nineteenth century to help fugitive slaves in America escape to freedom in the northern states and Canada.

While Thomas's father, a professor of history, relishes the opportunity to live in such a monumental site, Thomas is much more reluctant. The house has so many secret doors and passageways—it would be easy for one to get lost—and a series of strange events lead him to believe that the house may be haunted. Plus, their groundskeeper, an old, eccentric named Mr. Skinner, seems to be hiding something. Thomas is determined to get to the bottom of this mystery, but the more he pursues it, the deeper it becomes.

Hamilton is noted for her ability to capture the complex interior worlds of her characters. The anxiety and uncertainty that weigh on Thomas are physically manifested in the strange, unpredictable Drear House. As he uncovers the house's secrets, he discovers new ways of seeing.

**For those also seeking**: disinterested understanding of the world
**For those drawn to**: story
**Themes/subjects**: actors/acting, African American history, aging elders, anxiety/fears, buried/hidden treasure, churches, class differences, disguises, family, father-son relationships, fear, feuds, ghosts, haunted houses, insiders/outsiders, mysteries, midwestern United States, moving houses (relocating), otherness, secrets, stories and storytelling, Underground Railroad
**Reading interest level**: grades 6–8

**Curricular tie-ins**: Have students do some basic Internet research about slavery and/or the Underground Railroad. Ask them to explain how it illuminates the text and/or offers insight into current political events (e.g., Black Lives Matter and reparations).

**Adaptations & alternative formats**: audiobook read by Lynne Thigpen (1995); film directed by Allan A. Goldstein (1984)

**Read-alikes**: The sequel, *The Mystery of Drear House*, concludes the Dies Drear Chronicles and continues to explore themes of illness (particularly mental illness) and aging. Barbara Smucker's *Underground to Canada* is another book about the underground railway.

**Kadohata, Cynthia** (1956–)
**Kira-Kira** (2004). New York: Aladdin Paperbacks, 2006. 244pp. 978-0689856402.

Katie Takeshima's family moves from Iowa to Georgia when their Oriental grocery store fails. Although her mother and father find jobs in the chicken-processing industry, they work long hours in appalling conditions. As Japanese Americans living in the 1950s, they are shunned by those who are not Japanese. Although Katie's life is not easy, she adores her older sister, Lynn—a girl who is intelligent, kind, and caring. Life changes dramatically for the sisters the winter that Katie turns 10. Lynn begins suffering from periods of intense fatigue, and the doctors treat her for anemia. But Lynn does not get better. Although Katie does not guess for a while, readers begin to suspect that Lynn is suffering from something far more serious than anemia. As the novel progresses, it becomes evident that the girl is dying.

This gripping, intensely moving story won the Newbery Award in 2005. Katie's gradual understanding of life is conveyed in simple and, at the same time, profound language. Always struggling in school, and never sure how to identify themes in stories, Katie suddenly comprehends what a theme is after Lynn's death. In an essay for school, she writes, "Lynn could take a simple, everyday object like a box of Kleenex and use it to prove how amazing the world is. She could prove this in many different ways, with Kleenex or soap bubbles or maybe even a blade of grass. This is the main theme of my sister's life."

Never a person to work hard before Lynn's death, Katie cooks and cleans when she realizes her parents cannot cope. She also begins to work diligently at school since this was one of her sister's last wishes. Lynn's death

Historical Fiction

shapes Katie's development, inspiring her to become a person that she would never have thought possible before. Readers who are experiencing grief will find in Katie's story not just a very candid and moving depiction of the death of a sister but also a new way to look at the loss of a loved one.

Readers will also gain a deeply felt understanding of what it would have been like to be Japanese American during the 1950s. An emotionally stirring, memorable novel, *Kira-Kira* will resonate with readers who enjoy realistic fiction as well as those who love historical novels.

**For those also seeking**: disinterested understanding of the world
**For those drawn to**: character
**Themes/subjects**: sisters, 1950s (United States), Japanese Americans, grief, prejudice, family, moving houses (relocating), poverty, southern United States, illness, struggling or disinterested students, cancer, workers' rights/unionization
**Reading interest level**: grades 6–8
**Curricular tie-ins**: A novel that explores racism in the 1950s, *Kira-Kira* would tie in well with a social studies unit on post–World War II America. Ask students to work in groups to create presentations about postwar Japanese Americans. What issues did they face and why?
**Adaptations & alternative formats**: audiobook read by the author (2005)
**Translations**: Spanish: *Kira-Kira*
**Read-alikes**: Yoshiko Uchida's *Journey to Topaz* and *A Jar of Dreams* and Cynthia Kadohata's *Weedflower* are also historical novels about Japanese American families. Hà and her family in Thanhha Lai's *Inside Out and Back Again* relocate to Alabama after fleeing North Vietnam. Patrick Ness's *A Monster Calls* is about a boy who must face the cancer and death of a family member. Although Karen English's *It All Comes Down to This* is set a decade later than *Kira-Kira*, it is also a historical novel about racism and about the influence of an older sister.


**Taylor, Mildred D.** (1943–)
**Roll of Thunder, Hear My Cry** (1976). New York: Puffin Books, 2004. 276pp. 978-0142401125.

Whenever Cassie Logan and her three brothers make the long walk to their all-black elementary school, they are routinely harassed by the white school's bus driver, who spatters them with mud with his tires as he speeds past them. It's 1933, the Great Depression, and Cassie lives on a farm in rural Mississippi during a time of profound racial segregation. Cassie, though, is only nine years old and just beginning to recognize these problems. She can't understand why the bus driver would taunt her and her brothers this way.

As payback, Cassie's older brother, Stacey, convinces them to prank the driver. They dig a hole in the road and let it fill it with mud so that the next time the driver whips by, his wheels will get stuck. The plan works, and although no harm comes to the driver or the kids, the prank sets off racial tensions and leads to a series of events that put the Logans' lives in peril.

Set against the backdrop of the violent American South, Cassie's coming-of-age story is especially poignant as it highlights not only the otherness of race and gender but also the otherness of childhood. Segregation compels Cassie into premature political awareness, disrupting her childhood, forcing her to act more "grownup," more tolerant, when confronting her racist tormentors, most of whom are *actually* adults. Winner of the Newbery Award, this novel captures not only a realistic perspective of African Americans in the days of Jim Crow and the Great Depression but also the perspective of a child whose circumstances force her to grow up fast.

**For those also seeking**: models for identity
**For those drawn to**: story, character
**Themes/subjects**: African American history, aiding/helping, coming of age, corporeal punishment, guns, family, farm life, father-daughter relationships, feudal systems, friendship, grandmothers, Great Depression (United States), mob mentality, mother-daughter relationships, otherness, poverty, racial violence, racism, resistance, segregation, southern United States, white supremacists, workers' rights/unionization, wrongfully accused
**Reading interest level**: grades 4–8
**Curricular tie-ins**: Ask students to research Jim Crow laws and to find examples of how their legacy can still be felt in present-day America (e.g., in the criminal justice system, in education, in media) and possible solutions.
**Adaptations & alternative formats**: audiobook read by Lynne Thigpen (2005)
**Translations**: Spanish: *Lloro Por La Tierra*; French: *Tonnerre, Entends Mon Cri*
**Read-alikes**: Read the prequel, *Song of the Trees* (1975) or the companion novels, *The Friendship* (1987) or *Mississippi Bridge* (1990), or read in conjunction with *To Kill A Mockingbird*. Sharon M. Draper's *Stella by Starlight* is

Historical Fiction

also about an African American family battling prejudice during the Great Depression era.

**Peck, Richard** (1934–)
**A Long Way from Chicago: A Novel in Stories** (1998). New York: Puffin Books, 2004. 148pp. 978-0142401101.

Every summer since 1929, Joey and his younger sister, Mary Alice, have taken a train from their home in Chicago to visit their Grandma Dowdel in her tiny, middle-of-nowhere town, right off the railroad tracks. Grandma Dowdel isn't like most grandmothers, welcoming her grandchildren with hugs and kisses; rather, she is downright surly. But the somber expression is really just a mask with which she hides her roguish personality. By seeming so cool and unapproachable, no one would have the courage to accuse her of all the tricks and mischief that she does, indeed, commit.

While Grandma Dowdel makes and follows her own rules, she resorts to mischief only when it is for a good reason. It's the Great Depression, and times are hard. Grandma Dowdel does what she can to bring happiness and relief to her neighbors and community. For instance, she stays up all night frying catfish so that they can bring meals to the poor. So what if she poached the fish, temporarily stole a boat, and blackmailed the police in order to do so?

Each chapter in this hilarious novel is its own stand-alone short story that provides a vivid snapshot into Depression-era, rural America. Readers can better imagine this struggle as well as more fully appreciate the magnanimity it inspired. It shows how hardships, while difficult, can also be a unifying force. While readers could pick and choose stories, reading them together, chronologically, follows narrative arc that brings the grandmother's generous, albeit renegade, spirit into sharper relief.

**For those also seeking**: disinterested understanding of the world
**For those drawn to**: story, character
**Themes/subjects**: aiding/helping; airplanes; automobile industry (American); coming of age; community; country life; grandmothers; Great Depression (United States); gossip; guns; humor; midwestern United States; prank, tricks, and mischief; poverty; Prohibition/temperance movements; railroads; siblings and sibling issues, resourcefulness
**Reading interest level**: grades K–6

**Curricular tie-ins**: In addition to complementing studies about the Depression-era America, this novel would also support a unit on rail transportation and/or the rise of the automobile and how they have impacted the landscape (in terms of how cities are designed), the environment, and culture (the move toward convenience, fast food, etc.).
**Adaptations & alternative formats**: audiobook read by Ron Mclarty (2005)
**Read-alikes**: Grandma Dowdel's hijinks continue in the sequel, *A Year Down Yonder*, but these new adventures are told from the perspective of Mary Alice. Christopher Paul Curtis's *Bud, Not Buddy* is another story about a boy that is set during the Great Depression and is also humorously written.


**Schlitz, Laura Amy** (1955–)
**Good Masters! Sweet Ladies! Voices from a Medieval Village** (2007). Cambridge, MA: Candlewick Books, 2011. 95pp. 978-0763615789.

What was it like to be a child in the Middle Ages? Well, that depends on whose child you were. This collection of prose poem/monologues is a collage of children's and teen's voices in a single medieval village in England. Some are the sons or daughters of lords and ladies, some are knights; most are peasants. While the lord's daughter, Isobel, worries about her stained dress, Will, the plowboy, struggles to feed his family. Though, it becomes clear that no one exactly has it easy in medieval England.

In addition to being extremely well written, this collection of poems is also extremely well researched. Each monologue poem is its own self-contained vignette that provides a small but vivid glimpse into the actual daily existence of children living during the Middle Ages. Yet, at the same time, Schlitz still appeals to modern sensibilities with her fun use of language and accessible prose poem structure. Although each monologue can stand alone, reading them together is a much richer experience. Individual stories link together, providing readers' with multiple perspectives and a much more nuanced understanding of children during this period.

**For those also seeking**: connection with others/awareness of not being alone
**For those drawn to**: language
**Themes/subjects**: abused children, abuse (physical), alcohol/alcoholism, apprentices, body image, bullying, class differences, Christianity, coming of age, Crusades, cycles of abuse, disability, domestic abuse, England, etiquette

and customs, feudalism, fleas, food, gender roles, hunger, hunting, Judaism, justice and injustice, knights, low self-esteem, Middle Ages, monologues, prejudice, superstitions

**Reading interest level**: grades 5–8

**Curricular tie-ins**: Since this novel is so well footnoted, use this book to teach students the purpose and importance of citation. Discuss the role of research in the writing process. Or, ask students to draw a diagram of the caste structure in feudal Europe and to label where each character would belong in it. Moderate a discussion in which students compare children living in the medieval ages with children living throughout the world today.

**Adaptations & alternative formats**: a paperback edition (978-0763650940) is also available, but the hardback edition cited contains illustrations and footnotes that are easier to read; audiobook read by Christina Moore (2008)

**Read-alikes**: Marguerite de Angeli's *The Door in the Wall* and Karen Cushman's *Catherine Called Birdy*, *Matilda Bone*, and *The Midwife's Apprentice* all have medieval settings.


**Twain, Mark** (1835–1910)
**The Prince and the Pauper** (1889). New York: Vintage Books, 2015. 272pp. 978-1101873106.

The dirty, cramped slums of London during the mid-sixteenth century are a dire place to be. But poor, hungry Tom Canty knows nothing else. Though he is only about nine years old, he spends his days on the streets, begging for his family, constantly fearing the beating his father will give him should he come home empty-handed, though his father, a mean gangster and thief, is likely to beat him whether he delivers or not. On the other hand, Prince Edward, the son and heir of Henry VIII and soon-to-be king, cannot get dressed or eat his breakfast without a dozen or more servants waiting on him. Though he studies hard, and makes use of his privileges, he has never been able to do anything for himself, on his own, and wouldn't even know how to. He wonders and longs for such freedom.

When, by a chance encounter, the prince meets Tom, he realizes that they could pass for identical twins. Together, they decide to use this advantage to try out the other's life. They change clothes and Tom becomes a prince, and the prince becomes Tom. It's fun at first, but the novelty soon wears off when the king dies, and no one believes Edward when he says he is the king. Tom, still at the palace, is forced to manage the country but without knowledge of royal customs. So far out of their element, both boys are accused of madness by whomever they meet.

This story is all about shifting perspectives. For instance, once Tom has had a taste of respectability and luxury, he begins to forget and become out of touch, indifferent, to the commoner's daily sufferings. The prince, on the other hand, experiencing social class injustice and poverty's cruel realities for the first time, becomes much more sympathetic to their plight and, once his crown is restored, rules with compassion. The story remains timeless as it shows the different sides of privilege and of poverty and how, depending on the individual, either position can breed good or evil. Princeliness is more of an attitude, a state of mind, that one chooses to adopt rather than inherits by birthright. Anyone who has ever felt ashamed of his or her background may also find comfort and reassurance in this knowledge.

**For those also seeking**: reassurance/comfort/confirmation of self-worth/strength
**For those drawn to**: story
**Themes/subjects**: abused children, abuse (physical), adaptation/adjusting to change, alcohol/alcoholism, aiding/helping, capital punishment, class differences, cycles of abuse, disguises, domestic abuse, etiquette and customs, fashion/costume, father-son relationships, friendship, gangs and gangsters, humor, hunger, imposters, justice and injustice, kings/queens, kindness, London, madmen, mental illness, missing persons, money/debt, nurturers, sacrifice, satire, Tudor England, trauma
**Reading interest level**: grades K–8
**Curricular tie-ins**: To emphasize this novel's timeless applicability, ask students to research the personal and educational background of a local, state, and/or national leader and analyze how his or her background may inform his or her leadership and ability to rule for the people.
**Adaptations & alternative formats**: abridged edition by Puffin Classics (1997); audiobook read by (2014); film directed by Donna Deitch (1999)
**Read-alikes**: Sid Fleischman's *The Whipping Boy* is another story in which a prince and a pauper trade places.

**Yolen, Jane** (1939–)
**The Devil's Arithmetic** (1988). New York: Puffin Books, 2004. 170pp. 978-0142401095.

Thirteen-year-old Hannah is fed up with her Jewish family and all of their traditions. Every time there is a Jewish holiday, her parents and her younger brother have to travel all the way to her grandfather's apartment in the Bronx where she must endure endless conversations about the past. Hannah is sick of "remembering."

But the evening they come to celebrate Seder, the Jewish ritual feast that marks the beginning of Passover, something peculiar happens during the ceremony that causes Hannah to suddenly transform and enter the past. She is no longer Hannah, but Chaya, an orphaned Jew from Lublin, Poland, who is captured by the Nazis and experiences firsthand the brutal and dehumanizing world that was the German concentration camp. Hannah longs for her old life, but she does not know how to return to it, and as time passes, she begins to doubt it had ever existed.

While certainly a morality tale about the importance of remembering and honoring the past, this novel refrains from excessive didacticism. Rather, this revelation is earned as readers empathize with Hannah whose experience of Nazi persecution and camp life is depicted with heart-wrenching accuracy. This story is certain to expand readers' understanding not only of Jewish history and culture but also of the diversity of childhoods, bringing to light that not all of them are carefree and innocent.

**For those also seeking**: disinterested understanding of the world
**For those drawn to**: setting, character
**Themes/subjects**: authoritarian rule, concentration camps, courage, death, empathy, family, food, friendship, injustice, Judaism, magical transformations, marriage, memory, pain/suffering, Poland, portals/thresholds, racial violence, racism, rituals and traditions, trauma, sacrifice, soldiers, war crimes, World War II
**Reading interest level**: grades 5–8
**Curricular tie-ins**: In addition to complementing studies on Jewish culture and World War II, this novel would be an ideal springboard into an activity in which students are asked to interview their own family members and write a history of their past.
**Adaptations & alternative formats**: audiobook read by Barbara Rosenblat (2014); film directed by Donna Deitch (1999)
**Read-alikes**: The Holocaust is also captured in Jane Yolen's *The Devil's Arithmetic* and Lois Lowry's *Number the Stars*.

## Models for Identity

**Brink, Carol Ryrie** (1895–1981)
**Caddie Woodlawn** (1935). New York: Aladdin Paperbacks, 2006.
978-1416940289.

Caddie's yearlong chronicle of pioneer life begins in 1864, when she is eleven years old. Bright and energetic, Caddie much prefers roaming the Wisconsin prairie and going on adventures with her brothers than being inside with her mother and sisters. Surrounded by tall grass, pine trees, and lakes, there is always something to do. They especially like to sneak away to visit John, a native, and his tribe, who live nearby and watch him build canoes.

Frontier life is always exciting—sometimes too exciting. When a rumor spreads that the natives are going to attack the settlers, a mob gathers to strike the natives first, and Caddie fears for the life of her friend, John. Unable to reach her father, who is the only person the other men would listen to, Caddie must figure out how to warn John on her own.

As a determined, independent thinker, who cares more about doing right than conforming to convention, Caddie is a model for identity. She also demonstrates how even the smallest actions bear meaningful impact, reminding readers of their own agency and discouraging them from complacency. It should be noted that while Brink intends to preach peace and equality among whites and Native Americans, her descriptions of the latter are at times blatantly condescending and reveal her privileged status. For this reason, it would be an ideal text for teaching young readers how to uncover ideological bias.

**For those also seeking**: disinterested understanding of the world
**For those drawn to**: story, character
**Themes/subjects**: adventure, U.S. Civil War, being different, corporeal punishment, crushes, courage, cultural differences, dogs, empathy, family, frontier and pioneer life, gender roles, indigenous peoples (United States), mob mentality, midwestern United States, music, otherness, prejudice, racism, redheads, schools
**Reading interest level**: grades 3–6
**Curricular tie-ins**: To stress the importance of an author's point of view, ask students to rewrite a chapter from the story or write a new chapter from

Historical Fiction

the perspective of one of the Native American characters (e.g., John, the mixed-race Hankinson children or their Native American mother).
**Adaptations & alternative formats**: audiobook read by Roslyn Alexander (2012)
**Read-alikes**: Laura Ingalls Wilder's *On the Banks of Plum Creek* takes place at the about the same time, and Laura is about the same age and, like Caddie, a bit unconventional for girls at that time. Jo in *Little Women* is also a kindred spirit.

**Cushman, Karen** (1941–)
**Catherine, Called Birdy** (1994). New York: Houghton Mifflin Harcourt, 2012. 169pp. 978-0547722184.

Catherine is 12 years old when she begins her diary, which describes her growing up and becoming a noblewoman in medieval England. Though she is very young, her greedy father has already begun to entertain suitors, who are willing to pay for her hand in marriage. Catherine despises the thought and feels as though she were being sold like an animal or a piece of property. She yearns for independence and adventure and would much rather be a monk like her older brother, Edward, or join the Crusades like her uncle, George. Smart, spirited, and outspoken, Catherine could do anything she put her mind to—if only it weren't the year 1290. Since Catherine is a girl, marriage is her only option. The most she can do with her cleverness is use it to chase off potential husbands.

Then enters Shaggy Beard, an old, crude brute who, unsurprisingly, has a big, dirty, shaggy beard. Unlike Catherine's other suitors, Shaggy Beard is not deterred by her antics. Rather, he is determined to marry her, and Catherine's father is determined to sell her. As the day of her betrothal draws nearer, Catherine begins to despair. How can she escape this bitter fate?

Catherine's wit sparkles in these diary entries, giving contemporary readers greater insight into medieval life and culture. While Cushman exploits a contemporary voice that is anachronistic, her descriptions are historically authentic, and this contrast results in a novel that is deeply thought provoking. Readers, especially young female readers who have not yet recognized their own strength, will find a model in Catherine, who manages to maintain her own identity and sense of self-worth despite her being born into such a narrow world.

**For those also seeking**: connection with others/awareness of not being alone
**For those drawn to**: character, language
**Themes/subjects**: art (as coping mechanism), birds, Christianity, courtly love, Crusades, crushes, domestic abuse, England, feminism, feudalism, fleas, guilt, grief, hope, marriage, memoirs/diaries, Middle Ages, miscarriage, otherness, pain/suffering, pregnancy, spells/curses, superstitions, women's history
**Reading interest level**: grades 6–8
**Curricular tie-ins**: Invite students to research gender roles in the Middle Ages and compare and contrast them to today.
**Adaptations & alternative formats**: audiobook read by Jenny Sterlin (2008)
**Translations**: Spanish: El *Libro De Catherine*; French: *Le Livre De Catherine*
**Read-alikes**: Readers who are drawn to Catherine's determined character as well as the structure of this novel may also enjoy Jean Webster's *Daddy-Long-Legs*. Cushman's *The Midwife's Apprentice* and *Matilda Bone* are also stories of girls living in medieval England.

**Garfield, Leon** (1921–1996)
**Smith** (1967). New York: New York Review Books, 2013. 195pp. 9781590176757.

Twelve-year-old Smith is a pickpocket—but a brilliant one. Although it is not exactly the trade he would have chosen, there are few other options for a young, poor orphan living on the mean streets of eighteenth-century London. He lives in the basement of a seedy tavern, frequented by criminals of all kinds, along with his two older sisters, who barely earn their living mending and reselling the clothes of deceased felons.

But when this story begins, Smith has picked the wrong pocket. He swipes an older, wealthy-looking fellow who seems to have been visiting from the country. But when Smith looks in his hands, instead of cash, he discovers he is holding some kind of document. He's not sure what it is because he doesn't know how to read. But, he does know that it is important because a moment later, two mysterious men follow the stranger, murder him, and search him for the paper. Smith flees but determines to uncover the secret of the document, which he hopes can somehow help release him and his sisters from their hard life of indigence.

*Historical Fiction*

The discovery of the document sets a series of events that transform Smith and shape and expand his capacity for empathy. Fleeing from the murderers, Smith crosses paths with a sympathetic family, a retired, blind judge and his dutiful daughter, who takes Smith in and teaches him how to read. While recognizing their kindness as the product of their privilege, Smith nonetheless discovers, for the first time, humanity at its best. While already a model of cleverness and tenacity, Smith also becomes a model of empathy as he learns to look beyond his own self-interest.

**For those also seeking**: connection with others/awareness of not being alone
**For those drawn to**: character, language
**Themes/subjects**: adventure, buried/hidden treasure, capital punishment, class differences, criminals/thieves, ghosts, guilt, heroes, humor, inns/taverns, justice and injustice, London, literacy/illiteracy, missing persons, mysteries, murder, orphans, poverty, prison/incarceration, secrets, stealing, wrongfully accused, self-interest
**Reading interest level**: grades 5–8
**Curricular tie-ins**: Provide background information on the practice of public executions in eighteenth-century England, and ask students to discuss its modern-day counterparts (e.g., capital punishment today, global terrorism) and/or examine structural inequalities in prison systems.
**Read-alikes**: Leon Garfield's *John Diamond* and *Black Jack* also feature boy heroes living in eighteenth-century London, Laura Amy Schlitz's *Splendors and Glooms* shares its Gothic atmosphere, and Sid Fleischman's *Bandit's Moon* is also about an illiterate outlaw and shares Garfield's sense of humor.

**Hesse, Karen** (1952–)
**Stowaway** (2000). New York: Aladdin Paperbacks, 2002. 315pp. 978-0689839894.

Captain Cook began the first of three sea voyages in 1768, exploring and mapping unknown parts of the world. Historical records indicate that 11-year-old Nicholas Young was a stowaway on the first voyage. Using these historical facts, Levine depicts one of the voyages from the 11-year-old's perspective. Leaving a note for his father, Nicholas runs away from home, steals money from the butcher who employs him, and hides on the ship, *Endeavor*. When Captain Cook discovers that he has a stowaway, he tells Nicholas that he must prove himself an able-bodied seaman or be put ashore to fend for himself.

During the course of the three-year voyage, Nicholas endures violent storms at sea, the enmity of a midshipman who hates him, the drowning of shipmates, near-destruction of the ship, malaria of crew members, serious threats from indigenous peoples, and the death of a beloved friend.

In this coming-of-age story, Nicholas runs away from his problems at home only to encounter new versions of them at sea. Knowing that he is a disappointment to his father, Nicholas says to himself, "I shall prove to Father that I am not a quitter. That I am good for something. That I am more than a butcher's boy." Yet little could he anticipate the challenges that his life at sea would pose. Written in the form of entries in a ship's journal, Nicholas's notes reveal his inner thoughts and anxieties. Children who have made mistakes in life, have not lived up to other's expectations, or have little interest in school will find in Nicholas's story a model for moving forward with their lives.

Readers will gain deep personal knowledge of what it was like to live and work on a ship, to be a child in the eighteenth century, and to be an explorer at a time when parts of the world were still unknown.

**For those also seeking**: disinterested understanding of the world
**For those drawn to**: story, setting
**Themes/subjects**: sea voyage, Captain Cook, stowaways, explorers, memoirs/diaries, colonialism, indigenous peoples, adventure, cultural differences, coming of age, identity formation, sea and seashore, boats and ships, failure, runaway children, struggling or disinterested students, parental disapproval, illness, stealing
**Reading interest level**: grades 6–8
**Curricular tie-ins**: *Stowaway* will stimulate interest in Captain Cook and his voyages around the world. Ask students to form groups to research one of Captain Cook's three voyages. They could present their findings as questions and answers for a talk show interview.
**Adaptations & alternative formats**: audiobook read by David Cole (2012)
**Translations**: French: *Vers des Terres Inconnues*
**Read-alikes**: Paula Fox's *The Slave Dancer* is another historical novel set at sea. Sharon Creech's *The Wanderer* and Avi's *The True Confessions of Charlotte Doyle* are also exciting sea stories. Scott O'Dell's *The King's Fifth* is a tale about explorers who map unidentified parts of the world.

Historical Fiction

**Sutcliff, Rosemary** (1920–1992)
**Eagle of the Ninth** (1954). New York: Square Fish, 2011. 210pp.
978-0312564346.

Marcus Flavius Aquila is just a teenager when he leaves his home in the Etruscan countryside for the south of Britain to command his first cohort in the ancient Roman army. Marcus hopes to rise through the ranks and eventually become commander of an Egyptian Legion, like his father had been before he disappeared in battle over 10 years ago, when Marcus was just a little boy.

But the first time the fort is attacked, Marcus is wounded. Though he recovers and can still walk, his lame leg means that his dreams of becoming a camp commander are over. While recuperating at his uncle's, he considers his alternatives. But, being a freeman and a person with a disability, there are actually few options. Instead, he decides he will try to discover the truth of his father's disappearance. Along with his companion, Esca, he sets out on the long and dangerous journey. Disguising himself as a Greek eye doctor, Marcus is able to spy on enemy tribes and slowly piece the mystery together. Despite the danger and physical challenges, Marcus refuses to give up until he recovers the Eagle statue, the legion's emblem, and restores his father's honor.

This story is so complex, detailed, and richly described that it is hard to believe that Sutcliff had made it up. Combining the story of the discovery of a Roman eagle statue in the south of Britain during the early twentieth century and historical reports of the missing Ninth Legion from the early second century, Sutcliff weaves a timeless story about loss, resiliency, loyalty, and virtue. Despite broken dreams and physical challenges, Marcus refuses to succumb to despair and instead finds other ways to use his talents as a leader. In modeling mercy, justice, and courage, he is a model for identity. In addition, both Marcus (who has a disability) and Esca (who is a recently freed slave) are marginalized figures in their society, and thus, as outsiders, both provide connection with others.

**For those also seeking**: connection with others/awareness of not being alone
**For those drawn to**: story, language
**Themes/subjects**: ambition, ancient civilizations, battles/wars, circuses (Roman), courage, critical thinking/strategy, dead or absent father, death,

disability, disguises, duty, failure, fashion/costume, freedom, friendship, homesickness, horses, hunting, identity formation, indigenous peoples (Britain), loyalty, mythology, mysteries, occupied countries, otherness, pain/suffering, quests, resilience, rituals and traditions, Roman Empire, slavery, soldiers, spies and spying, sportsmanship, wolves

**Reading interest level**: grades 5–8

**Curricular tie-ins**: In addition to enhancing studies about the Roman Empire (particularly with regard to slavery and the military), this book can be used to stimulate thinking about the psychological effects of occupations. Ask students to compare and contrast Esca (who is enslaved, then freed) to examples of modern-day slavery (child labor, sex trafficking, etc.).

**Adaptations & alternative formats**: abridged audiobook read by Charlie Simpson (2006); film adaptation, *The Eagle*, directed by Kevin Macdonald (2011)

**Translations**: Spanish: *El Águila de la Novena Legión*; French: *L'aigle De La 9e Légion*

**Read-alikes**: This is the first of a sequence of novels about a family living in Roman Britain: *The Silver Branch*, *Frontier Wolf*, *The Lantern Bearers*, *Sword at Sunset*, *Dawn Wind*, *Sword Song*, and *The Shield Ring*. Her *Mark of the Horselord* also takes up these issues of liminality and otherness.

## Reassurance/Comfort/Confirmation of Self-Worth/Strength

### Avi
**Crispin: The Cross of Lead** (2002). New York: Hyperion, 2004. 310pp. 978-0786816583.

In a tiny medieval village in England, 13-year-old Crispin mourns the death of his mother. An orphan now, he goes into the forest to grieve alone. But there he accidentally stumbles upon his village's steward whom he finds conspiring with a stranger. He does not know yet what he hears, but when the steward discovers him listening, he tries to chase him down. Though Crispin manages to escape, the next day he finds himself accused of theft and then murder. He is declared a "wolf's head," which means he can be killed on sight, by anyone.

Crispin has no idea why he is being wrongfully accused, but he knows he must flee his village in order to live. As he runs, he crosses paths with Bear, a big, surly man who claims to be a jester. Upon discovering that Crispin is a runaway, Bear quickly claims him as an apprentice (as the medieval law allows). But Bear is a paradox. On the one hand, he is loud and demanding. At times, he even seems mad. But, on the other hand, he insists that Crispin think for himself, value himself, and stand up for himself. Thanks to Bear's guidance, Crispin begins to recognize his own strength and power, which he needs as the steward, along with his guards, continues his relentless pursuit.

This character-driven story tracks Crispin's transformation from total disenfranchisement to self-empowerment. As Crispin learns he can question and challenge authority, he realizes he must continue questioning, and trusting his own judgment, or else play a complicit role in his own oppression. In coming to recognize his own self-worth and accepting personal responsibility, he is finally able to stand up for himself and others. Readers in need of comfort and reassurance can draw on Crispin's resilience and strength.

**For those also seeking**: connection with others/awareness of not being alone
**For those drawn to**: character
**Themes/subjects**: adventure, agency and powerlessness, battles/wars, capital punishment challenging authority figures, Christianity, churches, courage, dead or absent father, death, depression, displacement (psychology), England, escape, fear, feudalism, friendship, grief, guilt, hunger, identity formation, independence, inns/taverns; justice and injustice, knives/daggers/swords, literacy/illiteracy, illegitimate children, loneliness, low self-esteem, Middle Ages, missing persons, moral dilemmas, music, mysteries, murder, names and naming, neglect, oppressive environments, orphans, outcasts/misfits, pain/suffering, political corruption, poverty, resilience, runaway children, secrets, self-confidence, self-esteem, slavery, soldiers, spies and spying, survival, trust, wrongfully accused
**Reading interest level**: grades 3–8
**Curricular tie-ins**: Crispin's inability to read at the beginning of the book is part of the reason he is so powerless. Ask students to research literacy in the Middle Ages and/or discuss the relationship between literacy and political and economic power.
**Adaptations & alternative formats**: audiobook read by Ron Keith (2006)
**Translations**: Spanish: *Crispín: La Cruz De Plomo*; French: *Le Dernier Seigneur*

**Read-alikes**: Two more novels complete the trilogy, *Crispin: At the Edge of the World* (2006) and *Crispin: The End of Time* (2010). Marguerite de Angeli's *The Door in the Wall* is also about a boy living in the fourteenth century who is discovering his own strength.

**Curtis, Christopher Paul** (1953–)
**Bud, Not Buddy** (1999). New York: Dell Laurel-Leaf, 2004. 243pp. 978-0553494105.

Bud Caldwell is only six years old when his mother dies, leaving him alone and homeless in Flint, Michigan, at the dawning of the Great Depression. For four years he is moved in and out of foster care until he is stuck with a family so mean and hypocritical that he decides he would rather run away. Bringing only a suitcase filled with mementos of his mother and a few possible clues about her past, he decides to look for his father. Bud has a reason to suspect that Herman E. Calloway, the famous jazz bassist, is him, so he maps his way to Grand Rapids, where Mr. Calloway lives, hoping to be reunited.

Despite this novel's difficult subject matter—child abuse, neglect, poverty, and family conflict—this novel is laugh-out-loud funny and, for this reason, completely compelling to read. Bud's past, though traumatic, has also gifted his keen observational skills, intuition, and sense of humor. He is a charismatic narrator. His unwillingness to tolerate abuse, his daring to seek out a better life, and his resilience can all be sources of hope for readers.

**For those also seeking**: connection with others/awareness of not being alone
**For those drawn to**: character
**Themes/subjects**: abused children, adventure, African American history, aiding/helping, anxiety/fears, automobile industry (American), books, bullying, dead or absent father, dead or absent mother, food, foster care, grandfathers, Great Depression (United States), grief, humor, hunger, illegitimate children, jazz, journeys, libraries/librarians, lies/lying, midwestern United States, missing persons, misanthropes, music, names and naming, only children, pain/suffering, poverty, racism, railroads, runaway children, secrets, trauma, resilience
**Reading interest level**: grades 3–8
**Curricular tie-ins**: Bud figures out how to go to Grand Rapids using the library. Use this story to segue into a discussion of the importance of

nurturing one's own curiosity. Allow students to explore their own interests by visiting a public library. This novel would also complement studies about jazz music and its contribution to American culture.
**Adaptations & alternative formats**: audiobook read by James Avery (2000)
**Translations**: Spanish: *Me Llamo Bud, No Buddy*
**Read-alikes**: Richard Peck's *A Long Way from Chicago* is also character driven and describes the Great Depression with humor. Sharon M. Draper's *Stella by Starlight* is about African Americans battling prejudice during the Great Depression. Katherine Paterson's *The Great Gilly Hopkins* is also about a child who does not want to live in a foster home.


**Curtis, Christopher Paul** (1953–)
**The Watsons Go to Birmingham—1963** (1995). New York: Dell Laurel-Leaf, 2000. 210pp. 978-0440228004.

Having a lazy eye and being super smart are liabilities at Clark Elementary School, where Kenny Watson attends the fourth grade in Flint, Michigan, in 1963. His odd looks and intelligence make him the constant target of Larry Dunn, the biggest bully in school. Luckily, Kenny has inherited a good sense of humor from his quirky father and wry mother, so he doesn't let Larry Dunn get him too down. He also has his best friend, Rufus, who just moved to Flint from the South and who also suffers taunting because of his southern accent and threadbare clothing.

Kenny's family is also loving and supportive. His little sister, Joetta, mothers him, and his older brother, Byron, stands up for him. But Byron is also a bit of a bully himself, a borderline "juvenile delinquent." Kenny's parents are so worried about Byron's behavior that they decide to take him to Birmingham, Alabama, to stay with his grandmother for the summer, with whom they hope he will straighten him out. After a long, scenic road trip, they find themselves in the hot, beautiful, muggy South. But their happy family reunion is cut short when the nearby 16th Street Baptist Church is bombed, a tragedy that changes the Watsons' lives forever.

With remarkable warmth and humor, Curtis depicts racism and its complexity, revealing the effects of segregation within African American communities and the reasons why prejudice persists. As Kenny, who witnesses the bombing, grieves and tries to grapple with this injustice, he models both resilience and strength.

**For those also seeking**: connection with others/awareness of not being alone
**For those drawn to**: character
**Themes/subjects**: African American history, automobile industry (American), being different, bullying, death, empathy, extrasensory perception, family, family conflict, father-son relationships, friendship, grandmothers, grief, humor, justice and injustice, midwestern United States, mother-son relationships, music, middle children, missing persons, pain/suffering, poverty, prejudice, racism, racial violence, road trips, segregation, self-blame (psychology), siblings and sibling issues, southern United States, terrorism, trauma, resilience
**Reading interest level**: grades 3–8
**Curricular tie-ins**: Motown and R&B songs feature strongly in this novel. Ask students to research and create a playlist of songs that capture the 1960s and the Civil Rights Movement.
**Adaptations & alternative formats**: audiobook read by Levar Burton (2003); film adaptation, *The Watsons Go to Birmingham*, directed by Kenny Leon (2013)
**Translations**: Spanish: *Los Watson Van a Birmingham-1963*; French: *Voyage À Birmingham, 1963*
**Read-alikes**: Another middle-grade-level novel with a funny protagonist who is also grappling with discrimination is Sherman Alexie's *The Absolutely True Diary of a Part-Time Indian*. William H. Armstrong's *Sounder* is also a story about an African American family facing prejudice and injustice.


**MacLachlan, Patricia** (1938–)
**Sarah, Plain and Tall** (1985). New York: HarperCollins, 2015. 67pp. 978-0062399526.

Anna and Caleb's mother died when Caleb was born, so for the last several years, they have lived on the vast, lonely prairie with only their papa to look after them. A pioneer family, they manage as they all work together to maintain the house and farm. Still, they are lonely. Anna and Caleb would like a mother, and their father would like a wife.

So their father decides to place an ad in the newspaper, asking for a wife. Sarah Elisabeth Wheaton, from the watery shores of Maine, replies. For a time, Sarah corresponds with the children and their father and then agrees to visit them for a month. Anna and Caleb, who have never seen the sea before, or known someone who has, love to listen to her tell stories about her home. They adore Sarah's lively spirit and creativity, her gentle, motherly ways, but they also know she is homesick, so both of them worry that she will decide that she does not like the prairie life and leave.

This gorgeous novella is a testament to the idea that less can be more. In spare, simple language, MacLachlan creates a vivid tableau of domestic and pioneer life that is realistic yet heartwarming without being sentimental. Readers who relate to Anna and Caleb's fears of abandonment will take comfort in Sarah who demonstrates maternal devotion.

**For those also seeking**: disinterested understanding of the world
**For those drawn to**: story
**Themes/subjects**: anxiety/fears, cooperation and teamwork, dead or absent mother, family, frontier and pioneer life, homesickness, midwestern United States, nurturers, prairies, stepparents
**Reading interest level**: grades K–5
**Curricular tie-ins**: To help students gain a deeper appreciation of the lives of pioneer children in comparison to their own, present or ask them to research and present on related topics (e.g., education, chores, gender roles, transportation, health care and medicine, recreation). Invite them to participate in a typical chore (e.g., candle making, bread baking) to demonstrate and emphasize these differences in lifestyle.
**Adaptations & alternative formats**: audiobook read by Glenn Close (2008); film directed by Glenn Jordan (1991)
**Translations**: Spanish: *Sarah, Sencilla y Alta*; French: *Sarah, La Pas Belle*
**Read-alikes**: The family saga of frontier life continues in four more books: *Skylark*, *Caleb's Story*, *More Perfect than the Moon*, and *Grandfather's Dance*. Laura Ingalls Wilder's *Little House on the Prairie* is another pioneer novel set in the prairies.


**Selznick, Brian** (1966–)
**The Invention of Hugo Cabret** (2007). Illustrated by the author. New York: Scholastic Press, 2007. 533pp. 978-0439813785.

It's the early 1930s, in Paris, France, when this mystery begins. Hugo Cabret, just 12 years old, lives all alone in his Uncle Claude's apartment inside the Montparnasse Train Station. After Hugo's father died, his uncle, who is a timekeeper at the station, takes him in as his apprentice. But when Uncle Claude, who is also a reckless alcoholic, goes missing, Hugo becomes

homeless. Since he would rather live alone than go to an orphanage, he continues to take care of the station's clocks, covering for his missing uncle. This solitude also allows him the freedom to continue piecing together the automaton he and his father had been working on before he died.
The automaton is a self-operating machine that, once it works, will write a message. Hugo is determined to fix the machine because he hopes that his father has programmed the automaton to write a secret, personal message just to him.

But, because Hugo has no income of his own and is unable to cash his uncle's paychecks, he is reduced to a life of thievery. One day, while trying to steal mechanical parts for his automaton from the toy booth inside the train station, toy makers catch him, and, in the scuffle, the toy maker snatches Hugo's notebook, which contains all of his father's drawings and diagrams of the automaton and which Hugo needs in order to finish building it. The toymaker, however, is gruff and unsympathetic. He refuses to return the notebook. Only with the help of the toymaker's god daughter, Isabelle, does Hugo stand a chance of rescuing his plans and finishing the machine. In this pursuit, however, they discover more than they bargained for, the secret of the automaton and also the secret of the toymaker.

Selnick's work is a masterpiece collage that combines text and story with his own gorgeous pencil illustrations, archival photographs, and silent film stills, including those from French illusionist and special effects innovator Georges Méliès, who is the toymaker in the story. This multimedium approach raises questions about the importance of art, especially art as a coping mechanism. Hugo, Isabelle, and Méliès all experience loss and seek comfort in art by either consuming it (in books or film) or creating it.
For readers who are struggling to possess a sense of agency, these characters provide models of comfort and strength.

**For those also seeking**: connection with others/awareness of not being alone
**For those drawn to**: story, character
**Themes/subjects**: alcohol/alcoholism, anxiety/fears, art (as coping mechanism), books, child neglect, clockwork and mechanical figures, dead or absent father, death, dreams, escape, film/film history, food, friendship, guilt, grief, homelessness, hunger, imagination, inventing/creating, magicians, museums, mysteries, orphans, prison/incarceration, self-blame (psychology), toy figures, libraries/librarians, lies/lying, mythology, only

children, pain/suffering, Paris, purpose in life, quarrels/fights, runaway children, secrets, stealing, survival, trains/subways, trauma
**Reading interest level**: grades K–8
**Curricular tie-ins**: To promote art appreciation, show Georges Méliès' film *A Trip to the Moon* in order to facilitate discussion and further probe the relationship between dreams and art and life and art. For example, would humans have ever actually gone to the moon if visionary artists like Méliès hadn't conceived of it? In other words, pose the old philosophical question, "Does life imitate art or does art imitate life?"
**Adaptations & alternative formats**: audiobook read by Glenn Close (2008); film directed by Martin Scorsese (2011)
**Translations**: Spanish: *La Invención De Hugo Cabret*; French: *L'invention De Hugo Cabret*
**Read-alikes**: Jules Verne's novels would be good companions as they are alluded to both in the novel and Méliès's films. Selznick's two subsequent historical novels, *The Marvels* and *Wonderstruck*, are also graphic novels.

**Wilder, Laura Ingalls** (1867–1957)
**Little House on the Prairie** (1935). New York: HarperTrophy, 2008. 352pp. 978-0064400022.

When Pa receives an offer on their house, he decides that the family should move west to a less crowded place. Leaving Wisconsin and traveling across Minnesota, Iowa, and Missouri by covered wagon, the Ingalls family arrives in Kansas. The dangerous journey across four states is a prelude to the many perils the family must face once they settle on the prairie. Living in the middle of a deserted landscape, the Ingalls have virtually no one to rely upon and nothing to call their own but a few possessions. Using what he can find on the bare prairie landscape, Pa must build the family a home, a barn, a well, and furniture. Life in this new landscape is threatened by fire, wild animals, unfriendly natives, and disease.

*Little House on the Prairie* is both a compelling historical novel and a thrilling story of survival in the wilderness. Using simple, spare language, Wilder describes complicated processes such as building a log house and complex issues such as settlement disputes and tense relations between pioneers and natives. Drawing upon her childhood memories of life in frontier America, Wilder creates an authentic account of pioneer existence. After reading the story, readers will not only understand the period of frontier expansion but be deeply moved by the challenges pioneers faced.

Although Laura fears many things on the prairies, she loves "the enormous sky and the winds, and the land that you couldn't see to the end of." Wilder conveys the complex emotions of a six-year-old in a way that is both accessible and compelling for young readers. Those who are facing a major change in their lives and readers who are moving to a new place will find the encouragement they need in Laura's story.

**For those also seeking**: disinterested understanding of the world
**For those drawn to**: setting, story
**Themes/subjects**: frontier and pioneer life, survival, wilderness survival, family, sisters, country life, farm life, prairies, indigenous peoples (United States), cultural differences, otherness, cooperation and teamwork, moving houses (relocating), wolves, illness, midwestern United States
**Reading interest level**: grades 3–6
**Curricular tie-ins**: Ask students to build a model of a pioneer house.
**Adaptations & alternative formats**: Disney mini-series directed by David Cunningham (2005); audiobook read by Cherry Jones (2003)
**Translations**: Spanish: *La Casa de la Pradera*; French: *La Petite Maison dans la Prairie*
**Read-alikes**: Readers who are interested in pioneer novels will also enjoy Patricia MacLachlan's Sarah, Plain and Tall series (*Sarah, Plain and Tall*; *Skylark*; *Caleb's Story*; *More Perfect than the Moon*; and *Grandfather's Dance*) and Sandra Dallas's *The Quilt Walk*. As an Ojiba girl, Omakaya's traditions in Louise Erdrich's *The Birchbark House* are different than Laura's, but both characters experience life as young girls in the nineteenth century.

**Wilder, Laura Ingalls** (1867–1957)
**On the Banks of Plum Creek** (1937). New York: HarperTrophy, 1971. 339pp. 978-0064400046.

Forced off their Kansas land by a change in settlement plans by government officials, the Ingalls move to Minnesota in their covered wagon. When Pa trades their wagon and animals for land, Ma is dismayed to find they must live in a dugout carved out of the side of a creek bank. After surviving in this primitive dwelling for the winter, Pa buys boards, window glass, and a new stove on credit, intending to pay for them after he sells his first crop. But a massive infestation of grasshoppers destroys all his wheat. Pa must walk 300 miles east to look for work, leaving Ma and the girls alone in Minnesota. A series of blizzards threaten their lives.

Historical Fiction

One of the most gripping stories in the Little House series, this fourth novel presents one crisis after another as the family tries to survive in the harshest of conditions. Laura repeatedly gets into trouble and must learn how to channel her desires and manage her impulsive emotions. She and her sister, Mary, start school in the nearby town, an experience that introduces them to children who make fun of their country ways. The novel will resonate with readers who fear the future, those who have difficulty managing their emotions, and children who live in poverty. Like Laura, readers can learn to accept adversity, making the best of what they cannot change.

**For those also seeking**: acceptance
**For those drawn to**: setting, story
**Themes/subjects**: frontier and pioneer life, wilderness survival, family, country life, farm life, prairies, cooperation and teamwork, moving houses (relocating), urban versus rural living, blizzards, winter, sisters, midwestern United States, poverty
**Reading interest level**: grades 3–6
**Curricular tie-ins**: Ask students to write a reflection in their reader response journals comparing children today with children in the novel. Ask students to consider what they would like and not like about being a child in pioneer times.
**Adaptations & alternative formats**: Disney mini-series directed by David Cunningham (2005); audiobook read by Cherry Jones (2003)
**Translations**: Spanish: *A Orillas del Río Plum*; French: *Au Bord du Ruisseau*
**Read-alikes**: Readers interested in stories set in an earlier era about girls the same age as Laura and would enjoy Patricia MacLachlan's *More Perfect than the Moon* and *Grandfather's Dance* as well as Maud Hart Lovelace's *Betsy-Tacy and Tib* and *Betsy and Tacy Go over the Big Hill*.


**Wilder, Laura Ingalls** (1867–1957)
**The Long Winter** (1940). New York: HarperTrophy, 1971. 352pp. 978-0644000697.

When Laura and Pa examine a muskrat's house, Pa notices that its walls are extra thick, a sign of a hard winter to come. Then one October morning, the Ingalls awaken to a blizzard, an event that surprises them all. A few days later, an elderly native man visits the local store and warns settlers to expect seven months of blizzards. Pa, who worries that they are too isolated on the outskirts of town and that their claim shanty is not sturdy enough to withstand extreme weather, moves the family to the small town of De Smet for the winter.

No sooner are they settled in town than a series of severe blizzards confine them indoors. All the settlers' provisions dwindle as the stores await stock that can only come by rail. But the trains have difficulty getting through to the town because blizzards block their paths. Eventually the railway announces that trains will not run until spring. The Ingalls' kerosene for light, coal for heat, and food supply eventually runs out.

As conditions deteriorate, they increasingly affect characters psychologically as well as physically. The constant shrieking of the wind makes Laura feel numb and listless: "She felt that the blizzard must stop before she could do anything, before she could even listen or think, but it would never stop." The winter of continuous blizzards is the biggest challenge Laura has faced up until now, and she realizes that she is old enough to stand by Pa and Ma during times of crisis. Readers who are experiencing hardship or deprivation will find guidance and inspiration in the novel. The family's patience and perseverance provide inspiration for readers who must accept difficulties that they cannot change. A compelling story of survival, the plot is even more riveting when readers realize that the story is based on the devastating American winter of 1880–1881.

**For those also seeking**: acceptance
**For those drawn to**: setting, story
**Themes/subjects**: winter, blizzards, frontier and pioneer life, prairies, survival, hunger, family, sisters, music, perseverance/determination, midwestern United States, trains/subways
**Reading interest level**: grades 4–8
**Curricular tie-ins**: *The Long Winter* depicts the "Snow Winter" of 1880–1881. Ask students to research blizzards, considering such aspects as conditions for their development, famous historical examples, and blizzard safety. Students could create a pamphlet using the information they find.
**Adaptations & alternative formats**: Disney mini-series directed by David Cunningham (2005); audiobook read by Cherry Jones (2005)
**Translations**: Spanish: *El Largo Invierno*; French: *Un Hiver sans Fin*
**Read-alikes**: Jean Craighead George's *Julie of the Wolves* is also about a 13-year-old girl who endures the harsh winter elements to survive.
The railway plays an essential role in the survival of a community in Geraldine McCaughrean's *Stop the Train!*

## Connection with Others/Awareness of Not Being Alone

**Armstrong, William H.** (1914–1999)
**Sounder** (1969). New York: HarperCollins, 2002. 116pp. 978-0064400206.

Somewhere in the rural American South, perhaps over a hundred years ago, a boy and his father spent their days working and farming a portion of land they rented from a wealthy landowner. This practice, called sharecropping, was common in the South after the American Civil War and the abolition of slavery. But it was a very difficult way for African Americans to earn a living and, in fact, really no different from slavery.

So when the boy's father is unable to support and feed his family on his meager sharecropper's earnings, he becomes desperate and steals a neighbor's pig. But, soon after he is caught. The police burst into their home before they violently arrest and take his father away. As the sheriff drives away in the wagon, the father's faithful coon dog, Sounder, chases after him. But one of the guards, overeager to wield his power, pulls out a gun and shoots the dog, injuring him. Like the boy's father, Sounder also disappears, and the boy doesn't know when he will see either of them again, if ever.

While this story gives a realistic depiction of the lives of African Americans living in the rural South at the turn of the twentieth century, it is also a universal story about loss, loneliness, and hope. That none of the characters, with the exception of Sounder, have names further emphasizes this universality. Any man, woman, or child who has felt helpless and alone in their grief will connect to this boy and remember they are not alone. Anyone who has ever striven for something that seems out of reach (the boy also desperately wants an education) will also find a model of determination and perseverance.

**For those also seeking**: models for identity
**For those drawn to**: character, language
**Themes/subjects**: African American history, anxiety/fears, books, death, dead or absent father, dogs, faith, family, farm life, feudal systems, food, grief, guns, injustice, loneliness, missing persons, names and naming, otherness, poverty, prison/incarceration, racism, racial violence, school, segregation, southern United States, survival
**Reading interest level**: grades 6–8

**Curricular tie-ins**: Use this book to bring the lives of African Americans living in the South during the Reconstruction and its relevance to present-day arguments for reparations.
**Adaptations & alternative formats**: film directed by Martin Ritt (1972); audiobook read by Stephen Fry (2005)
**Read-alikes**: Mildred Taylor's *Roll of Thunder, Hear my Cry* would be a perfect historical read to follow *Sounder* as it picks up African American history in the South in the early twentieth century. Also, Christopher Paul Curtis's *The Watsons Go to Birmingham* depicts racial injustice toward African Americans.

**Cushman, Karen** (1941–)
**The Midwife's Apprentice** (1995). New York: Clarion Books, 2012. 122pp. 978-0547722177.

The girl, who might have been 12 or 13, is discovered while sleeping on a dung heap. A peasant, with no parents or family, with no name even, the girl has no place in medieval England. Her whole life, she has been homeless and drifting, doing whatever she can to stave off hunger and keep warm (even if that means sleeping on a dung heap).

So, when the sharp-nosed midwife discovers her sleeping on the dung heap, the girl begs to be her apprentice so as to secure a little food and shelter. The midwife, being both mean and cunning, is happy to exploit this opportunity for cheap labor. So she takes the girl on and uses her as her assistant. Dubbing the girl Beetle, as in *dung beetle*, the midwife bosses her and constantly belittles her with harsh criticism. But Beetle has no better options, so she tolerates the abuse and tries to learn what she can so as to make the most of her situation. With this effort, though, she starts to discover her own gifts and her own desires, and, in knowing herself, she begins to create her own place in world.

While this novel is short, its depictions of the effects of childhood neglect are deeply thought provoking. Beetle, who later names herself Alyce, struggles with low self-esteem, doubts her authority (even when considering her own feelings), and lacks a sense of identity. Any reader who has had to face these challenges on his or her own will find in this book a kindred spirit as Alyce, who draws upon only her inner strength, finds the courage to persevere.

**For those also seeking**: reassurance/comfort/confirmation of self-worth/strength
**For those drawn to**: character, language
**Themes/subjects**: abused children, abuse (emotional), apprentices, agency and powerlessness, aiding/helping, babies, birth, body image, bullying, cats, child labor exploitation, child neglect, class differences, courage, depression, dreams, England, existentialism, gossip, heroines, homelessness, hope, hunger, identity formation, imagination, loneliness, low self-esteem, medicine, Middle Ages, misanthropes, missing persons, names and naming, orphans, oppressive environments, outcasts/outsiders, poverty, pregnancy, runaway children, self-knowledge, self-reliance, superstitions, survival, village/small-town life, women's history
**Reading interest level**: grades K–7
**Curricular tie-ins**: Use this book in conjunction with a unit on the history of medicine, particularly with respect to women's health.
**Adaptations & alternative formats**: audiobook read by Jenny Sterlin (2008)
**Translations**: Spanish: *Aprendiz De Comadrona*; French: *L'apprentie Sage-Femme*
**Read-alikes**: The protagonist of Kate Douglas Wiggin's *Rebecca of Sunnybrook Farm* faces a similar situation and learns to persevere without familial support. Karen Cushman's *Catherine, Called Birdy* and *Matilda Bone* are also both stories of girls living in medieval England.

**Hesse, Karen** (1952–)
**Out of the Dust** (1997). New York: Scholastic Inc., 1999. 227pp. 978-0590371254.

Billie Jo is a 15-year-old girl living on a farm in Oklahoma during the 1930s, one of the worst places to be. It is not only the Great Depression but also the center of the Dust Bowl. For years, severe dust storms have destroyed her father's farm and filled their home with layers of grime. She can't even sit down to a meal without getting the taste of dirt in her mouth. While friends and neighbors move out West, hoping for better luck in California, she watches her mother and father struggle through their days, trying to hold out for rain.

Then, a terrible accident happens. A fire takes away Billie Jo's mother and her newborn brother. Billie Jo survives, but her hands are burned so badly, she struggles to play her beloved piano. As she and her father grieve over their loss, they stop talking, and an icy distance grows between them. It seems Billie Jo has lost everything she has ever loved, and she no longer knows where to turn for hope.

Written in the first person, in free verse, this novel offers an intimate account of one of the worst periods during the Dust Bowl (1934–1936). Hesse's command of language, the music she creates through her words, and her precision of detail are outstanding. Readers who feel lonely, or abandoned, will quickly identify with Billie Jo as she struggles to find hope in the wake of a series of tragic events.

**For those also seeking**: acceptance
**For those drawn to**: language
**Themes/subjects**: accidents (major), art (as a coping mechanism), coming of age, death, depression, disability, environmentalism, farm life, father-daughter relationships, Great Depression (United States), grief, guilt, hope, loneliness, music, pain/suffering, poverty, pregnancy, self-blame (psychology), trauma
**Reading interest level**: grades 6–8
**Curricular tie-ins**: Use this story to interrogate how current industrial practices (such as fracking) threaten the environment.
**Adaptations & alternative formats**: audiobook read by Marika Mashburn (2007)
**Translations**: Spanish: *Lejos del Polvo*
**Read-alikes**: Sandra Cisneros's *A House on Mango Street* is another lyrically told novel featuring a coming-of-age, female protagonist. Clare Vanderpool's *Moon over Manifest* is another story of a girl during Great Depression. Dan Gemeinhart's *Scar Island* and Ann E. Burg's *All the Broken Pieces* both have main characters who feel responsible for a catastrophic accident to a family member, and both novels explore the theme of guilt.


**Speare, Elizabeth George** (1908–1994)
**The Witch of Blackbird Pond** (1958). Boston: Sandpiper, 2011. 255pp. 978-0547550299.

Orphaned and alone, 16-year-old Katherine "Kit" Tyler dares to sail from Barbados, the only home she has known, to America, where her only surviving relatives live in Connecticut Colony. The daughter of a wealthy plantation family, Kit had previously only known a life of beauty and luxury. She is hardly prepared for the bleak scene that is Wethersfield, the Puritan settlement where her aunt, uncle, and two cousins live. And, although her relatives welcome her to their home, they hardly know what to make of her extravagant wardrobe, her love of reading, her make-believe and other idle habits, and her outspoken, unconventional ways.

Though Kit learns to adapt to her new surroundings, she questions some of the Puritans' beliefs, which at times seem arbitrary, if not outright hypocritical. Kit continues to think for herself and make her own judgments. For instance, she befriends an old Quaker woman named Hannah who lives at Blackbird Pond—even though the rest of the town has shunned her for having different religious beliefs. But when a fever epidemic spreads throughout the town, the town looks for someone to blame. They point their finger at Hannah, convinced she is a witch, and Kit, because of her association with Hannah, also becomes accused. Jailed and awaiting trial, Kit fears for her life. How can she prove her innocence when everyone has already assumed her guilt?

While the characters and setting are fictionalized, Speare precisely conveys the emotional truth of this dark history. She depicts the dreariness of Puritan life (their strict attitudes; their long, labor-intensive routines; their superstitious, close-minded views) so as to reveal the dangers of mindlessness. As the New England witch trials demonstrate, such faith can create a vacuum for evil rather than good. Kit Tyler, in refusing to allow popular opinion to sway her convictions, demonstrates that thoughtful resistance is the only way to battle such madness and stands apart as a model of nonconformity. Treated as an alien outsider, and also accused, she also reminds readers they are not the only ones who feel alone.

**For those also seeking**: connection with others/awareness of not being alone
**For those drawn to**: story, character
**Themes/subjects**: adaptation/adjusting to change, beauty/ugliness, being different, books, colonial New England, crushes, courage, cultural differences, education, family, fashion/costume, friendship, heroines, homesickness, hypocrisy, insiders/outsiders, loneliness, conformity and nonconformity, Puritans, gender roles, mob mentality, otherness, outcasts/misfits, rituals and traditions, romance, school, slavery, superstitions, witch hunting, work (labor), wrongfully accused
**Reading interest level**: grades 5–8

**Curricular tie-ins**: Ask students to compare a current event in the news or other historical event that illustrates the power of mob mentality to the witch trials. As a further reflection, ask students to consider how or if mob mentality can be used for good.
**Adaptations & alternative formats**: audiobook read by Mary Beth Hurt (2003)
**Read-alikes**: Injustice toward witches is also explored in Sid Fleishman's *The 13th Floor* and Diana Wynne Jones's *Witch Week*.

**Paterson, Katherine** (1932–)
**The Master Puppeteer** (1975). Illustrated by Haru Wells. New York: HarperCollins, 1989. 179pp. 978-0064402811.

Thirteen-year-old Jiro is the only surviving son in his family. Born during the eighteenth century in Osaka, Japan, Jiro's three older siblings died in a plague when he was just an infant. Now in the wake of a five-year famine, the city is at war with itself. Poor, starving peasants, called "street rovers," are rioting in the streets and galvanizing behind a mysterious Robin Hood–like figure, Saburo, who is said to steal from the rich in order to feed the poor. Though, truth be told, no one has ever actually met him, and the poor do not seem to be profiting any from his help.

While Jiro is not well off, his situation is better than most. His father is a puppet maker who supplies many of the puppets at the Hanzana, the master pupeeteer Yoshida's theater. Jiro assists him, though he is not very skillful. Sensing his burden to his family, as both a poor apprentice and another hungry mouth to feed, Jiro decides to run away to the Hanzana and apprentice himself to Yoshida. While his new life at the theater provides him with both food and shelter, his desertion upsets his relationship with his family. After he leaves, his father disappears and his mother goes on starving, and as long as he remains at the Hanzana, he must live with this guilt.

Readers can easily empathize and connect with Jiro's tragic situation: On the one hand, his struggling, penurious parents make him feel like he is unwanted and a burden. Yet, once he leaves, his mother shames him for his disloyalty. As Jiro tries to reconcile his motivations and actions, he reveals the dark reality of our humanity—how we all share a tendency toward selfishness and self-interest and how an impoverished environment can bring out the desperate and worst in everyone.

**For those also seeking**: courage to make a change
**For those drawn to**: story, character
**Themes/subjects**: abused children, anxiety/fears, betrayal, courage, critical thinking/strategy, dead or absent father, feudal systems, food, friendship, guilt, justice and injustice, only children, Japanese history, loyalty, manipulation, missing persons, moral dilemmas, mother-son relationships, plays, poverty, puppets, riots, secrets, self-blame (psychology), survival, work (labor), self-interest
**Reading interest level**: grades 5–8
**Curricular tie-ins**: To heighten students' awareness of the puppeteer's political role, ask students to identify present-day analogies of puppeteering. For example, discuss bias and how it can be detected in the media.
**Translations**: Spanish: *El Maestro De Las Marionetas*; French: *Le Voleur Du Tokaïdo*
**Read-alikes**: Laura Amy Schlitz's *Splendors and Glooms* is about a boy and girl who are assistants to a puppet master.


**Yep, Laurence** (1948–)
**Dragonwings** (1975). New York: HarperCollins, 2000. 317pp. 978-0064400855.

Moon Shadow is eight years old when he leaves his mother and his home behind in China and crosses the Pacific to be with his father, whom he has never met before, in San Francisco. In search of a better living, his father left for America before Moon Shadow was born. Ever since, he has been working at a laundry, sending half his wages to his family in China and saving the remainder to bring them to the United States. But it's 1906, a time when the Chinese Exclusion Act is still in effect. Because the law prohibits Chinese laborers from immigrating to the United States, it is very difficult (and expensive) for his father to bring their family together again.

Moon Shadow lives in San Francisco's Chinatown, with other Chinese immigrants, and must adjust not only to his father and new surroundings but also to the constant threat of racial violence. Though Moon Shadow and his father find a friendly presence at the home they rent from an elderly white woman, their home is destroyed by the San Francisco earthquake and forces Moon Shadow and his father to move on and start over. Inspired by the Wright brothers, they decide to build an airplane. They hope that they can attract paying spectators so they can save enough money so their family can be reunited.

A masterful storyteller, Yep uses brilliant visual language that leaves a lasting impression. His narrative structure, the way he weaves in Chinese legends (dragon legends in particular) while simultaneously embracing the format of the American novel, further underscores his depiction of the immigrant experience. While Moon Shadow is an outsider, he eventually realizes that his own ethnocentrism is partly to blame. In this way, he reminds readers that they must also actively try to bridge differences if they want to connect with others.

**For those also seeking**: courage to make a change
**For those drawn to**: story
**Themes/subjects**: adaptation/adjusting to change, addiction, aiding/helping, airplanes, books, bullying, cultural differences, dragons, earthquakes/volcanoes, ethnocentrism, father-son relationships, fear, food, [the] immigrant experience, kites, language, literacy, missing persons, otherness, San Francisco, stories and storytelling, translation/translators, nurturers
**Reading interest level**: grades 4–7
**Curricular tie-ins**: As a tie-in with geometry, have students build and fly their own kites. To further emphasize cultural traditions and differences, ask them to compare and contrast the significance of kite flying or symbolism in other cultures.
**Read-alikes**: *Dragonwings* is a part of Laurence Yep's series, Golden Mountain Chronicles, which covers immigrant and Chinese American experiences between 1835 to the present. In Ann E. Burg's *All the Broken Pieces*, a boy immigrates to the United States from Vietnam and also faces racism.

## Courage to Make a Change

**Avi**
**The True Confessions of Charlotte Doyle** (1990). New York: Scholastic Inc., 2012. 215pp. 978-0545477116.

It's the summer of 1832 when 13-year-old Charlotte Doyle finishes her final year at the Barrington School for Better Girls and sets sail from Liverpool, England, to meet her family back home in Providence, Rhode Island. To her surprise, and horror, no other passengers are aboard the *Seahawk*—just the ship's captain and crew of poor, downtrodden men. At first, Charlotte, who has been taught to be a lady and never befriend those below her social station, spends the first weeks in miserable isolation.

Historical Fiction

But once she realizes that the ship's captain, Captain Jaggery, is not a gentleman, as she at first believed, but actually a deranged and deadly killer, she becomes disillusioned of social customs and casts them aside. Thus, she sheds her white gloves, skirts, and petticoats and dons a sailor's suit and joins the crew instead. In doing so, she protests Captain Jaggery's cruelty and demonstrates her solidarity with the other men. But Captain Jaggery will not tolerate rebellion of any kind. To punish her for her opposition, he accuses her of murder. Charlotte has just 24 hours to prove her innocence or else she will be hanged!

Avi has a special gift for getting into the minds of his characters and translating their thoughts with exacting detail. The solitary setting of the ship builds the novel's suspense as every character is completely vulnerable to the violent whims of the cruel captain. But it is Charlotte's transformation from an unthinking follower to a self-possessed, principled leader that leaves a lasting impression. Readers who feel as though they are powerless or lacking agency may think again once they meet Charlotte, who demonstrates that one is never too young to stand up for his or her own convictions and make his or her own choices.

**For those also seeking**: reassurance/comfort/confirmation of self-worth/strength
**For those drawn to**: character
**Themes/subjects**: adaptation/adjusting to change, authoritarian figures, being different, boats and ships, class differences, courage, cowardice, empathy, etiquette and customs, friendship, gender roles, guilt, humility, justice and injustice, knives/daggers/swords, loneliness, trust, missing persons, moral dilemmas, murder, otherness, prejudice, rebellions/coups, sea voyage, wrongfully accused, women's history
**Reading interest level**: grades 6–8
**Curricular tie-ins**: As a history lesson, research women's rights in the West during the nineteenth century. Ask students to reflect on why Avi would create a character like Charlotte Doyle even though it is unlikely such a person existed at that time.
**Adaptations & alternative formats**: audiobook read by Alexandra O'Karma (2011)
**Translations**: Spanish: *Las Verdaderas Confesiones De Charlotte Doyle*
**Read-alikes**: The female protagonist in Elizabeth George Speare's *The Witch of Blackbird Pond* is also a story about being wrongfully accused. Sharon Creech's *The Wanderer* is another sea adventure featuring a girl who crosses the Atlantic.

**Forbes, Esther** (1891–1967)
**Johnny Tremain** (1943). Boston: Graphia, 2011. 300pp. 978-0547614328.

Johnny Tremain is only 14 years old, but he is already one of the best silversmiths in the Massachusetts Bay Colony. Although he is still just an apprentice under the elderly Mr. Lapham, he boasts and bosses the other apprentices around as if he owns the shop. As the most promising apprentice, Johnny's fantasies are not far from reality; he will inherit the shop when Mr. Lapham dies.

But then a terrible accident occurs while he is melting silver at the shop, and his right hand becomes paralyzed and disfigured. Without the use of both his hands, he can no longer handle the delicate artistry and craftwork of silver sculpting, and his future as a silversmith is destroyed. In order to survive, he must find other work, but it seems no one will take him on because of his disability. He wanders from guild to guild, trying to find a job as a candlemaker, a sea hand, but no one will take him.

Finally, he wanders into the printing press of *The Observer* and is offered a job delivering papers. Riding horseback throughout Massachusetts, by delivering these papers, he helps spread the word of the coming rebellion against the British, as they continue to tax the colonists while refusing them political representation. As Johnny becomes more and more involved with the resistance, he finds a new sense of purpose, a higher cause, and at the same time discovers the secrets of his familial past.

This is a story about humility and the importance of thinking beyond individual self-interest to consider the political whole. After his accident, Johnny experiences the world of the disenfranchised for the first time, and this awakening propels him to social justice. He uses the skills he has—literacy, critical thinking—to serve his community and not just himself. Readers who are seeking the courage to change will find a model of transformation in Johnny.

**For those also seeking**: disinterested understanding of the world
**For those drawn to**: character
**Themes/subjects**: adaptation/adjusting to change, American Revolution, apprentices, Boston Tea Party, class differences, colonial New England, courage, cowardice, death, depression, disability, disfigurement, friendship, gender roles, horses, justice and injustice, literacy, loneliness, newspapers,

*Historical Fiction*

orphans, pride, rebellions/coups, romance, secrets, soldiers, slavery, spies and spying, self-interest
**Reading interest level**: grades 6–8
**Curricular tie-ins**: Ask students to research the role of the printing press (newspapers and pamphlets) and their role in democracy and to compare them to modern means of communication (e.g., social media and the Arab Spring).
**Adaptations & alternative formats**: audiobook read by Grace Conlin (2009); film adaptation directed by Robert Stevenson (1957)
**Read-alikes**: Daniel in Elizabeth George Speare's *The Bronze Bow* must also overcome personal pride. Jean Fritz's *Early Thunder* is about another 14-year-old boy living in 1770s, and *The Cabin Faced West* is also set during the American Revolution.

**Garfield, Leon** (1921–1996)
**John Diamond (United States: Footsteps)** (1980). London: Vintage Books, 2014. 238pp. 978-0099583271.

Twelve-year-old William Jones can't sleep. His father, whose bedroom is below his, paces back and forth all through the night, and his constant, dragging shuffle keeps William awake. When his father falls fatally ill, the pacing grows worse and then, one night, ceases completely. Fearing the worst, William goes to check on him and finds him alive but jittery and distraught. His father confesses the source of his trouble: guilt. He admits to William that he has swindled a business colleague Alfred Diamond and may be partially responsible for his death. His father dies soon after, before William can ask him questions.

Burdened with this disappointing revelation, William decides to run away to London and locate John Diamond, Alfred Diamond's son, to try to make amends on behalf of his father. Unfortunately, eighteenth-century London is not a friendly place to runaway children, and William, who appears obviously well-off, becomes the frequent target of swindlers and muggers. At least, though, he makes the acquaintance of a dwarf, Mr. Seed. Though a tad mercenary and opportunistic, Mr. Seed nonetheless helps William look for John Diamond, who proves very difficult to find, and unravel the mystery of the 10,000 pounds William's father is said to have stolen from Alfred Diamond.

A master of understatement, Garfield succeeds in turning what would otherwise be a dark, dangerous adventure into a light, fun, laugh riot. Garfield's humor, however, does not distract from more serious themes about guilt. As William initially takes on his father's guilt so as to assuage his own disillusionment, he begins to eventually realize that he is not his father and that he can *choose* to live his life differently. Through multiple trials, William shows that he possesses the strength of character his father lacked. Thus, he reminds readers that they, too, can choose who they want to be—if they show the courage.

**For those also seeking**: models for identity
**For those drawn to**: character, language
**Themes/subjects**: alcohol/alcoholism, anxiety/fears, buried/hidden treasure, class differences, courage, dead or absent fathers, dwarfs, fashion/costume, friendship, gambling, gangs and gangsters, good and evil, guilt, heroism, humor, inns/taverns, justice and injustice, language/communication, laws, London, missing persons, money/debt, mysteries, poverty, quarrels/fights, revenge, runaway children, secrets, self-blame (psychology), stealing,
**Reading interest level**: grades 4–7
**Curricular tie-ins**: Cockney rhyming slang is a pronounced feature of this novel. Teach students how to create their own cockney rhyming slang. For more advanced study, expand into a unit about language and class (i.e., how certain Englishes are privileged) with respect to the book and with respect to World Englishes.
**Adaptations & alternative formats**: audiobook read by Ron Keith (2013)
**Read-alikes**: Leon Garfield's *Smith* and *Black Jack* are both stories of boys in eighteenth-century London, and *The Strange Affair of Adelaide Harris* is probably his wittiest.

**Pullman, Philip** (1946–)
**The Ruby in the Smoke** (1985). New York: Ember, 2013. 978-0375845161.

The opening paragraph in *The Ruby in the Smoke* immediately captures the reader's attention. After describing a girl who lives in Victorian London, the narrator says, "Her name was Sally Lockhart; and within fifteen minutes, she was going to kill a man." Acting on the contents of a mysterious letter, Sally becomes involved in a highly dangerous intrigue. As she tries to find information about the death of her father, she unearths new facts about the past, learns that her inheritance has disappeared, and discovers that a priceless ruby is somehow involved in her fate. An orphan

# Historical Fiction

since her father's death three months earlier, Sally lives with a cruel distant relative. When this relative tries to bully Sally, she decides to leave for good. Alone, homeless, and frightened, Sally must figure out how to survive in a peril-filled world.

This historical mystery will attract readers who enjoy suspenseful, action-filled plots that contain many twists and turns. Pullman evokes a darkly brooding, Dickensian atmosphere in this first of four Sally Lockhart mysteries. Larger-than-life characters such as the inimitable Mrs. Holland could easily have walked out of a Dickens novel.

Readers looking for courage to make a change in their lives will find Sally's example a source of inspiration. When bullied by her guardian, she leaves despite the fact that she has nowhere to go and no one to help her. Undaunted, she moves steadily forward in the face of great personal danger. Although she would like to ignore the mysterious circumstances of her father's death, she tells herself that "something was wrong, and there was no one but her to set it right."

Because she was taught at home by her father, Sally's education is uneven and unconventional. Although she knows nothing about the arts, she has "a thorough grounding in the principles of military tactics and book-keeping, a close acquaintance with the affairs of the Stock Market, and a working knowledge of Hindustani." Constrained by the limited options available to women in the nineteenth century, Sally ignores convention and tries her hand at bookkeeping and business. Readers who feel inferior because they do not conform to the norm will see their differences as strengths after reading Sally's story.

**For those also seeking**: connection with others/awareness of not being alone
**For those drawn to**: story, setting
**Themes/subjects**: mystery/suspense, secrets, London, British history, orphans, dead or absent father, buried/hidden treasure, opium trade, photography (nineteenth century), gender roles, assertiveness, addiction
**Reading interest level**: grade 7 and up
**Curricular tie-ins**: Ask students to research the occupations open to females in the Victorian era. Students could pretend that they are nineteenth-century women and write an editorial about their plight. Alternatively they could research photography in the nineteenth century and present their findings as a YouTube video.

**Adaptations & alternative formats**: movie directed by Brian Percival (2006); audiobook read by Anton Lesser (2006)
**Translations**: Spanish: *Sally y la Maldición del Rubí*; French: *La Malédiction du Rubis*
**Read-alikes**: Readers who enjoyed this first book in the Sally Lockhart series will like its sequels (*The Shadow in the North*, *The Tiger in the Well*, and *The Tin Princess*). Leon Garfield's *John Diamond* and Jennifer Donnelly's *These Shallow Graves* are historical mysteries about a nineteenth-century youth who unravels the mystery of a father's past. Laura Amy Schlitz's *Splendors and Glooms* and Karen Foxlee's *A Most Magical Girl* are both gothic thrillers set in Victorian London.


**Speare, Elizabeth George** (1908–1994)
**The Bronze Bow** (1961). Boston: Houghton Mifflin, 1995. 255pp. 978-0395137192.

For five years, Daniel has been hiding in the mountains of Galilee, fighting a guerilla war against the Roman occupation. Daniel joined the resistance after the Romans crucified his father, devastating and destroying his family. His mother dies of heartbreak, and his sister, Leah, is so traumatized that she barely speaks and is afraid to step out of the house. His grandmother, Daniel and Leah's only remaining relative, tries to look after them, but poverty forces her to sell Daniel to a blacksmith as an indentured servant. Weary of the blacksmith's brutishness, Daniel escapes to the mountains, leaving behind what remains of his family in Ketzah.

But through a chance encounter with a twin brother and sister from his village, Joel and Malthace, he discovers that his grandmother is dying and his sister needs him. Although he returns to Ketzah, vengeance is still on his mind, and with the help of Joel and Malthace, he continues to plot against the Romans. At the same time, some villagers are losing faith in the guerilla war. It is said that their leader, Rosh, steals from the rich to give to the poor, but, for all his pillaging, the poor seem no better off. Daniel finds himself lured by a new leader, Jesus of Nazareth, who has come to his town preaching a message of love instead of violence. Daniel is captivated yet cannot reconcile Jesus's teachings with his own oath: How can he "live and die for God's victory" if he does not fight?

This action-packed story, rich in sensory details, is completely engrossing. On the one hand, it offers a vivid picture of life during the time of Christ.

But it also tells a more universal story about overcoming personal pride in order to become receptive and willing to change.

**For those also seeking**: acceptance
**For those drawn to**: story, language
**Themes/subjects**: battles/wars, Christianity, critical thinking/strategy, cultural differences, disability, duty, faith, fear, good and evil, hatred, hunger, illness, Jesus Christ, Judaism, leadership, loneliness, love, miracles, oaths, occupied countries, phobias, Roman Empire, revenge, romance, siblings and sibling issues, sacrifice, slavery, survival, trauma, war (psychological effects), violence, mountains, bible stories
**Reading interest level**: grades 3–7
**Curricular tie-ins**: To emphasize how the past shapes the present, ask students to identify current events in Israel that mirror the conflicts in the book.
**Adaptations & alternative formats**: audiobook read by Mary Woods (2006)
**Read-alikes**: Donna Jo Napoli's *Song of the Magdalene* is about a girl growing up in ancient Israel, and Geraldine McCaughrean's *Not the End of the World* tells the biblical story of Noah's Ark.

**Wilder, Laura Ingalls** (1867–1957)
**These Happy Golden Years** (1943). New York: HarperTrophy, 1971. 288pp. 978-0064400084.

Laura, who is almost 16, leaves home to board with homesteaders when she begins her career as a teacher in a one-room schoolhouse. After she arrives at her new home, she is shocked by Mrs. Brewster's mean spirit and lack of hospitality. Mrs. Brewster opens Laura's eyes to a way of life and type of thinking she never knew existed. Because it is the beginning of a cold, harsh winter, Laura expects to be trapped at the Brewster's home for six long weeks. Laura, who is small for her age and underage for a teacher, is also deeply fearful of teaching. She worries about managing children who misbehave and dealing with boys who are bigger and stronger than her. Although she receives unexpected help from Almanzo Wilder, she must also cope with unwanted attention from him.

In this eighth story in The Little House series, Laura enters the workforce as a teacher, seamstress, and lady's companion. She feels unprepared to do so and believes she lacks the skills to succeed. Nevertheless she perseveres and tries to make the best of adversity. Pa reminds her, "You've tackled every job that ever came your way . . . You never shirked, and you always stuck to it till you did what you set out to do."

The book is also about leaving home, each temporary relocation preparing Laura for her ultimate move to her own home. Readers who must face something that they think they cannot handle will gain courage from Laura's example. They will also realize that people who succeed often feel scared and unprepared for major changes and challenges.

**For those also seeking**: awakening/new perspectives/enlargement of possibilities
**For those drawn to**: setting, character
**Themes/subjects**: frontier and pioneer life, education, teachers, romance, family, horses, self-confidence, self-reliance, sisters, perseverance/determination, midwestern United States, work (labor)
**Reading interest level**: grade 5 and up
**Curricular tie-ins**: Divide students into small groups for a jigsaw activity. Each group could research one aspect of schools in the nineteenth century, exploring topics such as what students were taught, what type of books they used, how were they taught, what the classroom was like, how they were assessed, and what the occupation of teaching was like.
**Adaptations & alternative formats**: Disney mini-series directed by David Cunningham (2005); audiobook read by Cherry Jones (2006)
**Translations**: Spanish: *Aquellos Años Dorados*; French: *Ces Heureuses Années*
**Read-alikes**: Like Laura, Anne in L. M. Montgomery's *Anne of Avonlea* becomes a teacher in a one-room schoolhouse. Although set a couple of decades after *These Happy Golden Years*, Laura Amy Schlitz's *The Hired Girl* is about an adolescent girl getting her first full-time jobs.

## Acceptance

**Bawden, Nina** (1925–2012)
**Carrie's War** (1973). London: Puffin Books, 2014. 210pp. 978-0141354903.

When World War II breaks out, Carrie Willow and her little brother, Nick, are evacuated from their London home and sent to live with strangers in the quiet Welsh countryside where they can escape the danger of city bombings. But they miss their father, who is fighting in the navy, and their mother, who is an ambulance driver. A middle-aged brother, Mr. Evans, and his kind, younger sister, "Auntie Lou," take them into their home. But Mr. Evans, who is always scowling and criticizing, does not seem to want them around; only gentle Auntie Lou provides any comfort and solace.

But the clouds lift when Carrie and her brother discover the home of Mr. Evan's estranged sister, which is hidden in the forest in a place called "Druid's Bottom." There they meet Hepzibah, the help; an odd little man named Johnny; and another evacuee, about Carrie's age, named Albert. Together they gather in Hepzibah's kitchen, feast on pie, and listen to Hepzibah as she tells them stories, including the story of the "screaming skull" and the terrible curse that haunts Druid's Bottom. At first, Carrie thinks it is just a fiction, but a series of tragic events convince her that the curse is not only true but also she is to blame.

While set during World War II, this novel is more about the war's psychological effects and how it can be used as a metaphor for one's own ethical dilemmas. Carrie, who recounts the story as an adult and mother, continues to feel guilt for her childhood actions, which she wrongly believed led to her friends' destruction. Thus she reveals the complex, emotional dimensions of guilt—how *knowing* one is blameless does not necessarily make one *feel* blameless. Readers who are struggling with their own conscience may be moved by this story's tale of redemption toward self-acceptance. For the same reason, it also provides connection with others.

**For those also seeking**: connection with others/awareness of not being alone
**For those drawn to**: character, language
**Themes/subjects**: agency and powerlessness, aging elders, authoritarian figures, disability, dreams, family conflict, fear, guilt, haunted houses, homesickness, memory, moral dilemmas, nurturers, oppressive environments, secrets, self-blame (psychology), superstitions, trauma, war (psychological effects), Wales, World War II
**Reading interest level**: grades K–7
**Curricular tie-ins**: Define and discuss kinds of trauma. Then ask students to search for current examples of children who have been affected by war or terrorism countries and to reflect on the potential lifelong effects of unresolved trauma.
**Adaptations & alternative formats**: audiobook read by Jenny Sterlin (2008)

**Translations**: Spanish: *Aprendiz De Comadrona*; French: *L'apprentie Sage-Femme*
**Read-alikes**: Kimberly Brubaker Bradley's *The War That Saved My Life* and C. S. Lewis's *The Lion, the Witch & the Wardrobe* are both stories about war evacuees. The protagonist of Kate Douglas Wiggin's *Rebecca of Sunnybrook Farm* faces a similar situation and learns to persevere without familial support.


**Erdrich, Louise** (1954–)
**The Birchbark House** (1999). Illustrated by the author. New York: Hyperion Paperbacks for Children, 2002. 244pp. 978-0786814541.

When mid–nineteenth-century fur traders discover a baby on an island, they realize that the rest of her tribe must have died from smallpox. Afraid of contracting the disease, they leave the baby knowing that she will die. After they depart, one trader has second thoughts about this decision. The story then shifts to seven-year-old Omakaya, an Ojibwa girl living with her parents, grandmother, older sister, and two younger brothers. Her life is happy until her family contracts smallpox and her youngest brother dies of it.

Nothing in her eight years prepares Omakaya for the grief she suffers when her younger brother dies. Although she is supported by a wise grandmother and a close-knit family, Omakaya experiences a depression that totally engulfs her. As she gradually learns to cope, she begins to realize that, like her grandmother, she is a healer. A National Book Award finalist, *The Birchbark House* will resonate with readers who must accept something that they cannot change. Omakaya's story will also resonate with any child who has experienced depression or grief over the death of a loved one.

Readers who wonder what it would have been like to be an indigenous child in nineteenth-century America will learn about the household activities, the customs, and the traditions of the Ojibwa people. The last chapter—"Full Circle"—ties together strands of the plot in a surprising and satisfying way.

**For those also seeking**: disinterested understanding of the world
**For those drawn to**: character, setting
**Themes/subjects**: Native American history, indigenous peoples (United States), family, siblings and sibling issues, depression, nature, faith, illness,

Historical Fiction

smallpox, death, grief, rituals and traditions, cultural differences, grandmothers, stories and storytelling, work (labor), seasons, bears
**Reading interest level**: grades 2–6
**Curricular tie-ins**: Ask students to create questions and answers for a game-show quiz. These questions and answers could be about topics in the novel that they are curious about (e.g., smallpox, Ojibwa people, native folklore stories, fur trapping, maple syrup production).
**Adaptations & alternative formats**: audiobook read by Nicolle Littrell (2004)
**Read-alikes**: Readers who enjoyed this story will also like its sequels: *The Game of Silence, The Porcupine Year, Chickadee,* and *Makoons.* Laura Ingalls Wilder's *Little House on the Prairie* is another historical novel about a girl living in the nineteenth century, while Cynthia Kadohata's *Kira-Kira* is a story about the death of a sibling.


**Wilder, Laura Ingalls** (1867–1957)
**By the Shores of Silver Lake** (1939). New York: HarperTrophy, 1971. 290pp. 978-0064400053.

When Aunt Docia visits the Ingalls, she discovers that Ma and the girls are recuperating from scarlet fever, an illness that has left Laura's sister, Mary, blind and forced Pa into debt. Aunt Docia offers Pa a job with her husband, a contractor on the new railroad in South Dakota. Pa accepts and leaves right away with Aunt Docia. Ma and the girls join Pa later, traveling by train after Mary is stronger. Laura is excited to move; if she had her way, she acknowledges, she "would rather not stop anywhere. She would rather go on and on, to the very end of the road, wherever it was." Ma, on the other hand, does not want to move and is anxious about living in the "wild west."

Forced to live in a railway shanty among rough men, and then provide room and board to the droves of settlers moving into the area, Ma worries about the safety of the girls in this lawless Western frontier. When the family moves into a surveyor's empty house for the winter, their nearest neighbors are 40 miles away. Uncertainty about the future affects the entire family as Pa is unable to submit a claim for a homestead until spring when weather will allow him to travel. Since people from the East are rushing to settle in the West, Pa is afraid he might be too late to get the land he wants.

When Pa tells Laura that Ma expects her to follow in her footsteps and be a teacher, Laura thinks, "I won't! I won't . . . I don't want to! I can't." But she knows that she must, especially since the family needs the money she can earn to send Mary to a college for the blind. The story will resonate with readers who are struggling to accept situations they cannot change. They will find inspirational role models in both Laura and Mary.

**For those also seeking**: models for identity
**For those drawn to**: setting, story
**Themes/subjects**: frontier and pioneer life, wilderness survival, family, country life, prairies, cooperation and teamwork, sisters, moving houses (relocating), disability, blindness, winter, midwestern United States, trains/subways
**Reading interest level**: grades 4–8
**Curricular tie-ins**: Ask students to work in groups to create a diorama of a frontier village.
**Adaptations & alternative formats**: Disney mini-series directed by David Cunningham (2005); audiobook read by Cherry Jones (2004)
**Translations**: Spanish: *En las Orillas del Lago de Plata*; French: *Sur les Rives du Lac*
**Read-alikes**: Readers interested in stories set in an earlier era about girls the same age as Laura will enjoy Carol Ryrie Brink's *Caddie Woodlawn* and Karen Cushman's *The Ballad of Lucy Whipple* and *Rodzina*.

**Wilder, Laura Ingalls** (1867–1957)
**Little Town on the Prairie** (1941). New York: HarperTrophy, 2004. 307pp. 978-0060581862.

Fourteen-year-old Laura is surprised when Pa asks her if she would like to work in town. Pa tells her there is a job vacancy for a person to sew men's shirts, and Laura accepts, albeit hesitatingly. One of a limited number of jobs open to females in the 1880s, sewing shirts confines Laura indoors during the beautiful summer months. But the Ingalls need the money to send Mary to a college for the blind. Once harvest is over, the family moves from their claim shanty in the country to town for the winter to be close to school. Laura does not want to move, does not want to go to school, and does not want to become a teacher, as Ma expects her to be. Laura, in fact, "did not know what she wanted, but she knew she could not have it, whatever it was."

*Little Town in the Prairie* is about Laura's growing independence as a young woman. Having led a very sheltered life, Laura hates the thought of meeting strangers. But she develops socially throughout the novel and learns to cope with the loss of her beloved sister when Mary goes to college. Laura's growing independence parallels that of the new town and the young country. Just as she listens to the Declaration of Independence on the Fourth of July, and recites at an exhibition, the history of America and the beginnings of self-government, Laura too relies more on herself and less on her parents as she grows older. Readers who are separated from a loved one and those who find it difficult to accept circumstances that cannot be changed will find strength in Laura's example.

**For those also seeking**: reassurance/comfort/confirmation of self-worth/strength
**For those drawn to**: setting
**Themes/subjects**: frontier and pioneer life, family, sisters, urban versus rural living, work (labor), sacrifice, prairies, teachers, adaptation/adjusting to change, independence, shyness, self-confidence, midwestern United States
**Reading interest level**: grade 5 and up
**Curricular tie-ins**: In a think-pair-share activity, students could discuss the differences between easterners and westerners in the novel. Ask them, if they had lived during the time of the novel, which one they would have liked to be and why.
**Adaptations & alternative formats**: Disney mini-series directed by David Cunningham (2005); audiobook read by Cherry Jones (2005)
**Translations**: Spanish: *La Pequeña Ciudad en la Pradera*; French: *La Petite Ville dans la Prairie*
**Read-alikes**: Readers interested in stories set in an earlier era that are about 15-year-old girls will enjoy Louisa May Alcott's *Little Women*, Richard Peck's *A Year down Yonder*, and L. M. Montgomery's *Emily Climbs*.

## Disinterested Understanding of the World

**Lowry, Lois** (1937–)
**Number the Stars** (1989). Boston: Houghton Mifflin Harcourt, 2011. 137pp. 978-0547577098.

By the time Annemarie is 10 years old, the Germans have been occupying her homeland of Copenhagen, in Denmark, for three years. So, for three years, she has lived under the dark shadow of Nazi rule, an existence characterized by constant patrols, enforced curfews, and too little food.

Although Annemarie misses her freedom, she takes solace in her family (her mom and dad and little sister, Kirsti) and her neighbor and best friend, Ellen.

But when the Germans decide they will force all of the Jewish families out of their homes and "relocate" them, Ellen and her family, who are Jewish, must flee. Annemarie's family tries to help them escape, but the journey is wrought with danger; Germans soldiers are everywhere, spying and questioning. And when Annemarie's mother is injured, it is up to her to carry out the final plans of Ellen's and her family's escape.

This compelling narrative provides a realistic account of authoritarian rule from a child's perspective. While set during World War II, it can help readers appreciate the terror of living in war-torn conditions. As Annemarie demonstrates shrewd thinking and courage in the face of danger, she also stands out as a model for identity.

**For those also seeking**: models for identity
**For those drawn to**: character, story
**Themes/subjects**: aiding/helping, anxiety/fears, authoritarian rule, courage, Denmark, empathy, escape, faith, family, food, friendship, Judaism, loyalty, occupied countries, prejudice, racism, rationing, resistance movements, soldiers, secrets, survival, trauma, World War II
**Reading interest level**: grades K–6
**Curricular tie-ins**: While this text would obviously complement units on World War II history, it would be a particularly good segue into researching the ways in which children are affected by war (past and present).
**Adaptations & alternative formats**: audiobook read by Blair Brown (2004)
**Translations**: Spanish: *Quien Cuenta Las Estrellas?*; French: *Compte Les Étoiles*
**Read-alikes**: Yolen's *The Devil's Arithmetic* also offers a child's perspective, this time from a Jewish girl who is in a German concentration camp. Also, in Anne Holmes's *I Am David* is about a boy fleeing a camp in Eastern Europe, where he has spent most of his childhood.

**McCaughrean, Geraldine** (1951–)
**The Kite Rider** (2001). New York: Harper Trophy, 2003. 307pp. 978-0064410915.

Historical Fiction

When Haoyou is twelve years old, he watches his father die after being forced to be a "wind tester." Haoyou's father was lashed to a kite and flown in the air to test the favorability of the winds. The first mate of his father's ship had volunteered Haoyou's father for this barbaric practice in the hope that he would die, an action that would free Haoyou's mother for marriage. With the help of his cousin, Haoyou outwits the first mate's plans to marry his mother. Ironically, a circus then recruits Haoyou to work as a kite rider. This highly dangerous occupation introduces him to many people, including the legendary Kublai Khan.

Readers will experience what it was to live in thirteenth-century China and particularly what it was like to be trapped in a society that presented few opportunities for the poor and the disadvantaged. They will also gain insight into the prejudicial feeling that existed between Chinese and Mongolian peoples.

Raised in a culture that places high value on obedience and respect of elders, Haoyou never questions his dishonest uncle. But when blind obedience endangers the lives of those he cares about, Haoyou begins to challenge authority figures. Haoyou's story will resonate with readers whose parents expect unquestioning obedience.

**For those also seeking**: awakening/new perspectives/enlargement of possibilities
**For those drawn to**: setting
**Themes/subjects**: Kublai Khan, kites, Chinese history, circuses (animal), dead or missing father, cultural differences, poverty, gender roles, challenging authority figures, prejudice, superstitions, obedience, adventure, justice and injustice, gambling
**Reading interest level**: grades 5–8
**Curricular tie-ins**: Ask students to form groups for a jigsaw activity. Each group can research different aspects of thirteenth-century China (e.g., the Yuan dynasty, Kublai Khan, the invasion of the Mongols, customs and traditions, the everyday life of children).
**Adaptations & alternative formats**: audiobook read by Cynthia Bishop and cast (2004)
**Read-alikes**: Characters leave home and spend time at a circus in James Otis's *Toby Tyler*. Readers interested in early Oriental history will also enjoy Linda Sue Park's *A Single Shard* and Katherine Paterson's novels about Japan: *The Sign of the Chrysanthemum* and *Of Nightingales That Weep*.

**Paterson, Katherine** (1932–)
*Lyddie* (1991). New York: Puffin Books, 1995. 182pp. 978-0140373899.

After her father abandons the family and her mother becomes increasingly dysfunctional, Lyddie takes over parental chores and responsibilities. When a bear invades their cabin, Mama reaches a breaking point and takes the two youngest children to go and live with relatives. Thirteen-year-old Lyddie and 10-year-old Charlie stay behind to look after the family farm, enduring the harsh conditions of rural life in mid-nineteenth-century America. After the winter, Mama writes to say that she has hired out Lyddie to work in a tavern and Charlie to work in a mill. Although conditions in the tavern are substandard and the small amount of income that Lyddie earns goes straight to her mother, she perseveres. But when she is unfairly dismissed from her job, she decides to look for factory work in the textile mills of Lowell, Massachusetts. Although she finds work, the conditions are appalling and the 13-hour days exhausting. Lyddie's one hope is to make enough money to pay off the debt on the family farm.

Lowell, Massachusetts, as the cradle of the American Industrial Revolution, is a fascinating setting for those who are curious about what it would have been like to work in the early factories. Readers experience what Lyddie does as she battles injustice, poverty, harassment, and exploitation. The novel also provides a window into the lives of African American slaves and the mentally ill in nineteenth-century America.

Although Lyddie is determined, resourceful, and tough, she experiences doubt and confusion as she worries about her decisions and questions her motives. Readers who suffer from self-doubt or are unsure of their talents will not feel so alone after reading Lyddie's story.

**For those also seeking**: connection with others/awareness of not being alone
**For those drawn to**: character, setting
**Themes/subjects**: industrialization, factory work, work (labor), self-reliance, self-confidence, child labor exploitation, abandoned children, poverty, perseverance/determination, workers' rights/unionization, justice and injustice, money/debt, New England
**Reading interest level**: grades 6–8
**Curricular tie-ins**: *Lyddie* depicts the impact of the Industrial Revolution on nineteenth-century America. Issues such as unhealthy working conditions in factories, exploitation of child workers, harassment of women by

Historical Fiction

men in power, worker safety, and lack of worker rights are vividly portrayed in the novel. Ask students to form five groups. Each group can research one of these issues and compile their research into a companion booklet to the novel.
**Adaptations & alternative formats**: audiobook read by Melba Sibrel (2007)
**Translations**: Spanish: *Lyddie*
**Read-alikes**: Like Lyddie, Dicey in Cynthia Voigt's *Homecoming* must look after the family when her mother becomes increasingly dysfunctional. Although set half a century later, Laura Amy Schlitz's *The Hired Girl* is about a farm girl who leaves home to earn a living.


**Peck, Richard** (1934–)
**A Year Down Yonder** (2000). New York: Puffin Books, 2002. 130pp. 978-0142300701.

Mary Alice has been visiting her Grandma Dowdel in her middle-of-nowhere Illinois town every summer since the Great Depression started in 1929. After eight years, when Mary Alice is 15 years old, the nation is still struggling. In fact, her father loses his job. Unable to make ends meet, Mary Alice's parents send her away from her Chicago home to live with Grandma Dowdel until they can find work. As Grandma Dowdel is known for her roguish, nonconformist tendencies, Mary Alice is fully prepared for, and excited to participate in, her grandma's stunts. But she is less thrilled about adjusting to a new school and trying to make new friends, especially since she is an outsider and the people in Grandma Dowdel's community are not particularly welcoming.

Like the first book in this Grandma Dowdel series, *A Long Way from Chicago*, each chapter in this novel can be read as its own stand-alone short story—like a postcard from Depression-era, rural America—though the narrative impact is deeper when they are read together. It differs from the previous novel, however, by offering a female perspective of this period, particularly with respect to women's work. Mary Alice finds women tending to World War I veterans with PTSD and fundraising for the DAR and Legion Auxiliary Ladies to help support their community.

**For those also seeking**: awakening/new perspectives/enlargement of possibilities
**For those drawn to**: story, character

**Themes/subjects**: aiding/helping, cats, cliques (in school), coming of age, community, country life, grandmothers, Great Depression (United States), gender roles, gossip, guns, humor, insiders/outsiders, midwestern United States, prank tricks and mischief, Prohibition/temperance movements, romance, poverty, school, World War I, resourcefulness
**Reading interest level**: grades 5–8
**Curricular tie-ins**: To draw attention to the physical and psychological effects of war, do a close reading of "A Minute in the Morning." Have students do some background research on trench warfare, mustard gas, and the concept of "shell shock," or PTSD.
**Adaptations & alternative formats**: audiobook read by Lois Smith (2006)
**Read-alikes**: Another story that takes place during the same time, but in England, and that also features a charismatic female is Dodie Smith's *I Capture the Castle*.


**Peck, Richard** (1934–)
**The River Between Us** (2003). Toronto: Penguin, 2005. 164pp. 978-0142403105.

The novel begins and ends in 1916, the year that 15-year-old Howard, his twin brothers, and their father visit Grandma Tillie Pruitt in Grand Tower, Illinois. The novel then shifts to 1861 when Grandma Tillie was 15 years old. The Civil War breaks out and Tillie's mother worries that her son, Noah, will enlist. At first Noah remains home, captivated by a mysterious new boarder who arrives by boat from New Orleans. The Southern belle, Delphine, is accompanied by her dark-skinned companion, Calinda.
The townspeople suspect that Calinda is Delphine's slave and that the girls are spying for the south. Eventually Noah leaves for the war, and word arrives that the troops are ill with measles. Mrs. Pruitt sends Tillie and Delphine to find Noah and bring him home.

In this coming-of-age novel, the harsh realities of war shape the lives and fates of the characters that live through it. Delphine, Calista, and Tillie, each of whom appears ordinary and unheroic, are, in fact, models of courage and selflessness.

Children will gain a deep, emotional understanding of the impact of the Civil War on individuals, families, and communities when they read this novel. An intensely moving story, *The River between Us* captures readers' hearts in a way that nonfictional texts about the Civil War do not usually do.

Terms such as "abolitionism," "multiracialism," and "secession" can seem abstract until readers experience what it would have been like to live at a time when they affected individual lives.

The Mississippi River as both a dividing line between different states and a means of communication between the North and the South is a reverberating symbol in the novel. All strands of the story intersect and converge in the stirring, culminating chapters.

**For those also seeking**: models for identity
**For those drawn to**: character, setting
**Themes/subjects**: American Civil War, battles/wars, insiders/outsiders, outcasts/misfits, slavery, coming of age, poverty, racism, New Orleans, multiracialism, abolitionism, illness, soldiers, twins, village/small-town life, love, selflessness
**Reading interest level**: grade 7 and up
**Curricular tie-ins**: Ask students to pick one of the following topics and conduct further research about it: abolitionism, secession, and multiracialism in nineteenth-century America; Abraham Lincoln; Ulysses S. Grant. With what they learn, students could write an editorial for a Civil War–era newspaper.
**Adaptations & alternative formats**: audiobook read by Lina Patel and Daniel Passer (2006)
**Translations**: Spanish: *El Río Que nos Divide*
**Read-alikes**: Irene Hunt's *Across Five Aprils*, Avi's *Iron Thunder*, and Janet Lunn's *The Root Cellar* are also set during the American Civil War era. Ann E. Burg's *Unbound* is another story about slavery and racism during the 1860s. Katherine Paterson's *Jip: His Story* explores the theme of multiracialism.


**Ryan, Pam Muñoz** (1951–)
**Esperanza Rising** (2000). New York: Scholastic, 2007. 262pp. 978-0439120425.

In the 1930s, Esperanza grows up on a prosperous Mexican ranch and is supported by a loving, close-knit family. Just before she turns 13, bandits kill her father. Her uncle sets fire to the family ranch house in an effort to force Esperanza's mother to marry him. She realizes that her brother-in-laws will always control her future if she remains in Mexico. Sneaking out of the country and immigrating to California, mother and daughter become migrant farmworkers alongside their long-time servants Alfonso, Hortensia, and their son, Miguel. Although Esperanza realizes that they are peasants now, she is unprepared for the challenges they face as poverty-stricken immigrants.

When Esperanza leaves Mexico, her grandmother gives her a blanket to finish crocheting. Abuelita tells her granddaughter, "Look at the zigzag of the blanket. Mountains and valleys. Right now you are in the bottom of the valley and your problems loom big around you. But soon, you will be at the top of a mountain again." Having been accustomed to a life of privilege, Esperanza finds it difficult to adjust to her changed social and financial status. She must also cope with the death of her beloved father, the loss of her home and country, and the devastating illness of her mother. Readers who must accept parts of their life that they cannot change will find a model of how to do so in Esperanza.

Children who read this novel will experience vicariously the injustice and racism that migrant workers faced during this era, an experience that will impress upon them the hardships that these people endured. The novel will particularly resonate with readers who have experienced prejudice or economic hardship.

**For those also seeking**: acceptance
**For those drawn to**: character, setting
**Themes/subjects**: Mexican Americans, (the) immigrant experience, migrant farm workers, Great Depression (United States), class differences, cultural differences, prejudice, justice and injustice, mother-daughter relationships, family, grandmothers, only children, otherness, rituals and traditions, wealth, poverty, moving houses (relocating), workers' rights/unionization, illness, faith, work (labor), California
**Reading interest level**: grades 6–8
**Curricular tie-ins**: This novel would be an ideal resource for a lesson on migrant farmworkers in the United States in the 1930s, or on the immigrant experience, or on the repatriation of Mexican workers in the 1930s. Students could pretend they are a person in one of these groups and role play complaining about their condition with a group of like-minded individuals.
**Adaptations & alternative formats**: audiobook read by Trini Alvarado (2003)
**Translations**: Spanish: *Esperanza Renace*; French: *Les Roses du Mexique*

**Read-alikes**: The Chinese American immigrant experience is depicted in Laurence Yep's *Dragonwings*, the Vietnamese American immigrant experience in Thanhha Lai's *Inside Out and Back Again*, the Polish immigrant experience in Eleanor Estes's *The Hundred Dresses*, and the Russian immigrant experience in Karen Hesse's *Letters from Rifka*. Ann E. Burg's *Serafina's Promise* is about a girl who endures harsh poverty and hopes for a better future.

**Sutcliff, Rosemary** (1920–1992)
**The Mark of the Horse Lord** (1965). Chicago: Chicago Review Press, 2015. 293pp. 978-1613731543.

For the past four years, Phaedrus has lived a precarious, day-to-day existence. An enslaved combatant, a gladiator, he fights in a small frontier circus in the ancient, Roman-occupied city, Corstopitum, in the British Isles. But, having earned his freedom after winning a major contest, he finds himself wandering, not quite sure what to do with himself. As a gladiator, he lived life never knowing whether he would see tomorrow, so he never allowed himself the luxury of thinking about his future.

Then, just within a mere couple of days he has won his freedom, he gets into a drunken street brawl and goes to jail. A stranger called Gault, from the Dalriadain tribe in what is now modern-day Scotland, bails him out, on the condition that Phaedrus join him and his people by posing as their deposed King, Midir. The real Midir had disappeared, presumed dead, when the queen of the Caledones, the enemy tribe of the Dalriadain, usurped his throne. As Gault explains, because Phaedrus bears such an uncanny resemblance to the real king Midir, he can pose in his place and help the Dalriadain recover their kingdom and become their king.

Although very little is known about these two groups in the second century, Sutcliff takes what little evidence exists and manages to create a convincing account of how Roman-occupied Britain might have looked before Christianity. Propelled by a complex, richly detailed, action-packed narrative, it completely transports the reader. Given the sophisticated language and level of detail, it is most suited for advanced readers, but some might find it worth the attempt because of the subject matter or story alone. As Phaedrus assumes his role as king, ultimately sacrificing his own life to save the Dalriadain, he discovers true freedom in the willing performance of one's moral duty.

**For those also seeking**: models for identity
**For those drawn to**: story, language
**Themes/subjects**: ancient civilizations, battles/wars, blindness, British history, cats, critical thinking/strategy, death, disguises, duty, free will, freedom, friendship, gender roles, gladiators, horses, identity formation, inheritance and succession, Irish history, kings/queens, knives/daggers/swords, matrilineality, moral dilemmas, occupied countries, otherness, rebellions/coups, revenge, rituals and traditions, Roman Empire, romance, sacrifice, secrets, slavery, sportsmanship
**Reading interest level**: grades 7–8
**Curricular tie-ins**: Use this book to complement a unit on early Roman history. Ask students to do some background research on gladiators (their origins, purpose, etc.) and discuss how this knowledge changes or illuminates the text.
**Read-alikes**: Those drawn to its epic quality might also enjoy Adam's *Watership Down*. Those drawn to its setting should check out Sutcliff's sequence of novels about Roman Britain: *Eagle of the Ninth*, *The Silver Branch*, *Frontier Wolf*, *The Lantern Bearers*, *Sword at Sunset*, *Dawn Wind*, *Sword Song*, and *The Shield Ring*.


**Wilder, Laura Ingalls** (1867–1957)
**Little House in the Big Woods** (1932). New York: HarperTrophy, 2004. 238pp. 978-0060581800.

The pioneer world of the novel is presented through the eyes of five-year-old Laura Ingalls. Living isolated in a small house in the Wisconsin woods, the Ingalls and their three daughters depend upon themselves to survive. Laura describes the daily life, traditions, and celebrations of her family in the years 1882 and 1883. The family has no money, their work is never-ending, and they face continual threats from wild animals. Nevertheless they lead a fulfilling, pastoral life in harmony with the natural world.

The first of nine historical novels that increase in stylistic complexity as Laura ages, *Little House in the Big Woods* provides readers with in-depth knowledge about the day-to-day life of a pioneer family. Readers will see how children were expected to behave during this time ("Mary and Laura did not say a word at table, for they knew that children should be seen and not heard").

What particularly distinguishes the novel is the way Wilder describes what it felt like to be a young child in pioneer America. Living in a precarious environment, Laura feels snug and secure in the little log cabin: "Laura knew that wolves would eat little girls. But she was safe inside the solid log walls. Her father's gun hung over the door and good old Jack, the brindle bulldog, lay on guard before it." Readers who fear the future or those enduring poverty will be reassured by Laura's story.

**For those also seeking**: reassurance/comfort/confirmation of self-worth/strength
**For those drawn to**: setting
**Themes/subjects**: frontier and pioneer life, family, sisters, wilderness survival, country life, farm life, work (labor), wilderness survival, cooperation and teamwork, wolves, bears, rituals and traditions, seasons, midwestern United States
**Reading interest level**: grades 3–6
**Curricular tie-ins**: For a lesson on pioneers, classes could visit a local historic house that provides tours and hand-on activities for students.
**Adaptations & alternative formats**: Disney mini-series directed by David Cunningham (2005); audiobook read by Cherry Jones (2003)
**Translations**: Spanish: *La Casa del Bosque*; French: *La Petite Maison dans la Prairie*
**Read-alikes**: Although Maud Hart Lovelace's *Betsy-Tacy* provides less historical background than does *Little House in the Big Woods*, it is also about a five-year-old girl who lives in late nineteenth-century America. *The Birchbark House* by Louise Erdrich describes the customs and traditions of nineteenth-century family life as experienced by a seven-year-old Native American girl.

**Wilder, Laura Ingalls** (1867–1957)
**Farmer Boy** (1933). New York: HarperTrophy, 1971. 372pp. 978-0064400039.

Nine-year-old Almanzo, the youngest of four children, lives on a pioneer farm in New York State. His passion is horses, but his father thinks he is too young to help with the colts. The novel depicts a year in his life, one filled with numerous challenges and trials. Learning how to break in calves, watching the new teacher deal with bullies who severely beat previous teachers, falling through ice and nearly drowning, and helping with the never-ending work on the farm are some of the experiences that prepare Almanzo for making a momentous decision at the end of the novel.

Readers wondering what the day-to-day life of a pioneer child would be like will find a captivating, in-depth portrayal of it in this second novel in The Little House series. Wilder describes how to do such things as make whips and bobsleds, harvest crops, make butter and maple syrup, and cut and store blocks of ice to make ice cream. Descriptions of the farmhouse, the clothes, the meals, the routines, and the celebrations make children feel as if they truly understand what it would have been like to live in the 1880s. Readers will be surprised to learn that work on the farm took precedence over school. Particularly memorable is Wilder's depiction of the thoughts, anxieties, and passions of a nineteenth-century child.

Almanzo's desire to do what is right, even when he fails or makes mistakes, makes him an engaging and inspirational character. Readers who are driven by a single-minded pursuit of something they want will identify with Almanzo's all-consuming passion for horses. The novel will also appeal to those who wish that they could grow up faster or are frustrated at not being taken seriously because of their age.

**For those also seeking**: models for identity
**For those drawn to**: setting
**Themes/subjects**: frontier and pioneer life, farm life, country life, family, horses, work (labor), New York State history, self-reliance, bullying, independence, youngest sibling, rituals and traditions
**Reading interest level**: grades 3–6
**Curricular tie-ins**: Almanzo is passionate about horses. Ask students to create a scrapbook about horses, covering aspects of them such as breeds, life stages, history, as well as care and maintenance.
**Adaptations & alternative formats**: Disney mini-series directed by David Cunningham (2005); audiobook read by Cherry Jones (2004)
**Translations**: Spanish: *Un Granjero de Diez Años*; French: *Un Enfant de la Terre*
**Read-alikes**: Those who enjoy stories about boys growing up in pioneer America will like Avi's *The Barn* and Elizabeth George Speare's *Sign of the Beaver* while readers who are looking for stories about boys and horses will like Mary O'Hara's *My Friend Flicka* and Walter Farley's *The Black Stallion*.

**Yolen, Jane** (1939–)
**Briar Rose** (1992). New York: Tor, 2016. 270pp. 978-0765382948.

For as long as Becca Berlin could remember, whenever she and her sisters visited their Grandma Gemma, she would tell them the story of "Sleeping Beauty." But Grandma Gemma's version was different. In her version, only the princess, the Sleeping Beauty, wakes from the evil sleeping spell. This is because Grandma Gemma used the fairy tale to encode her own painful story of escape from Poland and Nazi persecution.

Unfortunately, Becca does not realize the truth in Grandma Gemma's fairy tale until she is a young woman, and Grandma Gemma has passed away. Devoted to her grandmother and determined to uncover her past, Becca gathers the few clues she has—immigration documents, some photographs, a ring—and puts her training as an investigative journalist to use. The trail leads her to Poland, to a town called Chelmno, once the site of a World War II German death camp and the final piece in her story's puzzle.

This is a fast-paced, compelling read that is structured as a story within a story. Once Becca reaches Poland, she meets Josef Potocki, who she knows had some connection with her grandmother. The voice then shifts to his and his story. Potocki was a young, aspiring playwright in Berlin when he was sent to a concentration camp because of his homosexuality. He eventually escapes and joins the partisan resistance, and through these events, he meets Becca's grandmother. While this story offers vivid depiction of the horrific events of the Holocaust (and, therefore, a disinterested understanding of the world), Potocki's story, his transformation from apathetic, apolitical observer to resistance leader, emphasizes the evil of ignorance and the importance of empathy and political vigilance.

**For those also seeking**: courage to make a change
**For those drawn to**: story
**Themes/subjects**: authoritarian rule, concentration camps, courage, death, family, grandmothers, homophobia, homosexuality, justice and injustice, Judaism, mysteries, occupied countries, pain/suffering, Poland, prejudice, racial violence, racism, resistance movements, romance, secrets, stories and storytelling, trauma, "Sleeping Beauty" (story), soldiers, war crimes, World War II
**Reading interest level**: grades 7–8
**Curricular tie-ins**: In addition to complementing studies on Jewish culture and World War II, this novel would be an ideal springboard into an activity in which students are asked to interview their own family members and write a history of their past.

**Adaptations & alternative formats**: audiobook read by Barbara Rosenblat (2014); film directed by Donna Deitch (1999)

**Read-alikes**: The Holocaust is also captured in Jane Yolen's *The Devil's Arithmetic* and Lois Lowry's *Number the Stars*. As *Briar Rose* borders children and young adult literature, mature readers may also be interested in Marcus Zusak's *The Book Thief*, which is set in Nazi Germany.

# CHAPTER NINE

# Myth/Legend

Myths are traditional stories rooted in folk beliefs and typically feature supernatural beings. They serve to explain or justify natural phenomena or social customs. Legends, unlike myths, focus on humans rather the gods. Although legendary heroes such as Robin Hood, King Arthur, Paul Bunyan, and others may have had some basis in historical facts, these facts are greatly embellished to create an extravagant tale.

Mythic and legendary stories are typically larger-than-life narratives characterized by heroic feats and dangerous adventures. Readers who are inspired by mythic or legendary protagonists believe that nothing is beyond their reach. Motivated by the feats of a character such as Perseus or Robin Hood, readers are ready to slay their own monsters and win their own battles, whether large or small.

Although folk literature such as myths and legends appeals to many children, it was never originally intended for them. Their themes resonate with the young because they empower them. Myths and legends often feature heroic characters who begin as underdogs—typically undervalued, ridiculed, or disdained by others. These underdogs must face powerful opponents and undergo testing which proves their worth.

For many centuries, folk literature was transmitted only one way—orally. When writers such as Charles Perrault and Thomas Malory wrote oral stories down, theirs was only one version of a narrative that had continuously changed over time. Stories that have been passed down through generations have stood the test of time. Honed over centuries, these tales of passed-down wisdom embody the essential, the significant, and the memorable.

The novels in this chapter vary in the ways they embody source material. Rosemary Sutcliff's books are skillful adaptations of literary predecessors such as Homer and Malory. T. H. White, on the other hand, invents a childhood for King Arthur that is completely new. Washington Irving uses German folktales, but transplants them to American soil and introduces local ideas. In the Prydain Chronicles, Lloyd Alexander bases names, characters, places, and events on Welsh mythology, but his intention, as he says, is to create "the feeling, not the fact, of the land of Wales and its legends." Diana Wynne Jones in *The Game* and Susan Cooper in her Dark Is Rising series both use a broad array of mythic sources, combining them in unique and original ways.

Mythic and legendary stories are typically set in the past. Children reading about Robin Hood, King Arthur, and Achilles will learn about British, Welsh, and Greek history. Mythic and legendary tales bring history to life, which makes them excellent resources for social studies units. Readers who enjoy the supernatural element in myths and legends typically like fantasy novels as well.

### Awakening/New Perspectives/Enlargement of Possibilities

**Alexander, Lloyd** (1924–2007)
**The Book of Three** (1964). New York: Henry Holt, 2006. 190pp. 978-0805080483.

Frustrated by his dull life at Caer Dallben and his boring job as Assistant Pig-Keeper, Taran yearns for a heroic life of adventure. The old enchanter Dallben sympathizes with his plight but also warns him that he is not, under any circumstances, to leave the boundaries of Caer Dallben. But Taran does leave the property and enters the forbidden forest in order to capture his escaped charge—the oracular pig, Hen Wen. During his chase, he catches sight of the terrifying Horned King and meets the renowned war leader, Prince Gwydion. Captured by the enemy, imprisoned in Spiral Castle, and separated from Prince Gwydion, Taran then undertakes a dangerous quest to save the people of Prydain. The exciting plot makes this novel a favorite novel with many readers.

This first book in the Prydain series is noteworthy for its many appeal elements. Characters such as the endearing King Fflewddur, the crusty dwarf Doli, the spunky girl Eilonwy, and the lovable creature Gurgi are truly unforgettable. Taran, the Assistant Pig-Keeper who longs to be a hero but fails at almost everything he does, will resonate with readers who have large ambitions but few accomplishments. The book will also appeal to those who have experienced repeated failure, encouraging them to view their lack of success as an essential part of the learning process. Readers may also have a kindlier, more accepting attitude toward the faults of others after they read the novel.

Those who view heroism in romanticized terms will discover that heroes can be found in unlikely places. The unassuming wisdom of elders such as Dallben and Medwyn will comfort readers looking for direction in their lives.

**For those also seeking**: reassurance/comfort/confirmation of self-worth/strength
**For those drawn to**: character, story
**Themes/subjects**: heroism, identity formation, castles, fairies, appearance versus reality, failure, cooperation and teamwork, courage, valleys, Welsh mythology, knives/daggers/swords
**Reading interest level**: grades 4–7
**Curricular tie-ins**: The castles of Wales, according to the author, were sources of inspiration for *The Book of Three*. Ask students to create a poster on medieval castles, addressing such questions as: what life was like inside them, how they were built, and what their purpose was?
**Adaptations & alternative formats**: audiobook read by James Langton (2004)
**Translations**: Spanish: *El Libro de los Tres*; French: *Le Livre des Trois*
**Read-alikes**: Those who want to read more about Taran will enjoy the sequels to the novel: *The Black Cauldron*, *The Castle of Llyr*, *Taran Wanderer*, and *The High King*. Readers who like quest narratives with unlikely heroes will enjoy J. R. R. Tolkien's *The Hobbit*.

**Alexander, Lloyd** (1924–2007)
**The Black Cauldron** (1965). New York: Holt, Rinehart and Winston, 1965. 224pp. 978-0805080490.

Arawn, the Lord of a death realm called Annuvin, uses a magical black cauldron to create zombie-like creatures who can never die. His plan is to increase their numbers so that he can assemble an army of warriors to overtake the kingdom of Prydain. In response, the war hero Gwdion calls a Council at Caer Dallben to reveal his plan for a counterattack. He asks for volunteers to enter Annuvin and destroy the black cauldron. Taran is paired with Ellidyr, a prince who despises him and calls him a lowly pig boy. Once the warriors set out for Annuvin, the plan goes wrong, band-members double-cross each another, and everyone's life is in peril. This rousing tale will appeal not only to readers who enjoy medieval legends but also to those who love tales of survival.

A Newbery Honor book, this second novel in the Prydain series is remarkable for both its astute psychological portraits and its daring adventures. As a boy on the threshold of manhood, Taran desperately wants to prove himself as a hero. Ironically, he loathes Prince Ellidry for wanting the same glory and honor that he does. Ellidry functions as Taran's dark double, representing the hidden desires of Taran's heart. Readers who long to be the best at something will find a new perspective on ambition in this novel. As Ellidry's behavior makes clear, some people who strive to win at all costs do so at the expense of others.

**For those also seeking**: reassurance/comfort/confirmation of self-worth/strength
**For those drawn to**: character, story
**Themes/subjects**: heroism, ambition, identity formation, cooperation and teamwork, humility, projection (psychology), vanity and pompousness, pride, survival, Welsh mythology, princes, Middle Ages
**Reading interest level**: grades 4–7
**Curricular tie-ins**: Set during the Welsh Middle Ages, the novel is a good choice for a jigsaw activity. Divide the class into four groups, each responsible for one of the following topics: life during the middle ages in Wales, the role of women in the Middle Ages, the geography of Wales, and the political organization of the country.
**Adaptations & alternative formats**: Walt Disney movie directed by Ted Berman and Richard Rich (1985); audiobook read by James Langton (2004)
**Translations**: Spanish: *El Caldero Negro*; French: *Le Chaudron Noir*
**Read-alikes**: Readers who enjoyed this novel will want to read the other books in the series: *The Book of Three*, *The Castle of Llyr*, *Taran Wanderer*, and *The High King*. Ged's ambition in Ursula K. Le Guin's *A Wizard of Earthsea* also leads him into serious trouble.

**Alexander, Lloyd** (1924–2007)
**Taran Wanderer** (1967). New York: Holt, Rinehart and Winston, 1967. 256pp. 978-0805080513.

Taran tells the wise enchanter Dallben that he wants to travel around Prydain to search for information about his identity. He needs to know who he is, who his parents are, and if he is "lowly born or nobly." Dallben tells him, "Your road indeed will not be easy . . . Though you may not find what you seek, you will surely return a little wiser." Orddu, Orwen, and Orgoch—the witches connected with fate and destiny—tell Taran that, in order to discover his true identity, he needs to find the Mirror of Llunet. The quest in search of this mirror becomes life-threatening. Taran meets people who try to rob him, bewitch him, and kill him. But he also meets others who need his help and some who become beloved friends.

A character-driven book, this fourth novel in the Prydain series will appeal to readers who are questioning their role and purpose in life. It will comfort readers to realize that others also struggle with this question. Taran longs to discover that he is descended from royalty but his quest changes his ideas about greatness. On his journey, Taran learns to appreciate a humble shepherd as truly noble, an idea that prepares him for what he sees in the Mirror of Llunet. Taran does not find what he expected, but he does fulfill his quest. His story will open reader's eyes to a new way of viewing others.

**For those also seeking**: connection with others/awareness of not being alone
**For those drawn to**: character, story
**Themes/subjects**: identity, identity formation, humility, quests, truth, orphans, poverty, Welsh mythology, witches, friendship
**Reading interest level**: grades 5–8
**Curricular tie-ins**: The search for identity is a key concern in the novel. Ask students to write a reflection in their reader response journals about how Taran's search for identity relates to their own lives.
**Adaptations & alternative formats**: audiobook read by James Langton (2005)
**Translations**: Spanish: *Taran el Vagabundo*
**Read-alikes**: Readers who enjoyed this novel will want to read the other books in the series: *The Book of Three*, *The Black Cauldron*, *The Castle of Llyr*, and *The High King*. Ojo the Unlucky also undertakes a quest in search of self-knowledge in L. Frank Baum's *The Patchwork Girl of Oz*. Boy 412 knows little about his true identity in Angie Sage's *Magyk*.

**Cooper, Susan** (1935–)
**The Grey King** (1975). New York: Aladdin Paperbacks, 2007. 165pp. 978-0689829840.

After a serious bout of hepatitis, Will Stanton awakens thinking, "I've lost something. It's gone. What was it? It was terribly important, I must remember it. I must!" Unable to retrieve the memory and in need of recuperation, Will visits his aunt, uncle, and cousin in Wales. As he approaches his uncle's farm, Will realizes that he is in an ancient part of Britain, "a secret, enclosed place, with powers hidden in its shrouded centuries." Exploring the Welsh landscape, Will meets a strange albino boy and his dog, both devoid of all color and suggestive of otherworldly beings.

With Bran's aid, Will embarks on a dangerous quest, his first one without help from the guardians of the Light. The boys' task is to retrieve a golden harp and awaken the legendary Sleepers—Arthur's knights who are trapped in spells within the Welsh mountains. Riddles from half-remembered chants provide clues. But the quest exposes the boys to the enmity of the Grey King, the powerful King of the Dark.

Winner of the Newbery Medal, *The Grey King* is an intense, dramatic story of a boy who is set apart from others and whose origin is cloaked in mystery. The tension in the brooding mountains reflects both the strained relations between Bran and his father and the emotions of a boy trapped in an existence he does not comprehend. This novel will appeal to readers who have experienced a particularly strict upbringing, those who feel unloved, and children who feel different from others. Bran's story may help children realize that they do not always know all the facts about those close to them. Although the book can be read as a standalone novel, it will resonate more deeply if read after *The Dark Is Rising*.

**For those also seeking**: connection with others/awareness of not being alone
**For those drawn to**: setting, character
**Themes/subjects**: quests, Arthurian legends, mythology, Wales, father-son relationships, adoption, good and evil, being different, family conflict, clues/riddles, anger/hostility, Welsh mythology
**Reading interest level**: grades 4–8
**Curricular tie-ins**: Ask students to create a script for a commercial about Wales.

*Myth/Legend*

**Adaptations & alternative formats**: audiobook read by Richard Mitchley (2007)
**Translations**: Spanish: *El Rey Gris*
**Read-alikes**: The other books in *The Dark Is Rising* series are: *Over Sea, Under Stone*, *The Dark Is Rising*, *Greenwitch*, and *Silver on the Tree*. Mythology also infuses an English landscape with strange power and tension in *The Weirdstone of Brisingamen* and *The Owl Service*, both by Alan Garner. Strained father-son relationships also dominate Grace Lin's *Starry River of the Sky*.

**Pyle, Howard** (1853–1911)
**The Merry Adventures of Robin Hood** (1883). Illustrated by the author. New York: Dover, 1968. 296pp. 978-0486220437. PD.

When foresters taunt 18-year-old Robin Hood, and one of them narrowly misses killing him with a bow and arrow, Robin retaliates with his own bow, killing his victimizer. An outlaw from that point on, Robin attracts followers who are similarly cast out of society. The Sheriff of Nottingham vows to hunt Robin down in revenge for killing his kin. But Robin continually outwits the sheriff, thereby putting himself at greater risk. He and his band of followers do not just hide from the law but also steal from the rich, powerful, and corrupt to help the poor and powerless.

Still the most popular edition of the Robin Hood legend, Howard Pyle's lavishly illustrated version will appeal to readers who love stirring adventures and heroic deeds. A distinguished Golden-Age illustrator of children's books, Pyle is the creator of beautifully stylized and highly decorative pen-and-ink illustrations that will attract readers to the medieval world. Although his use of archaic language such as "quoth" and "thou" may detract some readers, it adds an air of medieval grandeur to the tale.

*The Merry Adventures of Robin Hood* presents a more complex view of moral behavior than is typically seen in children's novels. After reading the book, children will realize that actions can be governed by complex motives.

Although Robin Hood's outlaws are continually threatened with capture and death, they live a joyous life, have few cares or responsibilities, and view their world as utopian. Robin Hood's merry disposition in the face of constant danger may show readers that they do not have to let external circumstances dictate their mood. As an underdog figure who fights the rich and powerful, Robin Hood will appeal to readers who feel powerless. The novel will also resonate with those who view themselves as outsiders or misfits in their families, classrooms, or societies.

**For those also seeking**: reassurance/comfort/confirmation of self-worth/strength
**For those drawn to**: story
**Themes/subjects**: outlaws, criminals/thieves, political corruption, outcasts/misfits, insiders/outsiders, forests, Middle Ages, adventure, friendship, stealing, disguises, justice and injustice, agency and powerlessness, revenge, rebelliousness
**Reading interest level**: grade 4 and up
**Curricular tie-ins**: Robin Hood kills two men and steals money, yet views his actions as justified. Students can debate whether he is a criminal or a hero.
**Adaptations & alternative formats**: movie starring Russell Crowe and directed by Ridley Scott (2010); movie starring Kevin Costner and directed by Kevin Reynolds (1991); audiobook read by David Thorn (2007); audiobook read by Christopher Cazenove (2009)
**Translations**: Spanish: *Las Alegres Aventuras de Robin Hood*
**Read-alikes**: Readers drawn to the Robin Hood legend will also enjoy Robin McKinley's *The Outlaws of Sherwood*, Roger Lancelyn Green's *The Adventures of Robin Hood*, and Paul Creswick's *Robin Hood*.

**Levine, Gail Carson** (1947–)
**Ever** (2008). New York: HarperCollins, 2010. 244pp. 978-0061229640.

Olus, the god of the wind, is hundreds of years younger than any of the other Akkan gods and goddesses. Feeling lonely, he leaves home to visit the world of mortals. Settling in the city of Hyte, he is attracted to Kezi, a girl who loves dancing and weaving. When Kezi's mother falls gravely ill, her father bargains with the god Admat, a god that the Hyte people believe is the one, true higher power. Kezi's father promises Admat that he can take as sacrifice the first person to congratulate him on his wife's recovery. By a bizarre twist of fate, that person turns out to be his own daughter.

With only a month to live, Kezi attends her cousin's wedding and meets Olus who is disguised as a mortal. Olus believes that if Kezi were to become immortal, she would escape her fate. But to become immortal she must

*Myth/Legend*

become a heroine and Olus, her champion. They undertake separate quests to achieve these goals.

This original mythological tale alternates between Olus's point of view and Kezi's, a technique that heightens the suspense in the story and highlights the different belief systems of the two characters. Before Kezi meets the god of wind, she never questions her faith in the god Admat. But once she encounters Olus, she reconsiders her ideas about spirituality, the afterlife, and immortality. A thought-provoking book, it will provide readers with a new perspective about faith. Kezi's search for answers never ends; her inquiring mind and questioning attitude provide an inspirational role model for readers filled with spiritual doubts and uncertainties.

**For those also seeking**: models for identity
**For those drawn to**: character, setting
**Themes/subjects**: fate/destiny, gods, sacrifice, faith and skepticism, immortality, loneliness, quests, romance, love
**Reading interest level**: grades 6–9
**Curricular tie-ins**: This novel would work well with a unit on belief systems and world religions. Ask students to write a reflection in their reader response journals about Kezi's ideas and their own regarding faith in a higher power.
**Adaptations & alternative formats**: audiobook read by Jenna Lamia and Oliver Wyman (2009)
**Read-alikes**: Gail Carson Levine's *Fairest* is also a romance between two characters from different spheres in life. Readers interested in stories about immortality will like Natalie Babbitt's *Tuck Everlasting*. Like Kezi, Mau in Terry Pratchett's *Nation* also questions his faith.

### Models for Identity

**Alexander, Lloyd** (1924–2007)
**The High King** (1968). New York: H. Holt, 2016. 253pp. 978-0805080513.

This final volume of The Chronicles of Prydain is a stirring culmination of the events in earlier novels. When Taran returns home after a quest in search of his parents, he hears that the evil Lord Arawn may be planning an attack on Prydain. Dallben turns to Hen Wen for insight, but the oracular pig's prophecy about Prydain is perplexing. Lord Gwydion then asks Taran to rally the people of the Free Commots and lead them into battle. But when the allies meet at Caer Dathyl, a traitor attacks, destroying the great stronghold of Prydain and killing its revered High King. The only remaining hope is for Taran to delay the Cauldron Born from returning home so that Lord Gwydion can defeat the evil Arawn and destroy his death realm, Annuvin.

Taran's life is dominated by a series of impossible choices—ones that define his character. His growth from impulsive boy to wise leader is both convincing and inspiring. Taran, Eilonwy, Gurgi, Fflewddur, Dallben, and Coll are some of the most likable and unique characters in children's literature. Their lives will provide hope and encouragement to readers who fall short of their own expectations.

Clever plotting, in which strands of the various stories converge in unexpected ways, is noteworthy in this last volume. Like the tapestry woven by the three witches, the novel celebrates interconnectedness on many levels. Winner of the Newbery Medal, *The High King* is a moving and satisfying conclusion to the series.

**For those also seeking**: reassurance/comfort/confirmation of self-worth/strength
**For those drawn to**: character, story
**Themes/subjects**: identity formation, coming of age, cooperation and teamwork, friendship, battles/wars, royalty, kings/queens, courage, romance, fate/destiny, fairies, betrayal, journeys, heroism, Welsh mythology, critical thinking/strategy
**Reading interest level**: grades 4–8
**Curricular tie-ins**: Ask students to find information about weapons used in medieval warfare and create a collage that includes explanatory captions.
**Adaptations & alternative formats**: audiobook read by James Langton (2005)
**Translations**: Spanish: *El Gran Rey*
**Read-alikes**: Readers who enjoyed this novel will want to read the other books in the series: *The Book of Three*, *The Black Cauldron*, *The Castle of Llyr*, and *Taran Wanderer*. The heroes in C. S. Lewis's *The Last Battle* and J. R. R. Tolkien's *The Hobbit* also engage in epic battles against forces of evil.

**Cooper, Susan** (1935–)
**The Dark Is Rising** (1973). New York: Aladdin Paperbacks, 2007. 244pp. 978-0689829833.

*Myth/Legend*

On the eve of his 11th birthday, Will Stanton observes unusual signs in the natural world. When he goes to bed that night, he experiences strange, nightmarish sensations. Looking out the window the next morning, Will is shocked to see a totally different landscape. He subsequently discovers that he is no ordinary boy, but the Sign Seeker who has a crucial role to play in the epic battle between the forces of Light and Dark. As the last of "Old Ones,"—magical beings on the side of the Light—Will's task is to find six ancient signs. He travels through time to accomplish his quest and is continually pursued by the forces of evil. The novel will appeal to readers who enjoy heroic fantasy quests and time-travel plots.

A Newbery Honor novel and Boston Globe-Horn Book Award winner, this second novel in *The Dark Is Rising* series is sweeping in time span and epic in scope. A richly detailed book, it will appeal to those who enjoy stories with a leisurely pace and strong sense of place. Hints of a mysterious otherworld are evocatively conveyed through poetic language.

As the youngest of nine children, Will does not believe he has special talents. But when he comes into his power as the last Old One, he begins to discover his skills. Will's life provides readers with an inspirational example to follow. This book will appeal to youngest children who feel inferior to their older siblings. It will also appeal to readers who feel different from those around them.

**For those also seeking**: reassurance/comfort/confirmation of self-worth/strength
**For those drawn to**: setting, language
**Themes/subjects**: quests, time travel, omens/prophecies, identity formation, good and evil, being different, youngest sibling
**Reading interest level**: grades 6–8
**Curricular tie-ins**: Merriman Lyons is Merlin, the famed enchanter from Arthurian legend. Ask students to find information about Merlin and create an obituary about this legendary character in the style of newspaper obituaries.
**Translations**: Spanish: *Los Seis Signos de la Luz*; French: *Les Portes du Temps: A L'assaut des Ténèbres*
**Adaptations & alternative formats**: movie called The Seeker: The Dark Is Rising directed by David L. Cunningham (2007); audiobook read by Alex Jennings (2007)
**Read-alikes**: The other books in *The Dark Is Rising* series are: *Over Sea, Under Stone, Greenwitch, The Grey King,* and *Silver on the Tree*. Readers who

enjoy time travel will also like Edith Nesbit's *The House of Arden* and its sequel *Harding's Luck*.

**Sutcliff, Rosemary** (1920–1992)
**The Sword and the Circle** (1981). New York: Dutton, 1981. 260pp. 978-0140371499.

This first novel in the King Arthur trilogy is about the legendary king and his Knights of the Round Table. Rosemary Sutcliff's depiction of Arthur's rise to power, the treachery of Arthur's half-sister Morgan La Fay, the romance of King Arthur and Guenever, and the dangerous adventures of his famous knights is majestic, impassioned, tragic, and inspirational.

Setting legendary events within the larger historical context of the Dark Ages, Sutcliff inspires readers to want to learn more about British history. The medieval, fairy-tale-like settings are utopian and enchanting, conveyed in spare, poetic language. At the end of the novel, Arthur says the knights served their purpose, making "a shining time between the Dark and the Dark."

Sutcliff is a master of telling details that convey mood, atmosphere, and personality. Using an economy of words, she depicts the essence of a character and what that character is feeling. Arthur and his knights are both human in their failings and motivational in their aspirations. Each of them faces moral dilemmas and undergoes testing of character. Readers who are looking for a purpose in life will be inspired by the vision of the novel.

**For those also seeking**: reassurance/comfort/confirmation of self-worth/strength
**For those drawn to**: setting, character
**Themes/subjects**: Arthurian legends, knights, battles/wars, castles, honor, courage, loyalty, moral dilemmas, Middle Ages, fate/destiny, heroism, courtly love, romance, class differences, knives/daggers/swords, utopian places
**Reading interest level**: grade 6 and up
**Curricular tie-ins**: This book would make an excellent accompanying text for a unit on Britain's Dark Ages. Students could look up information on heraldry and design a coat of arms for one of the knight's shields.
**Read-alikes**: Sutcliff's two sequels to the novel—*The Light Beyond the Forest* and *The Road to Camlann*—as well as Kevin Crossley-Holland's Arthur

trilogy (*The Seeing Stone, At the Crossing-Places,* and *King of the Middle March*) will appeal to readers of Arthurian legend. They will also like Katherine Paterson's *Parzival: The Quest of the Grail Knight,* a story about one of Arthur's knights.

**McKinley, Robin** (1952–)
**The Outlaws of Sherwood** (1988). New York: Firebird, 2002. 282pp. 978-0698119598.

After the death of his father, Robin Hood looks forward to the Nottingham Fair as one of the few breaks from his endless work. However, on his way to the fair, he is forced to use his longbow in self-defense. Horrified to realize that he has killed someone, Robin hides in the forest. When friends Marian and Munch find him, they suggest living in the forest with like-minded people who have also been victimized by the cruel Normans. Although Robin thinks it impracticable, he has no real alternative. Once he decides to live in the forest, he and his band of outlaws must find a way to survive the winter, feed and clothe themselves, and elude the capture of the cruel Sheriff of Nottingham.

McKinley skillfully depicts the realities of medieval life and in particular the injustice and oppression that the common people suffer during the reign of King Richard I. The novel also focuses on the practicalities of survival in an inhospitable outdoor environment. Readers who enjoy desert-island novels will love the ingenuity with which the outcasts manage to exist without homes.

Although the setting is compelling, the portrayal of characters is what really distinguishes McKinley's novel. The psychological motivations of the main characters are described with insight and understanding. We learn about Robin's fears, jealousies, and anxieties. Unlike other versions of the Robin Hood tales, McKinley focuses on the plight of women in this era, and provides an expanded role for them in the novel. Readers looking for role models will find in Robin and Marian sources of inspiration. The novel will also resonate with readers who have suffered from injustice or poverty.

**For those also seeking**: reassurance/comfort/confirmation of self-worth/strength
**For those drawn to**: character, setting

**Themes/subjects**: outlaws, criminals/thieves, political corruption, outcasts/misfits, insiders/outsiders, forests, Middle Ages, friendship, stealing, romance, disguises, justice and injustice, agency and powerlessness, homelessness
**Reading interest level**: grade 7 and up
**Curricular tie-ins**: This novel would work well as a supplementary resource on a unit on the Norman invasion of Britain. Ask students to form small groups. Each member could create a question about some aspect of the historical period that they are curious about. They would research their question or one of the questions that another member created, and present their findings to the group.
**Read-alikes**: Readers who love the Robin Hood legend will also enjoy Howard Pyle's *The Merry Adventures of Robin Hood*, Roger Lancelyn Green's *The Adventures of Robin Hood*, and Paul Creswick's *Robin Hood*.

## Reassurance/Comfort/Confirmation of Self-Worth/Strength

**Cooper, Susan** (1935–)
**Over Sea, Under Stone** (1965). New York: Aladdin Paperbacks, 2007. 196pp. 978-0689840357.

This first novel in *The Dark Is Rising* series is about the dangerous quest that the three Drew children undertake while on vacation in the English coastal area of Cornwall. Exploring a strange place called the Grey House, Simon, Jane, and Barney discover not only a secret room but also an ancient manuscript within it. Barney, who loves stories about King Arthur and his knights, believes that the manuscript is a clue to the whereabouts of the legendary Grail. When the children show the manuscript to Great-Uncle Merry, a renowned scholar who is a guide and mentor to them, he encourages them to follow the clues in the manuscript. In doing so, they are pursued by evil characters who disguise their true purpose.

A plot-driven novel, *Over Sea, Under Stone* is an exciting story about children who decipher clues and escape from enemies who will do anything to steal their manuscript. The Grey House, the Cornish landscape, and the characters the children meet are all strange and mysterious. Readers who enjoy solving clues will love this novel.

Children whose abilities are underestimated by others will identify with the Drew children. Although they demonstrate great ingenuity and reasoning, the siblings are not fully appreciated by anyone except their uncle. This quest for the missing Grail will also appeal to readers who are drawn to Arthurian tales.

**For those also seeking**: models for identity
**For those drawn to**: story
**Themes/subjects**: quest, buried/hidden treasure, Arthurian legends, good and evil, clues/riddles, courage, kidnapping, sea and seashore, Cornwall, mysteries
**Reading interest level**: grades 4–8
**Curricular tie-ins**: Ask students to create a travel brochure for Cornwall after researching it.
**Adaptations & alternative formats**: audiobook read by Alex Jennings (2007)
**Translations**: Spanish: *Sobre el Mar, Bajo la Tierra*
**Read-alikes**: The sequels to the novel are: *The Dark Is Rising*, *Greenwitch*, *The Grey King*, and *Silver on the Tree*. Readers who enjoy books about searching for hidden treasure will also like Robert Louis Stevenson's *Treasure Island*, while those who like stories about solving clues will enjoy Avi's *Midnight Magic*, Ellen Raskin's *The Westing Game*, Trenton Lee Stewart's *The Mysterious Benedict Society*, and Chris Grabenstein's *Escape from Mr. Lemoncello's Library*.

**Cooper, Susan** (1935–)
**Greenwitch** (1974). New York: Aladdin Paperbacks, 2007. 147pp. 978-0689840340.

The third novel in *The Dark Is Rising* series brings together the characters from the first two books. Simon, Jane, and Barney Drew are upset to learn that the grail they worked so hard to find has been stolen from the British Museum. When Great-Uncle Merry asks them to return with him to Cornwall to help find the grail, they are delighted. Meanwhile, Will Stanton's uncle asks his nephew to go to Cornwall with him and meet Merry and the Drew children. After the children arrive in Cornwall, Jane watches the villagers create, as an ancient rite of spring, a being called the Greenwitch from branches and leaves. This Greenwitch figure possesses strange power and a secret that becomes central to the children's quest for the missing grail.

The ancient rituals and folklore that underpin the story lend an aura of mystery and magic to it. Although set in the present, an otherworldly atmosphere permeates the novel. Not a fast-paced story, Greenwitch will appeal to readers who enjoy gradually unfolding quest narratives.

This story is about Jane's quest, one which she feels unprepared to conduct. Although she makes wise choices, she second-guesses them. Readers who lack confidence in their choices or do not recognize their own strengths will feel reassured by Jane's example.

**For those drawn to**: setting
**Themes/subjects**: quests, witches, good and evil, self-confidence, sea and seashore, Cornwall, Welsh mythology, superstitions, gods, rituals and traditions
**Reading interest level**: grades 4–8
**Curricular tie-ins**: Ask students to write a reflection in their reader response journals about the character they liked best in the novel or one who reminds them of someone they know.
**Adaptations & alternative formats**: audiobook read by Alex Jennings (2007)
**Translations**: Spanish: *Brujaverde*
**Read-alikes**: The other books in *The Dark Is Rising* series are: *Over Sea, Under Stone*, *The Dark Is Rising*, *The Grey King*, and *Silver on the Tree*. A mythic woman created from plants also plays a central role in Alan Garner's *The Owl Service*.


**Cooper, Susan** (1935-)
**Silver on the Tree** (1977). New York: Aladdin Paperbacks, 2007. 274pp. 978-0689840333.

On Midsummer Eve, Will Stanton is magically conveyed into an earlier era, one where he meets two of the Old Ones of the Light: Merrimam Lyon and King Arthur. Will learns of the great uprising of the Dark 15 centuries earlier, one that he must now reverse by traveling back in time. He and Bran—King Arthur's son—travel to the Lost Land in search of the crystal sword of the Light. This final book in *The Dark Is Rising* series is a satisfying finale to the first four books. Children from the previous novels all unite to try to defeat the powers of the Dark.

Fans of Arthurian legend will enjoy a novel in which a boy from the twentieth century meets Arthur, Guinevere, their son Bran, and Merlin (as Merrimam Lyon). Places such as the glass maze, the walled rose-garden, the Lost City, the glass towers, and the Empty Palace are especially memorable. When the characters accomplish their quest, Merrimam tells them that they will forget these places, and only receive hints of them hereafter in future dreams. Readers who feel overwhelmed by the challenges in their lives will find comfort in the fact that the characters in the novel accomplish nearly impossible feats. *Silver on the Tree* is best appreciated after reading the previous novels in the series.

**For those also seeking**: connection with others/awareness of not being alone
**For those drawn to**: setting
**Themes/subjects**: quests, Arthurian legends, mythology, good and evil, clues/riddles, time travel, Wales, Welsh mythology, knives/daggers/swords
**Reading interest level**: grades 5–8
**Curricular tie-ins**: Ask students to create an advertisement for the book, highlighting its strengths and appeals.
**Adaptations & alternative formats**: audiobook read by Alex Jennings (2003)
**Read-alikes**: The other books in *The Dark Is Rising* series are: *Over Sea, Under Stone*, *The Dark Is Rising*, *Greenwitch*, and *The Grey King*. Mythological stories also play a key role in Diana Wynne Jones's *The Game*.


**Irving, Washington** (1867–1939)
**Rip Van Winkle** (1819). Illustrated by Arthur Rackham (1905). Bristol, UK: Pook Press, 2015. 112pp. 978-1447449195. PD.

Feeling harassed by his domineering wife, Rip Van Winkle takes temporary refuge in the nearby Catskill Mountains. When evening approaches and he is about to return home, he hears his name called. Surprised to see a man in antique Dutch costume, he follows this stranger deep into the hills and finds a group of similarly dressed men playing nine pins. After the men share a keg of liquor with him, Rip Van Winkle falls asleep. Upon awakening, he returns to his village but finds no one that he knows. Originally published in *The Sketch Book of Geoffrey Crayon, Gent.*, *Rip Van Winkle* was marketed for children when Arthur Rackham illustrated the story in 1905.

In the introduction to the story, the narrator tells us that the tale was found among the papers of a deceased gentleman interested in the Dutch history of New York State. Having established the credibility of the tale, Irving is able to convince readers of the plausibility of this strange story. What distinguishes *Rip Van Winkle* is its extraordinary, unexplained events. The misty colors and Gothic atmosphere of Rackham's haunting illustrations accentuate the feeling of strangeness that the tale evokes.

Rip Van Winkle, in his dislike of work and desire to be free from authority, is a child-like character with whom young readers can identify. Those who feel entrapped in situations will find hope in this story.

Irving transplants this German folktale to American soil, establishing a distinctly American folklore. Rip Van Winkle's wish to be free from "petticoat rule" is echoed in the country's longing to be free from British domination. Readers interested in the American Revolution or New York State history will be interested in this tale.

**For those also seeking**: disinterested understanding of the world
**For those drawn to**: story
**Themes/subjects**: New York State history, American Revolution, independence, freedom, Dutch Americans, village/small-town life, authoritarian figures, stories and storytelling, idleness, mountains
**Reading interest level**: grades 4–8
**Curricular tie-ins**: This story could accompany a lesson on the Dutch colonial period in New York State. Students could research Henry Hudson and present their findings in a mock interview of the historic figure.
**Adaptations & alternative formats**: animated movie directed by Will Vinton (1978); audiobook by Curtis Sisco (2012)
**Translations**: Spanish: *Rip Van Winkle*; French: *Rip Van Winkle*
**Read-alikes**: Irving's *The Legend of Sleepy Hollow* is another strange story with folklore roots. Readers interested in stories about the Catsgill Mountains will enjoy Jean Craighead George's *My Side of the Mountain*. Margaret Mahy's *The Haunting* will appeal to those who like scary stories.

**Irving, Washington** (1867–1939)
**The Legend of Sleepy Hollow** (1820). Illustrated by Arthur Rackham (1928). New York: Universe, 2013. 88pp. 978-0789318435. PD (1820 version).

*Myth/Legend*

When Ichabod Crane moves to a sequestered valley in New York State called Sleepy Hollow, he falls in love with a farmer's daughter named Katrina. But the boisterous Brom Bones also loves Katrina, so he and his friends ridicule Ichabod and play practical jokes on him. During a visit to Katrina's farm, Ichabod listens as villagers tell stories about ghosts and apparitions, chief among them the tale of the headless horseman. When Ichabod leaves to go home, he must ride past the haunts of this horseman. He spots someone in the gloom and his worst nightmares materialize.

In *The Legend of Sleepy Hollow*, Irving Americanizes a European folktale by adapting it to colonial concerns and giving it a New York setting. Ichabod, like the newly independent country, succeeds despite earlier subjugation.

Sleepy Hollow with its "drowsy, dreamy influence," abounds in "local tales, haunted spots, and twilight superstitions." The eerie setting and ghostly apparition will appeal to readers of scary stories. Arthur Rackham's sinister illustrations skillfully evoke the menacing atmosphere of the tale.

Living in such a place, Ichabod yields to its influences and becomes an easy prey for local pranksters. Readers who are mocked or ridiculed by others will be reassured by rumors of Ichabod's survival and success.

**For those also seeking**: disinterested understanding of the world
**For those drawn to**: setting
**Themes/subjects**: New York State history, American Revolution, mystery/suspense, village/small-town life, prank tricks and mischief, superstitions, romance, teachers, valleys, anxiety/fears
**Reading interest level**: grades 4–8
**Curricular tie-ins**: This story could supplement a lesson on the history of New York State. Ask students to research the history of the Dutch settlers and write an article about it for a magazine such as *The New Yorker*.
**Adaptations & alternative formats**: movie directed by Tim Burton (1999); audiobook by Curtis Sisco (2012)
**Translations**: Spanish: *La Leyenda del Valle Dormir*; French: *La Légende de Sleepy Hollow*
**Read-alikes**: Sid Fleischman's *The Midnight Horse*, Washington Irving's *Rip Van Winkle*, and Phillip Pullman's *Clockwork* and *Count Karlstein* are all stories with folklore and supernatural elements.

**Sutcliff, Rosemary** (1920–1992)
**Black Ships before Troy: The Story of the Iliad** (1993). Illustrated by Alan Lee. Toronto: Stoddart Kids, 1993. 127pp. 978-0773731103.

A retelling of the legendary 10-year war between the Greeks and the Trojans, *Black Ships before Troy* begins with the myth of the golden apple. Paris must pick one of three goddesses as the fairest. He chooses Aphrodite, the goddess of beauty—a decision that eventually leads to the Trojan War. When Paris hears about the beauty of the wife of King Menelaus, he travels across the Aegean Sea to meet her. Once he sees Helen, he convinces her to leave her husband because "if Paris wanted a thing, then he must have it." Helen leaves her husband and baby "and from that came all the sorrows that followed after." The war that results is long, bitter, and costly.

This moving novel conveys the heroism, tragedy, drama, and irony of the Trojan War. Readers who enjoy war narratives or larger-than-life heroic stories will be inspired by Sutcliff's novel. Children who find success difficult to achieve will find inspiration in the Greeks, a people who take ten years to win victory. Winner of the Kate Greenaway Medal for the best-illustrated British children's book, *Black Ships before Troy* is attractively illustrated by Alan Lee.

**For those also seeking**: connection with others/awareness of not being alone
**For those drawn to**: story
**Themes/subjects**: battles/wars, honor, courage, fate/destiny, mythology, appearance (physical), self-centeredness, gods
**Reading interest level**: grades 5–8
**Curricular tie-ins**: Students can discuss Sutcliff's attitude toward war and debate whether they think war is ever justified.
**Adaptations & alternative formats**: audiobook read by Robert Glenister (2011)
**Translations**: *Naves Negras ante Troya: La Historia de la Ilíada de Homero*
**Read-alikes**: Nathaniel Hawthorne's *A Wonder Book for Boys and Girls* and his *Tanglewood Tales* and Sutcliff's *The Wanderings of Odysseus* are tales about the ancient Greeks.

## Connection with Others/Awareness of Not Being Alone

**White, T. H.** (1906–1964)
**The Sword in the Stone** (1938). New York: Philomel Books, 1993. 256pp. 978-0399225024.

*The Sword in the Stone* is a humorous depiction of the childhood of King Arthur. Foster child of Sir Ector and nicknamed the Wart, Arthur grows up in the shadow of his foster brother. Kay, who knows that he will become a knight and master of his father's estate, treats his foster brother as his inferior. One day when lost in the woods, the Wart meets Merlyn, an unconventional character who becomes his tutor. Merlin teaches the Wart about the world by transforming him into a variety of creatures. Despite the inequality between Kay and the Wart, the boys enjoy exciting adventures together, including visiting a giant, joining in a boar hunt, and meeting Robin Hood.

A witty satire, *The Sword in the Stone* pokes fun at the adventures of knights such as Sir Pellinor. Merlyn's role as a gifted but eccentric teacher is one of the most original and enjoyable parts of the novel. Readers who are familiar with the legends will especially enjoy the way White departs from the original.

By juxtaposing Kay as a rather ordinary knight apprentice with the Wart, White highlights the latter's exceptional traits. The Wart's compassion for all creatures helps him cope with his unjust circumstances and sets him apart as a model leader. Readers who feel inferior to a sibling will not feel so alone after reading the Wart's story.

**For those also seeking**: models for identity
**For those drawn to**: setting
**Themes/subjects**: Arthurian legends, Middle Ages, knights, castles, siblings and sibling issues, foster brothers, quests, magicians, magical transformations, knives/daggers/swords, humor, tutors
**Reading interest level**: grades 4–8
**Curricular tie-ins**: This novel is an excellent resource for a unit on the Middle Ages. White depicts different aspects of medieval life such as feudalism, hunting traditions, education, and manorial life. In a jigsaw activity, students could research and teach each other about these different aspects of medieval life.
**Adaptations & alternative formats**: animated Disney movie directed by Wolfgang Reitherman (1963); audiobook read by Neville Jason (2008)
**Translations**: French: *Excalibur: l'Épée dans la Pierre*
**Read-alikes**: *The Sword in the Stone* is the first book in the four-volume, *The Once and Future King*. Although Arthur is older in both Kevin Crossley-Holland's Arthur trilogy and Rosemary Sutcliff's *The Sword and the Circle*, fans of Arthurian legends will enjoy these books. They will also like

Katherine Paterson's *Parzival: The Quest of the Grail Knight*, a story about one of Arthur's knights.

## Acceptance

**Alexander, Lloyd** (1924–2007)
**The Castle of Llyr** (1966). New York: Holt, Rinehart and Winston, 1966. 201pp. 978-0805080506.

When Eilownwy is sent on a trip to the Isle of Mona to further her education as a princess, she is accompanied by her friend Taran and the creature Gurgi. Once they arrive, Taran is surprised to learn that King Rhuddlum and Queen Teleria expect their son to eventually marry Eilonwy. He is also surprised to discover that the shoemaker who visits him is Prince Gwydion in disguise. The prince tells Taran that the evil enchantress Achren intends to kidnap Eilonwy. Despite Taran's best efforts at protecting her, Eilonwy is abducted. The host of life-threatening situations that the characters face makes the novel an ideal choice for readers who enjoy narratives of suspense.

Beloved characters from earlier books in the Prydain Chronicles reappear in this third volume in the series. Characters in the novel must make a number of difficult decisions, ones that they agonize over. In the preface to the first book in the series, Lloyd Alexander observes, "The choices and decisions that face a frequently baffled Assistant Pig-Keeper are no easier than the ones we ourselves must make. Even in a fantasy realm, growing up is accomplished not without cost."

Both Taran and Eilonwy must come to terms with their lack of prestige and power—Taran as an assistant pig-keeper, not the person of noble birth he wishes to be; and Eilonwy as a girl, not the powerful enchantress that she has the power to be. Readers who feel inferior to those of greater wealth, social class, or talent will find comfort in the fact that esteemed characters in the novel experience the same insecurities.

**For those also seeking**: reassurance/comfort/confirmation of self-worth/strength
**For those drawn to**: character, story

*Myth/Legend*

**Themes/subjects**: cooperation and teamwork, royalty, princesses, kidnapping, missing persons, underground, castles, romance, jealousy, class differences

**Reading interest level**: grades 4–7

**Curricular tie-ins**: Characters make a number of difficult choices in the novel, for example, Taran's decision to continue to protect his rival Prince Rhun when he feels he should rescue Eilonwy; Gwydion's decision to give up the location of the book of spells and the bauble; Eilonwy's decision to give up her powers as an enchantress; Gwdion's decision to let the evil sorceress Lady Achren live; Taran's decision to go back for Glew after the giant betrayed everyone. Ask students to form pairs for a think-pair-share activity. They can discuss one of the decisions in the book, considering what they would have done or believe the character should have done.

**Adaptations & alternative formats**: audiobook read by James Langton (2004)

**Translations**: Spanish: *El Castillo de Llyr*

**Read-alikes**: Readers who enjoyed this novel will want to read the other books in the series: *The Book of Three*, *The Black Cauldron*, *Taran Wanderer*, and *The High King*. Angie Sage's *Flyte* and L. Frank Baum's *The Lost Princess of Oz* are also stories about the kidnapping of a princess.

CHAPTER TEN

# Realism/Everyday Life

"Everyday Life" is basically what it sounds like: fiction that portrays ordinary people living their ordinary lives. Literature scholars would categorize most of the novels included in this chapter as "realistic fiction." In sharp contrast to fantasy, realistic fiction depicts the world as it is, not as it could be. Characters in these stories are familiar rather than heroic, and mirror the prosaic, commonplace experiences of their readers. However, we have opted to call this chapter "Everyday Life" instead so as to draw attention to this genre's coming-of-age theme even when novels do not fit neatly in the "realistic fiction" genre. For example, we wanted to include David Almond's *Skellig* even though it features elements of fantasy because it primarily deals with life issues and Katherine Patterson's *Jacob Have I Loved*, even though it could also be categorized as historical fiction.

A key feature of realistic fiction is that its setting is contemporary with the author's writing. Writers of realistic fiction write about their own present, the time in which they are actually living (in contrast to historical fiction writers who write about a past that they could not have actually experienced themselves). So, writers of realistic fiction assume that the reader is familiar with the time period and therefore offer little cultural, social, or political explanation. For these reasons, Susan Coolidge's *What Katy Did* and Louisa May Alcott's *Little Women* are considered "realistic fiction" even though they occur long ago and offer historical insight to us now. However, because historical fiction and realistic fiction can be easily confused, we also wanted to call this chapter "Everyday Life" in order to help users clearly distinguish between the two genres.

Early "Everyday Life" stories, those written between the late nineteenth and early twentieth centuries, developed out of domestic fiction and so share many of its characteristics. These stories focus on interior worlds and familial relationships. For example, most of the action in *Little Women* takes place in the March household, in *The Secret Garden* on Misselthwaite Manor, and in *Anne of Green Gables* on the Cuthbert farm. The focus of these earlier novels is primarily on the problems of growing up. Some of these problems are universal, as when Jo March, described as "a colt in a flower garden," typifies the teenage awkwardness of changing and growing into one's new body, or when Anne Shirley, despairing of not having a dress with "puffed sleeves," typifies the common teenage fear of being unfashionable among one's peers. But, of course, not all of these realities are typical. Many of the children in these stories experience loss of a parent or become orphans, as is the case of Anne Shirley in *Anne of Green Gables*, Mary Lennox in *The Secret Garden*, and Jerusha Abbott in *Daddy-Long-Legs*. In these stories, the protagonists develop greater self-awareness and maturity as a result of overcoming their struggles.

Beginning in the 1970s, however, realistic fiction began to take a deeper look at these grim realities. In early realistic fiction, painful or traumatic events tend to occur off-stage, with little dramatization, and the focus is more on coping and building resilience after these events. "New Realism," on the other hand, acknowledges life's darker realities and the protagonist's suffering more vividly. For example, Katherine Paterson takes up sibling rivalry and parental favoritism in *Jacob Have I Loved*; Sharon Creech examines abandonment and loss in *Walk Two Moons*; and David Almond explores fear and anxiety in *Skellig*. In other words, newer fiction about everyday lives tends to more readily acknowledge and accept that children suffer, sometimes at the hands of adults, including their own parents.

For this reason, a lot of the novels in this chapter are also sometimes referred to as "social problem novels." For example, divorce is the social issue at hand in Anne Finch's *Madame Doubtfire*, child abuse in Sharon Creech's *Ruby Holler*, abandonment in Katherine Paterson's *The Great Gilly Hopkins*, and alcoholism and structural inequalities in Sherman Alexie's *The Absolutely True Diary of a Part-Time Indian*. In these stories, the children often have to learn to cope without a loving, supportive parent and instead must seek out their own support network.

A few notes on the series included in this section: only the first three novels of L. M. Montgomery's two series, *Anne of Green Gables* and *Emily of New Moon* are included. Although there are several more novels in each of these series, we do not consider them classics. *Anne of Green Gables* is followed by *Anne of Avonlea* and *Anne of the Island*. *Emily of New Moon* is followed by *Emily Climbs* and *Emily's Quest*. In both cases, major plot points will be spoiled by reading them out of order, so it is recommended that they are read chronologically.

## Awakening/New Perspectives/Enlargement of Possibilities

**Coolidge, Susan** (1858–1924)
**What Katy Did** (1872). New York: Puffin Classics, 2009. 211pp. 978-0141326719. PD.

"All legs and elbows, and angles and joints," Katy Carr is constantly tearing her dress and tangling her hair and bruising her knees in the rowdy games she invents. The oldest of five siblings, Katy lives in a small, country town in Ohio with her adoring, but often preoccupied, doctor father as well as her father's fastidious sister, Aunt Izzie, who joined the family when the children's mother died. While fun, imaginative, and popular with her friends—Katy intends to be famous when she grows up—she is also bossy and headstrong. At first, these faults cause only harmless scrapes, but as they go unchecked they eventually become the cause of a terrible accident that leaves Katy paralyzed from the waist down. She may never walk again and so is forced to reexamine and reinvent her future. Deeply embittered, she refuses to adjust until a chance visit from her favorite Cousin Helen, who is also paralyzed, helps guide her to strength and perseverance.

While modern readers will likely wince at Cousin Helen's "School of Pain" and Coolidge's unconcealed didacticism, her cautionary tale is nonetheless one of the first to explore children's disability. Not surprisingly, it is a character-driven story that tracks Katy's transformation from careless child to thoughtful young woman. She demonstrates how loneliness and suffering, once accepted, can be gifts, heightening one's depth of vision and one's depth of feeling.

**For those also seeking**: acceptance
**For those drawn to**: character
**Themes/subjects**: accidents (major), adaptation/adjusting to change, Christianity, dead or absent mother, depression, disability, games, humility, pain/suffering, school, siblings and sibling issues
**Reading interest level**: grades 6–8

**Curricular tie-ins**: Ask students to interrogate the lesson of Katy's accident to determine the values or beliefs that underlie it (e.g., girls are not supposed to be too lively or high-spirited) by writing a new episode or ending to the story. Then, as a class, discuss the paradox of ideology (how ideological assumptions, as assumptions, are taken as truth and therefore hard to recognize). Read aloud examples from students' work and ask them to discuss whether or not they can identify the presence of their own ideological influences.

**Adaptations & alternative formats**: audiobook read by Susan O'Malley (1997); TV movie directed by Stacey Curtis (1999)

**Read-alikes**: Readers can follow Katy's life in the two sequels to the novel: *What Katy Did at School* and *What Katy Did Next*. The protagonist in Dinah Maria Mulock Craik's *The Little Lame Prince* also learns to cope with a disability. *Little Women* is a good companion read not only because Katy resembles lively Jo but also because Coolidge and Alcott were contemporaries and shared the same editor.


**Hesse, Karen** (1952-)
**The Music of Dolphins** (1996). New York: Scholastic Press, 1996. 181pp. 978-0590897983.

When the coast guard spots a primitive-looking adolescent girl off the coast of Florida, they pick her up. Naked and unable to speak, Mila is identified as a feral child who has been living in the company of dolphins. Researcher, Dr. Elizabeth Beck, studies Mila in order to discover the role that language and socialization play in the development of humans. As Mila learns to speak English, she also becomes familiar with the customs and conventions of human beings. Although she makes friends with a research subject named Shay, Dr. Beck's research assistant Sandy, and Dr. Beck's son, Mila misses her dolphin family. After discovering that she is locked in her room in the research facility every night, Mila feels imprisoned and increasingly homesick. As a girl raised by dolphins, she feels trapped between two worlds.

Because Mila is an outsider to the human race, she has fresh insight and an unusual perspective about things readers take for granted. When the researchers tell her, for example, that she is making progress, she replies, "Making progress is when I wear clothes. Making progress is when I sleep in a bed and eat dead fish." Naive and lacking sophistication, Mila speaks simply yet wisely. Hesse's use of spare, poetic language is a strong appeal in the novel.

Mila is juxtaposed with Shay, another girl who is raised without human contact. But unlike Shay, Mila has experienced love and care, albeit with dolphins. Shay is never able to communicate with others or make connections with the people she meets. *The Music of Dolphins* presents a fresh perspective on the human condition; one that stresses love and caring as essential qualities for survival. Readers who are pulled strongly in two directions or those who feel like outsiders in their world will not feel so alone after reading this novel.

**For those also seeking**: connection with others/awareness of not being alone
**For those drawn to**: character, language
**Themes/subjects**: feral children, dolphins, music, language/communication, outcasts/misfits, imprisonment/entrapment, otherness, homesickness, non-traditional families, scholars/professors
**Reading interest level**: grades 5–8
**Curricular tie-ins**: Ask students to pretend they are social workers and write a report about Shay. Alternatively they could create group presentations about dolphins, focusing on their similarities with humans.
**Adaptations & alternative formats**: audiobook read by Michele McHall (2009)
**Translations**: French: *La Musique des Dauphins*
**Read-alikes**: Rudyard Kipling's *The Jungle Book* and *The Second Jungle Book* are also about a boy raised by animals. The mermaid in Randall Jarrell's *The Animal Family* is another sea-loving being who tries to adapt to life on land. Although not a serious novel like *The Music of Dolphins*, Maryrose Wood's *The Mysterious Howling* is also about feral children.


**Nesbit, Edith** (1858–1924)
**The Story of the Treasure Seekers** (1899). London: Hesperus, 2014. 140pp. 978-1843914747. PD.

"To restore the fallen fortunes of the House of Bastable" is how the treasure seeking all begins. The House of Bastable, located in the outskirts of London, consists of the six Bastable children and their father. Their mother has died and their father, who had become gravely ill after her death, lost all of his wealth. Now recovered, their father spends his days working anxiously in his office, leaving the children, who he can no longer afford to send to school, to occupy themselves.

Thus, the imaginative Bastables make use of their time by inventing ways to recover their riches. They dig for treasure, literally, and make several attempts as entrepreneurs, by selling cheap Sherry for instance, before resorting to more duplicitous schemes.

Initially published serial form, this novel is naturally episodic. But this formulaic structure is saved by its energetic narrator, Oswald Bastable, who recounts their shenanigans with unintentional humor. The first in the Bastable series (followed by *The Wouldbegoods* and *The New Treasure Seekers*), this novel is a testament to the power of ingenuity. Motivated by necessity—as "so many children with regular pocket-money have never felt it their duty to seek for treasure"—the Bastable children demonstrate that even in adverse circumstances children who are armed with imagination are never completely powerless and there is always treasure to be found.

**For those also seeking**: connection with others/awareness of not being alone
**For those drawn to**: character
**Themes/subjects**: adaptation/adjusting to change, adventure, dead or absent mother, humor, games, imagination, money/debt, siblings and sibling issues, single fathers, single-parent families, moving houses (relocating)
**Reading interest level**: grades 4–7
**Curricular tie-ins**: Ask younger students to write their own original episode about the Bastable children and their unsuccessful (or successful) attempts at making money for their family. Ask older students to contrast Nesbit's novel with contemporary or historical examples of children's labor (by finding news articles and/or conducting basic Internet research).
**Adaptations & alternative formats**: audiobook read by Simon Prebble (2001)
**Translations**: Spanish: *Los Buscadores De Tesoros*
**Read-alikes**: The mischief continues in *The Wouldbegoods* and *The New Treasure Seekers* (the more serious of the three). Arthur Ransome's *Swallows and Amazons* and E. Nesbit's *The Enchanted Castle* are also stories about the adventures of siblings.

**Nesbit, Edith** (1858–1924)
**The Railway Children** (1906). London: Puffin, 2010. 272pp. 978-0141321608. PD.

*Realism/Everyday Life*

Roberta (better known as "Bobbie"), Peter, and Phyllis "were not railway children to begin with." For all their young lives, they lived contentedly with their cheerful mother and father in their comfortable home situated in the center of hopping London. But one night, a mysterious visitor arrives and calls their father away—no one tells them why—and their mother packs up their house and moves them to the countryside. As the children observe their wealth suddenly diminish—though, again, no one tells them why—they must learn to make their own fun, and to take care of each other, as their mother now spends her days occupied, feverishly composing children's stories to make ends meet. So, alone, the children explore their picturesque surroundings and soon discover the railway station near their new home. The trains, the passengers, the station, and station workers—all become instant objects of fascination and lucky catalysts for friendship and adventure.

Originally published in serialized form in *The London* magazine, this novel is naturally episodic, but a narrative arc is built on the father's disappearance, the mystery of which propels the story until it is fully resolved in the final chapter. While the children are not particularly round characters, with the exception, perhaps, of Bobbie, this story retains its classic status as it exemplifies this one important reality: children can and *do* take responsibility for their own lives, and they are also capable of doing as much for others.

**For those also seeking**: connection with others/awareness of not being alone
**For those drawn to**: setting, character
**Themes/subjects**: adaptation/adjusting to change, adventure, dead or absent father, family, idleness and creativity, imagination, preoccupied parents, railroads, working mothers, siblings and sibling issues
**Reading interest level**: grades 3–7
**Curricular tie-ins**: Because trains and other modes of transportation figure so prominently in the novel's setting, reading it in conjunction with a unit on the history of transportation, urbanization, and/or consumption would be ideal. As an activity, ask students to compare and contrast the children's lives in an urban and rural setting.
**Adaptations & alternative formats**: abridged audiobook read by Jenny Agutter (2010) and unabridged audiobook read by Virginia Leishman (2013); film adaptation directed by Lionel Jeffries (1970)
**Translations**: Spanish: *Los Chicos Del Ferrocarril*

**Read-alikes**: Kenneth Oppel's *The Boundless* and Gertrude Chandler Warner's *Caboose Mystery* are also stories of railway adventures. The mother is the breadwinner and does not earn much in Eleanor Estes's *The Moffats* and Polly Horvath's *My One Hundred Adventures*.

**Patron, Susan**
**The Higher Power of Lucky** (2006). New York: Aladdin Paperbacks, 2008. 134pp. 978-1416975571.

Ten-year-old Lucky Trimble feels as if she has no control over events in her life. When she was eight, her mother died from electrocution. Her father, who left the family when Lucky was born, has no interest in raising her. He asks his first wife, Brigitte, to care for Lucky until a foster home is found for her. Leaving her native France to look after Lucky, Brigitte develops a close relationship with the girl. But Lucky is afraid that Brigitte will move back to France. Living in a trailer park in a California desert community, Lucky tries to cope with the unpredictability and uncertainty in her life.

Readers who love eccentric, endearing characters will enjoy this Newbery Medal–winning novel. Despite the fact that Lucky's mother died in a freak accident, her father abandoned her, her guardian may leave her, and her life is one of dire poverty, Lucky tries to be upbeat and hopeful. With a curious mind and a thoughtful disposition, she tries to figure out how to manage in the midst of all her challenges. Always carrying a survival kit backpack with her, and trying to glean tips from people in addiction recovery programs, Lucky manages to cope with a very difficult period in her life. Readers who have experienced loss and misfortune will see their situation in a new light after reading Lucky's story.

**For those also seeking**: reassurance/comfort/confirmation of self-worth/strength
**For those drawn to**: character
**Themes/subjects**: orphans, abandoned children, dead or absent mother, dead or absent father, runaway children, deserts, non-traditional families, grief, anxiety/fears, agency and powerlessness, poverty, village/small-town life, California, resilience
**Reading interest level**: grades 4–6
**Curricular tie-ins**: Lincoln is fascinated with tying knots. In small groups, students can look for information about knot tying. Ask one person in each group to teach the class how to tie a new knot and to explain what that knot

could be used for. Alternatively, read Miles's favorite picture book *Are You My Mother?* (by P. D. Eastman) to the class and ask students to discuss in small groups, then in a literature circle, why this particular picture book is included in the novel.
**Adaptations & alternative formats**: audiobook read by Cassandra Campbell (2007)
**Translations**: Spanish: *El Poder Superior de Lucky*; French: *Le Bonheur Selon Lucky*
**Read-alikes**: Readers interested in Lucky's story will also enjoy the sequels to the novel: *Lucky Breaks* and *Lucky for Good*. Ten-year-old girls also face adversity and loss in Kate DiCamillo's *Because of Winn Dixie*, *Flora and Ulysses*, and *Raymie Nightingale*.

## Models for Identity

**Burnett, Frances Hodgson** (1849–1924)
**A Little Princess** (1905). New York: Puffin Classics, 2008. 293pp. 978-0141321127. PD.

When Sara Crewe is seven years old, she says goodbye to her birthplace in India to begin her studies at Miss Minchin's boarding school in London. Accompanied by her loving and adoring father—as her mother died during childbirth—Sara is given the largest suite in the house and lavished with all kinds of material comforts: a pretty wardrobe, books, furnishings, and an exquisite doll named Emily, who she makes into her closest companion. Given such ease and luxury, one might expect Sara to be spoiled and aloof, but she is just the opposite. Gentle, generous, and empathetic by nature, she possesses a noble soul—hence her nickname, "the little princess." With a few jealous exceptions, Sara's classmates accept her immediately. In particular, Ermengarde, who is constantly ridiculed for her learning disability, and Lottie, a toddler who has also lost her mother, take to her motherly attention.

But, when Sara's father tragically dies, it is discovered that he has lost his fortune, and Sara is left penniless and alone—a bitter discovery for her avaricious headmistress who now must take Sara as her charge. Miss Minchin retaliates by making Sara into her drudge, stripping her of her possessions, and exiling her to the attic. To manage her grief and humiliation, Sara imagines herself actually a princess. In this way, she is able to maintain her goodness and not sink to Miss Minchin's level. A model of strength and perseverance, Sara uses her imagination to achieve agency, rising above her slavish, dehumanizing circumstances and Miss Minchin's cruelty.

**For those also seeking**: connection with others/awareness of not being alone
**For those drawn to**: setting, character
**Themes/subjects**: abused children, adaptation/adjusting to change, child neglect, courage, disability, dolls, empathy, father-daughter relationships, friendship, humility, community, imagination, loneliness, missing persons, only children, orphans, pain/suffering, poverty, stories and storytelling, school, resilience
**Reading interest level**: grades 3–7
**Curricular tie-ins**: Captain Crewe's diamond mine speculation and the depiction of the Indian manservant, Ram Dass provide entry points into discussions about the social and economic impact of colonial rule, bringing to life, in this case, British Imperialism.
**Adaptations & alternative formats**: film directed by Alfonso Cuarón (1995); audiobook read by Virginia Leishman (1999)
**Translations**: Spanish: *La princesita*; French: *La petite princesse*
**Read-alikes**: The protagonist in Susan Paton's *The Higher Power of Lucky* is also a poverty-stricken orphan whose future is uncertain.


**Burnett, Frances Hodgson** (1849–1924)
**Little Lord Fauntleroy** (1886). New York: Puffin Classics, 2010. 978-0141330143. PD.

When his father dies suddenly, young Cedric Errol tries his best to comfort his loving but heartbroken mother. Living in New York City, during the mid-nineteenth century, their small family is reduced to genteel poverty, though Cedric's cheerful influence helps lighten their burden. Charming and easy to love, Cedric is popular with his friends, especially the neighborhood grocer, Mr. Hobbes, and the bootblack, Dick.

Then, in an unbelievable twist of fate, Cedric's estranged grandfather, an English Earl who had never approved of his son's marriage to an American, sends news that he is his only living heir and to become the next Earl of Dorincourt. The Earl, a mean, stubborn man, arranges for Cedric and his mother to come to England but refuses to allow Cedric's mother to live with them. Although confused by this arrangement, Cedric, who has

Realism/Everyday Life

misinterpreted his grandfather's extravagances for generosity, withholds his doubts and instead idolizes him. In turn, the Earl, who is unaccustomed to such high esteem, finds himself trying to live up to Cedric's idealizations.

In this way, *Fauntleroy* challenges our conceptions and misconceptions about children and childhood. As the contrast between Cedric and the Earl's characters reveals, adults are not necessarily more evolved, more developed, or wiser by virtue of their age.

**For those also seeking**: connection with others/awareness of not being alone
**For those drawn to**: story
**Themes/subjects**: adaptation/adjusting to change, appearance versus reality, dead or absent father, aiding/helping, empathy, England, family, family conflict, father-son relationships, grandfathers, gratitude, humility, inheritance and succession, kindness, mother-son relationships, New York City, only children, primogeniture, royalty, wealth
**Reading interest level**: grades 2–5
**Curricular tie-ins**: Ask students to research primogeniture in Britain and, as a jigsaw activity, ask them to explain to their group different aspects of this law: history, purpose, gender discrimination, and current practices.
**Adaptations & alternative formats**: movie directed by Alfonso Cuarón (1995); audiobook read by Virginia Leishman (1999)
**Translations**: Spanish: *El Pequeño Lord*; French: *Le Petit Lord*
**Read-alikes**: The relationship between a child and grandfather is the focus of Patricia MacLachlan's *Caleb's Story* and Johanna Spyri's *Heidi*.


**Montgomery, L. M.** (1874–1942)
**Anne of Green Gables** (1908). New York: Aladdin Paperbacks, 2014. 440pp. 978-1442490000. PD.

Aging siblings Marilla and Matthew Cuthbert, living in a farmhouse in the lush, fictionalized community of Avonlea, on Prince Edward Island, decide that they will adopt a boy from the orphanage to help them manage the backbreaking routine of their rural life. But by some accident, 11-year-old, fiery-headed Anne arrives on their doorstep instead. The Cuthberts mean to correct the mistake but are soon so charmed by Anne's curiosity, exuberance, and relentless imagination, not to mention her ardent desire to live with them, that they decide to keep her after all. They give her the east gable room, a cozy nook overlooking cherry blossoms, and other natural delights.

This picturesque setting provides the perfect fodder for Anne's imagination. She spends much of her time daydreaming and trying to make her dreams a reality—with sometimes comic, but mostly successful, results. She also makes a best "bosom friend," excels at school (with the exception of geometry!), and forms an intellectual rivalry with the cutest boy in town.

Fast-paced, and episodic in style, this novel is also lengthy. The cumulative effect is a complete and richly textured narrative of Anne's transformation from poor, loveless waif to self-possessed, confident young woman. Yet, gifted as she is with the ability to make others "love her," Anne transforms those around her as well. Marilla, initially too firm and emotionally reserved, eventually melts with tenderness for her, and shy and taciturn Matthew glows with adoration. In the end, Anne builds for herself a loving and supportive community in Avonlea, a life so beautiful that the reader can't help but wonder if perhaps the worst kind of poverty might be poverty of the imagination.

**For those also seeking**: connection with others/awareness of not being alone
**For those drawn to**: setting, character
**Themes/subjects**: adaptation/adjusting to change, adoption, coming of age, courage, empathy, fashion/costume, friendship, grief, heroines, loneliness, only children, optimism, orphans, Presbyterianism, redheads, responsibility, imagination
**Reading interest level**: grades 4–6
**Curricular tie-ins**: Because Anne loves her natural surroundings, reading her story would complement a science unit focused on identifying and classifying trees, plants, and flowers. Students could look up one of the trees of flowers she mentions, do some background research about it, and write a description about it (characteristics, flowering season, native habitat and range, etc.).
**Adaptations & alternative formats**: abridged edition part of Puffin in Bloom series, illustrated by Anna Bond (2014); modern adaptation, *Ana of California*, by Andi Teran (2015); audiobook read by Mary Sarah (2013); *Anne of Green Gables*, a Canadian made-for-TV series (1985) was released by Sullivan Entertainment as a DVD (2002) and as part of a trilogy box set (2005); TV series adaptation, *Anne with an E*, produced by Netflix (2017) gives more attention to Anne's suffering.
**Translations**: Spanish: *Anne, la de tejados verdes*; French: *Anne, La Maison aux pignons verts*

**Read-alikes**: Readers who enjoyed this story will also enjoy the sequels, *Anne of Avonlea* and *Anne of the Island*. *Rebecca of Sunnybrook Farm* is the American equivalent of *Anne of Green Gables*. It follows a similar plot but Rebecca's guardian, unfortunately, is not as kind as the Cuthberts. Also, although Julie in Irene Hunt's *Up a Road Slowly* is not an orphan, she loses her mother when she is young and must learn to adjust to life in her aunt's house.

**Montgomery, L. M.** (1874–1942)
**Emily Climbs** (1925). Naperville, IL: Sourcebooks Fire, 2014. 344pp. 978-1402289156. PD.

At 14, Emily does not know everything her future holds, but one thing is for certain: she will be a writer. She even vows that she will never marry but would rather be "*wedded to [her] art.*" She thrives on "the flash" that thrilling moment of inspiration when a new poem or story begins to hold and take shape in her mind.

In pursuit of this ambition, Emily hopes to attend nearby Shrewsbury High School, along with her best New Moon friends, Ilse, Teddy, and Perry. But Aunt Elizabeth, fearful that Emily will fall in love and elope, just like her mother, staunchly refuses to send her. Eventually, she relents but on one impossible condition: Emily must give up her writing. Incapable of making such a promise, Emily agrees to a compromise. She will continue to write poems and true stories but *no* fiction. To Aunt Elizabeth and most of the other Murray relatives, fiction is considered frivolous, a waste of time.

Despite discouragement from her family, and even from some of her friends, Emily continues to climb the "Alpine path" until her literary aspirations are realized. Although she encounters failures and disappointments along the way, she accepts their inevitability, their necessity, and does not allow them to shake her faith in herself. Rather, it is success that proves to be her greatest challenge. Offered a position at a magazine in New York, Emily must make a difficult choice to pursue her dreams or to remain at New Moon, the home she has grown to love.

Of both the Anne and Emily series, this novel is the strongest in terms of narrative and character development and a bildungsroman in every sense. As Emily learns to trust in her own gifts and abilities, she offers a model for readers searching for the same strength.

**For those also seeking**: reassurance/comfort/confirmation of self-worth/strength
**For those drawn to**: character
**Themes/subjects**: ambition, authoritarian figures, body image, censorship, displacement (psychology), cliques (in school), coming of age, dreams, duty, extrasensory perception, feminism, fashion/costume, friendship, gossip, heroines, inventing/creating, mental illness, oppressive environments, perseverance/determination, projection (psychology), romance, wealth, writing, Presbyterianism, school
**Reading interest level**: grades 4–7
**Curricular tie-ins**: Emily's aunt considers fiction and art in general frivolous. Divide the classroom and ask students to debate this question: Is art frivolous, or is it essential to human happiness/flourishing?
**Adaptations & alternative formats**: audiobook read by Laural Merlington (2017)
**Translations**: Spanish: *Emily, Lejos de Casa*; French: *Émilie De La Nouvelle Lune 2*
**Read-alikes**: Like Emily, Rebecca in *Rebecca of Sunnybrook Farm* also copes with relatives who make judgments about her because of her parentage and who must also overcome challenges to become a writer.


**Wiggins, Kate Douglas** (1856–1923)
**Rebecca of Sunnybrook Farm** (1903). New York: Aladdin Classics, 2003. 341pp. 978-0689860010. PD.

When Rebecca's father dies, her mother is unable to care for both her seven children and the family's farm all on her own, so she sends Rebecca to live with her older sisters, Miranda and Jane, in another town. Aunt Miranda and Aunt Jane, who have never married or had children of their own, promise to be "the making of Rebecca" by providing and supervising her education. Inexperienced parents, both aunts, especially the severe and stern Aunt Miranda, who are taken aback by Rebecca's exuberance and energy, which they often mistake for wildness and impertinence—defects that she has inherited from her senseless dreamer of a father and that need constant correcting. Yet, so adored by her friends, teachers, and neighbors, Rebecca manages to endure her Aunt Miranda's cruelty and hard discipline while at the same time refusing to allow her to kill her spirit.

Rebecca's lively imagination and creative leanings render her a kind of American Anne of Green Gables. But, unlike L. M. Montgomery's stories, this one is quicker-paced and less episodic. At the conclusion, Rebecca is a young, self-assured woman, just graduated from school and in passionate pursuit of writerly ambitions. She is practically "made." Thus, Rebecca stands out as a model of courage in the face of loneliness and isolation and of perseverance in the face of constant criticism and condemnation. She reminds readers that no one knows oneself *better* than oneself, and her example empowers them to trust in this self-knowledge, to resist self-doubt, and, rather, to always follow one's heart.

**For those also seeking**: connection with others/awareness of not being alone
**For those drawn to**: character, language
**Themes/subjects**: adaptation/adjusting to change, art (as coping mechanism), authoritarian figures, being different, body image, clothing, community, dead or absent father, dead or absent mother, displacement (psychology), duty, friendship, gender roles, gossip, heroines, imagination, oppressive environments, perseverance/determination, projection (psychology), writing, moving houses (relocating)
**Reading interest level**: grades 6–8
**Curricular tie-ins**: Contemporary readers may find it strange that Rebecca's mother sent her away to live with her aunts. To help students appreciate the ways in which childhood is a social construct, shaped one's culture and history, ask them to research children's roles in the United States during the early twentieth century. Expand on this unit by assigning specific topics with regard to differences in roles dependent on location (urban versus rural children), race, gender, and class.
**Adaptations & alternative formats**: audiobook read by Lorna Raver (2007)
**Read-alikes**: Like Rebecca, Julie in Irene Hunt's *Up a Road Slowly* moves in with her aunt and grows to love her.

## Reassurance/Comfort/Confirmation of Self-Worth/Strength

**Birdsall, Jeanne** (1951–)
**The Penderwicks: A Summer Tale of Four Sisters, Two Rabbits, and a Very Interesting Boy** (2005). New York: Yearling, 2005. 262pp. 978-0440420477.

When the Penderwick sisters spend their summer vacation at a cottage on the Arundel estate, they meet 10-year-old Jeffrey, a likable boy who is pressured by his mother and her boyfriend to enroll in a military academy. The sisters, who range in age from twelve to four, are good-natured and well-meaning but prone to getting into trouble. Although the girls have great fun with Jeffrey, they dislike his snobbish mother and are upset that his mother does not care about his passion for music. Jeffrey's mother takes an instant dislike to the girls and believes they are a bad influence on her son.

Winner of the National Book Award, *The Penderwicks* is a highly readable, heart-warming story. Birdsall's penetrating insight into character and her comic depiction of the foibles of the girls are powerful appeals in the novel. The way that 12-year-old Rosalind, for example, tries to hide her interest in Cagney from herself is amusing. Penderwick customs and routines, such as calling MOOPS (meeting of older Penderwick sisters), swearing on the Penderwick family honor, and identifying the OAP (oldest available Penderwick) to perform certain jobs, bind the sisters together is a close-knit, supportive group. Although they complain at times, the girls accept each other's idiosyncrasies in a genial and magnanimous way. Their kindly father, who views his daughters' mishaps and shortcomings with a comic eye, is a reassuring figure in the novel. Readers who view their faults and problems as formidable may see them as more manageable after reading the novel. Jeffrey's story will resonate with children whose parents have decided their future for them.

**For those also seeking**: awakening/new perspectives/enlargement of possibilities
**For those drawn to**: character
**Themes/subjects**: sisters, summer vacations, single-parent dating, adventure, gardens/gardening, mansions, wealth, siblings and sibling issues, cottages, humor, parental disapproval, single-parent families
**Reading interest level**: grades 4–6
**Curricular tie-ins**: Ask students to pick a favorite character in the novel and create a scrapbook of the character's pastimes and interests.
**Adaptations & alternative formats**: audiobook read by Susan Denaker (2006)
**Translations**: Spanish: *Las Hermanas Penderwick*; French: *Les Penderwick: L'Été de Quatre Sœurs, de Deux Lapins et d'un Garçon Très Intéressant*
**Read-alikes**: Further adventures of the Penderwick family can be found in the sequels to the novel: *The Penderwicks on Gardam Street*, *The Penderwicks at Point Mouette*, and *The Penderwicks in Spring*. Edith Nesbit's Bastable novels (*The Story of the Treasure Seekers*, *The Wouldbegoods*, and

*The New Treasure Seekers*) are also stories about the comic adventures of four siblings.

**Burnett, Frances Hodgson** (1849–1924)
**The Secret Garden** (1911). New York: Penguin Books, 2011. 258pp. 978-0143106456. PD.

When her parents die in a cholera epidemic, Mary Lennox travels from her home in India to Misselthwaite Manor, on the Moorlands of England, to live with her uncle, her only surviving relative. Raised by wealthy but neglectful parents—her mother "had not wanted a little girl at all"—Mary has largely spent the first nine years of her life in isolation under the care of her Ayah, her nurse-servant. Thus, when Mary arrives to Misselthwaite, she appears spoiled and "quite contrary"—though, actually she is grieving and just beginning to confront the wounds of her neglect. In the beginning, Misselthwaite is lonely, too. Mary's uncle, Archibald Craven, is noticeably absent, and no other children appear as playmates. Eventually though, Mary does find friends on the manor and through these friendships develops an appetite for life and a sense of independence.

Misselthwaite Manor and the enclosed secret garden are markers of Mary's inner life in this character- and settings-driven novel. As Mary spends less time in the Gothic mansion "with a hundred rooms nearly all shut up," and more time weeding the tangled mass of plants in the secret garden, she clears the way for personal growth and development. So, while underscoring the importance of love and nurturing in a child's development, this story also exemplifies the possibility that children can find agency and a sense of self-worth in the face of adversity. Mary models perseverance and shows readers how they can seek and maintain nurturing relationships and support networks, for themselves—beyond their homes and families.

**For those also seeking**: models for identity
**For those drawn to**: character, setting
**Themes/subjects**: adaptation/adjusting to change, books, child neglect, class differences, death, depression, displacement (psychology), disability, empathy, education, friendship, grief, literacy/illiteracy, nature, only children, orphans, moving houses (relocating), resilience
**Reading interest level**: grades 4–7
**Curricular tie-ins**: The setting of this novel makes it the perfect complement for a unit on the plant life cycle and plant classification. Give students

their own mint plant or create a classroom herb garden. Celebrate their growth by using the herbs in food or drink (e.g., mint lemonade, rosemary shortbread).
**Adaptations & alternative formats**: audiobook read by Josephine Bailey (2003), movie directed by Agnieszka Holland (1993)
**Translations**: Spanish: *El Jardín Secreto*; French: *Le Jardin Secret*
**Read-alikes**: The garden in Philippa Pearce's *Tom's Midnight Garden* is also a healing place.

**Creech, Sharon** (1949–)
**Ruby Holler** (2002). New York: HarperCollins, 2012. 270pp. 978-0060560157.

At 13 years old, Florida and Dallas, also known as the "trouble twins," are the oldest children residing at the Boxton Creek Home for Children, where they have lived off-and-on, shuffled in-and-out of foster care, their entire lives. Repeatedly abused, both mentally and physically, by the Home's managers as well as their various foster parents, Florida and Dallas are more than a little skeptical when an aging, eccentric couple, Tiller and Sairy, invites them to their cozy cabin in beautiful Ruby Holler. Rustic and secluded, Ruby Holler is located in a valley whose hillsides are blanketed by ruby-leaved maple trees. Although Tiller and Sairy offer them many comforts—a snug, lofted bedroom like a "treehouse"; beds spread with soft, homemade quilts; warm, soulful meals—and invite them on an exotic summer vacation, Florida and Dallas, burned by past experience, resist their loving attentions and plot to run away together.

Groundbreaking in its depiction of the psychological effects of child abuse and foster care, this novel offers a realistic glimpse of these obstacles from the child's point of view. A nurturing home does not suddenly cure Florida and Dallas of their distrustfulness of adults, and up until the very end they struggle to form attachments to Tiller and Sairy. Yet, the progress they do make is a major testament to the transformative power of love. As Tiller and Sairy are unyielding in their devotion, Florida and Dallas begin to believe they really are worthy of love and reciprocate.

**For those also seeking**: connection with others/awareness of not being alone
**For those drawn to**: story, character
**Themes/subjects**: abandoned children, abused children, adaptation/ adjusting to change, agency and powerlessness, betrayal, camping,

*Realism/Everyday Life*

empathy, foster care, kindness, love, non-traditional families, orphans, runaway children, twins

**Reading interest level**: grades 4–7

**Curricular tie-ins**: This story provides a clear segue into introducing the concept of child abuse. As author suggests that the negligent foster home managers, Mr. and Mrs. Trepid, came from abusive backgrounds themselves, ask students to reflect on cycles of abuse and how they can be broken.

**Adaptations & alternative formats**: audiobook read by Donna Murphy (2007)

**Translations**: French: *Le Vallon Rouge*

**Read-alikes**: In Sharon Creech's *Walk Two Moons*, a 13-year-old copes with the loss of a parent.

## Connection with Others/Awareness of Not Being Alone

**Alexie, Sherman** (1966–)
**The Absolutely True Diary of a Part-Time Indian** (2007). Illustrated by Ellen Forney. New York: Little, Brown and Company, 1999. 978-0316013697.

Junior is a 14-year-old Spokane Indian living in Wellpinit, a tiny Indian Reservation in Eastern Washington State. Although Junior loves his family and friends on the reservation, his life there feels hopeless. All around him, all he ever sees, is poverty: joblessness, hunger, depression, and alcoholism. Although he tries to have a sense of humor about it—Junior was born with all sorts of physical problems and thus, as the object of teasing, has had to develop a thick skin—he flies into a rage when he realizes that his high school textbook is over 20 years old, the same textbook, in fact, that his mother used when she was in high school.

Convinced that the reservation offers no hope for a better future, Junior decides to "go where other people have hope." He quits the reservation school and instead attends a small, but better high school in the nearby suburban town of Reardan. But his decision is rife with internal conflict. On the one hand, he is grateful for the intellectual challenge and the likeminded friends he meets. On the other hand, he can't help resenting them a little for their privilege. Being poor and Spokane Indian, he feels like he can't relate to all of his rich, white classmates, and they can't relate to him. At the same time, his decision has alienated him from his friends on the reservation, who think he thinks he is better than them. When his best friend from the reservation, Rowdy, stops talking to him, Junior wonders if his decision to leave is worth it.

Winner of the 2007 National Book Award for Young People's Literature, this novel is groundbreaking in so many ways. At the same time he addresses the still-present effects of colonialism on Native Americans—structural inequalities (in terms of access to education, healthcare, and nutrition), alcoholism, and despair—he also manages to tell a story that almost anyone, at least anyone who has ever felt marginalized, can relate to. And yet he also tells it in a way that is both hugely funny and fun to read. It is, in a word, an absolute "masterpiece."

**For those also seeking**: reassurance/comfort/confirmation of self-worth/strength
**For those drawn to**: setting, language
**Themes/subjects**: adaptation/adjusting to change, abused children, alcohol/alcoholism, agency and powerlessness, anger/hostility, anxiety/fears, appearance versus reality, art (as a coping mechanism), body image, books, bullying, child neglect, class differences, cliques (in school), colonialism, coming of age, cycles of abuse, death, depression, disability, eating disorders, education, empathy, food, friendship, gifted children, grandmothers, hope, humor, hunger, indigenous people (the United States), insiders/outsiders, low self-esteem, mentality, memoirs/diaries, money/debt, moral dilemmas, Native American history, schools, outcasts/misfits, otherness, poverty, pain/suffering, perseverance/determination, racism, resourcefulness, sexual awakening, sports, teachers, Washington State
**Reading interest level**: grades 6–8
**Curricular tie-ins**: Discuss how media have influenced or shaped students' perceptions of Native Americans. Ask them to look for examples of stereotyping in the media. As a mathematics/statistics activity, have students compare and contrast income level, education achievement, and so on between Wellpinit and Reardan populations using online U.S. Census data.
**Adaptations & alternative formats**: audiobook read by Tom Parker (1997)
**Translations**: Spanish: *El Diario Completamente Verídico de un Indio a Tiempo Parcial*; French: *Le Premier qui Pleure a Perdu*
**Read-alikes**: Opal Buloni also copes with an alcoholic parent in *Because of Winn-Dixie*. Readers drawn to Alexie's humor should also check out books by Christopher Paul Curtis, Richard Peck, and Mark Twain.

**Almond, David** (1951–)
**Skellig** (1998). New York: Laurel-Leaf Books, 2008. 182pp. 978-0440229087.

In anticipation of the birth of his baby sister, 10-year-old Michael and his parents move into a new house. But the joy of her birth is shadowed by her premature arrival and delicate health. Fearful for her life, the family is constantly on edge. Young Michael feels especially helpless and finds himself withdrawing from the world of his friends, sports, and school.

One day, he wanders alone into the rickety toolshed in their backyard where he discovers a decrepit stranger—Skellig—lying on the floor. Creeping up next to him, Michael is at once fascinated by the Skellig's pallid, unearthly appearance and repulsed by his sickening stench. Distrusting his eyes, Michael invites his new neighbor and friend, a fiery spirit and independent thinker named Mina, to go to shed with him and help verify the creature's existence. Together, Michael and Mina come to Skellig's aid and try to penetrate his mystery. Uncovering his winged back, they wonder if, perhaps, he is an angel.

Profound and deeply spiritual, this narrative-driven novel meditates on questions related to life, death, and the divine. As the fate of Michael's sister remains uncertain for most of the novel, Michael's parents are necessarily preoccupied, and Michael must navigate his grief without them. In this way, Michael reminds readers that pain is a part of the human condition, unavoidable, and common to all.

**For those also seeking**: acceptance
**For those drawn to**: story, character
**Themes/subjects**: art (as coping mechanism), babies, birds, William Blake, Christianity, death, dreams, empathy, evolution, faith, friendship, grief, homeschool, illness, imagination, love, pain/suffering, sleepwalking
**Reading interest level**: grades 3–7
**Curricular tie-ins**: Read *Skellig* to complement a science unit on evolution and to draw out scientific and faith-based perspectives. For a literature-based activity, assign one of the Blake poems to which Almond alludes ("The School Boy," "The Angel," or "Night"). Then ask students to reread the excerpt in *Skellig* containing the allusion. Discuss how reading the poem illuminates or changes their reading of the text.
**Adaptations & alternative formats**: audiobook read by David Almond (2009)

**Translations**: French: *Skellig*
**Read-alikes**: Boys also worry about the health and safety of their younger sisters in Kenneth Oppel's *The Nest* and Kate DiCamillo's *The Magician's Elephant*.

**Cleary, Beverly** (1916–)
**Ramona the Pest** (1968). New York: HarperCollins, 2006. 211pp. 978-0380709540.

Ramona Quimby is a girl who can't wait. She can't wait to start kindergarten, and she can't wait to learn how to read and write so she can catch up with her fourth-grade sister Beezus. In other words, Ramona can't wait to grow up. But her first semester at Glenwood School on Klickitat Street turns into one blunder after another. First, some confusion about her teacher's use of the word *present* leads to some embarrassment—and disappointment. Then Davy, the cutest boy in her class, won't let her kiss him. But even worse, Ramona, fascinated by her classmate Susan's tightly wound, perfect curls, is unable to resist temptation and gives them a playful tug—an action that Susan takes for an attack and sends Ramona on suspension from school.

Each episode of this short novel captures, with humor, the daily humiliations of the playground and, for older readers especially, serves as a reminder for the scale with which these humiliations are often felt. It is impossible not to empathize with Ramona whose spiritedness is always well intentioned but often misunderstood. Thankfully, though, Ramona also demonstrates and confirms that one can always rise above these indignities and that enduring them helps strengthen one's character and defines it—helps one, in other words, "grow up." A truly timeless story and message.

**For those also seeking**: reassurance/comfort/confirmation of self-worth/strength
**For those drawn to**: character
**Themes/subjects**: adaptation/adjusting to change, growing up (apprehension), humor, identity formation, school, siblings and sibling issues, youngest siblings
**Reading interest level**: grades K–2
**Curricular tie-ins**: Read the excerpt from Chapter 1, "Ramona's Big Day," in which Ramona confuses the meaning of "present" to segue into a lesson or activity on homonyms.

Realism/Everyday Life

**Adaptations & alternative formats**: audiobook read by Stockard Channing (2013); film, *Ramona and Beezus* (2010), directed by Elizabeth Allen, is based on the entire Ramona series.
**Translations**: Spanish: *Ramona La Chinche*; French: *Ramona La Peste*
**Read-alikes**: Ramona's adventures continue in seven other books in the series.


**Fine, Anne** (1947–)
**Madame Doubtfire (US: Alias Madame Doubtfire)** (1987). London: Puffin Books, 2015. 228pp. 978-0141359755.

After the divorce of their parents, siblings Lydia, Christopher, and Natalie find themselves in the awkward position of managing the feelings of their antagonistic parents. While living full time with their mother, Miranda, in their suburban home in England, they visit their father, Daniel, an out-of-work actor, every other weekend at his shabby flat nearby. Although Daniel and the children wish that they could see more of each other, Miranda fiercely resists. So, when Daniel learns that Miranda plans to hire a cleaning lady to help her around the house, Daniel hatches a plan. He applies for the job, but not as himself, not as "Daniel." Rather, he disguises himself as a matronly old woman and puts his acting lessons to use by applying as Madame Doubtfire.

However funny and outlandish, this novel accurately depicts the situation that children of divorced parents commonly face. Caught between their fun-loving, albeit narcissistic father, and a protective, yet rigid and overly demanding, mother, the Hilliard children find themselves trying to accommodate both parents, reversing their child-parent roles. Luckily, Miranda and Daniel are not so caught up in their anger that they do not recognize the error of their ways, and the story ends "happily" with a compromise. Although some children readers may find it difficult to relate to this relatively mild domestic conflict, they will certainly find connection with the Hilliard children, who, recognizing the unfairness of their situation, learn to advocate for themselves. Children in similar situations can relate.

**For those also seeking**: reassurance/comfort/confirmation of self-worth/strength
**For those drawn to**: story, character

**Themes/subjects**: actors/acting, appearance versus reality, deception, disguises, displacement (psychology), divorce, family conflict, humor, narcissistic parents, child neglect, projection (psychology), single-parent families
**Reading interest level**: grades 4–6
**Curricular tie-ins**: Since so much of this story hinges on disguise and pretense, ask students to create a physical mask in which they symbolically capture the ways in which they feel like they have to "hide" themselves in their day-to-day lives, and to present their masks to each other.
**Adaptations & alternative formats**: movie directed by Chris Columbus (1993)
**Translations**: Spanish: *Señora Doubtfire*; French: *Madame Doubtfire*
**Read-alikes**: Following *Madame Doubtfire*, Fine wrote and published *Goggle-Eyes* (1989), which centers on another difficult aspect of divorce, divorced parents dating.

**Montgomery, L. M.** (1874–1942)
**Anne of the Island** (1915). New York: Aladdin Paperbacks, 2014. 358pp. 978-1442490048. PD.

The third book in the "Anne" series, the heroine now sails away from Avonlea—from Marilla and the twins and from her best friend Diana—to Nova Scotia where she will finally begin her university studies and pursue her literary ambitions. The changing setting corresponds to changes everywhere. A girlhood friend from Avonlea dies. Diana marries, launching a series of other friends' proposals and weddings. So too, Anne's relationship with close friend Gilbert Blythe becomes strained when he expresses his tender feelings for her, and she cannot reciprocate them.

Although embracing her new life and growing independence, Anne cannot help feeling a little unmoored by these rapid developments and also ambivalent about her own future wants. Although glad for her friends' fortunate couplings, she observes that "it is sometimes a little lonely to be surrounded everywhere by a happiness that is not your own." Thus, through the next four years spanning her university education, Anne learns about the "penalty" for growing up. Though she can finally make her youthful imaginings a reality, she realizes that achieving them can sometimes be a lonely pursuit. But, lucky for Anne, she is an inveterate dreamer. She is never sad for long because she wants to be happy and knows how to

Realism/Everyday Life

put herself in the way of happiness. Readers will relate to Anne's feelings of loneliness, but in her they will also find a model of how to tolerate them.

**For those also seeking**: reassurance/comfort/confirmation of self-worth/strength
**For those drawn to**: story, character
**Themes/subjects**: adaptation/adjusting to change, college/college life, commercialism, coming of age, courtship, loneliness, love, marriage, rejection, romance, writing, pride
**Reading interest level**: grades 4–7
**Curricular tie-ins**: In Chapter 15, "A Dream Turned Upside Down," Anne is mortified when a story she writes is published as a baking powder advertisement. Expand on this example by asking students to think of ways that advertising continues to shape the information they encounter (online, in print) and how/why this may be problematic.
**Adaptations & alternative formats**: audiobook read by Shelly Frasier (2006); *Anne of Green Gables: The Sequel*, a Canadian made-for-TV series (1987) was released by Sullivan Entertainment as a DVD (2004) and as part of a trilogy box set (2005)
**Translations**: French: *Anne Quitte Son Île*
**Read-alikes**: Readers who liked this novel may also enjoy the rest of the books in the series (*Anne of Windy Poplars*, *Anne's House of Dreams*, *Anne of Ingleside*, *Rainbow Valley*, and *Rilla of Ingleside*). Also, like *Anne of the Island*, Jean Webster's *Daddy-Long-Legs* is a story about a girl in college set in the early twentieth century.


**Montgomery, L. M.** (1874–1942)
**Emily of New Moon** (1923). Naperville, IL: Sourcebooks Fire, 2014. 368pp. 978-1402289125. PD.

At first, Emily Byrd Starr might not seem that different from Montgomery's more renowned, early twentieth-century heroine, Anne of Green Gables. Like Anne, she is an orphan who is deeply sensitive and drawn to the natural world and beauty that surrounds her. She is also bright, imaginative, artistic, and ambitious. She, too, wants to be a writer.

However, Emily's new living situation, with her Aunt Elizabeth at New Moon, is far less pleasant than Anne's with Matthew and Marilla Cuthbert. When they first meet, Emily instantly senses her aunt's resentment;

she knows she is received out of duty, not love. So wounded, Emily does not ingratiate herself, like Anne might have, but instead endures her aunt's rigid, sometimes cruel, discipline with quiet stoicism—but only to a point. Emily also possesses the "Murray pride" and so has the strength of mind to question authority when necessary.

Luckily though, New Moon is not without its redeeming qualities. Her Aunt Laura also lives with them, and she offers Emily the gentleness and warmth that her Aunt Elizabeth does not. There is also her odd, old cousin Jimmy, a kindred spirit, who is blessed with poetic gifts despite a childhood brain injury. Most importantly, she has her upstairs garret, where she can go to write. She journals every day, composing her entries as letters to her recently deceased father, who she misses.

Considered Montgomery's most autobiographical character, Emily is striking for her equanimity. She never wallows in self-doubt. She persists; she perseveres. Even by today's standards, Emily is remarkably self-possessed and a model of confidence for young girls.

**For those also seeking**: reassurance/comfort/confirmation of self-worth/strength
**For those drawn to**: story, character
**Themes/subjects**: art (as coping mechanism), authoritarian figures, challenging authority figures, body image, cliques (in school), death, disability, displacement (psychology), duty, friendship, heroines, letters, loneliness, mental illness, oppressive environments, orphans, pain/suffering, perseverance/determination, projection (psychology), Presbyterianism, school, wealth, memoirs/diaries
**Reading interest level**: grades 4–7
**Curricular tie-ins**: Use this novel to introduce daily journaling. Encourage students to address their journal entries, like Emily, to a friend, to a loved one, or to someone they admire.
**Adaptations & alternative formats**: audiobook read by Susan O'Malley (2009)
**Translations**: *Emily, la de Luna Nueva* (Spanish); *Emilie de la Nouvelle Lune* (French)
**Read-alikes**: Like Emily, Maia in Eva Ibbotson's *Journey to the River Sea* must adjust to life without parents, and Jean Webster's *Daddy-Long-Legs* also features an orphaned heroine and shares in this novel's epistolary style.

**Montgomery, L. M.** (1874–1942)
**Emily's Quest** (1927). Naperville, IL: Sourcebooks Fire, 2014. 241pp. 978-1402289187. PD.

Emily's decision to write *and* live at New Moon proves profitable—literally. Her poems and short stories are so frequently accepted for publication that she is able to make a small income and living of her own. But rather than content her, this success only fuels her ambition. Now she wants to write a novel.

But a series of events combine to hinder her progress. First, all of her childhood friends—Ilse, Perry, and Teddy—have, like her, grown up. They begin to depart, one-by-one, from Blair Water, leaving Emily feeling isolated and alone. Teddy's absence is particularly painful. She is in love with him, knows that he is her soul mate, and hopes that he will one day return to her after he has finished studies in Montreal to ask for her hand. But he becomes an almost instant success as an artist and his work keeps him away.

More disappointment: Publishers reject Emily's book. Then, misfortune: A freak accident leaves her bedridden for months and threatens her ability to ever walk again. Emily sinks into despair, and even as she recovers from her physical injuries, she cannot bring herself to write anymore. When Dean proposes marriage, she considers it, wondering if she ought to settle for this slice of contentment since Teddy, and bliss, seem impossible.

The third in the "Emily" series, the material in *Emily's Quest* is comparatively more mature than the first two books, but the novel's themes, especially surrounding alienation and loneliness, and the novel's accessible language make its appeal universal. (Note: Reading *Emily's Quest* before the second book, *Emily Climbs*, will spoil its ending.)

**For those also seeking**: reassurance/comfort/confirmation of self-worth/ strength
**For those drawn to**: story, character
**Themes/subjects**: adaptation/adjusting to change, courtship, depression, existentialism, feminism, friendship, heroines, marriage, romance, writing, quests
**Reading interest level**: grades 4–7
**Curricular tie-ins**: To teach students more about the publishing process, have students write, like Emily, poems or create other creative work and

self-publish them as a "zine." Use this activity to emphasize different aspects of information creation (e.g., copyright and intellectual property, the costs associated with publication, and the dissemination process and who gets information).
**Adaptations & alternative formats**: movie directed by Alfonso Cuarón (1995); audiobook read by Virginia Leishman (1999)
**Translations**: Spanish: *Emily, triunfa*; French: *Émilie De La Nouvelle Lune 3*
**Read-alikes**: Although Lyddie is in her mid-teens in Katherine Paterson's *Lyddie*, she too must learn how to support herself in nineteenth-century America.

**Smith, Dodie** (1896–1990)
**I Capture the Castle** (1948). New York: Saint Martin's Press, 2003. 343pp. 978-0312316167.

Seventeen-year-old Cassandra Mortmain lives in a beautiful, ancient castle outside of London with her gorgeous sister, Rose; her younger brother, Thomas; her eccentric but loving stepmother, Topaz; her father; and her former maid's son, Stephen. Stephen is also her age and also happens to be deeply in love with her. Although this setting sounds picturesque, Cassandra and her family have actually been penniless for years. Ever since her world-famous author father returned from prison and her mother died, her father has been unable to overcome his writer's block or work.

Then, two young Americans show up, brothers, Simon and Neil. Simon has inherited the castle from his father, who was an Englishman, and the brother comes to England to investigate it. When they are introduced, Rose is determined to win over Simon, whose wealth she knows can liberate her and her family from their impoverished surroundings. Cassandra, a penetrating observer with a great sense of humor, reflects on the saga with profound insight in her diary. Although, as she writes, she tries to curb her imagination (she harbors a slight superstition that if she imagines the things she wants, they won't come true), she can't help being a dreamer and a romantic. She thinks Rose ought to marry for love.

While the novel was not originally conceived as children's literature, audiences have received it as so due to its youthful narrator and its underlying coming-of-age themes. Children who are also trying to process the world around them, especially children who do not have adults in

*Realism/Everyday Life*

their lives who can help them with this process, will be able to connect to Cassandra who is trying, on her own, to make sense of adulthood and the adults around her. Beautifully written, this novel, once started, is truly hard to put down.

**For those also seeking**: acceptance
**For those drawn to**: character, language
**Themes/subjects**: castles, child neglect, class differences, coming of age, courage, crushes, dead or absent mother, dreams, faith, family, father-daughter relationships, gender roles, heroines, identity formation, imagination, inheritance and succession, jealousy, love, marriage, mental illness, memoirs/diaries, music, poverty, preoccupied parents, primogeniture, prison/incarceration, quarrels/fights, romance, secrets, sexual awakening, stepparents, sisters, wealth, writing, rejection
**Reading interest level**: grades 5–7
**Curricular tie-ins**: Because the plot of the story hinges so much on primogeniture and marriage, this novel offers an excellent way to introduce the implications of patriarchy and a point of comparison in terms of changing gender roles in the West.
**Adaptations & alternative formats**: audiobook read by Jenny Agutter (2006); BBC Radio dramatization staring Toby Jones and Holliday Grainger (2016); film directed by Tim Fywell (2003)
**Translations**: Spanish: *El Castillo Soñado*; French: *Le Château De Cassandra*
**Read-alikes**: Katherine Paterson's *Jacob Have I loved* also deals with jealousy between sisters.


**Paterson, Katherine** (1932–)
**Jacob Have I Loved** (1980). New York: HarperCollins, 2003. 263pp. 978-0064403689.

Louise Bradshaw returns to her home on Rass Island, a remote, isolated fishing village in the Chesapeake Bay, after many years of absence. As a grown woman now, she begins to recall her childhood days, during World War II, and the painful memories of living in the shadow of her more beautiful and musically gifted twin sister, Caroline.

Though she aches for the focused love and attention of just one person, *longs* for someone to look at her in the same way that her mother looked at Caroline, young Louise finds no relief. The entire town seems to fall under her sister's spell; no one can resist "light and gold" Caroline.

In gorgeous prose, Paterson explores this unfortunate but not uncommon reality of parental favoritism. Though Louise is not mistreated, she is often overlooked, and so forced to realize her own self-worth, without encouragement. The journey is long and difficult. Only after she stops comparing herself to Caroline and reflects inwardly on what *she* "really wants to do" does Louise begin to recognize her own gifts and grow into the self-possessed young woman she eventually becomes.

**For those also seeking**: reassurance/comfort/confirmation of self-worth/strength
**For those drawn to**: story, character
**Themes/subjects**: Christianity, coming of age, crushes, grandparents, heroines, dementia, favoritism, fishing, gender roles, jealousy, natural disasters, pain/suffering, projection (psychology), self-esteem, sisters, twins, hurricanes/cyclones, New England, sea and sea shore, fish and sea animals
**Reading interest level**: grades 5–8
**Curricular tie-ins**: Because the novel takes place in New England during World War II, reading it while studying the war's history would give insight into the everyday lives of ordinary Americans during the War. Create lessons that focus on differences in points of view. For instance, ask students to write a new scene or chapter from Caroline's point of view in order to stimulate thinking about how perspective affects perceptions and beliefs (sometimes leading to misunderstandings or even war).
**Adaptations & alternative formats**: abridged audiobook read by Moira Kelly (2009)
**Translations**: Spanish: *Amé a Jacob*
**Read-alikes**: Tenar in Ursula K. Le Guin's *The Tombs of Atuan* must also free herself from the grip of destructive emotions, and World War II is an important backdrop to the action in Lauren Wolk's *Wolf Hollow*.


**Spyri, Johanna** (1827–1901)
**Heidi** (1880–1881), translation. New York: Puffin Books, 2009. 294pp. 978-0141322568. PD.

Orphaned before she could even know her parents, Heidi is raised by her aunt Dete, her mother's sister, until she is five years old. But when Dete decides to take a job in Frankfurt, she leaves Heidi to live with Heidi's grandfather in his secluded mountaintop home in the Swiss Alps. Although Dete has heard rumors of the grandfather's questionable character, she does not want to be saddled with the responsibility for Heidi's care, and so she leaves Heidi with him anyway. Luckily, Heidi takes instantly to both her grandfather and her rustic surroundings. Cradled by steep, green slopes, Heidi loves to run alongside Peter, the 11-year-old goat herder, and pick wildflowers or sit and watch the sun sets the mountains "on fire" as it lowers in the sky.

Time passes easily until Dete returns several years later and insists on taking Heidi back with her to Frankfurt, where she has found her a "lucky" opportunity to serve as the companion of a young, wealthy invalid named Clara. Although Heidi befriends Clara and receives a free education as a result of her position, she remains profoundly homesick for her grandfather and her mountain home.

Traded off from home to home, Heidi's vulnerability is what makes her story so poignant and, at times, heartbreaking. As the narrative unfolds, Heidi's needs are often coopted by adult whims. Although they claim to act her best interests, they dismiss Heidi's feelings and the possibility that Heidi might know what is best for her. Children who can relate to her vulnerability will find a friend in Heidi.

**For those also seeking**: acceptance
**For those drawn to**: character, setting
**Themes/subjects**: art (as a coping mechanism), Christianity, civilization, community, country life, disability, dreams, grandparents, homesickness, mountain villages, nature, orphans, sleepwalking, only children, orphans, challenging authority figures, books, literacy/illiteracy, blindness, child neglect, moving houses (relocating), mountains
**Reading interest level**: grades 3–6
**Curricular tie-ins**: The transformative power of books and reading is a recurring theme in the novel. To help students appreciate the beauty of books and their power to build connections among people, create an assignment in which students interview a family member or relative about their favorite childhood book.
**Adaptations & alternative formats**: abridged edition part of Puffin in Bloom series, illustrated by Anna Bond (2014); audiobook read by Johanna Ward (2005) and abridged audiobook read by Sarah Greene (2009); movie directed by Allan Dwan, starring Shirley Temple (1937)
**Translations**: Spanish: *Heidi*; French: *Heidi*
**Read-alikes**: Although Miri in Shannon Hale's *Princess Academy* is older than Heidi, she too must leave her beloved mountain home, and Heidi's

orphan status, love of nature, and friendship with Clara have many parallels in Frances Hodgson Burnett's *The Secret Garden*.

**Webster, Jean** (1876–1916)
**Daddy-Long-Legs** (1912). London: Puffin, 2010. 181pp. 978-0141331119. PD.

Jerusha, "Judy," Abbott has lived all of her 17 years in the John Grier Home, a dreary children's orphanage, when she learns that a mysterious benefactor has decided to send her to college. The benefactor, a Grier Home trustee who wishes to remain anonymous, promises to pay for all of Judy's college expenses on one condition: she must write him a letter every month to keep him apprised of her academic progress. Because Judy does not know his name, but recalls having once caught a glimpse of his lanky backside as he was leaving the Grier Home, she decides to address him as "Daddy-Long-Legs." Judy's letters, which she often illustrates with charming, cartoonish doodles, comprise the rest of the novel.

While at first Judy struggles to relate to her wealthier, more entitled classmates, she delights in her studies and begins to cultivate her literary ambitions. As she succeeds, her confidence soars. She writes, "I am beginning . . . to feel at home in the world—as though I really belonged to it and had not just crept in on sufferance." She makes friends and takes risks, and in doing so her world expands. Thanks to Daddy-Long-Legs, she also finds the family and belongingness she has always longed for.

**For those also seeking**: reassurance/comfort/confirmation of self-worth/strength
**For those drawn to**: character
**Themes/subjects**: adaptation/adjusting to change, art (as coping mechanism), class differences, college/college life, coming of age, courtship, fashion/costume, heroines, letters, loneliness, missing persons, orphans, otherness, perseverance/determination, romance, school, socialism, writing
**Reading interest level**: grades 5–8
**Curricular tie-ins**: Jerusha's struggle to obtain an education and join the intellectual and political conversation captures the motivations behind the woman's suffrage movement and would bring to life a unit on this topic.
**Adaptations & alternative formats**: audiobook read by Julia Whelan (2011)

**Translations**: Spanish: *Papaito-Piernas-Largas*; French: *Papa Longues-Jambes*
**Read-alikes**: *Emily of New Moon* is about a younger orphan girl, also with literary aspirations, and shares *Long-Legs'* epistolary style as does Dodie Smith's *I Capture the Castle*. L. M. Montgomery's *Anne of the Island* is another story about a college girl at the turn of the twentieth century.

### Courage to Make a Change

**Dodge, Mary [Elizabeth] Mapes (1831–1905)**
**Hans Brinker, Or, the Silver Skates** (1865). New York: Aladdin Classics, 2002. 381pp. 978-0689849091. PD.

Set in Holland, where "ditches, canals, ponds, rivers, and lakes are everywhere to be seen," this Christmas story opens just as the holidays begin. And, because there are more waterways in Holland than there are roadways, the winter weather gives rise to a most unusual sight: men, women, and children travel to-and-fro on ice skates, using the frozen canals as if they were sidewalks. Fifteen-year-old Hans Brinker and his younger sister Gretl regret their wood rudders slow them down and squeak loudly on the ice, but they do not ask for better skates because they know their mother cannot afford them. Their father, who fell in a work-related accident 10 years earlier, has lost his senses and therefore cannot work.

Profoundly poor—schoolmates refer to them as the "ragpickers from the idiot's cottage"—Hans and Gretl take heart when they learn that there will be a skating competition, the prize of which is a new pair of silver skates. In pursuit of this chance, the Brinkers' luck begins to change.

Filled with gorgeous descriptions of the Netherlands, its landscape, history, and culture, this story is almost as much about the country as it is about Hans Brinker. Ultimately though, it is Hans who stands out. Modeling courage in the face of adversity, Hans shows readers that they, too, no matter who they are, or how old they are, can be brave and noble.

**For those also seeking**: disinterested understanding of the world
**For those drawn to**: character, setting
**Themes/subjects**: bullying, Christmas, competition, disability (of parent/guardian), Dutch people, family, ice-skating, Netherlands, poverty, responsibility, winter, museums

**Reading interest level**: grades 5–7
**Curricular tie-ins**: This novel complements units on transportation, world cultures, and/or the history/geography of the Netherlands. For example, ask students to pick out a detail mentioned in the story (e.g., a Dutch master painter mentioned in the chapter, "What the Boys Saw and Did in Amsterdamn," the legend of the boy and the dike) and do some basic, Internet background research about it. Ask them to explain how it illuminates the text and/or offers insight into other kinds of knowledge.
**Adaptations & alternative formats**: audiobook read by Christine Marshall (2006)
**Translations**: Spanish: *Los patines de plata* (abridged); French: *Les patins d'argent* (abridged)
**Read-alikes**: Minli also tries to help her poverty-stricken family in Grace Lin's *Where the Mountain Meets the Moon*. Mark Twain's *The Adventures of Huckleberry Finn* is another tale that unfolds along waterways but this time on the American Mississippi.


**Paterson, Katherine** (1932–)
**The Great Gilly Hopkins** (1978). New York: HarperCollins, 2004. 178pp. 978-0064402019.

In her 11 years, Gilly Hopkins has moved in-and-out of so many foster homes she has practically lost count. Longing for her real mother, who she has never met and who lives far away from Virginia, in California, Gilly purposefully and repeatedly sabotages her relationships with her foster parents. Although quick and savvy when it comes to reading both books and people, Gilly has become so focused on self-preservation, and so blinded by loyalty to her mother, that she struggles to form loving relationships with others. Rather, she thinks, "The trick was in knowing when to dispose of people when you were through with them . . ."

When she first meets her new foster mother, the aging Maime Trotter, Gilly disdains her soft, obese appearance and her sloppy, oversweet sentimentality. She is further disgusted by her younger foster brother, William Ernest, and disturbed by her African American neighbor, an elderly blind man with a penchant for poetry.

Set in the 1970s, this story represents the beginning of the breakdown of the traditional family. "God help the children of the flower children," Gilly's caseworker says. Yet, this story also advocates for alternative families by depicting their transformative power. Because of Trotter's demonstration of unconditional love, Gilly learns how to love others and also herself.

**For those also seeking**: connection with others/awareness of not being alone
**For those drawn to**: character, story
**Themes/subjects**: art (as coping mechanism), bullying, dead or absent father, dead or absent mother, foster care, heroines, illegitimate children, kindness, lies and lying, love, low self-esteem, missing persons, mother-daughter relationships, narcissistic parents, non-traditional families, nurturers, pain/suffering, poverty, racism, stealing, moving houses (relocating)
**Reading interest level**: grades 4–6
**Curricular tie-ins**: For a literature-based activity, read the William Wordsworth poem, "Ode: Intimations of Immortality from Recollections of Early Childhood" to which Paterson alludes. Discuss how reading the poem illuminates or changes their reading of the text.
**Adaptations & alternative formats**: audiobook read by Alyssa Bresnahan (2009); film directed by Stephen Herek (2016)
**Read-alikes**: Like Gilly Hopkins, Raymie Nightingale in Kate DiCamillo's novel of the same name hopes that a parent will return home to look after her, and Sharon Creech's *Ruby Holler* features protagonists, orphaned twins, who also learn how to trust adults despite terrible experiences in the foster care system.


**Paterson, Katherine** (1932–)
**Bridge to Terabithia** (1977). New York: HarperCollins, 2017. 176pp. 9780064401845.

Ten-year-old Jesse, "Jess," Aarons is the middle child in a brood of five all living in a farmhouse outside of Washington, DC. As the only boy, Jess handles the hard, manual chores, like milking the cow, while his dad is already at work. Though Jess would rather be upstairs in his room drawing or painting, he has learned, based on his parents' looks of disapproval, that he should keep this desire secret.

Then Jess meets Leslie, his new neighbor who has just moved with her parents from the city. Leslie's parents are artists and intellectuals, who actively encourage her curiosity. While initially repelled by her strange, outsider habits, Jess eventually discovers in her a kindred spirit, and they become friends. After school, they escape to Terabithia, an imaginary kingdom they have built between their houses, where they go to talk and draw—just be themselves. But when tragedy strikes, Jess must learn to preserve the magic of their imaginary sanctuary without her.

Character-driven, this novel will appeal to readers who have ever felt alone and alien in their own families, unaccepted, or creatively stifled. A black sheep, Jess models courage and tenacity, discovering and drawing on nurturing influences outside of his family in order to realize his best self.

**For those also seeking**: connection with others/awareness of not being alone
**For those drawn to**: character, language
**Themes/subjects**: abused children, art (as coping mechanism), being different, bullying, camping, class differences, crushes, death, friendship, gender roles, grief, imagination, otherness, pain/suffering, middle children
**Reading interest level**: grades 4–8
**Curricular tie-ins**: Part of the reason Jess and Leslie are drawn to each other is because they both defy gender expectations. Use this novel to introduce the concept of gender stereotypes and to challenge students' views of gender expectations.
**Adaptations & alternative formats**: audiobook read by Robert Sean Leonard (2009); film directed by Gabor Csupo (2007)
**Read-alikes**: Ten-year-old Katie must cope with the death of her 14-year-old sister in Cynthia Kadohata's *Kira-Kira*.

**Porter, Eleanor Hodgman (1868–1920)**
**Pollyanna** (1913). New York: Aladdin Classics, 2002. 287pp. 978-0689849107. PD.

First her mother and then her father dies, leaving 11-year-old Pollyanna orphaned but, fortunately, not alone. She travels from the West, where her father was serving as a minister, to stay with her Aunt Polly, her mother's sister, in New England. Although Aunt Polly lives alone in a lavish house on a hill, she does not receive Pollyanna out of generosity or love but merely "duty." Still embittered toward Pollyanna's father for taking her sister away, Aunt Polly refuses to allow Pollyanna to utter his name.

But ever-hopeful Pollyanna does not take notice of her aunt's severity but rather tries to find things to be "glad about." She shares the "glad game" with

*Realism/Everyday Life*

her neighbors and townspeople, many of whom do nothing but complain despite their affluent circumstances.

Although "Pollyanna," as a term, has come to describe a foolishly optimistic person, the actual Pollyanna faces real trials—the deaths of her parents, loneliness and isolation, a paralyzing accident—that test her confidence. In the end, even she realizes her naiveté, the fact that one cannot always be comforted by the "glad game." But, as the entire town is moved, and transformed, by Pollyanna's positive perspective, she also reveals the courage such an imagination requires.

**For those also seeking**: connection with others/awareness of not being alone
**For those drawn to**: character
**Themes/subjects**: accidents (major), adaptation/adjusting to change, Christianity, death, disability, displacement (psychology), duty, games, grief, heroines, imagination, optimism, pain/suffering
**Reading interest level**: grades 4–7
**Curricular tie-ins**: Watch the 1960s Disney film and ask students to compare and contrast the ways the film departs from the book (particularly with respect to depictions of Pollyanna's optimism) and what these choices may reveal about American culture during this time period.
**Adaptations & alternative formats**: audiobook read by Rebecca Burns (2005); film directed by David Swift (1960)
**Translations**: Spanish: *Pollyanna*; French: *Pollyanna*
**Read-alikes**: Readers interested in following Pollyanna's story will enjoy *Pollyanna Grows Up*. Julie in Irene Hunt's *Up a Road Slowly* is also raised by a strict aunt.

## Acceptance

**Creech, Sharon** (1949–)
**Walk Two Moons** (1994). New York: HarperCollins, 2012. 277pp. 978-0613002042.

Salamanca, "Sal," Hiddle is 12 years old when her mother suddenly deserts her and does not return. A year later, determined to start life anew, Sal's father relocates them from their farm home in Bybanks, Kentucky, to Euclid, Ohio. There, he starts up a relationship with a new woman named

Margaret Cadaver, who Sal can barely tolerate. She misses Bybanks, and her mother but she finds some consolation in her new friends, Phoebe, whose mother also abandons her and her family without explanation, and Ben, who lives with his extended relatives and does not seem to have a mother at all.

At the end of her first school year in Euclid, Sal's grandparents convince her to go on a road trip with them to Lewiston, Idaho, where Sal's mother was last heard from. As they travel across the country, Sal untangles the mystery of Phoebe's missing mother as well as her own. Heart wrenching and beautifully written, this coming-of-age story exemplifies empathetic growth and self-conviction as Sal imagines walking "two moons" in her mother's shoes and begins to accept her mother's disappearance and realize it's not her fault.

**For those also seeking**: reassurance/comfort/confirmation of self-worth/strength
**For those drawn to**: setting, story
**Themes/subjects**: abandoned children, death, dead or absent mother, empathy, friendship, grandparents, grief, miscarriage, missing persons, mother-daughter relationships, romance, school, single-parent dating, single-parent families
**Reading interest level**: grades 4–7
**Curricular tie-ins**: Since this story is structured around a road trip, ask students to map major plot points geographically and illustrate them with pictures or symbols in order to make connections between setting and story.
**Adaptations & alternative formats**: audiobook read by Hope Davis (2006)
**Translations**: Spanish: *Entre Dos Lunas*; French: *Le Voyage à Rebours*
**Read-alikes**: A grandparent also helps a grandchild cope with a tragedy in Sharon Creech's *The Wanderer*. The physical journey in both novels reflects psychological progression.


**Fitzhugh, Louise** (1928–1974)
**Harriet the Spy** (1964). Illustrated by the author. New York: Harper & Row, 1964. 298pp. 978-0440416791.

When 11-year-old Harriet M. Welsch goes to the movies with Ole Golly and the nanny's boyfriend, her parents arrive home early and find everyone gone. Mrs. Welsch is so upset at the unexplained disappearance of her daughter that she fires the nanny, a woman who has looked after Harriet since her birth. Harriet is devastated but carries on with her life, attending school and spying on her neighbors. Everywhere she goes, Harriet takes her writer's notebook with her, jotting down her thoughts and impressions. One day a couple of classmates find the book and start reading Harriet's private notes about everyone. All her classmates turn against her, including her best friends, Sport and Jamie.

Harriet is subsequently bullied, left out, and treated as an outcast. Trying to cope without her beloved Ole Golly to guide her is almost too much for Harriet to handle. She is a creature of habit, a girl who thrives on routine. She finds change difficult and must learn to deal with it on her own. Ultimately she must accept the loss of her nanny as part of the process of growing up and becoming more independent. Readers who have been bullied or left out by others will see themselves in Harriet. Those who are facing a major change in their lives or a significant loss will find guidance in Harriet's story.

*Harriet the Spy* is also the story of an aspiring writer, one who comes to realize how she processes her thoughts: "She found that when she didn't have a notebook, it was hard for her to think. The thoughts came slowly as though they had to squeeze through a tiny door to get to her, whereas when she wrote, they flowed out faster than she could put them down." Children with artistic and literary talents will identify with Harriet's story.

**For those also seeking**: connection with others/awareness of not being alone
**For those drawn to**: character
**Themes/subjects**: adaptation/adjusting to change, bullying, cliques (in school), art (as coping mechanism), identity formation, writing, nannies and caregivers, regression (psychology), self-reliance, spies and spying, outcasts/misfits, revenge, nurturers, school, city life, New York City
**Reading interest level**: grades 4–6
**Curricular tie-ins**: Harriet wants to be a writer when she grows up, and Sport, a professional baseball player. Knowing what they want to do motivates these characters to prepare for a future career. In their reading response journals, students could write about what they want to do when they grow up and what they could do now to prepare for it. Teachers might also want to suggest that creating a personal journal may help some students clarify their ideas and understand their emotions.
**Adaptations & alternative formats**: film directed by Bronwen Hughes (1996); audiobook read by Anne Bobby (1999)

**Translations**: French: *Harriet l'Espionne*
**Read-alikes**: Harriet's story is continued in *The Long Street*. Readers interested in aspiring writers will also enjoy L. M. Montgomery's *Emily of New Moon*, Irene Hunt's *Up a Road Slowly*, Sharon M. Draper's *Stella by Starlight*, and Jean Webster's *Daddy-Long-Legs*. Those interested in spies and spying should read Rebecca Stead's *Liar & Spy*. Like Harriet, Joan in Laura Amy Schlitz's *The Hired Girl* must deal with the consequences when someone reads her private diary.

**Montgomery, L. M.** (1874–1942)
**Anne of Avonlea** (1909). New York: Aladdin Paperbacks, 2014. 384pp. 978-1442490024. PD.

In the sequel to *Anne of Green Gables*, Anne is now "half-past sixteen" and about to begin teaching at the Avonlea schoolhouse that she attended herself not so very long ago. Although she received a scholarship to attend college, she delays her studies so that she can tend to Marilla, her adopted guardian, who is aging and cannot handle the household chores on her own. Undaunted, Anne finds other ways to learn and grow by investing in her community.

Along with friends Diana Barry and Gilbert Blythe, she initiates the Avonlea Village Improvement Society. She also embraces her role as schoolteacher with excited pleasure although, self-conscious of her inexperience, with trepidation as well. Meanwhile, Avonlea is abuzz with the sudden arrival of orphaned twins Davy and Dora. Although they are only her distant relatives, Marilla agrees to take them under her wing until they can be united with their uncle. Anne, ever empathetic to their plight as orphans, warms to them instantly and devotes herself to their care.

Aptly titled, the setting in this novel expands from the cozy interior world of Green Gables to the larger, but still small, world of Avonlea. A series of episodes and character sketches builds upon each other to reveal a larger narrative about the importance of friendship and community. While portraying the beauty of close, provincial society, this novel depicts its limitations as well: small-mindedness, conservatism, and impassivity. Though acknowledging the inevitability of (and need to accept) town gossips, curmudgeons, and eccentrics, this story also depicts provincialism as a choice, a state of mind that can be overcome, as Anne proves, with a little effort and imagination.

Realism/Everyday Life

**For those also seeking**: disinterested understanding of the world
**For those drawn to**: setting, character
**Themes/subjects**: citizenship, community, corporeal punishment, ethnocentrism, friendship, grief, school, teachers
**Reading interest level**: grades 4-7
**Curricular tie-ins**: Use the beginning chapters, in which Anne and her friends raise money for various town improvement projects, to introduce ideas of citizenship and the individual's ability to create change at local levels. Build into a civic learning project (in which the class identifies an improvement project of their own and chooses how to address it).
**Adaptations & alternative formats**: audiobook read by Shelly Frasier (2005); *Anne of Green Gables: The Sequel*, a Canadian made-for-TV series (1987) was released by Sullivan Entertainment as a DVD (2004) and as part of a trilogy box set (2005).
**Translations**: Spanish: *Anne, La De Avonlea*; French: *Anne D'avonlea*
**Read-alikes**: In addition to the sequel, *Anne of the Island*, a similar read is Laura Ingalls Wilder's *These Happy Golden Years* in which Laura, like Anne, begins her career as a teacher in a one-room schoolhouse.

### Disinterested Understanding of the World

**Alcott, Louisa May** (1832–1888)
**Little Women** (1868). New York: Penguin Books, 2014. 504pp. 978-0143106654. PD.

Set in a New England town during the American Civil War (1861–1865), *Little Women* is an intimate portrayal of the four March sisters and their "Marmee," as they wait for their father, a chaplain, to return from the front. Indeed, one of the reasons this novel enjoyed such popular reception—not only by women and girls but also by men and boys—was its domestic focus and female perspective, the way it provided a window into a picturesque, nineteenth-century middle-class American household.

Written in two parts, each chapter is its own self-contained episode, centering on one or more of the March sisters: Meg, the romantic; Jo, the individualist; Beth, the nurturer; and Amy, the aesthete. Although Alcott portrays four distinct, and also very *real*, personalities, Jo, short for Josephine, is the most rounded, complex, and memorable of them. An unapologetic tomboy—her best friend is the "Laurence boy" next door—Jo resists many of the gendered roles her sisters seem to more willingly accept.

She is awkward and clumsy, "a colt in a flower garden," who is more interested in reading, writing, and adventure than keeping her gloves clean. As she grows into a young woman, she also rejects a path of marriage and easy wealth—choosing instead to make her own living, to pursue her literary ambitions, and to hold out for true love.

In this way, Jo becomes not only a model of female independence—French feminist philosopher Simone de Beauvoir wrote that in Jo she found her "future self"—but also of American individualism. Certainly, *Little Women* is a very *American* book—some immigrant writers have even said that reading it taught them how to become more American, that is, how to become more a part of the American, white middle class. Although today's reader may at times find it excessively moralizing, its themes about family responsibility, about community, remain as relevant today as then, perhaps more so.

**For those also seeking**: models for identity
**For those drawn to**: story, character
**Themes/subjects**: American Civil War, art (as a coping mechanism), New England, community, courtship, death, disability, family, family conflict, fashion/costume, feminism, games, grief, heroines, illness, marriage, mistakes, money/debt, mother-daughter relationships, music, quarrels/fights, resourcefulness, romance, school, scholars/professors, seasons, siblings and sibling issues, sisters, teachers, transcendentalism, vanity and pompousness, women studies, work (labor), writing
**Reading interest level**: grades 5–8
**Curricular tie-ins**: Complement a unit on the American Civil War by asking students to compare and contrast gender role expectations between men and women during the mid-nineteenth century and today.
**Adaptations & alternative formats**: movie directed by George Cukor (1933); abridged edition part of Puffin in Bloom series, illustrated by Anna Bond (2014)
**Translations**: Spanish: *Mujercitas*; French: *Les Quatre Filles du docteur March*
**Read-alikes**: Readers who enjoyed this story will also like the sequels, *Little Men* and *Jo's Boys*. Although the girls are slightly younger in Jeannie Birdsall's *The Penderwicks*, the novel is also about four sisters.

CHAPTER ELEVEN

# Science Fiction

Science fiction and fantasy are commonly confused and understandably so, since there is a lot of crossover. In fact, science fiction fans have defined science fiction and fantasy in terms of each other, describing science fiction as "the left brain reaching out to the right brain (logic reaching towards the artistic) while Fantasy is the opposite."[1] Although these definitions help explain why science fiction and fantasy are so often used interchangeably, they are not particularly helpful for librarians, teachers, or parents who are trying to figure out which of these genres would appeal most to their children. For this reason, we defer to readers' advisory expert Joyce Saricks who says, "Science Fiction posits worlds and technologies which *could* exist. Science, rather than magic, drives these speculative tales, and the science must be accurate and true to key axioms of Newtonian (classical) and relative physics."[2] Put simply, for a book to earn the genre designation "science fiction," it must conform to physical laws, even if those laws are made up. While alternate worlds or realities in science fiction may seem magical or supernatural from our point of view, they nonetheless conform to a consistent order from the characters' point of view. Their reality cannot be explained through magic. If magic is used as a plot device, then it is no longer science fiction. It's fantasy.

As speculative fiction, stories in this genre generally pose moral, social, or ethical questions with regard to science and technology's ambiguous role in promoting human progress. For example, in *20,000 Leagues under the Sea*, Jules Verne seems prescient in his critique of scientific faith.

While conceding the wonders of scientific discovery and technology (it is, after all, a state-of-the-art submarine that allows the main characters to explore, discover, and learn about life never seen before), he also points out how the human drive for knowledge, exploration, and expansionism has also brought both human and environmental ruin. The hopeful intellectual curiosity of marine scholar Professor Aronnax is sharply contrasted with the skepticism of Captain Nemo, who is so traumatized and personally destroyed by humanity's destructive use of technology (his wife and child are casualties of modern warfare) that he is driven to underwater seclusion. In representing these two extremes, Professor Aronnax and Captain Nemo bring to light the tension and inherent paradox of scientific knowledge discovery—how, in the right hands, it can improve human lives and how, in the wrong ones, annihilate them.

Ideas, more than characters, drive these stories. The scenarios that play out inevitably raise more abstract, philosophical questions about what it means to be human. Questions about perception, what we can and cannot know, time and space, identity, freedom, free will, and faith frequently emerge in these stories. For example, in Peter Dickinson's *Eva*, the protagonist is spared death after a major car accident thanks to advanced medical procedures: her mind is transplanted into a chimpanzee's body. As Dickinson explores this possibility, and presses on its implications, he prompts questions about identity and how it is shaped by the relationship between the mind and body. This question draws out further ones about medical ethics, environmental ethics, and the effects of capitalism on society. In this way, this story is just as much an intellectual adventure as action adventure.

In order to explore these philosophical possibilities, science fiction also necessarily features alternate realities. Sometimes stories are set in some far-off, distant future, as is the case in Peter Dickinson's *Eva* and Jane Yolen's *Dragon Pit* series, but not always. Madeline L'Engle's *Wrinkle in Time* quintet is roughly set during the time in which each novel was published, a period that spans from the early 1960s to the late 1980s. Jules Verne's *20,000 Leagues under the Sea* also takes place at the same time of its publication during the late nineteenth century. And Rebecca Stead's *When You Reach Me* actually takes place in the past, during the 1970s. The reality, too, may be very close to our own, as in Stead's novel, or radically different, as in Jane Yolen's series. However, in science fiction, reality is always tweaked a little bit so as to produce this contrast and thus to challenge us to question our own conceptions of reality.

In presenting such complex worlds and ideas, science fiction demands an engaged intellect, a reader who wants to be challenged and is not only

Science Fiction

capable of but also enjoys abstract thinking and philosophical inquiry. So, given the genre's more mature themes and content, it is most likely to appeal to older children. With a couple of exceptions (Antoine de Saint-Exupéry's *The Little Prince* and Ted Hughes's *The Iron Giant*), all of the novels included in this chapter are written primarily for middle-grade readers.

A couple notes on the series listed in this section: all of the novels in Madeline L'Engle's *Wrinkle in Time Quintet*, which include, in chronological order, *A Wrinkle in Time*, *A Wind in the Door*, *A Swiftly Tilting Planet*, *Many Waters*, and *An Acceptable Time*, and Jane Yolen's original *Dragon Pit* trilogy, *Dragon's Blood*, *Heart's Blood*, and *A Sending of Dragons* can easily be read and enjoyed as standalone books. Though these novels definitely do build upon each other, and reading them in order can add nuance and depth, they do not need to be.

## Awakening/New Perspectives/Enlargement of Possibilities

**Pratchett, Terry** (1948–2015)
**Truckers**. (1989). In *The Bromeliad Trilogy: Truckers, Diggers, Wings*. New York: HarperCollins, 2003. 502pp. 978-006009493.

Masklin, who is only four inches tall, realizes that he and his fellow nomes can no longer live in their dangerous environment. Originally from another plane, these creatures have not adapted well to earth and have gradually died off. With only ten nomes left—and eight of them elderly—Masklin is forced to do all the hunting himself. Believing that they will not survive another winter, he persuades the nomes to climb aboard a transport truck, and trust that it will take them to a more suitable place to live. When the truck arrives at a mall, the nomes meet fellow creatures who are shocked to discover that anyone actually lives outside their mall. When calamity hits the stores, Masklin faces the impossible task of saving everyone from destruction.

The first novel in the Bromeliad trilogy (also known as the Nome trilogy), *Truckers* is a clever, witty story of a miniature race of creatures whose way of life is threatened. When a store nome first meets Masklin, he asks, "Are you trying to tell me you came from *Outside*? . . . There's nothing Outside!" The store nomes' night and day are Closing Time and Opening Time; their earth and sky are floor and ceiling. Arnold Bros (est. 1905) is their creator, a deity that the nomes believe will guide and protect them.

A very entertaining and thought-provoking novel, *Truckers* makes readers look at their consumer society with fresh eyes. Using biblically styled epigraphs such as "And the nomes grew fat and multiplied as the years passed, and spent their time in Rivalry and Small War, Department unto Department, and forgot all they knew of the Outside," Pratchett satirizes the pettiness and insular thinking of the status quo. The novel will appeal to readers who envision a better world. Masklin's role as reluctant leader will inspire readers with big dreams and ambitions.

**For those also seeking**: reassurance/comfort/confirmation of self-worth/strength
**For those drawn to**: setting, language
**Themes/subjects**: survival, miniature beings, consumerism, commercialism, leadership, cooperation and teamwork, faith and skepticism, moving houses (relocating), planetary travel, conformity and nonconformity, humor, aging elders, gnomes, stores
**Reading interest level**: grade 7 and up
**Curricular tie-ins**: In a think-pair-share activity, students can discuss what Pratchett is satirizing about modern society.
**Adaptations & alternative formats**: audiobook read by Stephen Briggs (2009)
**Translations**: Spanish: *Camioneros*
**Read-alikes**: Exodus and the search for a home are also key concerns in Richard Adams's *Watership Down*, Terry Pratchett's *The Carpet People*, and Mary Norton's *The Borrowers* series (*The Borrowers*, *The Borrowers Afield*, *The Borrowers Afloat*, *The Borrowers Aloft*, and *The Borrowers Avenged*). Pratchett's novel and Norton's series are also about a miniature race of people. Meg McKinlay's *A Single Stone* is a science fiction novel about people who stop believing in the existence of a world outside their own.

**Saint-Exupéry, Antoine de** (1900–1944)
**The Little Prince** (1943). Translated from the French by Richard Howard. San Diego: Harcourt, 2000. 83pp. 978-0156012195.

When a pilot crashes his plane, landing in the middle of the Sahara Desert, he realizes that he has enough drinking water to last eight days. Setting about the difficult task of fixing the engine of the plane, he does not expect to meet anyone. However, the next morning he is awoken by the Little Prince, a boy who has traveled to Earth from another planet. The Little Prince, who seems oblivious of the fact that they are a thousand miles from the nearest person and in danger of dying from thirst, asks the pilot to draw him a picture of a sheep. Although the pilot thinks the situation is absurd, he does so and then listens to the story of this strange character. The Little Prince tells the pilot that he left Asteroid B-612 and visited six small planets before coming to Earth.

According to bestseller lists, *The Little Prince* is one of the most popular stories of all time. Although an engaging story about both interplanetary travel and survival in an inhospitable environment, the novel is particularly notable for its arresting ideas about life. A philosophic book about life's big questions, the novel manages to appeal to readers of all ages. The Little Prince's ideas are simple, unconventional, and, at the same time, profound. Although the grown-ups in the novel have forgotten the wonders of living and the essential values of life, children such as the Little Prince have not. An outsider to our planet, he makes readers look anew at what they have taken for granted. Uninterested in money, power, prestige, and material goods, the Little Prince insists that "anything essential is invisible to the eye." Those who are struggling to find meaning in life will find much to ponder in their reading of *The Little Prince*.

**For those also seeking**: reassurance/comfort/confirmation of self-worth/strength
**For those drawn to**: character
**Themes/subjects**: princes, friendship, deserts, plane crashes, planetary travel, planets, survival, purpose in life, conformity and nonconformity, reptiles
**Reading interest level**: grade 4 and up
**Curricular tie-ins**: Ask students to create an infographic about asteroids.
**Adaptations & alternative formats**: movie directed by Mark Osborne (2015); audiobook read by Bower, Humphrey (2008); graphic novel by Joann Sfar (2010)
**Translations**: Spanish: *El Principito*; French: *Le Petit Prince*
**Read-alikes**: The characters in Terry Pratchett's *Wings* also return to their own planet. Pratchett's *Truckers* also questions the conventional assumptions of modern society.

**Yolen, Jane** (1939–)
**A Sending of Dragons** (1987). Orlando, FL: Harcourt, 2004. 296pp. 978-0152051280.

After Jakkin and his beloved Akki are accused of bombing their capital, Rokk, on the planet Austar IV, they are forced into hiding. They flee to wilderness, hiding in the Austarian mountainside. They would never have survived had it not been for Heart's Blood, Jakkin's loyal dragon. In fact, she saved them twice—first by taking a pursuer's bullet and then again when they used her body to shelter them from "Dark After," a period of time just before dawn when it is too cold for a human to stay outside on Austar IV. Fearing exposure, Jakkin and Akki were forced to cut open Heart's Blood's still-warm body and crawl inside her birth sac for safety. But this contact leads to a strange transformation. Now, both Jakkin and Akki can hear and send messages with their minds not only to dragons but also to each other. They also now have the power to withstand Dark After without shelter. They have, in other words, become part-human, part-Dragon.

This power, however, becomes a liability when they are captured by a cave society that does not permit the use of vocal language. Everyone in this dark city communicates only through their minds, and for this reason Jakkin and Akki have to be careful what they think, for deception is difficult without speech. Once Jakkin and Akki realize the cave people's brutal ritual of dragon sacrifice, they are determined to not only escape but also free their dragons. But the cave is an intricate labyrinth of pitch-black tunnels. Jakkin and Akki struggle not only to communicate, but also to figure out where to exit the cave in the first place.

The third book in the *Dragon Pit* saga raises questions about cultural traditions, tolerance, and ethnocentrism. Jakkin is at first disgusted by the ritualistic brutality of the cave people, but at the same time the experience forces him to recognize the monstrous ways in which his own society behaves. With this realization, he is motivated to return to his village and try to do the difficult work of changing cultural attitudes. In the same way, this novel can prompt an introspective look at oneself and one's culture and awaken self-awareness.

**For those also seeking**: disinterested understanding of the world
**For those drawn to**: story
**Themes/subjects**: adventure, animal sacrifice, birth, critical thinking/strategy, cultural differences, death, dragons, extrasensory perception, food, language/communication, telepathy, magical transformations, medicine, mountains, rituals and traditions, super powers (magical), survival, wrongfully accused, ethnocentrism
**Reading interest level**: grades 6–8

Science Fiction

**Curricular tie-ins**: Ask students to identify the different ways in which Austarian cultures treat the dragons and to compare and contrast this treatment to the way human beings treat animals on Earth.
**Adaptations & alternative formats**: audiobook read by Marc Thompson (2009)
**Read-alikes**: A fourth book, *Dragon's Heart*, was published much later, in 2009, and continues the series.

**Verne, Jules** (1828–1905)
**Journey to the Centre of the Earth** (1864). Translated from the French by Frank Wynne. London: Penguin Books, 2009. 252pp. 9780141441979. PD.

When Professor Lidenbrock discovers an old parchment that contains runic letters, he realizes it is a cryptogram. His 16-year-old nephew Axel cracks the code, uncovering a hidden message written by a sixteenth-century alchemist. The message provides clues to the location of the center of the earth, a place that can be reached by way of an Icelandic volcano. A wildly enthusiastic geologist, Professor Lidenbrock expects his nephew to accompany him on his scientific expedition to the earth's center. Although Axel is deeply fearful of the mission, he does not want to disappoint his uncle by refusing him. Traveling to Iceland, they hire a guide, and proceed to the volcano.

Never completely certain whether the volcano is extinct, and unsure how they will return to the surface, Axel, his uncle, and their guide proceed anyway. Their expedition involves the difficult climb up Mount Sneffels, and perilous descent into the crater. Axel becomes separated from the others and gets lost inside the maze-like tunnels. This plot-driven novel is also noteworthy for its remarkable subterranean setting.

Fearful every step of the way, Axel overcomes his panic, emerging stronger and more resilient in the process. Readers who are anxious about difficult challenges will find strength and inspiration in Axel's story.

The joy of scientific discovery is infectious in this novel, opening readers' eyes to the thrills and wonders of exploration. The novel also provides readers with an in-depth understanding of Icelandic peoples and their customs.

**For those also seeking**: disinterested understanding of the world
**For those drawn to**: story, setting
**Themes/subjects**: explorers, journeys, underground, clues/riddles, secrets, anxiety/fears, earthquakes/volcanoes, courage, Iceland, scholars/professors
**Reading interest level**: grade 6 and up
**Curricular tie-ins**: This novel could be used as a companion resource for lessons on either volcanoes or Iceland. In small groups, students could create a questions-and-answers form for a game about one of these topics.
**Adaptations & alternative formats**: movie directed by Eric Brevig and T. J. Scott (2008); audiobook read by Noel Gibilaro (2010); graphic novel by Fiona Macdonald (2007).
**Translations**: Spanish: *Viaje al Centro de la Tierra*; French: *Voyage au Centre de la Terre*
**Read-alikes**: Jules Verne's *20,000 Leagues under the Sea* and Edgar Rice Burrough's *At the Earth's Core* also depict underwater or subterranean explorations. Peter Dickinson's *The Tears of the Salamander* is another story about a volcanic mountain.

## Models for Identity

**Yolen, Jane** (1939–)
**Dragon's Blood** (1982). Orlando, FL: Harcourt, 2004. 303pp. 978-0152051266.

Jakkin is 15 years old, an orphan and "a bonder," or indentured servant, who lives and labors on a dragon nursery on Austar IV, a planet in another galaxy. Jakkin's master, Sarkkhan, breeds and trains the dragons for fighting in the dragon pits, which earns him his gold. While Jakkin does not mind his work, and loves the dragons, he hates his bondage. He longs instead to be a master and train his own dragon fighters.

When he happens upon an unaccounted for dragon hatchling, he seizes his opportunity. If he can secretly raise and train the dragon into a champion dragon fighter, then he can enter it into the pits and perhaps earn the money he needs to free himself from his bondage. With the help of Akki, a nurse who is also his age, he is able to rear his dragon and, after he has grown enough, register him for his first fight. However, Likkarn, another bonder, much older, has it out for him and poses a constant threat to his plans. When Jakkin reaches the pits, Likkarn is there, too, and ready to expose him as a dragon thief.

*Science Fiction* 409

In the first book in *The Pit Dragon Chronicles* series, Yolen creates a vivid imaginary world in which to pose universal questions about freedom and bondage: How easy is it to mistake captivity for powerlessness, to perceive lack of choice as *no* choice? As Jakkin steals the dragon hatchling, he dares to take a risk and demonstrates how barriers to one's freedom, though sometimes real, more often are perceived. As his boldness is rewarded, he serves as a model of courage, agency, and self-determination.

**For those also seeking**: courage to make a change
**For those drawn to**: story, character
**Themes/subjects**: adventure, animal sacrifice, breeding/genetics, bullying, caste systems, caves, coming of age, competition, courage, death, deception, dragons, freedom, hunting, indentured servitude, orphans, prostitution/human trafficking, romance, secrets, self-reliance
**Reading interest level**: grades 6–8
**Curricular tie-ins**: This novel would complement lessons on indentured servitude in the world today and in the past.
**Adaptations & alternative formats**: audiobook read by Marc Thompson (2009)
**Read-alikes**: In *The Hunger Games*, the protagonist also enters a competition that is far more than a game.

## Reassurance/Comfort/Confirmation of Self-Worth/Strength

**L'Engle, Madeleine** (1918–2007)
**A Swiftly Tilting Planet** (1978). New York: Square Fish/Farrar Straus Giroux, 2007. 309pp. 978-0312368562.

The Murray family has just sat down to a beautiful Thanksgiving spread when the President of the United States phones with a devastating announcement: The nation is on the brink of a nuclear war. Realizing that a nuclear attack would spell the complete and total destruction of the planet, Charles Wallace, now 15, slips outside to his favorite star-watching rock to be alone and think about what he can do to stop it from happening. While there, he repeats a cryptic message to himself, a "rune," that he was recently learned. When he completes the chant, he suddenly finds himself face-to-face with a winged unicorn who calls himself Gaudior. Together, they soar in and out of time, to different Whens and different Wheres, in the hope of decoding the message, which somehow connects to the impending war, and is the only way to put a stop to it.

The third novel in the *Time Quintet* contemplates the individual's interconnectedness with the world not only in the present but also throughout time. In depicting how the past is still felt in the present, L'Engle emphasizes how every individual's actions (or failures to act) impact our history and each other. As one character explains, "Nothing, no one is too small to matter. What *you* do is going to make a difference." Thus, in stressing the importance of taking responsibility for one's actions, she also stresses and confirms the importance of every individual life.

**For those also seeking**: awakening new perspectives/enlargement of possibilities
**For those drawn to**: story, language
**Themes/subjects**: anxiety/fears, battles/wars, clues/riddles, colonialism, cycles of abuse, disability, extrasensory perception, faith and skepticism, good and evil, free will, greed, indigenous peoples, journeys, love, paradox, portals/thresholds, technology and civilization, tests, time travel, magical transformations, unicorns, witch hunting, omens/prophecies
**Reading interest level**: grades 6–8
**Curricular tie-ins**: This novel intertwines several events from American History: the discovery of the New World, colonialism, the Salem Witch Trials, and the proliferation of nuclear weapons. To further underscore this theme of interconnectedness, ask students to do some background research on one of these events and to identify a current event in which this history makes itself present (e.g., the Native American protests at Standing Rock demonstrate the continuing effects of European expansionism).
**Adaptations & alternative formats**: audiobook read by Jennifer Ehle (2012)
**Read-alikes**: *Many Waters* is the next novel in the series. Readers drawn to the historical events alluded to in this novel may also enjoy Elizabeth George Speare's *The Witch of Blackbird Pond*.


**Pratchett, Terry** (1948–2015)
**Diggers** (1990). In *The Bromeliad Trilogy: Truckers, Diggers, Wings*. New York: HarperCollins, 2003. 502pp. 978-006009493.

*Diggers* begins where Terry Pratchett's *Truckers* left off—in the nomes' new home, an abandoned quarry. The leaders of the colony leave to explore a nearby airport, leaving the nome, Nisodemus, in charge. Apprehensive about the arrival of winter, the nomes face another challenge when they discover a sign announcing the reopening of the quarry. Nisodemus wants to return to their earlier life in the store but Grimma believes they should stay where they are and create a plan to outwit the humans.

Another very humorous book, *Diggers* will appeal to readers who enjoy stories presented from an unusual perspective. *Diggers* is filled with witty observations such as a store nome saying that nature "isn't natural. And there's a sight too much of it. 'S not like a proper world at all. You've only got to look at it. The floor's all rough, 'n' it should be flat. There's hardly any walls."

A story of underdogs fighting for their lives in an inhospitable environment, the novel will appeal to readers who face overwhelming challenges or difficult choices. Children who are fearful of change or are afraid they might fail will find reassurance and hope in *Diggers*.

**For those also seeking**: courage to make a change
**For those drawn to**: setting, language
**Themes/subjects**: survival, miniature beings, gnomes, feminism, leadership, adaptation/adjusting to change, faith and skepticism, winter, consumerism, romance, humor
**Reading interest level**: grade 7 and up
**Curricular tie-ins**: This novel would work well as a resource for a geology lesson. Ask students to create a slide presentation about quarries and how they tie in with the lithosphere.
**Adaptations & alternative formats**: audiobook read by Stephen Briggs (2007)
**Translations**: Spanish: *La Nave*
**Read-alikes**: Laura Ingalls Wilder's *The Long Winter* is another story about surviving in winter with limited supplies. Mary Norton's *The Borrowers* series (*The Borrowers*, *The Borrowers Afield*, *The Borrowers Afloat*, *The Borrowers Aloft*, and *The Borrowers Avenged*) is about a miniature race of beings who must survive in a world of human beings.

## Connection with Others/Awareness of Not Being Alone

**Dickinson, Peter** (1927–2015)
Eva (1988). New York: Random House Young Readers, 1990. 219pp. 978-0440207665.

Barely surviving a car accident, 13-year-old Eva lies in a hospital bed for months in a deep coma. When she finally wakes up, she can't feel her body. But even as physical sensation slowly begins to return, she realizes something is off, doesn't feel right. She reaches for a mirror and is horrified to discover her suspicions confirmed. In her reflection, she does not see her dark-haired, blue-eyed self but the face of a chimpanzee. Her dad, a primatologist, explains that because Eva's body was completely destroyed by the accident, this experimental surgery was their only hope. By transplanting her mind into the body of a chimpanzee they were able to keep her alive.

But even once Eva adapts to her body and accepts it, she finds that she is no longer herself, that is, the Eva before the accident. Although she still possesses Eva's memories and her consciousness, without her body, she is literally no longer herself. Her new body gives way to new thoughts, new desires. She longs to groom her loved ones' hair and sit in a high tree, and rather than spend time with her old friends she would rather go to her father's lab, where she can be with other chimpanzees. But, most of all, she longs for the freedom of the wild. With the help of a friend, an animal rights' advocate, she tries to make her escape.

While primarily a philosophical inquiry into the relationship between mind, body, and identity, this novel also, in imagining a future Capitalist society at its worse, offers a critique of it. Eva lives in a world that has been totally exploited by corporate greed. Haunting and thought provoking, this novel is sure to transport readers and stimulate the imagination.

**For those also seeking**: acceptance
**For those drawn to**: story, language
**Themes/subjects**: accidents (major), adaptation/adjusting to change, aiding/helping, anger/hostility, animal behavior, animals in captivity, animal ethics, animal testing/experiments, appearance (physical), beauty/ugliness, being different, bioethics, challenging authority figures, child labor exploitation, commercialism, consciousness, consumerism, courage, death, dreams, dystopia, environmentalism, father-daughter relationships, food, forests, freedom, human body, identity theory, intellectual property, language/communication, moral dilemmas, nature, overpopulation, purpose in life, quarrels/fights, self-acceptance, self-knowledge, survival, technology and civilization, monkeys/apes
**Reading interest level**: grades 6–8
**Curricular tie-ins**: Environmental destruction and corporate responsibility are major themes in this work. Provide a basic introduction of the

*Science Fiction*

relationship between capitalism and environment, such as *The Story of Stuff Project's* online video "Story of Stuff" and ask students to find and examine examples of how corporate interests have hurt and/or benefited the environment.

**Read-alikes**: Mila in Karen Hesse's *The Music of Dolphins* is also a character caught between two worlds, human and animal, and fitting into neither.

**L'Engle, Madeleine** (1918–2007)
**A Wind in the Door** (1973). New York: Square Fish/Farrar Straus Giroux, 2007. 245pp. 978-0312368548.

Meg Murry is worried about her little brother Charles Wallace. Intelligent and advanced for his age, Charles talks like their scientist parents—a quality, needless, to say that does not make him very popular. He hasn't made many friends since he started the first grade, rather he often comes home with bruises. However, the bullying isn't the only thing that has Meg concerned. Charles is also sick. It has something to do with his mitochondria and a dragon-like creature that keeps appearing in the Murry's garden.

As it turns out, the entire planet, not just Charles Wallace's life, is in peril. The enemies are Echthroi, who are the complete opposite of being. They are nothingness, despair, and they have ripped through the galaxy, bringing evil upon everyone. Meg, along with her close friend Calvin must travel with their new dragon-like companion, Proginoskes, to save Charles and to save the world.

The second novel in *The Wrinkle in Time* quintet stands out in the way that it offers as solid of an explanation of human suffering as is possible to put into words. L'Engle describes interdependence on the microcosmic (mitochondrial) and macrocosmic (universal) levels to reveal our interconnectedness with our planet and each other and to emphasize how protecting this interconnectedness ensures everyone's and everything's survival. Readers who have ever felt rejected or unwanted will take comfort in this reminder that every life matters and all lives are connected.

**For those also seeking**: reassurance/comfort/confirmation of self-worth/strength
**For those drawn to**: character, language
**Themes/subjects**: adaptation/adjusting to change, aliens (from space), angels/cherubs, anxiety/fears, being different, bullying, cell biology,

crushes, ecosystems, family, gifted children, good and evil, imagination, intelligence, interconnectedness, journeys, love, magical transformations, multiple worlds/universes, names and naming, nihilism, paradox, portals/thresholds, relativity, reptiles, school, scholars/professors, self-confidence, sensory perception, siblings and sibling issues, teachers, tests
**Reading interest level**: grades 6–8
**Curricular tie-ins**: This novel would easily enhance studies in cellular biology and/or ecosystems.
**Adaptations & alternative formats**: audiobook read by Jennifer Ehle (2012)
**Translations**: French: *Le Vent Dans La Porte*
**Read-alikes**: *A Swiftly Tilting Planet* is the next novel in the series.


**L'Engle, Madeleine** (1918–2007)
**Many Waters** (1986). New York: Square Fish/Farrar Straus Giroux, 2007. 357pp. 978-0312368579.

Twin teenagers Sandy and Dennys Murray aren't like the rest of the family. Their parents and their siblings Meg and Charles Wallace, all are exceptionally gifted scientific thinkers—extraordinary. Sandy and Dennys are smart enough, and capable, but they are ordinary. They much prefer *doing*, planting vegetables in their garden or playing ice hockey, than sitting around and theorizing. They are actually skeptical of theory (what does it matter in the *real* world?) and skeptical in general. They have to *see* things to believe them.

But snowed-in one afternoon, Sandy and Dennys find themselves alone casually tinkering in Mr. Murray's lab, where he has been experimenting with "tesseracts," or time travel. Suddenly, there is an explosion, and when the dust settles, they are no longer in Mr. Murray's lab but in a hot desert. It takes them a while to figure out where they are: the atmosphere is so different, the people are so small, and the animal life is so strange. But once they realize they are in Biblical times, their whole worldview is turned on its head, and only once they believe do they begin to figure out a way home.

The fourth novel in the *Wrinkle* quintet is primarily a story about faith. As Sandy and Dennys have compared themselves to the others members of their family, they have underestimated their own gifts and potential. This experience shakes and stretches their powers of belief in the world and in themselves. In learning faith, Sandy and Dennys also model acceptance in the face of difficult circumstances.

**For those also seeking**: acceptance
**For those drawn to**: story, language
**Themes/subjects**: adaptation/adjusting to change, aging elders, angels/cherubs, Bible stories, coming of age, crushes, cultural differences, death, deserts, faith and skepticism, family conflict, feuds, floods, gender roles, good and evil, love, magical transformations, portals/thresholds, pregnancy, rituals and traditions, temptation, terrorism, time travel, twins, unicorns
**Reading interest level**: grades 6–8
**Curricular tie-ins**: Terrorism is a major theme in this novel. Use it to segue into discussions and activities that explore the roots of terrorism. Ask students to compare and contrast current terrorist activities to the events in the story.
**Adaptations & alternative formats**: audiobook read by Ann Marie Lee (2009)
**Read-alikes**: *An Acceptable Time* follows this novel and is the final installment of the series. Geraldine McCaughrean's *Not the End of the World* is also a Noah's Arc story.

## Courage to Make a Change

**Lowry, Lois** (1937–)
**The Giver** (1993). Boston: Houghton Mifflin Harcourt, 2014. 225pp. 978-0544336261.

Jonas is about to celebrate the Ceremony of the Twelve, a major event in his community. During this ceremony, the leaders of the community, called "the committee," not only recognize those children who are celebrating their 12th birthdays but also announce their "Assignments," that is, the occupations they will have for the rest of their lives. Although Jonas knows the committee carefully observes each 12-year-old and tries to match them with the vocation that they seem most suited to, Jonas is apprehensive: What if he disagrees with the committee's choice?

Jonas's parents try to reassure him, pointing out that there are "very rarely disappointments." For instance, his father loves being a "Nurturer," a caretaker at the nursery where all of the children in the community are raised, and his mother likes the intellectual challenge that comes with her work in the Department of Justice—though neither chose these professions themselves. In the community, there is little choice. The committee makes most of the decisions. However, while the community is heavily regimented, it is also orderly and safe. No one ever has to feel pain or suffering. Once Jonas receives his Assignment and begins to learn the dark side of the committee's rules, he begins to doubt whether or not a life free of pain is really a life worth living. He longs to escape to Elsewhere, the world outside his community, and discover freedom.

The quiet, slow unfolding of Jonas's story gives way to an explosion of philosophical questions by the story's end. Jonas is assigned the role of Receiver, the task of which requires that he receive and bear the memories of all of humanity's past, both pleasure and pain, so that the rest of the community can be saved from suffering. As Jonas begins to recognize the meaningless in such painless living, and finds the courage to escape, forcing his community to grieve for itself but also the *freedom* to grieve, he demonstrates the necessity of and power of individual dissent. Jonas is a vivid reminder that even when one *feels* powerless and/or disenfranchised, he or she nonetheless does possess free will and the power of choice.

**For those also seeking**: acceptance
**For those drawn to**: story, language
**Themes/subjects**: aging elders, babies, being different, books, conformity and nonconformity, death, disability, dreams, dystopia, escape, existentialism, families, feelings/emotions, freedom, free will, gifted children, helping/aiding, identity, language/communication, lies/lying, loneliness, memory, murder, names and naming, outcasts/misfits, otherness, pain/suffering, privacy/surveillance, rituals and traditions, sexual awakening, purpose in life, sensory perception, survival, technology and civilization
**Reading interest level**: grades 6–8
**Curricular tie-ins**: Use this novel to complement a civics unit on government surveillance and/or censorship and how the threats they pose to democracy.
**Adaptations & alternative formats**: gift edition illustrated by Bagram Ibatoulline (2011; ISBN: 978-0547424774); film directed by Phillip Noyce (2014); audiobook read by Ron Rifkin (2006)
**Translations**: Spanish: *El Dador*; French: *Le Passeur*
**Read-alikes**: *The Giver* is the first novel in a quartet that includes *Gathering Blue* (2000), *Messenger* (2004), and *Son* (2012). Jeanne DuPrau's *The City of Ember* is another dystopian novel about a corrupt society that hides information from its citizens.

**Pratchett, Terry** (1948–2015)
**Wings**. (1990). In *The Bromeliad Trilogy: Truckers, Diggers, Wings*. New York: HarperCollins, 2003. 502pp. 978-006009493.

The third novel in the Bromeliad series, *Wings* is "the story of the going home"—in fact, "all the way home" to another planet. Four-inch high Masklin, Gurder, and Angalo decide to make the dangerous journey to an airport in order to fly to Florida and search for their spaceship. Doing so without the knowledge of the immensity of their task makes their journey laughably impossible. Guided by the Thing, an electronic box that communicates with them, the three nomes manage to hide on a plane and make their way to NASA where the Thing hopes to make contact with the spaceship that will take them back home.

A highly original story, *Wings* will appeal to those who love speculative fiction and novels about extraterrestrial life. Readers who are not content with their lives will find in Masklin's story the inspiration they need to make changes. The novel will also appeal to those with lofty but seemingly unattainable goals.

*Wings* is a very funny story told from the unusual perspective of miniature beings raised in unusual circumstances. Gurder, for example, who was brought up in a mall, says about the airplane food: "This is more like it, eh? ... Proper food the natural way, out of tins and things. None of this having to clean the dirt off it, like in the quarry." Readers will look at the world differently and not take it for granted as easily after seeing it through the eyes of the nomes. Although the prologue summarizes events from the first two books, *Wings* is better appreciated if read after the earlier novels.

**For those also seeking**: reassurance/comfort/confirmation of self-worth/strength
**For those drawn to**: setting, plot
**Themes/subjects**: miniature beings, survival, technology and civilization, spaceships, faith and skepticism, consumerism, journeys, planetary travel, humor, gnomes
**Reading interest level**: grade 7 and up
**Curricular tie-ins**: *Wings* will inspire curiosity about NASA. Ask students to create a webpage about NASA's space program.
**Adaptations & alternative formats**: audiobook read by Tony Robinson (2007)

**Read-alikes**: Antoine de Saint-Exupéry's *The Little Prince* is another novel about a character from beyond earth. Although not a book, the movie, E. T. the Extra-Terrestrial, will appeal to readers of *Wings*.

## Acceptance

**L'Engle, Madeleine** (1918–2007)
**A Wrinkle in Time** (1962). New York: Square Fish/Farrar Straus Giroux, 2012. 236pp. 978-1250004673.

For Meg Murray, nothing is right. She is not smart enough, or pretty enough, not like her mother, who is both a brilliant scientist and a violet-eyed beauty. At school, she is basically friendless, getting into fistfights with boys who poke fun at her youngest brother, Charles Wallace, and disappointing teachers by not "applying" herself. But, worse than all this, Meg's father is missing. He has been missing for years. And, while Meg's mother tries to comfort her and assure her of her father's return, Meg is losing hope.

Then, a mysterious stranger, calling herself Mrs. Whatsit, appears at the Murray's door, and a series of strange events begin to unfold. First, Calvin, a popular boy from school, randomly stumbles upon Meg and Charles Wallace, compelled, he says, by some unknown impulse. Quickly, the children begin to suspect that Mrs. Whatsit holds the secret to Dr. Murray's disappearance. Their suspicions confirmed; the three of them set out on a rescue mission, traveling through new dimensions to strange lands.

On this journey, Meg encounters several obstacles that force her to be brave and, most importantly, self-reliant. While before she blamed dissatisfaction with herself, and her life, on external causes—her plain looks, her father's absence—she discovers that she herself possesses agency over her own fate. No longer does she expect life to be easy or hope for others to make it easy for her, but instead she embraces the struggle of living and of making one's life one's own.

**For those also seeking**: reassurance/comfort/confirmation of self-worth/strength
**For those drawn to**: story, language
**Themes/subjects**: adventure, aliens (from space), anxiety/fears, being different, courage, dead or absent father, despair, faith and skepticism, free will, friendship, good and evil, heroines, hope, love, low self-esteem,

Science Fiction

magical transformations, missing persons, multiple worlds/universes, planetary travel, outer space, portals/thresholds, self-esteem, self-image, struggling or disinterested students
**Reading interest level**: grades 6–8
**Curricular tie-ins**: Cold War
**Adaptations & alternative formats**: graphic novel adapted and illustrated by Hope Larson (2015); audiobook read by Hope Davis (2012); film directed by Ava DuVernay (2018)
**Translations**: Spanish: *Una Arruga En El Tiempo*; French: *Un Raccourci Dans Le Temps*
**Read-alikes**: The second novel in the Wrinkle Quintet is *A Wind in the Door*. *A Wrinkle in Time* is also Miranda's favorite novel in Rebecca Stead's *When You Reach Me* and an excellent companion read.


**L'Engle, Madeleine** (1918–2007)
**An Acceptable Time** (1989). New York: Square Fish/Farrar Straus Giroux, 2007. 373pp. 978-0312368586.

Polly O'Keefe is just a teenager when she decides to move to Connecticut to live with her grandparents in the home where her mother, Meg Murray, grew up. The oldest of seven children, Polly treasures her picturesque surroundings, the quiet time to herself, and the opportunity to study under her brilliant scientist grandparents, Kate and Alex Murray. Still, she wouldn't mind having some people her own age around. Luckily, a friend and a seeming admirer, Zachary Gray, is working as an intern for his professor at an office nearby and sometimes comes to visit.

Then, while exploring her grandparents' orchard, she stumbles upon another young woman who is her same age. But right away, Polly notices that something is different, off. The other girl's hair, dress, and way of speaking all seem to belong to another time. Quickly, Polly realizes that this is because the girl *is* from another time. Polly has stumbled onto a tesseract, another dimension that allows her to travel through space and time to 3000 years ago. At first, Polly is able to easily move back-and-forth through time, meeting and communicating with some of the earth's earliest human inhabitants before meeting her grandparents for dinner back in the twentieth century. When Zach, who is ailing from a mysterious heart condition, discovers her special power, he tries to use it, and her, to search for a cure for his affliction. But, in the process, they both become trapped in time, and both their lives become endangered.

The final novel in the *Time Quintet* is also the darkest of the series, taking up such topics as abusive relationships and human sacrifice. L'Engle compares the sacrificial practices of early cultures to contemporary events in order to question the notion of human evolution and progress and reveal the problem of evil. Polly and Zach's relationship is a microcosm of this tension, and as Polly must learn to accept the evil, the weakness and selfishness of others, she also realizes that love, the act of it, is the only solution. This revelation, that we have free choice, the ability to choose our destiny and to choose love, may help other readers find a way to find ways to cope and accept with less than desirable circumstances.

**For those also seeking**: connection with others/awareness of not being alone
**For those drawn to**: story
**Themes/subjects**: aging elders, Christianity, cowardice, death, faith and skepticism, geology, human sacrifice, illness, indigenous peoples, language/communication, love, medicine, moral dilemmas, paradox, portals/thresholds, rituals and traditions, romance, sacrificial offerings, self-centeredness, space and time, time travel, translation/translators
**Reading interest level**: grades 6–8
**Curricular tie-ins**: L'Engle's focus on geological changes makes this novel a good complement to studies on geology/climate change. Researching ancient medicine traditions would also help shed light on L'Engle's critique of primitivism (i.e., how modern cultures tend to dismiss the views/contributions of earlier cultures by either labeling them as unevolved or fetishizing them).
**Adaptations & alternative formats**: audiobook read by Ann Marie Lee (2008)
**Read-alikes**: L. M. Montgomery's *Emily's Quest* is also a coming-of-age story of a young woman who must come to terms with some of life's dark realities.

**Stead, Rebecca** (1968–)
**When You Reach Me** (2009). New York: Dell Publishing, 2010. 199pp. 978-0375850868.

Miranda and Sal have always been best friends—ever since they were babies born in the late 1960s. Although Sal is a boy, and she is a girl, they have a lot in common. Both are only children. Both have single moms. Both live in the same crumbling apartment building in New York City. But one day in 1978, during the sixth grade, a bully comes out of nowhere and knocks Sal to the ground. Sal gets away uninjured, but afterward he completely avoids Miranda—but never explains why.

Miranda doesn't understand Sal's rejection, but she distracts herself by reading her favorite book, *A Wrinkle in Time* and by helping her mom prepare for her upcoming appearance on Dick Clark's game show, *The $10,000 Pyramid*, which they hope will help rid them of their money troubles. She also makes new friends. Then, though the puzzle of Sal's rejection still nags at her, other mysteries begin to trouble her as well. Suddenly, she begins to receive cryptic, handwritten letters sent from an unknown sender. At first, she isn't sure what they are about—though she suspects they might have something to do with Sal, the strange new kid who has moved on her block, and the madman who always seems to be screaming nonsense on her corner.

The creativity and careful skill in which Stead constructs this plot is praiseworthy in itself. Not a single detail distracts from the story; rather, they fit together into a kind of narrative Rubik's cube. While it is a great intellectual exercise, it is award winning no doubt because it is completely compelling—and fun—to read. The structure, a series of letters addressed to an unknown recipient, reflects and reinforces larger philosophical questions about the uncertainty that comes with living. As Miranda comes to recognize the limits of her reason, she is able to find acceptance.

**For those also seeking**: reassurance/comfort/confirmation of self-worth/strength
**For those drawn to**: story, language
**Themes/subjects**: anxiety/fears, being different, books, bullying, city life, class differences, cliques (in school), clues/riddles, coming of age, crushes, dead or absent father, death, disability, food, food allergies, friendship, games, grief, heroines, humor, jealousy, kindness, letters, madmen, money/debt, mother-daughter relationships, mysteries, New York City, only children, preoccupied parents, quarrels/fights, rejection, single-parent dating, school, single-parent families, space and time, time travel, work (labor), wrongfully accused
**Reading interest level**: grades 6–8
**Curricular tie-ins**: Assigning this novel in conjunction with L'Engle's *A Wrinkle in Time* would make for an excellent lesson on intertextuality. This intertexual relationship would also provide an excellent means of introducing how knowledge/information is created, a key information literacy concept.

**Adaptations & alternative formats**: audiobook read by Cynthia Holloway (2009)
**Translations**: Spanish: *Cuando Me Alcances*; French: *Hier Tu Comprendras*
**Read-alikes**: L'Engle's *A Wrinkle in Time* heavily influences this story and Fitzhugh's *Harriet the Spy* also takes place in New York, features a female protagonist, and focuses on friendships. Stead also takes up similar themes in *Liar & Spy* (2013) but through a male protagonist.

## Disinterested Understanding of the World

**Hughes, Ted** (1930–1998)
**The Iron Man** (1968) (US: The Iron Giant). Illustrated by Andrew Davidson. New York: Alfred A. Knopf, 1999. 96pp. 978-0375801532.

No one knows where the Iron Giant came from, or how he was made, but the steel creature stands as tall as a tree, and the earth shakes when he walks. His footprint is as wide and deep as your bed. Naturally, the Iron Giant frightens the townspeople, clawing and trampling upon their farms, hungrily eating their fences, their tractors—anything metal. Although the people try to trick and ensnare him, they cannot match his extraordinary strength. The giant is essentially indestructible. He can dismantle and reconstruct his body at whim.

Luckily, a clever boy named Hogarth has an idea. He meets with the giant and, instead of fighting him, proposes that he take the town's scrap metal yard, which, to a giant, is like an all-you-can eat buffet. The giant agrees, and the town and the giant live together peacefully, that is, until the awful space-bat-angel-dragon appears from outer space and threatens to lick, quite literally, every single person from the face of the earth.

A compelling plot drives this short, allegorical novel. The battle between the Iron Giant and the dragon monster captures not only the Cold War milieu in which the story was written but also poses timeless, universal questions about the origins of good and evil and man and woman's simultaneous life-giving and destructive impulses, the paradox that is the human condition.

**For those drawn to**: story, language
**Themes/subjects**: aliens (from space), anxieties/fears, battles/wars, clockwork and mechanical figures, cooperation and teamwork, dragons,

*Science Fiction*

existentialism, giants, good and evil, hunger, pain/suffering, outer space, peace, sea and seashore
**Reading interest level**: K-8
**Curricular tie-ins**: This novel would provide an ideal example for teaching students allegory and symbolism. Ask students to create an actual image/collage of the characters and what they represent. For older students, use this novel to complement studies on the Cold War. Discuss how this book is a product of this context.
**Adaptations & alternative formats**: art book edition (2010) contains gorgeous illustrations and paper art by Laura Carlin (978-0375871498), film adaptation directed by Brad Bird (1999)
**Translations**: Spanish: *El Hombre De Hierro*; French: *Le Géant De Fer*
**Read-alikes**: Ted Hughes's *The Iron Woman* is the perfect companion read. Readers drawn to the novel's allegorical characteristics might also like Kate Dicamillo's *The Tale of Desperaux*.


**Verne, Jules** (1828–1905)
**20,000 Leagues under the Sea** (1870). New York: Random House, 2003. 437pp. 978-0553212525. PD.

In the year 1866, news begins to spread across the world as several seafaring men report strange sightings of a sea monster, a massive, whale-like creature like nothing they have ever seen before. After it sinks several ships, an American navy sets out to pursue and destroy it. The crew invites Professor Aronnax, a marine scholar from France, as a consultant aboard the frigate to help lead the expedition.

But their ship is no match for the monster; they sink in the Pacific. Though Professor Aronnax and a couple of his shipmates survive—his assistant Conseil and a Canadian harpooner named Ned Land—they are all immediately taken hostage aboard an enormous submarine. Their captor, Captain Nemo, is a recluse. Weary of the hypocrisy and cruelty of human society, he has rejected it and decided to live the remainder of his days under water. Although Captain Nemo tries to make Professor Aronnax and his shipmates as comfortable as possible—feeding them all the bounty the sea has to offer, guiding them on underwater tours of sea life never before seen by the human eye—and though, for a while, they enjoy their underwater adventures, these rare glimpses of marine life, they are still, nonetheless, hostages. As Captain Nemo's behavior becomes increasingly erratic and hostile, they are put on alert and long to return to home. But the captain's craft is so expertly built, it is as tightly sealed as a prison. They don't know how, or if, they will ever escape.

This Odyssey-like adventure is not only fittingly episodic and action-packed but it also contains beautiful descriptions of marine life. Readers who are fascinated by the ocean or underwater exploration will find themselves easily transported to this world through this book. As the mysterious motivations of Captain Nemo's reclusiveness are revealed, readers will also obtain a disinterested understanding of grief and how, left unchecked, it can reduce to despair and hate.

**For those also seeking**: awakening/new perspectives/enlargement of possibilies
**For those drawn to**: story
**Themes/subjects**: adventure, anger/hostility, boats and ships, buried/hidden treasure, civilization, colonialism, critical thinking/strategy, death, despair, environmentalism, fish and sea animals, food, freedom, geography, grief, hatred, homesickness, hunting, hypocrisy, imprisonment/entrapment, journeys, justice and injustice, loyalty, misanthropes, murder, pain/suffering, scholars/professors, sea and seashore, sea voyage, survival, technology and civilization, underwater exploration
**Reading interest level**: grades 7–8
**Curricular tie-ins**: Teach/reinforce how to read geographic coordinates by asking students to plot and identify all or some of the locations Professor Aronnax mentions in the story.
**Adaptations & alternative formats**: abridged edition (ISBN: 978-0140367218); audiobook read by James Frain (2011); film directed by Richard Fleischer (1954)
**Read-alikes**: Edith Nesbit's *Wet Magic* and L. Frank Baum's *The Sea Fairies* are also novels about underwater marvels and adventures. Jules Verne's *Journey to the Centre of the Earth* is another novel of daring adventure into inaccessible places on the planet.

**Yolen, Jane** (1939–)
**Heart's Blood** (1984). Orlando, FL: Harcourt, 2004. 354pp. 978-0152051181.

Having become a dragon master, 15-year-old Jakkin has earned the money he needs to free himself from his indentured servitude at the dragon nursery. But, even though he can now remove the "bond bag," which all "bonders" on the planet Austar IV are required to wear, Jakkin continues to wear it around his neck. Though he knows he is a free man, he does yet feel comfortable with his freedom. He also does he feel like he is a man. Part of the reason is the caste system itself, which Jakkin cannot entirely embrace. When Errikkin, an acquaintance at the dragon nursery, begs to be his charge, Jakkin agrees, but finds his eagerness to submit disturbing. Why would he choose bondage over freedom?

Meanwhile, Jakkin begins to become aware of the growing political unrest in his capital, Rokk. Normally, Jakkin does not care much for political matters. He would much rather spend his time training Heart's Blood, his dragon, for the next pit match. But when Golden, a politician from Rokk, pays him a visit and explains that his beloved Akki, who Jakkin has not seen for over a year, is being held captive by a Austarian rebel sect, Jakkin is compelled to care. In order to save Akki, Jakkin becomes a rebel spy and must quickly decide who and who not to trust.

The sequel to *Dragon's Blood* continues to address themes related to freedom and oppression, but with a particular focus on tension between individual and group interests. Once Jakkin secures his own freedom, he initially resists political participation, adopting an isolationist's attitude. Only after politics affect him personally, when the life of his beloved is put at risk, does he see the connection between the personal and the political and does he realize he cannot avoid politics. In overcoming his own self-interests, Jakkin reveals to readers the importance of citizenship.

**For those also seeking**: courage to make a change
**For those drawn to**: story, character
**Themes/subjects**: addiction, adventure, aiding/helping, battles/wars, birth, breeding/genetics, caste systems, citizenship, colonialism, critical thinking/strategy, death, disguises, dragons, extrasensory perception, freedom, gambling, lies/lying, laws, magical transformations, medicine, missing persons, prostitution/human trafficking, politics, romance, secrets, self-interest, spies and spying
**Reading interest level**: grades 6–8
**Curricular tie-ins**: Ask students to compare and contrast the caste system on Austar IV to real life caste systems in India and/or explain caste-like features in their own countries.

**Adaptations & alternative formats**: audiobook read by Marc Thompson (2009)

**Read-alikes**: *A Sending of Dragons* is the next book in Jane Yolen's *Dragon Pit* series.

## Notes

1. Joyce Saricks, *Readers' Advisory Guide to Genre Fiction*, 2nd ed. (Chicago: ALA Editions, 2009), 244.

2. Ibid., 245.

CHAPTER TWELVE

# Toys/Games

Books about toys often resonate with children. Just as some of their most prized possessions are toys, some of the most popular classic books are about toys: *Pinocchio, The Velveteen Rabbit, Winnie-the-Pooh, Nutcracker.* Playing with toys is an activity that is remarkably universal. Despite changes over time, basic toys, according to toy historian Deborah Jaffé, "have retained the same shapes and functions for centuries, and that core group of the ball, spinner, rattle, doll, wheeled toy, pull-along and miniature replicas remain firmly in place."[1] Children who do not own toys create their own from natural and household objects. Playing with toys fulfills many needs for children, as does reading stories about them.

The most common toys in children's literature are dolls, action figures, war toys, games, stuffed animals, wind-up figures, and miniatures such as doll houses, toy cities, and small-scale trains. Since toys are often given as gifts to children, celebrations such as birthdays and holidays such as Christmas are key events in toy literature. Although stories about toys take place in a wide variety of locales, they are frequently set in toy stores, playgrounds, children's bedrooms, attics, dollhouses, and other child-centered and imagination-friendly retreats. Despite the fact that stories about toys tend to appeal to younger children, the genre includes books for older children as well (*The Homeward Bounders, Doll Bones*).

Dolls, toy animals, and action figures function as confidants, soul mates, and supports for characters. When children feel misunderstood or underappreciated by friends and family, they can count on their miniature friends to understand their problems, empathize with their plight, and even guide their actions. Children know what it is like to be small, powerless, and dismissed by those who are older and larger. The special bond that children form with human and animal replicas is a result of their shared size and mutual dependency on others. If children are diminutive in dimensions and limited in agency, their dolls, action figures, and stuffed toys are even smaller and more helpless.

Although many toy-centered books are fantasies in which toys are personified, realistic stories frequently depict toys as alive in young character's minds (*The Jamie and Angus Stories*, *The Fairy Doll*, and *Nutcracker*). Lines between reality and the imagination are often blurred in this genre. Readers who enjoy toy stories will enjoy novels in the fantasy chapters.

Authors use toy-centered narratives in a variety of ways. Some books about toys and games question life's meaning and explore existential issues (*Through the Looking-Glass*, *The Mouse and His Child*, *Homeward Bounders*, *The Mennyms*). Other toy books explore characters' fears and anxieties (*The House at Pooh Corner*), help them cope with difficulties (*The Magic City*), and prepare them for the future (*The Castle in the Attic*). Characters in these books learn to deal with life's challenges by proxy, using play as a simulator environment.

### Awakening/New Perspectives/Enlargement of Possibilities

**Burnett, Frances Hodgson** (1849–1924)
**Racketty-Packetty House** (1906). New York: Simon & Schuster Books for Young Readers, 2006. 96pp. 978-0689869747. PD.

When eight-year-old Cynthia receives Tidy Castle for her birthday, she relegates her former dollhouse to a corner behind a door, in "an unfashionable neighborhood." Ashamed of the old dollhouse, Cynthia starts calling it Racketty-Packetty House. The grand but haughty Tidy Castle dolls scorn their Racketty-Packetty neighbors, considering them beneath their notice. When an actual princess plans to visit, Cynthia decides that Racketty-Packetty House and the dolls within it must first be discarded and burnt.

Even though the Racketty-Packetty dolls live in a dilapidated house, wear shabby, tattered clothes, and endure the scorn of others, they use their imaginations to create a pleasant and enjoyable world. The dolls' lighthearted attitude towards their problems offers an alternative way of coping for children, one that can help them see their own difficulties in a more optimistic light. Readers who have been misjudged, treated unfairly, left out, or ridiculed by others will find a source of consolation and comfort in the book. The incongruity between the childlike dolls and adult issues such as social status is humorous and engaging for readers of all ages.

**For those also seeking**: reassurance/comfort/confirmation of self-worth/strength
**For those drawn to**: character, setting
**Themes/subjects**: dolls, dollhouses, class differences, optimism, inclusiveness, imagination, royalty, fairies, princesses, only children
**Reading interest level**: grades 2–5
**Curricular tie-ins**: Facilitate a literature circle discussion about social class and social equity in the novel. This discussion could be extended to a global community that students have studied.
**Read-alikes**: Rumer Godden's *The Doll's House*, Sylvia Waugh's *The Mennyms*, and Mary Norton's *The Borrowers Aloft* also explore discrimination against dolls or miniature beings.

**Carroll, Lewis** (1832–1898)
**Through the Looking-Glass** (1871). In *Alice's Adventures in Wonderland & Through the Looking-Glass*. Illustrated by John Tenniel. New York: Bantam, 1981. 223pp. 978-0553213454. PD.

Sitting at home with her cats, seven-year-old Alice wonders what it would be like to live in the room that is reflected in the drawing-room mirror. The glass immediately turns misty and she is transported to looking-glass house. After exploring this strange place that is populated with live chess pieces, Alice wanders outside and discovers an even more bizarre landscape. Once she realizes that the world is arranged as a giant chessboard, her goal is to get the eighth square and become queen. Along the way, she encounters memorable characters such as Tweedledum, Tweedledee, and Humpty Dumpty, all of whom say and do the oddest, most inexplicable things. A sequel to *Alice's Adventures in Wonderland* but a book that can be read on its own, *Through the Looking-Glass* is carefully constructed with the rules of chess in mind.

When Alice first sees the looking-glass house, she says that it is just the same as her drawing room, only the objects in it "go the other way." Carroll takes the idea of the reversing function of a mirror to absurd extremes. Everything in the fantasy world works in reverse and happens in the opposite manner to the usual or expected way. A witty, playful novel that uses the themes and techniques of postmodern literature, it is just as accessible to young children as older ones. Because nothing that happens in looking-glass World does so in the usual way, readers look at the world they have taken for granted with fresh insight.

Like *Alice's Adventures in Wonderland*, *Through the Looking-Glass* presents the confusing, intimidating adult world as it appears to an anxious seven-year-old. When Alice becomes a queen, she tries on a grown-up role and realizes that she can manage better than the adults she meets. If life in the grown-up world is depicted as a game, she wins this chess game. Readers who fear growing up will be reassured by Alice's story. John Tenniel's iconic illustrations to the novel are just as popular today as they were a century and a half ago when the novel was first published.

**For those also seeking**: reassurance/comfort/confirmation of self-worth/strength
**For those drawn to**: setting, language
**Themes/subjects**: games, identity, wordplay, malapropisms, language, nonsense, agency and powerlessness, royalty, kings/queens, knights, growing up (apprehension), dreams, repression (psychology)
**Reading interest level**: grades 2–7
**Curricular tie-ins**: Students in small groups could research dreams, especially their meaning and characteristics. Then in a large group, they could discuss their findings in relation to the novel.
**Adaptations & alternative formats**: movie directed by James Bobin (2016); audiobook read by B. J. Harrison (2014); graphic novel by Lewis Helfand and illustrated by Rajesh Nagulakonda (2010)
**Translations**: Spanish: *Alicia a Través del Espejo*; French: *Ce Qu'Alice Trouva de L'autre Côté du Miroir*
**Read-alikes**: Readers who enjoyed the novel will also like its companion, *Alice's Adventures in Wonderland*. Like Alice, Coraline in Neil Gaiman's novel by the same name enters a strange world that mirrors her own. L. Frank Baum's 14 Oz books are set in an odd, out-of-the-ordinary places that are populated with eccentric, highly unusual characters. Norton Juster's *The Phantom Tollbooth* is filled with witty, literary nonsense.

**Jones, Diana Wynne** (1934–2011)
**The Homeward Bounders** (1981). London: HarperCollins, 2000. 266pp. 978-0006755258.

Toys/Games

When 12-year-old Jamie climbs over a wall, he discovers a mysterious triangular castle. Upon entering it, he finds "*Them*"—cloaked figures playing intently with machines. *They* tell Jamie he is a "discard" and has no further use in "play." *They* banish him to the "Bounds," a strange liminal area that leads him to a new world. Just as he starts to familiarize himself with this place, he receives the "call," an overwhelming longing to head again for the Bounds. Henceforth, he is a pawn in *Their* game, repeatedly leaving worlds whenever one of *Them* finishes a game move. The only way that Jamie can enter play again is if he succeeds in returning home. After traveling through a hundred worlds, Jamie meets fellow homeward bounders, Helen and Joris, who convince him to rebel against *Them*.

*The Homeward Bounders* will appeal to gamers and those who enjoy vividly imagined fantasy/science fiction worlds. Narrated by a boy looking back at his radically altered life years after the story, the novel is a poignant account of someone who has been wrongfully treated. Readers who have suffered injustice or are trapped in hopeless situations will find a way of reframing their problems through Jamie's example. They will also learn how to accept situations where change is not possible.

The dual perspective of homeward bounders as characters on a journey and pawns in a game adds a rich layer of meaning to a book that can be enjoyed on many levels. This larger-than-life story about a boy at the mercy of forces beyond his control is both haunting and inspirational.

**For those also seeking**: acceptance
**For those drawn to**: setting
**Themes/subjects**: games, homesickness, homelessness, outcasts/misfits, hope, agency and powerlessness, purpose in life, journeys, loneliness, justice and injustice, multiple worlds/universes, memoirs/diaries, portals/thresholds, imprisonment/entrapment, oppressive environments
**Reading interest level**: grade 6 and up
**Curricular tie-ins**: "*They*" are depicted as cruel and uncaring gamers. In a think-pair-square activity, students could discuss and then join with a second pair to further discuss the following questions: Does video gaming lead to such callous behavior in some people? Is gaming unfairly depicted in this novel?
**Read-alikes**: Life is also depicted as an unfair game in Diana Wynne Jones's *The Game* and Suzanne Collins's *The Hunger Games*. The protagonist of Philip Pullman's His Dark Materials trilogy (*The Golden Compass, The Subtle Knife,* and *The Amber Spyglass*) also moves between different universes.

**Jones, Diana Wynne** (1934–2011)
**The Game** (2007). New York: Firebird, 2007. 179pp. 978-0142407189.

Raised by a busy grandfather and overly strict grandmother, Haley Foss is "always overflowing Grandma's edges." One day Grandma becomes so angry with Haley that she sends her off to live with her Irish cousins. Haley is not even sure what she did wrong. Nothing in her sequestered life with her grandparents prepares her for the host of "rushing, shouting" cousins that she encounters once she arrives in Ireland. When her older cousin Harmony suggests Haley play "the game" with them, Haley is intrigued. Each cousin enters a magical land called the "mythosphere" and follows a silvery, slippery strand of story in search of an object. It is in this mythosphere that Haley makes important discoveries about her identity and role in life.

Diana Wynne Jones has created an enchanting story about stories in *The Game*. Readers who enjoy out-of-the-ordinary fantasy worlds and memorable settings will lose themselves in the magical storyland of the game. Children familiar with mythical stories will recognize characters and situations; those new to myths will be inspired to read more. The book will also appeal to readers who feel as if they do not belong. The reader, like Haley, learns not only that there is nothing wrong with being different but also that uniqueness can be a source of strength.

**For those also seeking**: models for identity
**For those drawn to**: setting
**Themes/subjects**: games, stories and storytelling, mythology, loneliness, identity, identity formation, multiple worlds/universes, grandparents, only children, moving houses (relocating), nontraditional families, being different, comets
**Reading interest level**: grades 5–8
**Curricular tie-ins**: Myths are a key feature of the novel. Ask students to look up one of the myths referred to in the novel, and create a summary of it. The class can compile the myths for a companion book to the novel.
**Read-alikes**: Diana Wynne Jones's *The Homeward Bounders* is a novel about playing dangerous games. Salman Rushdie's *Haroun and the Sea of Stories* is a good choice for older readers who are looking for a novel about stories and the role that they play in life.


**Waugh, Sylvia** (1935–)
**The Mennyms** (1993). London: Red Fox, 2001. 236pp. 978-1782954323.

Toys/Games

A family of life-size rag dolls springs to life after their creator dies. The dolls live a secluded life in an empty house and, amazingly enough, manage to blend in with humans. By carefully disguising themselves and limiting their contact with people, the dolls manage, for 40 years, to keep up the pretense that they are humans. All goes well until they receive a letter from their landlord's nephew, a man who lives in Australia. He has inherited the house that the dolls inhabit and would like to visit them. Complications ensue as the doll family tries to discourage the visit and keep their secret hidden.

*The Mennyms* is a story of survival and suspense. Character- and family-centered, it depicts the lives of five doll children, their parents, and grandparents. Although the novel is about the entire family, it focuses on 15-year-old Appleby. She becomes entangled in a situation which grows worse the longer she keeps it secret. The novel will appeal to readers who face problems that they consider unsolvable.

Winner of the Guardian Award and short-listed for the Carnegie Medal, *The Mennyms* is a thought-provoking book that explores the role of pretense in life. After reading the novel, readers might think differently about the imaginative side of human existence. According to Grandpa, "We pretend to live and we live to pretend."

**For those also seeking**: acceptance
**For those drawn to**: character, story
**Themes/subjects**: appearance versus reality, dolls, being different, disguises, imagination, lies/lying, mistakes, immortality; family, outcasts/misfits, secrets
**Reading interest level**: grade 4 and up
**Curricular tie-ins**: Unlike the other Mennyms, Soobie finds no joy in pretending. In their reader response journeys, students can discuss Soobie's attitude toward pretense. Do they agree with it or not? Is pretending just a waste of time?
**Read-alikes**: Readers who enjoyed *The Mennyms* will like its sequels: *The Mennyms in the Wilderness*, *The Mennyms under Siege*, *The Mennyms Alone*, and *The Mennyms Alive*. Mary Norton's *The Borrowers* is a novel about another group of misfit creatures who live in a world of human beings. *The Doll People* and its sequels (*The Meanest Doll in the World*, *The Runaway Dolls*, and *The Doll People Set Sail*) by Ann M. Martin and Laura Godwin are also books about dolls who survive in the world of humans.

## Models for Identity

**Bailey, Carolyn Sherwin** (1875–1961)
**Miss Hickory** (1946). New York: Penguin Books, 1978. 120pp.
978-0140309560.

When Miss Hickory—the spunky doll with an applewood-twig body and hickory-nut head—discovers that her owners have gone away and left her outside for the winter, she is shocked. She knows that she cannot survive the bitter winter under a lilac tree in her corncob dollhouse. Leaving behind her well swept floors, neatly stored teacups, and life of tranquility, Miss Hickory looks for a more suitable place to weather the harsh New Hampshire winter.

Previously protected by her owners, Miss Hickory must now draw upon hidden stores of resourcefulness and courage to face life on her own. Despite being abandoned and losing all her possessions, this plucky little doll learns to adapt to a new life. With the help of her animal friends, Miss Hickory makes herself a winter wardrobe, creates a new home, and develops a resilience and toughness that she never realized she had.

Winner of the Newbery Medal, *Miss Hickory* is a character-driven novel that will comfort and guide readers faced with loss, poverty, or homelessness. Inspired by Miss Hickory, children will discover that they too are more resourceful than they think and that they could manage if they lost everything.

**For those also seeking**: courage to make a change
**For those drawn to**: character
**Themes/subjects**: dolls, country life, homelessness, adaptation/adjusting to change, independence, agency and powerlessness, resilience, resourcefulness, courage, self-reliance, winter
**Reading interest level**: grades 3–5
**Curricular tie-ins**: Ask students to create a miniature-sized figure such as Miss Hickory or a male equivalent using twigs, pinecones, nuts, leaves, and flowers. The novel can also be used as a springboard to a science unit on the adaptation of plants and animals to their environments.
**Read-alikes**: The protagonist in Laura Amy Schlitz's *The Night Fairy* must also create a home for herself in the natural world. The characters in Rachel Field's *Hitty, Her First Hundred Years*, J. R. R. Tolkien's *The Hobbit*, and

Kenneth Grahame's *The Wind in the Willows* must learn to adapt to the world after they leave their homes.

**Baum, L. Frank** (1856–1919).
**The Life and Adventures of Santa Claus** (1902). Potsdam, NY: Parkhurst Brook, 1985. 154pp. 978-0961566418. PD.

When Ak, the Master Woodsman of the World, walks through the Forest of Burzee one day, he finds an abandoned baby boy. The wood nymph Necile takes pity on the baby and asks Ak if she can raise him. Although immortal beings are not supposed to interfere with the lives of mortals, Ak grants her an exception. She names the baby Neclaus, which gets shortened to Claus. He grows up happy and content in the forest, beloved by all the immortals. But when the Master Woodsman shows him human beings, Claus decides to leave the immortals and take his place among fellow creatures. Settling in the Laughing Valley, he starts carving wooden animals for children in need. Because he was abandoned at birth, Claus is especially sympathetic to the sufferings of children. As his reputation as a toymaker grows, Claus faces a number of threats and difficulties.

Although Claus could have continued his utopian existence with the immortals, he willingly sacrifices his own comfort to help children who need him. Although he is not initially sure what he should do with his life, his natural affinity for deprived children helps guide his decision. Turning the negative experience of abandonment into something positive by helping disadvantaged children, Claus becomes an inspiring role model for readers who have been wronged or neglected. The depiction of the utopian setting and the traditions of the seasonal holiday are added appeals in the novel.

**For those also seeking**: reassurance/comfort/confirmation of self-worth/strength
**For those drawn to**: setting
**Themes/subjects**: Santa Claus, Christmas, toymakers, abandoned children, adoption, mythological creatures, purpose in life, forests, inventing/creating, selflessness, kindness, rituals and traditions, utopian places
**Reading interest level**: preschool–grade 3
**Curricular tie-ins**: Students could paint a picture of a holiday that they celebrate. In a large group, they could also describe the holiday and the traditions associated with it.

**Adaptations & alternative formats**: audiobook read by Bobbie Frohman (2013)
**Translations**: Spanish: *Vida y Aventuras de Santa Claus*
**Read-alikes**: E. T. A. Hoffmann's *The Nutcracker*, Dr. Seuss's *How the Grinch Stole Christmas*, and Rumer Godden's *The Story of Holly and Ivy* and the narrative poem " 'Twas the Night before Christmas" by Clement C. Moore are also stories about Christmas. James Thurber's *The Great Quillow* is a story about a lovable toymaker.

**Hoban, Russell** (1925–2011)
**The Mouse and His Child** (1967). Illustrated by David Small. New York: Arthur A. Levine Books, 2001. 244pp. 978-0439098267.

A clockwork mouse and his son who are attached to each other and dance in a circle live in a toy store. One Christmas they are sold and must leave the security of the store. The toy is eventually discarded by the children who own it. Despite the mouse child's fears, the pair set out on a dangerous journey in search of a house, family, and liberty. The dependence of the mice on other creatures bothers the mouse child, whose dream is to be autonomous. He tells his father, "Maybe we shan't always be helpless, Papa . . . Maybe we'll be self-winding someday." The mouse child's quest for independence is a long and difficult one. The story is by turns, witty, exciting, funny, charming, and philosophical.

When the novel was first published, *The Times Literary Supplement* insisted that Russell Hoban's earlier picture books gave no indication that he had such a "blockbuster of a book" in him. Indeed, *The Mouse and His Child* is one of those rare books that can be enjoyed on many levels by readers of all ages. It is just as much an engaging adventure story as it is an existential exploration of the meaning of life, one that is surprisingly accessible to children. When asked to teach a success course in life, the mouse and son refuse: "The whole secret of the thing, they insisted, was simply and at all costs to move steadily ahead."

The mouse child's life models the journey from childhood to maturity, and from powerlessness to autonomy, appealing to children who are anxious and even fearful of change. David Small's illustrations evoke the innocence and guilelessness of the mouse child's world.

**For those also seeking**: courage to make a change
**For those drawn to**: character, story

Toys/Games 437

**Themes/subjects**: clockwork and mechanical figures, agency and powerlessness, father-son relationships, family, journeys, mice, existentialism, self-reliance, justice and injustice, anxiety/fears, accidents (major), wordplay
**Reading interest level**: grade 4 and up
**Curricular tie-ins**: Students could look for a newspaper article about a marginalized group of people suffering from injustice. In a literature circle, they could discuss the articles they found.
**Adaptations & alternative formats**: play adapted by Tamsin Oglesby (2012) and first performed by the Royal Shakespeare Company in Stratford-upon-Avon in 2012; audiobook read by William Dufris (2003)
**Translations**: Spanish: *El Ratón y Su Hijo*; French: *Souris Père et Fils*
**Read-alikes**: The protagonist in *The Miraculous Journey of Edward Tulane* is another toy character who undertakes a long and difficult journey. A mouse family also goes on a journey in Richard Peck's *Secrets at Sea*.

## Reassurance/Comfort/Confirmation of Self-Worth/Strength

**DiCamillo, Kate** (1964–)
**The Miraculous Journey of Edward Tulane** (2006). Illustrated by Bagram Ibatoulline. Cambridge, MA: Candlewick Press, 2006. 198pp. 978-0763647834.

Edward Tulane, the china rabbit who considers himself to be "an exceptional specimen," lives a spoiled life with his owner, Abilene. When her family sets sail on the Queen Mary, the toy rabbit is accidently tossed overboard and sinks to the bottom of the ocean. Edward's privileged life changes dramatically as he undergoes a series of adventures and misfortunes with different owners. Mistaken for a female rabbit, tossed in the garbage, used as a scarecrow, and working as a puppet, Edward is beaten, battered, and gradually transformed.

Two-time Newbery Medal winner, and recipient of the Boston Globe-Horn Book Award for this novel, Kate DiCamillo has created a heart-warming story that readers of coming-of-age stories will enjoy. When a character as haughty as Edward Tulane manages to survive and prosper in the bleakest of circumstances, his story kindles faith and hope in readers. Children experiencing dejection or discouragement will find hope in this uplifting, character-centered story.

Bagram Ibatoulline's charming, muted-tone illustrations reinforce the book's message of reassurance and comfort. Spare language and a resonating narrative voice transform an engaging story into a timeless tale that will strike a chord with readers of all ages. The novel is an excellent choice to read aloud.

**For those also seeking**: courage to make a change
**For those drawn to**: character, language
**Themes/subjects**: toy animals, love, stories and storytelling, pride, journeys, hope, coming of age, appearance (physical), rabbits, vanity and pompousness, narcissism, adaptation/adjusting to change, accidents (major)
**Reading interest level**: grades 2–6
**Curricular tie-ins**: Ask students to create a timeline of the events in the story.
**Adaptations & alternative formats**: movie directed by Robert Zemeckis (2016); audiobook read by Judith Ivey (2006)
**Translations**: Spanish: *El Prodigioso Viaje de Edward Tulane*; French: *Le Miraculeux Voyage d'Édouard Tulane*
**Read-alikes**: The doll in Rachel Field's *Hitty, Her First Hundred Years* also falls overboard and is separated from her owner. A. A. Milne's *Winnie-the-Pooh* and *The House at Pooh Corner* are also about the lives of toy animals.


**Fine, Anne** (1947–)
**The Jamie and Angus Stories** (2002). Illustrated by Penny Dale. Cambridge, MA: Candlewick Press, 2007. 100pp. 978-0763633127.

Young Jamie knows immediately that the stuffed bull in the toy store is meant for him: "He gazed at Angus. Angus gazed at him." After Jamie takes the bull home, the pair becomes inseparable. In six intersecting stories, Anne Fine depicts Jamie's day-to-day life with his toy bull. Winner of the Boston Globe-Horn Book Award, the book is a humorous and endearing portrayal of the close attachment between a preschooler and his stuffed animal.

Jamie transfers his thoughts and feelings to Angus in a way that only children at this age can do. The toy bull "trembles" in Jamie's arms at the thought of the dry cleaners; he looks "anxiously" at Jamie when the boy has to go to the hospital; and he "keeps looking" at the big box of chocolates that do not belong to him.

Toys/Games 439

Like A. A. Milne, Anne Fine depicts the character of a young child with insight, gentle humor, and compassion. Young readers who have many fears and anxieties will find the light-hearted treatment of Jamie's worries comforting and reassuring. This skillfully written novel is an excellent choice for a read-aloud story. Penny Dale's illustrations evoke a world of innocent childhood foibles.

**For those also seeking**: connection with others/awareness of not being alone
**For those drawn to**: character, language
**Themes/subjects**: toy animals, imagination, friendship, projection (psychology), humor, anxiety/fears
**Reading interest level**: preschool–grade 3
**Curricular tie-ins**: Ask students to bring a favorite stuffed animal or doll to school for show and tell.
**Adaptations & alternative formats**: audiobook read by the author (2010)
**Read-alikes**: A. A. Milne's *Winnie-the-Pooh* and *The House at Pooh Corner* also depict the humorous adventures of a young boy and his stuffed animals.


**Hoffmann, E. T. A.** (1776–1822)
**Nutcracker** (1816). Illustrated by Maurice Sendak. Translated from the German by Ralph Manheim. London: Bodley Head, 1984. 102pp. 978-0385348645. PD.

On Christmas Eve, seven-year-old Marie notices a wooden nutcracker that captures her heart. She is upset when her brother breaks the nutcracker's teeth while cracking a nut, and worries about his "wounds." After everyone goes to bed, Marie watches as the nutcracker, toy soldiers, and mice come to life and engage in a dangerous battle. When she tries to convince her parents and her uncle that the nutcracker is a cousin who has been transformed into an inanimate object, they laugh at her. But Marie stays devoted to her beloved nutcracker and participates in stirring adventures with him at night.

Hoffman's magical fairy-tale world of marzipan castles, gingerbread cities, Christmas woods, and lemonade rivers will enchant young readers. Blurring the boundary between fantasy and reality, Hoffmann depicts a mesmerizing world that fantasy enthusiasts will love. The story within a story provides enriching parallels between real and magical worlds, parallels that expose Marie's hidden anxieties. Readers who are afraid of growing up will find reassurance and comfort in Marie's heartening story.

Hoffman's *Nutcracker* will also appeal to readers who enjoy thrilling battles and rousing adventures. Maurice Sendak's witty, otherworldly illustrations cast a magical spell over this traditional tale. Ralph Manheim, the highly praised translator of the Grimms' fairy tales, has captured the authentic voice of the original German tale.

**For those also seeking**: models for identity
**For those drawn to**: setting, story
**Themes/subjects**: toy figures, Christmas, royalty, kings/queens, princesses, clockwork and mechanical figures, toymakers, mice, battle/wars, growing up (apprehension), anxiety/fears, repression (psychology), beauty/ugliness, rituals and traditions, candy/chocolate
**Reading interest level**: grades 2–6
**Curricular tie-ins**: The novel could be used as a resource for a lesson about seasonal holidays around the world. Students could listen to the music from Tchaikovsky's ballet while creating their own nutcrackers.
**Adaptations & alternative formats**: movie directed by Carroll Ballard (based on the Maurice Sendak-Kent Stowell stage production, 1986); audiobook read by BBC full cast (2015); Tchaikovsky's *The Nutcracker and the Mouse King* ballet (1892)
**Translations**: Spanish: *Cascanueces*; French: *Le Casse-Noisette*
**Read-alikes**: Sherri L. Smith's *The Toymaker's Apprentice* is an imagined backstory to the novel. Lynne Reid Banks's *The Indian in the Cupboard* and Elizabeth Winthrop's *The Castle in the Attic* are also about the adventures and battles of toy figures. L. Frank Baum's *The Life and Adventures of Santa Claus* is another Christmas story. Eleanor Estes's *The Witch Family* is also about another seven-year-old girl who imagines a world that she then enters.

**Milne, A. A.** (1882–1956)
**Winnie-the-Pooh** (1926). Illustrated by Ernest H. Shepard. New York: Puffin Books, 2005. 161pp. 978-1415643716.

Based on the real-life experiences of Milne's son Christopher and his beloved teddy bear, *Winnie-the-Pooh* is a timeless fantasy story about a young boy and his toy animals. Winnie-the-Pooh, Owl, Eeyore the donkey,

Piglet, Kanga, and his son Roo face a host of adventures in the Hundred Acre Wood. What distinguishes *Winnie-the-Pooh* is the humorous and insightful portrayal of the foibles and anxieties of the animal characters.

Milne also skillfully captures the feelings of children on the verge of reading and writing. Christopher Robin and his child-like animals have not quite mastered these skills and are defensive about them. Pooh Bear tells Owl that his writing is "Wobbly. It's good spelling but it Wobbles, and the letters get in the wrong places." And Eeyore thinks, "This writing business. Pencils and whatnot. Over-rated, if you ask me. Silly stuff. Nothing in it." Young readers who feel anxious about the thought of school will find reassurance and humorous relief in *Winnie-the-Pooh*. Editions of the novel with the original whimsical illustrations by Ernest H. Shepard are still readily available.

**For those also seeking**: acceptance
**For those drawn to**: characters
**Themes/subjects**: toy animals, literacy/illiteracy, forests, projection (psychology), growing up (apprehension), anxiety/fears, tolerance, humor, bears, rabbits, owls, pigs, lions and tigers
**Reading interest level**: preschool–grade 3
**Curricular tie-ins**: Read the book aloud to the class and then show them the Disney movie. Ask students which one they like better and why.
**Adaptations & alternative formats**: Walt Disney movie directed by Stephen J. Anderson and Don Hall (2011); audiobook read by Peter Dennis (2004)
**Translations**: Spanish: *Winny de Puh*; French: *La Visite de Winnie l'Ourson*
**Read-alikes**: The characters in *Winnie-the-Pooh* appear in a sequel novel, *The House at Pooh Corner*, and two books of poetry—*When We Were Very Young* and *Now We Are Six*. Marjorie Williams's *The Velveteen Rabbit* is a story about a boy and his stuffed animal while Emily Jenkins's *Toys Go Out* is humorous story about the lives of toys.

**Milne, A. A.** (1882–1956)
**The House at Pooh Corner** (1928). Illustrated by Ernest H. Shepard. New York: Puffin Books, 1992. 180pp. 978-0140361223.

Although *The House at Pooh Corner* is a sequel to *Winnie-the-Pooh*, it can also be read as a stand-alone book. In this second novel, Milne introduces Tigger, the irrepressibly bouncy toy animal. The characters face new challenges and adventures such as losing a home, getting stuck in a tree, falling into an animal trap, getting lost in the forest, and nearly drowning. Christopher Robin plays a greater role in this book as the guide and protector of the animals. On the threshold between the carefree world of preschoolers and the more serious world of education, Christopher Robin warns Pooh, "I'm not going to do Nothing any more . . . Well not much. They don't let you."

Like *Winnie-the-Pooh*, *The House at Pooh Corner* is a humorous, character-driven book. It skillfully portrays the emotions, thoughts, and concerns of the child-like animals. Children who are apprehensive about starting school, or feel intimidated by older siblings' knowledge will feel less daunted and more reassured after reading *The House at Pooh Corner*.

**For those also seeking**: acceptance
**For those drawn to**: characters
**Themes/subjects**: toy animals, literacy/illiteracy, forests, friendship, projection (psychology), anxiety/fears, growing up (apprehension), lions and tigers, tolerance, humor, bears, rabbits, owls, pigs, lions and tigers
**Reading interest level**: preschool–grade 3
**Curricular tie-ins**: Ask students to create a billboard of the Hundred Acre Wood and the animals' homes within it as an advertisement for the novel.
**Adaptations & alternative formats**: audiobook read by Peter Dennis (2005)
**Translations**: Spanish: *El Rincon De Puh*; French: *Une Maison pour Hi-han*
**Read-alikes**: The characters in *The House at Pooh Corner* also appear in *Winnie-the-Pooh* and two books of poetry—*When We Were Very Young* and *Now We Are Six*. Kenneth Grahame's *The Wind in the Willows* also explores the amusing adventures of young animal friends.

**Raskin, Ellen** (1928–1984)
**The Westing Game** (1978). New York: Puffin Books, 2004. 182pp. 978-0142401200.

Preselected individuals are sent letters promoting affordable apartments in a luxury building called Sunset Towers. After touring the building, each of the individuals decides to move in. One day, tenants see smoke wafting out of the nearby Westing mansion. But the doorman tells the tenants that this mansion has been deserted for years and that Sam Westing is rumored to be dead. Some of the tenants believe that Westing's corpse is in the house. Thirteen-year-old Turtle enters the mansion on a dare and does indeed find the corpse of Mr. Sam Westing. Then all but two of the new tenants are sent letters identifying them as heirs and asking them to attend a meeting at the mansion. According to the executor of the will, Mr. Westing, before he died, suspected that one of his sixteen heirs would murder him. The job of these heirs is to find who among them is the murderer. The 16 people are divided into eight pairs, and each one is given $10,000 and a set of clues to the murderer's identity. The winner will receive 200 million dollars.

Sam Westing, "dedicated gamesman and master of chess," creates the ultimate game by pairing together strangers in order to find the murderer. In his will, Westing warns that the game will not be easy: "Some are not who they say they are, and some are not who they seem to be." The tension created by the game drives the heirs to steal from one another and even set off bombs. Greed, cruelty, and prejudice cause bitter rivalry both within and between the pairs. The novel will appeal to readers who enjoy deciphering clues and solving mysteries.

Playing the game forces characters to work with others, an activity that eventually brings them together in a variety of unexpected ways. The changed outlooks and new friendships that emerge will reassure readers that positive outcomes can emerge from unlikely sources. According to a poll in *School Library Journal*, this Newbery Medal winner still remains a highly popular book today.

**For those also seeking**: awakening/new perspectives/enlargement of possibilities
**For those drawn to**: story
**Themes/subjects**: mystery/suspense, appearance versus reality, clues/riddles, games, secrets, disguises, greed, class differences, prejudice, disability, mansions, murder, critical thinking/strategy
**Reading interest level**: grades 6–8
**Curricular tie-ins**: One of the biggest mysteries in the novel is the character of Sam Westing. In small groups, students can create a script for a talk show interview. The audience will especially want answers to the following questions: What do we know about his character? What motivated him to create such a strange game?
**Adaptations & alternative formats**: movie directed by Terence H. Winkless (1997); audiobook read by Eric Michael Summerer (2007)
**Read-alikes**: Readers who enjoy solving clues will also like Avi's *Midnight Magic*, Susan Cooper's *Over Sea, Under Stone*, Trenton Lee Stewart's *The Mysterious Benedict Society*, and Chris Grabenstein's *Escape from Mr. Lemoncello's Library*.

**Williams, Margery** (1922–1944)
**The Velveteen Rabbit, Or, How Toys Become Real** (1922). Illustrations by William Nicholson. New York: Doubleday, 1991. 44pp. 978-0385077255. PD.

For "at least two hours" on Christmas morning, the Boy really loved his new velveteen rabbit. But in the commotion of the holiday, the rabbit is forgotten and then relegated to a toy cupboard. While sitting on a shelf, he learns from the wise old Skin Horse about love, belonging, and the nature of reality. When asked how a toy becomes real, the horse replies, "It doesn't happen all at once. You become." The Boy subsequently rediscovers the velveteen rabbit, becomes intensely attached to it, and engages in many delightful adventures with the toy before they are forced to separate.

Stripped of extraneous detail, the novel focuses on the essential and universal. Williams' insight into the workings of a young child's mind is another strong attraction of the novel. *The Velveteen Rabbit* will appeal to readers who have felt left out or forgotten by others. Even though the rabbit is left behind twice by the Boy, he does find happiness and fulfillment. Based on Williams's memories of her rabbit Fluffy and the experiences of her children, the book skillfully captures the emotions of preschoolers and still resonates with readers today. The gentle humor and simple wisdom of the story appeals to children looking for reassurance and guidance.

**For those also seeking**: acceptance
**For those drawn to**: character, language
**Themes/subjects**: toy animals, existentialism, love, friendship, illness, rabbits
**Reading interest level**: preschool–grade 3
**Curricular tie-ins**: Ask students to imagine the velveteen rabbit's life after joining the other rabbits, and draw a picture of his new life.
**Adaptations & alternative formats**: movie directed by Michael Landon Jr. (2009); audiobook read by Meryl Streep (2007)
**Translations**: Spanish: *El Conejo De Felpa*; French: *Le Lapin en Peluche*
**Read-alikes**: *Poor Cecco* is another novel about toys by Marjorie Williams. Like the velveteen rabbit, the china rabbit in Kate DiCamillo's *The Miraculous Journey of Edward Tulane* deteriorates physically as the story progresses. Carl Collodi's *Pinocchio* is another story of a toy that comes to life.

## Connection with Others/Awareness of Not Being Alone

**Carroll, Lewis** (1832–1898)
**Alice's Adventures in Wonderland** (1865). In *Alice's Adventures in Wonderland & Through the Looking-Glass*. Illustrated by John Tenniel. New York: Bantam, 1981. 223pp. 978-0553213454. PD.

While Alice is sitting outdoors with her sister one summer day, a rabbit runs by taking a watch out of its jacket. Surprised and curious, Alice jumps into a rabbit hole in pursuit of the animal. When she reaches the bottom, she finds herself in a long, low hall that contains a series of locked doors. Behind a curtain, she spies a beautiful garden that she longs to enter. Finding herself too large to get through the door, she tries to change her size with magical food and drink. After finding herself either too big or too small, she creates a plan for herself. "The first thing I've got to do," says Alice, "is to grow to my right size again; and the second thing is to find my way into that lovely garden." But, in dream-like fashion, her goal seems just beyond her reach as she encounters a series of ludicrous creatures and bizarre, nonsensical situations.

Alice's physical journey is an exploration of her inner landscape, particularly her buried thoughts and subconscious fears. "Down, down, down" she goes below the surface, both literally and psychologically. "I wonder how many miles I've fallen by this time?" Alice asks, "I must be getting somewhere near the centre of the earth." Deep within the recesses of her mind is her fear of the adult world. The rules of law in particular ("The Queen had only one way of settling all difficulties, great or small. 'Off with his head!' she said, without even looking round") appear arbitrary and capricious to a seven-year-old. The Queen of Hearts is a playing card, and the world she oversees is as unpredictable and driven by chance as the game she plays.

But by playing at adult roles such as looking after a baby and participating in a trial, Alice becomes less fearful and more confident. When the Queen of Hearts threatens to cut off her head, Alice is able to say, "Who cares for you? . . . You're nothing but a pack of cards!" Readers who fear growing up will not feel so isolated or unusual after reading Alice's story. John Tenniel's original illustrations evoke the strange eccentricity of Wonderland so well that they remain the most renowned ones in editions of the novel today.

**For those also seeking**: reassurance/comfort/confirmation of self-worth/strength
**For those drawn to**: setting, story
**Themes/subjects**: underground, identity, wordplay, malapropisms, language/communication, nonsense, identity formation, games, royalty, kings/queens, gardens/gardening, growing up (apprehension), anxiety/fears
**Reading interest level**: grades 2–6
**Curricular tie-ins**: Ask students to create a scrapbook that Alice might have produced after returning from Wonderland.
**Adaptations & alternative formats**: Disney movie directed by Clyde Geronimi, Wilfred Jackson, and Hamilton Luske (1951); audiobook read by Scarlett Johansson (2016)
**Translations**: Spanish: *Alicia en el País de las Maravillas*; French: *Alice au Pays des Merveilles*
**Read-alikes**: Readers who enjoyed this story will like the sequel, *Through the Looking-Glass*. L. Frank Baum's *The Emerald City of Oz* and *Dorothy and the Wizard in Oz* are also set in strange and highly unusual underworlds. Norton Juster's *The Phantom Tollbooth* is another novel filled with witty, literary nonsense.

**Collodi, Carlo** (1826–1890)
**Pinocchio** (1883). Translated from the Italian by E. Harden. London: Puffin Books, 2011. 255pp. 978-0141331645. PD.

Geppetto is amazed when the wooden marionette he carves springs to life. The mischievous Pinocchio runs away from home, spreads lies that lead to Geppetto's arrest, kills a talking cricket with a mallet, burns his feet by falling asleep next to a heater, and consorts with swindlers. As the novel progresses, Pinocchio's adventures become wilder and more dangerous. Readers who love thrill-seeking adventures will enjoy this book.

When the talking cricket asks Pinocchio what he wants to do with his life, the puppet replies, "To eat, drink, sleep, and amuse myself, and to lead a vagabond life from morning to night." Although the novel is ostensibly about the value of hard work, honesty, and obedience, what really resonates with readers is the way the well-intentioned protagonist repeatedly backslides and gets into trouble. Throughout the novel, Pinocchio tries to turn his life around, only to give in to temptation and ignore his good intentions. Those who feel alone in their unsuccessful efforts to change their bad habits

Toys/Games

will find comfort and relief in Pinocchio's story. Readers will relate to this engaging character who knows his weaknesses and ever so gradually conquers them. Although changing undesirable traits can seem unattainable, Pinocchio proves it is possible. A century later, Collodi's humorous voice and penetrating insight into human nature still continues to attract readers.

**For those also seeking**: courage to make a change
**For those drawn to**: character, story
**Themes/subjects**: puppets, prank tricks and mischief, identity formation, idleness, empathy, work (labor), father-son relationships, rebirth, runaway children, mistakes
**Reading interest level**: grades 3-6
**Curricular tie-ins**: Ask students to create paper cut-out puppets and a stage for them. They could also perform a puppet show.
**Adaptations & alternative formats**: movie directed by Norman Ferguson (a 70th anniversary edition of the 1940 Disney movie); audiobook read by Robin Field and Kathy Aughenbaugh (2012); award-winning graphic novel by Winshluss (1993)
**Translations**: Spanish: *Pinocchio*; French: *Pinocchio*
**Read-alikes**: Margery William's *Poor Cecco* is another novel about a toy who engages in exciting adventures. Like Pinocchio, the china rabbit in Kate DiCamillo's *The Miraculous Journey of Edward Tulane* learns humility and kindness through his adventures.


**Godden, Rumer** (1907–1998)
**The Doll's House** (1948). Illustrated by Tasha Tudor. New York: Puffin Books, 1976. 126pp. 978-0140309423.

When Charlotte and Emily Dane receive Tottie Plantagenet, the sisters find a toy family for the tiny wooden doll. At first, the Plantagenet family must live in two drafty shoe boxes. "It doesn't feel like home," complains Mr. Plantagenet. When a great-aunt dies, relatives give Charlotte and Emily their heirloom dollhouse but it needs renovations. After the sisters refurbish the dilapidated house, a haughty china doll unexpectedly moves in. This doll usurps the Plantagenets and threatens their existence, introducing the children to a more complex adult world.

Like children, the dolls are utterly dependent on the actions of others. When Mr. Plantagenet feels hopeless about the plight of his home, he complains, "What shall we do? What can we?" Tottie, the stalwart doll made from "good strong wood," does not give up but insists, "Wish! Wish! Wish!" Emily Dane becomes less timid and more assertive as she follows Tottie's example. By imagining the doll's feelings, the children begin to understand their own emotions and clarify their own values. Readers who feel isolated and alone because of their timidity or shyness will feel relieved to know that they are not alone.

Tasha Tudor's depiction of the Victorian-looking dolls lends an old-world charm to the novel. The ingenious dollhouse setting is an additional appeal for readers who are attracted to miniatures.

**For those also seeking**: courage to make a change
**For those drawn to**: character, setting
**Themes/subjects**: dolls, dollhouses, homelessness, assertiveness, agency and powerlessness, family, shyness, wishes and wishing
**Reading interest level**: grades 2–5
**Curricular tie-ins**: Students could create a cardboard dollhouse or a home for toy animals.
**Translations**: French: *La Maison de Poupée*
**Read-alikes**: Readers will also enjoy Rumer Godden's other books about dolls: *Miss Happiness and Miss Flower*, *Little Plum*, and *The Fairy Doll & Other Tales from the Dolls' House*. Frances Hodgson Burnett's *Racketty Packetty House* is another tale about dolls and dollhouses.

**Godden, Rumer** (1907–1998)
**Miss Happiness and Miss Flower** (1961). London: Macmillan Children's Books, 2015. 128pp. 978-1447292746.

Like Mary Lennox in *The Secret Garden*, eight-year-old Nona Fells leaves behind her family, home, and country when she moves from India to England. Nona's aunt, uncle, and three cousins do not understand why she is so quiet, reserved, and sad. But Nona's spirits lift after a great aunt sends the Fells two Japanese dolls. Like Nona, the dolls are also anxious about moving countries. "No one will understand us or know what we want," complains Miss Flower to Miss Happiness. Nona learns to adapt to her new situation by creating a Japanese dollhouse for the dolls.

By imagining the emotions and thoughts of the displaced dolls, Nona learns to cope with her homesickness. Readers who have moved houses, experienced loneliness, or felt powerless in a situation will find inspiration and strength in Nona's example. Reading this story will help them recognize that others have also felt sadness and loneliness and have managed through such a difficult experience.

Nona's clever construction of a dollhouse and furnishings using such objects as a pencil case for a closet and a thimble for a vase will appeal to readers who enjoy such ingenuity. As Nona learns about Japanese customs and traditions, so too does the reader.

**For those also seeking**: disinterested understanding of the world
**For those drawn to**: character, setting
**Themes/subjects**: dolls, dollhouses, homesickness, loneliness, inventing/creating, agency and powerlessness, moving houses (relocating), Japanese social life and customs, cultural differences, honor, kindness, wishes and wishing
**Reading interest level**: grades 2–5
**Curricular tie-ins**: When studying communities around the world, students can read about the Japanese star festival. They can imitate Nona by creating a tree of wishes to celebrate the occasion.
**Read-alikes**: The story of *Miss Happiness and Miss Plum* is continued in *Little Plum*. Readers of these two novels will enjoy Godden's other doll stories: *The Doll's House* and *The Fairy Doll & Other Tales from the Dolls' House*. Frances Hodgson Burnett's *The Secret Garden* is a story about a girl who also finds it difficult to move from India to England.

## Courage to Make a Change

**Winthrop, Elizabeth** (1979–)
**The Castle in the Attic** (1985). New York: Yearling, 1994. 179pp. 978-0440409410.

When Mrs. Phillips—the housekeeper who has looked after 10-year-old William since his birth—announces that she is retiring and moving to England, the boy is deeply upset. Before she leaves, Mrs. Phillips presents William with a stone-and-wooden toy castle. After bringing the sole inhabitant of the castle to life by simply holding him in his hand, William discovers that the silver knight owns a magic token that can miniaturize people. William uses it to reduce Mrs. Phillips to toy size so that she is unable to leave. Then he too becomes a miniature figure and accompanies the silver knight on a magical adventure in search of an evil wizard. William and the knight travel to a castle to rescue the kingdom from the wizard's spell.

In this fairy-tale quest story, William visits an enchanted world of knighthood, sorcery, and dragons. Through imaginative adventures, he discovers that he possesses the necessary skills and abilities to face challenges, and that he can do so without the aid of his beloved housekeeper. A child facing a major change in life will find William's story a source of strength and courage. Through William's example, readers can learn to let go of the past and move on to new challenges. A character-driven novel, *The Castle in the Attic* is also noteworthy for its exciting plot.

**For those also seeking**: models for identity
**For those drawn to**: character, story
**Themes/subjects**: castles, knights, toy figures, quests, independence, agency and powerlessness, identity formation, courage, nannies and caregivers, preoccupied parents, battle/wars, self-reliance, spells/curses, portals/thresholds
**Reading interest level**: grades 3–7
**Curricular tie-ins**: As part of a unit on medieval times, students can create a miniature castle.
**Adaptations & alternative formats**: audiobook read by the author and a full cast (1996)
**Read-alikes**: Lynne Reid Banks's *The Indian in the Cupboard* is another story about boys and their toy figures, while Louise Fitzhugh's *Harriet the Spy* is a novel about a child who must learn to let go of her caregiver.

## Acceptance

**Nesbit, Edith** (1858–1924)
**The Magic City** (1910). Radford, VA: Wilder Publications, 2010. 158pp. 978-1617200892. PD.

Philip, a 10-year-old boy raised by his half-sister Helen, discovers that she is engaged to a man named Peter Graham. Although Helen reassurances Philip that she will continue to care for him, he is still upset. "It won't be just the two of us any more," he tells her. When Helen leaves on her honeymoon, Philip moves into the family's new home with Peter Graham's daughter, Lucy. Philip does not get along with his new half-sister and is miserable under the care of her strict nurse.

Toys/Games 451

An imaginative boy, he copes by creating a miniature city out of toys and household items. Pillars made from candlesticks, steps from dominoes, fountains from silver and glass ashtrays, canals from silver paper strips, and domes from brass finger bowls magically transform into a real city in the moonlight. Characters walk right out of the pages of books used as building props. Philip undertakes seven dangerous tasks in this fantasy realm.

Inside the magic city, Philip meets fantasy versions of real-world characters and regains control over his life as he moves from victim to victor. Children facing unwanted changes in their lives will find encouragement in Philip's example. Although he cannot change the fact that his sister has married, he learns to accept the change by controlling what is within his power. Renowned writer of children's fantasy novels, Edith Nesbit skillfully blends waking and dream worlds as well as everyday reality and fantasy. Readers who enjoy quest adventures and enchanted realms will love *The Magic City*.

**For those also seeking**: awakening/new perspectives/enlargement of possibilities
**For those drawn to**: setting, character
**Themes/subjects**: imagination, stories and storytelling, toy figures, toy animals, agency and powerlessness, moving houses (relocating), displacement (psychology), battle/wars, challenging authority figures, stepparents, inventing/creating, half siblings, siblings and sibling issues
**Reading interest level**: grades 2-6
**Curricular tie-ins**: Ask students to draw a detailed map of the magic city.
**Translations**: Spanish: *La Ciudad Mágica*
**Read-alikes**: The characters in Mary Norton's *The Borrowers Aloft* also move into a miniature village. Bastian in *The NeverEnding City* deals with his real-world problems by facing fantasy versions of them first in Fantastica.

**Field, Rachel** (1894–1942)
**Hitty: Her First Hundred Years** (1929). Illustrated by Dorothy P. Lathrop. New York: Aladdin, 1998. 235pp. 978-0689822841.

Hitty, a 100-year-old doll who lives in an antique shop, recounts her exciting life in this memoir. Originally carved by an itinerant peddler for seven-year-old Phoebe Premble, this wooden doll outlives many of her owners. Surviving such dangers as being abandoned in a forest, shipwrecked on a whaling ship, dropped under a pew and forgotten in a church, idolized by natives on a desert island, seized by a snake charmer in Bombay, and abandoned by a missionary's daughter, Hitty suffers one catastrophe after another.

Carved from mountain ash, a wood associated with good luck, Hitty is a resilient and optimistic doll who is beloved by her many owners. Hitty's equipoise through her misfortunes makes her an inspiring character, especially for readers who have little control over the circumstances of their lives. As Hitty demonstrates, when change is not possible, readers can find peace by accepting the inevitable.

Winner of the Newbery Medal, this story will appeal to those who love fast-paced adventures. *Hitty: Her First Hundred Years* is also a historical novel, reflecting cultural changes from pioneer times to the early twentieth century—especially those changes that would interest a child. What is particularly unique about this historical novel is that it is narrated from the unusual perspective of a doll. The edition in print today includes the charming illustrations of Dorothy P. Lathrop. Friend of the author, Lathrop was with her when they found the antique doll who inspired this story.

**For those also seeking**: disinterested understanding of the world
**For those drawn to**: story
**Themes/subjects**: dolls, frontier and pioneer life, resilience, optimism, adaptation/adjusting to change, memoirs/diaries, Christianity
**Reading interest level**: grades 3–5
**Curricular tie-ins**: Ask students to create a collage of the frontier setting of the novel for a unit on pioneers.
**Translations**: French: *Hitty: Ses Cent Premières Années*
**Read-alikes**: *The Doll People* and its sequels (*The Meanest Doll in the World*, *The Runaway Dolls*, and *The Doll People Set Sail*) by Ann M. Martin and Laura Godwin are also books about dolls who survive in the world of humans.

## Note

1. Deborah Jaffé, *The History of Toys: From Spinning Tops to Robots* (Phoenix Mill, UK: Sutton, 2006), 18.

# Appendix

# Key Children's Literature Awards for Fiction in English

## INTERNATIONAL

### The Hans Christian Andersen Medal

"The Hans Christian Andersen Award is the highest international recognition given to an author and an illustrator of children's books. Every other year IBBY presents the Andersen Award to a living author and illustrator whose complete works have made a lasting contribution to children's literature.... The Award recipients are selected by a distinguished international jury of children's literature specialists."

## AMERICAN

### The Newbery Medal

"It is awarded annually by the Association for Library Service to Children, a division of the American Library Association, to the author of the most distinguished contribution to American literature for children."

### The Laura Ingalls Wilder Award

"Administered by the Association for Library Service to Children, a division of the American Library Association, the Laura Ingalls Wilder Award was first given to its namesake in 1954. The award, a bronze medal, honors an author or illustrator whose books, published in the United States, have made, over a period of years, a substantial and lasting contribution to literature for children."

### The Boston Globe–Horn Book Award

"Winners are selected in three categories: Picture Book, Fiction and Poetry, and Nonfiction. ... The winning titles must be published in the United States but they may be written or illustrated by citizens of any country. The awards are chosen by an independent panel of three judges who are annually appointed by the Editor of the Horn Book."

### The National Book Award

"Established in 1950, the National Book Award is an American literary prize administered by the National Book Foundation, a nonprofit organization. ... Each year, the Foundation selects a total of twenty Judges, including five in each of the four Award categories: Fiction, Nonfiction, Poetry, and Young People's Literature."

## BRITISH

### The Carnegie Medal

"The CILIP Carnegie Medal is awarded by children's librarians for an outstanding book written in English for children and young people."

### The Costa Book Award (formerly called "The Whitbread Award")

"The Costa Book Awards honour some of the most outstanding books of the year written by authors based in the UK and Ireland. There are five categories - First Novel, Novel, Biography, Poetry and Children's Book. ... Launched in 1971 as the Whitbread Literary Awards, they became the Whitbread Book Awards in 1985, with Costa taking over in 2006."

### The Guardian Children's Fiction Prize

"The Guardian Children's Fiction Prize or Guardian Award is a literary award that annually recognises one fiction book written for children or young adults (at least age eight) and published in the United Kingdom. It is conferred upon the author of the book by *The Guardian* newspaper."

## CANADIAN

### Governor General's Award for Children's Literature

"The Governor General's Literary Awards are presented in recognition of the best Anglophone and best Francophone book in each of seven categories [one of them being Young People's Literature]."

# Themes/Subjects Index

Abandoned children, 83–84, 118–119, 324–325, 366–367, 376–377, 395–396, 435–436
Abolitionism, 326–327
Abuse (emotional), 77–78, 79–80, 153–154, 159–161, 178–179, 302
Abuse (physical), 67–68, 77–78, 79–80, 159–161, 280–281, 281–282
Abused children, 67–68, 77–78, 106–107, 153–154, 159–161, 292–293, 302, 367–368, 376–377, 377–378
Accidents (major), 72–74, 75–76, 81–82, 86–87, 88–89, 102–103, 112–113, 185–186, 203–204, 303–304, 361–362, 394–395, 411–413, 436–437, 437–438
Actors/acting, 275–276, 381–382
Adaptation/adjusting to change, 72, 81–82, 93–94, 110–111, 111–112, 113–114, 114–116, 123–124, 151–152, 186–187, 203–204, 219–220, 220–221, 222–223, 233–234, 239–240, 281–282, 304–306, 307–309, 310–311, 320–321, 361–362, 363–364, 364–366, 367–368, 368–369, 369–371, 372–373, 375–376, 375–376, 376–377, 377–378, 380–381, 382–383, 385–386, 390–391, 394–395, 396–398, 410–411, 411–413, 413–414, 414–415, 434–435, 437–438, 451–452
Addiction, 119–120, 211–212, 307–308, 312–314, 424–426
Adoption, 80–81, 110–11, 340–342, 369–371, 435–436

Adventure, 56–57, 58–59, 62–63, 63–64, 67–68, 69–70, 70–71, 74–75, 75–76, 76–77, 79–80, 80–81, 86–87, 88–89, 98–99, 105–106, 120–122, 124–125, 127–128, 128–129, 133–134, 135–136, 137–138, 139–141, 141–142, 146–147, 147–148, 152–153, 157–158, 158–159, 162–163, 165–166, 166–168, 171–172, 181–182, 182–183, 183–185, 191–192, 220–221, 284–285, 286–287, 287–288, 290–292, 292–293, 321–322, 341–342, 363–364, 364–366, 373–375, 405–406, 408–409, 418–419, 423–424, 424–426
African American history, 79–80, 275–276, 277–279, 292–293, 293–294, 301–302
Agency and powerlessness, 91–93, 156–157, 168–169, 169–170, 203–204, 207–208, 208–210, 210–211, 220–221, 264–265, 290–292, 302–303, 316–318, 341–342, 347–348, 366–367, 376–77, 377–378, 429–430, 430–431, 434–435, 436–437, 447–448, 448–449, 449–450, 450–451
Aging elders, 275–276, 316–318, 403–404, 414–415, 415–416, 419–420
Aiding/helping, 58–59, 102–103, 126–127, 127–128, 277–279, 279–280, 281–282, 292–293, 302–303, 307–308, 321–322, 325–326, 368–369, 411–413, 424–426
Airplanes, 279–280, 307–308. *See also* Plane crashes
Alaska, 85–86

# 458                                                                                   Themes/Subjects Index

Alcohol/alcoholism, 79–80, 118–119, 122–123, 130–131, 280–281, 281–282, 295–297, 311–312, 377–378

Aliens (from space), 413–414, 422–423

Amazon region, 62–63

Ambition, 207–208, 248–249, 268–269, 289–290, 337–338, 371–372

American Civil War, 102–103, 326–327, 399–400

American Revolution, 310–311, 351–352, 352–353

Amulets, 175–177, 271–272

Ancient civilizations, 271–272, 289–290, 329–330

Angels/cherubs, 223–234, 269–270, 413–414, 414–415

Anger/hostility, 71–72, 86–87, 190, 203–204, 340–341, 377–388, 411–413, 423–424

Animal abuse, 99–100, 102–103, 104–105, 111–112, 116–117, 120–122, 130–131

Animal behavior, 411–413

Animal ethics, 126–127, 411–413

Animal instinct, 102–103

Animals in captivity, 136–137, 411–413

Animal testing/experiments, 411–413

Anxiety/fears, 72–74, 79–80, 80–81, 110–111, 111–112, 112–113, 114–116, 126–127, 138–139, 169–170, 171–172, 181–182, 229–230, 234–235, 263–264, 266–267, 267–268, 275–276, 292–293, 294–295, 295–297, 301–302, 306–307, 311–312, 321–322, 352–353, 366–367, 377–378, 407–408, 409–410, 413–414, 418–419, 420–422, 436–437, 438–439, 439–440, 440–441, 441–442, 445–446

Appearance (physical), 188–189, 217–218, 353–354, 411–413, 437–438

Appearance versus reality, 164–165, 204–205, 215–216, 216–217, 250–251, 252–253, 254–255, 256–257, 264–265, 336–337, 368–369, 377–378, 381–382, 432, 444

Apprentices, 207–208, 264–265, 280–281, 302–303, 310–311

Arctic, 85–86, 88–89, 90–91

Art (as coping mechanism), 123–124, 285–286, 295–297, 373–375, 379–380, 384–385, 390–391, 392–393, 393–394, 396–398

Arthurian legends, 340–341, 346–347, 348–349, 350–351, 355–356

Assertiveness, 312–314, 447–448

Atomic bombing (Japan), 86–87

Authoritarian figures, 159–161, 208–210, 223–224, 231–232, 268–269, 269–270, 308–309, 316–318, 351–352, 371–372, 372–373, 383–384. *See also* Challenging authority figures

Authoritarian rule, 282–283, 321–322, 332–334

Automobile industry (American), 279–280, 292–293, 293–294

Babies, 97–98, 114–116, 302–303, 379–380, 415–416. *See also* Birth

Badgers, 96–97, 119–120

Balloons (hot-air), 75–76, 226–227

Bats, 104–105, 107–109, 112–113, 151–152

Battles/wars, 65–66, 89–90, 96–97, 98–99, 104–105, 113–114, 155–156, 157–158, 165–166, 212–214, 216–217, 224–225, 237–238, 253–254, 289–290, 290–292, 314–315, 326–327, 329–330, 343–344, 346–347, 354, 409–410, 422–423, 424–426

Bears, 93–94, 97–98, 110–111, 122–123, 268–269, 318–319, 330–331, 440–441, 441–442

Beauty/ugliness, 188–189, 190, 304–306, 411–413, 439–440

Being different, 106–107, 107–109, 109–110, 110–111, 114–116, 124–125, 151–152, 159–161, 224–225, 225–226, 227–228, 229–230, 230–231, 231–232, 232–233, 233–234, 249–250, 253–254, 254–255, 255–256, 256–257, 257–258, 258–259, 261–262, 263–264, 284–285, 293–294, 304–306, 308–309, 340–341, 344–346, 372–373, 393–394, 411–413, 413–414, 415–416, 418–419, 420–422, 432, 433–34

## Themes/Subjects Index

Betrayal, 204–205, 211–212, 243–244, 264–265, 268–269, 306–307, 343–344, 376–377
Bible stories, 211–212, 212–214, 214–215, 215–216, 216–217, 237–238, 238–239, 314–315, 414–415
Bioethics, 411–413
Birds, 98–99, 129–130, 151–152, 190, 285–286, 379–380. *See also specific species*
Birth, 99–100, 302–303, 405–406, 424–426,
Blindness, 187–188, 319–320, 329–330, 388–390
Blizzards, 298–299, 299–300
Boats and ships, 62–63, 68–69, 69–70, 70–71, 79–80, 80–81, 93–94, 98–99, 207–208, 214–215, 232–234, 287–288, 308–309, 423–424
Body image, 104–105, 114–116, 137–138, 188–189, 236–237, 280–281, 302–303, 371–372, 372–373, 377–378, 383–384
Books, 159–161, 200–201, 201–202, 292–293, 295–297, 301–302, 304–306, 307–308, 375–376, 377–378, 388–390, 415–416, 420–422
Boredom, 71–72, 139–141, 148–149
Boston Tea Party, 310–311
Breeding/genetics, 408–409, 424–426
British history, 56–57, 191–192, 271–272, 312–314, 329–330
Brothers, 93–94, 102–103, 148–149, 162–163
Bullying, 60–61, 77–78, 91–92, 105–106, 137–138, 159–161, 215–216, 241–242, 245–247, 263–264, 280–281, 292–293, 293–294, 302–303, 307–308, 331–332, 377–378, 391–392, 392–393, 393–394, 396–398, 408–409, 413–414, 420–422
Buried/hidden treasure, 57–58, 61–62, 62–63, 65–66, 70–71, 74–75, 91–92, 147–148, 182–183, 208–210, 275–276, 286–287, 311–312, 312–314, 348–349, 423–424

California, 57–58, 303–304, 327–329, 366–367

Camping, 68–69, 74–75, 79–80, 122–123, 376–377, 393–394
Cancer, 276–277
Candy/chocolate, 173–174, 439–440
Capital punishment, 281–282, 286–287, 290–292
Captain Cook, 287–288
Castaways, 64–65, 81–82, 86–87, 93–94, 123–124, 128–129
Caste systems, 408–409, 424–426. *See also* Feudal systems
Castles, 106–107, 144–146, 146–147, 147–148, 158–159, 181–182, 201–202, 203–204, 206–207, 211–212, 212–214, 215–216, 216–217, 226–227, 235–236, 236–237, 243–244, 250–251, 259–260, 264–265, 336–337, 346–347, 354, 356–357, 386–387, 439–440, 450–451
Cats, 116–117, 118–119, 127–128, 234–235, 265–266, 303–304, 326–327, 329–330. *See also* Wild cats
Caves, 65–66, 81–82, 93–94, 112–113, 131–132, 144–146, 408–409
Cell biology, 413–414
Cemeteries/tombs, 56–57, 104–105, 179–180, 208–210
Censorship, 371–372, 415–416
Challenging authority figures, 75–76, 100–101, 103–104, 135–136, 156–157, 159–61, 186–187, 190, 223–234, 290–292, 322–323, 383–384, 388–390, 411–413, 450–451
Child labor exploitation, 302–303, 324–325, 411–413
Child neglect, 77–78, 79–80, 106–107, 118–119, 159–161, 203–204, 204–205, 264–265, 268–269, 290–292, 295–297, 302–303, 367–368, 375–376, 377–378, 381–382, 386–387, 388–390
Chinese Americans, 117–118
Chinese history, 323–324
Chinese social life and customs, 141–142
Christianity, 64–65, 93–94, 211–212, 212–214, 214–215, 215–216, 216–217, 223–224, 237–238, 238–239, 269–270, 280–281, 285–286, 290–292, 314–315, 329–330, 361–362, 379–380, 387–388, 388–390, 394–395, 419–420, 451–452

Christmas, 391–392, 435–436, 439–440
Churches, 275–276, 290–292
Circuses (animal), 67–68, 165–166, 323–324
Circuses (Roman), 289–290
Citizenship, 398–390
City life, 71–72, 77–78, 110–111, 117–118, 130–131, 152–153, 175–177, 396–398, 420–422. *See also* Urban versus rural living
Civilization, 64–65, 72–74, 81–82, 84–85, 93–94, 116–117, 119–120, 388–390, 423–424
Class differences, 63–64, 76–77, 98–99, 105–106, 119–120, 123–124, 155–156, 171–172, 173–174, 204–205, 260–261, 268–269, 275–276, 280–281, 281–282, 286–287, 302–303, 308–309, 310–311, 311–312, 327–329, 346–347, 356–357, 375–376, 377–378, 386–387, 390–391, 393–394, 420–424, 428–429, 442–443
Cliques (in school), 174–175, 263–264, 325–326, 371–372, 377–378, 383–384, 396–398, 420–422
Clockwork and mechanical figures, 168–169, 250–251, 254–255, 295–297, 422–423, 436–437, 439–440
Clues/riddles, 56–57, 182–183, 215–216, 242–243, 244–245, 247–248, 248–249, 340–341, 348–349, 350–351, 407–408, 409–410, 420–422, 442–443
College/college life, 382–383, 390–391
Colonial New England, 62–63, 304–306, 310–311
Colonialism, 63–64, 64–65, 65–66, 90–91, 93–94, 98–99, 287–288, 377–378, 409–410, 423–424, 424–426
Comets, 228–299, 432
Coming of age, 72–74, 78–79, 88–89, 90–91, 102–103, 105–106, 122–123, 155–156, 157–158, 158–159, 179–180, 208–210, 210–211, 265–266, 266–267, 267–268, 277–279, 279–280, 280–281, 287–288, 303–304, 325–326, 326–327, 343–344, 369–371, 371–372, 377–378, 382–384, 386–387, 387–388, 390–391, 408–409, 414–415, 420–422, 437–438

Commercialism, 382–383, 403–404, 411–413
Community, 102–103, 118–119, 122–123, 279–280, 299–300, 325–326, 367–368, 372–373, 388–390, 398–399, 399–400
Competition, 105–106, 126–127, 128–129, 244–245, 391–392, 408–409
Concentration camps, 282–283, 332–334
Conformity and nonconformity, 74–75, 84–85, 90–91, 106–107, 151–152, 157–158, 266–267, 304–306, 403–404, 404–405, 415–416
Consciousness, 411–413
Consumerism, 403–404, 410–411, 411–413, 417–418
Cooperation and teamwork, 98–99, 99–100, 104–105, 107–109, 113–114, 153–154, 161–162, 234–235, 256–257, 294–295, 297–298, 298–299, 319–320, 330–331, 336–337, 337–338, 343–344, 356–357, 403–404, 422–423
Cornwall, 348–349, 349–400
Corporeal punishment, 67–68, 76–77, 173–174, 277–279, 284–285, 398–399
Cottages, 373–375
Country life, 103–104, 105–106, 114–116, 118–119, 130–131, 163–164, 219–220, 279–280, 297–298, 298–299, 319–320, 325–326, 330–331, 388–390, 434–435
Courage, 62–63, 63–64, 65–66, 81–82, 88–89, 100–101, 102–103, 103–104, 104–105, 107–109, 112–113, 114–116, 116–117, 117–118, 123–124, 124–125, 138–139, 151–152, 153–154, 154–155, 157–158, 165–166, 181–189, 200–201, 201–202, 202–203, 224–225, 226–227, 229–230, 233–234, 248–249, 250–251, 252–253, 255–256, 256–257, 265–266, 266–267, 267–268, 282–283, 284–285, 289–290, 290–292, 302–303, 304–306, 306–307, 308–309, 310–311, 311–312, 321–322, 332–334, 336–337, 343–344, 348–349, 354, 367–368, 369–371, 386–387, 407–408, 408–409, 411–413, 418–419, 434–435, 449–450
Courtly love, 285–286, 346–347

*Themes/Subjects Index*

Courtship, 382–383, 385–386, 388–390, 399–400
Cowardice, 226, 308, 310, 419
Criminals/thieves, 57–58, 79–80, 99–100, 162–163, 200–201, 201–202, 202–203, 286–287, 241–242, 347–248
Critical thinking/strategy, 98–99, 104–105, 107–109, 112–113, 113–114, 133–134, 134–135, 171–172, 288–289, 306–307, 314–315, 329–330, 343–344, 405–406, 423–424, 424–426, 442–443
Cruelty, 63–64, 67–68, 91–92, 99–100, 130–131, 190, 208–210, 442–443
Crusades, 279–280, 285–286,
Crushes, 284–285, 285–286, 304–306, 386–387, 387–388, 393–394, 413–414, 414–415, 420–422
Cults/sects, 208–210
Cultural differences, 63–64, 64–65, 65–66, 81–82, 85–86, 86–87, 88–89, 89–90, 98–99, 113–114, 133–134, 135–136, 284–285, 287–288, 297–298, 304–306, 307–308, 314–315, 318–319, 322–323, 327–329, 405–407, 414–415, 448–449. *See also* Ethnocentrism
Cycles of abuse, 280–281, 281–282, 376–377, 377–378, 409–410

Dead or absent father, 60–61, 107–109, 142–143, 147–148, 289–290, 290–292, 295–297, 301–302, 306–307, 311–312, 312–314, 364–366, 366–367, 368–369, 372–373, 392–393, 418–419, 420–422
Dead or absent mother, 79–80, 118–119, 137–138, 142–144, 156–157, 171–172, 174–175, 292–293, 294–295, 361–362, 363–364, 366–367, 372–373, 386–387, 392–393, 395–396
Death, 80–81, 81–82, 97–98, 100–101, 102–103, 105–106, 111–112, 122–123, 125–126, 126–127, 129–130, 132–133, 179–180, 186–187, 201–202, 202–203, 210–211, 214–215, 216–217, 223–224, 238–239, 243–244, 245–247, 247–248, 248–249, 265–266, 266–267, 267–268, 276–277, 282–283, 289–290, 290–292, 293–294, 295–297, 301–302, 303–304, 310–311, 312–314, 318–319, 329–330, 332–334, 341–342, 363–364, 375–376, 377–378, 379–380, 383–384, 393–394, 394–395, 395–396, 400–401, 405–406, 408–409, 411–413, 414–415, 415–416, 419–420, 420–422, 423–424, 424–426
Deception, 100–101, 103–104, 188–189, 235–236, 256–257, 268–269, 281–282, 408–409. *See also* Lies/lying
Deer, 122–123, 129–130, 177–178
Dementia, 387–388
Denial (psychology), 203–204
Denmark, 321–322
Depression, 79–80, 210–211, 243–244, 290–292, 302–303, 303–304, 310–311, 318–319, 361–362, 373–375, 377–378, 384–385
Deserts, 91–92, 237–238, 250–251, 366–367, 404–405, 414–415
Despair, 211–212, 418–419, 423–424
Detectives, 162–163
Diplomacy, 104–105, 116–117
Disability, 109–110, 118–119, 122–123, 151–152, 185–186, 187–188, 222–223, 280–281, 289–290, 303–304, 310–311, 314–315, 316–318, 319–320, 361–362, 367–368, 375–376, 377–378, 383–384, 388–390, 391–392, 394–395, 399–400, 409–410, 415–416, 420–422, 442–443
Disability (of parent/guardian), 391–392
Diseases/viruses, 102–103
Disfigurement, 310–311
Disguises, 57–58, 79–80, 175–177, 206–207, 215–216, 216–217, 236–237, 241–242, 275–276, 281–282, 289–290, 329–330, 341–342, 347–348, 381–382, 424–426, 432, 442–443
Displacement (psychology), 290–292, 371–372, 372–373, 375–376, 381–382, 383–384, 394–395, 450–451
Divorce, 72–74, 118–119, 381–382
Dogs, 90–91, 98–99, 99–100, 102–103, 103–104, 105–106, 111–112, 118–119, 120–122, 127–128, 284–285, 301–302
Dogsledding, 90–91, 111–112, 120–122
Dollhouses, 428–429, 447–448, 448–449
Dolls, 261–262, 367–368, 428–429, 432, 434–444, 447–448, 448–449, 451–452
Dolphins, 81–82, 362–363

Domestic abuse, 280–281, 285–286
Donkeys, 216–217, 227–228
Dragons, 137–138, 141–142, 158–159, 161–162, 181–182, 210–211, 307–308, 406–407, 408–409, 422–423, 424–426
Dreams, 80–81, 90–91, 106–107, 113–114, 133–134, 136–137, 150–151, 169–170, 210–211, 245–247, 295–297, 302–303, 316–318, 371–372, 379–380, 386–387, 388–390, 411–413, 415–416, 429–430
Dutch Americans, 351–352
Duty, 102–103, 289–290, 314–315, 329–330, 371–372, 372–373, 383–384, 394–395
Dwarfs, 161–162, 182–183, 211–212, 216–217, 311–312
Dystopia, 411–413, 415–416

Earthquakes/volcanoes, 75–76, 112–113, 252–253, 307–308, 407–408
Eating disorders, 377–378
Ecosystems, 85–86, 132–133, 413–414
Education, 63–64, 71–72, 105–106, 133–134, 139–141, 177–179, 179–180, 207–208, 315–316, 354, 375–376, 377–378
Elderly, 148–149, 187–188
Eldest siblings, 71–72, 83–84, 102–103, 236–237
Elephants, 136–137
Empathy, 103–104, 106–107, 114–116, 123–124, 126–127, 130–131, 151–152, 155–156, 226–227, 249–250, 252–253, 282–283, 284–285, 293–294, 308–309, 321–322, 367–368, 368–369, 369–371, 375–376, 377–378, 379–380, 395–396, 446–447
England, 130–131, 175–177, 280–281, 285–286, 290–292, 302–303, 369–371
Environmentalism, 81–82, 85–86, 113–114, 126–127, 129–130, 303–304, 411–413, 423–424
Escape, 112–113, 290–292, 295–297, 321–322, 415–416
Ethnocentrism, 64–65, 307–308, 398–399, 405–407. *See also* Cultural differences

Etiquette and customs, 79–80, 156–157, 174–175, 281–282, 308–309
Evolution, 111–112, 379–380
Existentialism, 119–120, 123–124, 302–303, 385–386, 415–416, 423–424, 436–437, 444
Explorers, 75–76, 287–288, 407–408
Extended families, 114–116, 224–225, 235–236
Extrasensory perception, 113–114, 293–294, 371–372, 405–406, 409–410, 424–426. *See also* Telepathy

Factory work, 324–325. *See also* Work (labor)
Failure, 207–208, 287–288, 289–290, 336–337
Fairies, 150–151, 156–157, 181–182, 183–185, 217–218, 218–219, 271–272, 336–337, 343–344, 428–429
Fairy godmothers, 156–157, 185–186
Faith, 112–113, 113–114, 116–117, 301–302, 314–315, 318–319, 321–322, 327–329, 379–380, 386–387, 414–415. *See also* Faith and skepticism
Faith and skepticism, 144–146, 164–165, 211–212, 212–214, 214–215, 216–217, 223–224, 237–238, 238–239, 269–270, 342–343, 403–404, 409–410, 410–411, 414–415, 417–418, 418–419, 419–420
Falcons, 84–85
Family, 83–84, 97–98, 99–100, 110–111, 124–125, 135–136, 142–143, 173–174, 275–275, 276–277, 282–283, 284–285, 293–294, 294–295, 297–298, 298–299, 299–300, 301–302, 304–306, 315–316, 318–319, 319–320, 320–321, 321–322, 327–329, 330–331, 331–332, 332–334, 364–366, 368–369, 371–372, 386–387, 391–392, 399–400, 413–414, 432, 436–437, 447–448. *See also* Non-traditional families
Family conflict, 260–261, 293–294, 316–318, 340–341, 368–369, 381–382, 399–400, 414–415
Farm life, 102–103, 122–123, 126–127, 277–279, 297–298, 298–299, 301–302, 303–304, 330–331, 331–332

## Themes/Subjects Index

Fashion/costume, 281/282, 289–290, 304–306, 311–312, 369–371, 371–372, 390–391, 399–400
Fate/destiny, 91–92, 141–142, 201–202, 204–205, 236–237, 342–343, 343–344, 346–347, 354
Father–daughter relationships, 85–86, 118–119, 156–157, 158–157, 174–175, 200–201, 201–202, 265–266, 268–269, 277–279, 367–368
Father–son relationships, 56–57, 60–61, 79–80, 109–110, 112–113, 122–123, 137–138, 171–172, 275–276, 281–282, 293–294, 307–308, 340–341, 368–369, 436–437, 446–447
Favoritism, 387–388
Fears. *See* Anxiety/fears
Feelings/emotions, 415–416
Feminism, 80–81, 249–250, 254–255, 285–286, 371–372, 385–386, 399–400, 410–411
Feral children, 362–363
Feudalism, 280–281, 285–286, 290–292
Feudal systems, 277–279, 301–302, 306–307
Feuds, 79–80, 122–123, 234–235, 235–236, 275–276, 414–415
Film/film history, 295–297
Fish and sea animals, 81–82, 93–94, 97–98, 98–99, 387–388, 423–424
Fishing, 387–388
Fleas, 280–281, 285–286
Floods, 414–415
Flying magically, 151–152, 185–186, 191–192, 206–207, 217–218, 218–219, 259–260, 263–264
Food, 96–97, 102–103, 110–111, 111–112, 120–122, 122–123, 126–127, 153–154, 171–172, 173–174, 178–179, 280–281, 282–283, 292–293, 295–297, 321–322, 377–378, 406–407, 411–413, 420–422, 423–24
Food allergies, 420–422
Forests, 60–61, 72–74, 96–97, 100–101, 107–109, 114–116, 119–120, 122–123, 129–130, 132–133, 163–164, 177–178, 182–183, 238–239, 341–342, 347–348, 411–413, 435–436, 440–441, 441–442

Foster brothers, 354
Foster care, 292–293
Foxes, 97–98, 114–116, 128–129, 227–228
Freedom, 79–80, 260–261, 289–290, 329–330, 351–352, 408–409, 411–413, 415–416, 423–424, 424–426
Free will, 116–117, 268–269, 329–330, 409–410, 415–416, 418–419
Friendship, 60–61, 65–66, 66–67, 68–69, 76–77, 79–80, 86–87, 104–105, 112–113, 114–116, 117–118, 118–119, 119–120, 124–125, 126–127, 127–128, 128–129, 142–143, 151–152, 153–154, 161–162, 174–175, 207–208, 224–225, 226–227, 241–242, 243–244, 244–245, 245–247, 247–248, 248–249, 249–250, 255–256, 277–279, 281–282, 282–283, 289–290, 290–292, 293–294, 295–297, 304–306, 306–307, 308–309, 310–311, 311–312, 321–322, 329–330, 338–339, 341–342, 343–344, 347–348, 367–368, 369–371, 371–372, 372–373, 373–375, 375–376, 377–378, 379–380, 383–384, 385–386, 388–390, 393–394, 395–396, 398–399, 404–405, 418–419, 420–422, 438–439, 441–443, 444
Frontier and pioneer life, 57–58, 284–285, 294–295, 297–298, 298–299, 299–300, 315–316, 319–320, 320–321, 330–331, 331–332, 451–452

Gambling, 311–312, 322–323, 424–426,
Games, 114–116, 138–139, 361–362, 363–364, 394–395, 399–400, 408–409, 420–422, 429–430, 430–431, 432, 442–443, 445–446
Gangs and gangsters, 281–282, 311–312
Gardens/gardening, 148–149, 373–375, 445–446
Geese, 155–156
Gender roles, 157–158, 158–159, 280–281, 284–285, 285–286, 294–295, 304–306, 308–309, 310–311, 312–314, 322–323, 325–326, 329–330, 372–373, 386–387, 387–388, 393–394, 414–415
Genies, 161–162, 175–177, 206–207

Geography, 423–424
Geology, 174–175, 410–411, 419–420
Ghosts, 62–63, 148–149, 166–168, 179–180, 275–276, 286–287
Giants, 133–134, 215–216, 257–258, 422–423
Gifted children, 159–161, 175–177, 377–378, 413–414, 415–416
Glaciers, 266–267
Gladiators, 329–330
Gnomes, 188–189, 250–251, 254–255, 403–404, 410–411, 417–418
Goblins, 144–146, 182–183, 230–231
Gods, 107–109, 112–113, 113–114, 264–265, 342–343, 349–350
Gold Rush, 57–58, 120–122
Good and evil, 104–105, 106–107, 107–109, 112–113, 113–114, 116–117, 120–122, 133–134, 135–136, 144–146, 164–165, 186–187, 187–188, 248–249, 253–254, 311–312, 314–315, 340–341, 344–346, 348–349, 349–350, 350–351, 409–410, 413–414, 414–415, 418–419, 422–423
Gossip, 245–247, 279–280, 302–303, 325–326, 371–372, 372–373
Governesses, 63–64, 163–164. *See also* Nannies and caregivers
Grandfathers, 187–188, 292–293, 368–370
Grandmothers, 83–84, 144–146, 150–151, 178–179, 186–187, 277–279, 279–280, 293–294, 318–319, 325–326, 327–329, 332–334, 377–378
Grandparents, 80–81, 173–174, 387–388, 388–390, 395–396, 432
Gratitude, 141–142, 368–369
Great Depression (United States), 277–279, 279–280, 303–304, 325–326, 327–329
Greed, 57–58, 70–71, 75–76, 79–80, 96–97, 99–100, 116–117, 120–122, 141–142, 159–161, 171–172, 173–174, 182–183, 219–220, 260–261, 409–410, 442–443
Grief, 102–103, 106–107, 112–113, 122–123, 129–130, 150–151, 153–154, 186–187, 243–244, 276–277, 285–286, 290–292, 292–293, 293–294, 295–297, 301–302, 303–304, 316–318, 366–367, 369–371, 375–377, 379–380, 393–394, 394–395, 395–396, 398–399, 399–400, 420–422, 423–424. *See also* Pain/suffering
Growing up (apprehension), 183–185, 380–381, 429–431, 439–440, 440–441, 441–442, 445–446
Guilt, 112–113, 207–208, 208–210, 211–212, 266–267, 285–286, 286–287, 290–292, 295–297, 303–304, 306–307, 308–309, 311–312, 316–318
Guns, 79–80, 102–103, 129–130, 190, 277–279, 279–280, 301–302, 325–326

Half siblings, 74–75, 450–451
Hatred, 175–177, 247–248, 314–315, 423–424
Haunted houses, 204–206, 275–276, 316–318
Heroines, 133–134, 159–161, 302–303, 304–306, 369–371, 371–372, 372–373, 383–384, 385–386, 386–387, 387–388, 390–391, 392–393, 394–395, 399–400, 418–419, 420–422
Heroism, 104–105, 106–107, 112–113, 186–187, 248–249, 311–312, 336–337, 337–338, 343–344, 346–347
Homelessness, 77–78, 83–84, 91–92, 151–152, 162–163, 295–297, 302–303, 347–348, 430–431, 434–435, 447–448
Homeschool, 379–380
Homesickness, 67–68, 114–116, 117–118, 123–124, 127–128, 174–175, 289–290, 294–295, 304–306, 316–318, 362–363, 388–390, 423–424, 430–431, 448–449
Homophobia, 332–334
Homosexuality, 332–334
Honor, 346–347, 354, 448–449
Hope, 106–107, 135–136, 173–174, 286–287, 302–303, 303–304, 377–378, 418–419, 430–431, 437–438
Horses, 102–103, 128–129, 130–131, 235–236, 237–238, 289–290, 310–311, 315–316, 329–330, 331–332
Hospitality, 99–100, 127–128
Human body, 411–413

*Themes/Subjects Index*

Humility, 308–309, 337–338, 338–339, 360–361, 367–368, 368–369, 446–447
Humor, 61–62, 71–72, 74–75, 75–76, 77–78, 79–80, 96–97, 98–99, 109–110, 110–111, 114–116, 116–117, 118–119, 119–120, 123–124, 124–125, 133–134, 135–136, 142–143, 143–144, 150–151, 159–161, 166–168, 169–170, 170–171, 173–173, 178–179, 190, 217–218, 218–219, 219–220, 220–221, 222–223, 229–230, 230–231, 231–232, 232–233, 233–234, 239–240, 260–261, 279–280, 281–282, 286–287, 292–293, 293–294, 311–312, 325–326, 354, 363–364, 373–375, 377–378, 379–380, 381–382, 385–386, 403–404, 410–411, 411–413, 420–422, 438–439, 440–441, 444
Hunger, 65–66, 72–73, 85–86, 88–89, 127–128, 173–174, 280–281, 281–282, 292–293, 295–297, 299–300, 302–303, 314–315, 377–378, 422–423, 430–431
Hunting, 85–86, 88–89, 90–91, 102–103, 105–106, 114–116, 122–123, 127–128, 129–130, 171–172, 190, 280–281, 289–290, 408–409, 423–424
Hurricanes/cyclones, 122–124, 226–227, 387–388
Hypocrisy, 79–80, 304–306, 423–424

Iceland, 406–407
Ice-skating, 233–234, 391–392
Identity, 71–72, 90–91, 157–158, 187–188, 257–258, 263–264, 266–267, 338–339, 415–416, 429–430, 431–432, 445–446
Identity formation, 123–124, 137–138, 151–152, 157–158, 174–175, 179–180, 187–188, 207–208, 208–210, 210–211, 230–231, 237–238, 263–264, 265–266, 266–267, 287–288, 289–290, 290–292, 302–303, 303–304, 329–330, 336–337, 337–338, 338–339, 343–344, 344–346, 380–381, 386–387, 396–398, 431–432, 445–446, 446–447, 449–450
Identity theory, 411–413
Idleness, 74–75, 168–170, 351–352, 446–447
Idleness and creativity, 114–116, 364–366

Illegitimate children, 290–292, 392–393
Illiteracy. *See* Literacy/illiteracy
Illness, 181–182, 276–277, 287–288, 297–298, 314–315, 318–319, 326–327, 327–329, 379–380, 399–400, 419–420, 443–444
Imagination, 114–116, 120–122, 134–135, 142–143, 144–146, 148–149, 173–174, 183–185, 200–201, 201–202, 202–203, 295–297, 302–303, 363–364, 364–366, 367–368, 369–371, 372–373, 378–379, 386–387, 393–394, 394–395, 413–414, 428–429, 432, 438–439, 450–451
(The) immigrant experience, 110–111, 117–118, 327–329
Immortality, 112–113, 132–133, 158–159, 201–202, 202–203, 210–211, 216–217, 223–224, 238–239, 241–242, 247–248, 248–249, 342–343, 432
Imposters, 58–59, 281–282
Imprisonment/entrapment, 91–92, 132–133, 165–166, 169–170, 208–210, 219–220, 220–221, 225–226, 239–340, 243–244, 250–251, 258–259, 260–261, 268–269, 362–363, 423–424, 430–431. *See also* Prison/incarceration
Inclusiveness, 224–225, 225–226, 227–228, 229–230, 230–231, 231–232, 232–233, 233–234, 249–250, 253–254, 254–255, 255–256, 256–257, 257–258, 258–259, 261–262, 428–429
Indentured servitude, 173–174, 408–409
Independence, 72–74, 83–84, 123–124, 142–143, 157–158, 179–180, 198–199, 219–220, 220–221, 222–223, 230–231, 233–234, 239–240, 260–261, 290–292, 320–321, 331–332, 351–352, 381–382, 399–400, 434–435, 449–500
Indigenous peoples, 99–100, 287–288, 409–410, 419–420
Indigenous peoples (Africa), 65–66
Indigenous peoples (Brazil), 63–64
Indigenous peoples (Britain), 289–290
Indigenous peoples (Canada), 88–89, 111–112, 127–128
Indigenous peoples (South Pacific), 64–65, 81–82

Indigenous peoples (United States), 86–87, 90–91, 284–285, 297–298, 318–319
Industrialization, 119–120, 130–131, 324–325
Inheritance and succession, 155–156, 158–159, 185–186, 212–214, 329–330, 368–369, 386–387
Injustice. *See* Justice and injustice
Inns/taverns, 56–57, 70–71, 166–168, 168–169, 188–189, 286–287, 290–292, 311–312
Insects, 117–118, 153–154
Insiders/outsiders, 74–75, 157–158, 275–276, 304–306, 325–326, 326–327, 341–342, 347–348, 377–378
Intellectual property, 173–174, 411–413
Intelligence, 107–109, 226–227, 227–228, 249–250, 413–414
Interconnectedness, 126–127, 132–133, 409–410
Inuit, 85–86, 88–89, 90–91
Inventing/creating, 75–76, 77–78, 84–85, 88–89, 93–94, 142–143, 171–172, 220–221, 222–223, 295–297, 371–372, 435–436, 448–449, 450–451. *See also* Idleness and creativity
Invisibility cloaks and rings, 146–147, 182–183, 241–242, 248–249
Irish history, 329–330
Islands, 61–62, 65–66, 68–69, 70–71, 75–76, 81–82, 86–87, 93–94, 128–129, 183–185, 207–208, 214–215, 224–225, 225–226, 231–232, 258–259
Italian Americans, 118–119
Italian Renaissance, 71–72
Italian social life and customs, 234–235

Japanese Americans, 275–276
Japanese history, 306–307
Japanese social life and customs, 86–87, 448–449
Jazz, 292–293. *See also* Music
Jealousy, 104–105, 188–189, 200–201, 202–203, 356–357, 386–387, 387–389, 420–422
Jesus Christ, 314–315
Journeys, 65–66, 71–72, 75–76, 79–80, 90–91, 99–100, 112–113, 120–122, 127–128, 140–141, 187–188, 227–228, 229–230, 230–231, 249–250, 252–253, 253–254, 254–255, 255–256, 256–257, 257–258, 258–259, 292–293, 343–344, 407–408, 409–410, 413–414, 417–418, 423–424, 430–431, 436–437, 437–438
Judaism, 280–281, 282–283, 314–315, 321–322, 332–334
Justice and injustice, 57–58, 62–63, 76–77, 91–92, 111–112, 155–156, 171–172, 173–174, 185–186, 241–242, 242–243, 243–244, 245–247, 263–264, 280–281, 281–282, 286–287, 290–292, 293–294, 306–307, 308–309, 310–311, 311–312, 323–324, 324–325, 327–329, 332–334, 341–342, 347–348, 423–424, 430–431, 436–437. *See also* Wrongfully accused

Kidnapping, 132–133, 150–151, 147–158, 200–201, 202–203, 206–207, 220–221, 256–257, 268–269, 348–349, 356–357
Kindness, 147–148, 281–282, 368–369, 376–277, 392–393, 420–422, 435–436, 448–449
Kings/queens, 133–134, 174–175, 188–189, 211–212, 212–214, 216–217, 250–251, 281–282, 329–330, 343–344, 429–430, 439–440, 445–446
Kites, 307–308, 322–323
Knights, 168–169, 214–215, 279–280, 280–281, 344–346, 346–347, 354, 429–430, 449–450
Knives/daggers/swords, 157–158, 248–249, 269–270, 290–292, 308–309, 329–330, 336–337, 346–347, 349–350, 354
Kublai Khan, 322–323

Language/communication, 61–62, 98–99, 113–114, 139–141, 152–153, 311–312, 362–363, 406–407, 411–413, 445–446
Laws, 111–112, 311–312, 424–426
Leadership, 104–105, 113–114, 153–154, 164–165, 225–226, 249–250, 253–254, 314–315, 403–404, 410–411
Letters, 114–116, 383–384, 388–390, 420–422

*Themes/Subjects Index* 467

Libraries/librarians, 118–119, 159–161, 200–201, 201–202, 259–260, 266–267, 290–292, 295–297
Lies/lying, 292–293, 295–297, 415–416, 424–426, 432
Lions and tigers, 211–212, 216–217, 226–227, 440–441, 441–442, 442–443. *See also* Wild cats
Literacy/illiteracy, 57–58, 78–79, 91–92, 122–123, 286–287, 290–292, 375–376, 388–390, 440–441, 441–442
London, 99–100, 110–111, 130–131, 133–134, 152–153, 175–177, 281–282, 286–287, 311–312, 312–314
Loneliness, 60–61, 72–74, 77–78, 81–82, 97–98, 111–112, 118–119, 122–123, 123–124, 138–139, 233–234, 290–292, 301–302, 302–303, 303–304, 304–306, 308–309, 310–311, 314–315, 342–343, 367–368, 369–371, 382–383, 383–384, 388–390, 415–416, 430–431, 432, 448–449
Love, 97–98, 99–100, 106–107, 109–110, 111–112, 112–113, 118–119, 120–122, 123–124, 126–127, 143–144, 156–157, 157–158, 158–159, 168–169, 170–171, 173–174, 177–178, 314–315, 326–327, 346–347, 376–377, 379–380, 382–383, 386–387, 392–3, 409–410, 413–414, 414–415, 418–419, 419–420, 437–438, 444. *See also* Courtly love
Low self-esteem, 79–80, 104–105, 106–107, 107–109, 280–281, 290–292, 295–297, 302–303, 377–379, 392–393, 418–419
Loyalty, 104–105, 124–125, 126–127, 127–128, 289–290, 306–307, 321–322, 346–347, 423–424
Luck/chance, 91–92, 123–124, 173–174, 187–188, 261–262

Madmen, 135–136, 173–174, 281–282, 420–422
Magic potions, 135–136, 173–174, 165–166, 178–179, 261–262
Magical transformations, 112–113, 135–136, 146–147, 153–154, 173–174, 177–178, 178–179, 186–187, 203–204, 206–207, 230–231, 235–236, 236–237, 243–244, 244–245, 249–250, 250–251, 257–258, 258–259, 259–260, 261–262, 282–283, 354–356, 405–407, 409–410, 413–414, 414–415, 418–419, 424–426
Magicians, 136–137, 175–177, 187–188, 204–205, 234–235, 235–236, 238–239, 261–262, 295–297, 354–356
Malapropisms, 98–99, 133–134, 429–430, 445–446
Manipulation, 306–307
Mansions, 204–205, 373–374, 442–443
Marriage, 282–283, 285–286, 382–383, 385–386, 386–387, 399–400
Math/numbers, 135–136, 139–141, 178–179
Matrilineality, 329–330
Mazes/labyrinths, 208–210, 244–245
Medicine, 302–303, 405–407, 419–420, 424–426
Memoirs/diaries, 231–232, 242–243, 285–286, 287–288, 377–378, 383–384, 386–387, 430–431, 451–452
Memory, 282–283, 316–318, 415–416
Mental illness, 83–84, 269–270, 281–282, 371–372, 383–384, 386–387
Mermaids, 97–98, 165–166, 183–185
Mexican Americans, 327–329
Mice, 100–101, 106–107, 117–118, 123–124, 124–125, 186–187, 214–215, 436–437, 439–440. *See also* Rats
Michelangelo, 71–72
Middle Ages, 106–107, 280–281, 285–286, 290–292, 302–303, 337–338, 341–342, 346–347, 347–348, 354–356
Middle children, 293–294, 393–394
Midwestern United States, 79–80, 275–276, 279–280, 284–285, 292–293, 293–294, 294–295, 297–298, 298–299, 299–300, 315–316, 319–320, 320–321, 325–326, 330–331
Migrant farm workers, 327–329
Mines/mining, 65–66, 144–146, 250–251, 253–254
Miniature beings, 219–220, 220–221, 222–223, 239–240, 260–261, 403–404, 410–411, 417–418

Miracles, 314–315
Misanthropes, 133–134, 190, 292–293, 302–303, 423–424
Miscarriage, 285–286, 395–396
Misopedists, 153–154, 159–161, 178–179, 186–187, 190
Missing persons, 57–58, 62–63, 65–66, 118–119, 133–134, 136–137, 150–151, 165–166, 200–201, 204–205, 254–255, 256–257, 265–266, 268–269, 281–282, 286–287, 290–292, 292–293, 293–294, 301–302, 302–303, 306–307, 307–308, 308–309, 311–312, 356–357, 367–368, 390–391, 392–393, 395–396, 418–419, 424–426
Mistakes, 67–68, 72–74, 110–111, 207–208, 208–210, 210–211, 211–212, 215–216, 399–400, 432–433, 446–447
Mob mentality, 79–80, 277–279, 284–285, 304–306
Modernization, 119–120, 130
Moles, 119–120
Money/debt, 62–63, 79–80, 98–99, 142–143, 281–282, 311–312, 319–320, 324–325, 363–364, 377–378, 399–400, 420–422
Monkeys/apes, 67–68, 86–87, 190, 216–217, 411–413
Monologues, 280–281
Moral dilemmas, 57–58, 74–75, 79–80, 96–97, 102–103, 103–104, 104–105, 114–116, 116–117, 122–123, 132–133, 171–172, 188–189, 238–239, 290–292, 306–307, 308–309, 316–318, 329–330, 346–347, 377–378, 411–413, 419–420
Mother–daughter relationships, 223–224, 277–279, 327–329, 395–396, 399–400, 420–422
Mother–son relationships, 269–270, 293–294, 306–307, 368–369
Mountains, 84–85, 141–142, 144–146, 174–175, 182–183, 314–315, 351–352, 388–389, 405–407
Moving houses (relocating), 138–139, 159–161, 163–164, 186–187, 219–220, 220–221, 222–223, 239–240, 275–276, 276–277, 297–298, 298–299, 319–320, 327–329, 363–364, 372–373, 375–376, 383–384, 388–389, 392–393, 403–404, 432, 448–449, 450–451
Multiple worlds/universes, 203–204, 204–205, 223–224, 238–239, 263–264, 264–265, 268–269, 269–270, 413–414, 418–419, 430–431, 432
Multiracialism, 326–327
Murder, 74–75, 179–180, 286–287, 290–292, 308–309, 415–416, 442–443
Museums, 71–72, 295–297, 391–392
Music, 106–107, 109–110, 117–118, 188–189, 284–285, 290–292, 292–293, 293–294, 299–300, 303–304, 362–363, 386–387, 399–400
Mysteries, 175–177, 200–201, 201–202, 202–203, 204–205, 241–242, 242–243, 243–244, 244–245, 245–247, 247–248, 248–249, 275–276, 286–287, 289–290, 290–292, 295–297, 311–312, 332–334, 348–349, 420–422, 442–443. *See also* Kidnapping; Missing persons
Mythological creatures, 161–162, 211–212, 212–214, 435–436
Mythology, 104–105, 107–109, 112–113, 113–114, 146–147, 211–212, 212–214, 289–290, 295–297, 340–341, 350–351, 354, 432. *See also* Welsh mythology

Names and naming, 207–208, 208–210, 290–292, 292–293, 301–302, 302–303, 413–414, 415–416
Nannies and caregivers, 152–153, 396–398, 449–450. *See also* Governesses
Narcissism, 119–120, 178–179, 203–204, 214–215, 437–438
Narcissistic parents, 79–80, 159–161, 264–265, 381–382, 392–393
Native American history, 318–319, 377–378
Natural disasters, 72–74, 81–82, 122–123, 123–124, 226–227, 232–233, 252–253, 254–255, 255–256, 387–388
Nature, 64–65, 81–82, 98–99, 114–116, 126–127, 129–130, 132–133, 219–220, 230–231, 231–232, 232–233, 233–234, 239–240, 318–319, 375–376, 388–390, 411–413

## Themes/Subjects Index

Nature versus nurture, 111–112
Neglect. *See* Child neglect
Netherlands, 391–392
New England, 58–59, 324–325, 387–388, 399–400. *See also* Colonial New England
New Orleans, 326–327
Newspapers, 310–311
New York City, 71–72, 77–78, 117–118, 124–125, 368–369, 396–398, 420–422
New York State history, 331–332, 351–352, 352–353
Nihilism, 413–414
1950s (United States), 276–277
Nonsense, 133–134, 135–136, 139–141, 429–430, 445–446
Non-traditional families, 83–84, 85–86, 88–89, 136–137, 162–163, 179–180, 362–363, 366–367, 376–377, 392–393, 432
Northern Canada, 72–74, 88–89
Northern settings, 72–74, 85–86, 88–89, 90–91, 111–112, 120–122, 127–128, 215–216, 237–238, 268–269
Nurturers, 56–57, 122–123, 126–127, 159–161, 171–172, 186–187, 281–282, 294–295, 307–308, 316–318, 396–398

Oaths, 314–315
Obedience, 156–157, 322–323
Obsessions, 56–57, 175–177, 247–248
Occupied countries, 289–290, 314–315, 321–322, 329–330, 332–334
Omens/prophecies, 107–109, 112–113, 161–162, 181–182, 187–188, 188–189, 206–207, 210–211, 223–224, 237–238, 243–244, 245–247, 247–248, 248–249, 266–267, 268–269, 269–270, 344–346, 409–410
Only children, 79–80, 114–116, 118–119, 122–123, 138–139, 142–143, 153–154, 171–172, 173–174, 200–201, 201–202, 202–203, 219–220, 220–221, 222–223, 224–225, 239–240, 259–260, 260–261, 292–293, 295–297, 306–307, 327–329, 367–368, 368–369, 369–371, 375–376, 388–390, 420–422, 428–429, 432,
Oppressive environments, 203–204, 204–205, 208–210, 234–235, 260–261, 263–264, 264–265, 290–292, 302–303, 316–318, 371–372, 372–373, 383–384, 430–431
Optimism, 224–225, 255–256, 369–371, 394–395, 428–429, 451–452
Orphans, 56–57, 57–58, 60–61, 62–63, 63–64, 67–68, 77–78, 79–80, 80–81, 88–89, 133–134, 136–137, 153–154, 157–158, 161–162, 162–163, 163–164, 166–168, 179–180, 185–186, 186–187, 203–204, 231–232, 241–242, 243–244, 263–264, 286–287, 290–292, 295–297, 302–303, 310–311, 312–314, 338–339, 366–367, 367–368, 369–371, 375–376, 376–377, 383–384, 388–390, 390–391, 408–409
Otherness, 110–111, 111–112, 124–125, 152–153, 275–276, 277–279, 284–285, 285–286
Outcasts/misfits, 56–57, 79–80, 151–152, 155–156, 157–158, 231–232, 266–267, 290–292, 302–303, 304–306, 326–327, 341–342, 347–348, 362–363, 377–378, 415–416, 430–431, 432–433
Outer space, 418–419, 422–423
Outlaws, 56–57, 57–58, 76–77, 200–201, 201–202, 202–203, 341–342, 347–348
Overprotective parents, 132–133, 144–146, 179–180, 219–220, 220–221, 239–240, 259–260, 260–261
Overweight children, 137–138
Owls, 100–101, 104–105, 129–130, 440–441, 441–442

Pain/suffering, 105–106, 106–107, 111–112, 112–113, 122–123, 123–124, 130, 153–154, 282–283, 285–286, 289–290, 290–292, 292–293, 293–294, 295–297, 303–304, 361–362, 367–368, 377–378, 379–380, 383–384, 387–388, 392–393, 393–394, 394–395, 415–416, 422–423, 423–424
Palaces, 133–134, 234–235
Paradox, 409–410, 413–414, 419–420
Parental disapproval, 141–142, 206–207, 219–220, 220–221, 222–223, 239–240, 260–261, 287–288, 373–375
Paris, 295–297

Peace, 422–423
Perseverance/determination, 71–72, 83–84, 89–90, 100–101, 103–104, 128–129, 158–159, 299–300, 315–316, 324–325, 371–372, 372–373, 377–378, 390–391
Phobias, 80–81, 181–182, 266–267, 314–315
Pigs, 126–127, 440–441, 441–442
Pirates, 61–62, 62–63, 70–71, 183–185
Plane crashes, 72–74, 404–405
Planetary travel, 403–404, 417–418, 418–419
Planets, 404–405
Plays, 306–307
Poisoning, 164–165, 268–269. *See also* Magic potions
Poland, 282–283, 332–334
Political corruption, 164–165, 175–177, 187–188, 202–203, 216–217, 223–224, 268–269, 269–270, 290–292, 341–342, 347–348
Politics, 89–90, 135–136, 175–177, 424–426
Porcupines, 100–101
Portals/thresholds, 138–139, 211–212, 212–214, 214–215, 215–216, 216–217, 238–239, 264–265, 265–266, 266–267, 267–268, 271–272, 282–283, 409–410, 413–414, 414–415, 418–419, 419–420, 430–431, 449–450
Poverty, 58–59, 79–80, 83–84, 91–93, 98–99, 102–103, 103–104, 105–106, 118–119, 122–123, 141–142, 155–156, 162–163, 171–172, 173–174, 219–220, 239–240, 276–277, 277–279, 279–280, 286–287, 290–292, 292–293, 293–294, 298–299, 301–302, 302–303, 303–304, 306–307, 311–312, 314–315, 322–323, 324–325, 325–326, 326–327, 327–329, 338–339, 366–367, 367–368, 377–378, 386–387, 391–392, 392–393, 434–435
Prairies, 294–295, 297–298, 298–299, 299–300, 319–320, 320–321. *See also* Frontier and pioneer life
Prank tricks and mischief, 74–75, 79–80, 96–97, 190, 279–280, 325–326, 352–353, 446–447

Predators, 96–97, 100–101, 111–112, 113–114, 127–128, 129–130
Pregnancy, 285–286, 302–303, 303–304, 414–415. *See also* Miscarriage
Prejudice, 109–110, 116–117, 174–175, 175–177, 242–243, 276–277, 280–281, 284–285, 293–294, 308–309, 321–322, 322–323, 327–329, 332–334, 442–443. *See also* Racism
Preoccupied parents, 118–119, 138–139, 204–205, 264–265, 364–366, 386–387, 420–422, 449–450
Presbyterianism, 369–371, 371–372, 383–384
Pride, 207–208, 310–311, 337–338, 383–384, 437–438
Primogeniture, 368–369, 386–387
Princes, 76–77, 156–157, 168–169, 170–171, 177–178, 185–186, 188–189, 210–211, 212–214, 224–225, 266–267, 337–338, 404–405
Princesses, 106–107, 143–144, 144–146, 155–156, 158–159, 164–165, 165–166, 170–171, 174–175, 177–178, 181–182, 225–226, 249–250, 256–257, 356–357, 428–429, 439–440
Prison/incarceration, 91–93, 119–120, 243–244, 286–287, 295–297, 301–302, 386–387. *See also* Imprisonment/entrapment
Privacy/surveillance, 415–416
Prohibition/temperance movements, 279–280, 325–326
Projection (psychology), 80–81, 247–248, 337–338, 371–372, 372–373, 381–382, 383–384, 387–388, 438–439, 440–441, 441–442
Prostitution/human trafficking, 408–409, 424–426
Puppets, 234–235, 306–307, 446–447
Puritans, 62–63, 304–306
Purpose in life, 90–91, 295–297, 404–405, 411–413, 415–416, 430–431, 435–436

Quarrels/fights, 163–164, 234–235, 235–236, 248–249, 295–297, 311–312, 386–387, 399–400, 411–413, 420–422
Quarries, 174–175

## Themes/Subjects Index

Quests, 104–105, 113–114, 136–137, 137–138, 141–142, 150–151, 158–159, 161–162, 170–171, 177–178, 181–182, 182–183, 210–211, 214–215, 215–216, 226–227, 237–238, 238–239, 248–249, 261–262, 289–290, 338–339, 340–341, 342–343, 344–346, 349–350, 350–351, 354–356, 385–386, 449–450

Rabbits, 113–114, 129–130, 437–438, 440–441, 441–442, 444
Raccoons, 105–106
Racial violence, 277–279, 282–283, 293–294, 301–302, 332–334
Racism, 57–58, 91–93, 242–243, 276–277, 277–279, 282–283, 284–285, 292–293, 293–294, 301–302, 321–322, 326–327, 327–329, 332–334, 377–378, 392–393. *See also* Prejudice
Railroads, 279–280, 292–293, 364–366
Rain/storms, 123–124
Rationing, 321–322
Rats, 104–105, 106–107, 116–117, 126–127
Rebellions/coups, 308–309, 310–311, 329–330
Rebelliousness, 74–75, 100–101, 341–342
Rebirth, 111–112, 126–127, 129–130, 216–217, 244–245, 446–447
Redheads, 142–143, 284–285, 369–371
Refugees, 89–90
Regression (psychology), 396–398
Rejection, 241–242, 382–383, 386–387, 420–422
Relativity, 413–414
Repression (psychology), 80–81, 429–430, 439–440
Reptiles, 91–93, 93–94, 242–243, 404–405, 413–414
Resilience, 72–74, 83–84, 118–119, 123–124, 151–152, 153–154, 156–157, 159–161, 186–187, 207–208, 208–210, 210–211, 224–225, 232–233, 233–234, 255–256, 289–290, 290–292, 292–293, 293–294, 366–367, 367–368, 375–376, 434–435, 451–452. *See also* Resourcefulness
Resistance, 277–279
Resistance movements, 321–322, 332–334

Resourcefulness, 60–61, 79–80, 83–84, 156–157, 279–280, 325–326, 377–378, 399–400, 434–435. *See also* Resilience
Responsibility, 102–103, 103–104, 105–106, 116–117, 117–118, 128–129, 369–370, 391–392
Revenge, 57–58, 81–82, 112–113, 143–144, 175–177, 179–180, 190, 203–204, 243–244, 311–312, 314–315, 329–330, 341–342, 396–398
Riots, 306–307. *See also* Rebellions/coups
Rituals and traditions, 282–283, 289–290, 304–306, 318–319, 327–329, 329–330, 330–331, 331–332, 349–350, 405–407, 414–415, 415–416, 419–420, 435–436, 439–440
River rats, 119–120
Road trips, 227–228, 293–294
Robots. *See* Clockwork and mechanical figures
Roman Empire, 289–290, 314–315, 329–330,
Romance, 56–57, 109–110, 143–144, 155–156, 156–157, 157–158, 158–159, 163–164, 174–175, 177–178, 181–182, 188–189, 201–202, 202–203, 206–207, 223–224, 236–237, 247–248, 265–266, 304–306, 310–311, 314–315, 315–316, 325–326, 329–330, 331–334, 342–343, 343–344, 346–347, 347–348, 352–353, 356–357, 371–372, 382–383, 385–386, 386–387, 390–391, 395–396, 399–400, 408–409, 410–411, 419–420, 424–426
Royalty, 76–77, 133–134, 143–144, 155–156, 164–165, 174–175, 185–186, 188–189, 211–212, 212–213, 216–217, 224–225, 225–226, 237–238, 250–251, 266–267, 343–344, 356–357, 368–369, 428–429, 429–430, 439–440, 445–446
Runaway children, 67–68, 71–72, 74–75, 76–77, 77–78, 79–80, 84–85, 85–86, 162–163, 287–288, 290–292, 292–293, 295–297, 302–303, 311–312, 366–367, 376–377, 446–447

Sacrifice, 112–113, 116–117, 143–144, 211–212, 223–224, 248–249, 281–282, 282–283, 314–315, 320–321, 329–330, 342–343, 419–420

Sailing, 64–65, 68–69, 69–70, 80–81. *See also* Sea voyage
San Francisco, 307–308
Santa Claus, 435–436
Satire, 79–80, 135–136, 281–282, 354–356
Scholars/professors, 362–363, 399–400, 407–408, 413–414, 423–424. *See also* Teachers
School, 105–106, 156–157, 176–177, 203–204, 207–208, 241–242, 242–243, 243–244, 244–245, 245–247, 247–248, 263–264, 264–265, 284–285, 301–302, 304–306, 325–326, 361–362, 367–368, 371–372, 377–378, 380–381, 383–384, 390–391, 395–396, 396–398, 398–399, 399–400, 413–414, 420–422. *See also* Education
Sea and seashore, 58–59, 97–98, 165–166, 214–215, 231–232, 232–233, 287–288, 348–349, 349–350, 422–423, 423–424
Seasons, 318–319, 330–331, 399–400. *See also* Rebirth
Sea voyage, 62–63, 69–70, 70–71, 80–81, 98–99, 128–129, 207–208, 210–211, 214–215, 224–225, 231–232, 232–233, 255–256, 287–288, 308–309, 423–424
Secrets, 58–59, 71–72, 72–73, 75–76, 103–104, 132–133, 148–149, 163–164, 171–172, 204–205, 235–236, 242–243, 248–249, 249–250, 275–276, 286–287, 290–292, 292–293, 295–297, 306–307, 310–311, 311–312, 312–314, 316–318, 321–322, 329–330, 332–334, 386–387, 407–408, 408–409, 424–425, 432–433, 442–443
Segregation, 277–279, 293–294, 301–302
Self-acceptance, 188–189, 411–413
Self-blame (psychology), 112–113, 207–208, 208–210, 266–267, 293–294, 295–297, 303–304, 306–307, 311–312, 316–318
Self-centeredness, 126–127, 250–251, 354, 419–420. *See also* Self-interest
Self-confidence, 100–101, 142–143, 181–182, 182–183, 188–189, 226–227, 236–237, 241–242, 259–260, 261–262, 290–292, 315–316, 320–321, 324–325, 349–350, 413–414. *See also* Low self-esteem
Self-interest, 116–117, 286–287, 306–307, 310–311, 424–425. *See also* Self-centeredness
Self-knowledge, 241–242, 257–258, 261–262, 269–270, 302–303, 411–413
Selflessness, 141–142, 326–327, 435–436. *See also* Sacrifice
Self-reliance, 68–69, 69–70, 72–74, 81–82, 84–85, 100–101, 105–106, 128–129, 129–130, 151–152, 201–202, 230–231, 265–266, 302–303, 315–316, 331–332, 396–398, 408–409, 434–435, 436–437, 449–450
Sensory perception, 413–414, 415–416
Servants, 166–168, 204–205. *See also* Slavery
Sexual awakening, 377–378, 386–387, 415–416
Shipwrecks, 64–65, 93–94, 98–99, 128–129
Shyness, 236–237, 266–267, 267–268, 320–321, 447–448
Siblings and sibling issues, 57–58, 71–72, 74–75, 102–103, 147–148, 218–219, 279–280, 293–294, 314–315, 318–319, 354–356, 361–362, 363–364, 364–366, 373–375, 380–381, 399–400, 413–414, 450–451
Single-parent dating, 373–375, 395–396, 420–422
Single-parent families, 58–59, 118–119, 363–364, 373–375, 381–382, 395–396, 420–422
Sisters, 181–182, 276–277, 297–298, 298–299, 299–300, 315–316, 319–320, 320–321, 330–331, 373–374, 386–387, 387–388, 399–400
Slavery, 79–80, 242–243, 289–290, 290–292, 304–306, 310–311, 314–315, 326–327, 329–330
"Sleeping Beauty" (story), 332–334
Sleepwalking, 378–380, 388–390
Smallpox, 318–319
Smugglers, 56–57

*Themes/Subjects Index*

Soldiers, 282–283, 289–290, 290–292, 310–311, 321–322, 326–327, 332–334, 373–374, 386–387, 387–388
Southern United States, 60–61, 102–103, 105–106, 118–119, 122–123, 276–277, 277–279, 293–294, 301–302
Space and time, 135–136, 419–420, 420–422
Spaceships, 417–418
Spells/curses, 143–144, 156–157, 186–187, 187–188, 203–204, 206–207, 225–226, 226–227, 234–235, 238–239, 244–245, 245–247, 247–248, 248–249, 249–250, 250–251, 258–259, 285–286, 449–450
Spiders, 126–127, 151–152. *See also* Insects
Spies and spying, 161–162, 187–188, 223–224, 235–236, 289–290, 290–292, 310–311, 396–398, 424–426
Spoiled children, 76–77, 173–174, 186–187, 214–215, 259–260
Sports, 241–242, 242–243, 243–244, 244–245, 245–246, 247–248, 248–249, 377–378
Sportsmanship, 105–106, 244–245, 289–290, 329–330
Squirrels, 129–130
Stealing, 57–58, 76–77, 91–93, 96–97, 99–100, 137–138, 162–163, 171–172, 175–177, 182–183, 264–265, 286–287, 287–288, 295–297, 311–312, 341–342, 347–348, 392–393
Stepparents, 156–157, 236–237, 294–295, 386–387, 450–451
Stepsisters, 156–157
Stores, 236–237, 403–404
Stories and storytelling, 80–81, 106–107, 113–114, 116–117, 123–124, 137–138, 141–142, 159–161, 168–169, 171–172, 173–174, 183–185, 186–187, 187–188, 200–201, 201–202, 202–203, 212–214, 217–218, 218–219, 259–260, 260–261, 271–272, 275–276, 307–308, 318–319, 332–334, 351–352, 367–368, 432, 437–438, 450–451. *See also* Books
Stowaways, 287–288

Struggling or disinterested students, 139–141, 234–235, 276–277, 287–288, 418–419
Subways. *See* Trains/subways
Sudan, 89–90
Summer vacations, 114–116, 146–147, 191–192, 373–375
Super powers (magical), 104–105, 159–161, 405–407
Superstitions, 62–63, 79–80, 166–168, 280–281, 285–286, 302–303, 304–306, 316–318, 322–323, 349–350, 352–353
Survival, 60–61, 64–65, 69–70, 72–74, 75–76, 77–78, 79–80, 81–82, 83–84, 85–86, 86–87, 88–89, 89–90, 90–91, 91–93, 93–94, 98–99, 100–101, 102–103, 104–105, 111–112, 112–113, 113–114, 123–124, 128–129, 200–201, 201–202, 202–203, 219–220, 229–230, 245–247, 247–248, 248–249, 252–253, 290–292, 295–297, 297–298, 301–302, 302–303, 306–307, 314–315, 321–322, 337–338, 403–404, 405–407, 410–411, 411–413, 415–416, 417–418, 423–424. *See also* Wilderness survival
Swans, 109–110
Sweden, 142–143
Swords. *See* Knives/daggers/swords

Teachers, 75–76, 159–161, 263–264, 315–316, 320–321, 352–353, 377–378, 398–399, 399–400, 413–414
Technology and civilization, 409–410, 411–413, 415–416, 417–418, 423–424
Telepathy, 174–175, 405–407. *See also* Extrasensory perception
Temptation, 211–212, 414–415
Terrorism, 293–294, 414–415
Tests, 409–410, 413–414
Time travel, 62–63, 147–148, 148–149, 191–192, 218–219, 271–272, 344–346, 350–351, 409–410, 414–415, 419–420, 420–422
Toads, 119–120
Tolerance, 133–134, 229–230, 231–232, 232–233, 234–235, 249–250, 253–254, 258–259, 261–262, 440–441, 441–442
Tornados, 64–65, 72–74

Toy animals, 437–438, 438–439, 440–441, 441–442, 444, 447–448, 450–451
Toy figures, 295–297, 439–440, 449–450, 450–451
Toymakers, 435–436, 439–440
Traditions. *See* Rituals and traditions
Trains/subways, 77–78, 117–118, 295–297, 299–300, 319–320
Translation/translators, 97–98, 307–308, 419–420
Trauma, 80–81, 266–267, 281–282, 282–283, 292–293, 293–294, 295–297, 303–304, 314–315, 316–318, 321–322, 332–334
Trust, 308–309
Truth, 256–257, 338–339
Tudor England, 281–282
Tutors, 174–175, 175–177, 203–204, 212–214, 264–265, 354–356
Twins, 63–64, 326–327, 376–377, 387–388, 414–415

Underground, 96–97, 100–101, 113–114, 117–118, 119–120, 208–210, 215–216, 223–224, 250–251, 252–253, 254–255, 266–267, 356–357, 407–408, 445–446
Underground Railroad, 275–276
Underwater exploration, 165–166, 225–226, 423–424
Unfairness. *See* Justice and injustice; Wrongfully accused
Unicorns, 216–217, 235–236, 409–410, 414–415
Urban versus rural living, 84–85, 117–118, 217–218, 298–299, 320–321
Utopian places, 68–69, 75–76, 216–217, 220–221, 239–240, 253, 346–347, 435–436

Valleys, 161–162, 163–164, 187–188, 352–353
Vanity and pompousness, 242–243, 254–255, 256–257, 337–338, 399–400
Venice, 162–163
Verbal abuse. *See* Abuse (emotional)
Village/small-town life, 56–57, 58–59, 74–75, 163–164, 166–168, 174–175, 326–327, 351–352, 352–353, 366–367

Wales, 316–318, 340–341, 350–351
War crimes, 282–283, 332–334
War (psychological effects), 60–61, 136–137, 289–290, 314–315, 316–318, 325–326
Washington State, 377–378
Water shortages (drinking), 89–90
Wealth, 65–66, 75–76, 171–172, 173–174, 217–218, 249–250, 254–255, 264–265, 327–329, 368–369, 371–372, 373–375, 383–384, 386–387. *See also* Buried/hidden treasure
Welsh mythology, 336–337, 337–338, 338–339, 340–341, 349–350, 350–351
White supremacists, 277–279
Wild cats, 97–98. *See also* Lions and tigers
Wilderness survival, 60–61, 64–65, 65–66, 72–74, 81–82, 84–85, 85–86, 88–89, 90–91, 93–94, 111–112, 120–122, 127–128, 129–130, 182–183, 297–298, 298–299, 319–320, 330–331
William Blake, 379–380
Winter, 85–86, 88–89, 90–91, 107–109, 211–212, 233–234, 268–269, 298–299, 299–300, 319–320, 391–392, 410–411, 434–435
Wishes and wishing, 146–147, 175–177, 185–186, 206–207, 217–218, 218–219, 271–272, 447–448, 448–449
Witches, 150–151, 158–159, 179–180, 186–187, 191–192, 203–204, 211–212, 215–216, 223–224, 226–227, 235–236, 236–237, 238–239, 259–260, 263–264, 268–269, 269–270, 338–339, 349–350
Witch hunting, 62–63, 191–192, 263–264, 304–306, 409–410
Wizards, 177–178, 182–183, 207–208, 210–211, 241–242, 242–243, 243–244, 244–245, 245–247, 247–248, 248–249, 252–253, 259–260, 264–265
Wolves, 85–86, 111–112, 120–121, 122–123, 182–183, 289–290, 297–298, 330–331
Women's history, 285–286, 302–303, 308–309

*Themes/Subjects Index*

Wordplay, 61–62, 135–136, 139–141, 143–144, 170–171, 173–174, 177–178, 241–242, 429–430, 436–437, 445–446
Work (labor), 304–306, 306–307, 315–316, 318–319, 320–321, 324–325, 327–329, 330–331, 331–332, 399–400, 420–422, 446–447
Workers' rights/unionization, 276–277, 277–278, 324–325, 327–329
World War I, 325–326
World War II, 211–212, 282–283, 316–317, 321–322, 332–334

Writing, 371–372, 372–373, 382–383, 385–386, 386–387, 390–391, 396–397, 399–400
Wrongfully accused, 57–58, 62–63, 79–80, 244–245, 245–246, 277–278, 286–287, 290–291, 304–305, 308–309, 420–421

Youngest sibling, 169–170, 331–332, 344–345, 380–381
Yukon Territory, 111–112, 120–121

# Author/Title Index

Adams, Richard: *Watership Down* (1972), 113–114
Alcott, Louisa May: *Little Women* (1868), 399–400
Alexander, Lloyd: *The Book of Three* (1964), 336–337; *The Black Cauldron* (1965), 337–338; *The Castle of Llyr* (1966), 356–357; *Taran Wanderer* (1968), 338–339; *The High King* (1968), 343–344
Alexie, Sherman: *The Absolutely True Diary of a Part-Time Indian* (2007), 377–378
Almond, David: *Skellig* (1998), 379–380
Armstrong, William H.: *Sounder* (1969), 301–302
Avi: *The True Confessions of Charlotte Doyle* (1990), 308–309; *Poppy* (1995), 100–101; *Crispin: The Cross of Lead* (2002), 290–292

Babbitt, Natalie: *Tuck Everlasting* (1975), 132–133
Bailey, Carolyn Sherwin: *Miss Hickory* (1946), 434–435
Ballantyne, R. M.: *The Coral Island* (1858), 64–65
Barrie, J. M.: *Peter and Wendy* (1911), 183–185
Baum, L. Frank: *The Wonderful Wizard of Oz* (1900), 226–227; *The Life and Death of Santa Claus* (1902), 435–436; *The Marvelous Land of Oz* (1904), 249–250; *Ozma of Oz* (1907), 250–51; *Dorothy and the Wizard in Oz* (1908), 252–253; *The Road to Oz* (1909), 227–228; *The Emerald City of Oz* (1910), 253–254; *The Patchwork Girl of Oz* (1913), 261–262; *Tik-Tok of Oz* (1914), 254–255; *The Scarecrow of Oz* (1915), 255–256; *Rinkitink in Oz* (1916), 224–225; *The Lost Princess of Oz* (1917), 256–257; *The Tin Woodman of Oz* (1918), 257–258; *The Magic of Oz* (1919), 258–259; *Glinda of Oz* (1920), 225–226
Bawden, Nina: *Carrie's War* (1973), 316–318.
Birdsall, Jeanne: *The Penderwicks: A Summer Tale of Four Sisters, Two Rabbits, and a Very Interesting Boy* (2005), 273–275
Bond, Michael: *A Bear Called Paddington* (1958), 110–111
Brink, Carol Ryrie: *Caddie Woodlawn* (1935), 284–285
Burnett, Frances Hodgson: *Little Lord Fauntleroy* (1886), 368–369; *A Little Princess* (1905), 367–368; *Racketty-Packetty House* (1906), 428–429; *The Secret Garden* (1911), 375–376
Burnford, Sheila: *The Incredible Journey* (1961), 127–128
Byars, Betsy: *The Midnight Fox* (1968), 114–116

Carroll, Lewis: *Alice in Wonderland* (1865), 445–446; *Through the Looking Glass* (1872), 429–430

Cleary, Beverly: *Ramona the Pest* (1968), 380–381
Collodi, Carlo: *Pinocchio* (1883), 446–447
Coolidge, Susan: *What Katy Did* (1872), 361–362
Cooper, Susan: *Over Sea, Under Stone* (1965), 348–349; *The Dark Is Rising* (1973), 344–346; *Greenwitch* (1974), 349–350; *The Grey King* (1975), 340–341; *Silver on the Tree* (1977), 350–351
Craik, Dinah Maria Mulock: *The Little Lame Prince* (1875), 185–186
Creech, Sharon: *Walk Two Moons* (1994), 395–396; *The Wanderer* (2000), 80–81; *Ruby Holler* (2002), 376–377
Curtis, Christopher Paul: *The Watsons Go to Birmingham—1963* (1995), 293–294; *Bud, Not Buddy* (1999), 292–293
Cushman, Karen: *Catherine, Called Birdy* (1994), 285–286; *The Midwife's Apprentice* (1995), 302–303

Dahl, Roald: *James and the Giant Peach* (1961), 153–154; *Charlie and the Chocolate Factory* (1964), 173–174; *Fantastic Mr. Fox* (1970), 96–97; *Charlie and the Great Glass Elevator* (1972), 135–136; *Danny, Champion of the World* (1975), 171–172; *The Twits* (1980), 190; *George's Marvellous Medicine* (1982), 178–179; *The BFG* (1982), 133–134; *The Witches* (1983), 186–187; *Matilda* (1988), 159–161
DiCamillo, Kate: *The Tale of Despereaux* (2003), 106–107; *Because of Winn-Dixie* (2004), 118–119; *The Miraculous Journey of Edward Tulane* (2006), 437–438; *The Magician's Elephant* (2009), 136–137
Dickinson, Peter: *Eva* (1988), 411–413; *The Ropemaker* (2001), 187–188
Dodge, Mary [Elizabeth] Mapes: *Hans Brinker, Or, the Silver Skates* (1865), 391–392
Du Bois, William Pène: *The Twenty–One Balloons* (1947), 75–76

Ende, Michael: *The Neverending Story* (1979), 137–138
Erdrich, Louise: *The Birchbark House* (1999), 318–319

Falkner, J. Meade: *Moonfleet* (1898), 56–57
Farley, Walter: *The Black Stallion* (1941), 128–129
Field, Rachel: *Hitty, Her First Hundred Years* (1929), 451–452
Fine, Anne: *Madame Doubtfire* (United States: Alias Madame Doubtfire) (1987), 381–382; *The Jamie and Angus Stories* (2002), 438–439
Fitzhugh, Louise: *Harriet the Spy* (1964), 396–398
Fleischman, Sid: *The Whipping Boy* (1987), 76–77; *The 13th Floor: A Ghost Story* (1995), 62–63; *Bandit's Moon* (1998), 57–58
Forbes, Esther: *Johnny Tremain* (1943), 310–311
Funke, Cornelia: *Dragon Rider* (1997), 161–162; *The Thief Lord* (2000), 162–163; *Inkheart* (2003), 200–201; *Inkspell* (2006), 201–202; *Inkdeath* (2008), 202–203

Gaiman, Neil: *Coraline* (2002), 138–139; *The Graveyard Book* (2008), 179–180
Garfield, Leon: *Smith* (1967), 286–287; *John Diamond* (United States: Footsteps) (1980), 311–312
George, Jean Craighead: *My Side of the Mountain* (1959), 84–85; *Julie of the Wolves* (1972), 85–86
Gipson, Fred: *Old Yeller* (1956), 102–103
Godden, Rumer: *The Doll's House* (1958), 447–448; *Miss Happiness and Miss Flower* (1961), 448–449
Goudge, Elizabeth: *The Little White Horse* (1946), 163–164
Grahame, Kenneth: *The Wind in the Willows* (1908), 119–120

Haggard, H. Rider: *King Solomon's Mines* (1885), 65–66

## Author/Title Index

Hale, Shannon: *The Goose Girl* (2003), 155–156; *The Princess Academy* (2005), 174–175

Hamilton, Virginia: *The House of Dies Drear* (1968), 275–276

Hesse, Karen: *The Music of Dolphins* (1996), 362–363; *Out of the Dust* (1997), 303–304; *Stowaway* (2000), 287–288

Hoban, Russell: *The Mouse and His Child* (1967), 436–437

Hoffmann, E. T. A.: *The Nutcracker and the Mouse King* (1816), 439–440

Holman, Felice: *Slake's Limbo* (1995), 78–79

Horvath, Polly: *My One Hundred Adventures* (2008), 58–59

Hughes, Ted: *The Iron Man* (1968), 422–423

Ibbotson, Eva: *Journey to the River Sea* (2001), 63–64

Irving, Washington: *Rip Van Winkle* (1819), 351–352; *The Legend of Sleepy Hollow* (1819), 352–353

Jansson, Tove: *Comet in Moominland* (1946), 229–230; *Finn Family Moomintroll* (1948), 230–231; *Moominsummer Madness* (1954), 232–233; *Moominland Midwinter* (1957), 233–234; *Moominpappa's Memoirs* (1960), 231–232

Jarrell, Randall: *The Animal Family* (1965), 97–98

Jones, Diana Wynne: *Charmed Life* (1977), 203–204; *The Magicians of Caprona* (1980), 234–235; *The Homeward Bounders* (1981), 430–431; *Witch Week* (1982), 263–264; *The Lives of Christopher Chant* (1988), 264–265; *Conrad's Fate* (2005), 204–205; *The Pinhoe Egg* (2006), 235–236; *Howl's Moving Castle* (1986), 236–237; *Castle in the Air* (1990), 206–207; *The Game* (2007), 432; *House of Many Ways* (2008), 259–260

Juster, Norton: *The Phantom Tollbooth* (1961), 139–141

Kadohata, Cynthia: *Kira-Kira* (2004), 276–277

Key, Watt: *Alabama Moon* (2006), 60–61

Konigsburg, E. L.: *From the Mixed-Up Files of Mrs. Basil E. Frankweiler* (1967), 71–72

Le Guin, Ursula: *A Wizard of Earthsea* (1968), 207–208; *The Tombs of Atuan* (1970), 208–210; *The Farthest Shore* (1972), 210–211

L'Engle, Madeleine: *A Wrinkle in Time* (1962), 418–419; *A Wind in the Door* (1973), 413–414; *A Swiftly Tilting Planet* (1978), 409–410; *Many Waters* (1986), 414–415; *An Acceptable Time* (1989), 419–420

Levine, Gail Carson: *Ella Enchanted* (1997), 156–157; *The Two Princesses of Bamarre* (2001), 181–182; *Fairest* (2006), 188–189; *Ever* (2008), 342–343

Lewis, C. S.: *The Lion, the Witch and the Wardrobe* (1950), 211–212; *Prince Caspian* (1951), 212–214; *The Voyage of the Dawn Treader* (1952), 214–215; *The Silver Chair* (1953), 215–216; *The Horse and his Boy* (1954), 237–238; *The Magician's Nephew* (1955), 238–239; *The Last Battle* (1956), 216–217

Lin, Grace: *Where the Mountain Meets the Moon* (2009), 141–142

Lofting, Hugh: *The Voyages of Doctor Dolittle* (1922), 98–99

London, Jack: *Call of the Wild* (1903), 120–122; *White Fang* (1906), 111–112

Lowry, Lois: *Number the Stars* (1989), 321–322; *The Giver* (1993), 415–416

MacDonald, George: *The Light Princess* (1864), 143–144; *The Princess and the Goblin* (1872), 144–146; *The Princess and Curdie* (1882), 164–165

MacLachlan, Patricia: *Sarah, Plain and Tall* (1985), 294–295

McCaughrean, Geraldine: *The Kite Rider* (2001), 322–323

McKinley, Robin: *The Blue Sword* (1982), 157–158; *The Hero and the*

*Crown* (1984), 158–159; *The Outlaws of Sherwood* (1988), 347–348

Milne, A. A.: *Winnie-the-Pooh* (1926), 440–441; *The House at Pooh Corner* (1928), 441–442

Montgomery, L. M.: *Anne of Green Gables* (1908), 369–371; *Anne of Avonlea* (1909), 398–399; *Anne of the Island* (1915), 382–383; *Emily of New Moon* (1923), 383–384; *Emily Climbs* (1925), 371–372; *Emily's Quest* (1927), 385–386

Morpurgo, Michael: *Kensuke's Kingdom* (1999), 86–87

Mowat, Farley: *Lost in the Barrens* (1956), 88–89

Naylor, Phyllis Reynolds: *Shiloh* (1991), 103–104

Nesbit, Edith: *The Story of the Treasure Seekers* (1899), 363–364; *Five Children and It* (1902), 217–218; *The Phoenix and the Carpet* (1904), 218–219; *The Railway Children* (1906), 364–366; *The Story of the Amulet* (1906), 271–272; *The Enchanted Castle* (1907), 146–147; *The House of Arden* (1908), 147–148; *The Magic City* (1910), 450–451; *Wet Magic* (1913), 165–166

Nix, Garth: *Sabriel* (1995), 265–266; *Lirael* (2001), 266–267; *Abhorsen* (2002), 267–268

Norton, Mary: *The Borrowers* (1952), 260–261; *The Borrowers Afield* (1955), 219–220; *Bedknob and Broomstick* (1957), 191–192; *The Borrowers Afloat* (1959), 239–240; *The Borrowers Aloft* (1961), 220–221; *The Borrowers Avenged* (1982), 222–223

O'Dell, Scott: *Island of the Blue Dolphins* (1960), 81–82

Oppel, Kenneth: *Silverwing* (1997), 107–109; *Sunwing* (2000), 104–105; *Firewing* (2007), 112–113

Otis, James: *Toby Tyler; or, Ten Weeks with a Circus* (1881), 67–68

Park, Linda Sue: *A Long Walk to Water* (2009), 89–90

Paterson, Katherine: *The Master Puppeteer* (1975), 306–307; *Bridge to Terabithia* (1977), 393–394; *The Great Gilly Hopkins* (1978), 392–393; *Jacob Have I Loved* (1980), 387–388; *Lyddie* (1991), 324–325

Patron, Susan: *The Higher Power of Lucky* (2006), 366–367

Paulsen, Gary: *Dogsong* (1985), 90–91; *Hatchet* (1987), 72–74

Pearce, Philippa: *Tom's Midnight Garden* (1958), 148–149

Peck, Richard: *A Long Way from Chicago: A Novel in Stories* (1998), 279–280; *A Year Down Yonder* (2000), 325–326; *The River Between Us* (2003), 326–327

Porter, Eleanor Hodgman: *Pollyanna* (1913), 394–395

Pratchett, Terry: *Truckers* (1989), 403–404; *Diggers* (1990), 410–411; *Wings* (1990), 417–418; *The Amazing Maurice and His Educated Rodents* (2001), 116–117; *The Wee Free Men* (2003), 150–151

Pullman, Philip: *Count Karlstein* (1982), 166–168; *The Ruby in the Smoke* (1985), 312–314; *The Golden Compass* (1995), 268–269; *Clockwork* (1996), 168–169; *The Subtle Knife* (1997), 269–270; *The Amber Spyglass* (2000), 223–224

Pyle, Howard: *The Merry Adventures of Robin Hood* (1883), 341–342

Ransome, Arthur: *Swallows and Amazons* (1930), 68–69; *We Didn't Mean to Go to Sea* (1937), 69–70

Raskin, Ellen: *The Westing Game* (1978), 442–443

Rawlings, Marjorie Kinnan: *The Yearling* (1938), 122–123

Rawls, Wilson: *Where the Red Fern Grows* (1961), 105–106

Richler, Mordecai: *Jacob Two-Two and the Hooded Fang* (1975), 169–170

Rowling, J. K.: *Harry Potter and the Philosopher's Stone* (1997), 241–242; *Harry Potter and the Chamber of Secrets*

## Author/Title Index

(1998), 242–243; *Harry Potter and the Prisoner of Azkaban* (1999), 243–244; *Harry Potter and the Goblet of Fire* (2000), 244–245; *Harry Potter and the Order of the Phoenix* (2003), 245–247; *Harry Potter and the Half-Blood Prince* (2005), 247–248; *Harry Potter and the Deathly Hallows* (2007), 248–249

Ryan, Pam Muñoz: *Esperanza Rising* (2000), 327–329

Sachar, Louis: *Holes* (1998), 91–92
Saint-Exupéry, Antoine de: *The Little Prince* (1943), 404–405
Salten, Felix: *Bambi: A Life in the Woods* (1923), 129–130
Schlitz, Laura Amy: *Good Masters! Sweet Ladies! Voices from a Medieval Village* (2007), 280–281; *The Night Fairy* (2010), 151–152
Selden, George: *The Cricket in Times Square* (1960), 117–118
Selznick, Brian: *The Invention of Hugo Cabret* (2007), 295–297
Sewell, Anna: *Black Beauty* (1877), 130
Smith, Dodie: *I Capture the Castle* (1948), 386–387; *The One Hundred and One Dalmatians* (1956), 99–100
Speare, Elizabeth George: *The Witch of Blackbird Pond* (1958), 304–306; *The Bronze Bow* (1961), 314–315
Spyri, Johanna: *Heidi* (1880–1881), 388–390
Stead, Rebecca: *When You Reach Me* (2009), 420–422
Steig, William: *Abel's Island* (1976), 123–124
Stevenson, Robert Louis: *Treasure Island* (1885), 70–71
Stroud, Jonathan: *The Amulet of Samarkand* (2003), 175–177
Sutcliff, Rosemary: *Eagle of the Ninth* (1954), 289–290; *The Mark of the Horse Lord* (1965), 329–330; *The Sword and the Circle* (1981), 346–347; *Black Ships before Troy: The Story of the Iliad* (1993), 354

Taylor, Mildred D.: *Roll of Thunder, Hear My Cry* (1976), 277–279
Thurber, James: *The White Deer* (1945), 177–178; *The 13 Clocks* (1950), 170–171; *The Wonderful O* (1957), 61–62
Tolkien, J. R. R.: *The Hobbit* (1937), 182–183
Travers, P. L.: *Mary Poppins* (1934), 152–153
Twain, Mark: *The Adventures of Tom Sawyer* (1876), 74–75; *The Adventures of Huckleberry Finn* (1884), 79–80; *The Prince and the Pauper* (1889), 281–282

Verne, Jules: *Journey to the Centre of the Earth* (1864), 407–408; *20,000 Leagues under the Sea* (1870), 423–424
Voigt, Cynthia: *Homecoming* (1981), 83–84

Waugh, Sylvia: *The Mennyms* (1993), 432–434
Webster, Jean: *Daddy-Long-Legs* (1912), 390–391
White, E. B.: *Stuart Little* (1945), 124–125; *Charlotte's Web* (1952), 126–127; *The Trumpet of the Swan* (1970), 109–110
White, T. H.: *The Sword in the Stone* (1938), 354–356
Wiggins, Kate Douglas: *Rebecca of Sunnybrook Farm* (1903), 372–373
Wilder, Laura Ingalls: *Little House in the Big Woods* (1932), 330–331; *Farmer Boy* (1933), 331–332; *Little House on the Prairie* (1935), 297–298; *On the Banks of Plum Creek* (1937), 298–299; *By the Shores of Silver Lake* (1939), 319–320; *The Long Winter* (1940), 299–300; *Little Town on the Prairie* (1941), 320–321; *These Happy Golden Years* (1943), 315–316
Williams, Margery: *The Velveteen Rabbit, Or, How Toys Become Real* (1922), 444
Winthrop, Elizabeth: *The Castle in the Attic* (1985), 449–450

Wyss, Johann David: *The Swiss Family Robinson* (1812-13), 93–94

Yep, Laurence: *Dragonwings* (1975), 307–308

Yolen, Jane: *Dragon's Blood* (1982), 408–409; *Heart's Blood* (1984), 424–426; *A Sending of Dragons* (1987), 405–407; *The Devil's Arithmetic* (1988), 282–283; *Briar Rose* (1992), 332–334

## About the Authors

**Meagan Lacy**, MLIS, is an information literacy librarian at Stella and Charles Guttman Community College, CUNY, New York. She is the editor of Library Unlimited's *The Slow Book Revolution: Creating a New Culture of Reading on College Campuses and Beyond*, which is a librarian's response to the Age of Digital Distraction. She also studies children's literature, and in 2015, she received the Emerging Scholar Award from Children's Literature in Education for her article, "Portraits of Children of Alcoholics: Stories that Add Hope to Hope." Lacy received her Master of Library and Information Science from the University of Washington (Seattle) and her master's degree in English from Indiana University–Purdue University Indianapolis.

**Pauline Dewan**, PhD, is a reference librarian at the Brantford, Ontario campus of Wilfrid Laurier University. She has published two books about children's literature and a number of articles about reading for pleasure. Dewan served for five years on the Readers' Advisory Committee of the Ontario Library Association. She won the 2015 RUSA Press Award for her article, "Reading Matters in the Academic Library: Taking the Lead from Public Librarians." Dewan received her doctorate in English from York University (Toronto).